THE JEWS OF ITALY 1848–1915

THE JEWS OF ITALY 1848–1915

Between Tradition and Transformation

Elizabeth Schächter

VALLENTINE MITCHELL
LONDON • PORTLAND, OR

First published in paperback in 2015 by Vallentine Mitchell

Catalyst House, 720 Centennial Court
Centennial Park, Elstree
WD6 3SY, UK

920 NE 58th Avenue, Suite 300
Portland, Oregon,
97213-3786 USA

www.vmbooks.com

Copyright © 2011 Elizabeth Schächter
First printed in hardback in 2011

British Library Cataloguing in Publication Data
An entry can be found on request

ISBN 978 0 85303 903 7 (cloth)
ISBN 978 0 85303 953 2 (paper)
ISBN 978 1 910383 03 2 (ebook)

Library of Congress Cataloging-in-Publication Data
An entry can be found on request

All rights reserved. Without limiting the rights under copyright reserved alone, no part of this publication may be reproduced, stored in or introduced into a retrieval system, or transmitted, in any form or by any means (electronic, mechanical, photocopying, recording or otherwise), without the prior written permission of both the copyright owner and the above publisher of this book.

Printed by Edwards Brothers Malloy Inc, Ann Arbor, MI

*In memory of my grandparents
Amalie and Emil Mahler
Anna and Adolf Schächter*

*With the exception of Adolf
they perished in the Shoah*

Contents

Acknowledgements	ix
List of Abbreviations	x
1. Introduction: Methodologies and Mise en Scène	1
2. Reshaping Identities	13
3. Social and Demographic Change in the Jewish Communities	63
4. The Longest Hatred	97
5. 'We are a people – one people'	152
6. A Jewish Renaissance	206
Conclusion	231
Bibliography	235
Index	262

Acknowledgements

My interest in the Jews of Italy developed out of my research on Italo Svevo and the Jewish community of Trieste. A grant from the British Academy funded several visits to Italy, and a travel bursary from the School of European Culture and Languages at the University of Kent enabled me to spend ten days in Jerusalem.

There are a number of people who encouraged me in varied ways. In Italy, I have been enriched by the scholarly friendship of Alberto Cavaglion, Liana Funaro and Lionella Viterbo; with Lionella, I spent many pleasant and productive hours in the archives of the Jewish Community in Florence. I would like to acknow-ledge Daniel Vogelmann's generosity in giving me relevant volumes from his publishing house, La Giuntina. From my own institution, David Shaw, dear friend and colleague, read the entire manuscript correcting, inter alia, my propensity for lengthy parentheses and also offered valuable technical assistance. Axel Stähler commented constructively on the chapter on Zionism and shared with me his extensive knowledge of European Judaism.

I am indebted to my daughter Luisa and to Alun Jones for their perceptive suggestions. I would also like to thank the anonymous reader for detailed comments, and the editor Heather Marchant for her help at each stage of the publication process.

Many institutions made their facilities available to me and I am most grateful to their staff, in particular Irene Battino of the Svevo Museum in Trieste, who always ensured that I was provided with the requisite volumes of *Il Corriere Israelitico*; Angela Faunch, document delivery supervisor in the Templeman Library of the University of Kent; Miriam Hassid of the Jewish Community in Trieste; Dr Renato Spiegel at the Central Archives for the History of the Jewish People, and the kind lady at the main desk of the Central Zionist Archives in Jerusalem who gave me chocolate so I could work through lunchtime.

Elizabeth Schächter
February 2010

Abbreviations

ACDEC	Archivio del Centro di Documentazione Ebraica Contemporanea, Milan
ASCEF	Archivio Storico della Comunità Ebraica di Firenze
CAHJP	Central Archives for the History of the Jewish People, Jerusalem
CI	*Il Corriere Israelitico*
CZA	Central Zionist Archives, Jerusalem
EI	*L'Educatore Israelita*
IS	*L'Idea Sionista*
LBIYB	*Leo Baeck Institute Year Book*
RMI	*Rassegna Mensile di Israel*
SI	*La Settimana Israelitica*
VI	*Il Vessillo Israelitico*

1

Introduction: Methodologies and Mise en Scène

Much has been written about the Jews in Italy during the fascist regime, but the period from the second emancipation (1848) until the First World War is largely uncharted territory in the English-speaking world. The notable exception is Cecil Roth's *The History of the Jews of Italy*, which appeared more than sixty years ago.[1] Moreover, in David Vital's seminal work, *A People Apart: The Jews in Europe 1789–1939*, published in 1999 as part of the series 'Oxford History of Modern Europe', the fate of Italian Jews is almost absent. Furthermore, it is only in the last decades of the twentieth century that Einaudi produced the two volumes of its *Storia d'Italia Annali*, which are devoted to the Jews; that Olschki initiated the series *Storia dell'ebraismo in Italia*; and that Italian scholars began to publish on this subject.[2] A substantial part of this research relates to specific communities of which the emancipatory epoch is but one aspect.[3] Gadi Luzzatto Voghera claims that it is impossible 'to write the history of Jewish emancipation in Italy on the assumption of a unified Jewish experience common to all Jews ... The political, economic and jurisdictional fragmentation of the peninsula does not allow it', and that this lack of unity of purpose persisted throughout the nineteenth century.[4] As Luzzatto Voghera's statements reveal, contemporary Italian historiography foregrounds the heterogeneous nature of Italian Judaism, the myriad modalities following emancipation. Thus one of the questions still open to reinterpretation relates to the way these processes are assessed. The aim of this book is to redress the imbalance, fill a major gap in our knowledge of liberal Italy, and to present Italian Jewry, the largest ethnic minority in the nineteenth century, to a wider public within a European context.[5] It reveals the unifying elements that bound Italian Jews on a communal level, the cohesions and continuities which existed within the diversity and multiplicity of transformation.

The intention is not to present a comprehensive, chronological survey of political and social development, but to examine the issues which were considered the principal areas of concern to the Jews themselves. The primary focus is the integration – in the sense of a previously segregated group entering society in equal participation – of the Jews from *their* perspective: their response to the changing patterns of their lives recorded in memoirs, autobiographies, oral testimony, private correspondence, and the views of their religious leaders. It is an area that is little studied.[6] Augusto Segre's recollections, for example, were not destined for publication, but the distinguished historian Renzo De Felice encouraged him and established a series, 'I fatti della storia' (The Facts of History), in order that memories such as these are retained for posterity;[7] Rodolfo De Benedetti wrote his first and only book, *Nato ad Asti: vita di un imprenditore*, at the age of 97.[8] What of the poor and the unlettered who left little or no written testimony? They are not neglected. Through sources such as census data, judicial records, interviews and archival material, their presence is also preserved, although it has to be said that the focus will inevitably favour the middle classes, whose legacy is more voluminous. In treating their evocations, I have subscribed to the 'revival of the narrative ... the most traditional form of historical writing'.[9] The limitations, distortions and omissions of this kind of historical evidence are critically evaluated in the following chapters.

Alongside these 'familial and individual microrealities',[10] another fundamental contemporary source is the Jewish periodical press which played a key role in the dissemination of ideas. Two journals spanned the nineteenth and twentieth centuries, *L'Educatore Israelita* (The Jewish Educator) (later *Il Vessillo Israelitico* [The Jewish Banner], 1853–1922) and *Il Corriere Israelitico* (The Jewish Courier, 1862–1915). The former, which changed its name, editor and place of publication in 1874, was published in Piedmont; the latter in Trieste, which presents an anomaly within the context of Italian Jewry, being the main port of the Austro-Hungarian Empire, but also a city culturally and politically oriented towards Italy, to which it was annexed in 1918. In addition, two other influential publications are considered: *La Settimana Israelitica* (The Jewish Weekly, 1910–15), which signalled an intellectual and spiritual renewal initiated by the chief rabbi of Florence, Samuel Hirsch Margulies; and *L'Idea Sionista* (The Zionist Idea, 1901–11), published in Modena, reflecting to a large extent the activities of the Federazione Sionistica Italiana, also founded in 1901. These journals testify to initiatives on the part of individual members from disparate Jewish communities to communicate with their co-religionists and thus shape the cultural and religious development of Italian Jews during this crucial period of change.

With the exception of the Triestine journal, the other periodicals were published in northern and central Italy, and it is on these regions of the peninsula that this study will concentrate, in particular Piedmont, which was not only the cradle of the Risorgimento, but also the provenance of many influential Jewish figures and of the most enduring journalistic activities.

At the period of the Italian Unification, Italian Jewry were some 40,000 in number (with a further 6,000 in Trieste); 1.44 Jews per 1,000 Italians.[11] These figures are comparable with those of France and Germany: in the 1890s, 570,000 German Jews and 75,000 French Jews comprised 1 per cent of the total population of each country.[12] However, mere numbers can be misleading, as the Jews were not evenly dispersed: in Italy they were scattered among sixty-seven communities, a third of which contained fewer than 200 people, whereas in others, such as Ancona, Livorno and Rome, they constituted 4.6 per cent, 4.06 per cent and 2.2 per cent respectively of the total population. The large settlements of southern Italy and Sicily had been expelled in the sixteenth century during the Spanish occupation; they were also kept out of Lombardy until Austrian rule replaced the Spanish in 1714.[13]

The date of the Jews' re-entry into Italian history is 29 March 1848,[14] when Carlo Alberto, king of Piedmont and Sardinia, granted them civil and political equality, the Statuto Albertino, which was extended to the whole of Italy as it became unified, concluding in 1870 with the annexation of the Papal States and the abolition of the Jewish ghetto in Rome. The Waldensians, Italian Protestants of western Piedmont, had been given the same rights a month earlier; they too had effectively remained outside the course of Italian history until that date.[15] Between 1800 and 1815, during Napoleon's rule of Italian territories, both minorities had enjoyed the freedoms accorded to the French Jews and Protestants in 1791. This is known as the first emancipation. The status quo ante was restored after Napoleon's expulsion with the exception of the Duchy of Parma. I have chosen as the end date 1915, the year that Italy entered the First World War, to signify the culmination of Jewish patriotism: for the many Jews who were ready to sacrifice their lives for their country, the war would be the ultimate demonstration of their unqualified *italianità*.

In Italy, the premises which resulted in Jewish emancipation were no different from those in the rest of western Europe.[16] Citizenship came at a price. The demands and expectations were high: they included renunciation of any separate national identity, of any distinctiveness; radical transformation; regeneration; re-education; *Bildung* ('self-formation'); civic improvement; religious conversion. All this would lead to fusion with Christian society. These were the central assumptions of the various debates in the eighteenth and nineteenth centuries. The fundamental text on the emancipation of European Jewry, *Ueber die bürgerliche Verbesserung der Juden* (On the Civil Improvement of the Jews), by Christian Wilhelm von Dohm, published in 1781, was translated into Italian in 1807.[17] Emancipation was an inherent feature of emerging nation states such as Germany and Italy; their creation and stability necessitated integration, homogeneity and uniformity; the construction of a national identity was predicated on inclusive similarity and the rejection of diversity. Massimo d'Azeglio's statement of 1860 – 'We have made Italy; now we must make the Italians' – subsequently became famous.[18] Assimilation – in the sense of absorbing, incorporating, making alike, conforming, the disappearance of difference – was the prevailing ideology; a linear, unidirectional trajectory, a monocultural ethos. These universalizing objectives were a legacy of the French Enlightenment.[19] This was the utopia. What was the reality?

Assimilation remains the key concept in any attempt to examine Jewish experience at the individual and collective level.[20] It is also 'a problematic term', 'a blunt term':[21] its ever-changing usage over the centuries has led to a multiplicity of meanings which has rendered it increasingly inadequate as a useful analytical tool.[22] Not only has it acquired pejorative connotations, particularly within Zionist historiography but, as an example of its limitations, David Sorkin cites new terms introduced by historians to describe neglected aspects of assimilation: Steven Aschenheim's 'dissociation' and Shulamit Volkov's 'dissimilation'.[23] Thus, as an 'undifferentiated'[24] concept, assimilation has little value. However, there is consensus that Milton M. Gordon's pioneering and influential study of assimilation in American life offers a rigorous analysis which has been acknowledged by Jewish historians.²⁵ He has distinguished seven major factors to describe the gradual stages of the assimilation process. They include: acculturation or 'cultural assimilation' – adoption of the language, behaviour patterns and education of the host society; 'structural assimilation' – large-scale entry into the institutional framework of the host society at the primary group level; 'marital assimilation' – intermarriage on a large scale; 'identificational assimilation' – 'development of a sense of peoplehood based exclusively on the host society'; and 'civic assimilation' – 'absence of value and power conflict'. Structural assimilation is 'the keystone of the arch of assimilation', the crucial intermediary stage between acculturation and marital assimilation. Gordon emphasizes that acculturation does not necessarily lead to structural assimilation, but *'once structural assimilation has occurred, either simultaneously with or subsequent to acculturation, all of the other types of assimilation will naturally follow'*, resulting in 'the disappearance of the ethnic group as a separate identity and the evaporation of its distinctive values'.²⁶ This sociological paradigm is taken up by other sociologists to deconstruct assimilation into discrete variables, 'the core measurable aspects of assimilation': socio-economic status, residential location, generational change, language use, and intermarriage.²⁷ I shall adopt where relevant Gordon's terminology, using the generic term 'assimilation' to refer to 'the entire continuum'²⁸ of the process; nevertheless, the methodological approach of this study privileges an eclectic interpretation of individual and collective experience rather than abstract theoretical discourse.²⁹

The second chapter explores the complex process of 'the anguish of assimilation', as Fritz Stern and David Sorkin describe it:³⁰ the tensions and pressures arising from acceptance in the host society and retention of Jewish patrimony; the relationship between Jewish identity and nascent national identity which has recently become problematic within Italian historiography. The shared aspirations of Jews and non-Jews in the emerging Italian nation led to active participation in public life. However, 'the classic list of prominent Jews in liberal Italy ... is only one side of the coin'.³¹ The other side, as Stefano Caviglia and others have commented, is the erosion of the traditional bonds that bound the individual Jew to his community, and the abandonment of religious practices, leading, in some cases, to mixed marriages and conversion. Thus the perception of the untroubled integration of the Jews into the national structure, propounded by earlier histories,³² is irrevocably undermined. The hypothesis expounded and illustrated in this chapter is 'the profound mutability', the 'hybridity', the reshaping of Jewish identity and the coexistence of a plurality of identities.³³

A fundamental and controversial methodological problem has to be addressed: to attempt to define what is meant by Jewish identity in the post-emancipation period – a problem compounded by the fact that the Jews of the Diaspora were geographically dispersed in very varied cultural and political conditions. The traditional definition according to rabbinical law, Halakah, states that a Jew is anyone born of a Jewish mother or who converted to Judaism. According to Halakah, the condition of being a Jew is irreversible, even with conversion to another religion. Based solely on this ruling, in theory there could be, as Sergio Della Pergola points out, large groups of people and their descendants who were

INTRODUCTION: METHODOLOGIES AND MISE EN SCÈNE

unaware of their Jewish origins; therefore, as a definition in empirical research, it is of limited value. Bearing this in mind, one could adopt Della Pergola's concept of *la popolazione ebraica allargata* (enlarged Jewish population), which comprises four principal categories: demographic – individuals within a family where at least one member is Jewish; organizational – membership of a Jewish community or association; rabbinical – the Halakic precept; and socio-psychological – those who identify themselves as Jewish. Compliance with all four criteria constitutes the nucleus of the Jewish population. In statistical surveys, such as the one carried out in Italy in 1965, those who fulfil the first three of these components are defined as Jews.[34]

Other definitions prioritize religion or ethnicity as the dominant characteristic. The latter term also has multifarious meanings. Yulian Bromley's primordialist position appears to be the most apposite: he defines ethnos as being 'a historically formed community of people characterised by common, relatively stable cultural features, certain distinctive psychological traits, and the consciousness of their unity as distinguished from other similar communities ... it is strongly resilient, persisting through generations'.[35] Interestingly, Della Pergola uses the epithets *minoranza etnico-religiosa* elsewhere in his analysis.[36] Closely associated with ethnicity is nationality, presupposing that Jews were a national group, a stance which was adopted by the Zionist movement. The impact of modern political anti-Semitism is also taken into account in that ethnic identity assumes fundamental significance when it is threatened. Furthermore, there is the problem of the 'marginal' Jews who refused to disclose their group identity for official purposes. A preferable strategy, as Della Pergola suggests, is to use different criteria where appropriate.[37] Anthropological approaches to the term 'identity' draw attention to the ambiguity of its usages which allow for individuals' 'conscious self-typifications'.[38] The criterion of subjective perception is of particular relevance when bearing in mind the encroachments of assimilation in an increasingly secular society. What is left of identity, asks Stuart Hughes, when language and religion are gone? To which he answers: 'some submerged thread ... a shared sensibility'; what others have called 'an unmeltable ethnic'; or, in Freud's words, 'many dark emotional powers ... the clear consciousness of an inner identity, the familiarity of the same psychological structure'.[39] The problematic of Jewish identity is yet to be resolved.[40]

Whatever their responses, western European Jews in the post-emancipation period found themselves placed between the new opportunities of Gentile society and the traditional security of their communities. The individual, the focus of Chapter 2, is not the only unit of analysis in the process of integration: the communities and the roles they played in relation to the host society are also key indicators and an appropriate component of assessment. Prior to emancipation, autonomous communities in central and western Europe constituted the centre of Jewish life. Their governing bodies regulated religion, education and welfare; they registered births, deaths and marriages, and held judicial courts. With the new political order of the emerging nation states, the tendency was to transform these communities into purely religious entities, the individual members of which were citizens whose only difference was that they practised a minority religion.

The third chapter examines the ways in which the Jewish communities were modified by these changes. They lost their jurisdictional status but retained control over the other areas, although state education diminished the influence of the confessional schools. In Italy, in an attempt to harmonize their activities into a central organization as in France and England, two conferences were held, in 1863 and 1867. What were the outcomes, which were reported in detail by *L'Educatore Israelita* and *Il Corriere Israelitico*? Did the religious reforms taking place in Germany and Austria-Hungary have any impact in Italy? How did the communities combat a growing indifference to religion? As a result of internal migration to the principal cities, which occurred throughout emancipated Europe, small communities were depleted. What measures were taken to assist them? How did they retain their corporate structure? As a manifestation of their success and collective identity, the larger communities constructed monumentally magnificent synagogues in, for example, Brussels, Budapest, Florence, Paris, Rome and Turin. Continuities were maintained through many institutions, especially the traditional philanthropic associations, and other forms of cohesion evolved around new causes. One prominent example was the transnational Alliance Israélite Universelle established in Paris in 1860, with branches throughout central and western Europe. As Sorkin and others have argued, 'the very process of emancipation paradoxically served both as the basis for a new sort of community solidarity and provided new forms of Jewish self-understanding'.[41] The shared concerns about Jewish activities and the problems of participation in the modern era formed a common bond between the Jewish communities of the whole of Europe, despite the many differences.[42]

It is no longer the case that the history of Italian Jews since Unification can be described in terms of unqualified success and therefore as an anomaly with regard to European Jewry. This uncritical and hagiographic interpretation has been challenged. The introduction of the Racial Laws of 1938 can only be completely understood if considered not as a break with the past, but as a continuation of a tradition of discrimination and clerical anti-Judaism deriving from the consequences of emancipation. Chapter 4 evaluates the contemporary debates on this major issue in Italian Jewish historiography.

The pivotal role of the Roman Catholic Church in disseminating anti-Semitism through its publications such as the authoritative Jesuit journal, *Civiltà Cattolica*, is examined. The series of articles in the 1880s on ritual murder as a 'well-known Jewish practice' based on 'authentic' historical evidence, fostered belief in and contributed to renewed intolerance of the Jews. Accusations of blood libel, as it is also called, were exploited by the Nazi propaganda machine and have currently resurfaced in the Middle East crisis. The views of the papacy are also of significance. Pope Pius IX reimposed the Rome ghetto after the first emancipation; Leo XIII, who succeeded him, was reticent on the Dreyfus Affair; Pope Pius XII's silence on the Holocaust has been contextualized in the light of his profound aversion to the Jews early in his career at the turn of the twentieth century.[43] On 12 March of the Jubilee year 2000, in an unprecedented mea culpa, Pope John Paul asked for pardon in the name of the Roman Catholic Church on many counts, including that of anti-Semitism. During his historic visit to Israel a week later, at a ceremony at Yad Vashem, Israel's memorial to the dead, the Pope spoke of the Church's sadness regarding Christian anti-Semitism. He was, however, unwilling to ask forgiveness for Catholic silence during the Holocaust. A critic of the Pope, Rabbi Shalom Gold, expressed the opinion that the pontiff had not said 'enough to eliminate 2,000 years of hatred and distrust'.[44]

Catholic antipathy towards the Jews fed into and was nourished by political anti-Semitism, which began to manifest itself in Italy – as in other western European countries – at the time of the emancipation. Such incidents as occurred are disclosed, and the Jewish response in their press is analysed, thus filling another lacuna in the documentation of this epoch. Trieste's proximity to anti-Semitic Vienna, it is argued, gave a sharper insight and perception to the articles of *Il Corriere Israelitico*. There is scholarly consensus that anti-Semitism had far less impact in Italy than elsewhere in Europe. Nevertheless, it was present in the Liberal Party and became integral to the Italian Nationalists' ideology.

The most international, transformative and cohesive Jewish movement of the late nineteenth century was Zionism. It propelled European Jews into world politics under the charismatic leadership of its founder, Theodor Herzl (1860–1904). *Il Corriere Israelitico* was the first Jewish journal to publicize the Zionist movement to Italian readers; its unqualified support for the political Zionism of Herzl was in marked contrast to the ambivalent stance of the Federazione Sionistica Italiana, *L'Idea Sionista*, and the initial opposition adopted by *Il Vessillo Israelitico*. These conflicting views are discussed and interpreted within the European context. The forceful figure of Rabbi Dante Lattes (1876–1965), principal editor of the Triestine periodical between 1903 and 1915, may account to some extent for this ideological divergence, but the anomalous position of Trieste also has to be taken into consideration. It is, perhaps, at this point that an explanation for the inclusion of an 'Austrian' publication in a study of Italian Jewry is of relevance.

Il Corriere Israelitico was published monthly between 1862 and 1908 and bi-monthly from 1909 to 1915. It ceased publication when Italy declared war on Austria-Hungary in that year, and Dante Lattes, who was an Italian citizen, fled to Florence where he co-founded the journal *Israel* in 1916. *Il Corriere Israelitico* is generally considered to be the most influential Jewish journal in the Italian language: 'the only Jewish journal admired and widely read in Italy', to quote its editor.[45] Its main objective was to promote Jewish culture and religion, and to keep its reading public informed of Jewish activities worldwide. Over the years, more space was devoted to Italian Judaism and, as such, it became a banner of *italianità* for Triestine Jews. Moreover, between 1885 and 1896, Leone Racah of Livorno was part of the editorial team. Under Lattes's editorship and pro-Zionist position, it attained an international reputation.

Trieste at that time was the principal seaport of Austria-Hungary, and a flourishing banking and insurance centre. Emperor Joseph II's Edict of Tolerance of 1781 had encouraged people of many nationalities to settle there, including Jews, and by the end of the nineteenth century they were the largest single ethnic minority (3.23 per cent of the total population). They contributed immeasurably to the intellectual, social and economic life of the city, which was essentially

Italian in its cultural and political aspirations.[46] *Il Corriere Israelitico* was pro-Italian, and the editors considered the Jewish community of Trieste as Italian; it was perceived as such by the public and also by the Jews in Italy: in 1873, the editor of *L'Educatore Israelita* (*EI*) wrote: 'from Trieste we receive news of that great community. Trieste is Italian and therefore we feel that we are not going outside the peninsula' (*EI*, 1873, p.150). As a thriving cosmopolitan metropolis at the centre of Europe, Trieste stood at a crossroads of three main languages and cultures: Italian, German and Slav; it was also the port of embarkation for many of the emigrants from central and eastern Europe. The first-hand accounts of persecuted Jews from these regions imbued the Zionist views of the Triestine journal with a sense of urgency. The city itself functioned as a kind of observatory of European politics, looking both eastwards and to the west. Thus Jews living in Trieste were uniquely placed to monitor and record events. Throughout *Il Corriere Israelitico*'s fifty-three years of existence, one can see reflected in its pages the changing currents, contingencies and attitudes that affected the Jews of the Diaspora.

At the beginning of the twentieth century, in reaction to the prolonged propaganda of patriotism and *italianità* of the communities' leaders, the young Jews of Florence, under the guidance of an east European rabbi, Samuel Hirsch Margulies, began to reassert their ethnic and national identity and reconnect with their Jewish heritage. Their initiatives – organizing national conferences and producing their own journal, *La Settimana Israelitica* – and their effect on Italian Jewry as a whole is the subject of the sixth chapter, which addresses a problematic within recent Italian historiography concerning the role of Margulies and the impact of the cultural revival. The ideology of this group must also be perceived within the context of Zionism.

All the issues outlined in this introductory chapter are analysed in the light of recent historiographical debates in Italian and European scholarship and are presented in a comparative context. I have adopted what Endelman calls an 'internal' comparison between Italian Jewry and other Jewries, in order to establish similarities and differences ('external' comparisons with other minority religious groups are fleetingly acknowledged).[47] Thus the question of whether the experience of Italian Jews after 1848 was qualitatively different from that of other countries in western Europe can be addressed.

NOTES

1. Cecil Roth, *The History of the Jews of Italy* (Philadelphia, PA: Jewish Publication Society of America, 1946). *The Italian Jewish Experience* (Stony Brook, NY: Forum Italicum Publishing, 2000), edited by Thomas P. DiNapoli, and *The Most Ancient of Minorities: The Jews of Italy* (Westport, CT, and London: Greenwood Press, 2002), edited by Stanislao G. Pugliese, are collections of conference papers, mainly on the twentieth century. *Acculturation and Its Discontents: The Italian Jewish Experience between Exclusion and Inclusion* (Toronto: University of Toronto Press, 2008), edited by David N. Myers, Massimo Ciavolella, Peter H. Riell and Geoffrey Symcox, is a volume of essays by different authors covering the Renaissance to the twentieth century, while David I. Kertzer's *The Kidnapping of Edgardo Mortara* (London: Picador, 1997) examines one – albeit important – aspect of the period.
2. Corrado Vivanti (ed.), *Storia d'Italia, Annali 11, Gli ebrei in Italia*, vol. 1, *Dall'alto Medioevo all'età dei ghetti*; vol. 2, *Dall'emancipazone a oggi* (Turin: Einaudi, 1996/97). This was the first scholarly general history of Italian Jewry since Attilio Milano's *Storia degli ebrei in Italia* (Turin: Einaudi, 1963). The Olschki series edited by Pier Cesare Ioly Zorattini, *Storia dell'ebraismo in Italia*, 24

INTRODUCTION: METHODOLOGIES AND MISE EN SCÈNE 9

volumes (Florence: Olschki, 1980–), has mainly concentrated on individual communities and trials of the Inquisition against the Jews in the sixteenth and seventeenth centuries. Maurizio Molinari's slim monograph, *Ebrei in Italia: un problema di identità (1870–1938)* (Florence: Giuntina, 1991), contains three chapters relevant to this period. Mario Toscano's edited volume *Integrazione e identità: l'esperienza ebraica in Germania e Italia dall'Illuminisimo al fascismo* (Milan: FrancoAngeli, 1998) is a collection of conference papers which, given the extensive period covered, offers a broad perspective with greater emphasis placed on the German experience. Toscano's *Ebraismo e antisemitismo in Italia: dal 1848 alla guerra dei sei giorni* (Milan: FrancoAngeli, 2003) is an anthology of articles dating from 1982 to 1998. Aldo A. Mola (ed.), *Isacco Artom e gli ebrei italiani dai Risorgimenti al fascismo* (Foggia: Bastogi, 2002), is also a collection of conference papers, the focus of which is on individual Jews. Ester Capuzzo's *Gli ebrei nella società italiana: comunità e istituzioni tra Ottocento e Novecento* (Rome: Carocci, 1999) considers the Jewish institutions and communities within a changing legal framework. By the same author is *Gli ebrei italiani dal Risorgimento alla scelta sionista* (Florence: Le Monnier, 2004), which contains two relevant chapters. Giampiero Carocci's *Storia degli ebrei in Italia: dall'emancipazione a oggi* (Rome: Newton & Compton, 2005) focuses mainly on the period from fascism to the present day.
3. For example, Acqui, Asti, Bologna, Florence, Gorizia, Livorno, Mantua, Milan, Modena, Pisa, Rome, Trieste, Turin, Venice and Verona. In addition, there is the ongoing project, directed by Shlomo Simonsohn, to collate documentation on each region of Italy: *A Documentary History of the Jews in Italy*, 19 volumes (Jerusalem and Leiden: Israel Academy of Sciences and Humanities and E.J. Brill, 1982–).
4. Gadi Luzzatto Voghera, 'Italian Jews', in Rainer Liedtke and Stephen Wendehorst (eds), *The Emancipation of Catholics, Jews and Protestants: Minorities and the Nation State in Nineteenth-Century Europe* (Manchester and New York: Manchester University Press, 1999), pp.169, 171.
5. See Guri Schwarz, 'A proposito di una vivace stagione storiografica: letture dell'emancipazione ebraica negli ultimi vent'anni', *Memoria e Ricerca*, 19 (2005), p.169: 'despite progress in recent years, studies on Jews and anti-semitism in liberal Italy are few. The process of integration of the [Jewish] minority ... is mostly uncharted territory.'
6. See Alberto Cavaglion, 'L'Autobiografia ebraica in Italia fra Otto e Novecento. Memoria di sé e memoria della famiglia: osservazioni preliminari', *Zakhor. Rivista di Storia degli Ebrei D'Italia*, 3 (1999), pp.171–7.
7. Augusto Segre (1915–80), *Memorie di vita ebraica: da Casale a Gerusalemme* (Rome: Bonacci, 1979), with a preface by Renzo De Felice in which he states that Segre had written 'an historical, human document ... of real importance ... to know and understand contemporary Italian Judaism' (p.15).
8. Rodolfo De Benedetti, *Nato ad Asti: vita di un imprenditore* (Genoa: Marietti, 1989).
9. John Tosh, *The Pursuit of History: Aims, Methods and New Directions in the Study of Modern History*, third edn (London and New York: Longman, 2000), p.99.
10. Michele Luzzati, 'Integrazione e assimilazione nella Livorno ebraica: proposte per una discussione', in Michele Luzzati (ed.), *Ebrei di Livorno tra due censimenti (1841–1938): memoria familiare e identità* (Livorno: Belforte, 1990), p.10. One striking example of 'microhistory' is Elena Rossi Artom's research on her own family from the sixteenth to the twentieth century, through sixteen generations: *Gli Artom: storia di una famiglia della comunità ebraica di Asti attraverso le sue generazioni (XVI–XX secolo)* (Turin: Zamorani, 1997).
11. Andrew M. Canepa, 'Considerazioni sulla seconda emancipazione e le sue conseguenze', *Rassegna Mensile di Israel* [hereafter *RMI*], 47, 1–3 (1981), p.85; and Sergio Della Pergola, 'La popolazione ebraica in Italia nel contesto ebraico globale', in Vivanti (ed.), *Storia d'Italia, Annali 11, Gli ebrei in Italia*, vol. 2, p.933. In the 1871 census, the number of Italian Jews living abroad, many of Livornese origin, was as follows: 2,347 in Egypt; 1,086 in Constantinople and Smirne; 427 in Salonica; 307 in Syria. See Gadi Luzzatto Voghera, *Il prezzo dell'eguaglianza: il dibattito sull'emancipazione degli ebrei in Italia (1781–1848)* (Milan: FrancoAngeli, 1998), p.25. In 1895, there were also about 2,000 in Tunisia: see Elia Boccara, 'La comunità ebraica portoghese di Tunisi (1710–1944)', *RMI*, 66, 2 (2000), pp.25–98. See also Liana Elda Funaro, 'A Mediterranean Diaspora: Jews from Leghorn in the Second Half of the Nineteenth Century', in Marta Petricioli (ed.), *L'Europe méditerranéenne: Mediterranean Europe* (Brussels: Peter Lang, 2008), pp.95–110.
12. See Jacques Ehrenfreund, 'Citizenship and Acculturation: Some Reflections on German Jews during the Second Empire and French Jews during the Third Republic' in Michael Brenner, Vicki Caron and Uri R. Kaufmann (eds), *Jewish Emancipation Reconsidered: The French and German Models* (Leo Baeck Institute, London: Mohr Siebeck, 2003), p.156.
13. Jews had lived in Sicily for fourteen centuries until their expulsion – fifty communities, estimated by some scholars at 10 per cent of the island's total population – and yet there seem to be no physical signs of their inhabitation, as if those many years 'had been erased from the consciousness of Sicilians'. See

Gaetano Cipolla, 'The Jews of Sicily', in DiNapoli (ed.), *Italian Jewish Experience*, p.52.
14. Yosef Hayim Yerushalmi, *Zakhor: Jewish History and Jewish Memory* (Seattle, WA, and London: University of Washington Press, 1982), p.99: 'As a result of emancipation ... Jews have fully re-entered the mainstream of history.'
15. Giorgio Spini, *Risorgimento e protestanti* (Turin: Claudiana, 1998), pp.28, 32, 45; and Gian Paolo Romagnani, 'Italian Protestants', in Liedtke and Wendehorst (eds), *Emancipation of Catholics, Jews and Protestants*, p.162. In the 1861 census, they numbered nearly 33,000 (Spini, *Risorgimento e protestanti*, p.310). Austrian and Hungarian Jews achieved full emancipation in 1867, and those in Germany in 1871. See, for example, Werner E. Mosse, 'From "Schutzjuden" to "Deutsche Staatsbürger Jüdischen Glaubens": The Long and Bumpy Road of Jewish Emancipation in Germany', in Pierre Birnbaum and Ira Katznelson (eds), *Paths of Emancipation: Jews, States, and Citizenship* (Princeton, NJ: Princeton University Press, 1995), pp.58–93; Robert S. Wistrich, *Socialism and the Jews: The Dilemmas of Assimilation in Germany and Austria-Hungary* (London and Toronto: Associated University Presses, 1982); and Christopher Clark, 'German Jews', in Liedtke and Wendehorst (eds), *Emancipation of Catholics, Jews and Protestants*, pp.122–47.
16. See Jacob Katz, *Out of the Ghetto: The Social Background of Jewish Emancipation, 1770–1870* (Cambridge, MA: Harvard University Press, 1973), p.4; Liedtke and Wendehorst, *Emancipation of Catholics, Jews and Protestants*, p.197; and Paul Mendes-Flohr and Jehuda Reinharz (eds), *The Jew in the Modern World: A Documentary History*, second edn (New York and Oxford: Oxford University Press, 1995), Chapters 1–3.
17. Dohm's book was published in Berlin and Stettin, two volumes, 1781 and 1783. The seminal French text is Abbé Gregoire's *Essai sur la régénération physique, morale et polititque des Juifs* (1788). For a summary of the debates on emancipation of the Jews in Italy from the lay, Roman Catholic and Jewish perspectives, see, for example, Canepa, 'Considerazioni sulla seconda emancipazione'; Andrew Canepa, 'Emancipation and Jewish Response in Mid-Nineteenth-Century Italy', *European History Quarterly*, 16, 4 (1986), pp.403–39; Paolo Bernardini, *La questione ebraica nel tardo illuminismo tedesco: studi intorno allo 'Ueber die bürgerliche Verbesserung der Juden' di C.W. Dohm (1781)* (Florence: Giuntina, 1992); Franco Della Peruta, 'Gli ebrei nel Risorgimento fra interdizioni ed emancipazione', in Vivanti (ed.), *Storia d'Italia, Annali 11, Gli ebrei in Italia*, vol. 2, pp.1135–67; Giorgina Arian Levi and Giulio Disegni, *Fuori dal ghetto: il 1848 degli ebrei* (Rome: Riuniti, 1998); Luzzatto Voghera, *Il prezzo dell'eguaglianza*; Capuzzo, *Gli ebrei nella società italiana*, Chapters 1–4; and Valerio De Cesaris, *Pro Judaeis: il filogiudaismo cattolico in Italia (1789–1938)* (Milan: Guerini, 2006). See also Liedtke and Wendehorst, *Emancipation of Catholics, Jews and Protestants*, pp.207–10, for a chronology of formal emancipation for British Catholics and Jews; French Protestants and Jews; German Catholics and Jews; Italian Protestants and Jews.
18. See Martin Clark, *Modern Italy 1871–1982* (London and New York: Longman, 1984), p.30.
19. See Albert Russell Ascoli and Krystyna Von Henneberg (eds), *Making and Remaking Italy* (New York and Oxford: Berg, 2001); E.J. Hobsbawm, *The Age of Capital 1848–1875* (London: Abacus, 1995), Chapter 5, 'Building Nations'; Zygmunt Bauman, *Modernity and Ambivalence* (Cambridge: Polity Press, 1991), Chapter 4, 'A Case Study in the Sociology of Assimilation'; Marcus Banks, *Ethnicity: Anthropological Constructions* (London and New York: Routledge, 1996), Chapter 5, 'Ethnicity and Nationalism'; and Thomas Hylland Eriksen, *Ethnicity and Nationalism: Anthropological Perspectives* (London and East Haven, CT: Pluto Press, 1993), Chapter 6.
20. See Amos Morris-Reich, *The Quest for Jewish Assimilation in Modern Social Science* (London: Routledge, 2008), p.8.
21. Marsha L. Rozenblit, *The Jews of Vienna 1867–1914: Assimilation and Identity* (Albany, NY: State University of New York Press, 1983), p.3; Paula E. Hyman, *Gender and Assimilation in Modern Jewish History: The Roles and Representation of Women* (Seattle, WA, and London: University of Washington Press, 1995), p.11.
22. See, for example, David N. Myers, ' "The Blessing of Assimilation" Reconsidered: An Inquiry into Jewish Cultural Studies', in David N. Myers and William V. Rowe (eds), *From Ghetto to Emancipation: Historical and Contemporary Reconsiderations of the Jewish Community* (Scranton, PA: Scranton University Press, 1997), p.20; David Sorkin, 'Emancipation and Assimilation: Two Concepts and their Application to German-Jewish History', *Leo Baeck Institute Year Book*, 35 (1990), p.17; Morris-Reich, *Quest for Jewish Assimilation*, pp.9; 10, and Sergio Della Pergola, 'Quantitative Aspects of Jewish Assimilation', in Bela Vago (ed.), *Jewish Assimilation in Modern Times* (Boulder, CO: Westview Press, 1981), pp.185–6.
23. Sorkin, 'Emancipation and Assimilation', pp.28–9. See also Ritchie Robertson's use of the term 'dissimilation' in *The 'Jewish Question' in German Literature 1749–1939: Emancipation and its Discontents* (Oxford: Oxford University Press, 1999), Chapter 5.
24. Sorkin, 'Emancipation and Assimilation', p.30.

25. See, for example, Hyman, *Gender and Assimilation*, p.13; Della Pergola, 'Quantitative Aspects of Jewish Assimilation', p.187; Rozenblit, *The Jews of Vienna*, pp.3–4; Myers et al., *Acculturation and its Discontents*, p.7. Jonathan Frankel, 'Assimilation and the Jews in Nineteenth-Century Europe: Towards a New Historiography?', in Jonathan Frankel and Steven J. Zipperstein (eds), *Assimilation and Community: The Jews in Nineteenth-Century Europe* (Cambridge: Cambridge University Press, 2004), p.21; and in the same volume, Michael K. Silber, 'The Entrance of Jews into Hungarian Society in *Vormärz*: The Case of the "Casinos" ', p.285.
26. Milton M. Gordon, *Assimilation in American Life: The Role of Race, Religion, and National Origins* (New York: Oxford University Press, 1964), pp.61, 70–1, 81. Italics in the original text.
27. Mary C. Waters and Tomás R. Jiménez, 'Assessing Immigrant Assimilation: New Empirical and Theoretical Challenges', *Annual Review of Sociology*, 31 (2005), p.106.
28. Rozenblit, *The Jews of Vienna*, p.4.
29. See Frances Malino and David Sorkin (eds), *From East and West: Jews in a Changing Europe, 1750–1870* (Oxford: Blackwell, 1990), Introduction, p.7: 'the undeniable conclusion: the inviolability of individual experience foils the presumptions of grand teleology'; and Alexander Stille, *Benevolence and Betrayal: Five Italian Jewish Families Under Fascism* (London: Jonathan Cape, 1992), p.16: 'The complexity of individual experience ... can be a useful touchstone for the abstract, linear theories of history.'
30. Fritz Stern, *Gold and Iron: Bismarck, Bleichröder, and the Building of the German Empire* (London: Allen & Unwin, 1977), p.11; also of relevance is Stern's phrase 'the anguished ambiguity of Jewish success' (p.xv); Sorkin, 'Emancipation and Assimilation', p.29. Note also Michael Gold's expression, 'the anguish of becoming American', in his autobiographical novel *Jews without Money* (New York: Horace Liveright, 1930), on immigrant life in New York, cited in the introduction of Michael D'Innocenzo and Josef P. Sirefman (eds), *Immigration and Ethnicity: American Society – 'Melting Pot' or 'Salad Bowl'* (Westport, CT, and London: Greenwood Press, 1992), p.ix.
31. Stefano Caviglia, *L'identità salvata: gli ebrei di Roma tra fede e nazione: 1870–1938* (Rome-Bari: Laterza, 1996), p.xxi.
32. Milano, *Storia degli ebrei in Italia*, p.693: 'the Jews' residence in Italy has been ... one of the happiest that any Jewish group has encountered in the Diaspora'; and Roth, *History of the Jews of Italy*, p.474: 'the Jews were accepted freely, naturally and spontaneously as members of the Italian people'.
33. Michael A. Meyer, *The Origins of The Modern Jew: Jewish Identity and European Culture in Germany, 1749–1824* (Detroit, MI: Wayne State University Press, 1967), p.8; Esther Benbassa and Jean-Christophe Attias (eds), *The Jew and the Other* (Ithaca, NY, and London: Cornell University Press, 2004), p.x; Myers, ' "The Blessing of Assimilation" Reconsidered', p.24.
34. Sergio Della Pergola, *Anatomia dell'ebraismo italiano: caratteristiche demografiche, economiche, sociali, religiose e politiche di una minoranza* (Assisi and Rome: Carucci, 1976), pp.9–11, 28–30. The methodological premises of Werner E. Mosse and Werner Sombert take no account of individual self-perception. See Ilaria Pavan, ' "Ebrei" in affari tra realtà e pregiudizio: paradigmi storiografici e percorsi di ricerca dall'Unità alle leggi razziali', *Quaderni storici*, 38, 3 (2003), p.779.
35. Banks, *Ethnicity*, pp.17, 19.
36. Della Pergola, *Anatomia dell'ebraismo italiano*, p.53.
37. Ibid., p.37.
38. Alan Barnard and Jonathan Spencer (eds), *Encyclopedia of Social and Cultural Anthropology* (London and New York: Routledge, 1998), p.292.
39. H. Stuart Hughes, *Prisoners of Hope: The Silver Age of the Italian Jews 1924–1974* (Cambridge, MA, and London: Harvard University Press, 1983), pp.9, 28; D'Innocenzo and Sirefman, *Immigration and Ethnicity* (eds), p.x; Freud's address to members of the B'nai B'rith Lodge of 6 May 1926, in Ernst L. Freud (ed.), *Letters of Sigmund Freud 1873–1939* (London: Hogarth Press, 1961), p.367. Freud expressed similar sentiments in letters to Sándor Ferenczi and Arnold Zweig, cited in Peter Gay, *Freud: A Life for Our Time* (London and Melbourne: Dent, 1988), pp.601–2.
40. See, for example, Jonathan Freedland, *Jacob's Gift: A Journey into the Heart of Belonging* (London: Hamish Hamilton, 2005): 'what category did Jews most naturally occupy? Were they a religion ... a nation ... a race? ... Or were they all of the above, all at the same time? ... They are a civilization, a culture, a people and a tribe' (pp.29, 365; see also Chapter 14).
41. Sorkin, 'Emancipation and Assimilation', p.32. See also John F. McClymer, 'The Paradox of Ethnicity in the United States: The French-Canadian Experience in Worcester, 1870–1914', in D'Innocenzo and Sirefman (eds), *Immigration and Ethnicity*, pp.15–23; and Katz, *Out of the Ghetto*, p.215: 'thus not only the persistence of old habits, but paradoxically, the very attempts at integration ... reinforced a sense of international community'.
42. See S.N. Eisenstadt, *Jewish Civilization: The Jewish Historical Experience in a Comparative Perspective* (Albany, NY: State University of New York Press, 1992), pp.91–118.
43. See John Cornwell, *Hitler's Pope: The Secret History of Pius XII* (London: Viking, 1999).

44. *The Times*, 24 March 2000, p.17. The words of Pope Benedict XVI, during his visit to Israel in May 2009, also failed to heal the rift between the Catholic Church and the Jewish people. See *The Times*, 12 May 2009, p.31.
45. *Il Corriere Israelitico*, 1875, p.221. There is a complete run of the journal in the Biblioteca Civica of Trieste and in the archive of the Jewish community of Trieste. The British Library holds volumes 14–20 (1875–1882).
46. See, for example, Elio Apih, *Trieste* (Rome-Bari: Laterza, 1988); Tullia Catalan, *La comunità ebraica di Trieste (1781–1914): politica, società e cultura* (Trieste: Lint, 2000); Elizabeth Schächter, *Origin and Identity: Essays on Svevo and Trieste* (Leeds: Northern Universities Press, 2000), Chapters 1 and 2; and Lois C. Dubin, 'The Jews of Trieste: Between Mitteleuropa and Mittelmeer, 1719–1939', in Charles Klopp (ed.), *Bele Antiche Stòrie: Writing, Borders, and the Instability of Identity: Trieste, 1719–2007* (New York: Bordighera, 2008), pp.69–90.
47. Todd M. Endelman (ed.), *Comparing Jewish Societies* (Ann Arbor, MI: University of Michigan Press, 1997), pp.14–16. With regard to the comparative dimension, reliance has necessarily been made on secondary sources.

2
Reshaping Identities

Jews have been living in various regions of Italy for over 2,000 years, since the second century BCE at the time of the Roman Republic; the community of Rome is the oldest in the European Diaspora. Successive migrations came from the Mediterranean in the first century CE; from France and Germany in the fourteenth century; from the Iberian Peninsula in the fifteenth; from the Balkans at the end of the nineteenth and beginning of the twentieth centuries; the notable exception was eastern European Jews during the period of mass emigrations from the 1880s.[1] Two factors in particular facilitated the Jews' ability to adapt during their lengthy residence in Italy despite regional and political divergences prior to Unification: their exiguous number, and linguistic homogeneity in the sense that they spoke the same dialect as other inhabitants – Venetian Jews spoke Venetian, Piedmontese Jews spoke Piedmontese. These dialects have been defined as Judeo-Italian, further divided into Judeo-Venetian, Judeo-Piedmontese, and so on. They were firmly established by the thirteenth century and evolved from Judeo-Latin as Italian became a vernacular. Their linguistic base was the dialect of the place of residence, infused with liturgical Hebrew and archaisms from previous settlements: for example, Spanish, Provençal or Yiddish. There was no literary tradition to speak of in Judeo-Italian.[2] A disincentive to any literary development in Judeo-Italian was the fact that, before emancipation, Jews were taught to read and write Italian in Jewish schools as part of an educational programme to assist active participation in the host society, in contrast to schools in central and eastern Europe where instruction was in Hebrew and Yiddish. A positive evaluation was placed on Italy's cultural heritage, which was studied alongside Jewish culture, whereas in central Europe, Jewish and secular studies were separate; indeed, religious scholars in eighteenth-century Germany who only spoke Yiddish 'condemned as heretics all who attempted to acquire a secular education'.[3] In the late eighteenth century, the Italian Jewish educational system was upheld as a pedagogic model and the collaboration of Italian Jewish leaders was considered crucial by the European *Haskalah* movement centred in Berlin within the ambit of the German Enlightenment. This influential group of Jewish scholars campaigned for radical cultural reforms, and their founder, Moses Mendelssohn (1729–86), promoted the study of secular culture, of which he became a prominent figure.[4] 'Italian supporters of *Haskalah* were not a peripheral coterie of radical intellectuals but the rabbinic and communal élite.'[5] The noted historian Raphael Mahler commented that at this period, Jews in Italy were better integrated than anywhere else in Europe.[6]

The life of the ghettos reduced, but did not eliminate, contact between Jew and non-Jew, and in Livorno, one of the largest communities, a ghetto was never constituted. To encourage development in this major port, concessions, known as the *Livornina*, were accorded the Jewish inhabitants by King Ferdinand I on 10 June 1593.[7] Consequently the Livornese Jews lived 'in exceptional conditions of religious and civil liberty'.[8] Isaac Euchel, a leading figure of the *Haskalah*, visiting Livorno in 1769, noted with satisfaction that his Livornese brothers inhabited fine houses, engaged in every occupation and lived securely among the Gentiles, speaking the same language and wearing similar attire.[9] Thus acculturation had already taken place among the wealthy Jews of northern and central Italy. This openness and sensitivity towards the cultural environment, the ability to mediate between tradition and modernity, characterized Italian Jewry and assisted them in the transition from the ghetto to emancipation. Furthermore, there were no significant linguistic barriers: Jewish adherents of emancipationist ideology emphasized the fact that Italian Jews and non-Jews shared the same language. After the acquisition of civil and political equality, many Jews sought to distance themselves from their past by rejecting Judeo-Italian in favour of what they considered to be correct spoken Italian – one of the aspects of cultural assimilation.[10] It was only at the beginning of the twentieth century, as part of the Jewish cultural revival, that there was renewed interest in Judeo-Italian, of which lexical and semantic elements had survived in the spoken form. The continuous transformation of the Italian Jewish experience is reflected in the representation and memory of their language: 'a residual linguistic identification with all its cultural, emotional and psychological components'.[11] Knowledge of Yiddish was rare among Italian Jews: in his memoirs, Augusto Segre (1915–80), a rabbi and a Zionist, recalls his student days in Rome when he lodged at the Jewish Pensione Pines, then full of Russian, German, Hungarian and Polish Jews. They were surprised that Segre did not speak Yiddish and doubted the authenticity of his Jewish identity. At meetings his ideas were not taken seriously, indeed almost ignored, 'for the simple fact that the person presenting them was a Jew born in Italy who did not even know Yiddish'.[12]

PARTICIPATION IN THE RISORGIMENTO

Italian Jews who had experienced freedom during the first emancipation – many had joined Masonic lodges, some aptly named 'Napoleonic' – perceived in the Risorgimento ideals the prospect of once more acquiring equality and liberty.[13] Extensive documentary evidence attests to their active involvement – as soldiers, writers and financiers – in every stage and political aspect of the Risorgimento from the earliest manifestations until its culmination with the liberation of Rome in 1870. They became members of the secret revolutionary Carbonari sects in Tuscany, the Veneto and the Papal States; they fought in the uprisings of 1820/21 in Piedmont.[14] In cafés, clubs, universities and opera houses – places 'where "Italians" were "made"'[15] – young educated Jews met with liberals to discuss politics. They were indispensable in Giuseppe Mazzini's republican 'Young Italy' (*La Giovine Italia*) movement, initiated in 1831; one of its principal centres was a bookshop in Vercelli belonging to Salvador Vita Levi and his son Giuseppe, who acted as an intermediary between Mazzinian supporters in Marseilles and Lugano. Clandestine documents and books were transported in baskets hidden beneath Abram Lazzaro Levi's goose salamis, and when in June 1833 the police arrested 'Young Italy' sympathizers, Giuseppe managed to evade capture and escape to Switzerland where he joined Mazzini in exile.[16] David Levi (1816–98) poet, playwright and patriot, served as a key contact between 'Young Italy' groups in Piedmont, Tuscany and the Romagna. Tullo Massarani (1826–1905) and Giuseppe Finzi (1815–86) held meetings with Mazzini in London, smuggling into Italy important papers sewn inside their clothes. Massarani and David Levi were among the first Jews to be elected to the Italian parliament in 1860.[17] Another Jew, Angelo Usiglio, followed Mazzini into exile in Switzerland and England; he was, in Mazzini's words, 'his guardian angel'.[18] The Nathan-Rosselli family, many of whose members were to figure prominently in Italian public life, were close allies and intimate friends of Mazzini; he was often their guest, and he died in the home of Giannetta Nathan Rosselli on 10 May 1872. The house was subsequently donated to the nation, and Giannetta's son was named Giuseppe in his memory.[19] The poet and dramatist Giuseppe Revere (1812–89) was also an ardent Mazzinian, contributing articles to various journals in Milan and Turin; so too was Salvatore De Benedetti (1818–91), who was to hold the first Chair of Hebrew Studies at the University of Pisa from 1862.[20]

Count Camillo Benso di Cavour, founder of *Il Risorgimento* (1847), prime minister of Piedmont from 1852 and briefly of the kingdom of Italy in the last months of his life in 1861, also numbered Jews among his closest collaborators: Isacco Artom (1829–1900), his private secretary; Giacomo Dina (1824–79), editor of *L'Opinione*, 'Cavour's mouthpiece',[21] and Alessandro D'Ancona (1835–1914) who, when a student at the University of Turin, acted as a conduit between the liberals of Tuscany and Cavour;[22] D'Ancona was to become a central figure of Italian culture. The Jews of Turin within Cavour's constituency were instrumental in returning him to parliament in 1852.[23] There were links between Piedmont's Jews and the royal House of Savoy dating back to the sixteenth century, and converging interests with the emerging Piedmontese bourgeoisie which contributed to the shaping of mid-nineteenth-century nationalism.[24] Lelio Cantoni (1801–57), chief rabbi of Piedmont, was deeply involved from 1845 in the discussions that led to the promulgation of the Statuto Albertino three years later.[25] In 1847, the young Isacco Rignano (1824–96), who was to become a distinguished lawyer in Livorno, wrote a pamphlet, *Sull'attuale posizione giuridica degli israeliti in Toscana*, in which he anticipated a new dawn for the Jews, who would be 'devoted sons of Italy'.[26] For Giacomo Dina, 'Jewish redemption' (*il riscatto israelitico*) was an 'essential component of the Italian Risorgimento'[27] – a reiteration of Massimo D'Azeglio's position in his essay 'On the Civil Emancipation of the Jews' (1848): 'the cause for the regeneration of the Jews is closely linked to that of the Italians'.[28] D'Azeglio was the first prime minister of the new Piedmontese parliament (1849) and one of the architects of the Statuto Albertino. Two prominent figures of nineteenth-century Italian Judaism, Rabbi Elia ben Abraham Benamozegh (1823–1900) of the Rabbinical College of Livorno and Samuel

David Luzzatto (known by his Hebrew acronym Shadal, 1800–65), professor of the Rabbinical College in Padua, endorsed their co-religionists' love of Italy. In an impassioned speech in the synagogue of Livorno on 8 September 1847, Benamozegh exhorted his congregation 'to love Italy after God above all other earthly affections'; in another peroration of 22 September 1848, he declaimed with all the ardour and emotion of youth: 'swear [*giurate*], o Israelites, swear that you will always love Italy ... with all your heart and soul, with all your might ... with an immense and insuperable love'.[29] In this manner, Benamozegh participated in the 'patriotic festivities of brotherhood' of 7 and 8 September in Livorno between Christians and Jews.[30] Luzzatto, privately in a letter in Hebrew (to avoid censorship) to his Hungarian friend David Schwarz, exulted in Italy's potential freedom, referring to a recently published poem: 'the whole of Italy is united [*fraterna*] as one man; the spirit of the Lord urges her to throw off the foreigners' yoke'.[31] Luzzatto was at the centre of a group of friends and former students who exchanged views and ideas particularly during the heady revolutionary years of 1848/49; these included Graziadio Isaia Ascoli (1829–1907) who was to become the greatest Italian philologist of the nineteenth century, and Isacco Pesaro Maurogonato (1817–92), a promising politician.[32]

The process of the Jews' emancipation occurred in conjunction with the emerging Italian nation: the Italian state liberated them and they in turn participated in the wars of independence to liberate and unite Italy. They fought against the Austrians during the 'five glorious days', as the insurrection in Milan between 17 and 22 March 1848 became known. In the short-lived republics of Venice (22 March 1848 to August 1849) and Rome (9 February 1849 to June 1849), Jews played a prominent part in their governance, elected to the assemblies and appointed as ministers, such as Leone Pincherle, minister of agriculture, and Isacco Pesaro Maurogonato, minister of finance in Venice. Jews from all over Italy and from abroad flocked to both cities in order to enrol in the civic guard to defend their freedom and that of their fellow Italians – for some at the cost of their lives, an emblematic case being that of Giacomo Venezian (1824–49) from Trieste who was killed in Rome.[33] They willingly absorbed the nationalist rhetoric of sacrificing their lives for their country.[34] In the subsequent campaigns, they fought heroically and in disproportionately high numbers in relation to the population as a whole: 213 in the battles of 1859/60; eight, three of them officers, in Garibaldi's 'Thousand' who liberated Sicily in 1860; 174 volunteers in the 1866 offensive in the Veneto. By 1869, there were eighty-seven Jewish officers among 14,108 and three hundred soldiers out of 170,000.[35] In 1870, the Italian artillery which breached the walls of Porta Pia in Rome was under the command of Captain Segre, and the first combat unit to enter the city was led by another Jewish officer, Captain Mortara.[36]

Rabbis also contributed to the formation of a national conscience within their communities: for example, the words of Marco Mortara, chief rabbi of Mantua, in 1866: 'Children of ancient Judea, citizens of the newly redeemed [*risorta*] Italy ... we will be worthy of the grave task entrusted to us by Divine Providence ... we will join with our brothers to defend ... and fortify ... the *patria* that God has given us, the great nation of which we are a part.'[37] Such expressions of gratitude were not merely 'part of a prescribed ritual ... developed during centuries of Jewish submission'.[38] On the contrary, it can be argued that Jewish participation in the Risorgimento and the celebration of their freedom alongside their Christian brothers 'had no precedent in Italian history'.[39] *L'Educatore Israelita* (*EI*) promoted patriotic zeal in reports on the struggle for Italian independence: 'In this year [1860], Italian Jews gave proof that their ancient valour is not spent; from all parts of the country we have seen brave young volunteers rush to fight under the Savoyard banner' (*EI*, 1860, p.21).[40] In the war for the liberation of the Veneto (1866), the editor proclaimed: 'Your great country calls to you! ... respond to the appeal and show that you are worthy of your country and the freedom given to you'.[41] A sense of worthiness was part of the ideal of *Bildung*, which combined moral education with notions of character formation, integral to emancipationist teleology. In the first Jewish journal published in German from 1806, the *Sulamith*, a co-editor exhorted his readers: 'Show that you are worthy of the name citizen and subject.'[42]

It is the case that Italian Unification was achieved by a political elite of northerners and that only 2 per cent of the population were eligible to vote in the elections, but within that narrow band the Jews were a significant presence, as they possessed in a far higher proportion than non-Jews the requisites of electoral law: literacy, a taxable income or a recognized professional qualification. Thus, in some electoral colleges, their vote was influential.[43] With the electoral reform of 1882 when male suffrage was extended to all those who were literate, most Jews were able to vote and, with this 'political legitimization', it could be said that they gained admission to the middle class.[44] For the rest of the populace, mostly illiterate peasant farmers, unity meant very little.[45] Nevertheless, the Risorgimento ideals of this first period of liberalism (the Liberal State was to last until 1922) united a coterie of Christians and Jews. The latter, mainly middle class but not entirely so,[46] played a decisive role in the military conquests and political movements, demonstrating their *italianità* to the extent that they, in particular Piedmontese Jews such as Dan Vittorio Segre's great-grandfathers and grandfathers, felt themselves to be 'not only citizens but also the founding fathers of a new nation'.[47] The sense of a shared destiny, of common goals, of forging an Italian identity, however fragile,[48] was a turning point for Italian Jews. Elia Tagliacozzo, a 25-year-old Jew from Rome who was a *garibaldino* in 1866, kept a diary of his experiences which reveal the passionate patriotism of the volunteers. His parting telegram to his fiancée read: 'A greater duty calls me: MY COUNTRY' (*Un dovere più alto mi chiama: LA PATRIA*).[49] Similar sentiments consoled Eugenio Artom (1896–1975) during the dark days of the early 1940s when he began to write his own history of the period:

> The Risorgimento made Jews into citizens equal to all others; and they proved themselves worthy ... It is an exceptional episode because for the first time since the Diaspora, Jews have taken part in the life of another people, without limitations or restrictions ... it is an episode that has great significance in the history of Italy, since Italy is the only European nation that was unified in freedom and for freedom ... victory was achieved without religious oppression.[50]

This idealized Jewish perception had no 'corresponding image' on the Italian side, as large swathes of the population persisted in their hostility towards the Jews.[51]

A decade earlier, in 1933, the distinguished historian Arnaldo Momigliano (1908–87), then a young academic, wrote a short book review in which he presented his thesis of 'parallel nationalization' as an essential prerequisite in order to understand the integration of the Jewish minority:

> The development of an Italian national conscience for Jews is parallel to the formation of a national conscience by the Piedmontese, the Neapolitans, or the Sicilians; it is part of the same process and characterizes the process itself. Just as from the beginning of the seventeenth to the nineteenth century … the Piedmontese and the Neapolitans have become Italian, Jews living in Italy have at the same time become Italian … The major political figures of the Italian Risorgimento proved with facts that they understood that the emancipation of Jews vis-à-vis other Italian citizens was a major step for the creation of the Italian state. This slow but ultimately resolute acquisition of an Italian conscience, for which there is plenty of evidence, explains that throughout the Italian Risorgimento Jews were in the forefront.[52]

This passage has been quoted at some length since, more recently, Italian historians have reiterated the assertion in their own accounts of Jewish participation in the Risorgimento.[53] There has also been a critical re-evaluation of Momigliano's theory within Italian historiography that has been obfuscated to some extent by having been conflated with Gramsci's own immediate endorsement in an article entitled 'Judaism and Anti-Semitism', in which he inferred two fallacious corollaries from Momigliano's observations: that there was no anti-Semitism in Italy and that Jews abandoned Judaism.[54] Placing these views together as cause and effect is 'erroneous and misleading'.[55] Mario Toscano's observations on the subject have oscillated between acceptance and rejection in different publications;[56] for Michele Sarfatti, Momigliano's thesis still poses an open question in the reconstruction of events.[57] Simon Levis Sullam suggests that it owes much of its *fortuna* to Gramsci's citation. He holds the view that the contextualization of the review needs to be considered – the patriotic dimension and the rhetoric of the period in which it was written.[58] This revisionist perspective is problematic in that it challenges the theory on the basis of its composition in the fascist era and Momigliano's own political affiliations at that time. An evaluation based on documentary evidence of the Risorgimento, on the other hand, corroborates Momigliano's thesis, at least for the first phase of Unification (1821–70).[59]

In their sustained *italianità* in the post-Unification period, described by the poet David Levi as 'the religion of the Nation',[60] the Jews of Italy contributed to the foundation myths of their national history and the shaping of Italian identity.[61] Arnaldo Momigliano writes that 'this patriotism, this devotion to the new Italy of the Risorgimento, has been in our blood since the days of our great-grandfathers', adding, on a lighter note, that his grandmother wept every time she listened to the Italian national anthem.[62] Marianna Foà Uzielli, an inspector of Jewish schools and a central figure in Livornese society of the late nineteenth century, was so patriotic that her loyalty to Cavour was likened to that of a religious cult.[63] In

Michele Luzzati's edited volume on the Jews of Livorno, largely based on interviews, the picture emerges of a profound allegiance to Italy transmitted from generation to generation among the middle class.[64] Rita Castelli, born in 1913, recalls the pivotal influence of her father (born in 1865) who imbued his family with love for *la patria* and pride in their *italianità*. Among the cherished documents in the Ottolenghi household were a portrait of Mazzini and articles from *Il Pensiero Mazziniano*.[65] Gadi Luzzatto Voghera's great-grandfather made his family stand to attention in the railway carriage every time they crossed the river Piave by train when they were on holiday in the Dolomites, out of respect for the river 'that had saved' Italy.[66] In many of Massarani's speeches, which were published posthumously, there is conveyed 'an unshakeable devotion to the fatherland and the king'.[67] Towards the end of his life he wrote to Felice Momigliano that 'the ideal of the fatherland is equal to that of humanity'.[68] Felice Momigliano (1866–1924) was a teacher of philosophy, a socialist and a Zionist, who made his academic reputation with a monograph on Mazzini published in 1905.[69]

The family of Ernesto Nathan (1845–1921), who was the famous and popular Jewish mayor of Rome from 1907 to 1913, was steeped in the Risorgimento; their homes in London, Florence and Milan were 'open to patriots of democracy'. One evening in 1862, Garibaldi and his son dined at the Nathan's residence in Milan. When people in the neighbourhood heard about this momentous event, they begged to be given 'the cigar butts that the Hero had smoked in order to preserve them as precious relics'. Ernesto Nathan venerated Garibaldi; he was devoted to the 'Maestro' (Mazzini), considering him to be 'the new Moses'; he also befriended the Irredentist Felice Venezian.[70] The family of the two Rosselli brothers Carlo and Nello, murdered by the fascists in 1937, was staunchly patriotic: their maternal grandfather fought to defend Venice – at home he kept a piece of black bread 'like a relic', a symbol of the city besieged by the Austrian army in 1849 – and their cousin was Leone Pincherle, a minister in the provisional government. One of their mother's plays, *San Marco* (1913), was based on the events in Venice of 1848/49; in her memoirs she wrote of 'that sacred *italianità*', 'the pride of our *italianità*', of feeling 'first and foremost Italian'.[71] Cesare Lombroso (1835–1909), the renowned criminal anthropologist, came from a patriotic Piedmontese family. His mother gave shelter to political dissidents in the family house at Chieri. Lombroso himself, while a student at the University of Milan, engaged in clandestine activities and narrowly escaped arrest by the Austrian authorities.[72] Alexander Stille, in his study of five Italian Jewish families, writes that 'the star of the Ovazza family and that of the Italian nation rose together on a parallel course. As the war for Italian unification began, Ettore's grandfather, Vitta Ovazza, started life as a free man. For him, as for all Italian Jews, the processes of national unity and freedom were synonymous.' In 1860 the Ovazzas, prominent bankers from Turin, raised money to help finance Garibaldi's invasion of Sicily.[73] On 25 September 1870, five days after the breach of Porta Pia which brought an end to papal rule, the Jews of Rome sent a message to King Vittorio Emanuele II in which they stated that as 'a debt of gratitude' on attaining civil liberty, they would use the name *Israelita* for the last time; outside the synagogue they would remember that they were and would always be *Italiani e Romani*.[74]

Allegiance also extended to the royal family: 'On the death of Carlo Alberto, the Jews of Turin painted the sacred ark holding the Torah scrolls black.'[75] A non-Jew, Eugenio Righini, observed that Jews were more affected by the death of King Vittorio Emanuele II than the Gentiles. During a ceremony to commemorate the asassination of Umberto I in 1900, Giuseppe Foà, chief rabbi of Turin, went as far as to declare: 'we feel ourselves to be firstly Italians rather than Jews' (*Sentiamo di essere più che Israeliti, anzitutto Italiani*).[76] Enzo Levi (1889–1947), a lawyer from Modena who wrote his memoirs while in exile in the early 1940s, states that among 'very many middle-class Italian families, particularly Jewish ones', there was a blind veneration (*una venerazione cieca*) for the House of Savoy, and he was told that the Dreyfus case could not occur in Italy where equality was guaranteed by the Statute and 'by THE KING!' [*sic*]. His parents' genuine grief at Umberto I's untimely death was experienced as if it had been a family bereavement.[77] *Il Vessillo Israelitico* (*VI*) reported King Vittorio Emanuele III's visit to the new synagogue in Rome on 2 July 1904 in the following terms: many had tears in their eyes; most certainly they were comparing the present with the inequalities of the past. There was no doubt that the royal presence would increase, if that were possible, the 'deep affection' and the 'profound reverence for His Majesty the King and for the whole Royal Household' (*VI*, 1904, pp.345–8). The king, in his turn, in recognition of the Jews' entry into the new nation, conferred the titles of Grandi Ufficiali della Corona d'Italia on the president of the Jewish Community, Angelo Sereni, and on the architect and the civil engineer of the synagogue.[78] Jemolo recalls a Jewish family in Rome whose devoted affection towards the royal family could be traced for three generations from the 1840s.[79]

Royal names were popular among Jewish families of all classes. Many Jewish boys born between 1860 and 1864 in Ancona were called Carlo Alberto, Vittorio Emanuele and Umberto; girls were Margarita or Regina, even 'Italia'.[80] Members of the Di Veroli family of Rome, peddlers and shopkeepers for many years, were Umberto and Elena; Vittorio Foà of Turin was named after his maternal grandfather (born in 1850): 'Had King Vittorio Emanuele not confirmed the emancipation of the Jews, I would have been called Samuele or Abramo.'[81] Another indicator of Italianization was the adoption of a 'dual identity' in the register of births, a Jewish name combined with a non-Jewish one: Tedida alias Ida, Mardocheo alias Attilio, Mosè alias Marco;[82] and in some instances, the omission, later in life, of the Jewish name: for example, Israele Luigi Pisa, a successful banker in Milan, was known as Luigi Pisa in all official papers from the 1880s.[83] In census registers such as the one for Pitigliano of 1886, it is evident that a number of families dispensed with Jewish names in favour of ones that embodied *italianità* such as Dante, Regina, Garibaldi, Italo and, to reflect the first emancipation, Napoleone.[84] Marco Soria, in researching his antecedents, was able to document the transition from strong Sephardic traditions, typical of Livornese Jews, to those of Italy, reflecting the process of acculturation: the family trees of the nineteenth century that he found were written in Italian and all his ancestors had Italian names.[85]

INTEGRATION

With their patriotic commitment to a united Italy, Jews integrated into Italian society swiftly and effectively, despite entrenched discrimination. Arnaldo Momigliano describes this integration as 'the sudden explosion of initiative, creativity, intellectual and political responsibility'.[86] There was an exodus from the small semi-rural communities of central and northern Italy, where the Jews had been forced to live during the period of the ghettos, to cities such as Bologna, Florence, Genoa, Milan, Rome and Turin. Jewish contribution to the Italian nation was out of all proportion to their small number; they were prominent in every profession. Giuseppe Ottolenghi (1838–1904) became the first (unconverted) Jewish general in Europe in 1888 and later minister of war (1902/03) – the Jews' involvement in the wars of independence facilitated admission to the armed forces at the highest level with far less hostility than in other western European countries.[87] Italy also boasted the first Jewish prime minister, Luigi Luzzatti (1841–1927), who served from 1910 to 1911. They entered the civil service and politics: eleven Jewish members of parliament in 1871, compared to five in Austria, six in France, and eight in England, all countries with much larger Jewish populations; the first two Italian senators, nominated in 1876, were Isacco Artom and Tullo Massarani. Jews' participation in local and national politics reflected the whole political spectrum from the Historical Right of the Liberal Party to the Socialist and Communist Parties; nevertheless, the majority, as in other western European countries, remained moderate liberals.[88] In Italy they did not speak on Jewish affairs; indeed, they publicly avoided privileging their own social and religious specificity.[89] The editor of *Il Vessillo Israelitico* proudly listed the names of the Jewish members of parliament at national elections: 'the Jewish deputies ... are there to witness the equality that has been achieved' (*VI*, 1879, p.179).

Jews were also successful in higher education: of the 550 students attending the University of Pisa in 1872, 8 per cent were Jewish (*Il Corriere Israelitico* [*CI*], 1872, p.140), and by 1919, 6.3 per cent of university teachers were Jews (they comprised 1 per cent of the total population).[90] They contributed, in other words, to the national structure and economy of the country that had effected their emancipation. There are strong parallels with the Jews of France who were instrumental in 'constructing the Republic'; one has only to think of Adolphe Crémieux (1796–1880) and the Reinach brothers: 'so many state Jews pursued brilliant careers ... in the heart of the republican government, becoming deputies or ministers, generals, judges or prefects'.[91] By the end of the nineteenth century the Jewish elite had penetrated the upper echelons of Italian society and many had been ennobled for services to king and country. Toscano cites two emblematic figures: Graziadio Isaia Ascoli (1829–1907), considered to be the founder of modern Italian linguistics, and Ludovico Mortara (1855–1937), son of the chief rabbi of Mantua, who became not only a distinguished professor of law at several universities but also a senator (1910), head of the Supreme Court (1915), minister of justice (1919) and deputy prime minister (1919/20). They thus played a central role in two fundamental aspects of nation building, language and the law.[92] Of significance are the opening lines of Mortara's *Pagine autobiografiche*, written when he was in his seventies, as they document one Jew's experience of successful integration into the national life of his country: 'The story of my life is not worth keeping for posterity, but it may be interesting to recall the events that led the son of a rabbi ... who had no other prospect but to be either a rabbi or a businessman, to the position of Procurator General, the first President of the Supreme Court.'[93]

The Jewish press expressed pride in the achievements of their co-religionists in the intellectual and political life of the newly unified Italy. In every issue of *Il Vessillo Israelitico*, under the rubric 'News Items', correspondents' reports on their communities were published, detailing significant events and individuals who had distinguished themselves and were rewarded for so doing, thus recording the extent and level of social and cultural integration. For example, the editor enthused about the Milanese Jews' collaboration in the organization of the 1881 Industrial Exhibition: 'we are brothers, we are Italian' (*VI*, 1881, p.170).[94]

Fabio Levi dissents from what he calls the hasty and a priori interpretation of those who ascribe to the 'rapid and "natural" assimilation of the Jews in conjunction with the process of Unification'.[95] He argues that the phenomenon was not uniform, that it was geographically diverse and that much is not yet known for areas outside the principal cities. He provides statistics from the 1911 census which illustrate the uneven dispersion within the various employment sectors compared with the population as a whole: 8.15 per cent of Jews in agriculture (55.5 per cent of non-Jews); of that small percentage none were agricultural workers (*contadini*), but landowners; 27.19 per cent in industry (30.19 per cent); 41.57 per cent in commerce (5.63 per cent), a massive presence in the traditional Jewish occupation, though the level will have largely been transformed from peddler to shop owner, from usury to banking; 23.9 per cent in public administration and the liberal professions (8.6 per cent). Illiteracy accounts for the disparity in these last figures: in the 1901 census, 50 per cent of the non-Jewish population was recorded as illiterate in contrast to 5 per cent of Jews.[96] Studies on individual communities confirm Levi's data: for example, in Ancona, Livorno, Pisa and Turin the increase in the professions between 1861 and 1901 is striking, whereas the percentage engaged in commerce did not diminish; in fact, it was the major source of income for Jewish families.[97] Furthermore, the socio-economic conditions of the Jews of Rome support Fabio Levi's non-linear thesis. After over three centuries of a ghetto existence, from 1555 to 1870, the Jewish community of Italy's capital city was one of the largest and the most impoverished, numbering 4,705 in 1871, equivalent to 2.2 per cent of the population, approximately half of whom depended partially or entirely on charity. Contemporary accounts attest to the dank, dark and overcrowded dwellings near the river Tiber. Even by 1889, after the demolition of the ghetto and the formal establishment of the Jewish community, there was great deprivation: in that year 600 families received subsidies from charitable organizations. The poorest continued to live in the ghetto area, engaged in the stereotypical trade of the Jews, that of the itinerant peddler selling second-hand goods. In 1914, nearly 14 per cent of Rome's Jews were still in that occupation, demonstrating not only that many had not progressed beyond the centuries-old tradition of their ancestors, but also the lower level of social and economic integration. There was an elite which ran the community and participated in the life of the nation.[98]

However, it can be argued that the Jews of Rome constituted an anomaly: elsewhere in Italy, the transition from artisan to small business to professional class was effected within one or two generations of emancipation.[99] In Livorno, for example, by 1861, five of the forty-one surgeons were Jews and six of the twenty-four general practitioners.[100] In Florence, according to figures published in *Il Corriere Israelitico*, in a community of 2,359 in 1870, 4 per cent belonged to the professions; a third were engaged in business, and there was a very small 'working class', fifty-six Jews in total (*CI*, 1872, pp.109–10). In a recent study, it has been shown that 'the structure of the wealth of the [Florentine] nobility ... and that of the Jewish bankers ... followed the same tendencies'.[101] In Pisa, many Jews were doctors, lawyers or engineers; four were university professors, and the local textile industry was largely Jewish owned (*CI*, 1872, pp.139–40); by the beginning of the twentieth century, the public image of middle-class Jews in Pisa was indistinguishable from that of others in the same social stratum.[102] On a micro-level, Funaro cites the case of Angiolo Funaro, a dyer from Livorno married to the daughter of a butcher (in 1853), who ensured that his own offspring, male and female, gained professional qualifications: his three sons studied at university and his three daughters became primary schoolteachers. Through his correspondence, 'Angiolo reveals great awareness of the value of education as a factor in personal and social development.'[103] In the 1860s, Vitta Ovazza, who was born in the ghetto of Turin, founded a successful bank and purchased not only an elegant townhouse in the city but also an eighteenth-century villa in the countryside that had once been the property of a member of the royal family. The Ovazzas 'assimilated rapidly, living a life virtually indistinguishable from that of other Italian upper middle-class families'.[104]

For the first time since the establishment of the ghettos in the sixteenth century, Jews in many regions of Italy had the possibility of becoming landowners (they had been permitted to own property in some Habsburg areas since the eighteenth century). Dan Vittorio Segre's grandfather bought a castle that had belonged to the dukes of Genoa; his father was also a landowner and became mayor of a small village in Piedmont where the majority of the population were peasants working on his land.[105] Wealthy Milanese Jews invested in landed property, hunting lodges, country mansions and seaside villas in the most desirable locations. By the end of the nineteenth century, their ownership of real estate was comparable in value to that of members of the Lombard aristocracy. They also acquired the most sought-after boxes at the opera house of La Scala, adjacent to those of the nobility and high-ranking government officials; to own one in the first row was symbolic of one's social status.[106] Important business decisions were often made within the confines of exclusive clubs, and by the 1890s the Jews of Milan comprised 2.5 per cent of the membership of the Union Club (Circolo dell'Unione), and 2.7 per cent of the Garden Society (Società del Giardino); in short they had become 'bourgeois par excellence in the most bourgeois of Italian cities'.[107] In these ways – and the same can be said of the Jews of other conurbations – they contributed to the creation of the modern bourgeoisie of Italy. Upward socio-economic mobility and integration were shared by all the emancipated, urbanized Jews of western Europe.[108] The sons of Jewish businessmen no longer wished to follow in their fathers' footsteps and strove to achieve intellectual and professional status, which was often combined with a rejection of the habitual mores.[109] One striking and emblematic case is that of Alfred Dreyfus: the grandson of a peddler and a kosher butcher, the son of a successful textile manufacturer from eastern France, Dreyfus was trained at the École Supérieure de Guerre and became an infantry captain bound for a glittering career at the centre of France's military machine.[110] Migration to the cities and new opportunities – educational, occupational, political and cultural – transformed the traditional life of the Jewish people in nineteenth-century Europe.[111] Luzzatto Voghera sounds a note of caution against a too bland and even distorted analysis of the consequences of emancipation: in many of the large communities in Italy, for example, not only in Rome, but also in Livorno, Turin and Venice, throughout the period under discussion, there remained sections of the Jewish population who were poor and had to rely on charitable institutions for survival.[112]

The journey from tradition to modernity, from the enclosed and unchanging world of the ghetto to the acquisition of civic and political equality, posed dangers for the ancient rituals and beliefs of Judaism. The transformation, over several generations, of moving from segregated Judaism to a fusion with society at large, was complex and challenging, and it was central to the experiences of western European Jews in the second half of the nineteenth century. In David Vital's view, 'the process of assimilation hinged on retaining membership in two, in important respects incompatible and traditionally hostile, cultures – or, with greater traumatic effects, seeking to pass from one to the other entirely'.[113] Rather than interpreting the process of assimilation in opposition to traditional Judaism – the position of Vital, Zygmunt Bauman and others[114] – recent historiography has eschewed this dichotomous vision to make allowances for a multilayered approach: Jewish identity, with modernity, was not irrevocably eroded, but was transformed and redefined in myriad ways.[115]

'From Italian Jews to Jewish Italians' (*da ebrei italiani a italiani ebrei*) is the expression used by three Italian writers to illustrate the emergence of a new kind of Jew: the emancipated, liberal Jew for whom affiliation to traditional mores was altered.[116] According to Maurizio Molinari, Italian Jews faced three choices with regard to their identity: to assimilate to the detriment of their Jewishness; to retreat into their communities to the detriment of their *italianità*; to attempt the path of integration while retaining their ethnic and religious diversity: in other words, to endeavour to cultivate a dual identity, Italian and Jewish, the latter being retained through the celebration of the major religious festivals, endogamy and the practice of circumcision.[117] One can note the parallel transformation in the nineteenth century of the term *Israélite français* to *Français israélite*, reflecting not only the integration of Jews into French society but also their allegiance to France: 'Jewish spokesmen ... objected to using *Israélite* as a noun, precisely because it conveyed an ethnic meaning, whereas the adjectival form had the reduced connotation of a religious affiliation.'[118] During the first emancipation, in order to encourage a positive perception of the Jews in France, Berr Isaac Berr, in an essay of 1805, advocated the replacement of *Juif*, which had negative connotations, with the term *Israélite*. This change of collective name to designate their new role in French society was also favoured by the editor of the first Jewish periodical in French, *L'Israélite français*, in 1817, reiterating Berr's views.[119] The term *Israélite* was adopted for official institutions and publications in France and elsewhere in Europe, as exemplified in the titles of Italian Jewish periodicals and their communities, which were renamed *Università israelitica*. In Austria and Germany there was a sustained effort to adopt this terminology, but it was not so widespread; both *Israelitischer* and *Jüdischer* were used in the names of Jewish organizations.[120] In practice it proved problematic to avoid the word *juif/ebreo* in sustained prose, and in fact these nouns and their derivatives were used interchangeably with *israélite/israelita* with no semantic differentiation, sometimes within the same paragraph. However, it was the case that anti-Semites did not speak or write of *Israélites/Israeliti*.[121]

INDIVIDUAL NARRATIVES

The study of individuals is a useful methodological tool to illustrate the plurality of approaches in the reformulation of Jewish identity.[122] Within that framework, three broad groups emerge: those who were young adults in 1848 and aspired to 'normalization', for whom 'the first commandment was integration into the liberal fatherland'.[123] Dan Vittorio Segre boldly declares that the 'exhilarating situation' experienced by his Piedmontese forbears psychologically and morally justified 'abandonment of their ancestral traditions'. They believed they were both ' "true Italians" and "true Jews" – a hybrid situation'.[124] The second group, those who reached maturity between 1855 and 1875, thought they had achieved 'normalization' and were fully integrated; and the third category, born between 1875 and 1910, developed a sense of unease and disaffection with the consequences of emancipation; they either detached themselves from Judaism completely through intermarriage and conversion, or re-engaged with their Jewish heritage through Zionism.[125]

Caviglia suggests that the price of high office was the diminution of Judaism in its traditional forms, borne out by an editorial comment from *Il Corriere Israelitico* when General Giuseppe Ottolenghi was promoted to minister of war: 'Jews, dazzled by success, have assimilated in word and soul. We ask that they retain a Jewish soul where neither politics nor economics enters ... we do not ask much if we hope that General Ottolenghi, amongst his thoughts about the army, does not forget the synagogue.'[126] In some cases, patriotism and citizenship replaced religious faith. Enrico Fano, member of parliament and senator, stipulated in his will of 1899 that he should be buried in the part of the cemetery common to all religions, as 'the only religion I have ever professed is that of love for my country and my fellow men'. The list of bequests were not the religious objects often itemized in the wills of preceding generations, but those of a man who had actively participated in the national life of his country, which included five medals as a member of parliament for Milan, a portrait given to him by Umberto I, and an edition of Dante's *Divine Comedy*.[127]

TULLO MASSARANI

Tullo Massarani (1826–1905), literary critic, art historian, *assessore* of the Milan council, secretary and then president of the provincial council, member of parliament and senator, was one of the most prominent Jews in public life, but he did not write on Jewish matters unless pressed to do so, and his responses were evasive. For example, when in 1892 the lawyer Leone Ravenna requested him to formally protest to the editor of a Milanese newspaper who had published anti-Semitic remarks containing references to ritual murder, Massarani, in his reply, refused to do so, stating that he was of the opinion that it was not 'opportune to raise a controversy on a past matter'. He would ask another co-religionist to speak to the editor. He added that the only way for persecuted races to combat intolerance was to emulate good citizenship and, without ostentation, to demonstrate in word and deed that they could surpass others in honesty, charity and patriotism. To be esteemed by others, one had to 'be worth more' (*valere di più*). In 1893, he rejected a request to assist in the publication of an article on the Jewish poet David Levi, stating that the tenor of his work was not 'opportune in these times'. In the same letter he expressed the view that the reason anti-Semitism had not taken root in Italy was due to the fact that Italian Jews had not accentuated a distinctive appearance of a race apart which would harm 'that complete assimilation which must be the desire of every citizen who is loyal to his country'. In another letter of the same year, he wrote that he hoped the new synagogue of Rome would be of modest and restrained proportions and that it should not, even in a symbolic way, give expression to a past of 'extinct nationalities'. To Dante Lattes, editor of *Il Corriere Israelitico*, who had sent him some of his Zionist publications, he replied that although he was filled with admiration for Lattes's erudition, he could not share his ideas, as Italy was a country where 'assimilation of all its citizens is close to achievement in both customs and legislation'.[128] Massarani did not deny his Jewish faith; it was a private matter.[129] The identity Massarani wished to convey in the public domain was that of a fully integrated, patriotic Italian citizen, an identity without diversity.

ALESSANDRO D'ANCONA

For Alessandro D'Ancona (1835–1914), who was professor of Italian at the University of Pisa (1860–1900), director of the Scuola Normale di Pisa (1893–1900), the first editor of the daily newspaper *La Nazione* of Florence (1859/60), founder of the *Rassegna bibliografica della letteratura italiana* (1893), senator (1904) and mayor of Pisa (1906/07), his Jewishness, 'the race to which, not of my choice, I belong ... that Semitic name ... that fate has imposed on me',[130] was imbued with ambivalence. At every stage of his career he experienced discrimination, and it was for this reason that he refused to enter national politics; the idea that he would always be publicly referred to as a Jew in election campaigns was insufferable to him.[131] His detachment from religious practices occurred early in his life and is evident in his private correspondence. There was also tension in his marriage, as his wife was strictly orthodox (her parents had initially opposed the match), yet somewhat reluctantly he permitted her to keep a kosher kitchen.[132] D'Ancona's views on religion are conveyed in several of his essays: although born into a specific religion, he practised no rites, but had great respect for all religions, which with mutual tolerance would eventually converge 'in a common house of God'.[133] Thus he did not take up Dante Lattes's invitation to contribute to *Il Corriere Israelitico* and, like Massarani, expressed his absolute dissension from Lattes's Zionist ideology;[134] nor, despite living in Florence later in life, did he have any contact with the young disciples of Rabbi Margulies's circle. As Mauro Moretti states, not much is known about his relationship with the Jewish community of Pisa, although among those who subscribed to his Festschrift in 1900, there were several leading members of the community, and some information emerges from his correspondence with his wife. *Il Vessillo Israelitico* regularly reported on his activities, emphasizing 'our illustrious co-religionist's' integration into the national and social life of Italy (*VI*, 1914, p.637): at his daughter's wedding it was noted that the best of Pisa society attended; his funeral cortège was accompanied by eminent figures both Jewish and Catholic.[135] Nevertheless, although his prolific scholarly output contains few Jewish themes, there is a certain attention to anti-Semitism in previous centuries and in his own times. As editor of *La Nazione*, he wrote several articles about the Mortara case in order to put pressure on European public opinion, and he closely followed the Dreyfus Affair, expressing (both publicly and privately) admiration for a spirited defence of the Jewish race by his French colleague Gaston Paris, a leading medieval philologist.[136] In his *Ricordi ed Affetti*, two aspects are striking: D'Ancona's complete identification with Italian culture and his total commitment to the Italian nation and the House of Savoy, epitomized in his patriotic speech delivered on 20 September 1892 at the inauguration of a monument to Vittorio Emanuele II in Pisa.[137] In a letter to Gaston Paris he stated: 'Questioning myself, I find neither drop of blood ... nor feeling or thought that is not wholly and sincerely Italian.'[138] Lattes observed in his obituary of D'Ancona that his roots were too deep in the historical spirit of his country, in the Risorgimento ideals of tolerance and equality for which he had fought, to conceive the necessity for a resurgence of Jewish nationalism.[139]

LUIGI LUZZATTI

There is a consensus that Luigi Luzzatti (1841–1927), Italy's first and only Jewish prime minister, represents arguably the most famous and 'classic' case of assimilation.[140] In his memoirs, dictated in 1926 towards the end of his life, Luzzatti carefully cultivated his public persona for posterity: from his religious and patriotic upbringing in Venice (when the brief republic fell, an Austrian officer housed in the family home referred to 8-year-old Luigi as 'the little rebel') to his rational decision, at the age of 16, to abandon Judaism in favour of deism combined with a deep respect for all religions.[141] He also accounted for the reassertion of his Jewish identity which only becomes significant in the face of anti-Semitism: 'I was born Jewish and I proudly return as such every time I am attacked for so being ... there is dignity in withstanding the weight of persecution and it would be cowardly to eschew it. But apart from this, my education, my aspirations are directed towards a broadly-based Christianity, as is evident in my writings.'[142] Dante Lattes was scathing in his attacks on Luzzatti for this stance: in one article, he writes: 'Luigi Luzzatti, in spite of his fear of being a Jew, often finds himself in the presence of some troublesome person who reminds him of this little misfortune in his life' (*CI*, 1912, pp.59–60). Another piece is 'The honourable Luzzatti for the Catholic League and against the Jewish religion' (*CI*, 1909, pp.361–2), and 'Luzzatti against Buddhism and for Christianity ... Luzzatti was not in one of those moments when *he returns to being a Jew*' [sic] (*CI*, 1913, pp.191–3). However, in the same year Lattes praised him for his public defence of Romanian Jews (*CI*, 1913, pp.211–13), and his obituary of Luzzatti of 31 March 1927 in *Israel* is muted with melancholy that such a great man, 'this wonderful product of his race ... was unable to ... understand ... the universal values of Israel'.[143] Luzzatti, like most Jews, was deeply affected by the Dreyfus case, to the point that he wrote to his friends in France that he would not set foot 'in a country from which human justice had been banished', until Dreyfus was rehabilitated.[144] In 1921, Luzzatti addressed a 'Message to the Jews of Palestine, with special greetings to the agricultural cooperatives'. Their reply was in Hebrew, with instructions for it to be translated in Rome and sent on to Luzzatti. This deliberate use of Hebrew was 'to emphasize their own religious, ethnic and also national identity'.[145] A year after his death, in an article in *Israel*, Sabatino Lopez, a Jewish scholar and playwright, suggested that Luzzatti's defence of other religions and the freedom of worship 'was very Jewish ... it could be said ... that he was more Jewish than he thought'.[146]

THE ARTOM FAMILY

In 1981, Guido Artom (1906–82) published a historical novel based on the lives of his paternal and maternal great-grandfathers, Raffaele Artom (1795–1859) and Zaccaria Ottolenghi (1797–1868), who came from Asti. In his meticulous reconstruction of this Jewish community based on archival research, the main theme is the transformation of their world from the ghetto to the European political stage. Born just before the first emancipation, they were the only Jewish boys to attend the local grammar school, where they excelled. They had barely taken the final examinations before Napoleon was defeated and Austrian rule reimposed the former restrictions on the Jews. Consequently, Raffaele's plans to study law at the University of Turin were thwarted. During that brief period of freedom (1800–15), Raffaele's father had rented a house in the countryside during the spring and summer; thus, after many centuries, the children of the ghetto could breathe the fresh air and sit beneath the shade of a tree to read and play (the house, known as il Chiossetto, was later purchased by the family). While Zaccaria entered his father's business, eventually becoming an extremely wealthy man, Raffaele harboured dreams of liberty and equality, the right to serve one's country as an equal citizen. These ideals were realized through his sons, for whom he ensured the educational opportunities denied to him. And it was his youngest son, Isacco Artom (1829–1900), who fulfilled them at the highest level: he was the first Jew to pursue a diplomatic career; he became Cavour's private secretary in 1858; a member of staff of the Italian embassy in Paris; chief secretary at the Italian Foreign Office; from 1870 to 1876, Under-Secretary of State for Foreign Affairs; and, in 1876, one of the first senators of the Italian parliament.[147] His son was, in other words, one of the protagonists in the making of the new Italy. He was the embodiment of the emancipated Jew who had made the transition from the ghetto to the modern world.[148] However, in so doing, Isacco Artom distanced himself from religious orthodoxy. In the year of national Unification, he wrote to Alessandro D'Ancona that if Jews were no longer needed to teach Hebrew, they had a clearly defined mission: to be open to the free exchange of ideas; to place their abilities at the service of everyone, leaving behind vain nostalgia for a vanished past.[149] In another letter to D'Ancona, he light-heartedly suggested that they would both benefit from re-reading the Bible.[150] Nevertheless, Artom remained loyal to his Jewish origins, becoming a member of the Alliance Israélite Universelle from its inception in 1860 and, together with Sansone D'Ancona (Alessandro's brother) who was a member of parliament, he put pressure on the ministry of foreign affairs on behalf of the Alliance regarding the persecution of the Jews in Romania, Russia and Morocco.[151] In 1865, he wrote to a member of the Rothschild family to obtain financial support for the construction of a new synagogue in Turin.[152]

Moreover, when *Il Vessillo Israelitico* congratulated him on becoming a senator, he responded by saying: 'I hope my co-religionists' support will always abide with me' (*VI*, 1876, p.205). In his will, dated 26 October 1892, he bequeathed considerable sums to four kindergartens, Jewish and non-Jewish and, as a further gesture of his *italianità*, he stipulated that a scholarship of 1,000 lire was to be awarded to a young man of Asti from a poor family, to enable him to study either mathematics or medicine at the University of Turin. His Jewish identity is expressed through his bequest to a Jewish charitable organization and his desire to be buried in the family tomb in the Jewish cemetery of Asti.[153]

MEMOIRS AND AUTOBIOGRAPHIES

Like Isacco Artom, both Giuseppe Levi (1814–74) and Salvatore De Benedetti (1818–91) defined themselves in terms of what each individual could offer in the formation of the new Liberal State.[154] While Artom's vision was essentially secular, the other two believed that the dissemination of their Jewish cultural heritage was a valid contribution. Thus Levi became the founder editor of the first important Jewish periodical, *L'Educatore Israelita*, and De Benedetti became the first professor of Hebrew Studies. Levi wrote two autobiographies, one in the form of letters in the periodical itself and the other in book form, *Autobiografia di un padre di famiglia*, and De Benedetti provided further information on Levi in his biographical note, published two years after Levi's death. While Levi's *Autobiografia* focuses on the family as the locus and cornerstone of civilized society, permeated with patriotic sentiment – one chapter is entitled 'Family and Country' – the epistolary version aimed to present the positive role of the Jew in the present in contrast to the difficulties and obstacles encountered in the past.[155] Thus it was left to De Benedetti to record Giuseppe Levi's many achievements: rabbi, editor of the aforementioned journal until his death; president of the Jewish community of Vercelli; president of the first conference of Jewish communities, held in Ferrara in 1863; teacher at the prestigious Collegio Foa in Vercelli; influential member of the Alliance Israélite Universelle; author of scholarly and pedagogic works on Judaism; translator from and into Hebrew; nominated *Cavaliere* by the Italian government. At his death, citizens of all faiths attended his funeral; in his will, he left bequests to both Catholic and Jewish charities. He was, states De Benedetti, an example to the young, working for Jewish integration as a Jew within the new Italy.[156] Alberto Cavaglion argues for a rediscovery, a reappraisal of 'the wisdom of the generation that came out of the ghetto: Isacco Artom, David Levi, Marco and Ludovico Mortara, Salvatore De Benedetti, David Castelli and Graziadio Isaia Ascoli, men who cultivated the hope of making their Jewish patrimony accessible to everyone'.[157]

Whereas neither Giuseppe Levi nor De Benedetti wished to return to the days when the only avenues open to Jews were either commerce or the rabbinate,[158] for Marco Mordechai Momigliano from Mondovì (1825–1900), who became chief rabbi of Bologna, the past was everything: in his *Autobiografia di un Rabbino italiano*, first published in 1897 to mark his fiftieth year as a rabbi and to celebrate the inauguration of the new synagogue in Bologna, he candidly and nostalgically recalls the happy times of his youth when religious faith and traditions were upheld. He laments the passing of the security and spirituality of the ghetto that for centuries had defined Jewish identity. The didactic aim of his memoir is 'to reignite the spark of that faith which every day is unfortunately being extinguished' in his fellow Jews, whom he saw moving towards a pernicious assimilation. He notes with regret that the Sabbath is profaned; the Sabbath lamp is not lit in the family home; religious instruction is neglected; Hebrew is no longer studied; no one knows the history of their people; children grow up deprived of any religious feeling.[159] As Cavaglion remarks, Marco Momigliano seemed unaware of significant political events and had no intention of relating that many of his nephews became socialists, so immersed was he in the pre-1848 world.[160]

Through the stories of his mother and grandmother, Arturo Carlo Jemolo (1891–1981), the noted historian and jurist, portrays a nostalgic evocation of the confined world of the ghetto areas of Mondovì and Ceva (Piedmont) where religious traditions remained unchanged within the 'security of isolation', even thirty years or so after emancipation. He also succinctly conveys the poverty, the ill-health, generational conflicts and the stifling atmosphere where the slightest infringement of ritual was condemned.[161]

Marco Besso (1843–1920), in contrast to Marco Momigliano, criticized those who had 'a blind respect for the past', arguing that many orthodox practices which in the earlier times of exclusion had their significance were no longer relevant to the social and public life of civilized countries.[162] He recalls his youthful 'indifference … even repugnance' to all that was religious, yet in middle age, between 1889 and 1890, he had daily Hebrew lessons with a rabbi, based on the Pentateuch which he had hated studying as a boy.[163] Besso was born in Trieste and pursued a successful career in the Assicurazioni Generali of Venice, eventually becoming president in 1909. He also played his part in the unification of Italy and records his involvement with the National Committee in Rome in the 1860s – 'I participated with that fervour borne of intense faith ... and love that aspired to the liberation of Rome';[164] his reputation as an Irredentist in his relations with the Austrian government; and his marriage to Ernesta Pesaro Maurogonato, daughter of the 'illustrious patriot'.[165] He had been encouraged to write his memoirs by his wife and son, and his aim was to narrate his own experiences which might assist future generations. The legacy he bequeathed his beloved country is the Fondazione Marco Besso, established in 1918 and still thriving today as one of the most richly endowed libraries in private hands. By the end of his life, Besso had reconciled his dual identity as a Jew and as an Italian, reconnecting with the ancient language of his forbears that he had repudiated as a boy; he opened his library, specializing in Dante studies and the history of Rome and Etruscology, to the nation to disseminate Italian culture.[166]

THE FRANCHETTI FAMILY

Mirella Scardozzi, in her study of members of the Franchetti family, presents 'the gamut of different possible ways of living their Jewishness'.[167] Raimondo Franchetti (1829–1905) inherited a baronetcy from his father in 1858 and in the same year married Sara Louise Rothschild of the Vienna branch, thus entering the European Jewish élite; among his many attributes, he is credited with saving the glass industry of Murano. His son Giorgio bought and restored Ca' d'Oro, the fifteenth-century palazzo on Venice's Grand Canal, bequeathing it to the nation in 1916; another son, Alberto, was a noted composer, admired by Verdi and D'Annunzio.[168] Raimondo's cousin Augusto (1840–1905), a lawyer, seemed to embody 'the perfect conciliation between Jewish identity and civil, patriotic commitment':[169] from 1872 to 1899, he was president of the Jewish community of Florence, overseeing the inauguration of the magnificent new synagogue in 1882, and honorary president of the Rabbinical College when it was transferred from Rome. Also in 1872, he became secretary of the Philological Society (Circolo filologico), one of the most influential cultural associations of its day, founded by the noted politician Ubaldino Peruzzi de' Medici with whom Augusto became close friends. In his role as mediator between the Jewish minority and Florentine society, Augusto Franchetti was able to assist the former through his contacts with the latter. Thus he introduced his younger cousin Leopoldo (1847–1917) to Ubaldino Peruzzi in November 1872, no doubt a useful connection to launch a promising parliamentary career. Leopoldo Franchetti's report on Sicily (1876), co-written with the politician Sidney Sonnino, is still considered an authoritative source, especially with regard to Leopoldo's analysis of the Mafia. Leopoldo Franchetti became a member of parliament in 1882 and a senator in 1909. In addition, he engaged in paternalisitic philanthropy: at his country villa in Umbria, he established a primary school with free tuition for the children of his estate employees; it was there that Maria Montessori tested her innovative pedagogic methods. In his will, he left the villa to a charity and the land to those who worked it. His connections with Judaism were tenuous, although he made a late marriage to a young woman of Jewish origins.[170] The Franchetti family thus reflected their integration in Italian society through the myriad avenues of economics, philanthropy, politics, culture, the liberal professions and the landed aristocracy, retaining at the same time their Jewish identity, however marginal in some cases.

CARLO ALBERTO VITERBO, ARNALDO MOMIGLIANO AND ENZO LEVI

In 1898 a group of Jewish students from Turin invited eminent writers to contribute articles to mark the occasion of the fiftieth anniversary of their emancipation; these included the prominent Zionist Max Nordau (1849–1923). He wrote:

> Up to 1848, you Jews of Italy were Italian Jews [*italienische Juden*]. Since then you have been Jewish Italians [*jüdische Italiener*]. What will you be in the future, purely and simply Italians, without even the adjective "Jewish" which is a reminder of your past? People ... tell me that the majority of Italian Jews – excuse me – of Jewish Italians, have forgotten their origins, have no longer any Jewish interest, do not know or want to know the history of their people ... Is this true?[171]

'For my family, at least, this was perfectly true', writes Dan Vittorio Segre. His parents (second-generation post-emancipation), although proud of being Jewish, had little knowledge of Jewish culture; his mother was not taught Hebrew. They grew up 'in a climate of obsolete Judaism and of vigorous Italian nationalism'.[172] Carlo Alberto Viterbo (1889–1974) recalls his complete ignorance of Judaism which, in his assimilated (*assimilatissima*) family, was considered something that had been left behind (*cosa superata*) belonging to a recent past of discrimination and humiliation which must never return (*che non dovevano ritornare*). It was indeed as if the adjective 'Jewish' had been expunged from his upbringing: 'I was full of prejudice and hostility, almost an "anti-semite" without realizing it. My brother and I barely knew that we were Jewish.'[173] Arnaldo Momigliano (1908–87) notes that among his own generation he was one of the few to have had a strictly orthodox education, and that 'the need to create a balance between the Jewish and the Italian side of ourselves conditioned our lives on a daily basis'.[174]

For Enzo Levi, the changes between 1880 and 1910 were perceived in a positive and, in some respects and with hindsight, an overly optimistic light: his father could study and qualify as a lawyer; there was closer integration between Jews and Catholics, not only on a professional level but also socially. Consequently, the antagonism and hostility, causing Catholics to regard Jews as inferior and Jews to see Catholics as persecutors and enemies, gradually disappeared: 'Jews were like freed prisoners who had to forget their cruel and unjust imprisonment.' This 'fusion' between Catholics and Jews was, in his view, fully developed by 1920. In order, perhaps, to affect his own 'fusion' with the host society, he eschewed religious practices that seemed to him unjustifiable, even absurd. He did not have a religious marriage; his sons were not circumcised; he did not provide a religious education for his children. The repercussions caused much pain to his parents and relatives, and personal inner turmoil – later in exile he returned to the faith of his forbears and expressed pleasure that his children became observant Jews.[175]

The effects of assimilation had a totally different impact on Carlo Alberto Viterbo – both he and Enzo Levi were born in the same year, 1889. Viterbo was brought up in almost total ignorance of Judaism. At university he met Alfonso Pacifici (1889–1981), a fellow undergraduate from a similar middle-class background who had rediscovered his Jewish identity. Viterbo was, in his words, 'shaken, awakened and guided' (*scosso, risvegliato, guidato*) by his friend, who in turn introduced him to the charismatic chief rabbi of Florence, Samuel Hirsch Margulies: 'Margulies took it upon himself to make of me a Jew ... with all the affection a father has for a son who had gone astray.'[176] Viterbo not only pursued his legal profession but also his Jewish activities, much to the consternation and disapproval of his parents, who 'barely tolerated my deviation from the assimilatory line ... believing that I was compromising my career as a lawyer'.[177] In 1920, he was a member of the short-lived Zionist administrative council of the Florence Jewish community. He later became president of the Italian Zionist Federation and editor of *Israel* until his death in 1974.[178] In Augusto Segre's opinion, through his presence at conferences and his contributions to *Israel*, Viterbo 'gave lustre and distinction to the whole of Italian Judaism';[179] Zionism reshaped his identity.

AUGUSTO SEGRE, GIANCARLO SACERDOTI AND MEMO BEMPORAD

Augusto Segre (1915–80), a rabbi and son of a rabbi, also espoused the Zionist cause in reaction to the environment of Casale Monferrato where 'assimilation entered Jewish homes with the fury of a flood', and where even the president of the Jewish community married out and 'succeeded in being accepted by the local bourgeoisie' who retained, in Segre's view, 'some reservations about the Jews, not devoid of envy'.[180] In his ideological orientation, Segre was influenced by his father's Zionist activities and contacts with Dante Lattes – Segre was to become a close friend when a student in Rome – and others in Europe and Palestine. Segre's first Zionist activity was to open the blue collection boxes of the Jewish National Fund which were distributed to a few families, since others 'refused to have such a compromising object in their homes'. Segre describes Casale Monferrato as 'the national centre and promoter of anti-Zionism',[181] due in part to the fact that *Il Vessillo Israelitico* was published there and its first editor was hostile to the Zionist movement. Thus, in his memoirs, apart from many pages on Dante Lattes whom he calls 'Maestro', Segre devotes the first section to a nostalgic narrative of the older members' recollections of the Jewish community and its traditions, an account 'so rare that it is bound to acquire historical significance for Italian Jews'.[182] In the post-Second World War period, among the positions Segre held were professor of Jewish History and Thought at the Rabbinical College in Rome, Secretary General of the Italian Zionist Federation, and editor of the *Rassegna Mensile di Israel* (Jewish Monthly Review); he was also the author of scholarly works on various aspects of Judaism.

The memoirs of Giancarlo Sacerdoti (1929–) were published in the same series as those of Segre, 'The Facts of History', edited by Renzo de Felice. Sacerdoti's details of various family members who became doctors, lawyers, civil servants, literary scholars and academics – an aunt married Attilio Momigliano – indicate successful integration. The same can be said for Rodolfo De Benedetti's account of his own family, which included two uncles who carried out radical agrarian reforms in Piedmont, and also for that of Memo Bemporad, born in 1905, whose paternal great-grandfather had set up a textile factory and a small village, called La Briglia, for the employees, with a school and theatre, seven kilometres from Prato in Tuscany.[183] Bemporad says of his grandfather and father who expanded the factory, 'the intention of these new citizens ... was to do well', citing Dante's phrase *ben fare*.[184] In his preface to Sacerdoti, De Felice posits the view that had it not been for the racial persecution of the 1930s, the Jewish middle class in Italy would be completely assimilated. This emerges from Sacerdoti's pages 'unequivocally'.[185] In his recollections of his family history, Sacerdoti does not dwell on his Jewishness except with respect to the racial laws and the war. However, he discloses that his maternal grandmother's will – she died in 1942 – contained the words 'I beseech my children and grandchildren to always retain the Jewish faith in which Providence has placed them.'[186]

FAMILY LIFE

What emanates most forcefully from the pages of these memoirs is the parents' role in religious education: for example, Besso's father made him read passages from the Pentateuch every day after school, and Luigi Luzzatti's father's life 'alternated between work and the synagogue'.[187] The role of the family as custodian of Jewish traditions, as 'the sphere of religious rituals',[188] 'where Jewish identity is shaped',[189] was fundamental. As Della Pergola observes, Judaism is more than a theological doctrine, it is a way of life; thus it is possible to measure 'the modalities of religious intensity' of groups and individuals.[190] Paula Hyman, Monica Miniati and Marion Kaplan privilege the role of women in the domestic sphere in the preservation and transmission of Judaism. Kaplan argues that women, as well as retaining their rich cultural and religious legacy, were also 'agents ... of integration', ensuring that their children adopted the manners and speech 'crucial to bourgeois class formation', and that they 'forged a modern Jewish identity'.[191] Through articles in the Jewish press, in sermons and pedagogical publications, rabbis expounded on the ideal qualities that a woman should possess in her traditional roles of wife and mother; on the importance of sound religious instruction in order to fulfil 'her saintly mission', her 'sacred duties' within 'the sanctuary of the family' for 'the preservation of the highest spiritual values'.[192] The Bat Mitzvah was introduced to Italian communities from the 1840s.[193]

Through the examination of individual cases, it is clear that in the post-emancipation period there was a wide range of religious views from the orthodox to the merely residual vestiges of a Jewish *quid*. Arnaldo Momigliano writes: 'our religion was all in the family ... I cannot separate my domestic feelings from the everyday religious ceremonies that our family celebrated ... My real experience with Judaism consists in an intense, austere, domestic piety: children who are blessed by their fathers on Friday nights; mothers who embrace their husbands and children.'[194] Fausto Coen recalls that one of his earliest memories was his mother making him repeat the *Shema* every night.[195] In Dan Vittorio Segre's household, it was the devoted family servant Annetta, a devout Christian, who presided over the Passover celebrations and ensured that as a child he recited the *Shema*.[196] Memo Bemporad's maternal grandparents were very religious, and thus three or four times a year, he was taken by his parents to Florence where they lived to attend synagogue.[197] From the oral family histories of Livornese Jews, a fairly uniform picture was conveyed to the interlocutors which, Luzzati suggests, reflected the majority position at the end of the nineteenth century: a detachment from orthodoxy; very little knowledge of Hebrew; infrequent use of Jewish terminology in daily language; Jewish names no longer adopted; kosher dietary rules not adhered to; few religious objects in the home; but religious rites observed at birth and death; attendance at the main religious festivals; and importance given to the Bar Mitzvah. This could be conflated into the definition 'good Jews, but not orthodox', combined with strong links to the Jewish community from all social classes. Every one wished to convey a sense of religiousness, however tenuous, as the essential characteristic of being Jewish, defined by Herbert Gans as 'symbolic Judaism',[198] even among those who had contracted exogamous marriages.[199] In the Sereni extended family, which included a royal physician, the leader of the Rome community/president of the Consortium of Jewish communities, and the pioneer of emigration to Palestine, Enzo Sereni (1905–44), Alfonsa (Enzo's mother) educated him and his siblings within traditional Jewish parameters, but also ensured that they looked and behaved like other middle-class children.[200]

From the examination of the wills of members of the Artom family, it emerges that the rituals of mourning, such as the recitation of the Kaddish and the lighting of candles, were still adhered to in the 1890s.[201] Dan Vittorio Segre's father, in spite of being 'totally ignorant of Jewish culture', carried the text of the Kaddish in his wallet with the names and dates of deceased relatives to remind him to attend synagogue on the anniversaries of their deaths.[202] The birthday celebrations of Samuel Levi of Asti in 1883 detailed in the handwritten invitation, partly composed in Hebrew – prayers in the synagogue on the Friday and Saturday, two dinners, and Levi's blessing of the guests who would have gathered from different parts of the country – attested to the close family ties and also deep attachment to and observance of Jewish ritual.[203]

For Nello Rosselli (1900–37), the religious sense of the family was one of the three fundamental tenets of his Jewish identity. He made a significant and much applauded speech at the Jewish youth congress in Livorno (1924) in which he stated:

> I am a Jew who does not go to the synagogue on the Sabbath, who does not know Hebrew, who observes no rites ... for me Judaism is a religious concept of life ... I declare myself a Jew ... because the monotheistic conscience is ineradicable within me ... because I have a profound sense of personal responsibility ... because I have that religious sense of the family which ... is a fundamental and indestructible characteristic of Jewish society.[204]

Both Enzo Levi and Elena Rossi Artom comment on a thread of continuity uniting Jews through the generations transmitted by Jewish nursery rhymes which could be traced back to the time before the expulsion of the Jews from Spain. In exile in

Argentina, both Enzo's wife and a Chilean Jewish friend would sing the same *ninna nanna* to their children, taught to them by their mothers and grandmothers.[205] Perhaps the most tenacious example of the retention of familial Jewish identity, which cultural anthropologists define as the power of deep primordial attachments that have survived through time,[206] is recounted by Elio Toaff (chief rabbi of Rome in the 1980s): a rabbi in Liège contacted him because eighty Italians had visited his synagogue claiming they were Jews from Calabria, yet they knew nothing of Judaism. Toaff travelled to Belgium to talk to them and discovered they were descendants of Marrano Jews (Spanish Jews forced to convert in the sixteenth century) who had sworn from father to son to keep the faith. This oath entailed them not to reveal their Jewish identity until they were in a free country. They returned to Italy, received religious instruction from Toaff and emigrated to Israel.[207]

NATIONAL CULTURE

In the post-Unification period, freed from former constraints, Italian Jews not only contributed to the political and economic structure of the young nation state, but also to the development of the nascent national culture.[208] Identification with Italy forged the careers of Tullo Massarani and Alessandro D'Ancona, the patriotic poetry of Giuseppe Revere and David Levi, the journalistic endeavours of Giacomo Dina. Several members of the Momigliano family distinguished themselves within mainstream culture, Attilio Momigliano (1883–1952) becoming one of the foremost literary scholars of Italian literature. Graziadio Isaia Ascoli and Cesare Lombroso were internationally innovative within the fields of linguistics and criminal anthropology. The Jewish publishers Paggi/Bemporad, Formiggini, Olschki, Rosenberg and Sellier, and Treves (the largest at the end of the nineteenth century) were instrumental as disseminators of Italian and European culture. Angiolo and Adolfo Orvieto were 'cultural operators' in their role as founders of literary periodicals such as the influential *Marzocco* (1896–1932) which helped to launch the careers of many writers later to become seminal figures – Aleramo, Capuana, D'Annunzio, De Amicis, Pascoli and Pirandello.[209] To take Roberto Salvadori's analogy with regard to Florence: 'the *Christian* banker Emanuele Fenzo, for example, behaves in a similar way to the *Jewish* banker Giacomo Servadio. The two are interchangeable … the same phenomenon occurs in the cultural sector. The Jews of Florence begin to find their place in *Tuscan* journalism, in *Italian* literature, in *Italian* and *European* painting.'[210] Among the many examples he gives is that of Augusto Franchetti: his scholarly pursuits of philosophy, bibliography, history and medieval literature were those of any other Jewish or non-Jewish intellectual. This analogy can be extended to any part of Italy where Jews resided. Thus the three families from the small town of Terni near Perugia also illustrate the three principal facets of integration – commerce, public administration and culture: the generational progression of the Sciunnachs, from their *bottega* in the Rome ghetto to their large modern stores on the new main street of Terni; the Beers who produced civil engineers and teachers; and the Coens whose members were leading lights of the local literary journals and exponents of dialect poetry.[211]

JEWISH CULTURE

Where, we can ask, in this plethora of Italian creativity, are the distinctive *Jewish* literary voices, writing as Jews in the mainstream? To be sure, there was much cultural activity within Judaism at this time, from the Jewish periodicals to the scholarship of Luzzatto, Della Torre, Benamozegh, Dante Lattes and, later, Margulies and Cassuto.[212] The answer to this question is that there were very few. Gaio Sciloni singles out three names: Alberto Cantoni (1841–1904), the humourist admired by Pirandello; Angiolo Israele Orvieto (1869–1967), the poet, and Enrico Castelnuovo (1839–1915), the novelist. The others, to emphasize their marginality, are placed in a footnote.[213] Cantoni can be discounted, as he did not treat Jewish themes in his major works.[214] Angiolo Orvieto, as a publisher of periodicals, articulated his *italianità*, and the *Marzocco* rarely contained articles on Jewish themes;[215] however, in his poetry he gave expression to the tension and anguish he felt, torn between his Jewish and Italian soul, aspiring to unite the two. In the collection *Il vento di Sion* (The Wind of Zion), in a poem composed around 1910, he writes: 'Who will give me peace?/Who will teach me/to recompose into a serene unity/my groaning soul that is divided in two?'[216] Orvieto also wrote the libretto for an opera on a biblical theme, *Mosè*, with music by his brother-in-law Giacomo Orefice, which was premiered in Genoa in 1905 and well reviewed.[217] According to Boralevi, Orvieto portrays Moses as 'a Jew "assimilated" to Eygptian culture', reflecting the poet's own condition.[218] Orvieto was gradually drawn into the Jewish milieu through the cultural revival initiated in Florence by Margulies, and later, in the 1930s, he took an active part in the Union of Italian Jewish Communities.[219] His friend Aldo Neppi Modona recalls that after the Second World War, Orvieto returned to religious observance 'in all its particulars'; he learnt Hebrew and attended Zionist meetings.[220]

Castelnuovo's novel *I Moncalvo* (1908) is comparable to that of Schnitzler, *Der Weg ins Freie*, published in the same year, in its treatment of the complexities of contemporary Jewish life. Set in Rome, the work focuses on two brothers, Gabrio and Giacomo Moncalvo: the former is a wealthy and opportunistic financier whose vain and socially ambitious wife Rachele is determined to marry her daughter off to the sickly scion of an impoverished aristocratic family, and in so doing has no qualms about her daughter's conversion to Catholicism. Giacomo is a professor of mathematics who has a studious only son Giorgio; they both live modestly and seem to embody moral integrity and an adherence to the traditions of their forbears who were strictly orthodox. The marriage goes ahead despite the virulent anti-Semitism of the bridegroom's mother, and Giorgio – who had loved his cousin in vain – leaves Italy. It is, as Dante Lattes notes in his review, a bleak depiction of Italian Judaism in the Giolittian era, when ancestral values are sacrificied on the altar of capitalist greed and apostasy: 'in the absence of any good Jewish modern literature of superior quality, this novel should find its way into Jewish homes' (*CI*, 1909, p.295). Indeed, apart from the poet Rachele Morpurgo (1790–1871), Italo Svevo (1861–1928), the novelist Ida Finzi (1867–1946), the poet Umberto Saba (1883–1957) and novelist and essayist Giorgio Voghera (1908–99), who were all from Trieste, it was not until after the Second World

War that in Italy Jewish authors were published to great acclaim.[221] One anomalous voice of the 1990s is the cultural phenomenon of the writer, director, actor and musician Moni Ovadia (1946–), a Sephardic Jew born in Bulgaria, but brought up in Italy. His performances do not belong to the regional theatre of Eduardo de Filippo or Dario Fo, but have everything to do with pre-war Yiddish theatre, and his success has become a reference point for Jewish culture in present-day Italy, supplying, in some way, the missing link of the mass emigration of eastern European Jews which transformed the milieus of Paris, London and Vienna at the end of the nineteenth century.[222]

EASTERN EUROPEAN JEWS

The political, socio-economic, demographic, cultural and psychological impact of the *Ostjuden* bypassed Italy entirely. From the pogroms of 1881 until 1914, approximately two-and-a-half million Russian Jews fled to the West, mainly to the United States of America. In addition, more than 400,000 Jews from Romania, Bohemia, Galicia and Moravia migrated to Vienna and beyond. By 1918, immigrants totalling 150,000 formed nearly half of the Jewish population of Paris; a similar number arrived in London between 1881 and 1906. In Germany there were only about 70,000 Jewish aliens dispersed among a dozen or so cities, the largest contingent being of 13,000 in Berlin.[223] This immense influx of eastern European Jews raised issues of assimilation and integration, contributed to the upsurge of anti-Semitism and compelled their co-religionists in western Europe to confront and reflect upon their own Jewish identity. Distaste, shame, embarrassment, alarm, anxiety and hostility were some of the emotions aroused by the *Ostjuden*: 'with their language, their religious expression, their appearance, dress, and dietary practices, the eastern Jews became the essential "bad" Jews'.[224] They threatened the image of the assimilated, emancipated Jew and were a painful reminder of the forbears whom western Jews wished to disavow.[225] Strenuous efforts were made to transform them into French, German and English Jews, even to the point, in the last case, of introducing them to the quintessentially English game of cricket![226] With the advent of the Zionist movement, Yiddish culture and customs were celebrated rather than denigrated.

THE JEWISH PERIODICAL PRESS

The debates on integration and assimilation continued in Italy until the promulgation of the Racial Laws in 1938, particularly in the pages of the Jewish periodicals which were 'part of the equipment of the emancipated Jewish community'.[227] The development and expansion of a periodical press edited by Jews for a specifically Jewish readership in the language of the country of publication was a distinctive aspect of Jewish public life in all western European countries,[228] and Italy was no exception. The first attempt to produce an Italian Jewish periodical dates from 1845: *La Rivista Israelitica* (Jewish Review, 1845–47), a monthly publication, was edited by a former army colonel who had fought in the 1866 war of independence, Cesare Rovighi (1820–70). It was published in Parma, where much of the liberal French legislation towards Jews had been retained under the enlightened rule of Maria Luisa of Austria. The full title of the journal, *La Rivista Israelitica. Giornale di morale, culto, letteratura e varietà* (Journal of Morality, Religion, Literature and News), is illustrative of the editor's approach. He initiated the debate on Jewish emancipation, steering a course between the ultra-traditionalists and those who expressed growing indifference to their religious faith. Several of the leading Jewish thinkers contributed to the journal, but it was too short-lived to have any lasting impact.[229] Between 1853 and 1867 six other periodicals were produced but only two survived, and they were to continue publication into the twentieth century: *L'Educatore Israelita–Il Vessillo Israelitico* (1853–1922) and *Il Corriere Israelitico* (1862–1915). The former was founded by Giuseppe Levi and Esdra Pontremoli, both of whom were rabbis and teachers, in Vercelli (Piedmont). It began life as an educational magazine, and then developed into a publication on moral and religious issues, inviting distinguished contributors. As its subtitle suggests, *Giornale mensile per la storia e lo spirito del Giudaismo* (Monthly Journal for the History and Spirit of Judaism), the principal aims were to interpret Judaism and inform its readers of the merits of Jewish history and rabbinical literature, aspects of which could be useful for the construction of the new Italy.[230] The editors also engaged in contemporary political and civil questions, and Levi in particular was instrumental in promoting cohesion between the communities through his support for the Alliance Israélite Universelle and the 1863 Congress of Ferrara.

With the death of Levi in 1874 (he had been sole editor since 1871), the periodical changed its name, direction and place of publication and became *Il Vessillo Israelitico. Rivista mensile per la storia, la scienza e lo spirito del Giudaismo* (The Jewish Banner. Monthly Journal for the History, Knowledge and Spirit of Judaism) edited by the rabbi of Casale Monferrato, Flaminio Servi (1841–1904) and then by his son Ferruccio with additional collaborators. Attilio Milano is dismissive of its new incarnation: 'the many volumes leave no trace of a direction, a particular ideality, or programme ... the *Vessillo* is but the mirror image of the religious and spiritual decadence of a prevalent part of Italian Judaism ... whose only aspiration was to succeed in public life'.[231] Cavaglion is also negative: in his judgement there was a loss of commitment regarding the dissemination of Jewish culture through translations and annotated editions; instead, defensive apologetics were frequently published.[232] Other scholars are more positive: the aims of the journal were to uphold the Jewish faith through debate, discussion and education. Moreover, the decision to monitor Jewish presence in Italian society through the regular rubric on the communities and individual attainments provides a continuous and significant record with which to reconstruct social relations, institutional activities and daily life, especially in cases where archival documentation has been lost or destroyed.[233] The journal, which was financed through subscriptions and later also through advertising, reached every community and was the most widely read until the First World War; thus it was 'the voice of the majority of Italian Jews of the period'.[234] The journal aspired to become 'the friend of all families and the organ of the Italian communities' (*VI*, 1876, p.3). Throughout the period of his editorship, Flaminio Servi reiterated that 'our sole aim is to endorse religious sentiment among the Jews and at the same time to ensure that they are upright, hard-working citizens, worthy of the country in which they were born' (*VI*, 1896, p.3); 'Patriotism and religious faith, charity and brotherhood, study and hard work; this is what we wish to inspire in our young readers and to retain in the older ones' (*VI*, 1885, pp.3–4). With regard to the didactic objective to transmit fundamental precepts of Judaism in a direct and easily comprehensible way, short stories, plays and dialogues were regularly published.[235] Initially there was little difference in format, structure and content between *Il Vessillo Israelitico* and *Il Corriere Israelitico*; the contributors, mostly rabbis, wrote for both journals. However, whereas the former promoted the image of the Italian citizen of the Jewish faith, the latter, from the late 1890s, adopted an ethnic and nationalist dimension of Jewish identity through its adherence to political Zionism.[236]

From 1862, with the newly elected liberal municipal government in Trieste and less stringent censorship, there occurred a veritable boom in journalistic initiatives, one of these being *Il Corriere Israelitico*.[237] The founding editor was Abram Vita Morpurgo. A devoutly religious man, a scholar and a teacher, he saw a pressing need for a periodical which would disseminate Jewish culture and religion, particularly among those who were gradually distancing themselves from their heritage.[238] At his death in 1867, his son-in-law, Aron di Shemuel Curiel, took over and remained editor for thirty-six years until he died in 1903 (he was also secretary to the Jewish community for over fifty years). From that date until it ceased publication, Rabbi Dante Lattes and Riccardo Curiel were the editors. Riccardo was Aron's son and Lattes was his brother-in-law, and he too served as secretary to the community for over half a century. Under Lattes's editorship *Il Corriere Israelitico* was the first and for many years the only Italian Jewish journal to promote political Zionism.

The full title of the journal attests to its aims: *Il Corriere Israelitico. Periodico mensile per la storia e la letteratura israelitica* (The Jewish Courier. Monthly Periodical for Jewish History and Literature) which, under the editorship of A. di S. Curiel, became the more assertive *Periodico per la storia, lo spirito ed il progresso del Giudaismo* (Periodical for the History, Spirit and Progress of Judaism). In his first editorial, Morpurgo outlined his programme: 'an educational objective ... to treat history and literature in such a way that the eternal principles of truth, righteousness and good emanate from them' (*CI*, 1862, p.7). He acknowledged the difficulties in engaging with the readership, a 'very restricted public' (*CI*, 1862, p.255),[239] for whom emancipation had wrought radical changes, leaving little time for study and prayer. Therefore, the role of the Jewish press was to offer co-religionists an effective way of continuing their religious education, of appreciating and taking pride in their cultural heritage, and also to encourage the young to participate in the institutional activities of their communities (*CI*, 1862, pp.285–8). Thus edifying, moralistic articles, essays on Jewish history and literature, uplifting sermons, biblical exegeses, extracts from plays and novels, and literary reviews were regularly published.

The same distinguished collaborators who had written for *La Rivista Israelitica* and *L'Educatore Israelita* were invited to contribute authoritative pieces on theological themes. The most eminent among them was Samuel David Luzzatto whose 'Lezioni di teologia dogmatica' appeared in many issues in 1862; his scholarship and erudition were internationally renowned. Another prominent contributor was Lelio Della Torre (1804–76); his 'Thoughts on the Lessons of the Pentateuch' were published in 1862 and in subsequent years. He, like Luzzatto, taught at the Rabbinical College in Padua and contributed in a decisive way to the historical perspective of Italian Judaism.[240] Both Luzzatto and Della Torre saw no conflict between civil equality and strict observance of Jewish law. However, they were critical of the reformist and assimilatory tendencies of the German Wissenschaft des Judentums.[241] Luzzatto's objectives were the renewal of Judaism through, inter alia, the study of Hebrew language and literature: 'the School of Padua ... prefers to conserve rather than to destroy', he wrote to Ascoli. To Lelio Cantoni, he commented: 'the Germans could not do much to publicly promote Judaism since they, or most of them, sacrificed everything to emancipation'.[242]

Over the years, both *Il Corriere Israelitico* and *Il Vessillo Israelitico* treated the problematic subject of assimilation and the various forms in which it manifested itself: the diminution of and indifference to traditional customs and religious practices; a deliberate non-disclosure or repudiation of the individual's Jewish origins both in public and private life, in extreme cases leading to self-hatred, epitomized in the tragic fate of the Viennese Jewish intellectual Otto Weininger;[243] renunciation of the faith; intermarriage; abandonment of Judaism through conversion to another religion and therefore total assimilation to the host society. In 1868, Giuseppe Levi of *L'Educatore Israelita* outlined his journal's stance on the fundamental issue of assimilation in a significant article entitled 'Neither Isolation nor Fusion' (*Nè isolamento, nè fusione*).[244] He argued that the history of the Jews from Biblical times to the Middle Ages demonstrated that neither isolation nor fusion worked: the former weakened and the latter destroyed. The ideal way forward was to 'assimilate the progress of the centuries and at the same time preserve Judaism's distinctiveness ... to progress without merging [*senza fondersi*] is vital' (*EI*, 1868, pp.13, 36). Flaminio Servi advocated a reappraisal of the role of Judaism in the light of emancipation, since religion 'was no longer everything' and commitment must also be directed to 'public life'.[245] Other contributors wrote on the necessity of Jews maintaining their individuality as a 'religious society', while also fulfilling their patriotic role as citizens (*VI*, 1879, pp.33–6). By 1910, within the context of political and racial anti-Semitism, the lawyer Moise Foà robustly rejected the prevalent opinion among 'European Aryans' (*ariani europei*) that Jews should assimilate to the point of disappearance: 'Why should we disappear? ... Are we an obstacle to the progress of humanity? We must show by word and deed that we are not on the point of distintegration ... The bright flame of Jewish culture must not be extinguished' (*VI*, 1910, pp.62–5).

Abram Morpurgo adopted a cautious and moderate approach in this debate as in all others by publishing many articles on the Jewish faith, civilization and history, including 'ghetto' stories, nostalgic evocations of authentic Jewish life of the pre-emancipation period, as he saw 'all the most venerable traditions of our fathers falling away'.[246] Subsequent editors warned of the dangers of assimilation, which they perceived as a process of erosion and disintegration of Jewish mores, in articles such 'The Harm of Assimilation' and 'Subversive Assimilation': 'Italy is the country where assimilation has caused the greatest damage and where Jewish sentiment has been destroyed sooner and more effectively' (*CI*, 1899, p.178). Dante Lattes was more polemical and vitriolic in his diatribes against assimilationist Jews, whom he perceived as enemies of Zionism and dangerous instigators of anti-Semitism: 'they are the anarchists of Judaism ... mad delinquents ... Are you not the dregs of the Jewish people? ... Are you or are you not Jews? For us you are anti-semites' (*CI*, 1901, pp.101–3, 129). From the ideological perspective of Zionism, 'assimilation' was an extremely negative and politicized term used to describe non-Zionist and anti-Zionist Jews. Lattes also railed against those rabbis who privileged patriotism over the Jewish faith. He had in mind Giuseppe Foà, the chief rabbi of Turin's statement at the service for King Umberto I: 'We feel ourselves to be firstly Italian rather than Jews.' This 'exaggeratedly assimilationist' utterance coming from a rabbi was, in Lattes's opinion, 'incomprehensible and monstrous', as if God's word were to be subjected to that of a temporal leader. There appeared to be a conflict between the principles of *italianità* and those of Judaism, and for the rabbi it was Judaism that would succumb: 'so assimilation triumphs even among orthodox rabbis' (*CI*, 1900, pp.105–6).

The Jewish journals expressed disquiet at the growing indifference to religion: 'a general apathy' (*EI*, 1872, p.185); 'Jewish Italy ... is slumbering' (*CI*, 1875, p.27). Flaminio Servi, on his visits to various communities, noted the decreasing numbers in the synagogues: in Ancona 'just four older men studying the sacred texts', and very few in Parma (*VI*, 1879, pp.41–4).[247] To combat this trend, the editors published articles on Jewish ritual, on the central role of women in transmitting a moral and religious education to successive generations, and short dialogues and essays on the importance of regular attendance. Another post-emancipation tendency was non-disclosure on census forms of religious affiliation, the most significant factor in the definition of minority groups in nineteenth-century nation states. From the 1870s to the 1900s, the Jewish press commented on this failure and the possible motives: unease, fear, shame, social servility, the desire to conform, and ignorance. Rabbi Lazzaro Ottolenghi's dialogue between Isaac and Joseph encapsulates some of these causes: Isaac changes his name to Ildebrando because he is ashamed of being called a Jew. Joseph asks him how he would react if his religion was being vilified: 'I would remain silent' (*EI*, 1873, pp.112–14). In 1911, the executive committee of Jewish communities sent out a circular to encourage co-religionists to declare their faith in the forthcoming census which would then provide reliable data on the number of Jews in Italy (*VI*, 1911, pp.202, 231). Tullia Catalan suggests that the main reason for non-disclosure was that the younger generation perceived themselves to be citizens of a secular, liberal state; they had never lived a segregated existence and thus, for them, religious faith was a wholly private matter.[248]

MARITAL ASSIMILATION

A phenomenon prevalent from the second half of the nineteenth century among wealthy, professional Jews in western Europe was that of mixed marriages, which constituted a significant step towards assimilation; in David Vital's words, 'the most acute of all modern indicators of social and cultural breakdown in Jewry'.[249] Social mobility; residential dispersal; living away from the traditional centres of the Jewish communities; an elevated socio-economic integration; cultural and ideological factors – all these components made exogamy virtually inevitable.[250] Until 1867, marriage between a Jew and a Catholic had been forbidden by law in Habsburg Austria, but with the new legislation of 1868 such unions were permitted if the couple did not profess different religious faiths. Therefore one of the partners had to renounce their faith and declare themselves to be *konfessionslos*, that is, without a confessional affiliation.[251] The Jewish press waged a long campaign against intermarriage: 'a real danger for our race and our faith'; 'the blight of mixed marriages that is corroding the body of Judaism'; 'the rodent worm of mixed marriages'; 'the terrible scourge'.[252] The passionate and forceful nature of the many articles on this subject from 1870 reflects that exogamy was on the increase within the Jewish communities.[253] One of the complications of such unions was the religious education of the children, which caused dissension within the family; for the most part, the offspring either became part of the Catholic majority or remained on the margins of both groups.[254] In its 1873 issues, *L'Educatore Israelita* published instalments of a play by Rabbi Lazzaro Ottolenghi to illustrate the negative aspects.[255] Guglielmo Lattes, a regular contributor to *Il Vessillo Israelitico*, published a novel in 1903, *Tra la fede e l'amore: scene della vita ebraica moderna*, on the anguish caused by these marriages.[256] A year later, Arturo Foà's play *The Daughter*, about a Catholic who marries a Jew, was performed to critical acclaim at the National Theatre of Rome (*VI*, 1904, pp.165–6). In 1903, *Il Vessillo Israelitico* reported the case of the dying wish of a Jewish husband that his 9-year-old daughter continue to worship in his faith, which was overturned by his Catholic widow who had her baptized even though she had received monies from Jewish charities in Modena. Two similar cases were also mentioned with 'these distressing consequences' (*VI*, 1904, pp.356–7). A further predicament of mixed marriages was the growing number of uncircumcised male children whose parents nevertheless wished to register them with the Jewish community.[257] For example, in Ancona between 1903 and 1920, approximately thirty were not circumcised; prior to 1901, only one was recorded.[258] The editors of the Jewish journals acknowledged one positive aspect of intermarriage: Catholic families, hitherto ignorant of Judaism, came to appreciate its values, customs and precepts; in some cases this led to conversion of the Christian bride or groom.[259]

In 1914, the executive committee of the Jewish communities in Italy commissioned a survey to collect data on mixed marriages. It was found that among the Jews of Bologna there were approximately 20 per cent of such marriages; from Modena came the response that 'the distressing phenomenon had been noted and deplored for some time, revealing a progressive increase in the last forty years', and from Ferrara the rabbi reported on the widespread practice in his community.[260] In the small Tuscan community of Pitigliano, the first one dated from 1876; there were twenty-two by 1931 (in the same period there were sixty-three Jewish marriages). In Ancona, they do not appear in the registers of the Jewish community until the 1870s and there was a sharp rise in numbers from the last decades of the nineteenth century.²⁶¹ In her analyses of the marriages in Turin, Chiara Foà demonstrates the growing tendency of exogamy. In her conclusion, she notes that in the majority of cases it was the women who were of the Jewish faith and that they retained links with the community: 'the stimulus towards assimilation and the desire to retain their [Jewish] identity seemed to coexist'.²⁶²

Among the Jews of Asti, Rossi Artom found no record of a mixed marriage before 1862. In his will of 24 January 1888, Giuseppe Ottolenghi, son of Zaccaria from Asti, stated that his heirs must not turn away from the Jewish faith or contract mixed marriages, 'as he is convinced that such unions are the cause of family dissension', otherwise the depositions contained in the will would not be valid. In addition, he bequeathed 300 lire to the editors of the Jewish press 'to encourage them to persevere in their enlightened efforts to ensure that our religion is appreciated'.²⁶³ Enzo Levi recalls that among his father's relatives (his father was born in 1859) only one of the fifteen marriages was exogamous and it caused endless critical comments, even though no conversion had taken place. This number increased and objections diminished due to the impact of the tragic suicide, within a short period of time, of two young couples (Jewish males, Catholic women) whose families had opposed their union. Among his own generation such marriages were more frequent and the majority of the children were brought up as Catholics.²⁶⁴ Three of Rabbi Lazzaro Ottolenghi's grandchildren married Catholics.²⁶⁵ In spite of this growing trend, the majority of marriages were endogamous, continuing the centuries-old tradition of consolidating and expanding family and professional ties. It is also the case that exogamy was confined largely to the professional classes; the poor tended to marry within the same ethnic group which gave them security and a sense of identity.²⁶⁶

RELIGIOUS CONVERSION

Religious conversion was the final step towards complete assimilation and abandonment of Judaism. David Vital estimates the total number of conversions in the nineteenth century among the Jews of western and central Europe to be 100,000 in a population that rose from 0.4 million to approximately 1.3 million by the close of the century. Paradoxically, among the Jews of eastern and southeastern Europe – 2 million rising to 7.4 million – the number of conversions has been calculated at 85,000. He cites an English observer in 1900 who remarked that it was among the most wretched and persecuted Jews that religious faith remained steadfast.²⁶⁷ Among the emancipated Jews of western Europe it was ambition – social, political and professional – and access to a wider, culturally richer world that drove them to embrace Christianity,²⁶⁸ 'the ticket of admission to European culture', as Heine called the baptismal certificate.²⁶⁹

The judgement of *Il Corriere* towards converted Jews was severe. The editors, inter alia, pointed out the futility of apostasy as a protection against anti-Semitic attacks: 'anti-semites still consider them [converted Jews] to be Jews, and Jews no longer acknowledge them, but they continue nevertheless to be targets of hatred and conflict'.²⁷⁰ As early as 1843, the founding editor of the journal had written a pamphlet entitled *L'Apostata smascherato* which expressed 'all the pain which a conversion could still bring to a family and the hatred the convert aroused among his former co-religionists'.[271] Religious conversion was less prevalent in Italy than in Germany or Austria-Hungary. When it did occur it was among patriotic Jews who were convinced that their religion was an obstacle to total identification with the newly unified nation.[272] For example, Giacomo Venezian, a Triestine Jew, identified Catholicism with *italianità*, and converted in 1889.[273] According to Caviglia, there were cases of Jews from Rome who converted due to poverty. In the first two decades after emancipation, almost all of the thirty-three conversions in the capital city were of women from the lowest socio-economic stratum.[274] There was also the case, in 1897, of four motherless children whose impoverished father sent them to a Catholic institution (*CI*, 1898, pp.40–1). In 1885, *Il Corriere Israelitico* reported on the initiative of the Society of Used Goods Buyers to stem the tide of female conversions by handing out every year at the festival of Pentecost a number of dowries to those daughters of its members who had shown exemplary moral and religious conduct (*CI*, 1885, pp.156–9). A threefold objective was thus achieved: financial assistance to ensure exogamous unions; diminution of conversions; incentive for religious observance.

THE FIRST WORLD WAR

This chapter began with detailed evidence of Jews and non-Jews sharing the same Risorgimento ideals, and it ends with the culmination of Jewish identity in the national and patriotic fervour engendered by the First World War, experienced as the fourth war of independence.[275] As Augusto Segre observes, for many Jews the 1914–18 war was 'the great test that would show everyone that the Jews were now really equal to others, Italian soldiers fighting side by side with other Italian soldiers, committed to the supreme sacrifice in the defence of their country'. He adds that the Jewish press, in particular *Il Vessillo Israelitico*, exalted this historic event, encouraging Jews to give their lives, as if the 'tests' hitherto taken for the *patria* were not sufficient and only death on the battlefield 'would put the seal of authencitity on the certificate of *italianità* for emancipated Jews'.[276] Indeed, the pages of the Piedmontese journal are filled with such exhortations. For example: 'the hour has come ... Italy is at war and we will give ourselves to Italy entirely. Every sacrifice will be sweet ... we – Jews – will give everything to our country: we will give our sons, our propery, our lives ... we must show that our feelings of gratitude are deeply rooted within us' (*VI*, 1915, p.261).[277] Jews in Italy – and this was also the case for those in Austria, England, France and Germany – 'felt a special obligation ... to prove their patriotism', betraying a sense of insecurity, 'an unspoken fear that if they fell short in their national duties, the gates of the ghetto might again swing shut on them'.[278] It was a fervent and joyful patriotism; the aspiration of the Jewish soldiers was to sanction with their blood their identity with the motherland and with the royal House of Savoy, dispenser of equality and liberty.[279] In 1915, Angelo Sereni, president of the Italian Jews, instructed the communities to collect information on those who had fought so that after the war it would serve 'as evidence of pride for our race'. This idea was taken up by the editor of *Il Vessillo Israelitico* who proposed a book of honour,

'Italian Jews in the war of redemption', as 'the most worthy monument to the fallen'.[280] Rabbis up and down the land gave patriotic prayers, as they had done during the wars of independence; in every issue of *Il Vessillo Israelitico*, there appeared lists of Jewish soldiers – names, rank and community – and details of those who had 'fallen gloriously' for their beloved country.[281]

Fifty Jewish generals served in the First World War; more than a thousand Jews were awarded medals; both the youngest and oldest to win the highest military honour were Jews; 261 died.[282] Italian Jews living in Tunisia, Turkey, Tripoli, Algeria, Morocco and Egypt returned to fight for their country.[283] Individual cases illustrate the depth of patriotism: Ernesto Ovazza, from Turin, and his three sons, Alfredo, Ettore and Vittorio, volunteered. They celebrated with a photograph of them all resplendent in their uniforms; as did the four Falco brothers, also from Turin; from Livorno the three Belforte siblings; Lello Sereni and his son, still a student, from Rome.[284] Even Ernesto Nathan, then 70 years old and on a government mission in the United States, volunteered; he sent a telegram to his old friend Sidney Sonnino who was foreign minister – 'I offer my old bones to my country' – and the offer was accepted.[285] For Enzo Levi, a lawyer from Modena, confirmation of his *italianità* was 'the joy to take part ... in years of war against Austria and Germany to complete the liberation of Irredentist Italy'.[286] Eugenio Levi, a 30-year-old mathematician at the University of Genoa, gave up his brilliant career to enlist, and a young Italian starved to death rather than serve in the Austrian army.[287]

However, there were those who felt anguish that Jew fought against Jew. There were stories that Jewish soldiers on both sides displayed their Star of David to avoid killing each other. The young editors of *La Settimana Israelitica* poignantly articulated this torment in a leading article: 'in the hour of our tragedy two hundred thousand Jews on the battlefield fighting against each other'. When Italy entered the war, they wrote another piece which encapsulated the tension between *italianità* and Jewish identity.[288]

The Jewish press played a vital role throughout emancipated Europe: it provided a public arena in which key questions and issues were debated; it was concerned with the ongoing transformation of Jewish identity; it was a forum in which the fate of Jews throughout the world was reported and thus fostered ties of solidarity.[289] *Il Vessillo Israelitico*, in its regular rubric on Jewish achievements, cultivated *italianità*; through its publicity and advertisements, it offered a crucial communication resource for institutions and businesses. Like its English counterpart, it became part of the communities as chronicler of those communities.[290] The unique contribution of *Il Corriere Israelitico* was its support of the Zionist movement; the editor of *L'Educatore Israelita* played a significant part in encouraging cohesion and cooperation between the Jewish communities in Italy.

NOTES

1. See Sergio Della Pergola, *Anatomia dell'ebraismo italiano: caratteristiche demografiche, economiche, sociali, religiose e politiche di una minoranza* (Assisi and Rome: Carucci, 1976), p.253. Subsequent groups were refugees from Nazi regimes and, in the 1950s and 1960s, immigrants – the majority of Italian nationality – from North Africa (p.254).
2. See, for example, Arnaldo Momigliano, 'The Jews of Italy', *New York Review of Books*, 24 October

1985, p.22; Nora Galli de' Paratesi, 'Il giudeo-italiano e i dialetti giudeo-italiani', in Bice Migliau (ed.), *La cultura ebraica nell'editoria italiana (1955–1990)* (Rome: Ministero per i Beni Culturali e Ambientali, 1992), pp.131–48; Maria Mayer Modena, 'Le parlate giudeo-italiane' in Corrado Vivanti (ed.), *Storia d'Italia, Annali 11, Gli ebrei in Italia*, vol. 2 (Turin: Einaudi, 1997), pp.937–63; in the same volume, Luisa Mortara Ottolenghi, 'Figure e immagini dal secolo XIII al secolo XIX', pp.965–1008. However, see also Giulio Lepschy, *Mother Tongues and Other Reflections on the Italian Language* (Toronto: University of Toronto Press, 2002): 'Judeo-Italian of debated nature and extension' (p.41). Some expressions of Hebrew origin passed into the local dialects and were adopted by Christians, an indicator of social interaction. See Attilio Milano, *Storia degli ebrei in Italia* (Turin: Einaudi, 1963), p.574; Roberto G. Salvadori, *La comunità ebraica di Pitigliano: dal XVI al XX secolo* (Florence: Giuntina, 1991), pp.131–2.
3. Amos Elon, *The Pity Of It All: A Portrait of Jews in Germany 1743–1933* (London: Allen Lane, 2003), pp.34–5.
4. See, for example, ibid., pp.33–64.
5. Lois C. Dubin, 'Trieste and Berlin: The Italian Role in the Cultural Politics of the Haskalah', in Jacob Katz (ed.), *Toward Modernity: The European Jewish Model* (New Brunswick, NJ, and Oxford: Transaction Books, 1987), p.209; also by Lois C. Dubin, *The Port Jews of Habsburg Trieste: Absolutist Politics and Enlightenment Culture* (Stanford, CA: Stanford University Press, 1999), Chapter 5. See also Paolo S. Colbi, 'Un "capitolo glorioso" di vita culturale ebraica triestina dei secoli passati', *Rassegna Mensile di Israel* [hereafter *RMI*], 66, 1 (2000), pp.105–17.
6. Cited by Andrew M. Canepa, 'Emancipation and Jewish Response in Mid-Nineteenth-Century Italy', *European History Quarterly*, 16, 4 (1986), p.429.
7. Francesco Ruffini, *La libertà religiosa: storia dell'idea* (Milan: Feltrinelli, 1967), pp.258–9. See also Attilio Milano, 'La Costituzione "Livornina" del 1593', *RMI*, 34, 7 (1968), pp.394–410; and Lucia Frattarelli Fischer, 'Reti toscane e reti internazionali degli ebrei di Livorno nel Seicento', *Zakhor*, 6 (2003), pp.93–116. The *Livornina* also applied to the Jews of Pisa.
8. Paolo Castignoli, 'Fonti per la storia degli ebrei a Livorno: gli archivi locali', in Isotta Scandaliato Ciciani (ed.), *Italia Judaica: gli ebrei in Italia dalla segregazione alla prima emancipazione. Atti del III convegno internazionale* (Rome: Pubblicazioni degli Archivi di Stato, 1989), p.183.
9. Dubin, 'Trieste and Berlin', p.206. In the seventeenth-century Venetian ghetto, the sermons of the chief rabbi, Leone Modena, were delivered in Italian and attended by non-Jews; Modena in turn went to hear the finest Christian preachers. See Michael A. Meyer, *Response to Modernity: A History of the Reform Movement in Judaism* (New York and Oxford: Oxford University Press, 1988), p.8.
10. See Mayer Modena, 'Le parlate giudeo-italiane' p.944.
11. Simon Levis Sullam, '"La loro *vera* lingua": storia e memoria linguistica degli ebrei in Italia tra Ottocento e Novecento', *RMI*, 69, 1 (2003), p.61. Levis Sullam observes that more research is needed on the language of the Jews of Italy as a central site of religious and cultural identity. See also Umberto Cassuto's article on the 'Parlata ebraica' (the Jewish way of speaking) of Florentine Jews in *Il Vessillo Israelitico* [*VI*], 1909, pp.254–60; see Levis Sullam for other essays on the subject in the Piedmontese periodical (p.52). The English version of Levis Sullam's article, '"Their *True* Tongue": History, Memory, Language, and the Jews of Italy', is published in David N. Myers, Massimo Ciavolella, Peter H. Riell and Geoffrey Symcox (eds), *Acculturation and Its Discontents: The Italian Jewish Experience between Exclusion and Inclusion* (Toronto: University of Toronto Press, 2008), pp.183–202. See also Augusto Segre, *Memorie di vita ebraica: da Casale a Gerusalemme* (Rome: Bonacci, 1979), on Judeo-Piedmontese lexis spoken by non-Jewish shop assistants and domestic servants working for Jewish employers (p.140); and Raniero Speelman, 'La lingua della letteratura italo-ebraica contemporanea fra prestiti e traduzione', *RMI*, 70, 1 (2004), pp.47–77.
12. Segre, *Memorie*, p.157. Through Pines and his circle, Segre came into contact, for the first time, with a much wider, more international Jewish world. See also Primo Levi in *The Drowned and the Saved*: 'Yiddish was in effect the second language of the camp ... Not only did I not speak it, I only vaguely knew of its existence ... The Polish, Russian and Hungarian Jews were amazed that we Italians could not speak it; we were suspect Jews, not to be trusted.' See Judith Woolf's translation, cited in her monograph *The Memory of the Offence: Primo Levi's If This is a Man* (Market Harborough: Troubador, 2001), p.30.
13. See Ester Capuzzo, *Gli ebrei italiani dal Risorgimento alla scelta sionista* (Florence: Le Monnier, 2004), pp.6–12; 95, n.71; Liana Elda Funaro, 'Massoneria e minoranze religiose nel secolo XIX', in Fulvio Conti (ed.), *La massoneria a Livorno: dal Settecento alla Repubblica* (Bologna: Il Mulino, 2007), pp.343–416; and Geoffrey Symcox, 'The Jews of Italy in the *Triennio Giacobino* 1796–1799', in Myers, Ciavolella, Riell and Symcox (eds), *Acculturation and Its Discontents*, pp.148–63.
14. See Capuzzo, *Gli ebrei italiani*, pp.12–20.
15. Martin Clark, *Modern Italy 1871–1982* (London and New York: Longman, 1984), p.42. See also Arturo Carlo Jemolo, in his preface to Guido Fubini, *La condizione giuridica dell'ebraismo italiano* (Turin: Rosenberg and Sellier, 1998), p.14; and Bruno Di Porto, 'Gli ebrei a Pisa dal Risorgimento al

fascismo tra identità e integrazione', in Michele Luzzati (ed.), *Gli ebrei di Pisa (secoli IX–XX)* (Pisa: Pacini, 1998), pp.294–5.
16. See Alberto Cavaglion (ed.), *La moralità armata: studi su Emanuele Artom 1915–1944* (Milan: FrancoAngeli, 1993), p.92. The importance of the Vercelli bookshop is related by David Levi, the poet, whose biography Emanuele Artom was preparing for publication. Nello Rosselli had donated Levi's papers, which included his unfinished autobiography, to the Museo del Risorgimento of Turin.
17. See Capuzzo, *Gli ebrei italiani*, Chapter 2, 'Mazzini e l'ebraismo italiano'; Alberto Cavaglion, *Gli ebrei in Piemonte* (Turin: AEC, 2003), p.50; Salvatore Foà, *Gli ebrei nel Risorgimento italiano* (Assisi and Rome: Carucci, 1978), pp.33–44, 54. On Massarani and Finzi's other patriotic activities during this period, see Francesca Cavarocchi, *La comunità ebraica di Mantova fra prima emancipazione e unità d'Italia* (Florence: Giuntina, 2002), pp.51–4. See also Tullo Massarani, 'Notizie autobiografiche d'un patriota', in Raffaello Barbiera (ed.), *Ricordi cittadini e patriottici* (Florence: Le Monnier, 1908), vol. 2, pp.3–20. The volume also contains Massarani's many patriotic manifestos and formal addresses, written on behalf of the *Comune* of Milan. David Levi composed numerous patriotic poems, including those dedicated to Massimo d'Azeglio and Garibaldi. See Augusto Comba, 'Giuseppe David Levi profeta del Risorgimento', in Aldo A. Mola (ed.), *Isacco Artom e gli ebrei italiani dai Risorgimenti al fascismo* (Foggia: Bastogi, 2002), pp.109–16. See also the relevant entries in the volumes of the *Dizionario biografico degli italiani* and the *Dizionario del Risorgimento Nazionale: dalle origini a Roma capitale*.
18. Eugenio Artom, *Un compagno di Menotti e di Mazzini: Angelo Usiglio* (Modena: Soliniani, 1949), p.5.
19. See Capuzzo, *Gli ebrei italiani*, pp.41–2; and Gina Formiggini, 'Documenti e Testimonianze: ricordo di Carlo e Nello Rosselli', *RMI*, 34, 6 (1968), p.351. A grim postscript to this family's support of one of the great architects of the Risorgimento: on 13 April 1921 in Pisa, a group of female fascist students, led by Mary Nissim Rosselli, was involved in the murder of the 24-year-old Jewish teacher and socialist leader Carlo Cammeo; he was called out of his class and shot. See Michele Sarfatti, *Gli ebrei nell'Italia fascista: vicende, identità, persecuzione* (Turin: Einaudi, 2000), pp.24–5; and di Porto, 'Gli ebrei a Pisa', pp.330–1.
20. See Capuzzo, *Gli ebrei italiani*, p.77. Like Massarani and David Levi, Revere took part in the Milan uprising of 1848; he also went to Venice and Rome during the brief republics. On De Benedetti, see Ulrich Wyrwa, 'Jewish Experiences in the Italian Risorgimento: Political Practice and National Emotions of Florentine and Leghorn Jewry (1849–1860), *Journal of Modern Italian Studies*, 8, 1 (2003), p.18.
21. Dan V. Segre, 'The Emancipation of the Jews in Italy', in Pierre Birnbaum and Ira Katznelson (eds), *Paths of Emancipation: Jews, States, and Citizenship* (Princeton, NJ: Princeton University Press, 1995), p.232. Dina was editor of *L'Opinione* from 1853 to1878; he was elected to parliament between 1867 and 1876. Artom was a volunteer in the first war of independence: see Elena Rossi Artom, *Gli Artom: storia di una famiglia della comunità ebraica di Asti attraverso le sue generazioni (XVI–XX secolo)* (Turin: Zamorani, 1997), p.152.
22. Foà, *Gli ebrei nel Risorgimento italiano*, p.55.
23. D.V. Segre, 'Emancipation of the Jews in Italy', p.232.
24. Ibid., pp.214–16, 221–2.
25. Bruno Maida, *Dal ghetto alla città: gli ebrei torinesi nel secondo Ottocento* (Turin: Zamorani, 2001), pp.205–7. Alberto Cavaglion describes Cantoni as 'the secret redactor of the Statute [of 1848], the silent weaver of emancipation', in *ebrei senza saperlo* (Naples: l'ancora del mediterraneo, 2002), p.101.
26. Liana Elda Funaro, '"Vita e legge": note per una storia della comunità ebraica livornese nel secondo Ottocento', *Rassegna Storica Toscana*, 48, 1 (2002), p.147.
27. Gadi Luzzatto Voghera, *Il prezzo dell'eguaglianza: il dibattito sull'emancipazione degli ebrei in Italia (1781–1848)* (Milan: FrancoAngeli, 1998), p.102. These words were published in 1848. On Dina, see also Canepa, 'Emancipation and Jewish Response', pp.425–6. Dina was a close friend of Lelio Cantoni, who valued his presence during the crucial phase of deliberations on emancipation (see Cavaglion, *Gli ebrei in Piemonte*, p.53).
28. Franco Della Peruta, 'Gli ebrei nel Risorgimento fra interdizioni ed emancipazione', in Vivanti (ed.), *Storia d'Italia, Annali 11, Gli ebrei in Italia*, vol. 2 (1997), p.1159.
29. Cited in Roberto G. Salvadori, *Gli ebrei di Firenze: dalle origini ai giorni nostri* (Florence: Giuntina, 2000), p.71; and Carlotta Ferrara degli Uberti, 'La questione dell'emancipazione ebraica nel biennio 1847–1848: note sul caso livornese', *Zakhor*, 6 (2003), p.87. Ferrara degli Uberti comments that such patriotism (of the second speech) could not have been expressed more powerfully, recalling the most important of all Jewish prayers, the *Shema* (p.88): 'Hear, O Israel: The Lord our God is one Lord; and you shall love the Lord your God with all your heart, and with all your soul, and with all your might' (Deuteronomy, 6: 4–6). On Benamozegh's speeches, see also Ferrara degli Uberti, *La 'Nazione Ebrea' di Livorno dai privilegi all'emancipazione (1814–1860)* (Florence: Le Monnier, 2007), pp.103–21. In a letter to Isacco Artom of 18 May 1876, Benamozegh stated that Cavour was 'the Italian Moses': cited by Mario Toscano, 'Italian Jewish Identity from the Risorgimento to Fascism, 1848–1938', in Joshua D. Zimmerman (ed.), *Jews in Italy under Fascist and Nazi Rule, 1922–1945* (Cambridge: Cambridge

University Press, 2005), p.51, n.27. Benamozegh, born in Livorno of a Sephardic family originally from Morocco, was the leading figure in the Rabbinical College of Livorno, of the Kabbala tradition, and as such was in opposition to the teachings of Luzzatto in Padua; nevertheless, the two men exchanged a correspondence of mutual esteem. On Benamozegh, see, for example, Maddalena Del Bianco Cotrozzi, *Il Collegio Rabbinico di Padova: un'istituzione religiosa dell'ebraismo sulla via dell'emancipazione* (Florence: Olschki, 1995), pp.225–6; Luzzatto Voghera, *Il prezzo dell'eguaglianza*, pp.150–3; see also Gadi Luzzatto Voghera, 'Aspetti della cultura ebraica in Italia nel secolo XIX', in Vivanti (ed.), *Storia d'Italia, Annali 11, Gli ebrei in Italia*, vol. 2, pp.1226–30. Benamozegh was marginalized in his own lifetime, and only recently has been the subject of scholarly reappraisal, as in the Livorno conference of 2000 to celebrate the centenary of his death. His most well-known student was Dante Lattes. See Asher Salah, 'Livorno: un convegno internazionale di studi su Elia Benamozegh', *RMI*, 66, 3 (2000), pp.113–24. See also Alessandro Guetta, *Filosofia e qabbalah: saggio sul pensiero di Elia Benamozegh* (Milan: Thalassa de Paz, 2000); and Liana Elda Funaro, '"Speculiamo, amiamo, combattiamo": lettere inedite di Elia Benamozegh', *Nuovi Studi Livornesi*, 10 (2002–03), pp.131–48 (p.137, n.3, contains a select bibliography of recent publications on Benamozegh).
30. See Ferrara degli Uberti, *La 'Nazione Ebrea' di Livorno*, pp.102–3.
31. Cited in Luzzatto Voghera, *Il prezzo dell'eguaglianza*, p.96. The letter is dated 13 April 1848.
32. See Tullia Catalan, 'La "primavera degli ebrei": ebrei italiani del Litorale e del Lombardo Veneto nel 1848–1849', *Zakhor*, 6 (2003), pp.35–66. Note 1 (p.25) contains a useful bibliography on the 1848 European revolutions with regard to the Jews.
33. See Capuzzo, *Gli ebrei italiani*, Chapter 3, 'A Venezia con Manin': Daniele Manin, the president, was of Jewish origin. The Jewish banker Cesare Levi financed and equipped an entire infantry regiment; he was described by the *Gazzetta Di Venezia* as 'an incomparable citizen' (p.63). On the Roman republic, see, for example, Ester Capuzzo, *Gli ebrei nella società italiana: comunità e istituzioni tra Ottocento e Novecento* (Rome: Carocci, 1999), pp.79–91. In these campaigns of 1848/49, the number of Jewish volunteers is given as 235 (p.87). See also Tullia Catalan, 'Il Quarantotto fra Austria e Italia: le lettere alla famiglia di Giacomo Venezian', in Maria Luisa Betri and Daniela Maldini Chiarito (eds), *'Dolce Dono Graditissimo': la lettera privata dal Settecento al Novecento* (Milan: FrancoAngeli, 2000), pp.254–70. In one of his letters of 1848, Venezian wrote: 'I glory in, I feel blessed to be Italian ... Italy is great, it is strong and true' (p.268). Livornese Jews living in Tunisia, where there was great enthusiasm for the successes of the Risorgimento, also volunteered from 1860; see Elia Boccara, 'La comunità ebraica portoghese di Tunisi (1710–1944)', *RMI*, 66, 2 (2000), pp.25–98.
34. See, for example, Wyrwa, 'Jewish Experiences in the Italian Risorgimento', p.24.
35. See Foà, *Gli ebrei nel Risorgimento italiano*, pp.67 (the names and place of residence of the Garibaldi eight are given), 71, 76: 'the Jews contributed an extraordinary contingent of officers and soldiers, being only thirty thousand in number in a population of twenty-five million'. See also Angelo Scocchi, *Gli ebrei di Trieste nel Risorgimento italiano* (Trieste: Mazziniana, 1952); Tullia Catalan, 'Una scelta difficile: gli ebrei triestini fra identità ebraica e identità nazionale (1848–1914)', *Annali dell'Istituto storico italo-germanico in Trento*, 23 (1997), pp.335–57; Elizabeth Schächter, *Origin and Identity: Essays on Svevo and Trieste* (Leeds: Northern Universities Press, 2000), pp.18–25. The Irredentist struggle for the annexation of Trieste to Italy, achieved in 1918, was dominated by three Jews: Salvatore Barzilai, Teodoro Mayer and Felice Venezian. Irredentism was also deep-rooted among the Jews of Gorizia, birthplace of Graziadio Isaia Ascoli. See Carlo Dionisotti, 'Appunti su Ascoli', in Franco Gavazzeni and Guglielmo Gorni (eds), *Le tradizioni del testo: studi di letteratura offerti a Domenico De Robertis* (Milan and Naples: Ricciardini, 1993), pp.419–32; and Adonella Cedarmas, *La comunità israelitica di Gorizia (1900–1945)* (Pasian di Prato: Istituto Friulano per la Storia del Movimento di Liberazione, 1999), pp.50–1. Italian Protestants also fought in the 1866 war of independence: 1,000 in the regular army; see Giorgio Spini, *Risorgimento e protestanti* (Turin: Claudiana, 1998), p.323.
36. See D.V. Segre, 'Emancipation of the Jews in Italy', p.232. See also Roberto Maria Dainotto, 'The Jewish Risorgimento and the Questione Romana', in Thomas P. DiNapoli (ed.), *The Italian Jewish Experience* (Stony Brook, NY: Forum Italicum Publishing, 2000), p.108.
37 Cited in Sarfatti, *Gli ebrei nell'Italia fascista*, p.4.
38. Canepa, 'Emancipation and Jewish Response', p.419; see also Luzzatto Voghera, *Il prezzo dell'eguaglianza*, p.100: 'they represent no great innovation in the usual ritual ... of submission'.
39. Wyrwa, 'Jewish Experiences in the Italian Risorgimento, p.27.
40. Cited in Maida, *Dal ghetto alla città*, p.293.
41. Cited in Foà, *Gli ebrei nel Risorgimento italiano*, p.7. There is a complete run of *L'Educatore Israelita–Il Vessillo Israelitico* in the library of the Jewish Community of Turin, an almost complete run in the Biblioteca Nazionale in Florence, and the British Library holds issues for 1853 to 1856. *Il Vessillo Israelitico* regularly published articles on Jewish participation in the Risorgimento: for example, the Jews who joined Garibaldi in Sicily (*VI*, 1879, p.318); Leone Ravenna's eyewitness

account of the demolition of the gates of the ghetto of Ferrara and the scenes of fraternization between Catholics and Jews, '22 March 1848 in Ferrara' (*VI*, 1898, pp.109–12); 'The Plebiscite of 1860' for the annexation of Tuscany to the Kingdom of Sardinia and the Jewish vote from Livorno (*VI*, 1906, p.474); the Jews' participation in the 1859 war (VI, 1908, pp.105–7; 1910, pp.246–8).

42. *Sulamith*, 6 (1807), cited in David Sorkin, 'The Impact of Emancipation on German Jewry: A Reconsideration', in Jonathan Frankel and Steven J. Zipperstein (eds), *Assimilation and Community: The Jews in Nineteenth-Century Europe* (Cambridge: Cambridge University Press, 2004), p.186. On *Bildung* and *Sittlichkeit* (proper moral comportment and decent behaviour), see, for example, George L. Mosse, 'Jewish Emancipation: Between *Bildung* and Respectability', in Jehuda Reinharz and Walter Schatzberg (eds), *The Jewish Response to German Culture: From the Enlightenment to the Second World War* (Hanover, MD, and London: University Press of New England, 1985), pp.1–16.

43. See Sarfatti, *Gli ebrei nell'Italia fascista*, p.6.

44. See Marco Meriggi, 'Bourgeoisie, bürgertum, borghesia: i contesti sociali dell'emancipazione ebraica', in Francesca Sofia and Mario Toscano (eds), *Stato nazionale ed emancipazione ebraica* (Rome: Bonacci, 1992), p.158; and Ester Capuzzo, 'La famiglia Sereni e l'ambiente ebraico italiano', *Clio*, 41, 3 (2005), p.470.

45. See, for example, Nicholas Doumanis, *Italy* (London: Arnold, 2001), p.47.

46. From police and other official records, it is clear that Jews from the 'lower' classes also played their part. See, for example, Capuzzo, *Gli ebrei italiani*, p.20; Cavarocchi, *La comunità ebraica di Mantova fra prima emancipazione e unità d'Italia*, p.58; Di Porto, 'Gli ebrei a Pisa', pp.288, 298–9; Gioietta Plati and Carmela Sturmann, 'I Piperno, i Cave e i Disegni: storie di famiglia', in Michele Luzzati (ed.), *Ebrei di Livorno tra due censimenti (1841–1938): memoria familiare e identità* (Livorno: Belforte, 1990), p.72; Ercole Sori, 'Una "comunità crepuscolare": Ancona tra Otto e Novecento', in Sergio Anselmi and Viviana Bonazzoli (eds), *La presenza ebraica nelle Marche: secoli XIII–XX* (Ancona: Quaderni monografici 'Proposte e ricerche', 1993), p.221; Wyrwa, 'Jewish Experiences in the Italian Risorgimento', p.21; Liana Elda Funaro, 'Il ruolo degli ebrei livornesi: due percorsi individuali su uno sfondo mediterraneo', in Laura Dinelli and Luciano Bernardini (eds), *I laboratori toscani della democrazia e del Risorgimento: la 'repubblica' di Livorno, 'l'altro' Granducato, il sogno italiano di rinnovamento* (Pisa: ETS, 2004), p.84: 'the butcher Samuel Morais, freemason and fervent Republican, was famous for his interjection "even the boards of my bed are republican!"' His funeral oration in 1862 was read by Salvatore De Benedetti (p.84).

47. Dan Vittorio Segre, *Memoirs of a Fortunate Jew: An Italian Story*, translated by the author (London: Paladin, 1988), p.20. See also D.V. Segre, 'Emancipation of the Jews in Italy': 'during the Risorgimento, the Italian Jews had the feeling that they … had created' the political system and 'that they were cofounders together with other Italian patriots of something totally new' (p.229).

48. See Alberto Cavaglion, 'Una famiglia ebraica fra Risorgimento e Resistenza', *RMI*, 64, 1 (1998), pp.23–9: 'The post-unification national identity which Italian Jews wanted to make their own soon revealed its cracks … It was neither compact nor solid … succumbing to the brutality of the fascist dictatorship' (p.26).

49. See Roberto Milano, 'Dal diario di Elia Tagliacozzo volontario garibaldino', *RMI*, 64, 1 (1998), p.91. Tagliacozzo describes himself as coming from 'the lower classes' (*basso popolo*) (p.88).

50. Cited in Mario Toscano, 'Storiografia e identità: revisione e critica dell'autorappresentazione degli ebrei in Italia: alcune considerazioni introduttive', in Cristina Benussi (ed.), *Storie di ebrei fra gli asburgo e l'Italia: diaspore/Galuyyot* (Udine: Gaspari, 2003), pp.50–1. Toscano states that this unfinished piece, 'Per una storia degli ebrei nel Risorgimento', published posthumously in the *Rassegna storica toscana*, January–June 1978, was 'a significant historiographical contribution' (p.50). See also Sandro Rogoni, 'Eugenio Artom', in Pier Luigi Ballini (ed.), *Fiorentini del Novecento* (Florence: Polistampa, 2002), pp.11–21. Artom was born in Asti; in his home 'one breathed the Risorgimento' (p.11). During the Second World War, he was one of the leaders of the Resistance in Florence and also a member of the council of the Florentine Jewish community (see Salvadori, *Gli ebrei di Firenze*, p.91). See also Ester Capuzzo, 'Risorgimento, liberalismo e ebraismo nell'esperienza di Eugenio Artom', *Clio*, 43, 2 (2007), pp.207–27: 'The Resistance was, for Artom, like a second Risorgimento', (p.219).

51. D.V. Segre, 'Emancipation of the Jews in Italy', p.230.

52. Arnaldo Momigliano, *Essays on Ancient and Modern Judaism*, edited and with an introduction by Silvia Berti, translated by Maura Masella-Gayley (Chicago, IL, and London: University of Chicago Press, 1994) (*Pagine ebraiche*, Turin: Einaudi, 1987), Appendix 1, pp.225–7. The book under review was Cecil Roth's *Gli ebrei di Venezia*; the review was first published in *La Nuova Italia*, April 1933. As evidence of the Jews 'in the forefront', Momigliano mentions the Venetian Republic with Manin, Pincherle and Maurogonato; Jews as members of the national assembly and in the National Guard.

53. See, for example, Maurizio Molinari, *Ebrei in Italia: un problema di identità (1870–1938)* (Florence: Giuntina, 1991), pp.25–7; Luisa Mangoni in her introduction to David Bidussa, Amos Luzzatto and Gadi Luzzatto Voghera, *Oltre il ghetto: momenti e figure della cultura ebraica in Italia tra l'Unità e*

il fascismo (Brescia: Morcelliana, 1992), p.7; Francesca Sofia, 'Su assimilazione e autocoscienza ebraica nell'Italia liberale', in Liliana Mezzabotta (ed.) *Italia Judaica: gli ebrei nell'Italia unita 1870–1945. Atti del IV convegno internazionale* (Rome: Pubblicazioni degli Archivi di Stato, 1993), p.33: 'no one equal to Arnaldo Momigliano has been better able to define the terms of the issue'; Luzzatto Voghera, *Il prezzo dell'eguaglianza*, p.101; Salvatore Mazzamuto, 'I giuristi dell'ateneo pisano e la questione ebraica', in Luzzati (ed.), *Gli ebrei di Pisa*, p.215; in the same volume, Di Porto, 'Gli ebrei a Pisa', p.294; Ester Capuzzo, *Gli ebrei nella società italiana: comunità e istituzioni tra Ottocento e Novecento* (Rome: Carocci, 1999), pp.119, 165; Cavarocchi, *La comunità ebraica di Mantova fra prima emancipazione e unità d'Italia*, pp.viii, 8; Enzo Collotti, *Il fascismo e gli ebrei: le leggi razziali in Italia* (Rome-Bari: Laterza, 2003), p.10; Monica Miniati, *'Les Emancipées': les femmes juives italiennes aux XIXe e XXe siècles (1848–1924)* (Paris: Honoré Champion, 2003), p.30; Giampiero Carocci, *Storia degli ebrei in Italia: dall'emancipazione a oggi* (Rome: Newton & Compton, 2005), pp.22, 48; and Ferrara degli Uberti, *La 'Nazione Ebrea' di Livorno*, pp.4–5, 15, 155.
54. See Momigliano, *Essays on Ancient and Modern Judaism*, Appendix 2, A. Gramsci, 'Judaism and Anti-Semitism', pp.228–9.
55. Canepa, 'Emancipation and Jewish Response', p.432.
56. See Mario Toscano, *Ebraismo e antisemitismo in Italia: dal 1848 alla guerra dei sei giorni* (Milan: FrancoAngeli, 2003). This volume contains articles published from 1982. Thus we read: 'at sixty years' distance, Momigliano's formulation is still valid' (p.26, 1994); 'Momigliano's famous interpretation' is 'optimistic ... it does not correspond to historical reality' (p.15, 1998). See also Mario Toscano (ed.), *Integrazione e identità: l'esperienza ebraica in Germania e Italia dall'Illuminismo al fascismo* (Milan: FrancoAngeli, 1998), Introduction by Toscano: Momigliano's theory 'is still in my opinion a very useful starting point in the study of the process of their [the Jews'] national integration, provided that it is separated from Gramsci's exegesis' (p.17).
57. Sarfatti, *Gli ebrei nell'Italia fascista*, p.5.
58. Simon Levis Sullam, 'Arnaldo Momigliano e la "nazionalizzazione parallela": autobiografia, religione, storia', *Passato e presente*, 25, 70 (2007), pp.59–82. This is not only Levis Sullam's view but also that of Michele Sarfatti, in a conversation with the author in Milan on 11 November 2005.
59. This is also Cavaglion's assessment. See Maida, *Dal ghetto alla città*, p.7, n.2.
60. David Levi, *Ausonia: vita d'Azione (dal 1848–1870)* (Rome: Loescher, 1882), p.130, cited by Dainotto, in DiNapoli (ed.), *The Italian Jewish Experience*, p.112. See also Andrew Canepa, 'Emancipazione, integrazione e antisemitismo liberale in Italia: il caso Pasqualigo', *Comunità*, 29, 174 (1975), pp.166–203: 'a religious duty' (p.196); Caviglia's phrase 'the cult of the new fatherland', p.121; Capuzzo, 'Risorgimento, liberalismo e ebraismo nell'esperienza di Eugenio Artom': 'the Risorgimento tradition [was] ... almost a religion of the soul' (p.215); and George L. Mosse, 'Gli ebrei e la religione civica del nazionalismo', in Sofia and Toscano (eds), *Stato nazionale ed emancipazione ebraica*, p.143. Similar sentiments were expressed by French Jews who venerated the country that emancipated them: their *culte dévot* for the French Revolution and their *ferveur pour la nation est quasi religieuse*. See Ilan Greilsammer, 'Réflexions sur l'identité juive de Léon Blum', in Patrick Cabanel and Chantal Bordes-Benayoun (eds), *Un modèle d'intégration: juifs et israélites en France et en Europe (XIX–XX siècles)* (Paris: Berg, 2004), p.159. See also Pierre Birnbaum, 'Between Social and Political Assimilation: Remarks on the History of Jews in France', in Birnbaum and Katznelson (eds), *Paths of Emancipation*, pp.94–127; and Pierre Birnbaum, *The Jews of the Republic: A Political History of State Jews in France from Gambetta to Vichy* (Stanford, CA: Stanford University Press, 1996), p.117, Joseph Reinach's speech in the Chamber of Deputies in 1891: 'If there is anyone who worships the French Revolution deep in his heart, it is the man who stands before you.'
61. Doumanis, *Italy*, p.48: 'the symbolic importance of the Risorgimento myth'; see also p.105: 'As the Italian public grew increasingly disenchanted with the nation's ... manifest level of political corruption and ineptitude ... nostalgia for the mythical Risorgimento grew stronger.' See also Leon Roth, *Jewish Thought as a Factor in Civilization* (Paris: Unesco, 1961), p.11: 'It is in such "myths" that a people's character and aims are most intimately reflected.'
62. Momigliano, 'The Jews of Italy', p.23. See also his *Essays on Ancient and Modern Judaism*, p.xxvii: 'for us [our family], Mazzini represented the link between Judaism and the Italian Risorgimento; our patriotism was never questioned'.
63. See Salvatore De Benedetti, *Marianna Foà Uzielli: Ricordo biografico* (Livorno: Vigo, 1880), p.22. See also Foà Uzielli's correspondence with Emilia Peruzzi, the basis of which was 'passionate patriotism': Mirella Scardozzi, 'Amiche: lettere di Marianna, Regina e Lina Uzielli a Emilia Toscanelli Peruzzi', in Michele Luzzati and Cristina Galasso (eds), *Donne nella storia degli ebrei d'Italia. Atti del IX convegno internazionale Italia Judaica* (Florence: Giuntina, 2007), p.386. Marianna's son Gustavo was a volunteer in the 1859 war of independence (pp.389–90).
64. Luzzati, 'Integrazione e assimilazione', in Luzzati (ed.), *Ebrei di Livorno*, p.14: 'The Risorgimento and post-Risorgimento traditions ... predominate unopposed and the Jews' identification with the

65. Rita Castelli, 'Una testimonianza', in Luzzati (ed.), *Ebrei di Livorno*, p.121; and Daniela Pesciatini, 'Tra emancipazione e assimilazione: i Cingholi-Ottolenghi', also in Luzzati (ed.), *Ebrei di Livorno*, p.168.
66. Luzzatto Voghera, 'Aspetti della cultura ebraica in Italia nel secolo XIX', p.1232, n.54.
67. Massarani, *Ricordi Cittadini*, vol. 2, p.69.
68. Tullo Massarani, *Una nobile vita: carteggio inedito*, edited by Raffaello Barbiera (Florence: Le Monnier, 1909), vol. 2, p.482. The letters, published posthumously, attest to his friendship with patriots, politicians, poets, philosophers and novelists. In his preface Barbiera describes Massarani as 'this most noble [*nobilissimo*] Italian of the Risorgimento whom Italians should not forget' (p.xviii).
69. See Alberto Cavaglion, *Felice Momigliano (1866–1924): una biografia* (Naples: Il Mulino, 1988). See also Arnaldo Momigliano's essay on his relative, whom he called 'his second teacher', in *Essays on Ancient and Modern Judaism*, pp.144–7: 'Felice's books on Mazzini and other figures of the Italian Risorgimento have their place in Italian culture' (p.146). Felice Momigliano regularly contributed to the Jewish press.
70. Alessandro Levi, *Ricordi della vita e dei tempi di Ernesto Nathan* (Florence: La Nuova Italia, 1927), pp.10, 32, 99, 150. Ernesto Nathan was the executor of Mazzini's will (Capuzzo, *Gli ebrei italiani*, p.42), and in his own will, made on 9 August 1917, he wrote: 'I die as I have lived, keeping faith with Giuseppe Mazzini' (Levi, *Ricordi della vita*, p.269).
71. Amelia Rosselli, *Memorie*, edited by Marina Calloni (Bologna: Mulino, 2001), pp.52, 128. See also Zeffiro Ciuffoletti, 'Amelia Rosselli', in Ballini (ed.), *Fiorentini del Novecento*, vol. 2, pp.147–8, and Alessandro Levi, *Ricordi dei fratelli Rosselli* (Florence: La Nuova Italia, 1947).
72. Paola and Gina Lombroso, *Cesare Lombroso: appunti sulla vita. Le Opere* (Milan, Turin and Rome: Bocca, 1906), pp.8, 41.
73. Alexander Stille, *Benevolence and Betrayal: Five Italian Jewish Families Under Fascism* (London: Jonathan Cape, 1992), p.24. Rich Jewish families from Acqui, Casale Monferrato and Turin donated funds to Cavour. See Germano Maifreda, *Gli ebrei e l'economia milanese: L'Ottocento* (Milan: FrancoAngeli, 2000), p.250. The Orvieto family from Florence boasted ancestors who had fought to defend the short-lived Venetian Republic of 1849 and were volunteers alongside Garibaldi. See Alberto Boralevi, 'Angiolo Orvieto, "il Marzocco", la società colta ebraica', in Caterina Del Vivo (ed.), *Il Marzocco: carteggi e cronache fra Ottocento e Avanguardie (1887–1913). Atti del seminario di studi (12–14 dicembre 1983)* (Florence: Olschki, 1985), p.218.
74. Stefano Caviglia, *L'identità salvata: gli ebrei di Roma tra fede e nazione: 1870–1938* (Rome-Bari: Laterza, 1996), p.55. On September 1895, the twenty-fifth anniversary of this important date in Italian national history, the Jewish community in Rome held a commemorative religious service to celebrate the double significance that it held for them: they had attained their freedom at the same time as the aspirations of national unity had been fulfilled. They also set up a committee to plan activities which would demonstrate the civil and patriotic ideals that they shared with all Roman citizens (ibid., p.71).
75. Stille, *Benevolence and Betrayal*, p.24. There was a cult of veneration among the Jews of Austria for the Emperor Franz Joseph. See Robert S. Wistrich, *The Jews of Vienna in the Age of Franz Joseph* (Oxford: Oxford University Press, 1989), pp.272–3, 284, 298. The *Jewish Chronicle* devoted many pages to the important events of the royal family, occasions for 'enormous outpourings of patriotic feeling', and also to 'crystallize' the identity of Jewishness and Englishness. See David Cesarani, *The Jewish Chronicle and Anglo-Jewry, 1841–1991* (Cambridge: Cambridge University Press, 1994), p.94.
76. Canepa, 'Il caso Pasqualigo', p.196.
77. Enzo Levi, *Memorie di una vita (1889–1947)* (Modena: STEM Mucchi, 1972), pp.13–14. These memoirs were edited posthumously by his son Arrigo Levi for his mother, children and grandchildren.
78. Caviglia, *L'identità salvata*, pp.90–1.
79. Jemolo, Preface to Fubini, *La condizione giuridica dell'ebraismo italiano*, p.14. On the Waldensians' protestations of loyalty to the Italian monarchy, see Gian Paolo Romagnani, 'Italian Protestants', in Rainer Liedtke and Stephen Wendehorst (eds), *The Emancipation of Catholics, Jews and Protestants: Minorities and the Nation State in Nineteenth-Century Europe* (Manchester and New York: Manchester University Press, 1999), pp.159–60.
80. Sori, 'Una "comunità crepuscolare"', p.223. See also Natalia Ginzburg, *Lessico famigliare* (Turin: Einaudi, 1963), p.9.
81. See Stille, *Benevolence and Betrayal*, pp.95, 179. Roberto was a popular name among Italian Protestants in homage to Roberto D'Azeglio who in December 1847 presented a petition to King Carlo Alberto in favour of their emancipation. See Spini, *Risorgimento e protestanti*, pp.215–16.
82. See Sori, 'Una "comunità crepuscolare"', p.214.
83. Maifreda, *Gli ebrei e l'economia Milanese*, p.140.
84. Salvadori, *La comunità ebraica di Pitigliano*, pp.123–6. See also Sergio Della Pergola's study of the names given to the Jewish children of Pitigliano between 1808 and 1886 (by 1886 only 14 per cent of Jewish boys had a Jewish/biblical name), in Sergio Della Pergola, 'Quantitative Aspects of Jewish Assimilation', in Bela Vago (ed.), *Jewish Assimilation in Modern Times* (Boulder, CO: Westview

Press, 1981), pp.187–90.
85. Marco Soria, 'I (De) Soria di Livorno: genealogia e storia famigliare', *RMI*, 72, 1 (2006), p.142.
86. Momigliano, 'The Jews of Italy', p.23. See also Sergio Della Pergola, 'La popolazione ebraica in Italia nel contesto ebraico globale', in Vivanti (ed.), *Storia d'Italia, Annali 11, Gli ebrei in Italia*, vol. 2: 'the process of emancipation and acculturation of the Jews in Italy ... reached levels of intensity rarely encountered in other countries ... an active Jewish presence in the socio-economic, intellectual and administrative elites of the country' (p.929).
87. See Fabio Levi, 'Gli ebrei nella vita economica dell'Ottocento', in Vivanti (ed.), *Storia d'Italia, Annali 11, Gli ebrei in Italia*, vol. 2, p.1190.
88. See Mosse, 'Gli ebrei e la religione civica', p.147. See also Roth, *The History of the Jews in Italy*, pp.476–85; Attilio Milano, *Storia degli ebrei*, pp.382–91; D.V. Segre, 'Emancipation of the Jews in Italy', p.227; Massimo Livi Bacci, 'La demografia degli ebrei italiani agli inizi del secolo, *RMI*, 47, 7–12 (1981), p.85; Momigliano, 'The Jews of Italy', pp.23–6; Bruno Di Porto, 'Apporti e posizioni di ebrei nella vita e nella cultura politica italiana', in Mola (ed.), *Isacco Artom e gli ebrei italiani*, pp.59–107; Alberto Cavaglion, 'Gli ebrei e il socialismo: il caso italiano', in Sofia and Toscano (eds), *Stato nazionale ed emancipazione ebraica*, pp.377–92: and Luzzati (ed.), *Ebrei di Livorno*, p.14. For a European dimension, see also Robert S. Wistrich, *Revolutionary Jews from Marx to Trotsky* (London: Harrap, 1976).
89. See Della Pergola, *Anatomia dell'ebraismo italiano*, p.283; and Gadi Luzzatto Voghera, 'Per uno studio sulla presenza e attività di parlamentari ebrei in Italia e in Europa', *RMI*, 6, 1 (2003), pp.73–92. Luzzatto Voghera provides a useful alphabetical list of more than one hundred Italian Jewish members of parliament from 1848 to the present.
90. See also *VI*, 1887, pp.95–6; 1902, pp.166–8.
91. Pierre Birnbaum, 'Exile, Assimilation, and Identity: from Moses to Joseph', in Elisheva Carlebach, John M. Efron and David N. Myers (eds), *Jewish History and Jewish Memory: Essays in Honour of Yosef Hayim Yerushalmi* (Hanover, MD, and London: Brandeis University Press, 1998), p.256. See also Birnbaum, *The Jews of the Republic*, pp.229, 145–6: Joseph Reinach (1856–1921), 'the quintessence of the emancipated and republican state Jew'. Crémieux was given a national funeral (p.221). Elsewhere, Birnbaum contrasts Crémieux with Bleichröder, Bismarck's banker and confidant, ennobled by the Emperor in 1892: whereas the former's power and influence had an institutional and legitimate basis, the latter's remained outside the state and was vulnerable to an entirely personal connection. See Pierre Birnbaum, *Anti-Semitism in France: A Political History from Léon Blum to the Present* (Oxford: Blackwell, 1992), pp.29–30. See also David Vital, *A People Apart: The Jews in Europe, 1789–1939* (Oxford: Oxford University Press, 1999), pp.229–32: Crémieux was 'the most eminent Jew in nineteenth-century France' (p.230).
92. Toscano, 'Italian Jewish Identity from the Risorgimento to Fascism', p.44. On the many Jewish jurists who collaborated in laying the foundations of the legal system in Italy, see Salvatore Mazzamuto, 'Ebraismo e diritto dalla prima emancipazione all'età repubblicana', in Vivanti (ed.), *Storia d'Italia, Annali 11, Gli ebrei in Italia*, vol. 2, pp.1767–827; see also, by the same author, 'I giuristi dell'ateneo pisano e la questione ebraica', in Luzzati (ed.), *Gli ebrei di Pisa*, pp.211–39.
93. Cited in Renzo De Felice, 'Stato, società e questione ebraica nell'Italia unita', in Sofia and Toscano (eds), *Stato nazionale ed emancipazione ebraica*, p.423. The autobiographical pages were published posthumously in *Quaderni del diritto e del processo civile* (1969), pp.34–65.
94. *L'Educatore Israelita* had done the same in a regular column, 'Cronaca d'Italia': 'the history of our days teaches us what roles our co-religionists play in the events of our country Italy and in the cities where they live' (*EI*, 1873, p.373). The French journal *L'Univers israélite* also reported in every issue promotions and honours accorded to the Jews to attest to their integration as citizens of France. See Pierre Birnbaum, 'Les Juifs et L'Affaire', in Jean-Jacques Becker and Annette Wieviorka (eds), *Les Juifs de France de la Révolution française à nos jours* (Paris: Editions Liana Levi, 1998), p.77. Similarly, the Jewish communal leadership in England was 'obsessed with projecting positive images of "good" citizenship'. See Geoffrey Alderman, 'English Jews or Jews of the English Persuasion?', in Birnbaum and Katznelson (eds), *Paths of Emancipation*, p.140.
95. Fabio Levi, 'Gli ebrei nella vita economica dell'Ottocento', p.1172.
96. Ibid., pp.1181–5. He also points out that Italian Jews did not become great capitalists or industrialists; there was no Italian equivalent of the Rothschilds (p.1181). See also Eitan F. Sabatello, 'Trasformazioni economiche e sociali degli ebrei in Italia nel periodo dell'emancipazione', in Mezzabotta (ed.), *Italia Judaica ... Atti del IV convegno internazionale*, pp.114–24; the gap was still wide with regard to literacy in 1938; 85 per cent of Jewish children attended secondary school compared with 12 per cent of non-Jews (p.117). See also Clark, *Modern Italy*, for regional illiteracy rates in Italy for 1871, 1881, 1901 and 1911 (far higher in the south in all cases), pp.35–6. It is of relevance to mention that the other religious minority in Italy, the Protestants, also had a higher level of literacy: 'the village schools transformed the Waldensian valleys [in western Piedmont] into a tiny island of literate peasants in a sea of illiterates' (Romagnani, 'Italian Protestants', p.152).

97. See Sori, 'Una "comunità crepuscolare"', pp.240–3; Di Porto, 'Gli ebrei a Pisa', pp.304–7; Mirella Ronchetti Vitaloni, 'Fonti archivistiche sull'evoluzione demografica economica e culturale della comunità israelitica di Livorno tra '800 e '900', in Mezzabotta (ed.), *Italia Judaica ... Atti del IV convegno internazionale*, pp.253–4; and Maida, *Dal ghetto alla città*, pp.101–5.
98. See Caviglia, *L'identità salvata*, pp.7–39; Della Pergola, *Anatomia dell'ebraismo italiano*, pp.146–7; Fabio Levi, 'Gli ebrei nella vita economica dell'Ottocento', p.1186; and Stille, *Benevolence and Betrayal*, pp.173–5, 178.
99. See Sabatello, 'Trasformazioni economiche e sociali degli ebrei in Italia', p.121.
100. See Funaro, 'Il ruolo degli ebrei livornesi', p.86. See also pp.96–7.
101. See Raffaele Romanelli, 'Urban Patricians and "Bourgeois" Society: A Study of Wealthy Elites in Florence, 1862–1904', *Journal of Modern Italian Studies*, 1, 1 (1995), p.3.
102. See Laura Savelli, 'Una città e i suoi ebrei: Pisa tra le due guerre mondiali' in Luzzati (ed.), *Gli ebrei di Pisa*, p.347. See also, in the same volume, Mirella Scardozzi, 'Da merciai "con fagotto" a industriali del cotone', pp.177–83.
103. Funaro, 'Il ruolo degli ebrei livornesi', pp.84–7. Angiolo was also sensitive to political issues: in 1899, he gave the additional name of Alfreda to his elder daughter in honour of Dreyfus (p.89).
104. Stille, *Benevolence and Betrayal*, pp.23–4. See also Maida, *Dal ghetto alla città*, pp.170–4, on the status symbol of the house in the country and noble titles for the Jews of Turin; and Primo Levi, 'Preface', in Luciano Allegra (ed.), *Ebrei a Torino: ricerche per il centenario della sinagoga 1884–1984* (Turin: Allemandi, 1984), p.12: 'their upward social mobility was parallel to that of the Christian bourgeoisie'. See also Esther Benbassa, *The Jews of France: A History from Antiquity to the Present* (Princeton, NJ: Princeton University Press, 1999), p.105: in the 1880s, the way of life followed by bourgeois Jews in Paris 'hardly differed from that of their non-Jewish counterparts'.
105. D.V. Segre, *Memoirs of a Fortunate Jew*, p.26.
106. Maifreda, *Gli ebrei e l'economia milanese*, pp.149, 187, 215–18, 236–7, 257–8. On the Jews of Mantua and their bourgeois lifestyle with boxes at the opera and membership of the Accademia Virgiliana, see Cavarocchi, *La comunità ebraica di Mantova fra prima emancipazione e unità d'Italia*, pp.92–3; on those of Ancona, see Sori, 'Una "comunità crepuscolare"', pp.231–3; on the various branches of the Franchetti family in Livorno, Pisa, Turin and Venice, see Mirella Scardozzi, 'Una storia di famiglia: i Franchetti dalle coste del Mediterraneo all'Italia liberale', *Quaderni storici*, 38, 3 (2003), pp.697–740; on the Jews of Livorno, see Luzzati (ed.), *Ebrei di Livorno*, p.13.
107. Meriggi, 'Bourgeoisie, bürgertum, borghesia', p.167.
108. See, for example, Reinhard Rürup, 'Verso la modernità: l'esperienza ebraica in Europa dagli inizi dell'emancipazione', in Toscano (ed.), *Integrazione e identità*, pp.41–2.
109. See Riccardo Calimani, *Di ebrei, di cose ebraiche e del resto* (Florence: Giuntina, 1984), p.89; Stefan Zweig, *The World of Yesterday* (Lincoln, NE, and London: University of Nebraska Press, 1964), p.12; Scardozzi, 'Da Merciai "con fagotto" a industriali del cotone', p.177; and Maifreda, *Gli ebrei e l'economia milanese*, p.162.
110. See Michael Burns, *France and the Dreyfus Affair: A Documentary History* (Boston, MA, and New York: Bedford/St Martin's, 1999), pp.16–17.
111. See Frankel and Zipperstein (eds), *Assimilation and Community*, pp.18–19; David Feldman, 'Was Modernity Good for the Jews?', in Bryan Cheyette and Laura Marcus (eds), *Modernity, Culture and 'the Jew'* (Cambridge: Polity Press, 1998), pp.171–2.
112. Luzzatto Voghera, *Il prezzo dell'eguagliana*, p.18. See also Barbara Armani and Guri Schwarz, 'Ebrei borghesi: identità famigliare, solidarietà e affari nell'età dell'emancipazione', *Quaderni storici*, 38, 3 (2003), p.640: 'The dearth of studies on the Jewish poor is not only a consequence of a lack of sources but originates also in the persistent tendency to consider the Jewish bourgeois identity ... as the only one with a numerical consistency and therefore worthy of study.'
113. David Vital, *The Origins of Zionism* (Oxford: Oxford University Press, 1975), p.26.
114. See Feldman, 'Was Modernity Good for the Jews?', pp.173–5.
115. Ibid., p.176: 'the writings of critics such as Bauman ... underestimate the extent to which Jewish interests were pursued and Jewish identities were articulated in Germany, France and Britain in the nineteenth century', to which we can add Italy. See also Frankel, in Frankel and Zipperstein (eds), *Assimilation and Community*, p.16: 'Instead of the one basic conflict between centrifugality and centripetality, now a great variety of ... processes ... variables are traced as they interact in constantly new permutations'; and the Introduction, in Birnbaum and Katznelson (eds), *Paths of Emancipation*, pp.20–3.
116. Molinari, *Ebrei in Italia*, p.31; Luciano Tas, *Storia degli ebrei in Italia* (Rome: New Compton, 1987), p.105; and Salvadori, *Gli ebrei di Firenze*, p.64. See also Barbara Armani, 'L'identità sfidata: gli ebrei fuori dal ghetto', *Storica*, 5, 15 (1999), pp.69–103. See also Marsha L. Rozenblit, 'Jewish Assimilation in Habsburg Vienna', in Frankel and Zipperstein (eds), *Assimilation and Community*, p.226: 'Jewish integration ... generated a new kind of Jew'; and David N. Myers, '"The Blessing

of Assimilation" Reconsidered: An Inquiry into Jewish Cultural Studies', in David N. Myers and William V. Rowe (eds), *From Ghetto to Emancipation: Historical and Contemporary Reconsiderations of the Jewish Community* (Scranton, PA: University of Scranton Press, 1997), who writes of 'a new Jewish type, at once observant and enlightened, Jewish and German' (p.24).
117. See Molinari, *Ebrei in Italia*, p.119. See also Carocci, *Storia degli ebrei in Italia*, p.35; Allegra, *Ebrei di Torino*, p.34, and D.V. Segre, *Memoirs of a Fortunate Jew*, pp.22–3.
118. Phyllis Cohen Albert, 'Israelite and Jew: How did Nineteenth-Century French Jews Understand Assimilation?', in Frankel and Zipperstein (eds), *Assimilation and Community*, p.93.
119. See Cohen Albert, 'Israelite and Jew', p.93, and Cabanel, in Cabanel and Bordes-Benayoun (eds), *Un modèle d'intégration* pp.8–9. See also the negative definition of the word *juif* in two French dictionaries of 1800 and 1828 in Georges-Elia Sarfati, *Discours ordinaires et identités juives: la représentation des Juifs et du judaisme dans les dictionnaires et les encyclopédies de langue français (du Moyen Age au XX siècle)* (Paris: Berg, 1999), p.130.
120. See, for example, the list of organizations in Marsha L. Rozenblit, *The Jews of Vienna 1867–1914: Assimilation and Identity* (Albany, NY: State University of New York Press, 1983), Appendix 2; and Sanford Ragins, *Jewish Responses to Anti-Semitism in Germany, 1870–1914: A Study in the History of Ideas* (Cincinnati, OH: Hebrew Union College Press, 1980), p.6.
121. See Cohen Albert, 'Israelite and Jew', pp.92, 94–6; 106, n.27.
122. See Armani and Schwarz, 'Ebrei borghesi: identità famigliare, solidarietà e affari nell'età dell'emancipazione': 'the history of Jewish integration is above all a history of individuals, at its centre must be the sphere of subjectivity, the behaviour and emotions of those who were emancipated and their descendants should be reconstructed' (p.624). See also Werner E. Mosse, 'Integration and Identity in Imperial Germany: Towards a Typology', *Leo Baeck Institute Year Book* [hereafter *LBIYB*], 42 (1992), pp.83–93: he rejects 'sweeping, ill-conceived generalizations ... of an alleged "symbiosis", whether "failed" or otherwise', in favour of looking at the evidence of individual families and the differentiated patterns and degrees of integration and identities (p.83). See also, by the same author, 'Problems and Limits of Assimilation: Hermann and Paul Wallich 1833–1938', *LBIYB*, 33 (1988), pp.43–65; 'Terms of Successful Integration: The Tietz Family 1858–1923', *LBIYB*, 34 (1989), pp.131–61; and 'Integration through Apartheid: The Hirschs of Halberstadt 1780–1930', *LBIYB*, 35 (1990), pp.133–50.
123. Luzzatto Voghera, 'Italian Jews', in Liedtke and Wendehorst (eds), *Emancipation of Catholics, Jews and Protestants*, p.172.
124. D.V. Segre, *Memoirs of a Fortunate Jew*, p.20. See also Stille, *Benevolence and Betrayal*: 'the Ovazzas ... were proud of being Jewish the way they were proud of being Italian and Piedmontese – and for the Ovazzas these identities were all interconnected' (p.27).
125. See David Bidussa, *Il sionismo politico* (Milan: Edizioni Unicopli, 1993), p.19.
126. *CI*, 1902, pp.6–7. See also Caviglia, *L'identità salvata*, p.xxi.
127. Maifreda, *Gli ebrei e l'economia milanese*, p.130.
128. Massarani, *Una nobile vita*, pp.195–7, 230–1, 221, 502–4.
129. See his letter to Dante Lattes in ibid., p.504.
130. See Mauro Moretti, 'La dimensione ebraica di un maestro pisano. documenti su Alessandro D'Ancona', in Luzzati, *Gli ebrei di Pisa*, p.271. These sentiments are contained in a letter dated 10 December 1894 to his friend and colleague, the French philologist Gaston Paris.
131. See Moretti, 'La dimensione ebraica', pp.268–9.
132. See ibid., pp.253–4. Disparity in religious beliefs featured prominently in D'Ancona's correspondence with his wife Adele Nissim; in several letters he shows sensitivity to her religious observance that did not permit her to write to him on the Sabbath (p.253). Of D'Ancona's nine brothers, only one was said to be orthodox (p.247).
133. Ibid., pp.256–7. In this essay, he referred with great optimism to the World's Parliament of Religions held in Chicago in 1893. See also his letters to the daughter of Giovan Battista Giorgini and to Ruggiero Bonghi (pp.249–50, 310).
134. See his letter to Lattes of 1901, cited in Moretti, 'La dimensione ebraica', pp.276–7.
135. See Moretti, 'La dimensione ebraica', pp.244–5, 266–7, 278. See also Birnbaum, *The Jews of the Republic*, p.222, on such occasions as indicators of integration: 'the funeral ceremonies symbolized the deep symbiosis existing between state Jews and the political class of the Republic'.
136. See Moretti, 'La dimensione ebraica', pp.264–5, 270–1, 274–6. In one essay, D'Ancona recalled that his own family had been forced to flee the Papal States and seek refuge in Tuscany (p.265).
137. See Alessandro D'Ancona, *Ricordi ed Affetti: in memoria d'illustri italiani. Ricordi di Maestri, Amici e Discepoli. Ricordi di Storia. Ricordi Autobiografici e Affetti* (Milan: Treves, 1902), pp.59–66.
138. Cited in Moretti, 'La dimensione ebraica', p.270. The letter is dated 10 December 1894.
139. See ibid., pp.278–9. Lattes made similar comments in his obituary of Tullo Massarani (*CI*, 1905, p.120).

140. Capuzzo, *Gli ebrei italiani*, p.86; Marino Berengo, 'Luigi Luzzatti e la tradizione ebraica', in Pier Luigi Ballini and Paolo Pecorari (eds), *Luigi Luzzatti e il suo tempo* (Venice: Istituto Veneto di scienze lettere ed arti, 1994), p.527.
141. Luigi Luzzatti, *Memorie autobiografiche e carteggi* (Bologna: Zanichelli, 1929), vol. 1, pp.1–12. See also his *Dio nella libertà: studio sulle relazioni tra lo Stato e le Chiese* (Bologna: Zanichelli, 1926).
142. Luzzatti, *Memorie*, vol. 2, pp.553–4, cited in Capuzzo, *Gli ebrei italiani*, pp.87–8, and Berengo, 'Luigi Luzzatti', p.527, n.1. This statement was first published in an open letter to Leonida Bissolati in *Avanti*, 15 April 1909. See also Isaac Deutscher, *The Non-Jewish Jew and other Essays*, edited with an introduction by Tamara Deutscher (London: Oxford University Press, 1968): 'He saw himself belonging to that breed of non-Jewish Jews who transcended Judaism ... I am, however, a Jew by force of my unconditional solidarity with the persecuted and exterminated' (pp.22, 51).
143. Cited in Berengo, 'Luigi Luzzatti', p.538.
144. Cited in Capuzzo, *Gli ebrei italiani*, p.89. The letter is dated 2 October 1899 and is published in Luzzatti's *Memorie*, vol. 2, p.555.
145. Berengo, 'Luigi Luzzatti', p.537.
146. Cited in ibid., p.539. Bruno Di Porto has an interesting thesis regarding Luzzatti's campaign to establish people's banks in Italy: it was partly based on a desire to counteract the stereotypical figure of the Jewish usurer. See Bruno Di Porto, 'Dopo il Risorgimento, al varco del '900: gli ebrei e l'ebraismo in Italia', *RMI*, 47, 1–6 (1981), p.30.
147. See Cecil Roth, *The History of the Jews of Italy* (Philadelphia, PA: Jewish Publication Society of America, 1946), p.477: 'The most important Jew in Italian public life in the age of the *Risorgimento* and for some time after was Isacco Artom.' See also Filomena Del Regno, 'Un archivio ottocentesco: le carte di Isacco Artom presso il centro bibliografico', *RMI*, 64, 1 (1998), pp.13–22.
148. Guido Artom, *I giorni del mondo* (Brescia: Morcelliana, 1997). Zaccaria's wealth transformed him into a very influential figure; he built a theatre, a new synagogue, schools and other public buildings in Asti. His eldest son, Leonetto, who completed some of his projects, was given the title of Count (p.299). See also *Il Vessillo Israelitico*, which regularly reported on the largesse of members of the Ottolenghi family: *VI*, 1889, pp.159–61; *VI*, 1898, pp.162–4 on the inauguration of a monument to the Risorgimento, designed and paid for by Leonetto Ottolenghi, whose name 'will be blessed for generations'; *VI*, 1903, p.229 on the newly restored birthplace of Alfieri financed by Leonetto Ottolenghi; *VI*, 1903, p.304 on the equestrian statue of Umberto I, also funded by Leonetto Ottolenghi, 'a peerless patron'. More recently, in 2000, Leonetto Ottolenghi has been described as 'the greatest benefactor that the city of Asti has ever had'; see Luigi Florio, mayor of Asti, in Mola (ed.), *Isacco Artom e gli ebrei italiani*, p.23. In his memoir, *Nato ad Asti: vita di un imprenditore* (Genoa: Marietti, 1989), Rodolfo De Benedetti recalls the prestige of the Jewish community in the nineteenth century due to Jewish families such as the Artom, the Ottolenghi and the Treves who distinguished themselves in the public life of the nation, an indicator of successful integration (pp.24–5). Rodolfo's paternal grandmother Dolcina was Isacco Artom's sister.
149. See Alberto Cavaglion, *ebrei senza saperlo* (Naples: l'ancora del mediterraneo, 2002), pp.13–14, and by the same author, *il senso dell'arca: Ebrei senza saperlo: nuove riflessioni* (Naples: l'ancora del mediterraneo, 2006), p.12. The letter is dated 21 October 1861 and is also cited by Moretti in 'La dimensione ebraica', pp.243–4.
150. See Moretti, 'La dimensione ebraica', p.252. The letter is dated 10 January 1869.
151. See Luisa Levi D'Ancona, '"Notabili e dame" nella filantropia ebraica ottocentesca: casi di studio in Francia, Italia e Inghilterra', *Quaderni storici*, 38, 3 (2003), pp.752, 772, n.73.
152. See Del Regno, 'Un archivio ottocentesco', p.21.
153. See Rossi Artom, *Gli Artom*, p.103, and Levi D'Ancona, '"Notabili e dame" nella filantropia ebraica ottocentesca', p.776, n.156.
154. See Capuzzo, *Gli ebrei italiani*, pp.80–1; and Alberto Cavaglion, 'Introduction', in Giuseppe Levi, *Autobiografia di un padre di famiglia* (Florence: Le Monnier, 2003; first edn 1868), p.ix.
155. See Cavaglion, 'Introduction', p.xviii.
156. Salvatore De Benedetti, *Giuseppe Levi: ricordo biografico*, published in the volume with Levi's autobiography (see note 154 above), pp.119–43.
157. Cavaglion, *il senso dell'arca*, p.12. He adds that Artom's name is difficult to find in Einaudi's history of the Jews; indeed it is absent from the index of Vivanti (ed.), *Storia d'Italia, Annali 11, Gli ebrei in Italia*, vol. 2.
158. See De Benedetti, *Giuseppe Levi*, p.120.
159. Marco Momigliano, *Autobiografia di un Rabbino italiano* (Palermo: Sellerio, 1986), pp.13, 16, 30, 33. A note on micro- and macro-history coming together: when Momigliano went to Turin to take his rabbinate exams in October 1848, they were delayed owing to the fact that 'the Chief Rabbi Lelio Cantoni who was due to examine me was very preoccupied on account of the Emancipation of the Jews' (p.20). Cantoni was a member of the Commissione Speciale Israelitica, set up in 1845;

he worked closely with Massimo and Roberto D'Azeglio. Marco Momigliano, of the illustrious Momigliano family, was Felice Momigliano's uncle and Arnaldo Momigliano's great-uncle.
160. Cavaglion, *Felice Momigliano*, pp.14–16.
161. Arturo Carlo Jemolo, *Anni di prova* (Verona: Pozza, 1969), pp.49–59. His mother, who was a Momigliano, converted on her marriage to a Sicilian Catholic.
162. Marco Besso, *Autobiografia* (Rome: Fondazione Marco Besso, 1925), p.8.
163. Ibid., pp.7, 22.
164. Ibid., p.50.
165. Ibid., Preface, p.vi.
166. The Marco Besso Foundation has an impressive website with online catalogue, its own publications list, and information on seminars and conferences.
167. Scardozzi, 'Una storia di famiglia: i Franchetti', p.698.
168. Ibid., pp.698, 721–2.
169. Ibid., p.725.
170. See ibid., pp.726–9. The Franchettis were rarely absent from the pages of *Il Vessillo Israelitico*, especially Raimondo's family (see ibid., pp.723–4). See also Paolo Pezzino and Alvaro Tacchini (eds), *Leopoldo e Alice Franchetti e il loro tempo* (Città di Castello: Petruzzi Editore, 2002), and the several entries on the influential members of the Franchetti family in the *Dizionario biografico degli Italiani* (Rome: Istituto della Enciclopedia Italiana, 1998), vol. 50.
171. Max Nordau, *Zionistische Schriften* (Cologne and Leipzig: Jüdischer Verlag, 1909), pp.372–3. Nordau, journalist, essayist and playwright, born Simcha Südfeld, was a German-speaking Hungarian Jew who became the second most influential figure of the Zionist movement. See *Il Vessillo Israelitico* praising the young Turinese Jews' patriotic initiative (1898, p.103).
172. D.V. Segre, *Memoirs of a Fortunate Jew*, p.23.
173. Carlo A. Viterbo, 'Un Maestro ancora presente', *RMI*, 38, 4 (1972), p.199, and by the same author, 'Una vita per l'Ebraismo', *Israel*, December 1974, p.6. The first piece is the text of the speech Viterbo gave at the fiftieth anniversary of Rabbi Margulies's death (the latter was chief rabbi of Florence from 1890 to 1922) in the synagogue of Florence. The second is an extract from Viterbo's notes on his life, published posthumously in a special edition of *Israel*, of which he had been editor. I am grateful to his son, Dr Giuseppe Viterbo, for bringing these articles to my attention.
174. Arnaldo Momigliano, *Pagine ebraiche*, p.xxix. The quotation is from an after-dinner speech made at Brandeis University in May 1977, cited in Levis Sullam, 'Arnaldo Momigliano e la "nazionalizzazione parallela"', p.59. See also Momigliano's comments from the 1930s, in Levis Sullam, 'Arnaldo Momigliano e la "nazionalizzazione parallela"', p.70.
175. Enzo Levi, *Memorie di una vita*, pp.20–32. This increase in socializing, as an indicator of structural assimilation, is corroborated by Luciano Allegra's research on the Jews of Turin: he notes that from 1910, Jews participated in greater numbers in workers' clubs, sports associations and other forms of group activities. See Allegra, *Ebrei a Torino*, pp.34–6. See also Tullia Catalan on Triestine Jews' social activities in *La comunità ebraica di Trieste (1781–1914): politica, società e cultura* (Trieste: Lint, 2000), pp.232–4.
176. Viterbo, 'Un Maestro ancora presente', p.199.
177. Ibid., p.199. One can note similar disapproval from Gershom Scholem's assimilated parents when he became deeply interested in Judaism and Zionism: 'This aroused the vehement opposition of my father ... discussions at our family table became heated'; Zionism 'promoted the rediscovery by the Jews of their own selves and their history'. See Gershom Scholem, *From Berlin to Jerusalem: Memories of My Youth*, translated from German by Harry Zohn (New York: Schocken Books, 1980), pp.40, 54. Scholem (1897–1982) emigrated to Palestine in 1923 and became the first professor of Jewish mysticism at the Hebrew University of Jerusalem in 1933. See also Arnaldo Momigliano, 'L'autobiografia di Gershom Scholem', in *Pagine ebraiche*, pp.201–10.
178. Francesco Del Canuto dedicates his article 'La soppressione della stampa ebraica in Italia e la sua ripresa (1938–1944)' in Mezzabotta (ed.), *Italia Judaica ... Atti del IV convegno internazionale*, pp.464–73, to the memory of 'one of the most representative figures of Italian Judaism and Zionism, to my Maestro, Carlo Alberto Viterbo' (p.464).
179. A. Segre, *Memorie*, pp.372–3.
180. Ibid., pp.74, 42; elsewhere he writes of their 'fanaticism to assimilate' which was like an epidemic (pp.31–2).
181. Ibid., pp.107, 101.
182. Momigliano, *Essays on Ancient and Modern Judaism*, p.138.
183. De Benedetti, *Nato ad Asti*, pp.82–5. Other family members were doctors and lawyers, and one was an army officer. Memo Bemporad, *La Macine: storia di una famiglia israelita negli ultimi 60 anni di vita italiana* (Rome: Carucci, 1984), pp.7–9. Lawyers and bankers also figured. Bemporad began his memoir as a diary during the war.

184. Dante, *La Divina Commedia*, 'Inferno', Canto 6.81.
185. Giancarlo Sacerdoti, *Ricordi di un ebreo bolognese: illusioni e delusioni 1929–1945* (Rome: Bonacci, 1983), p.5. See also Deutscher, *The Non-Jewish Jew*, p.47: 'Had anti-semitism not proved so deep-rooted, the Jews ... would have become completely assimilated.'
186. Sacerdoti, *Ricordi di un ebreo bolognese*, p.102. All immediate family members survived the war; his grandmother was protected by the local fascist commander of Cortemaggiore who played poker with her on a regular basis and told her she was the best player in Italy. Sacerdoti adds that she always let him win (p.168).
187. Besso, *Autobiografia*, p.22; Luzzatti, *Memorie*, vol. 1, p.2.
188. David Bidussa, 'Luoghi della memoria e percorsi della identità: note di lavoro', *RMI*, 71, 1 (2005), p.135. See also Della Pergola, *Anatomia dell'ebraismo italiano*, p.226.
189. Miniati, *Les 'émancipées'*, p.38; also Monica Miniati, 'Le "emancipate": le ebree italiane fra Ottocento e Novecento', in Claire E. Honess and Verina R. Jones (eds), *Le donne delle minoranze: le ebree e le protestanti d'Italia* (Turin: Claudiana, 1999), pp.243–54.
190. Della Pergola, *Anatomia dell'ebraismo italiano*', p.157.
191. Marion A. Kaplan, *The Making of the Jewish Middle Class: Women, Family and Identity in Imperial Germany* (Oxford: Oxford University Press, 1991), pp.3–4, 9. See also Miniati, *Les 'émancipées'*: 'women had a double responsibility ... a double "mission", that of Jewish mother and of "Italian" mother' (p.264); and Paula E. Hyman, *Gender and Assimilation in Modern Jewish History: The Roles and Representation of Women* (Seattle, WA, and London: University of Washington Press, 1995), pp.22–7.
192. The words of rabbis David Graziadio Viterbi, Giuseppe Modena and Samuel Hirsch Margulies. See Maddalena Del Bianco Cotrozzi, 'Ebraismo italiano dell'Ottocento: *la educazione della donna* di David Graziadio Viterbi', in Luzzati and Galasso (eds), *Donne nella storia degli ebrei d'Italia*, pp.341–2; in the same volume, Carlotta Ferrara degli Uberti, ' "Laboriose, educatrici e saggie": sulla corrispondenza femminile al "Vessillo Israelitico" all'alba del Novecento', p.405. Women contributors to *Il Vessillo*, such as Bettina Levi, did not deviate from the rabbinical stance. See also Milka Ventura Avanzinelli, 'Gravidanza, parto, allattamento: testimonianze di donne ebree fiorentine del Novecento', in Luzzati and Galasso (eds), *Donne nella storia degli ebrei d'Italia*, p.520. See also Miniati, 'Le "emancipate": le ebree italiane fra Otto e Novecento', pp.243–54; and Hyman, *Gender and Assimilation*, pp.27–9, 45–9, on the role of women in the Jewish periodical press in England, France and Germany.
193. See Ventura Avanzinelli, 'Gravidanza, parto, allattamento', p.530, n.105.
194. Momigliano, *Essays on Ancient and Modern Judaism*, p.xxvi.
195. Fausto Coen, *Una vita tante vite* (Catanzaro: Rubbettino, 2004), p.8. He wrote his memoir at the age of 89 (he was born in 1914) for his grandchildren 'who know little about me' (p.5).
196. D.V. Segre, *Memoirs of a Fortunate Jew*, p.28.
197. Bemporad, *La Macine*, p.17.
198. Cited in Milton M. Gordon, *Assimilation in American Life: The Role of Race, Religion and National Origins* (New York: Oxford University Press, 1964), p.194.
199. Luzzati, 'Integrazione e assimilazione', in Luzzati (ed.), *Ebrei di Livorno*, pp.12–21. Similar views were expressed by the women interviewed in Florence: see Ventura Avanzinelli, 'Gravidanza, parto, allattamento', pp.529–32.
200. Capuzzo, 'La famiglia Sereni', pp.477–9.
201. Rossi Artom, *Gli Artom*, pp.89, 96, 101.
202. D.V. Segre, *Memoirs of a Fortunate Jew*, p.22.
203. Rossi Artom, *Gli Artom*, pp.150–1 and Plate 13 (a facsimile of the invitation).
204. Cited in Molinari, *Ebrei in Italia*, pp.39–40. For a more complete version of the speech, see Toscano, *Ebraismo e antisemitismo*, pp.104–5.
205. Enzo Levi, *Memorie di una vita*, p.109; Rossi Artom, *Gli Artom*, p.155.
206. See Marcus Banks, *Ethnicity: Anthropological Constructions* (London and New York: Routledge, 1996), pp.17, 39.
207. In Stefano Jesurum, *Essere ebrei in Italia* (Milan: Longanesi, 1987), pp.155–6. *Il Vessillo Israelitico* reported on the first Chair of Hebrew Studies established in Spain after seven centuries; the successful candidate was of Spanish descent (*VI*, 1916, pp.45, 76–8).
208. See, for example, C. Roth, *History of the Jews of Italy*, p.479: 'Released from the Ghetto, Jewish genius became apparent in every aspect of Italian life ... There was thus no country of Europe where the Jewish contribution to cultural life was proportionately so great.' Other historians might dispute this statement and suggest Germany and Austria-Hungary for such an accolade. See, for example, Frederic V. Grunfeld, *Prophets without Honour: A Background to Freud, Kafka, Einstein and Their World* (New York: Holt, Rinehart & Winston, 1979), p.1: but for the 'infamous finale ... cultural historians would now be writing' of the German and Jewish intellectual traditions 'as a golden age second only to the Italian Renaissance'.

209. Gaio Sciloni, 'Scrittori ebrei nell'Italia dell'Unità: reciproche influenze o assimilazione? Un caso Pascoli-Orvieto', in Mezzabotta (ed.), *Italia Judaica ... Atti del IV convegno internazionale*, p.97; see also Boralevi, 'Angiolo Orvieto, "il Marzocco"', pp.213–33; Donald Sassoon, *The Culture of the Europeans: From 1800 to the Present* (London: Harper, 2006), pp.620–3. On Formiggini, see, for example, Luigi Balsamo and Renzo Cremente (eds), *Angelo Fortunato Formiggini un editore del Novecento* (Bologna: Il Mulino, 1981). Formiggini (1878–1938) also edited the periodical *L'Italia che scrive*. He committed suicide in 1938. The Belforte printers and publishers, established in Livorno in the nineteenth century (1834–1938) and reopened in 2001, specialized mainly in Jewish prayer books which were used throughout the Mediterranean.
210. Salvadori, *Gli ebrei di Firenze*, p.84. The italics are in the original text.
211. Paolo Pellegrini, 'Una storia, tante storie. Famiglie ebraiche a Terni fra Otto e Novecento', *RMI*, 70, 2 (2004), pp.63–114.
212. See, for example, Luzzatto Voghera, 'Aspetti della cultura ebraica in Italia nel secolo XIX', pp.1211–41. There was also a strong tradition of Hebrew poetry in Italy from the eleventh century to the beginning of the twentieth century. See, for example, Dan Pagis, 'Caratteri generali della poesia ebraica italiana', *RMI*, 60, 1–2 (1994), pp.6–21.
213. See Sciloni, 'Scrittori ebrei nell'Italia dell'Unità', p.100, n.6. Alberto Cantoni was Orvieto's maternal uncle.
214. See ibid., p.99.
215. See Boralevi, 'Angiolo Orvieto, "il Marzocco"', p.225.
216. Cited in Sciloni, 'Scrittori ebrei nell'Italia dell'Unità', p.102. The whole collection, writes Sciloni, is permeated with the wind that buffets the poet between his love for Florence and for Zion (ibid.). Orvieto wrote that *Il Vento di Sion* was 'an expression of my profound Jewish soul' (cited in Boralevi, 'Angiolo Orvieto, "il Marzocco"', p.231). Other collections such as *Verso L'Oriente* also treat the theme of Orvieto's love for both the Italian and Jewish cultures. See, for example, Angiolo Orvieto, *Poesie scelte*, with an introduction by Carlo Pellegrini (Florence: Olschki, 1979). Significantly, Orvieto had his first collection of poems published by the Casa Editrice Israel.
217. See Boralevi, 'Angiolo Orvieto, "il Marzocco"', pp.227–8.
218. Ibid., p.228. Boralevi sees affinities between Orvieto's and Freud's Moses in *Moses and Monotheism* (1937).
219. See Boralevi, 'Angiolo Orvieto, "il Marzocco"', pp.216–17.
220. Aldo Neppi Modona, 'Ricordo di Angiolo Orvieto', *RMI*, 34, 1 (1968), p.3.
221. See, for example, Stuart Hughes, *Prisoners of Hope: The Silver Age of the Italian Jews 1924–1974* (Cambridge, MA, and London: Harvard University Press, 1983). The authors he focuses on are Italo Svevo, Alberto Moravia, Carlo Levi, Primo Levi, Natalia Ginzburg and Giorgio Bassani.
222. See, for example, Laura Mincer, 'La tradizione rivisitata nel teatro Yiddish di Moni Ovadia', *RMI*, 66, 20 (2000), pp.145–54.
223. See Jack Wertheimer, *Unwelcome Strangers: East European Jews in Imperial Germany* (New York and Oxford: Oxford University Press, 1987), p.12; Frances Malino, 'French Jews', in Liedtke and Wendehorst (eds), *Emancipation of Catholics, Jews and Protestants*, p.97; Todd M. Endelman, 'Native Jews and Foreign Jews in London, 1870–1914', in David Berger (ed.), *The Legacy of Jewish Migration: 1881 and its Impact* (New York: Brooklyn College Press, 1983), pp.109–29.
224. Sander L. Gilman, *Jewish Self-Hatred: Anti-Semitism and the Hidden Language of the Jews* (Baltimore, MD, and London: Johns Hopkins University Press, 1986), p.270.
225. See Wertheimer, *Unwelcome Strangers*, pp.160–1. On Freud's and Mahler's 'revulsion', see Peter Gay, *Freud: A Life for Our Time* (London and Melbourne: Dent, 1988), p.19; Elon, *The Pity Of It All*, p.271. See also the German novelist Jakob Wassermann (1873–1934), *My Life as German and Jew* (London: Allen & Unwin, 1934 [1921]), p.152; Besso, *Autobiografia*, p.162; Benbassa, *The Jews of France*, pp.134–7; Cesarani, *Jewish Chronicle and Anglo-Jewry*, pp.75–8.
226. Endelman, 'Native and Foreign Jews', p.117.
227. C. Roth, *History of the Jews of Italy*, p.499.
228. See Vital, *People Apart*, pp.235–6. Vital gives details of the principal publications in England, France and Germany.
229. It closed through lack of funds and readership. See Rovighi's letter to Samuel David Luzzatto of February 1848, cited in Catalan, 'La "primavera degli ebrei"', p.54. See also Attilio Milano, 'Un secolo di stampa periodica ebraica in Italia', *RMI*, 12, 7–9 (April–June 1938), pp.99–100, and Francesco Del Canuto, 'La stampa ebraica in Italia dall'emancipazione alla seconda guerra mondiale', in Miglau (ed.), *La cultura ebraica nell'editoria italiana*, p.70.
230. See Giuseppe Levi, *Autobiografia*, Introduction by Cavaglion, p.xiv.
231. Milano, 'Un secolo di stampa', pp.107–8. Flaminio Servi was nominated Cavaliere della Corona D'Italia in 1877. This assessment was reiterated by Dan Vittorio Segre: see 'L'emancipazione degli ebrei in Italia', in Toscano (ed.), *Integrazione e Identità*, p.111. Flaminio Servi was a member of

many patriotic and philanthropic societies. He also published *Gli Israeliti d'Europa nella civiltà* (Turin, 1871).
232. Giuseppe Levi, *Autobiografia*, Introduction by Cavaglion, p.xiii.
233. See Maida, *Dal ghetto alla città*, p.292; and Schwarz, 'A proposito di una vivace stagione storiografica', p.168.
234. Carlotta Ferrara degli Uberti, 'Rappresentare se stessi tra famiglia e nazione: Il "Vessillo Israelitico" alla soglia del '900', *Passato e Presente*, 70 (2007), p.41. The archives of the journal and Flaminio Servi's personal papers have been lost, thus it is impossible to know details of the quality or quantity of the readership (p.40). See also Bruno Di Porto, 'Il giornalismo ebraico in Italia: un primo sguardo d'insieme al "Vessillo Israelitico"', *Materia giudaica*, 6, 1 (2001), pp.104–9.
235. For an analysis of some of these narratives, see Ferrara degli Uberti, 'Rappresentare se stessi', pp.46–52.
236. In support of *Il Vessillo Israelitico*'s editorial perspective, Marco Mortara, chief rabbi of Mantua from 1842 to 1894 and an influential figure, wrote: 'as is the case with our co-religionists of other nations, Italian Jews ... will have the courage to show that they are citizens everywhere, but Jews in the synagogues ... and in their homes' (*VI*, 1881, p.132), cited in Ferrara degli Uberti, 'Rappresentare se stessi', p.42.
237. Silvana Monti Orel, *I giornali triestini dal 1863 al 1902* (Trieste: Lint, 1976), p.10.
238. For biographical details of the first editor, see Lelio Della Torre, 'A.V. Morpurgo', *CI*, 1867, pp.102–6.
239. Despite being read throughout Italy and Europe, each issue did not exceed 500 copies and was limited to intellectual circles. See Catalan, 'La "primavera degli ebrei"', p.54.
240. Milano, *Storia degli ebrei*, p.376. See also C. Roth, *History of the Jews of Italy*, pp.496–7; Luzzatto Voghera, 'Aspetti della cultura ebraica in Italia nel secolo XIX', pp.1215–26; by the same author, *Il prezzo dell'eguaglianza*, pp.140–6; Del Bianco Cotrozzi, *Il Collegio Rabbinico di Padova*, pp.216–27; Morris B. Margolies, *Samuel David Luzzatto: Traditionalist Scholar* (New York: Ktav, 1979); *RMI*, 32, 9–10 (1966), in which all the articles are in commemoration of the first centenary of Luzzatto's death. On *Il Corriere*'s obituary and homages to Luzzatto, see *CI*, 1865, pp.199–203, 209–23, 261–4; 1866, pp.17–24. On Della Torre, see, for example, Aldo A. Mola, 'Lelio Della Torre: un rabbino tra Risorgimento e Terza Italia', in Mola (ed.), *Isacco Artom e gli ebrei italiani*, pp.27–38.
241. The Verein für Cultur und Wissenschaft der Juden (Society for the Culture and Scientific Study of the Jews) was founded in Berlin in 1819. In essence, it was the inauguration of modern, secular Jewish historiography and therefore a deliberate departure from the rabbinic tradition of scholarship. See, for example, Vital, *People Apart*, pp.139–41; Meyer, *Response to Modernity*, pp.75–97; Mendes-Flohr and Reinharz, *The Jew in the Modern World*, pp.211–30; Elon, *The Pity Of It All*, pp.110–16.
242. Isacco Garti, 'Il carteggio Ascoli-Luzzatto', *Italia*, 1, 1 (1976), p.72; they corresponded between 1849 and 1854; Samuel David Luzzatto, *Epistolario italiano francese latino pubblicato da' suoi figli* (Padua: Fratelli Salmin, 1890), vol. 1, p.520; the letter is dated 27 December 1847. See also Shadal's letter of 5 June 1860 to Salomon J. Rappaport, chief rabbi of Prague and one of the founders of the Wissenschaft des Judentums, in Mendes-Flohr and Reinharz (eds), *The Jew in the Modern World*, pp.235–7; Canepa, 'Emancipation and Jewish Response', pp.427–8: 'Luzzatto ... consistently opposed the secularizing rationalism, the historical relativism and the open assimilationism of his German colleagues in the Wissenschaft des Judentums movement.'
243. See, for example, Gilman, *Jewish Self-Hatred*, pp.244–8; Allan Janik, 'Viennese Culture and the Jewish Self-Hatred Hypothesis: A Critique', in Ivar Oxaal, Michael Pollak and Gerhard Botz (eds), *Jews, Antisemitism and Culture in Vienna* (London and New York: Routledge & Kegan Paul, 1987), pp.75–88.
244. On the nineteenth-century concept of 'fusion', see Cohen Albert, 'Israelite and Jew', pp.96–7.
245. Flaminio Servi, 'Giudaismo passato e presente', *VI*, 1877, pp.335–6. See also Molinari, *Ebrei in Italia*, p.32.
246. *CI*, 1867, p.329. See also Richard I. Cohen, 'Nostalgia and "Return to the Ghetto": A Cultural Phenomenon in Western and Central Europe', in Frankel and Zipperstein (eds), *Assimilation and Community*, pp.130–55.
247. See also *CI*, 1874, pp.154–7; 1892, pp.246–8. In 1891 in Rome, for example, the council of the community closed three of the five synagogues because of low attendance; in 1900, one of these councillors identified three categories of Jews: a devout minority; the majority who were not religious but felt themselves to be Jewish; and a small group who were completely indifferent to all aspects of Judaism (Caviglia, *L'identità salvata*, pp.42–3, 100); on religious indifference in Livorno, see Ferrara degli Uberti, *La 'Nazione Ebrea' di Livorno*, pp.35–7.
248. Tullia Catalan, 'L'organizzazione delle comunità ebraiche dall'Unità alla prima guerra mondiale', in Vivanti (ed.), *Storia d'Italia, Annali 11, Gli ebrei in Italia*, vol. 2, p.1279.
249. Vital, *People Apart*, p.262. He provides statistics for German Jews. On Germany, see also Monika

Richarz, 'Un profilo sociale degli ebrei tedeschi 1850–1933', in Toscano (ed.), *Integrazione e identità*, pp.81–2.
250. See Della Pergola, *Anatomia dell'ebraismo italiano*, pp.230–7.
251. On the figures for Trieste, see Catalan, *La comunità ebraica di Trieste*, pp.241–4.
252. *CI*, 1881, pp.221–2; *CI*, 1900, p.161; *VI*, 1909, p.570; *VI*, 1914, p.656.
253. Between 1853 and 1874, *L'Educatore Israelita* devoted twenty-four articles to the subject; *Il Vessillo Israelitico* published forty-one between 1875 and 1902, and *Il Corriere Israelitico* forty-seven. See Chiara Foà, *Gli ebrei e i matrimoni misti: l'esogamia nella comunità torinese (1866–1898)* (Turin: Zamorani, 2001), p.47.
254. See Della Pergola, *Anatomia dell'ebraismo italiano*, p.235.
255. Entitled *Il matrimonio misto*, it is reprinted as Appendix 1 in Chiara Foà, *Gli ebrei e i matrimoni misti*, pp.161–90. It centres on the marriage between a Jew, Davide, and a Catholic, Adele. She tries to convert her husband; they nevertheless agree to bring up the twins in both their religions – the boy as a Jew, the girl as a Catholic – but it ends in conflict and tragedy with the premature death of Adele. It was favourably reviewed in *Il Corriere Israelitico* (1873, pp.257–9). Interestingly, a more positive outcome was experienced by Rodolfo De Benedetti, whose father married a Catholic in 1884 in Asti. Neither of their families approved and there was initial disharmony. Both religions were celebrated in the home and he recalls that he preferred the Jewish rituals. See his memoir, *Nato ad Asti*, pp.46–8.
256. Guglielmo Lattes, *Tra la fede e l'amore: scene della vita ebraica moderna* (Florence: Paggi, 1903). He was the older half-brother of Dante Lattes, a teacher and rabbi by profession and author of numerous pedagogic works.
257. See *CI*, 1886, 'The Rite of Circumcision', pp.229–30.
258. Sori, 'Una "comunità crepuscolare"', p.214.
259. *VI*, 1885, p.133; *CI*, 1890, p.86, cited in Chiara Foà, *Gli ebrei e i matrimoni misti*, pp.97–8.
260. Catalan, 'L'organizzazione delle comunità ebraiche italiane', pp.1284–5. The president of the Jewish community of Casale Monferrato in the 1920s contracted a mixed marriage. See A. Segre, *Memorie*, p.41.
261. See Salvadori, *La comunità ebraica di Pitigliano*, p.250.
262. Chiara Foà, *Gli ebrei e i matrimoni misti*, p.157.
263. Rossi Artom, *Gli Artom*, pp.105, 95.
264. Enzo Levi, *Memorie di una vita*, pp.21–2.
265. Pesciatini, 'Tra emancipazione e assimilazione', p.165.
266. See, for example, Maifreda, *Gli ebrei e l'economia milanese*, pp.71–5; Scardozzi, 'Da merciai "con fagotto" a industriali del cotone', pp.191, 200; and Catalan, *La comunità ebraica di Trieste*, p.244.
267. Vital, *People Apart*, p.124. Vital provides conversion figures for Germany and Austria-Hungary, pp.124–5. In France, approximately 100 families converted between 1808 and 1840; fewer in the Second Empire, and none by the end of the century. See Malino, 'French Jews', p.94.
268. See Canepa, 'Il caso Pasqualigo', p.192. On the figures for Trieste, and the case of one of the city's most famous literary figures, see Schächter, *Origin and Identity*, pp.49–54. See also Catalan, *La comunità ebraica di Trieste*, p.243.
269. Grunfeld, *Prophets Without Honour*, p.2.
270. *CI*, 1899, p.157. See, for example, Heine's letter to Moses Moser of 1826: 'I am now hated by Christian and Jew alike. I am truly sorry that I permitted myself to be baptized. I do not see that my lot has improved', and in another letter to Moser, he wrote of his 'personal suffering' and 'the never removable Jew'. Marx, a child convert, who wished to distance himself from his Jewish identity, was still seen as a Jew (Gilman, *Jewish Self-Hatred*, pp.188, 196).
271. Paolo Bernardini, 'The Jews in Nineteenth-Century Italy: Towards a Reappraisal', *Journal of Modern Italian Studies*, 1, 2 (Spring 1996), p.297.
272. Ibid.
273. See Andrew M. Canepa, 'Reflections on Antisemitism in Liberal Italy', *Wiener Library Bulletin*, 31, 47–8 (1978), p.104.
274. Caviglia, *L'identità salvata*, p.15; on conversions through poverty in Livorno, see Ferrara degli Uberti, *La 'Nazione Ebrea' di Livorno*, pp.43–4.
275. See Toscano, *Ebraismo e antisemitismo*, p.116.
276. A. Segre, *Memorie*, pp.52, 54. See also Stille, *Benevolence and Betrayal*: 'by signing up in record numbers for the war, the Jews acted like citizens on probation ... they felt a special obligation to show their gratitude, to prove their ... *italianità*' (p.30).
277. Similar sentiments were expressed by Jews of the other nations at war. See, for example, the statement published in the *Verband der deutschen Juden* (Association of German Jews) on the day Russia declared war: 'It is self-evident that every German Jew is prepared to sacrifice his property and blood ... Brethren ... rush voluntarily to the banners!' The Zionists also declared: 'In this hour we

must show again that we ... belong to the best sons of the fatherland.' Cited in Jehuda Reinharz, *Fatherland or Promised Land: The Dilemma of the German Jew, 1893–1914* (Ann Arbor, MI: University of Michigan Press, 1975), p.222. See also the patriotic rhetoric of the *Archives israélites* in Birnbaum, *The Jews of the Republic*, pp.185–6; that of the Israelitische Kultusgemeinde, the Jewish community of Vienna, in Marsha L. Rozenblit, *Reconstructing a National Identity: The Jews of Hapsburg Austria during World War I* (Oxford: Oxford University Press, 2001), and the *Jewish Chronicle* in Cesarani, *Jewish Chronicle and Anglo-Jewry*, pp.115–17.
278. Stille, *Benevolence and Betrayal*, p.30. See also David Cesarani, 'British Jews', in Liedtke and Wendehorst (eds), *Emancipation of Catholics, Jews and Protestants*, p.44: 'English Jewry still felt itself to be on trial'.
279. See Toscano, *Ebraismo e antisemitismo*, p.114.
280. *Settimana Israelitica* [*SI*], 3 (1915); ASCEF, Attività Culturali-Enti Vari Ebraici, E. 19.1. 1918–1935, and Caviglia, *L'identità salvata*, pp.168–9. See also *The British Jewry Book of Honour* (London: Caxton, 1922), cited in Jonathan, Freedland, *Jacob's Gift: A Journey into the Heart of Belonging* (London: Hamish Hamilton, 2005), p.311, and *Les Israélites dans l'armée française, 1914–1918* (Angers: Gaultier and Thébert, 1920); see Paula Hyman, *From Dreyfus to Vichy: The Remaking of French Jewry, 1906–1939* (New York: Columbia University Press, 1979), p.57.
281. The editor of the *Jewish Chronicle* regularly published the number of Jews in the armed forces, listing their names in an Honour Record. See Cesarani, *Jewish Chronicle and Anglo-Jewry*, p.117; *Archives israélites* also published the names of Jews in the armed forces; see Birnbaum, *The Jews of the Republic*, pp.185–6.
282. Stille, *Benevolence and Betrayal*, p.30; Caviglia, *L'identità salvata*, p.168; Toscano, *Ebraismo e antisemitismo*, p.110.
283. Funaro, '"Vita e Legge"', p.172. German Zionists returned from Palestine to enlist; see Reinharz, *Fatherland or Promised Land*, p.223.
284. Stille, *Benevolence and Betrayal*, pp.17, 30. Ettore and his wife and daughter were brutally murdered by the Nazis in 1943 (pp.88–9); Allegra, *Ebrei di Torino*, photograph 287; Francesca Belforte, 'Una famiglia medio-borghese: i Belforte', in Luzzati (ed.), *Ebrei di Livorno*, p.94; Capuzzo, 'La famiglia Sereni', p.481.
285. A. Levi, *Ricordi della vita e dei tempi di Ernesto Nathan*, p.262.
286. Enzo Levi, *Memorie di una vita*, p.29. Jewish women also did their bit for the war effort: in Pisa, Eloisa Sarfatti was vice-president of the Comitato femminile pro-Patria; there were also other associations to which women contributed. See Savelli, 'Una città e i suoi ebrei', pp.354–5. See also Miniati, *Les 'émancipées'*, pp.221–33.
287. These last two cases were related to the author by surviving relatives during a meeting of the Gruppo Storico of the Jewish Community of Florence in October 2003.
288. *SI*, 32 (1914); *SI*, 21 (1915). See also Toscano, *Ebraismo e antisemitismo*, pp.92, 112–13. There is a complete run of *La Settimana Israelitica* in the Biblioteca Marucelliana, Florence. At its meeting on 6 December 1914, the executive committee of the Jewish communities agreed to send 'a note of condolences to all those co-religionists who are forced to fight against each other' (*VI*, 1914, p.656).
289. See Cesarani, *Jewish Chronicle and Anglo-Jewry*, pp.248–50.
290. Ibid., p.253.

3

Social and Demographic Change in the Jewish Communities

Until recently, the established historiography of this period privileged the processes of disintegration and the negative impact of modernization on Jewish communities, perceived as 'a clash between centrifugal and centripetal forces'.[1] Jacob Katz and others have argued for an analysis not in terms of fragmentation but of a 'thorough transformation', which was complex, multidimensional and multi-directional.[2] Emancipation and Italy's political Unification brought profound social and demographic change to the Jewish communities. After centuries of isolation and autonomy, the scattered congregations attempted to unify and create a central association along the lines of the English and French models — the Board of Deputies of British Jews (1760) and the Central Consistory (1808). The aspiration towards collective cohesion was motivated by a desire to pay homage to the Unification of Italy. There was also a pressing need for such a body to represent the Jews at government level, to ensure that all legislation was being applied equitably – in short, the need for a new relationship with the new Italy on the part of its Jewish citizens. To this end two conferences were organized, one in 1863 and the other four years later. In 1860, Leone Ravenna, a young lawyer from Ferrara who was to play an influential role in Italian Jewish life until his death in 1920, wrote in *L'Educatore Israelita* (*EI*) that the creation of such an organization would enhance the public image of the Jews and also protect them against intolerance.[3]

Formal initial contact between individual communities[4] was through the network of committees of the Alliance Israélite Universelle, an institution founded in Paris in 1860 by the leading French Jew Adolphe Crémieux. This was a philanthropic, voluntary institution primarily concerned with the welfare, security and education of less fortunate Jews throughout the world in their struggle for emancipation. It was the first international body committed to the protection of Jews and, as such, was able to exert political and economic pressure, as in the case of the plight of the Romanian Jews.[5] The genesis of the organization dates from the Damascus Affair (1840), in which Crémieux was closely involved, and the Mortara case (1858); in both, the imperative for a global coordinated Jewish response was made manifest. The efficacy of Jewish intervention with regard to the Damascus crisis was acclaimed not only by Jewry worldwide but also by liberal public opinion, despite doubts about Jewish solidarity beyond national boundaries. Moreover, the Alliance's 'message of modernity' through its main activity of education, designed 'to remake Jews everywhere in the image of the emancipated French Jew', would be perceived by the French government as a most laudable objective.[6] In 1862, elementary and secondary schools were established in Morocco; by 1913, there were schools, youth clubs, vocational courses and libraries for 43,700 students in eastern Europe, the Middle East and beyond; the principal language of instruction was French. The Alliance pursued an emancipationist and integrationist ideology, opposed to political Zionism.[7] *Il Corriere Israelitico* (*CI*) regularly reported on the meetings of its central committee, held each month in the French capital; *L'Educatore Israelita* was also in favour of such cooperation and saw it as a preliminary step towards consensus between Italian Jewish communities: 'Our century ... is one of cohesion ... it has given life to this universal alliance ... which could be a precedent for a robust internal constitution of our communities'.[8] Vercelli, where the journal was published, was the location of the Alliance's regional committee for Piedmont and Lombardy, and its chief rabbi was the president; Vercelli alone had twenty members. By 1875, the Alliance had over 18,000 members – 1,180 in Austria-Hungary and 723 in Italy.[9] The Alliance still exists; it is promoted on its website as one of the major international organizations in the field of Jewish education and culture.

THE CONFERENCE OF FERRARA

The first Italian affiliation to the Alliance was established in Ferrara in 1861, and it was Ferrara which hosted the conference of the Italian Jewish communities, held from 12 to 17 May 1863. The initiative had come from the Jewish community of Ancona for the specific purpose of forming a deputation to obtain a government subsidy for 'the Jewish religion'.[10] Subsequently, the aims of the conference broadened to include other issues which were publicized by *L'Educatore Israelita* (having invited readers to send in their proposals);[11] in effect, the Piedmontese journal became the fulcrum for the conference, as it was for Italian membership of the Alliance, and one of its editors, Professor Giuseppe Levi, was unanimously elected president of the Ferrara conference (Leone Ravenna, one of the secretaries, remained in that post for the 1867 conference in Florence).[12] Fifty-seven communities, then called *Università*, were invited, including those from the Veneto, Trieste, Gorizia and Rome (during the first session, it was agreed to send greetings to fellow Jews in those regions 'which do not yet belong to the kingdom of Italy').[13] In a letter of 4 May 1863, the leaders of the Triestine community had thanked the organizers for the invitation, adding that although they could not attend, they were very interested in the deliberations that would take place and would postpone their own discussions 'in order to draw on those of the conference'. Such sentiments indicated the extent to which the Triestine community identified with its counterparts in Italy. Two members of the Rome community had expressed similar views in a letter of 6 May, concluding: 'the circumstances that prevent our acceptance are evident'.[14]

Twenty-two delegates participated, representing thirty-two communities, all from within Italy as it then was. Several of them deputized for more than one community – in the case of Dr Gabriele Sacerdoti of Parma it was seven – while Ferrara, Turin and Modena had more than one representative.[15] Each participant was entitled to only one vote.[16] A twelve-point programme, drawn up by *L'Educatore Israelita,* formed the basis of the conference, and it included the following: government subsidies for 'the Jewish religion'; legislation against enforced religious conversion; the question of a new rabbinical college and an Italian rabbinical synod; the establishment of a society for the publication of 'good Jewish books' in Italian, and of a central Jewish agency.[17]

The first session and part of the second one were principally taken up with the question of religious conversion. Delegates were unanimous in their agreement that the Italian government should institute laws for the protection of children against abduction; issue safeguards for non-Catholic adults in hospitals and prisons in order that they did not fall victim to proselytism and that they would be granted access to ministers of their own religion; accord the same guarantees as other liberal governments to Jewish adults in the Houses of the Catechumens (Catholic institutions for the conversion of Jews and others); and ensure that minors held there were returned to their families.[18] These demands were prompted not only by the desire for civic and religious equality, but also by the persistence of the practice of clandestine baptism of Jewish children who were then taken from their families: the notorious case of Edgardo Mortara, a 6-year-old Jewish boy who was abducted from his home in 1858, would have been fresh in their minds. This had occurred in the Papal States which were as yet outside the jurisdiction of the new Italy, but a similar case had taken place three years later in 1861, involving a 16-year-old girl, Rosa Sadun, from Pitigliano in Tuscany.[19]

On the question of government subsidies for the Jewish religion, there was a heated discussion and the delegates were divided. Those in favour cited the example of the Waldensians (Italian Protestants), who had been granted a subsidy of 6,462.20 lire by the Subalpino parliament on 10 March 1856. It was agreed that an approach would be made to the government on the grounds of parity with other non-Catholic religions.[20] There was no consensus on a new rabbinical college, a rabbinical synod and a central Jewish organization: thus it was decided to defer these weighty matters to an elected executive committee which would oversee all the deliberations of the conference. Almost a whole day was devoted to the discussion of article eight of the programme: 'on a central Jewish representative body based on English Judaism, leaving maximum freedom to the local councils' (*lasciando la massima libertà ai Consigli locali*). The very formulation of this fundamental issue revealed a major concern of many conference delegates: the retention of autonomy enjoyed by individual communities for centuries. Several argued that membership of the Alliance Israélite Universelle was sufficient; others suggested waiting until Rome was united to Italy, and setting up a committee (*Commissione*) to formulate a proposal based on responses from the communities. Even this last idea was viewed with suspicion by some, in case the *Commissione* was given too much latitude and therefore compromised the communities' self-sufficiency.[21] There was agreement, however, that representatives should meet every three years (it was to be four until the Florence congress, owing to the war of 1866). Agreement was also reached on the need for the publication of 'good Jewish books' in Italian, and a committee of three was set up to promote this project, with funding to be provided by each community according to its size.

The conference ended on a positive and patriotic note: the last item, approved amidst 'loud applause', was that 'the same spirit of accord and moral intent which have motivated the delegates … should be evident in all the communities, in order that the deliberations may be realized to the full advantage and honour of Italian Judaism'. In his concluding remarks, Giuseppe Levi, the president, stated unequivocally: 'The conference has been a labour of faith and patriotism; the unity of Italian Judaism is a solemn homage to the unity of Italy' and, with shouts of 'Viva l'Italia!' and 'Viva il Re!', the last session drew to a resounding close on 17 May 1863.[22] In a printed circular of 18 May sent to all the communities, Giuseppe Levi reiterated the seriousness of the proceedings, which had ushered in 'a new era in the destiny of Italian Judaism'. With this circular was a document containing the twelve-point programme, a summary of the decisions which, it was stated, would be acted upon by the named executive committee only if ratified by three-quarters of the communities; they were requested to inform the president of their views.[23] Levi also published an editorial in *L'Educatore Israelita* on the positive outcomes of the conference: 'this was an historic moment … a beautiful bust of our beloved Sovereign rose behind the presidential chair as a witness to our discussions … as an enduring monument of love and freedom' (1863, pp.161–4). A detailed report was also published in *Il Corriere Israelitico*; the editors approved of the prudence and wisdom of the deliberations, particularly those relating to the Catechumens (*CI*, 1863, pp.94–101).

Two distinct features emerged from this first conference of Italian Jews, particularly with reference to the proposals for a central organization and a rabbinical synod: in the discussions of the former, repeated claims were articulated concerning the independence of individual communities, to the extent that the report sent out on 18 May contained the statement that 'the present considerations in no way prejudice the autonomy of the individual Italian Jewish communities sanctioned by the laws that govern them'. This defence of autonomy, which many thought would be undermined by a central agency, proved to be one of the principal impediments to any significant future collaboration for many years.

The three rabbis at the conference were in favour of a rabbinical synod: Rabbi David Terracini from Asti spoke emphatically and at length on the need for reform: 'everywhere it is demanded that the rabbis must take action; this demand is justified'.[24] Others were fearful about the idea of change. The proposal was defeated by eleven votes to five. This dissension was not recorded in the report of 18 May: 'the conference declares that no deliberations of article 10 took place' (Article 10: Italian Rabbinical Council – on whether it is necessary to promote a rabbinical synod, and in what way).[25] The religious reforms taking place in Germany and Austria-Hungary did not find fertile ground in Italy. The majority of Italian rabbis were opposed to any alteration, however moderate, to Judaism and its practices; among the exceptions to this position was Marco Mortara (1815–94), chief rabbi of Mantua.[26]

The only proposal for reform was put forward by the chief rabbi of Turin, Samuele Salomone Olper (1811–77). On 5 April 1865 he published his recommendations to reduce the period of strict mourning from seven days to three and to permit men to shave after seven days; all other external signs of mourning were to be voluntary. These modest modifications engendered a fierce debate among the Italian rabbinate: fourteen rabbis, led by Rabbi Benamozegh from Livorno, opposed them; seven others, guided by Marco Mortara, who were in favour of reform in principle, declared that all decision-making should devolve to a rabbinical synod; only one rabbi (from Biella) approved them. A rabbinical conference did not take place, and thus the opposition won. The editor of *Il Corriere Israelitico* publicized the polemic; in his stance and coverage he was on the side of the opponents to reform, as was *L'Educatore Israelita*.[27]

Thirty-six communities gave their support to the deliberations of the Ferrara conference, pledging funds for the publication of new books and for subsequent meetings, in proportion to their population. In many of the responses there was a sense of optimism for the future, epitomized in the letter from Lugo (province of Modena) of 3 July 1863: 'who could not see the supreme good that will come to all the Jews of Italy from the implementation of this programme?'[28] The list of these communities is revealing, as it provides information about their size: Livorno was the largest (4,340), followed by Florence and Modena (each 2,000), and Turin (1,990). Colorno (province of Parma) was the smallest, with forty; over half comprised 200 members or fewer.[29]

The new president, David Levi from Florence, also nominated to organize the next conference, sent out a handwritten circular dated 1 November 1866, addressed to representatives of the Jewish communities, in which he reported on the progress made so far with the programme of the 1863 conference. The salient points can be summarized: the government had given assurances that new legislation would safeguard religious minorities against enforced conversions and similar abuses; publication of new books for kindergartens had commenced; no subsidy for religious purposes had been requested, as this proposal had not been ratified by the required majority; parliamentary debates on the separation of Church and State had given rise to a climate of uncertainty as the provisional government of Tuscany had cancelled subsidies to the Jewish communities in that region in 1866, having halved them the previous year; divorce was not permitted under the Italian Civil Code although there had been discussions to apply for exemption, divorce being permitted under Judaic law. This request for exemption, as Tullia Catalan observes, is evidence of the difficulty some Jews had in accepting the new condition of citizenship with all its advantages and drawbacks.[30] Levi concluded his report by expressing the desire that all the Jewish communities of Italy would be represented at the next conference devoted to 'the discussion of the principles of freedom of worship and civil equality in order to derive full benefit for our cause'.[31]

THE CONFERENCE OF FLORENCE

The second conference was held in Florence between 30 April and 5 May 1867. Florence was then the capital of Italy, and thus the hosts, the Florentine Jewish community, were determined to impress: each delegate was invited not only to a special religious ceremony to inaugurate the conference, but also to a banquet to be held on 2 May in Via della Nave, one of the principal streets of the ghetto area before it was demolished in the 1880s.[32] To this effect, candelabra, velvet and silk drapes, flowers and champagne were ordered. We even know the flavours of the ice-cream they ate, made by Louis Normand & Fils! A choir and pianist were engaged; waiters and cleaners were hired; the premises were newly painted and decorated; and all the expense was borne by the president and the principal organizers.[33]

Of the sixty-four communities invited, forty-three replied, only twenty of which sent delegates, including those from the recently annexed Veneto region, Padua, Venice and Verona, and also the newly re-emerging Neapolitan community.[34] This was a reduction in number in contrast to the thirty-two represented at Ferrara. Comparing the two lists, it is clear that the smaller communities stayed away, with the exceptions of Novellara and Scandiano (province of Reggio Emilia). The reasons for the absence of Casale, Cuneo (Piedmont), Colorno and Soragna were financial constraints and in some cases also diminishing numbers: 'our community has almost dissolved', wrote Moisè Levi from Soragna on 28 April 1867. Colorno's population of forty had been reduced further by the departure of two families, and therefore they could not send a delegate, but expressions of support for the work of the congress that would contribute to the 'splendid ancient tradition of fraternity' were conveyed (letter of 22 April 1867). Rome once again could not attend for political reasons, but expressed solidarity (letter of 8 April 1867). Pisa, on the other hand, decided not to send a delegate as only one item of the conference programme was of interest (letter of 19 April). Fossano was even more negative: there was no point in participating 'in an enterprise that was destined to fail' (letter of 22 April).[35]

There was, however, some continuity as several representatives had also attended the Ferrara meeting: Alessandro Liuzzi (Reggio Emilia and Scandiano); Moisè Malvano (Turin); Leone Ravenna (Ferrara); and Rabbi David Terracini (Asti). The seven-point programme, which had been sent out prior to the conference, contained the following items: the steps to be taken in the interests of Italian Judaism should the government proceed with its policy of a free Church in a free State; a proposal to sanction a compulsory tax for religious and educational purposes; recognition of the Rabbinical College of Padua as the Italian rabbinical college and its funding as such; discussion of the principles of freedom of worship and civil equality; and the election of a permanent executive committee.[36] The question of a central organization was absent from the agenda of the second conference.

In a circular of 4 March 1867, David Levi, president of the executive committee, had requested that representatives of the communities should 'take note of incidents that endorsed or breached civil liberties in order to report to the conference'.[37] Thus, after the formalities of the opening session, the second meeting was devoted to instances of discrimination in hospitals and similar institutions where Jews were denied dietary and religious provision. Such cases were cited in Ferrara and Florence. Positive policies in Ancona and Asti were upheld as examples of 'a real triumph of religious freedom'.[38] In subsequent meetings there was dissension among the delegates in their discussions of the compulsory tax, in their recognition of the Paduan Rabbinical College as the national institution, and on the proposal for a rabbinical synod, put forward again by Rabbi Terracini 'outside the official programme' with additional support from members of the Italian rabbinate who were persuaded by the need for reform. Furthermore, the final session questioned the need for triennial conferences, and thus no date was fixed.[39] As one delegate remarked at the closing session, 'the poor attendance at the conference shows that not all the communities were convinced of the need to have one'. There were no patriotic speeches from the president or shouts of 'Long live the King!' from the floor, as there had been in Ferrara four years earlier.

The report of the 1867 conference, which was sent out to the communities for their ratification, contained the following resolutions on which the delegates had reached consensus: the elected executive committee would monitor the government's policies on religion and liaise with the communities; it would also deal with any cases of discrimination, appealing when appropriate to ministers and the liberal press; it would seek to promote voluntary, not compulsory, contributions to provide additional resources for religious and educational purposes; and validation would be sought for the Rabbinical College of Padua as the national institution, funded principally by the communities of Padua, Venice, Mantua, Verona and Rovigo. On the proposal for a rabbinical synod, the majority of delegates agreed that 'the Italian rabbis, in accord with their respective communities, may draw up a programme of intended reforms that would be sent to the executive committee, which would instigate a rabbinical conference where they would be discussed'.[40] There was unanimous agreement to revoke the 1863 decision to hold conferences every three years; a further meeting would be called if communities whose populations exceeded 3,000 requested it. In the interim, the executive committee would send out annual reports, serve as a contact for the communities on all matters, consult with them and be funded by them. Finally, greetings were to be sent to the Alliance Israélite Universelle in recognition of its work for the progress of Judaism.[41] In his reply, Adolphe Crémieux acknowledged this gesture from emancipated Jews as a sign of encouragement, the cooperation of Italian Jews being a crucial factor in the success of the institution's operations.[42]

The response from the various communities to the report of the 1867 conference was, on the whole, dispiriting. There was little support for the Rabbinical College in Padua, either in financial terms or as the national rabbinical college: the leaders of the communities of Vercelli and Livorno pointed out that they too boasted similar institutions and therefore would not endorse either measure. To further its case, Livorno sent Levi an eleven-page document on the excellence of their rabbinical college, opening with the words 'Livorno's fame as a seat of illustrious scholars'.[43] Further reasons may also have had to do with the death of Luzzatto in 1865, and the fact that by then the college had few students – only three in the final year and one in the second, according to *Il Corriere Israelitico* (*CI*, 1865, p.29). Such was the opposition from Livorno that De Rossi felt compelled to resign from the executive committee. Turin expressed reservations, as did Verona and Mantua; other communities – the smaller ones – felt that they could not sustain the funding asked of them. For example, the correspondent from the 'Council of the nascent community of Naples' replied that he was supportive 'in spirit', but their financial situation was 'very precarious'. Giuseppe Levi's account of the 1867 conference lacked his former optimism: he queried the decisions that were taken, and the composition of the executive committee as 'guardians of our cause'; he deplored the fact that Leone Ravenna, 'indefatigable in the interests of Italian Judaism and as a promoter of the Alliance in Italy', was excluded from the committee (*EI*, 1867, pp.172–5).

The proposal for a rabbinical synod received scant approval. David Almagià, a member of the executive committee, wrote that it was an unrealizable dream, a utopia; the community of Cento unequivocally rejected the idea, as it was against reform of any kind; Padua and Siena also vetoed it; the president of the administrative council of Sinigaglia was of the opinion that such a convocation with its reformist objectives would introduce 'a seed of schism that would produce discord and division'.[44]

The most sustained, articulate and perspicacious response came from the pen of Marco Mortara, chief rabbi of Mantua, graduate of the Rabbinical College of Padua, scholar, regular contributor to *Il Corriere Israelitico*[45] and *L'Educatore Israelita*, and a much respected figure in the world of Italian Judaism. In a long letter addressed to the Commissione Rabbinica of Livorno written at the request of Rabbi Costa of Livorno in order to influence opinion to reject Terracini's proposal, Mortara dismissed the commission's conviction that reform would be divisive and alienate congregations. On the contrary, in his opinion it was precisely the outdated practices that discouraged attendance, and he would urge his community to adhere to the proposal for a rabbinical synod. It was imperative, he argued, that the rabbis should come together out of their isolation, to unite and respond to the needs of Italian Judaism: 'perhaps Italian national unification could have a salutary and harmonizing influence on our affairs'. He invited the Rabbinical Commission of Livorno to organize 'this friendly and fraternal preparatory conference'; no institution was more worthy or authoritative to undertake such a grave responsibility.[46] He did not receive a reply.

Mortara continued his campaign in *Il Corriere Israelitico* throughout that year. The Triestine periodical opened its pages to debate the issue, inviting contributors from both sides to express their views in a civilized manner, avoiding controversy.[47] The editor, Aron di Shemuel Curiel, who had just taken over from the founder (his father-in-law), initially adopted a neutral stance, but as the debate unfolded he publicly defended Mortara's position (*CI*, 1867, p.299). Thus on this, as on other fundamental questions, he was in direct conflict with the editors of *L'Educatore Israelita*, who opposed it (*EI*, 1867, p.341). The two principal adversaries in the debate were Rabbi Lelio Della Torre, professor at the Rabbinical College of Padua, and his former student, Rabbi Marco Mortara. As one might expect, the level of discussion was scholarly and expertly exegetic, but also passionate, polemical and personal. Della Torre argued that a rabbinical synod would have no authority or mandate and it had few adherents among the Italian rabbinate; it was therefore a sterile, divisive (he cited the example of

Germany) and dangerous exercise, 'an indecorous and sacrilegious comedy' (*CI*, 1867, pp.170–4, 234–42). Mortara countered that it was essential to attempt to 'renew our ritual ... consonant with the times', exemplifying the flexibility of the liturgy in earlier centuries as a model for the present and advocating a wise council of rabbis which could open up a new glorious era for Judaism and humanity.[48] Rabbi Terracini also participated, with a letter to the editor reiterating his absolute conviction that Italian rabbis must form 'a collective force' to combat 'the undeniable decline in communal religious sentiment' and to debate religious issues in a mature, enlightened way: 'I aspire ... *for now* to a preliminary rabbinical convention' (*CI*, 1867, pp.211–13). These aspirations were never met in the nineteenth century; their negation was confirmed by the outcome of the second conference.

Italian Jewish liturgy had undergone modernization in the eighteenth century, with Italian translations of Hebrew prayers, sermons in Italian (since the sixteenth century in some communities) and the introduction of the organ and choirs for the major festivals. However, as Flaminio Servi observed in the pages of *L'Educatore Israelita*, no two communities were alike in their religious services, adopting the Spanish, Portuguese or German (Ashkenazi) ceremonial in addition to the Italian or 'Roman'; the larger ones contained several synagogues each observing different practices, and the Spanish or Castilian (Sephardic) was further divided into Catalan-Aragonese and Levantine. In three small congregations in Piedmont, Asti, Fossano and Moncalvo, the Italian *Appam* was preserved, a version of the French medieval rite combining elements of Ashkenazi and Sephardic origin. These variations reflected the diverse origins of the Jews in Italy. 'When will these anomalies disappear?' Servi enquired. Citing Della Torre and Luzzatto, he promoted the idea that there should be 'a fusion of all the rites' and in one place in the smaller communities. Divergent ceremonies in the same country were an anachronism; they recalled the exile, emigration and nomadic life of the past.[49] Harmonization of the liturgy would serve as a model of communal cohesion, a modest modification towards modernity which Della Torre supported; it did not impinge on his traditionalist position, which he affirmed in his debate with Mortara. With regard to religion, Italian Jews adhered to the practices of their forbears. Orthodox Judaism, which eschews any deviation of dogma or observance, has prevailed in Italy until the present time. The first Reform synagogue was opened in Milan in 2001; the first woman rabbi Barbara Aiello, an American of Italian origin, was appointed in Milan in 2004.[50]

In January 1868, David Levi, president of the executive committee, sent out information on the consequences of the Florence congress: of the responses thus far received, no majority had been reached in favour of either a rabbinical synod or for the conversion of the Paduan Rabbinical College into the national one (figures were attached). Only five communities (Ferrara, Reggio, Scandiano, Venice and Vercelli) with a population totalling 4,946 supported the former proposal. A particular blow had been the reaction from Livorno, the largest community (4,340 in 1867 – one must exclude the Jewish community of Rome, 4,490, not yet part of Italy), and the resignation of De Rossi.[51] Thus, on the two most significant proposals of the 1867 conference, no consensus had been achieved. Nevertheless, the executive committee persevered and, in June of the same year, another report was published by Levi on the activities of the remaining five members (Almagià had died). The three-man subcommittee, all from Turin, was continuing its project for the publication of 'good Jewish books', and detailed plans had been submitted to fund the Rabbinical College in Padua for a further three-year period commencing 1 November 1868. It would, stated Levi, be a 'grave dishonour to the Jews of Italy' if such a renowned institution could flourish 'under foreign domination', only to be condemned to close 'under the regime of freedom and after the triumph of independence'.[52] In the previous year, *Il Corriere Israelitico* had also voiced its support: 'we implore our brethren in Italy ... to be united ... and support those institutions that ... promote ... the development of European Judaism' (1867, p.5).

The Collegio Rabbinico of Padua had been founded in 1829 with the approval of the Habsburg government, and from its inception it was an international centre of excellence, largely through the reputation of its two professors, Samuel David Luzzatto and Lelio Della Torre. It was the first institution of its kind, established to meet the needs of the rabbinate in the changing climate of emancipation: a model on which others were based throughout Europe, training some of the finest students who would distinguish Italian Jewry (Cantoni, Olper, Mortara). On becoming Italian, its administrative staff resigned and its precarious financial situation foundered; the consortium of five communities (Padua, Venice, Mantua, Verona and Rovigo) which had been agreed at the Florence congress was disbanded at a meeting of 9 January 1870. By 1872 the college had closed and the palazzo had been sold. The fact that only six other communities had favoured its continuation as the national rabbinical college hastened its demise.[53] In this, too, the 1867 conference and executive committee had failed.

The final circular of the executive committee dated 15 March 1871 and filed appropriately under the heading 'Dissolution of the Executive Committee', contained the sad news of David Levi's death and the reasons for the termination of the committee's activities: very few communities had paid their subsidies since 1868 to the extent that 'he [Levi] lacked the courage to reclaim them'; thus the validity of its very existence was undermined. The paucity of funds demonstrated, in the words of the report, 'the insufficient support for the Committee's mandate'. No future conferences were envisaged. This circular was published in the name of Giuseppe di Salomone Orefice, the outgoing president, and the four remaining committee members.[54]

Reasons for the failure of the Jewish communities to organize themselves are many and complex. They are partly contained in a letter from the community of Ancona to David Levi: the two conferences had achieved very little, apart from the publication of 'good books' and financial support for the Rabbinical College in Padua, but even in these two areas the outcome was unsatisfactory. Resources for the latter were lacking and few books had been produced: 'it therefore appears to this administrative council that the Consortium of Communities has no longer any reason to exist'.[55] They were also to do with the lack of unity and leadership among the Italian rabbinate, so divided on reform and the question of a national college; there was no position of chief rabbi of Italy as in France and

England, for example. Doubts about the concept of a central organization on the part of individual Jewish communities also had a major part to play – the consequence of centuries of autonomous self-government, of diversity borne of the varied history of the different regions of the Italian peninsula.

REGULATIONS OF THE COMMUNITIES

There had been various attempts to regulate the Jewish communities prior to the two conferences, but they had not been able to achieve a coordinated and uniform structure, with the exception of the brief period of the first emancipation for certain areas of Italy. Between 1808 and 1815, the Jews of Piedmont, Liguria and Tuscany were subjected to the rigidly hierarchical French system: this comprised a Central Consistory in Paris of three rabbis and two lay members, and regional consistories of two rabbis and three lay members, which replaced the former communities of at least 2,000 Jews. Smaller consistories had to concede authority to larger ones, which in turn deferred to Paris where Napoleon's directives were issued. Thus, for example, the twenty communities of Piedmont and Liguria were grouped into two consistories.[56] In 1848, Rabbi Lelio Cantoni (1801–57) formulated a proposal for the Piedmontese communities which was to be based on the Napoleonic model, with a central consistory in Turin and with himself as chief rabbi, his role since 1834. Among his ideas were that rabbis should be appointed by the state, removing them from financial dependence on communal administration, and universal voting rights were not to be based on income, thus making the organization more democratic (executive control was in the hands of the wealthy elite). This scheme was fiercely resisted by the community leaders who perceived the hegemony of the regional capital as a threat to their independence and power, and thus the idea was abandoned.[57]

Another attempt was made in 1849 for the Jews and the Waldensians of Piedmont, but persistent opposition to centralization led yet again to withdrawal. A conference in Vercelli in 1856 drew up a further plan, conceding some authority to the communities, which formed the basis for the bill that Urbano Rattazzi, minister of the interior, presented to parliament the following year. It comprised thirty articles, with a supplement of eighty-two, which became law on 4 July 1857. Its principal features were the following: communities were designated as autonomous corporations – no distinction was made between large and small congregations; they could own property; were responsible for religious worship and instruction; and each elected council had the authority to impose means-assessed levies on its members, control the finances, appoint the rabbis and preside over the charitable institutions. There were detailed procedures on membership, elections (based on income), and other matters – in essence the communities would be subject to 'the regulations in force for municipal administrations' (Article 29); the minister of the interior had the power to dissolve the councils and authorize new elections (Article 16). Consequently a uniform legislation was conferred on the communities of the kingdom of Sardinia, but no specific provision was made for a central representative body, as this facet had been repeatedly rejected in previous years, although Article 27 provided for the possibility of councils setting aside funds 'for the common interest', for which 'special unions' could be established. Cantoni's democratic recommendations regarding elections to the councils were excluded, and thus communal power remained in the hands of the bourgeois oligarchy; indeed, this was the state of affairs throughout the Jewish communities of western Europe.[58] The policy was to extend the Rattazzi law to the rest of Italy as it became unified. During the 1863 Ferrara conference, the decree was discussed and criticized; the committee nominated to consider whether it was indispensable concluded in the affirmative and accepted the status quo.[59]

In the liberal atmosphere of the times, the Rattazzi law was not uniformly applied and communal administrations functioned under diverse systems. In Tuscany, several opted to remain for a period under Austrian regulations, and later underwent various transformations: for example, Florence changed its regulations in 1868, 1883 and 1898; Pisa initially adhered to the Rattazzi law, but jettisoned it in 1901; Bologna chose to have no formal constitution until 1928; Mantua and Rome operated as voluntary associations; the principle of affiliation to Siena and Milan was based on an annual and triennial financial commitment respectively. Anomalies occurred, such as the case brought to the Supreme Court of Turin in 1872 by the Jewish community of Ancona. One of its members decided not to pay the compulsory tax, declaring that he no longer wished to belong to the Jewish faith, and the Court of Appeal endorsed his decision within the context of a 'free Church in a free State'. The Supreme Court overturned that judgement on the grounds, inter alia, that a mere declaration of intent was not in itself sufficient reason for exemption from payment. As *Il Corriere Israelitico* observed, the outcome was of significance to all those communities under the Rattazzi legislation (*CI*, 1872, pp.205–8). However, in similar cases subsequently brought before the courts, the original ruling was upheld: in Modena, the sentence of 8 March 1886 stated that 'every citizen is at liberty to relinquish the religion of his ancestors, and the Rattazzi law ... has in no way obstructed that freedom'. The declaration of the Court of Appeal in Turin in 1892 was even more explicit: 'The obligation to pay contributions imposed by the Rattazzi law ceases when an individual declares his intention not to profess the Jewish faith.'[60] Thus the lack of uniformity amongst the Jewish communities in Italy was in sharp contrast to those of France where codification was imposed from above. Nevertheless, the necessity for appropriate coordination which the Rattazzi law had attempted to enshrine resurfaced in the first decade of the twentieth century on the part of the Jews; the Italian government made no further legislative effort to ratify their communal status until, irony of ironies, 1930.[61]

Nonetheless, there was some consistency. The tradition of Jewish descent and birth according to Mosaic Law continued to be the criterion of communal membership. Prior to emancipation, Jewish communities in Italy had various nomenclatures such as *comunioni*, *comunità*, *nazione ebrea* – in pre-Napoleonic France, *nation juive*, 'Jewish nation'; the last was not acceptable to liberal nation-state ideology as it implied internal divisions, 'A State within the State'. Jewish communities had constituted a separate 'nation' with their own laws, distinct from the rest of the population. With the homogeneous designation of *Università israelitiche*, a legacy from the first emancipation, emphasis was on the Jewish faith rather than ethnicity; thus the transformation indicated Italian Jewry's continued collective willingness to respond to their new role as citizens.[62] In 1868, Rabbi Olper, chairman of the publications committee established at the 1863 conference, planned a competition to attract authors to treat 'the arduous and serious theme of the ways in which the rights and duties of citizenship can be exercised and fulfilled by us in conjunction with our obligations as Jews', to be based on individual cases 'of lives as Citizens. ... Religion and the Motherland [*Religione e Patria*], the Motherland and Religion, that is our ensign'.[63] Rabbi Flaminio Servi was awarded the prize with his book, *The Jews in European Civilization: Historical Events, Biographies and Statistics from 1789 to 1870*. It was one of the first historical accounts of the Jews' emancipation and contribution to all areas of public life. By Servi's own admission, the statistical data were incomplete. There were also glaring omissions: since the aim of the work was to present 'noble actions and fraternal accord [between Jews and Christians], we must be silent about acts of intolerance or barely mention them'.[64] A few years later, Rabbi Mortara wrote a circular which was sent out to all the members of his Mantuan community on the importance of educating children 'never to separate [*disgiungere*] devotion to the *patria* from religious sentiment, never to consider that the duties of citizenship are incompatible with the humanitarian commitments of the Jewish faith' (*CI*, 1872, p.199). *Il Corriere Israelitico* published the letter under the title, 'An example to follow' (p.197).

Tullia Catalan suggests that the annexation of the Papal States in 1870 and the consequent extension of civil and political equality to the Jews of Rome had so reassured the representatives of Italian Jewry that they were of the opinion that even the existence of an executive committee was unnecessary; she cites the views of Alessandro Malvano and Marco Treves, both members of the committee.[65] However, while they both approved the termination of the executive committee, they did so with regret. In Treves's words, it was a committee 'without arms or funds'; for Malvano, this was 'a momentous decision' and he expressed the hope that in the future 'we will be able to revive operations and a new congress'.[66] On 18 March 1871, during a parliamentary debate on the Law of Guarantees, the chamber voted in favour of the motion not to interfere in any way in the religions professed in the State. This was more of an appeasement to the papacy than a manifestation of solidarity towards the minority religions which were still only 'tolerated in conformity with the law', in the words of the first article of the Statutes.[67] Thus any optimism on the part of the Jewish communities would have been ill-founded.

A postscript to these nineteenth-century attempts to unify Italian Jewry in synchrony with Italian Unification was Marco Mortara's open letter to *L'Educatore Israelita* (1873, pp.333–6), also published in *Il Corriere Israelitico*, under the title 'A new project for an association of Italian Jewish communities' which would oversee the needs of every community with regard to religion and religious education. He set out detailed plans which the editors of the Triestine journal invited their readers to examine (*CI*, 1873, pp.190–2). This proposal, as Catalan succinctly puts it, 'had no outcome'.[68] No further attempt was made to reconstitute a central Jewish organization until 1909. Mortara also persisted with his ideas on religious reform and a rabbinical synod (*CI*, 1873, pp.36–42). The latter was taken up by Rabbi Flaminio Servi: he publicized his 'Programme for a Rabbinical Association in Italy' in the Triestine periodical (*CI*, 1874, p.68), which continued to publish supportive articles. By 1880, Servi was not so sanguine about the possibility of even a Rabbinical Congress: administrative councils would obstruct it in a thousand ways; of the thirty rabbis in post, two-thirds of them were too infirm or too old; the other ten, if they did meet, would find themselves in total opposition (*Vessillo Israelitico* [*VI*], 1880, p.74). Thus it was not until 1917 that the Federazione Rabbinica Italiana (Italian Rabbinical Federation) was established, holding its first congress in Bologna in June of that year. This forum was part of the revival of Jewish culture and identity in Italy, initiated in Florence during the first two decades of the twentieth century. The two key speakers were Rabbi Samuel Hirsch Margulies and his former student, Rabbi Angelo Sacerdoti, chief rabbi of Florence and Rome respectively.[69]

EDUCATION

A central function of the Jewish community was education; in the nineteenth and twentieth centuries it was not only the conduit for the transmission of traditional values but also a major agent of social change. In Italy, as elsewhere in western and central Europe, in preparation for emancipation and eventual integration, emphasis was placed on modernizing the scholastic system and founding new establishments, both academic and vocational. Many were funded partly or wholly by private bequests, with the institutions bearing the names of the principal benefactors. Thus the Collegio Colonna e Finzi in Turin (1823), the Collegio Foa in Vercelli (1829)[70] and the Collegio Levi in Acqui (1837) were set up, offering both religious and secular subjects such as Italian history, geography and literature. They became 'formative academies for the élite of Piedmontese Jewry': Giacomo Dina and Isacco Artom were graduates of the Turin and Vercelli colleges respectively; grants were given to those who could not afford the fees.[71] Schools of crafts and trades (*arti e mestieri*) were formed by many communities: Mantua (1825), Padua (1841), Florence (1843), Modena (1846), Casale (1848), Turin (1853), Pitigliano (1854) and Verona (1865). Stefano Caviglia documents the initiatives to assist the newly emancipated Jews of Rome: for example, the Fraternal Society for the Civil Progress of Poor Jews (Società di Fratellanza per il Progresso Civile degli Israeliti Poveri, 1876) and the Society of Buyers of Used Goods (Società dei Compratori di Generi Usati, 1879).[72] The aim was to transform young Jews from itinerant peddlers to productive, skilled workers. Occupational regeneration was widespread throughout Europe: 'from Alsace to Hungary there was no community of any standing which did not have such an institution'.[73] Jews were thus fulfilling the stipulation for self-improvement (*Bildung*) demanded by Christian emancipationist ideology.

Pedagogic consideration was also given to the very young of both genders, aged between 3 and 6, with the creation of kindergartens (*asilo infantile*), and primary schools (*scuole elementari*), often called Talmud Torah. By 1850, the *asilo* of Florence was frequented by forty children who received free meals and clothing.[74] The wealthy were educated in private schools, such as the Istituto Convitto Coen in Livorno, founded in 1849; apart from religious instruction, the curriculum included foreign languages (French, English and German) and preparatory courses for the military and naval academies. The Istituto Ravà in Venice (1850) specialized in civil service entry (*VI*, 1894, p.247); the Collegio Convitto Femminile Israelitico Olimpia Paggi in Florence (1852), which offered languages, dance, music, gymnastics and 'women's work' (*VI*, 1880, p.69 – these schools placed regular advertisements in the periodical).

During the 1863 conference, delegates were taken to visit the *asilo* in Ferrara attended by sixty pupils who sang a song especially composed for the occasion; one child recited a poem in praise of 'our magnanimous Sovereign ... we praised the teachers who instilled such reverence for the first citizen of Italy in those young minds', wrote the conference president, Giuseppe Levi (*EI*, 1863, p.164). The leitmotifs of Guglielmo Lattes's many texts for primary pupils were *ebraismo* and *italianità*: devotion to the traditions of one's forbears and patriotic loyalty to one's country. These parallel themes are emblematically illustrated in his *Heart of Israel*, which opens with the celebration of 'two beautiful festivals', the Jewish New Year and 20 September (anniversary of the liberation of Rome in 1870, the culmination of the Unification of Italy). The two protagonists, young Jewish schoolboys, are given names that encapsulate this twofold objective – Vittorio (the name of the king) and biblical Elijah; through dialogue and exempla, the importance of religious faith, tolerance and moral rectitude are reinforced.[75]

Once emancipation had been achieved, a fundamental facet of the scholastic curriculum was citizenship and patriotism, and in this the rabbis had a crucial and constructive role to play, not only as the principal teachers in the schools, but also through their sermons. In this way they contributed to the formation of a national identity. In synagogues throughout the various Italian states, rabbis gave thanks for the freedom of their people and offered prayers for the success of the Italian armies. Rabbi Giuseppe Lattes's two sermons of 1848 were published by several of his 'beloved students' at their own expense.[76] Rabbi Beniamin Artom composed a 'Poem on the Emancipation of the Jews' which was performed by the choir in the synagogue of Saluzzo on 29 March 1860, and Marco Tedeschi, the rabbi of Asti from 1849 to 1858, wrote a 'Hymn on 29 March'; his patriotic verses 'were on everyone's lips in Piedmont'.[77] In his memoirs, Augusto Segre evokes the inauguration of the restored and enlarged synagogue of Casale Monferrato (Piedmont) in 1866 which was reported in *L'Educatore Israelita*. The rabbi exhorted the congregation to be upright and useful citizens, as he stood beneath the engraving in gold lettering on marble in Hebrew and Italian bearing the date of emancipation and the words, 'in order that you forget the past interdictions, and in equality and patriotic loyalty, you grow to be free citizens'. Segre comments: 'first and foremost, *la patria italiana*, then the Jewish faith'.[78] In 1893, in the evening of Yom Kippur, the rabbi of Pitigliano (Tuscany), Donato Camerini, gave an impassioned sermon on the Jews' *italianità*: 'What fate awaited our beloved country had not our fathers faced the enemies' swords, had they not with their blood given us the right to be called Italians, had they not, with their arms, driven the barbarous oppressors from our lands?'[79] Similarly, in 1898, solemn ceremonies were held in many synagogues to celebrate the fiftieth anniversary of the statute that had given civil rights to the Italian Jews: for example, in Florence the chief rabbi spoke of the 'great age of the Italian Risorgimento ... we rejoice in our beloved *patria* ... we citizens of a country where tolerance, freedom and justice are so deeply rooted' and for which they were ready to shed their own blood and that of their children.[80] *Il Vessillo Israelitico* published details of the ways in which communities throughout Italy marked the occasion, including the inauguration in Asti on 3 May of a monument to the Risorgimento, designed and paid for by Leonetto Ottolenghi, 'a generous and ardent patriot', attended by King Umberto I, and a letter from the sovereign thanking the Jewish communities for the 'demonstration of their devoted love to king and country'.[81] The Waldensian Church also fulfilled this role commemorating 17 February 1848; by the end of the century, that date (of their emancipation) became known as the 'Waldensians' national festival'.[82]

The establishment of schools and colleges for all social classes reflected the Jewish communities' commitment to education; their activities, achievements and progress were regularly reported in the Jewish press. Livorno, for example, was proud of its pedagogic tradition and its many educational institutions; in 1844, in addition to the community's Talmud Torah, it could boast of nineteen private establishments, eleven of which had women head teachers.[83] Nevertheless, one of the effects of civil equality was access to state education: aspirational and economically advantaged Jewish families began to avail themselves of this opportunity from primary level, as a means of more rapid integration.[84] To combat this withdrawal and consequent diminution of Jewish culture, communities endeavoured to amend the curriculum of their own schools and, in some cases, set up new ones. In Asti (Piedmont), a community of 500 in 1867, the chief rabbi, David Terracini (1811–92), founded the Istituto Clava (combining an *asilo* and a primary school for boys and girls) in 1866 which, alongside its religious programme, provided courses to prepare pupils for state secondary education – free for those who could not pay the fees. Initially it was successful and much praised for high standards and excellent results, opening with 112 enrolments in the first year, whereas in the community's elementary school there were only twenty-eight pupils (*CI*, 1865, pp.182). However, by 1881 there were seventy, fifty-five in 1886 and thirteen in 1911; it closed its doors in 1930. The reasons for its demise were the continuing trend for state education and demographic decline of the community due to exodus to the cities; ninety Jews lived in Asti in 1930;[85] 'unfortunately', commented the editor of *Il Vessillo Israelitico*, 'our schools are almost deserted' (*VI*, 1897, p.3). When Rabbi Terracini died, aged nearly 80, he had witnessed the disappearance of his world, and at his funeral the chief rabbi of Turin spoke of 'a Judaism which was now bloodless [*esangue*] ... of a cultural climate of scepticism, free thinkers and religious indifference'.[86]

A survey of Jewish schools commissioned by the Jewish Youth Conference of 1911 provided problematic results. Communities were sent a questionnaire and replies received from all of them apart from Genoa, Siena and Vercelli. In 1912 there was a total of 1,493 pupils (approximately 1600, taking into account the missing information), representing 4 per cent of the Jewish population. Fourteen of the twenty-five schools which sent in data on the number of enrolments had between 50 per cent and 75 per cent of pupils from poor families; in one school in Mantua and two in Florence, the figure was almost 100 per cent (*quasi tutti/tutte*). Only two primary schools, Florence and Livorno, had six classes; only two cities, Livorno and Turin, had Jewish secondary schools; two communities, Reggio Emilia and Parma, had no Jewish school. *Tout court*, there were few pupils and the majority were poor; their families sent them to these schools solely for financial reasons. Many teachers were not properly qualified; in several cases there was only one teacher for all classes; curricula were inadequately structured; post-biblical history was rarely taught; and in nearly every subject good textbooks were lacking. The statistics of the study clearly revealed the almost total absence of the middle classes: access to state education, where the secular curriculum was at a higher standard, and neglect of religious instruction had removed these groups from the communities' educational provision.[87]

In 1917, the executive committee of Italian Jewish communities carried out another questionnaire survey, to investigate the conditions of religious instruction and religious observance. Eighteen responses were returned, representing 30 per cent of the Jewish population; Bologna, Ferrara, Florence, Genoa, Padua and Rome inexplicably failed to reply (they had done so in 1912, with the exception of Genoa). Several of the smaller communities such as Cento, Sinigaglia and Fiorenzuola d'Arda were so reduced in numbers that there was no point in complying; this was revealed in their correspondence. The lacunary information presented an even more desolate picture than five years earlier: none of the communities offered a complete Jewish education (the best was in Turin); in several schools, elementary classes were barely in double figures; and most pupils were from poor families.[88] These two reviews reveal a reversal of the situation of the previous century when Jewish schools provided, prior to 1848, the only possibility for excellent academic and vocational preparation for entry into the host society. The decline of the Jewish schools demonstrates that 'the process of integration was immense, indubitable'.[89] From the point of view of social cohesion and national unity, it can be argued that the transition from Jewish to Italian schools was a positive one. On the other hand, the transmission of the rich heritage of Judaism was inevitably diminished: for the middle-class majority, *italianità* prevailed over *ebraismo*; the latter was not rejected, but rather relegated to the privacy of the home.[90]

PHILANTHROPY

Another primary responsibility of the communities was philanthropy, one of the fundamental precepts of Jewish law. Such material and moral assistance was an obligation, not defined as charity in Hebrew, but deriving from the word justice (*zedaqàh*). Thus every Jew was obliged to contribute within his/her means; on this basis, charitable organizations, *Opere pie* or *Confraternite*, were established, some as old as the communities themselves, others of the post-emancipation era. They offered a wide range of services such as funeral expenses, dowries, medical and financial assistance, and food and clothing; many were devoted to religious education.[91] Their activities were a regular item of regional reports in the Jewish press, and prominent wealthy individual philanthropists, such as members of the Rothschild families and Sir Moses Montefiore (1784–1885), also featured extensively: 'a venerated name ... one of those prodigious men ... with a holy mission to do good ... to help and console the suffering of others wherever they are ... such a man is Sir Moses Montefiore whose virtue is venerated throughout the world' (*CI*, 1867, p.133). On the occasion of Sir Moses's hundredth birthday, Flaminio Servi sent him a magnificent album of greetings, verse and prose written by many eminent Italian Jews (*VI*, 1885, p.14). At his death, when it was said that 'the greatest Jew of the century is dead', *Il Corriere Israelitico* (and *Il Vessillo Israelitico*) printed a black border on the first page of the issue containing his obituary, and set up a charitable foundation in his name.[92] Appeals for charity were also made in the press, consequent to personal tragedy or public disaster: for example, in 1872 *Il Corriere Israelitico* published one from the deputy rabbi of Trieste on behalf of the persecuted Jews of Romania, and also a letter from Professor Salvatore De Benedetti requesting financial assistance for the family of the chief rabbi of Pisa, who had died suddenly, leaving a widow and seven children (*CI*, 1872, pp.55–6, 291–2).

The *Opere pie* formed the infrastructure of the communities; they were a manifest indicator of collective cohesion and solidarity and, given that the welfare system was everywhere similar, they conferred a substantial homogeneity across the disparate Jewish groups: 'a special place was occupied by the burial society, which was ubiquitous'.[93] Time and money were voluntarily given to the poor who existed in every community, and an impecunious Jewish traveller would always find sustenance and lodgings. A key indicator of indigence was the number of charitable institutions: for example, in Livorno, with 4,771 Jews in 1846, there were reported to be seventy; by 1880 they were reduced to forty-five.[94] These associations were financed partly by communal taxation; by private donations made to celebrate a marriage; on the death of a family member, or at the time of the main religious festivals; and by testamentary bequests, such as that of Salomone Lampronti (1806–65) of Florence. Among his many legacies was a capital sum of 7,560 lire, the income of which was to provide two annual prizes for the best Hebrew composition or biblical translation into Italian and the best essay in literature or science written by 'poor (male) Jews' aged between 13 and 19. The *Opera pia* established by him was implemented by a committee formed from members of the Jewish community.[95] Dr Alberto Levi left money 'for impoverished Jews of Florence who had no means of providing shelter for their families', to be administered by the community according to specific conditions. On a more modest scale, Giuseppe Vivanti, also of Florence, bequeathed an annual sum for the purchase of a sewing machine to be given to a Jewish widow who had no means of support; the first recipient was Sara Belgrado who was living in 'absolute poverty with her three children'.[96] In Livorno, many bequests were left by wealthy widows: in 1863, of the thirty-six *Opere pie* registered in their names, twenty were specifically to assist women in various ways, including their education.[97] *Il Corriere Israelitico* gives an example, which should be 'in the golden book of charity', of three members of the Society of Used Goods Buyers who rented a small house and called it a hospital; within three years it was relocated to a comfortable, spacious building with twenty beds.[98] In each of these cases – and they were repeated throughout the Diaspora – the bequest was made in order to improve the educational, social and moral conditions of the recipients.

A phenomenon of the late nineteenth century was involvement in non-Jewish associations: in this manner successful Jewish businessmen, who were members of the Chambers of Commerce, and their wives were able to demonstrate their identification with the social fabric of the Italian nation. Thus among the 130 patronesses who formed the 'Municipal Committee for the Livornese Festivals' (1906), there numbered thirty-three upper-class Jewish *signore*.[99] Both *Il Corriere Israelitico* and *Il Vessillo Israelitico* were often critical of what was perceived as neglect of Jewish charities.[100] Just as the Jewish schools diminished in number, so did the charitable associations, as the result of demographic decline in particular areas, and social integration.

INTERNAL MIGRATION

From the period of Unification, exodus from the small semi-rural communities intensified, provoking a crisis in their very existence. In 1850, there were some fifty of these communities in northern and central Italy, containing 7,700 Jews or approximately one-fifth of the population. By 1931 this figure had fallen to 1,150 or one-fortieth of the population, which is to say, in effect, that many of them had disappeared.[101] Thus one of the consequences of emancipation was the demise of these small, traditional, religious centres where Jews had taken refuge for centuries, usually under the patronage of the local ruler. Internal migration to the cities was a phenomenon that affected Jews throughout Europe; parallel to this demographic transformation and greater mobility were the changes in their professional lives, as urbanized Jews became increasingly middle class. These changes began in the second half of the nineteenth century and reached their peak between 1890 and 1930. In 1860 the Jewish populations of Berlin, Vienna and Warsaw were 19,000, 6,000 and 41,000 respectively; by the 1920s they were 173,000 (4.3 per cent of the total population), 201,000 (10.8 per cent), and 350,000 (30 per cent). Other capital cities where the Jewish communities represented a significant part of the population in the twentieth century were Paris with 140,000 – that is, 70 per cent of the Jews resident in France – and London with 200,000.[102] These considerable increases also included the massive influx of persecuted Jews fleeing from the Russian pogroms.

In a series of articles entitled 'A Survey of the Jewish Communities of Italy', published in *Il Corriere Israelitico* between 1865 and 1867, Flaminio Servi provided the following information on each of them: population; name of rabbi (if there was one); membership of the council; schools (if any) and enrolments; particulars of the synagogue and religious rites; other notable monuments; details of the charitable associations; and prominent individuals. Thus on Pitigliano (Tuscany), where a Jewish presence dates back to the sixteenth century, Servi noted that the council was one of the richest due to the many legacies. Sixty-three pupils attended the primary school; the synagogue, which practised the Italian rite, was elegant and beautifully proportioned (Pitigliano was Servi's birthplace and that of Dante Lattes). According to his figures, Jewish residents numbered 280; other sources give 400 for 1867, 10 per cent of the total population.[103] In the decade 1870–80, several enterprises reflected the cohesion of the community; in 1871 a mutual aid society (Società di Mutuo Soccorso fra Israeliti) was established, which by 1879 had fifty members, and in the following year a *Confraternita*, funded by bequests and subscriptions; it provided flour for unleavened bread, clothing for primary schoolchildren, transport and burial for funerals, and assistance to the sick. The Istituto Consiglio (1854), despite administrative and financial problems in the 1860s, was crucial to the educational transformation of the young at primary and secondary level, offering vocational training in arts and crafts, technical design and science, with workshops and laboratories; its varied and intensive activities gave Pitigliano the appellation of 'Little Jerusalem' (*Piccola Gerusalemme*). Salvadori argues that the delayed decline of Pitigliano as a community was due, in great measure, to the Istituto, which closed after the First World War.[104] However, the tendency to emigrate could not be prevented, and the decreasing figures speak for themselves: in 1900, 250; in 1925, 120; in 1938, 70.[105] In 1931, Pitigliano lost its autonomy and merged with Livorno. The younger generations had moved to Florence and Rome: they could no longer live in 'a little town almost cut off from the world, fifty kilometres from the nearest railway station' (*La Settimana Israelitica* [*SI*], 30 [1910]).

Even today one senses the isolation of the place: in the midst of the Tuscan countryside, Pitigliano rises dramatically out of the tufa rocks from which the houses seemed carved; one can also appreciate that to the persecuted Jews of the sixteenth century it was indeed a 'a place of refuge', as Davide de Pomis called it (he was personal physician to Count Niccolò Orsini IV from 1556–62). Now only a few remain: Signora Elena Servi (born in 1930) is the custodian of its Jewish heritage, and the finely reconstructed synagogue (opened in 1995) and its small museum bear testimony to a once thriving community. The cemetery is also newly restored, with recent burials; many who emigrated chose Pitigliano as their final resting place – one plaque, for Alberto Servi (1909–88), bears the words 'with feelings of religious affection for the community of his ancestors'. Other parts of the old ghetto that lie below the synagogue have also been renovated: the first oratory, the ritual baths, the bakery, the wine-cellars, 'a unique historical patrimony of our region'.[106] These are initiatives of the Associazione La Piccola Gerusalemme set up by Elena Servi, its president, with funding from various regional councils. To talk to Elena Servi was to step back into history: her ancestors were patriotic Garibaldini; her paternal grandmother, Adele Servi Debenedetti, corresponded with Flaminio Servi, providing him with information for his article on Pitigliano's Jewish community in *Il Corriere Israelitico*. She also spoke of her own childhood memories of fascism and the family's flight to the countryside where they were hidden by peasant families until the end of the war.

The history of Soragna (province of Parma) survives through the ruins of its once magnificent synagogue inaugurated in 1855, 'one of the most beautiful in

Italy', and a newly established Jewish museum. In 1867 it had a population of seventy-four, the post of rabbi had been vacant since 1862, religious instruction was neglected, and there was no *confraternita*, but among 'the martyrs of the independence of Italy is numbered Folia Levi of Soragna' (*CI*, 1867, pp.222–4). Scandiano, near Reggio Emilia, can document Jewish inhabitants from the fifteenth century; by 1795 there were 122 Jews in a population of 929, but once again the 'phenomenon of urbanization'[107] caused a rapid depopulation. In 1867 only thirty-eight Jews remained, 'many families having emigrated'; there was no rabbi and a malfunctioning charitable association; by 1925 there were no Jews and the last Jewish burial took place in 1936 (some families who had left chose to be buried in their place of birth). There is a poignant description by Enzo Levi of the abandoned synagogue of Scandiano in the spring of 1934, when a friend asked him if he wished to purchase some of the Sabbath lamps; he gave one to the synagogue in Modena and took the other with him to Buenos Aires.[108] The synagogue was destroyed in the 1950s, but the house of the most influential family, the Almansi, and the cemetery were renovated in the 1990s.[109]

Jews had also been living in Carpi (Emilia Romagna) since the fifteenth century; in 1867 they numbered 100, but by 1898 this figure had been reduced to thirty-one. The last religious service in the synagogue took place in 1907, and in 1910 the president of the Modena community, concerned about the precariousness of Jewish life in Carpi, requested that its patrimony should devolve to Modena, its community be dissolved, and the remaining families to be under his guidance. Discussions on this crucial issue were protracted and divisive; nevertheless in 1913 Ubaldo Urbini, the administrator of Carpi's finances, was ordered to relinquish control to Modena. He refused, citing various laws in his defence, but in 1915 he was forced to concede. In 1921 the synagogue was sold and, apart from one or two objects which are in Modena and Israel, nothing remains of its contents.[110] Thus another small Jewish community was extinguished. Jews migrated to Sabbioneta (near Mantua) from Rome and Germany from the thirteenth century to escape persecution. In the sixteenth century a Jewish press was established by the Foà family; by 1820 its Jews numbered 113, reduced to seventy by 1867 and to zero in the 1930s. Its synagogue, constructed in 1824, still exists, having been recently renovated.[111]

Controversy surrounded the fate of Pomponesco (also near Mantua), which in 1867 was described by Servi as 'microscopic', with twenty-five members; he added that the mayor of the town was Jewish and 'a real patriot' (*CI*, 1867, p.118). By the beginning of the twentieth century, it was discovered that the few remaining Jews had appropriated everything that had belonged to their community, sold it and divided up the proceeds: 'a sad state of affairs', concluded *La Settimana Israelitica* in its report (38 [1910]). In their series of articles entitled 'The Small Communities', the editors of this journal investigated the situation in Piedmont. There were three categories of community: those that were flourishing and well organized – Alessandria, Asti, Casale Monferrato, Cuneo, Turin and Vercelli; those with limited activity – Acqui, Chieri, Moncalvo, Saluzzo and Trino Vercellese; and those with resources, but where 'Jewish life is completely spent' – Biella, Carmagnola, Cherasco, Fossano, Ivrea, Mondovì and Nizza Monferrato. In Mondovì, for example, no community had existed for nine years, the 'religious objects' were abandoned and the considerable funds of a charitable organization were being privately managed.[112] Asti, with 400 residents, 'one of the most distinguished communities', in Servi's words (*CI*, 1865, pp.182–4), was the birthplace of several Jewish families, many of whose members held prominent positions in Italian society: the Artom, De Benedetti, Ottolenghi and Treves. Rabbi Beniamin Artom (1833–79) was called to Naples in 1864 to assist in the organization of the new community, and in 1866 was nominated rabbi of the Bevis Marks synagogue in London, where he excelled also as a composer and musician.[113] These small and well-organized communities also eventually succumbed to the urban phenomenon as the younger generation moved to the regional capital of Turin: for example, as Asti declined, it was merged with Alessandria and later with Turin.[114]

Internal migration to the principal cities also affected the moderate-sized towns: within the four-year period that separated the two conferences of Ferrara and Florence (1863 to 1867), Modena's Jewish population was reduced from 2,000 to 1187 and Verona's was halved from 1,200 to 600. From 1870, many educated Jews from central and northern Italy – 180 families in 1883 alone – migrated to Rome, owing to the greater possibilities that the capital had to offer, thus increasing its size from 4,700 to 11,000.[115] On the regeneration of Rome's community, with modern housing, a large primary school and imposing synagogue, banishing the memory of the dank, dark dwellings of the ghetto, the correspondent of *La Settimana Israelitica* exclaimed: 'If I think of the past and the present quality, I am filled with emotion – everyone should recognise and understand the importance of such a beneficent transformation' (4 [1910]). In the case of Livorno, which in the eighteenth century was the largest community in Italy and one of the major centres in Europe, with a population of over 5,000,[116] the loss of free port status in 1868 and consequent economic decline caused the exodus of many, including Jews, who left for Tunisia, Tripoli, Smyrna and Alexandria where they had business connections.[117]

Thus while the smaller regional communities struggled to survive, the growing Jewish populations in the major conurbations thrived, celebrating their well-being and prosperity in the construction of magnificent synagogues: 1882 in Florence; 1884 in Turin; 1892 in Milan; 1904 in Rome; 1912 in Trieste. From the 1870s, many articles appeared in *Il Corriere Israelitico* on the significance of the synagogue for the local community in Trieste and the various projects for its construction, and an entire issue was devoted to the inauguration on 27 June 1912. Trieste's synagogue, the largest in Europe, replacing four smaller ones, was financed by generous individual donations, as were the others. David Levi, president of the 1867 Congress, bequeathed a million lire for the construction of the Florence synagogue (*CI*, 1872, p.108), and 3,000 people attended the ceremonial laying of the first stone for the Rome synagogue in June 1901, many of whom, rich and poor, had made donations.[118] These places of worship represented the public, physical manifestation of Jewish emancipation, and pride in the vitality of their communities. The Jews of Turin wished their synagogue to be 'the most grandiose (*vistoso*) and majestic ... symbolic of the social position they had attained ... of their definitive and irrevocable integration in the social fabric of their city'.[119] Among the numerous restrictions of the past, synagogues had to remain hidden and were modest buildings. Liberated from these constraints, architects adopted flamboyant, eclectic styles – gothic, Byzantine, oriental, Renaissance, even Christian, such as the Paris synagogue of Rue Victoire and that of České Budejovice in Czechoslovakia. To conform to the post-emancipation terminology of Jews as *Israélites/Israeliti*, the synagogue became a temple (*temple israélite/tempio/tempel*), not only recalling the Temple of Jerusalem, but also conveying a new sense of dignity, of official recognition, 'the symbol of the redemption of Judaism in a free country … an instrument of transformation'.[120]

Life in a metropolis gave emancipated Jews greater educational, economic, professional and social opportunities, and they began to return to those cities from which they had been banished in the past: Bologna, Milan and Naples. Thus new communities were reborn. The statistics from the 1867 conference give their respective populations as 600, 650 and 350. It was at the beginning of the nineteenth century that Jews moved to Milan in significant numbers from the small centres in Piedmont and Emilia, from the towns in the Veneto and in 1842 also from Mantua, fleeing from violent anti-Semitic demonstrations. The Milanese Jewish community was officially recognized in 1866 and by 1881 had grown to 1,000, increasing to 10,000 in 1938, equal to 4.7 per 1,000 of the city's population. Its members were principally engaged in business and banking – by 1861, one in three bankers was of Jewish origin. A contemporary account in *L'Educatore Israelita* reports on the extreme wealth of many, borne out by recent research which indicates that in the period 1862–90 the fortunes of certain Milanese families were among the largest in Italy.[121] Close ties were often retained to the place of origin, in the form of property, but the principal place of residence remained Milan. The community of Bologna was also re-established in 1866; Rabbi Marco Mordechai Momigliano was sent there for that purpose. He immediately set about raising funds for a synagogue; two Rothschild brothers who were 'passing through' donated 1,000 lire, and he recalls 'the noble satisfaction of inaugurating the new sacred temple' in 1877.[122] Jews began returning to Naples in the 1830s; the prolonged sojourn of members of the Rothschild family contributed to the revival of the community, with substantial funds towards a cemetery and synagogue. In 1894, at a meeting of the administrative council, it was agreed that on every Sabbath the chief rabbi would recite a special prayer and benediction for the deceased Baron Carlo Mayer De Rothschild and his heirs for their generous donations (*VI*, 1894, p.383). The community was formally constituted in 1862; by 1911, there were 1,000 members.[123]

CONFERENCES, 1909–14

The depopulation of the small communities, the migration to the principal cities, the advent of Zionism, the increase in anti-Semitism, and the Jewish cultural revival in Florence affected all Italian Jews, and once again there came the call for a central organization, this time from *L'Educatore Israelita*'s successor, *Il Vessillo Israelitico*. In 1908, under the exhortatory title '*Comunità d'Italia, raggruppatevi!*', it urged its co-religionists to shake off their torpor, discard their conservatism and individualism and work together. In 1909, the journal expressed its support for a conference, and in the editorial of June of that year, addressed to the 'The Honourable Presidents of the Italian Jewish Communities', the need – indeed the urgency – for cooperation. For too long, it argued, Jewish communities in Italy had been independent from and indifferent to each other, some thriving, others in decline; the regulations were 'in real chaos', with some communities adhering to the Rattazzi law, others to Austrian legislation or their own ordinances.[124]

The call was answered, and on 14 and 15 November 1909, twenty-three communities (including Gorizia and Trieste) were represented at a congress organized by the Società Israelitica di Beneficenza in Milan. A representative of the Italian Zionist Federation, Angelo Sullam, was also present. There was only one survivor from the 1863 and 1867 conferences, Leone Ravenna, described by *La Settimana Israelitica* as 'a venerable veteran of the struggles' (9 [1911]). He recalled those earlier aspirations, his own support for them and his satisfaction at the 'salutary revival' of the Jewish leadership, the solidarity and collaboration reflected in their participation.[125] Two important decisions were reached at the conference: a committee (*Commissione*) was nominated to carry out a detailed financial and statistical survey of all communities with the objective of merging the smaller, ailing ones with their larger neighbours (during the discussion on this matter, Angelo Sullam reminded the delegates that it was the Italian Zionists at their conference in 1904 who had highlighted the parlous state of the smaller communities);[126] and a mandate was given to the same committee to present to the next conference a plan for a Federation – *una Federazione di tutte le Comunità Israelitiche italiane* – which was to be based in Rome. The five members of the committee were: Avv. Elia Vitale (Alessandria), comm. Leone Ravenna (Ferrara), cav. Moisé Foligno (Milan), Rabb. Giuseppe Cammeo (Modena), and sig. Abramo Moscato (Pitigliano) (*VI*, 1909, pp.545–51).

The Piedmontese journal hailed the proposal for a union as 'the beginning of a real risorgimento for Italian Judaism ... a patriotic aspiration' (*il principio di un vero risorgimento per l'ebraismo italiano*) (*VI*, 1909, p.49); parallels were drawn between the unity 'of our beloved country' and the unity of Judaism (*VI*, 1911, p.142), sentiments echoing those enunciated nearly half a century earlier at the 1863 conference. *Il Corriere Israelitico* also endorsed 'the new and important event' (*CI*, 1909, pp.150–2). However, as before, there was opposition, this time from the community in Rome, the largest in Italy. At its council meeting on 18 February 1911, the members declared that a federation was neither opportune nor essential; an elected committee resident in Rome would suffice the needs of Italian Jewry. It is clear from the minutes of the meeting that there was apprehension regarding the political leverage and autonomy of a federation.[127]

At the second conference, held in Milan between 26 and 27 February 1911 and attended by representatives of twenty-four communities, the views of the Rome Jews prevailed. After heated and lengthy discussions, a compromise was reached: it was agreed that an eleven-man committee be appointed, the Comitato delle Università Israelitiche Italiane, with its centre in the capital. Angelo Sereni was elected president and Anselmo Colombo secretary; they were president and vice-president of the Rome community; Leone Ravenna was also selected. Communities were to contribute a subsidy according to their size. The only concession to those who pressed for the formation of a federation was that it would be discussed at the subsequent congress. Despite this unresolved issue, press reports conveyed a sense of purpose and union, especially with regard to assisting the smaller communities. Leone Ravenna was optimistic that his youthful dream, launched half a century earlier in the pages of *L'Educatore Israelita*, was about to be fulfilled (*CI*, 15 April 1915). The other vital item was the survey of the communities. The *Commissione* responsible for this task informed the delegates that they had been hampered by the refusal of many communities to take part in the investigation; they were unwilling to disclose their fragile financial situation.[128]

The deterioration of the smaller communities continued to be a cause for grave concern, with abandoned and derelict synagogues vulnerable to vandalism, neglected cemeteries, and income from charitable institutions and other sources falling into the wrong hands.[129] And yet, at the meetings of the Comitato delle Università Israelitiche Italiane in November 1911 and 1912, it was reported that there were difficulties in effecting the merger of Pesaro and Sinigaglia with Ancona; that Pitigliano continued to insist on its independence; that no agreement had been reached regarding Chieri's union with Turin; that attempts were being made to amalgamate Scandiano and Correggio to Reggio. Leone Ravenna was sent to Parma to assist and advise; Musatti, another committee member, attempted to consolidate the organizational structures of the new community in Udine, without much success (*CI*, 15 December 1912). In addition, some communities had not signed up to the new *Comitato,* and others had not sent their subvention. Discussions regarding the merger of the rabbinical colleges of Florence and Livorno and a rabbinical synod, two of the unresolved problems from the 1867 conference, ran aground yet again.[130]

Furthermore, the committee found itself facing unforeseen issues resulting from Italy's foreign policy: the acquisition of Libya in 1911 as an Italian colony, the trophy of the war with Turkey in September of that year. According to the 1911 official Turkish census, 14,282 Jews lived there, of whom 8,609 were in Tripoli (*CI*, 15 April 1914). Contact was made with the local rabbis who, according to *Il Vessillo Israelitico*, expressed fervent patriotism towards Italy (*VI*, 1912, p.634). In November 1912, the secretary of the *Comitato*, Anselmo Colombo, was despatched to Tripoli; Rabbi Margulies also visited in an official capacity to assess the religious and educational situation; and procedures were set up to appoint a chief rabbi for Tripoli.[131] Both the Piedmontese and the Triestine journals included a regular report on Libya from this period, the former stressing the civilizing Italian influence on the colony so heroically captured, the latter foregrounding the flourishing Jewish life, perceived as 'a corner of Palestine'.[132] The committee had to respond to other sensitive matters: the critical situation of the Romanian Jews during the Balkan wars of 1912 and 1913, and the Beilis trial in Kiev. It did so through public appeals, the lobbying of government ministers, and collaboration with the Alliance Israélite Universelle. *Il Corriere Israelitico* applauded 'this revival of Jewish solidarity'.[133] Other issues it had to confront were the problematic relationship with the Italian Zionist Federation, nascent Italian nationalism, and growing anti-Semitism.[134]

By 1913, both Sereni and Colombo had changed their views: their experience had taught them that a committee with no statutes or official recognition could not function fully or effectively.[135] Thus, in May 1914 at the conference held in Rome, the proposal to form a Consorzio delle Università e Comunità Israelitiche Italiane based in the capital was finally approved. Twenty-six communities were represented, including that of Tripoli. During the two-day meeting, there were fierce debates, carried over from the committee meetings, about the wording of one of its main objectives: to 'make provision for all that is considered of common interest to the communities and to Judaism in general according to their statutory aims, in particular with regard to the conservation of the religious, historical and artistic patrimony' (*provvedere a tutto ciò che si ritenga di comune interesse delle Comunità e dell'ebraismo in genere, secondo i loro fini statutari specialmente per la coltura ebraica e per la conservazione del patrimonio sacro, storico ed artistico*). The wording 'of Judaism in general' engendered in the more timorous delegates the fear that the consortium would be perceived as having political aspirations which would conflict with patriotic sentiments and would incite anti-Semitism. One delegate stated: 'the Rome council was seriously concerned that this kind of call to arms by the Jews of Italy could be interpreted in a dangerous way'.[136] The offending words were deleted from the final version of the statutes, together with many other amendments. The youthful editors of *La Settimana Israelitica* were scornful of the 'exasperating prudence' of their elders at the conference – indeed, the words 'caution' and 'prudence' permeated the proceedings – in sharp contrast to their own dynamic ideals and Zionist aspirations. They perceived that between the two generations 'an abyss has opened which perhaps nothing can fill ... Above all we want Israel to live; if we left it up to you, Israel would die' (*SI*, 22 [1914]). In the same issue of the journal, Anselmo Colombo wrote an open letter pointing out that in fact, during the previous three years, the committee had been active in matters of 'Judaism in general', and he called upon the young to participate in their communities' administrations and cooperate with the consortium; there should not be a division, but a concerted effort to work together. In a series of articles in *Il Vessillo Israelitico*, entitled 'Let us make the Jews' (*Facciamo gli ebrei*), he reiterated these themes.[137]

The consortium elected a fourteen-member executive committee (once again Leone Ravenna was of its number) which was engaged in prolonged bureaucratic procedures to obtain official recognition. This was achieved on 6 May 1920 by royal decree. After the First World War, the consortium, the rabbinate and the Italian Zionist Federation agreed to cast aside their animosities and work together for the future of Italian Jewry.[138] Zionist-oriented Jewish nationalism, emphasizing a revival of Jewish culture, was one of the principal responses among western European Jewry to the threatening danger of political and social anti-Semitism. One could argue that it was precisely these challenges that stimulated the twentieth-century attempts at collaboration and cohesion between the Italian Jewish communities, leading them to function as a collective, an aspiration that had eluded them in the previous century. Despite the disappearance of the smaller communities, there remained in Italy in the post-emancipation period a full range of communal, institutional and associational activities to provide Italian Jews with corporate structures within which they could live as Jews, should they wish to do so, and at the same time participate fully as citizens of their country. It could be asserted that among the educated younger generation there was a renewed vitality and enhancement of values specific to Judaism in the first two decades of the twentieth century; the tragedy was that this spark would be extinguished by the Shoah.

NOTES

1. Jonathan Frankel, 'Assimilation and the Jews in Nineteenth-Century Europe: Towards a New Historiography?', in Jonathan Frankel and Steven J. Zipperstein (eds), *Assimilation and Community: The Jews in Nineteenth-Century Europe* (Cambridge: Cambridge University Press, 2004), p.5.
2. Jacob Katz, *Out of the Ghetto: The Social Background of Jewish Emancipation, 1770–1870* (Cambridge, MA: Harvard University Press, 1973), p.2. See also Pierre Birnbaum and Ira Katznelson, 'Emancipation and the Liberal Offer', in Pierre Birnbaum and Ira Katznelson (eds), *Paths of Emancipation: Jews, States, and Citizenship* (Princeton, NJ: Princeton University Press, 1995), p.15; Frankel, 'Assimilation and the Jews', p.16; and Stephen Wendehorst, 'Emancipation as a Path to National Integration', in Rainer Liedtke and Stephen Wendehorst (eds), *The Emancipation of Catholics, Jews and Protestants: Minorities and the Nation State in Nineteenth-Century Europe* (Manchester and New York: Manchester University Press, 1999), p.196.
3. See also Tullia Catalan, 'L'organizzazione delle comunità ebraiche italiane dall'Unità alla prima guerra mondiale', in Corrado Vivanti (ed.), *Storia d'Italia, Annali 11, Gli ebrei in Italia*, vol. 2 (Turin: Einaudi, 1997), p.1246.
4. 'Channels of contact' through business transactions, from bankers to peddlers, marriages and cultural exchanges, between communities in Europe were a characteristic of Jewish society and remained so. See, for example, Katz, *Out of the Ghetto*, pp.22–3, 215.
5. See Michael Graetz, 'Jewry in the Modern Period: The Role of the "Rising Class" in the Politicization of Jews in Europe', in Frankel and Zipperstein (eds), *Assimilation and Community*, pp.173–4.
6. Aron Rodrigue, 'Totems, Taboos, and Jews: Salomon Reinach and the Politics of Scholarship in Fin-de-Siècle France', *Jewish Social Studies: History, Culture and Society*, new series, 10 (Winter 2004), p.2. Also by Aron Rodrigue, 'From *Millet* to Minority: Turkish Jewry', in Birnbaum and Katznelson (eds), *Paths of Emancipation*, pp.238–61: 'the Alliance played an important role in the Westernization process of Sephardi Jewry' (p.248); see also Aron Rodrigue, 'Abraham de Camondo of Istanbul: the Transformation of Jewish Philanthropy', in Frances Malino and David Sorkin (eds), *From East to West: Jews in a Changing Europe, 1750–1870* (Oxford: Blackwell, 1990), pp.46–56. See also Jacob Katz, *Emancipation and Assimilation: Studies in Modern Jewish History* (Farnborough: Gregg, 1972), pp.7–8.
7. See Jonathan Frankel, *The Damascus Affair: 'Ritual Murder', Politics, and the Jews in 1840* (Cambridge: Cambridge University Press, 1997), p.435.
8. *L'Educatore Israelita* [*EI*], 1861, pp.401–6; see also pp.84–6, 254, 257, 589; and Catalan, 'L'organizzazione delle comunità ebraiche italiane', p.1247.
9. *Il Corriere Israelitico* [*CI*], 1875, p.50. The figures for all member countries are given: 18,226, of whom sixty-nine were in England, 4,934 in France and 5,413 in Germany.
10. Archivio Storico della Comunità Ebraica di Firenze [hereafter ASCEF], Congresso di Firenze, D.8.2, file 6. In a letter dated 17 September 1870, the president of the Ancona Jewish community wrote to the president of the executive committee of the Florence Conference: 'It is well known that … the stimulus for the conference in Ferrara came from this community.'
11. ASCEF, Congresso di Ferrara, D.8.1, file 2. In the circular of 15 April 1863, Leone Borghi, president of the Jewish Community of Ferrara, wrote: 'the worthy editor of *L'Educatore Israelita* … has already begun to work on a programme'.
12. See ASCEF, Congresso di Ferrara, D.8.1, file 2, Minutes of the first meeting, 12 May 1863.
13. ASCEF, Congresso di Ferrara, D.8.1, file 2 and file 5, 'List of the Jewish Communities invited to the Conference'. An invitation had also been extended to the Rabbinical College of Padua.
14. ASCEF, Congresso di Ferrara, D.8.1, file 5, Correspondence relating to the conference.
15. ASCEF, Congresso di Ferrara, D.8.1, file 2, 'List of delegates'. Sacerdoti was nominated to represent Monticelli, Fiorenzuola, Cortemaggiore, Colorno, Bussetto and Soragna, all small communities in the province of Parma (file 5, Correspondence).
16. See the Minutes of the first meeting, 12 May 1863.
17. ASCEF, Congresso di Ferrara, D.8.1, file 2, Programma pel Congresso Israelitico Italiano.
18. ASCEF, Congresso di Ferrara, D.8.1, file 2, Minutes of the meetings of 12 and 13 May 1863.

19. ASCEF, Catecumeni 1831–1874, D.2.3, file 1. See also *CI*, 1867, pp.67–8: 'Attempts at conversion are unfortunately still operating ... we wish to use our voice to oppose this shameful market of human souls'; and Roberto G. Salvadori, *Gli ebrei di Firenze: dalle origini ai giorni nostri* (Florence: Giuntina, 2000), p.49, where he notes that these abductions were common in the southern part of Tuscany in the nineteenth century.
20. See ASCEF, Congresso di Ferrara, D.8.1, file 2, Minutes of the meeting of 13 May; file 5, letter of 7 May 1862 from the president of the Ancona community to his counterpart in the community of Ferrara on the subsidy to the Waldensians. See also Catalan, 'L'organizzazione delle comunità ebraiche italiane', p.1252.
21. ASCEF, Congresso di Ferrara, D.8.1, file 2, Minutes of the meeting of 14 May.
22. ASCEF, Il Congresso di Ferrara, D.8.1, file 2, Minutes of the meeting held on 17 May, 1863. One of the items on the conference programme was to devise a uniform system for all communities to celebrate the Italian national festivals. There was no need for any discussion or provision since the festivals were already commemorated in an appropriate manner by each community (Article 11), an indication of their leaders' patriotism.
23. ASCEF, Il Congresso di Ferrara, D.8.1, file 2.
24. ASCEF, Congresso di Ferrara, D.8.1, file 2, Minutes of the meeting of 15 May 1863.
25. ASCEF, Il Congresso di Ferrara, D.8.1, file 2, Minutes of the meeting of 15 May, 1863, and Deliberazioni relative. See also Catalan, 'L'organizzazione delle comunità ebraiche italiane', pp.1255–6.
26. Michael A. Meyer, *Response to Modernity: A History of the Reform Movement in Judaism* (New York and Oxford: Oxford University Press, 1988), pp.164–71, 433; also by Michael A. Meyer, *Judaism within Modernity: Essays on Jewish History and Religion* (Detroit, MI: Wayne State University Press, 2001), Part 3, Chapters 13–18. See also Alberto Cavaglion, 'Qualche riflessione sulla "mancata Riforma" ', in Mario Toscano (ed.), *Integrazione e identità: l'esperienza ebraica in Germania e Italia dall'Illuminismo al fascismo* (Milan: FrancoAngeli, 1998), pp.152–66; Maddalena Del Bianco Cotrozzi, *Il Collegio Rabbinico di Padova: un'istituzione religiosa dell'ebraismo sulla via dell'emancipazione* (Florence: Olschki, 1995), pp.255–9; Bruno Maida, *Dal ghetto alla città: gli ebrei torinesi nel secondo Ottocento* (Turin: Zamorani, 2001), pp.299–301; Attilo Milano, *Storia degli ebrei in Italia* (Turin: Einaudi, 1963), p.374; Arnaldo Momigliano, 'The Jews of Italy', *New York Review of Books*, 24 October 1985, p.26. On the similar position among French Jews, see Meyer, *Response to Modernity*, pp.164–71, and Michael Graetz, 'The History of an Estrangement between Two Jewish Communities: German and French Jewry during the Nineteenth Century', in Jacob Katz (ed.), *Toward Modernity: The European Jewish Model* (New Brunswick, NJ, and Oxford: Transaction Books, 1987), pp.165–7. Samuel David Luzzatto was not in favour of a rabbinical synod and, with regard to reforms of the liturgy, he was opposed to any that merely aped current practice elsewhere. See his letter of 26 December 1850 to his former student, Lelio Cantoni, chief rabbi of Turin, in Samuel David Luzzatto, *Epistolario italiano francese latino pubblicato da' suoi figli* (Padua: Fratelli Salmin, 1890), vol. 2, pp.586–89.
27. *CI*, 1865, pp.67–75, 150–60, 187–90; *EI*, 1873, pp.374–9, on 'these highly pernicious innovations' (p.374). See also Gadi Luzzatto Voghera, *Il prezzo dell'eguaglianza: il dibattito sull'emancipazione degli ebrei in Italia (1781–1848)* (Milan: FrancoAngeli, 1998), pp.183–5; and Umberto Nahon (ed.), *Scritti in memoria di Sally Mayer (1875–1953): saggi sull'Ebraismo italiano* (Jerusalem: Fondazione Sally Mayer, 1956), p.351; Catalan, 'L'organizzazione delle comunità ebraiche italiane', pp.1258–9.
28. ASCEF, Congresso di Ferrara, D.8.1, file 5.
29. ASCEF, Il Congresso di Ferrara, D.8.1, file 2, Tabella delle Università Israelitiche aderenti alle deliberazioni del Congresso di Ferrara, loro popolazione, e quota di riparto assegnata alle medesime. In the expanded list of the communities invited to the 1867 conference, Pomponesco (Lombardy) had the fewest members – thirty; the figures for the Veneto are: Venice 2,200; Verona 1,223; Padua 800 (D.8.2, file 11).
30. Catalan, 'L'organizzazione delle comunità ebraiche italiane', p.1258. See also Ester Capuzzo, *Gli ebrei nella società italiana: comunità e istituzioni tra Ottocento e Novecento* (Rome: Carocci, 1999), Chapter 8 on marriage and divorce. Legislation in Austria-Hungary permitted divorce.
31. ASCEF, Congresso di Ferrara, D.8.1, file 11.
32. ASCEF, Congresso di Firenze, D.8.2, file 1.
33. ASCEF, Congresso di Firenze, D.8.2, file 4.
34. ASCEF, Congresso di Firenze, D.8.2, files 2, 11 and 12.
35. ASCEF, Congresso di Firenze, D.8.2, file 12, Replies to the invitation to the Conference.
36. ASCEF, Congresso di Firenze, D.8.2, file 10.
37. ASCEF, Congresso di Firenze, D.8.2, file 10.
38. ASCEF, Congresso di Firenze, D.8.2, file 16, Minutes of the meeting of 1 May 1867. See also the letter of 1 July 1863 from the president of the community of Ancona to Giuseppe Levi on the estab-

lishment of a Jewish kindergarten: 'I can only attribute the highest praise to the management of the city's kindergartens ... they demonstrated a real sense of solidarity and civil equality' (D.8.1, file 5).
39. ASCEF, Congresso di Firenze, D.8.2, file 16, Minutes of the meetings of 2, 3, 4 and 5 May 1867. See also Catalan, 'L'organizzazione delle comunità ebraiche italiane', pp.1261–4.
40. ASCEF, Congresso di Firenze, D.8.2, file 17, Deliberazioni del Congresso. In a letter to David Levi of 16 May 1867, David Amalgià, a member of the executive committee, queried the wording of the motion (D.8.2, file 1). Rabbi Terracini responded on 20 May that because the deliberations were already published and the matter would 'arouse many susceptibilities', nothing could be altered (D.8.2, file 1). Such minutiae were in the end of no consequence as Terracini's cherished objective once again came to naught.
41. ASCEF, Congresso di Firenze, D.8.2, file 17, Deliberazioni del Congresso. The members of the committee in addition to the president, David Levi, were: Cav. Avv. Marco Diena (Venice); Avv. Alessandro Liuzzi (Reggio); David Almagià (Ancona); Alessandro Malvano (Turin); Avv. Vittorio de Rossi (Livorno); Cav. Ing. Marco Treves (Florence).
42. ASCEF, Congresso di Firenze, D.8.2, file 1. The letter is dated 21 July 1868.
43. ASCEF, Congresso di Firenze, D.8.2, file 18.
44. ASCEF, Congresso di Firenze, D.8.2, files 1 and 2. These letters were written between May and December 1867. A proposal for a synod of rabbis and lay people was put to the communities of Lombardy and the Veneto in 1851, but nothing came of it (*CI*, 1862, p.339).
45. For example, in every issue of 1866, Mortara had contributed a series of articles entitled 'Judaism and Progress'.
46. ASCEF, Congresso di Firenze, D.8.2, file 1. The letter is dated 4 June 1867. This exchange of letters was subsequently published in *CI*, 1867, pp.207–10.
47. *CI*, 1867, pp.136–7. In 1865 there had been two articles on the subject by Rabbi D.I. Maroni, chief rabbi of Florence, condemning it (pp.297–301, 329–34).
48. See *CI*, 1867, pp.205–6, 266–73, 299–302, 330–1.
49. *EI*, 1866, pp.313–14. See also similar views expressed in *Il Corriere Israelitico* by Guglielmo Lattes, chief rabbi of Reggio Emilia (*CI*, 1880, pp.16–17). In Rome, until the inauguration of the new synagogue in 1904, five smaller places of worship existed, each with different rituals (see Paolo Pellegrini, 'Una storia, tante storie: famiglie ebraiche a Terni fra Otto e Novecento', *Rassegna Mensile di Israel* [hereafter *RMI*], 70, 2 (2004), p.69. See also Edwin Seroussi, 'Singing Modernity: Synagogue Music in Nineteenth- and Early Twentieth-Century Italy', in David N. Myers, Massimo Ciavolella, Peter H. Riell and Geoffrey Symcox (eds), *Acculturation and Its Discontents: The Italian Jewish Experience between Exclusion and Inclusion* (Toronto: University of Toronto Press, 2008), pp.164–82.
50. See Gadi Luzzatto Voghera, 'L'Israélitisme en Italie aux xix e xx siècles', in Patrick Cabanel and Chantal Bordes-Benayoun (eds), *Un modèle d'intégration: juifs et israélites en France et en Europe (XIX–XX siècles)* (Paris: Berg, 2004), p.202; and Marina Morpurgo, 'Ebraismo reform: un'ora con rabbi Barbara', *Keshet*, 3, 1 (2005), pp.75–8.
51. ASCEF, Congresso di Firenze, D.8.2, file 6.
52. ASCEF, Congresso di Firenze, D.8.2, file 6. In the same report, Levi invites those communities who have not yet done so to pay their subsidies. Leone Ravenna expressed similar sentiments in his article, 'The Closure of the Rabbinical College of Padua', *EI*, 1872, pp.69–74.
53. See Gadi Luzzatto Voghera, *Il prezzo dell'eguaglianza*, pp.140–8; and by the same author, 'Aspetti della cultura ebraica in Italia nel secolo XIX', in Vivanti (ed.), *Storia d'Italia, Annali 11, Gli ebrei in Italia*, vol. 2 (1997), pp.1215–26, 1237–8; Del Bianco Cotrozzi, *Il Collegio Rabbinico*. The idea of a national rabbinical college was resurrected by a committee chaired by Marco Mortara; such an institution was set up in Rome in 1887, but ran into difficulties – few funds and fewer students – and was transferred to Florence in 1899 under the directorship of Rabbi Samuel Hirsch Margulies. It returned to Rome in 1934 (Del Bianco Cotrozzi, *Il Collegio Rabbinico*, pp.331–6). See also Stefano Caviglia on the problems in Rome, in *L'identità salvata: gli ebrei di Roma tra fede e nazione: 1870–1938* (Rome-Bari: Laterza, 1996), p.45.
54. ASCEF, Congresso di Firenze, D.8.2, file 8.
55. ASCEF, Congresso di Firenze, D.8.2, file 6. The letter is dated 17 September 1870.
56. See Milano, *Storia degli ebrei in Italia*, p.469; Capuzzo, *Gli ebrei nella società italiana*, p.30; Guido Fubini, *La condizione giuridica dell'ebraismo italiano* (Turin: Rosenberg and Sellier, 1998), p.28.
57. See Luzzatto Voghera, *Il prezzo dell'eguaglianza*, pp.132–3.
58. See, for example, Robert S. Wistrich's comments on the leadership of the Viennese Israelitischen Kultusgemeinde, in *The Jews of Vienna in the Age of Franz Joseph* (Oxford: Oxford University Press, 1989), pp.88–97: 'Ever since 1852 [until 1914] ... the *Gemeinde* had been run by an oligarchy of rich bankers, industrialists, merchants, and lawyers' (p.88). The Jewish community of Vienna was the largest in western Europe.

59. ASCEF, Congresso di Firenze, D.8.1/11. The report is dated 23 March 1866. This decision was confirmed, despite reservations, at the 1867 conference. See Congresso di Firenze, D.8.2, file 16, Minutes of the meeting of 2 May 1867. See also Catalan, 'L'organizzazione delle comunità ebraiche italiane', pp.1253–4.
60. Cited in Fubini, *La condizione giuridica dell'ebraismo italiano*, p.48.
61. On the various legislations, see Capuzzo, *Gli ebrei nella società italiana*, Chapter 6; Fubini, *La condizione giuridica dell'ebraismo italiano*, pp.46–8. This volume contains appendices of the laws governing the Jewish communities of Italy from 1770 to 1996; Carlo Ghisalberti, 'Sulla condizione giuridica degli ebrei in Italia dall'emancipazione alla persecuzione: spunti per una riconsiderazione', in Liliana Mezzabotta (ed.), *Italia Judaica: gli ebrei nell'Italia unita 1870–1945. Atti del IV convegno internazionale* (Rome: Pubblicazioni degli Archivi di Stato, 1993), pp.19–31; Milano, *Storia degli ebrei in Italia*, pp.459, 471–2; Maria Fausta Materini Zotta, *L'Ente comunitario ebraico. La legislazione negli ultimi due secoli* (Milan: Giuffrè, 1983).
62. See Capuzzo, *Gli ebrei nella società italiana*, pp.39, 99–100; Luzzatto Voghera, *Il prezzo dell'eguaglianza*, pp.130–1; and Bruno Di Porto, 'Gli ebrei a Pisa', in Michele Luzzati (ed.), *Gli ebrei di Pisa (secoli IX–XX)* (Pisa: Pacini, 1998), pp.289–90.
63. ASCEF, Congresso di Firenze, D.8.2/16, Lettere della Commissione per la diffusione dei buoni libri.
64. Flaminio Servi, *Gli Israeliti d'Europa nella civiltà: memorie storiche, biografie e statistiche dal 1789 al 1870* (Turin: Tipografia Foa, 1871), p.17. It was intended to be an informative and popular account, interspersed with anecdotes and dramatic patriotic episodes, a panegyric to the success of Jewish emancipation – in Luzzatto Voghera's words, a 'historiographical fiction' (*Il prezzo dell'eguaglianza*, p.167). It received a favourable review in *Il Corriere Israelitico*, which praised in particular the historical and biographical sections, as an inspiration to young Jews to follow the example of the many illustrious figures mentioned by Servi (*CI*, 1872, pp.52–4). See also *EI*'s positive evaluation, 1872, pp.113–14.
65. Catalan, 'L'organizzazione delle comunità ebraiche italiane', p.1265.
66. ASCEF, Congresso di Firenze, D.8.2, file 9. Malvano's and Treves's letters are dated 15 and 21 February 1871. Others expressed similar sentiments: the administrative council of Vercelli received the last report of the executive committee 'with the greatest regret' and praised its 'intelligent activities' in representing the interests of Italian Jewry (letter of 16 April 1871). The report itself makes no mention of the Jews of Rome; the reasons for the dissolution of the committee were wholly negative.
67. In the 1889 penal code, the distinction between the official state religion and 'tolerated creeds' was abolished; all were placed in the same category of 'religions accepted in the State' (*culti ammessi nello Stato*). In the following year there was a new law of 17 July 1890 for all charitable institutions, irrespective of religious difference. See Fubini, *La condizione giuridica dell'ebraismo italiano*, p.45; and Capuzzo, *Gli ebrei nella società italiana*, p.110, n.24. On the concept of toleration in liberal theory, see Zygmunt Bauman, *Modernity and Ambivalence* (Cambridge: Polity Press, 1991), p.8, n.4.
68. Catalan, 'L'organizzazione delle comunità ebraiche italiane', p.1265. These proposals included: a membership fee per individual; an elected executive committee; the association to meet every two years and to finance an Italian rabbinical college.
69. See Caviglia, *L'identità salvata*, pp.161–2.
70. On the Collegio Colonna e Finzi, see Maida, *Dal ghetto alla città*, pp.70–83. The Collegio Foa was housed in Elia Emanuel Foà's spacious home, which also served as the location for the general assembly of the Jewish community of Vercelli (*CI*, 1866, p.173). Distinguished pupils of this *collegio* included Salvatore De Benedetti and David Levi the poet. One of the teachers was Giuseppe Levi, editor of *L'Educatore Israelita*; see his own recollections of the Collegio Foa in Salvatore De Benedetti, *Giuseppe Levi: ricordo biografico*, published in the same volume with Giuseppe Levi, *Autobiografia di un padre di famiglia* (Florence: Le Monnier, 2003; first edn 1868), pp.120–3.
71. Andrew M. Canepa, 'Emancipation and Jewish Response in Mid-Nineteenth-Century Italy', *European History Quarterly*, 16, 4 (1986), pp.417, 425. Boys were educated in these colleges from the ages of 7 to 18.
72. See ibid., p.417; Salvadori, *Gli ebrei di Firenze*, pp.78–9; Luzzatto Voghera, *Il prezzo dell'eguaglianza*, pp.124–8: the institute in Modena, Pio istituto israelitico d'istruzione, was based on class lines – literary studies for the wealthy, commercial for the middle class, and apprenticeships for the poor (p.128); Caviglia, *L'identità salvata*, pp.31, 36. The societies in Rome were much praised by the Jewish press: *CI*, 1876, pp.174–6; *Vessillo Israelitico* [*VI*], 1876, pp.51–2; *VI*, 1879, pp.80–2, 272–3; *CI*, 1885, pp.133–5. In the article on the Society of Used Goods Buyers, the editor stated that this group was not diminishing fast enough; one benefactor who had dedicated himself to 'this redemptive work', Pellegrino Pontecorvo, had become known as 'the friend of the poor'. *Il Corriere Israelitico* also reported on good practice elsewhere: for example, the Scuola israelitica di lavoro in Paris where, in one year, seventeen students had qualified as printers, mechanics and blacksmiths; sixty-one apprentices

began their training. The director, in his address, spoke of the fight against poverty and hunger; qualifications signified dignity and independence, and the Jewish worker would find his respectable place within the Parisian proletariat (*CI*, 1907, p.259).
73. Katz, *Emancipation and Assimilation*, p.99. For example, the modern schools for the Jews of Alsace, set up by the 1850s to promote emancipationist values; see Paula E. Hyman, 'The Social Contexts of Assimilation: Village Jews and City Jews in Alsace', in Frankel and Zipperstein (eds), *Assimilation and Community*, p.123. From the 1880s, in London and Paris in particular, schools and various other institutions were established to assist, educate and westernize the massive influx of eastern European Jews.
74. See Salvadori, *Gli ebrei di Firenze*, p.78. See also Luzzatto Voghera, *Il prezzo dell'eguaglianza*, p.128: attached to the *asilo* in Padua (1846) was an establishment for Jewish girls trained to be domestic servants; the one in Venice was for dressmakers.
75. Guglielmo Lattes, *Cuore d'Israele. Libro per ragazzi israeliti* (Livorno: Belforte, 1908). The title was inspired by Edmondo de Amicis's classic children's book, *Cuore* (1886). See also Luzzatto Voghera, 'L'Israélitisme en Italie aux xix e xx siècles', pp.205–6; and Teresa Salzano, 'Un "libro cuore" ebraico', *RMI*, 47, 7–12 (1981), pp.159–66. Lattes was one of the collaborative editors of *Il Vessillo Israelitico* after Flaminio Servi's death. Lattes also wrote didactic short stories and plays for children, such as *Dall'East End ... al Cantico dei Cantici: scritti e racconti del Novellatore Israelita* (Casale Monferrato: Rossi and Lavagno, 1910). This collection contains a story entitled 'The Itinerant Peddler', on the iniquities of peddling, the regenerative value of manual work and the key to moral progress, education. His *Catechismo israelitico pratico proposto per le scuole elementari religiose* (Livorno: Belforte, 1895) is also infused with patriotic injunctions. See also his article 'Education and Instruction in Jewish schools', in *VI*, 1879, pp.235–7, and the positive review of *Cuore d'Israele* (*VI*, 1907, pp.681–4).
76. Giuseppe Lattes, *Due Discorsetti letti nel tempio israelitico di Chieri dal Rabbino Giuseppe Lattes richiesti da alcuni suoi diletti Alunni e stampati a loro diligenza e spese in atto di stima* (Turin: Tipografia di Giuseppe Coen, 1848).
77. See Elena Rossi Artom, *Gli Artom: storia di una famiglia della comunità ebraica di Asti attraverso le sue generazioni (XVI–XX secolo)* (Turin: Zamorani, 1997), Table 11; and Maria Luisa Giribaldi Sardi, *Scuola e vita nella comunità ebraica di Asti (1800–1930)* (Turin: Rosenberg and Sellier, 1993), p.52.
78. Augusto Segre, *Memorie di vita ebraica: da Casale a Gerusalemme* (Rome: Bonacci, 1979), p.30.
79. Cited in Roberto G. Salvadori, *La comunità ebraica di Pitigliano: dal XVI al XX secolo* (Florence: Giuntina, 1991), p.88.
80. S.H. Margulies, *Parole dette dal Rabb. Magg. Cavaliere Dott. S.H. Margulies nella solenne commemorazione del 50 anniversario dello Statuto nel tempio israelitico di Firenze* (Florence: Galletti e Cassuto, 1898), pp.3, 7. In France, on 12 May 1889, 'prayers of gratitude' were heard in the synagogues throughout France to honour the centenary of the Revolution. See Frances Malino, 'French Jews', in Liedtke and Wendehorst (eds), *Emancipation of Catholics, Jews and Protestants*, p.83.
81. *VI*, 1898, pp.162–4; 1898, p.109. See also *VI*, 1898, pp.3–4, 37–8, 86–95, 126–7, 129–30.
82. Gian Paolo Romagnani, 'Italian Protestants', in Liedtke and Wendehorst (eds), *Emancipation of Catholics, Jews and Protestants*, p.161.
83. See Liana Elda Funaro, '"Compagna e partecipe": donne della comunità ebraica livornese nel secondo Ottocento', in Lucia Frattarelli Fischer and Olimpia Vaccari (eds), *Sul filo della scrittura: fonti e temi per la storia delle donne a Livorno* (Pisa: Edizione Plus, 2005), pp.324–8; Carlotta Ferrara degli Uberti, *La 'Nazione Ebrea' di Livorno dai privilegi all'emancipazione (1814–1860)* (Florence: Le Monnier, 2007), pp.52–5.
84. There are several articles in the 1872 issues of *L'Educatore Israelita* on the growing trend for state education, the consequent decline of Jewish studies, young people's ignorance of Judaism, and the importance of knowing the Hebrew Scriptures. The main thrust of the argument is that it is fine to aspire to professional attainment if young Jews 'can reconcile their duties as citizens with those as Jews' (p.246); see also pp.89, 110–12, 153.
85. On the Istituto Clava, see Giribaldi Sardi, *Scuola e vita nella comunità ebraica di Asti*. One of its most famous pupils was the literary scholar Attilio Momigliano. See also Rossi Artom, *Gli Artom*, pp.145–52.
86. Giribaldi Sardi, *Scuola e vita nella comunità ebraica di Asti*, p.124.
87. *La Settimana Israelitica* [*SI*], 3–5 (1913). See also the statistical tables in Mario Toscano, *Ebraismo e antisemitismo in Italia: dal 1848 alla guerra dei sei giorni* (Milan: FrancoAngeli, 2003), pp.145–7.
88. See Toscano, *Ebraismo e antisemitismo*, 2003), pp.138–44, 148–50.
89. Ibid., p.143.
90. See ibid., pp.143–4.

91. Katz, *Out of the Ghetto*, p.21. *Il Corriere Israelitico* published a brief report on the Jewish Free School in London, attended by 1,000 boys and 800 girls. What impressed the editor in particular was that it was funded entirely by private subscription: at the annual banquet in 1863, presided over by the president of the school, Baron A. de Rothschild, donations amounted to £6,000 (*CI*, 1863, p.94).
92. *CI*, 1885, pp.25–6, 73–99; *VI*, 1885, p.241. *Il Vessillo* also published details of Sir Moses's will, including the large sums left to various charitable institutions in England and Palestine (*VI*, 1885, p.262). Servi was proud to recall that over the years his journal had received 100 letters from the English philanthropist (*VI*, 1885, p.241). On Lord Nathaniel Rothschild of the London branch of the family, see, for example, *VI*, 1911, p.31: 'Few men enjoy such universal esteem … this year is the centenary of the Rothschild London office'.
93. Katz, *Out of the Ghetto*, p.21. See Milano, *Storia degli ebrei in Italia*, pp.503–10; Sergio Della Pergola, *Anatomia dell'ebraismo italiano: caratteristiche demografiche, economiche, sociali, religiose e politiche di una minoranza* (Assisi and Rome: Carucci, 1976), pp.205–6. Salvadori, *Gli ebrei di Firenze*, pp.80–1 on the *Opere pie* of Florence; Maida, *Dal ghetto alla città*, pp.53–70, on those in Turin; on those of Trieste, see Tullia Catalan, *La comunità ebraica di Trieste (1781–1914): politica, società e cultura* (Trieste: Lint, 2000), Chapter 6. On the many associations in Vienna, see Marsha L. Rozenblit, *The Jews of Vienna 1867–1914: Assimilation and Identity* (Albany, NY: State University of New York Press, 1983), Chapter 7 and Appendix 2; *VI* reported on those of Paris in the ten-year period up to 1880 (1880, p.363).
94. Luzzatto Voghera, *Il prezzo dell'eguaglianza*, p.126; and Mirella Ronchetti Vitaloni, 'Fonti archivistiche sull'evoluzione demografica, economica e culturale della comunità israelitica di Livorno tra '800 e '900', in Mezzabotta (ed.), *Italia Judaica ... Atti del IV convegno internazionale*, p.252.
95. ASCEF, Sezione Opere Pie; Classificazione Lampronti, B.8.1–5, 1865–1938. The prizes were awarded throughout that period. Among the papers are examples of the essays submitted for consideration.
96. ASCEF, Sezione Opere Pie; Classificazione Alberto Levi; B.13.1, 1888–1939; Classificazione Vivanti, B.123, 1884–1923; file 107/18. This bequest was carried out between 1885 and 1919.
97. See Funaro, '"Compagna e partecipe"', pp.330–1.
98. *CI*, 1885, pp.205–6. See also Caviglia, *L'identità salvata*, p.14. The areas of philanthropy, education and the role of rabbis have yet to be fully researched; the archival sources are there 'to be tilled': see Giovanna Tosatti, 'Comunità israelitica ed amministrazione pubblica nei documenti dell'Archivio Centrale dello Stato', in Mezzabotta (ed.), *Italia Judaica ... Atti del IV convegno internazionale*, p.146. See also Funaro's comments on the lack of specific studies on the Jewish poor in the nineteenth century who formed a large segment of communities such as those of Rome, Trieste and Livorno, in her article, '"Compagna e partecipe"', p.322.
99. See Funaro, '"Compagna e partecipe"', p.321. See also Rossi Artom, *Gli Artom*, pp.72–102, on bequests to Christian charities and institutions.
100. See, for example, 'The Paradoxes of the Jewish Heart', *CI*, 10 (1910), cited in Catalan, *La comunità ebraica di Trieste*, p.132, and *VI*, May 1888, cited in Mirella Scardozzi, 'Una storia di famiglia: i Franchetti dalle coste del Mediterraneo all'Italia liberale', *Quaderni storici*, 38, 3 (2003), p.724.
101. Milano, *Storia degli ebrei in Italia*, p.378. See also Massimo Livi Bacci, 'La demografia degli ebrei italiani agli inizi del secolo', *RMI*, 47, 7–12 (1981), pp.81–5; Maurizio Molinari, *Ebrei in Italia: un problema di identità (1870–1938)* (Florence: Giuntina, 1991), pp.35–7; Sergio Della Pergola, 'Precursori, convergenti, emarginati: trasformazioni demografiche degli ebrei in Italia, 1870–1945', and Eitan F. Sabatello, 'Trasformazioni economiche e sociali degli ebrei in Italia nel periodo dell' emancipazione', in Mezzabotta (ed.), *Italia Judaica ... Atti del IV convegno internazionale*, pp.48–91 and pp.114–24 respectively.
102. See Reinhard Rürup, 'Verso la modernitá: l'esperienza ebraica in Europa dagli inizi dell'emancipazione', in Mario Toscano (ed.), *Integrazione e identità: l'esperienza ebraica in Germania e Italia dall'Illuminismo al fascismo* (Milan: FrancoAngeli, 1998), p.39.
103. *CI*, 1865, pp.279–80. See ASCEF, Congresso Israelitico Italiano 1867, D.8.2.2, and Salvadori, *La comunità ebraica di Pitigliano*, p.10; Livi Bacci's figure for 1860–69 is 323 (in Salvadori, p.111).
104. Salvadori, *La comunità ebraica di Pitigliano*, p.96; see also pp.92–5. The institute was established as a result of the generous legacy of Affortunata Consiglio, who had inherited her brother's large fortune. Both lived in Florence but were from Pitigliano.
105. See Giuseppe Celata, *Gli ebrei a Pitigliano: i quattro secoli di una comunità diversa* (Pitigliano: Laurum, 1995), p.143.
106. Elena Servi, *Pitigliano ebraica* (Pitigliano: 2002), second edition of a pamphlet, November 2002, p.6. I am grateful to Lionella Viterbo, archivist of the Jewish community of Florence, for my initial contact with Elena Servi, whose courtesy and kindness were much appreciated during my visit to Pitigliano in March 2003.

SOCIAL AND DEMOGRAPHIC CHANGE 95

107. Daniela Bergonzoni, *Storia degli ebrei di Scandiano* (Florence: Giuntina, 1998), p.43.
108. Enzo Levi, *Memorie di una vita (1889–1947)* (Modena: STEM Mucchi, 1972), pp.82–4.
109. See Daniela Bergonzoni and Lazzaro Padoa, *Le comunità ebraiche di Scandiano e di Reggio Emilia* (Florence: Giuntina, 1993).
110. See Franco Bonilauri and Vincenza Maugeri (eds), *Le comunità ebraiche a Modena e a Carpi* (Florence: Giuntina, 1999); and *SI*, 21 (1914).
111. See Vittore Colorni, *Judaica Minora: saggi sulla storia dell'ebraismo italiano dall'antichità all'età moderna. Nuove Ricerche* (Milan: Giuffrè, 1991), pp.99–111.
112. *SI*, 46 (1910). See also Flaminio Servi in *Il Corriere Israelitico*, on Vercelli, 'one of the oldest and most influential of Piedmont ... one of the best with regard to education and charity', with 500 residents (1866, pp.171–6); Casale Monferrato, 700 strong and thriving (1866, pp.203–6); Cuneo, 320 individuals (1866, p.239); Fossano, a community of 120, no school (1867, pp.19–20); Saluzzo, 300 members (1867, pp.278–80). See also *VI*, 1910, pp.499–503 on the small communities of Piedmont.
113. See Rossi Artom, *Gli Artom*, p.176. For his obituary, see *CI*, 1878, pp.217–19, and *VI*, 1879, pp.20–3.
114. See Rodolfo De Benedetti, *Nato ad Asti: vita di un imprenditore* (Genoa: Marietti, 1989), pp.24–8; and Luciano Allegra (ed.), *Ebrei a Torino: ricerche per il centenario della sinagoga 1884–1984* (Turin: Allemandi, 1984), p.32.
115. See Caviglia, *L'identità salvata*, p.25. These recent migrants had little in common with the mass of poor Jews emerging from the ghetto, many of whom relied on charity.
116. See Jean-Pierre Filippini, 'La nazione ebrea di Livorno', in Vivanti (ed.), *Storia d'Italia, Annali 11, Gli ebrei in Italia*, vol. 2, pp.1053–4. Livorno's Jewish population in 1901 was 2,636.
117. The number of shipping agents fell from 190 in 1850 to thirty-one in 1869. See Jean-Pierre Filippini, 'Il ceto mercantile ebraico di Livorno dall'Unità d'Italia alle leggi razziali del 1938', in Mezzabotta (ed.), *Italia Judaica ... Atti del IV convegno internazionale*, pp.240–1. Preference was given to the port of Genoa.
118. On the Rome synagogue, see Caviglia, *L'identità salvata*, pp.81–95. The Italian liturgy was chosen, partly in homage to Rome as Italy's capital (pp.94–5).
119. Tullio Levi's words, president of the Jewish community of Turin in 1984, cited in Allegra, *Ebrei di Torino*, p.9. The Mole Antonelliana (Antonelli's Pile), named after the architect Alessandro Antonelli, was considered by many as too ostentatious; it was substituted, after much dissension, by another edifice, also of grand proportions. The Mole Antonelliana was bought by the city council; with its roof and spire soaring to 167 metres, it has become a major landmark of Turin, and since 2000 it has housed the national film museum. See also Maida, *Dal ghetto alla città*, pp.34–41, 49–50.
120. See Dominique Jarrassé, 'Le temple israélite: approche comparative d'un symbole et d'un instrument de l'israélitisme dans l'Europe et l'Amerique du XIX siècle', in Cabanel and Bordes-Benayoun (eds), *Un modèle d'intégration*, pp.68–9. The term 'temple' was adopted from 1809 – the first French temple was inaugurated in 1812 (p.67) – and became diffuse throughout emancipated Europe and also the USA.
121. *EI*, 1855, pp.107–11; Maifreda, *Gli ebrei e l'economia milanese*, pp.251–3.
122. Marco Momigliano, *Autobiografia di un rabbino italiano* (Palermo: Sellerio, 1986), pp.31–3. See also his appeal for donations in *CI*, 1866, pp.313–14; *CI*, 1867, p.45. Jews had been expelled from Bologna, as from most of the Papal States, in 1593.
123. See *EI*, 1861, pp.388–9; *CI*, 1864, p.209; *SI*, 11 (1913).
124. *VI*, 1908, pp.253–4, 472–4; 1909, pp.213–14; 1909, p.213; 1911, p.232.
125. *CI*, 1909, p.150; *VI*, 1910, pp.4–7. In 1916 the Ferrara community celebrated Leone Ravenna's forty years as president; *Il Vessillo Israelitico* commissioned a gold medal to be presented to him to commemorate his many activities in the service of Italian Jewry (*VI*, 1916, pp.173–83).
126. See the published summary of the conference proceedings, ACDEC, Fondo Sullam, 1.3.1, Enti ebraici e/o sionistici italiani, B.18, file 214. At the Zionist meeting of 1904, Bettino Levi gave a lecture entitled 'Measures regarding the Jewish communities that are about to disappear'; this should be a matter for the communities' leaders, he stated, 'but it is clear that Zionism has to rouse the administrators' apathy' (*L'Idea Sionista*, 1904, pp.60–3).
127. See Caviglia, *L'identità salvata*, p.131.
128. See *VI*, 1911, pp.98–100, 136–42; *SI*, 6, 8, 9 (1911); Catalan, 'L'organizzazione delle comunità ebraiche italiane', pp.1276–80; Caviglia, *L'identità salvata* p.132.
129. See, for example, *VI*, 1912, pp.514–16, 525–7; *CI*, 15 October 1912.
130. See *VI*, 1911, pp.623–5; 1912, pp.514–16, 633–5, 765–71; *CI*, 1911, pp.131–4; *CI*, 15 December 1912. The merger was still being discussed in 1922 (*VI*, 1922, p.155). Both periodicals praised the work of the committee. At their meetings, parallels were drawn between the Italian Risorgimento and the rebirth of Italian Judaism. See, for example, Rabbi Margulies's speech in November 1911 (*CI*,

1911, p.133; *VI*, 1911, pp.623–5). Both journals also reported that on 4 May 1913, committee members had been received by the king, who had congratulated them on the reorganization of the communities (*CI*, 15 May 1913).
131. See *CI*, 15 January 1913; *SI*, 1 (1913); Catalan, 'L'organizzazione delle comunità ebraiche', p.1280; Caviglia, *L'identità salvata*, pp.148–9.
132. *CI*, 15 April 1912. See also *VI*, 1911, pp.505–6, 581–4; 1914, pp.322, 350.
133. *CI*, 1912, pp.211–17. See also *CI*, 15 February 1913; 15 March 1913.
134. See Catalan, 'L'organizzazione delle comunità ebraiche italiane', pp.1281–3; Caviglia, *L'identità salvata*, pp.134–7.
135. Caviglia, *L'identità salvata*, p.134.
136. *CI*, 15 May 1914; see also *VI*, 1914, pp.237–51; Catalan, 'L'organizzazione delle comunità ebraiche italiane', p.1286; Caviglia, *L'identità salvata*, pp.134–5.
137. See, for example, *VI*, 1915, p.173.
138. Catalan, 'L'organizzazione delle comunità ebraiche italiane', p.1289; Caviglia, *L'identità salvata*, p.139.

4

The Longest Hatred[1]

'For many Jews ... whatever the larger historical balance, anti-semitism is the heart of the matter.'[2]

There has been a plethora of publications on the rise of racial and political anti-Semitism in the nineteenth century, with particular reference to Austria-Hungary, France, Germany and Russia, but the consensus in non-Italian historiography is that 'anti-Jewish sentiments ... played almost no role in modern Italian history'.[3] Until recently, scholars of Italian history also subscribed to the view that Italy was an oasis of peaceful coexistence between the Jews and the host society.[4] In the two last decades, a reappraisal of the Racial Laws of 1938 has led several historians to consider their implementation not as a rupture with the past, but as a continuation of a tradition of clerical anti-Judaism arising from the consequences of emancipation.[5]

The historiography of anti-Semitism in nineteenth-century Italy has been problematic and complex. Renzo De Felice, in the third enlarged and revised edition of his classic study *Storia degli ebrei sotto il fascismo* published in 1972, reiterates the stance of Attilio Milano (1963): a tranquil integration of the Jews; they were welcomed 'without reservation and without prejudice ... we can say that from the second half of the nineteenth century there no longer existed among us a Jewish question ... we repeat – there was no Jewish question'.[6] De Felice acknowledges that there were a few anti-Semitic episodes (*singoli episodi e singoli casi*) within the Catholic sphere, but these were not part of a general malaise; anti-Semitism was 'alien to the Italian mentality and sensibility', and thus had no wider impact, although there was some intensification of an anti-Semitic campaign within the Catholic Church at the end of the century. Racist anti-Semitic incidents were minimal, of little significance and almost all of foreign import (*sono poche e scarsamente significative ... e pressoché tutte d'importazione*). He epeats several times that anti-Semitism was almost totally lacking in Italy until the First World War, when it was manifest in a contradictory and confused ideology within nationalist milieus.[7] There is, in other words, a tendency to minimize and undervalue the presence of anti-Semitism in order not to discredit his principal thesis of an untroubled integration. Interestingly, in his preface to the 1972 edition, Delio Cantimori seems to disagree with De Felice: 'I could not defend the view ... that from the Unification onwards there were no anti-semitic manifestations in Italy.'[8] Cantimori also comments on the difficulties of writing such a book for Italian historians of his generation: 'there is a sense of shame and personal remorse, also civil and national ... that one is ... in some measure responsible ... in such cases the best thing is silence'.⁹

Thus it took someone outside Italy, the American scholar Andrew Canepa, to document and analyse both religious and political anti-Semitism during the period under discussion, in a series of articles published in the 1970s and 1980s. He too alluded to the silence on these issues from Italian historians due, in his opinion, to their intention not to 'spoil the edifying story they were telling'.¹⁰ Mario Toscano in 1994 was still tenaciously clinging to that reticence when he wrote of 'the weakness of anti-Semitism in liberal Italy ... a subterranean vein and politically insignificant' and suggested that it was 'a sort of Catholic monopoly'.¹¹ In a footnote, Toscano states that only Canepa has published on this topic, but he finds that the American author places excessive emphasis on the political dimension 'of a problem which appears marginal'.¹² In his 1996 study of the Jewish community of Rome, Stefano Caviglia does not conceal his anger with those historians (he cites De Felice as an example) who persist in denying and ignoring the many manifestations of political and cultural anti-Semitism in favour of those aspects that promote the harmonious integration of the Jews. He perceives this attitude as being conditioned by an anxiety (*ansia*) to exculpate Italians from anti-Jewish prejudice, resulting in an incomplete representation of the post-emancipation period. To understand the fascist regime, it was necessary to analyse the liberal period.¹³ A year later, this historical perspective had gained currency and was reiterated by Gadi Luzzatto Voghera and Ester Capuzzo.¹⁴ This continues to be the view held by those historians working in the field, with the qualified exception of Toscano who, in 2003 and again in 2005, was still cautious about the presence of anti-Semitism in the pre-fascist period.¹⁵ Indeed, Enzo Collotti writes of a total revision of the historiography of Italian racism. He adds that there is still research to be done on the influence of the provincial Catholic press on the local populace.¹⁶ However, Alberto Cavaglion is critical of an 'excessively recriminatory historiography' in which the origins of fascism are attributed to liberalism.¹⁷ There are three excellent studies of the Catholic Church and the Jewish question: by Giovanni Miccoli as part of Einaudi's *Storia d'Italia*; Ruggero Taradel and Barbara Raggi's monograph; and David Kertzer's volume on the Vatican.¹⁸ The many memoirs that have been published in Italy in the last two decades also attest to individual experiences of racial discrimination. There appears to be a retrograde note in Romano Canosa's 2006 study of Mussolini and Preziosi in which he replicates De Felice's position on the lack of political anti-Semitism in nineteenth-century Italy.¹⁹ A new approach draws parallels between anti-Semitism and recent Islamophobia.²⁰ The majority of the above-mentioned publications do not present an overall perspective of the post-emancipation period to the First World War; most of them focus on the early nineteenth century or the fascist regime.

There is consensus that anti-Semitism had far less impact in Italy than in other European countries: there was no mass violence against the Jews, and no political party adopted anti-Semitic policies as an integral part of their ideology, in spite of the fact that several leading Italian nationalists displayed anti-Semitic tendencies. Anti-Semitism resurfaced in a tenacious and virulent manner where the new nationalism, in its rejection of the universalism of the Enlightenment in favour of an exclusivist ethnic ethos, took the form of organized political movements, such as those in Austria-Hungary and Germany.[21] It was a German, the journalist Wilhelm Marr (1819–1914), who is credited with inventing the term 'anti-Semite' and introducing it into general use: in 1879 he founded an anti-Semitic journal and an association which became known as the Antisemiten-Liga (Anti-Semitic League); 'thus the fateful word anti-semite was started on its way ... marking the beginning of modern anti-semitism'.[22] Several reasons have been put forward for the absence of such movements in Italy prior to fascism: the successful degree of social, political and cultural integration of Italian Jews from the time of the Unification; the demographic factor – the Italian Jewish population was one of the smallest in Europe; also, the self-exclusion of Catholics from national elections until 1913 constrained, in part, widespread political anti-Semitism and prevented the formation of a conservative Catholic party.[23] In contrast, in other Catholic countries such as Austria, the anti-Semitism of the Church underpinned the ideology of the new nationalist movements.[24]

Nevertheless, in Italy as elsewhere in western and central Europe, the 'social utopia' that emancipation would dissolve all differences between citizens apart from religious faith was not realized; critics began to voice their reservations that the Gentiles 'had got a bad bargain'.[25] The controversial and lengthy debates on equal rights for the Jews which raged throughout western Europe from the end of the eighteenth century 'bequeathed a potent legacy of anti-semitic sentiment and literature'.[26] To take but one example from Italy: Francesco Gambini, an economist and civil servant, published two pamphlets against the Jews, in 1815 and 1834. In the latter, reprinted in 1857 and described as 'one of the classic texts of modern anti-semitism',[27] Gambini articulated ideas that became central to later anti-Semitic manifestations: the innate incompatibility of the pernicious Jewish nation with the concept of citizenship; the Jews as a threat to society; and alarm at their financial domination.[28] During the initial phase of the first emancipation between 1799 and 1801, many Italian Jewish communities were attacked by the local populace and, where French troops were not present to protect them, the ghettos were sacked and destroyed by 'Viva Maria' bands, stirred up by the anti-Jacobin clergy. In June 1799, they entered the ghetto of Sinigaglia, leaving twelve dead and many injured; a few days later, 500 Jews fled to Ancona. In the same month, the ghetto of Siena was raided, Jews were killed – including a pregnant woman and a man who had sought refuge in a church – and the tree of liberty was burnt down; the neighbouring community of Monte San Savino was literally wiped out. In the same year, Jews were attacked in Pitigliano and Arezzo.[29] The ghetto of Ferrara was threatened; in Acqui and Verona groups of *contadini* (agricultural workers) terrorized the Jews. The Christian populace identified the Jews en masse as Jacobins, although certain sections of the Jewish communities remained loyal to the old regime. The assaults were also motivated by religious anti-Judaism.[30] Similar violence occurred in Germany; the *Hep! Hep! Jude verreck!* (Death to the Jews) riots of 1819 that spread throughout many towns in the south and west, and involved all social classes, were also instigated by religious prejudice and as a reaction to the Napoleonic era. Another wave of rioting took place in Germany in 1830.[31]

At the outset of the second emancipation, although not so widespread, there were episodes of hostility against the Jews: between 23 and 25 April 1848 the Jews of Acqui were subjected to intimidation by groups of workers, merchants and artisans, and Bonajut Ottolenghi was a victim of the accusation of ritual murder; in Rome, in response to concessions accorded to the Jews by Pope Pius IX between 1847/48, such as the abolition of the ghetto, acts of physical violence were committed against them.[32] Enzo Levi, in his memoirs, gives a graphic account of his paternal grandparents' flight from Modena to Bologna in 1858; one detail fascinated him as a boy, that the horses' hooves were *fasciati* (bound) when they crossed the border to the Papal States. His own family was reluctant to speak of the past, of the suffering and privations of the ghetto, which he suggests was a defence mechanism borne of fear of future persecution and injustice. He, on the other hand, expresses his deep conviction that silence is harmful and that it is his duty to record the facts for posterity.[33] Such reticence was the advice given to Jews by their leaders, and they were also advised to 'remain in the shadow ... to be as inconspicuous as possible in order not to arouse either the resentment or the hatred of the neighbouring Gentiles'.[34] Augusto Segre recalls being taught to behave 'so as not to be noticed', and he observes that some Jews were willing, if necessary, to 'swallow the bitter pill of anti-semitism, in silence'. Older members of the Jewish community related to him the tradition of verbal insults and stone-throwing during Catholic religious festivals such as Easter.[35]

Canepa distinguishes two distinct strands of anti-Semitism during this period in Italy: the political strand of the Liberal Party and that of the Roman Catholic Church, both of which fed into the nationalist and later fascist parties of the twentieth century.[36] Clerical anti-Semitism had the greater impact, given the number of Catholics who adhered to it throughout Europe, the intensity with which it was disseminated and the international role of the papacy in condoning it. However, in view of the similar rhetoric of religious, political and racial anti-Semitism of the late nineteenth century, it could be argued that it is specious to attempt to separate them. The links between religious Judeophobia and secular anti-Semitism are illustrated through, for example, the persistence of the allegations of ritual murder, the idea of a Jewish–Masonic conspiracy, and fear of Jewish ascendancy. The concept of racial inferiority can be traced back to the fifteenth-century laws of blood purity of Catholic Spain (*Estatutos de limpieza de sangre*) which excluded newly converted Christians of Jewish descent from entering universities, guilds, the military, and religious orders – in short, preventing them from attaining powerful positions in Spanish institutions. This legislation effectively created a despised lower caste in Spanish life, and the necessity to prove one's purity of blood became an obsession, permeating – not to say blighting – Spanish society until the seventeenth century: 'the statutes of *limpieza de sangre* were ... the first example in history of legalized racism'.[37] Catholic iconography depicting negative images of Jews was subsumed into the political sphere, and Catholic belief in the Jewish stench (*foetor judaicus*) was revived by the Nazi regime.[38] Much of modern anti-Semitism and the new nationalism were founded on Christian theology, and the anti-Semitism of the Catholic Church in the nineteenth century was predominantly political: 'the notion that the Church fostered only negative "religious" views of the Jews ... is clearly belied by the historical record ... As modern anti-Semitic movements took shape ... the Church was a major player in them.'[39]

Christianity brought into the nineteenth century a patrimony of prejudice against the Jews: they were the alien 'other', the outsider to be held in perpetual servitude and set apart through a distinguishing hat or badge (Fourth Lateran Council, 1215); they were deicides, and ritual murderers – it was believed that they killed Christian children whose blood they drank or used to make unleavened bread during the Passover celebrations; they were unscrupulous usurers; perpetrators of the Black Death (1348); they were in ghettos to protect the Christian population from contamination (the first ghetto in Venice 1516, then Rome, the latter instigated by the papacy in 1555).[40]

In the debates on emancipation of the Jews, the Catholic Church maintained an intransigent position: integration would only be considered if preceded by conversion. In 1825, Ferdinando Jabalot (1780–1834), procurator general of the Dominican order, published a pamphlet which was reprinted at least four times; the views therein would have aroused horror and hatred. The Jews were a barbarous and rebellious people who vented their cruelty in execrable excesses: in the past 'they killed Greeks and Romans; they fed on their flesh; they daubed themselves in their blood; they bound themselves with their entrails; they covered themselves in their skins'. He asked whether a people who made a religious duty of cursing the Christians on a daily basis could be obedient and loyal citizens. He observed how wealthy and influential they had become: 'they have infected Europe by their example [*il loro esempio ha sparso in Europa il contagio*], and have transmitted that accursed greed for gold'; there would be a time when Christians were enslaved by them, their churches burnt, children kidnapped and slaughtered, virgins raped; their domination 'will be hard, inflexible, tyrannical'. Current legislation to protect Christians should remain in force. His conclusion was unequivocal: 'never, never will the Jews [he uses the derogatory term *giudei*] be able to become citizens among Christians until they themselves become Christian'.[41] Pope Leo XII approved of this publication and rewarded Jabalot by appointing him director of the Dominican order worldwide.[42]

THE CASE OF EDGARDO MORTARA

When Pope Pius IX returned to Rome in April 1850, after the very brief Roman Republic during which he took flight, his previous tolerance was transformed into intransigence, and the Jews were once more banished to their ghetto. In 1858, almost as a manifestation of his resistance to emancipation, he endorsed the kidnapping of a 6-year-old Jewish boy who had been secretly baptized by a Christian servant five years previously. The case of Edgardo Mortara from Bologna caused a public outcry throughout the world – even Napoleon III and the Austrian emperor Franz Josef intervened – against the Catholic Church and Pope Pius IX. In spite of these protestations and pleas, Edgardo remained in the pontiff's custody, was adopted by him, given the name Pius, and became a priest.[43] In April 1859, while Sir Moses Montefiore was in Rome regarding the abducted boy, there were several incidents in the Rome ghetto involving the alleged disappearance of

Christian children, and consequently an angry populace. Of one such episode, Sir Moses wrote: 'had the beadle not seen the child ... the lives of hundreds of innocent persons would have been sacrificed'.⁴⁴ Among those who campaigned for Edgardo's release was the Florentine newspaper *La Nazione*, whose editor was then Alessandro D'Ancona. The response from *Civiltà Cattolica* was derisory: 'You *Nazione* are Jewish ... and all your writers are rabbis.'⁴⁵ The case resurfaced in 2000 due to the decision, which Italian Jews denounced, to beatify Pius IX. Indeed, Elena Mortara, Edgardo's great-great-niece, also publicly spoke out against the Vatican's proposal.⁴⁶ Pius IX was beatified on 3 September 2000. The legacy of the Mortara case lives on in the collective memory of Italian Jews: the writer Alberto Vigevani (1919–99) recalled his habitual anxiety until his children returned home at night – a normal reaction, except that his paternal grandmother was a Mortara.⁴⁷

The practice of abducting Jewish children was a common one in the Papal States and throughout Italy. They were placed in a House of the Catechumens, an institution founded in the sixteenth century for the conversion of Jews and other infidels. Adults spent on average forty days there, children longer. Edgardo Mortara was taken to the one established in Rome in 1540 by Ignatius Loyola, founder of the Jesuit order. The editors of *Civiltà Cattolica* always reported on recent conversions. Noble families often sponsored converted Jews, offering their names and financial welfare (many such Jews came from the poorest families); large processions and celebrations accompanied these events.⁴⁸ A lengthy article, 'The Child Neophyte Edgardo Mortara', appeared in *Civiltà Cattolica* in October 1858 and was reprinted in Catholic newspapers throughout Europe. It recounted the miraculous transformation of Edgardo, who manifested 'such a full and clear understanding of his new state, such a resolute sentiment, such unwavering determination to remain Christian',⁴⁹ and reiterated a central theme of Catholic narrative, that Edgardo had a new father, the pope, a new mother, the Virgin Mary, and a new family, the 'great Catholic family'.⁵⁰ According to Edgardo's father's deposition of 6 February 1860, 'after some time living in Rome, we lost all hope when we read in the *Civiltà Cattolica* that our son would not be returned to us, and so we went back to Bologna where my wife fell seriously ill'.⁵¹

The last reported case occurred in 1864 in Rome: 11-year-old Giuseppe Coen, an apprentice to a Catholic shoemaker, was sent on an errand by his employer to a priest's house, put in a carriage and taken to a House of the Catechumens. In vain his parents waited for their only son to return home: 'the too recent memory of the Mortara case made them suspect the fate of their child', wrote the editor of *Il Corriere Israelitico* [*CI*] (1864, p.147). The father was denied access, the boy's mother became insane and his eldest sister died of grief. It was to be hoped, commented the Triestine journal, that worldwide condemnation would put an end to 'these shameful acts that sully civilization and discredit religion itself' (*CI*, 1864, p.160). The French ambassador to Rome intervened on the family's behalf; the Alliance Israélite Universelle proposed raising funds to assist the emigration of the Jews of Rome en masse, who were still in the ghetto under papal rule; Coen's family moved to Livorno where a subscription was set up by the local Jewish community to assist them financially.⁵²

THE CATHOLIC PRESS

By 1870, the papacy lost its remaining territories, seized by Italian troops, and the Jews of Rome were freed from their ghetto. Thus weakened and diminished, its temporal power reduced to the 100 or so acres of the Vatican City, the Catholic Church's relationship with the secular liberal government of the newly unified Italy was one of hostility and estrangement. In a series of decrees between 1871 and 1881, the Holy See forbade Italian Catholics from voting or standing as candidates in parliamentary elections, although both were permitted at a local level where anti-Semitism played its part. It was not until the 1913 national elections that mass Catholic support was influential through the Gentiloni Pact, by which Count Gentiloni, president of the Catholic Electoral Union, made a secret deal with Liberal Party candidates in return for Catholic votes; the anti-Semitic card was used on a number of occasions.[53] In those intervening years, the Catholic Church attacked what it perceived to be the two principal causes of anti-clericalism of the liberal regime: the Freemasons and the Jews.

The Church possessed a formidable weapon with which to denounce these enemies of Christianity: 'it was in no small part through the press ... that traditional Church hostility toward the Jews was transformed into modern anti-Semitism'.[54] Not only were books and pamphlets published, but also 130 periodicals, including twenty dailies, were in print at this time, rising to 500 periodicals and thirty dailies by 1900.[55] Many were regional publications, but two attracted an international readership: the Jesuit periodical *Civiltà Cattolica*, founded in 1850, which became the most authoritative organ of the Catholic Church, 'faithful interpreter of the Pope's ideas',[56] and *L'Osservatore Romano* (1861), the official daily of the Vatican, both still in print, the former in six foreign languages. Such was the importance of *Civiltà Cattolica* that in 1866 Pius IX created a writers' residence (Collegium Societatis Iesu Scriptorum) for the contributors, with special privileges within the Jesuit order. In 1899, on the fiftieth anniversary of its publication, Pope Leo XIII, who succeeded Pius IX in 1878, publicly praised the 'beloved children' (*figli diletti*) for having responded so perfectly to the desires and expectations of the Holy See.[57] Its influence was far-reaching for Catholic public opinion throughout Europe and the world.

In the editorial of the first issue, Father Carlo Maria Curci outlined the principal objectives of the journal: to defend Catholicism and ensure its place at the centre of European civilization, and to combat the blasphemous and anti-Christian ideas promoted by an agnostic and liberal European press. Initially it campaigned against liberalism, secularization and the principles of the French Revolution; the first article on the Jews concerned the Mortara case – after all, at this time, Rome's Jews were safely constrained within the ghetto, as yet denied civic rights. In the 1870s, the focus of attention turned to the Freemasons – the seizure of Rome and the loss of temporal power were perceived as part of a demonic Liberal–Masonic conspiracy to destroy the spiritual power of the papacy.[58] Sinister connections were made between the Freemasons and the Jews, who craved world domination: 'that malevolent sect' of Freemasons and Jews, 'the Synagogue of Satan' with its army ready to attack not only the Church of Christ, but the whole of humanity.[59] The first international anti-Semitic conference in Dresden in 1882 was reported in detail and its resolutions applauded, reflecting as they did the journal's views. By 1884, *Civiltà Cattolica* was firming up its ideological position regarding the Jews: they formed not just a religious group, but a national and a racial one, extraneous to all other nations; they could never be Italians, Spanish, and so on, only Jews. In 1890, three articles from the journal, entitled 'On the Jewish Question in Europe', were also published as a ninety-page pamphlet to maximize dissemination; they contain, *in nuce*, the Vatican's attitude regarding the Jews. The usual themes, publicized throughout the 1880s, were reiterated: world supremacy through the press and finance – even regions of Italy were becoming 'a kingdom of the Jews'; the Jewish–Masonic cabal; endorsement of political anti-Semitic movements in Austria, France and Germany. The pressing need to restrain 'the Jewish race' (*la razza giudaica*) permeates the piece as a leitmotif, couched in a lexis of provocation and hatred: the 'evil flood', 'this scourge', 'rapacious vultures', 'insatiable locusts'; 'all populations are infected' by 'the Jewish disease' (*morbo giudaico*). The only solution was to abrogate civil equality; deny them citizenship; confiscate their property; remove them from schools; wrest back control of the press; and introduce special legislation. In this way Europe would be saved from them and they in turn would be protected from Christian anger.[60] Elsewhere, it was argued that the Jews brought the violence of the Russian pogroms upon themselves through their unscrupulous exploitation of the peasants.[61] In 1898, a presciently prophetic utterance was expressed: 'the excessive power that has raised the Jews to such heights is excavating an abyss beneath their feet. And if the turbulence they are whipping up in France, Germany, Austria, Romania and Italy erupts, they will fall into a precipice that will be without precedent.'[62] This unremitting campaign against the Jews was repeated in *L'Osservatore Romano*, often on a daily basis.[63]

BLOOD LIBEL

The western European emancipated Jew, assimilated and successful, was perceived as an even greater threat to Christian society than the orthodox Jew isolated in his ghetto. Fears of Jewish world domination led to the composition of many articles in the Catholic journals on this new enemy: the 'modern Jew', the 'enlightened Jew', the 'reformed Jew'.[64] It was the ancient accusation of ritual murder, or blood libel as it is also called, that *Civiltà Cattolica* in particular pursued with venomous intensity. Between the 1880s and 1890s no fewer that thirty-three articles were published on this subject. The first documented case occurred in 1144 in Norwich, England; these allegations, which often resulted in arrest, torture and death, 'spread eastward like an epidemic' and were 'particularly prominent in the German-speaking lands of Central Europe'.[65] Belief in this practice, fostered by popular preachers, plays, songs and woodcuts, reached its peak in the fifteenth and sixteenth centuries. The most infamous case in an Italian city was that of Simon of Trent in 1475: the Jews were accused of the boy's ritual murder; all the men in the community were massacred; their property was confiscated by the Catholic Church; and Simon was beatified.

In spite of a series of Papal Bulls denouncing specific cases from the thirteenth to the eighteenth century – no general refutation was ever issued[66] – the calumny persisted and resurfaced in the nineteenth century as a powerful weapon with which to demonize the Jews and foment anti-Semitism. Accusations of blood libel, followed by criminal charges and court cases, were numerous, including Damascus (1840), Tisza-Eszlar, Hungary (1882/83), Xanten and Konitz, Germany (1891 and 1900), Polna, Bohemia (1899) and Kiev, Russia (1911–13).[67] The Damascus and Kiev cases attracted international press coverage, parliamentary debates and eventual condemnation, although initially credence was given to the Damascus case.[68] The Catholic Church neither repudiated the Syrian allegations nor endorsed previous Papal Bulls; on the contrary, they were widely and publicly reinforced, and the inscription on the tomb in the Capuchin church in Damascus – 'Here lie the remains of Father Thomas … murdered by the Jews on 5 February 1840' – has not been erased.[69]

Despite a sense of betrayal, disillusionment and despair expressed in the emerging Jewish press of France and Germany and in private correspondence, the Damascus case also acted as a stimulus to western European Jews, leading them to act collectively in an unprecedented and impressive manner: public meetings, press campaigns, lobbying parliaments and fundraising.[70] The most prominent Jews of England and France, Sir Moses Montefiore (then president of the Jewish Board of Deputies) and Adolphe Crémieux (vice-president of the Central Consistory), led a diplomatic deputation to Egypt – Syria was then under the control of the Egyptian viceroy financed by subscriptions collected from as far afield as the West Indies, and they eventually secured the release of those Jews who had survived the ordeal. On their outward journeys in Europe (they travelled separately), each Jewish community they encountered greeted them with enthusiasm and great interest; on their return, wherever they stopped, they were treated like royalty and showered with gifts and honours: 'The triumphal progress of Crémieux and his wife across Europe could have had no precedent in modern Jewish history.'[71] The Damascus affair sowed the seeds of the Alliance Israélite Universelle, established twenty years later, the brainchild of Crémieux; in 1840 he remained a month in Alexandria and Cairo setting up Jewish elementary schools along modern, European lines.[72] In this unparalleled response to the crisis of 1840 which later led to the establishment of the first international Jewish organization, we witness what Dan Cohn-Sherbok has controversially called the paradox of anti-Semitism: that there are positive effects of adversity which unite the Jewish people in actions of renewal, and thus Jewish survival and anti-Semitism are interrelated.[73] In his presidential address to mark the fifteenth anniversary of the Alliance Israélite Universelle, Crémieux stated: 'We are brothers in this long and cruel persecution of our race' (*CI*, 1875, p.50).

Il Corriere Israelitico published accounts of the principal ritual murder cases, including the Damascus Affair, through the series of 'Jewish Letters' by Albert Cohn, translated from the French; Cohn had assisted Crémieux in the preparation of written responses in his capacity as an advisor on Jewish matters.[74] The extraordinary events of the trial in Tisza-Eszlar included the perjured evidence of Maurice Scharf, the 14-year-old son of one of the accused, who had been held in police custody for over a year and primed to tell his story of the ritual murder of Esther Solymossi; the intimidation of witnesses by the president of the court; the violent anti-Semitic outbursts of those in the public gallery; and the anti-Semitic riots in Budapest following the acquittal, causing the authorities to declare a state of emergency.[75] The Polna case also received detailed coverage, and this time a 3,000-strong Jewish demonstration in Vienna 'bore witness to our great and noble sense of solidarity and brotherhood',[76] as did the trial of Mendel Beilis in Kiev.[77] Italian Jews publicly protested for the first time, and it was the Italian Zionists of Milan who took the lead with a series of posters inviting all citizens to unite against the infamous calumny.[78] 'We are writing for posterity', commented the editor of the Triestine journal, 'so that our children will have knowledge of the facts, dispassionately recorded, and they will be able to judge' (*CI*, 1883, p.49). *Il Vessillo Israelitico* also published on the Beilis case, documenting the protests, letters and exchanges in addition to reports from the Catholic press in support of the practice of ritual murder, accusing the Florentine *Unità Cattolica* of conducting an anti-Semitic campaign. Through the auspices of the journal, Italian Jews set up a fund for Beilis's family.[79] After he was acquitted, Beilis emigrated to Palestine, embarking from Trieste where, he recounts, 'a reception was tendered me in a big hotel and thousands of people came to see me. I was besieged with requests for autographs and in the end I stayed in Trieste for a whole month.'[80]

In every blood libel brought to trial, the accusations were proved unfounded despite many distinguished 'expert' witnesses, such as Professor Ivan Alexeyevitch, psychiatrist and professor emeritus of the University of Kiev, in the case against Beilis,[81] and the defendants were acquitted and released.[82] The objective of the numerous articles on the subject in *Civiltà Cattolica* was to provide readers with irrefutable evidence and authentic proof drawn from secret archives of the existence of this depraved Jewish practice. Contemporary cases as well as past ones were analysed in often nauseating detail and, in a long essay published in 1893, the editors helpfully listed sixty of them dating from the twelfth to the nineteenth centuries in order to demonstrate the accuracy of their information; they dismissed the acquittals as further proof of Jewish supremacy, capable of corrupting judge and jury.[83]

Throughout Europe, Catholic propaganda at all levels publicized ritual murder, taking its cue from the Jesuit journal. In France, the Catholic review *La Croix* (1880), an influential popular daily from 1883 with many regional editions, fed its wide readership on a rich anti-Semitic diet, including ritual murder accompanied by illustrations; it was directly influenced by *Civiltà Cattolica*.[84] *L'Osservatore Cattolico*, the Milanese version of the Rome daily, *L'Osservatore Romano*, whose editor had close links with Pope Leo XIII, became obsessed with Jewish ritual murder; its Berlin correspondent noted in 1892 that the subject aroused great interest and selections from the journal would be published in German; in the same year in Austria, extracts were cited by members of parliament.[85] Karl Lueger, the notoriously anti-Semitic mayor of Vienna (in office from 1897 until 1910) and his Christian Social Party exploited it in their propaganda.[86] They in turn were praised by *Civiltà Cattolica* for their 'positive programme' against 'the corrupt Jewish tyranny of the press and the Bourse', and for their resounding victory in the municipal elections of 16 September 1895 which 'signals an historic day of the highest importance, not only for the capital, but also in the history of the Austrian monarchy'. A fulsome obituary was accorded Lueger: 'his name will remain for ever illustrious for having freed Vienna from Jewish economic and political enslavement'.[87] The noted French anti-Semite, Edouard-Adolphe Drumont (1844–1917), editor of the daily *La Libre Parole* (1892) – 'the flagship of French anti-semitism' – and author of the 'best-selling catalogue of Jewish iniquities', *La France juive: essai d'histoire contemporaine* (1886),[88] commented that ritual murder was 'a fact as clear as day' (*un fait aussi évident que la lumière du jour*).[89] He based many of his ideas on articles from *Civiltà Cattolica*. To reciprocate the compliment, as it were, Father Raffaele Ballerini, author of the key 1890 articles, lamented that 'there was no one yet in Italy who has written a work that can compete with those of Edoardo Drumont'.[90] The rhetoric of 'the smoothly and carefully written pages of *Civiltà Cattolica* differed in no real sense from the verbal *and* visual portrayal of "the Jew" in ... Drumont's *Libre Parole* newspaper, as a member of a knife-wielding, sub-human species, his disproportionately long, clawed fingers dripping blood'.[91]

The regional Catholic press in Italy was far from reticent in its anti-Semitic stance. For example, Umberto Benigni, a priest, professor of ecclesiastical history at the Roman Pontifical Seminary (1902) and confidant of Pope Pius X, wrote prolifically on anti-Semitic themes, including ritual murder, for such clerical publications as *Il piccolo monitore* of Perugia: 'that worthy rabbinical race that even today in 1891 slits the throats of little Christians for the synagogue Passover'.[92] *Il Corriere Israelitico* published anti-Semitic extracts from *Unità Cattolica* of Turin (founded in 1863), one of the most popular Catholic dailies, accusing the editor, don Giacomo Margotti, of inciting hatred and intolerance rather than preaching peace and harmony.[93] *L'Educatore Israelita* also condemned the Turinese Catholic journal for encouraging belief in ritual murder in its report of the Smirne case.[94] In Padua in 1884, an anti-Semitic society was formed with the support of the local Catholic journal, which in turn was praised by *Civiltà Cattolica*.[95] *La Croce pisana* (The Pisan Cross) regularly published articles hostile to the Jews, with titles in 1889 such as 'The Jewish Invasion' and 'Jewish Supremacy'.[96] The editor of *Il Corriere Israelitico* reported what he believed to be the first prosecution for anti-Semitism in Italy: in 1900, the Catholic daily, *La Patria* (My Country), based in Ancona, published an article entitled 'Jewish Statistics' which encouraged its readers to boycott Jewish businesses in the hope that the ensuing economic decline would bring about the destruction of their race. A lawsuit was brought against the newspaper by the local Jewish community, which resulted in a fine and a four-month prison sentence for the editor, Andrea Orciani. During the trial, the public prosecutor stated that Ancona was a hostile environment for the Jews and thus such articles could cause serious harm. The author was the noted anti-Semite Rocca d'Adria, pseudonym for Cesare Algranati (1865–1925), a converted Jew from Ancona. *La Patria* was one of many publications associated with the Catholic Church in which Algranati expressed his virulent anti-Semitism.[97] A few years later, he published a novel about a young Jew who converted to Christianity and became a monk, which was so imbued with 'anti semitic calumnies' that in the reviewer's opinion it should be banned: 'a voice of protest must be raised against this defamation and it should not be said that Jews are afraid to defend themselves ... We protest ... We protest ... We protest' (*CI*, 1904, pp.99–102). However, as Canepa points out, the Ancona case was 'almost unique in the Post-Risorgimento period of energetic and dignified self-defence on the part of an Italian Jewish community'.[98]

Another scandal which illustrates the extent to which anti-Semitism had pervaded Catholic society in Italy was the performance of 'The Fake Beggar' (*La falsa mendicante*) in 1904 at the Istituto clericale of Verona, a girls' school. The play, written by a priest, deals with the theme of ritual murder and contains such lines as: 'This year we are fortunate that our unleavened bread will be made with the fresh and pure blood of a Christian girl'; one of the Jewish characters, Rebecca, says: 'I myself will sharpen the sacerdotal knife' (*L'Idea Sionista* [*IS*] 1904, p.27). The Jewish press protested vigorously at this incitement to racial hatred in an educational establishment, referring to 'the clerical-anti-semitic propaganda of the Istituto Seghetti' (*CI*, 1904, p.196). Their voices were heard: questions were raised in parliament, teaching was suspended and an enquiry was set up.[99] In Germany, according to press reports, a similar situation prevailed: children in Catholic schools were being taught about ritual murder through books on the lives of saints, several of whom were purportedly murdered by Jews; even in the university town of Innsbruck in Austria, scholastic texts contained passages on the subject.[100] In 1909, *Il Corriere Israelitico* published a case of anti-Semitism in a grammar school in Milan: a priest had set an essay title on how to behave with children of criminals, and in the class discussion he had stated that compassion was a fine sentiment, but not for the offspring of deicides (*CI*, 15 June 1909). In the following year, *Il Vessillo Israelitico* uncovered what it claimed to be a further example of anti-Semitism infiltrating the scholastic curriculum: the publication of a dictionary for primary schools in which the word 'Jew' was defined, inter alia, as 'avaricious', 'usurer', 'greedy for gain'.[101]

What of the pontiffs' reactions during this period, apart from their patronage of the two leading Catholic journals? Pope Gregory XVI had not repudiated the blood libel allegations during the Damascus Affair; on the contrary, according to Sir Moses Montefiore who had gone to Rome hoping for just such a refutation, 'all the people about the pope were persuaded that the Jews had murdered Father Tommaso'.[102] Pope Pius IX had reimposed the Rome ghetto, and his speeches were replete with anti-Semitic rhetoric: 'the nation of Israel is a fomenter of lies and insults against Catholicism' is an example quoted in *Il Corriere Israelitico*.[103] In 1869, on the publication of a major work on ritual murder, Pius IX acclaimed the author, the French Catholic scholar Henri Gougenot des Mousseaux, and awarded him a high honour; his text was an inspiration to many others, and the pope's personal endorsement was subsequently cited, thus imbuing the calumny with 'papal backing'.[104] Leo XIII, who succeeded Pius IX, criticized certain aspects of *Civiltà Cattolica*, but never its anti-Semitic campaign. He too approved of publications on ritual murder, such as the 1889 book entitled *The Mystery of the Blood among the Jews* by the priest Henri Desportes.[105] In 1892 he sent a personal blessing to Karl Lueger and two years later a letter in which he expressed great sympathy for the Viennese mayor's Christian Social aims; the Vatican Secret Archives reveal the extent to which Leo XIII actively supported Lueger and his party, even ignoring the pleas of the archbishops of Prague and Vienna to condemn Lueger's anti-Semitic ideology.[106]

It is, therefore, not surprising that in 1899, in an interview granted to the influential French newspaper *Le Figaro*, his position on the Dreyfus Affair – which had polarized French society from 1894, when Alfred Dreyfus (1859–1935), a Jewish captain in the French army, was first falsely accused of high treason – was one of ambivalence and masterful circumlocution. He mentioned neither Dreyfus nor the Jews, but spoke of 'this cosmopolitan scandal', 'this dreadful affair'; he praised the French prime minister Dupuy for introducing special legislation for the retrial (which took place in June of that year); he stated that some people might wish to turn the affair into a religious controversy, but in his opinion it was political. Should the Catholic Church come under attack, it had a long tradition of martyrs and victims. He hoped that one day the voice of a pope who loved France 'will be better understood by these men whose high intelligence will free them from retrograde prejudice'. In other words, he made an indirect denial of anti-Semitism on the part of the Catholic Church.[107] It was thus also predictable that in 1899 he would refuse to accede to the request of the Catholic minority in England, led by the archbishop of Westminster, to denounce publicly the accusation of ritual murder. The Holy See procrastinated and in 1900 eventually responded with the statement that the declaration could not be made: '*Respondeatur ... petitam declarationem dari non posse.*' The cardinal appointed to deal with the matter was perceived as an extremely appropriate choice, since one of his ancestors had been crucified by the Jews.[108] Canepa attempts to make a case for Pius X's sympathy for the Jews on the grounds that he numbered several Jews as close friends, including Leone Romanin Jacur, a prominent Italian politician, to whom he wrote in a private letter at the time of the Beilis case, assuring him 'that the Holy See will study every means to prevent the fatal consequences of the infamous fanaticism of those populations ... I pray that the trial will end without harm to the poor Jews'.[109] However, as Kertzer argues, although he allowed certain Vatican documents of the thirteenth and seventeenth centuries defending Jews against accusations of ritual murder to reach Russia, he did not issue a public statement repudiating the calumny. Thus the international Catholic press, naturally including *Civiltà Cattolica*, continued reporting on the Kiev trial in gruesome detail, exploiting it to reaffirm yet again barbaric Jewish practices.[110]

The sustained campaign against the Jews conducted at the heart of Rome through its journals and reinforced in priestly sermons and teachings throughout Catholic Europe clearly demonstrate that not only did the Church utilize anti-Semitism to reinforce Christian traditions in an increasingly secular society but, more importantly, it promoted and shaped the ideology of anti-Semitism in the political arena, fostering a general criminalization of the Jews.[111]

THE PASQUALIGO CASE

Although emancipation of the Jews was one of the pillars of the newly formed democratic nation state, liberal Italy found itself grappling with the consequences in a manner that engendered tensions and ambivalence from the outset. In July 1860, Cavour was criticized in the newspaper *L'Armonia* for the trust he placed in a Jew – a reference to his private secretary Isacco Artom. Cavour's reply praised Artom and expressed the hope that public opinion would seek justice for the ignoble attacks of those who regretted the times when religious difference prevented the best from gaining government posts. *L'Armonia* responded by stating that they did not deny Artom's abilities, but they were saddened that 'Christian Piedmont was so lacking in capable young men that Count Cavour was obliged to look to Israel for a close and competent collaborator.'[112] In the first Italian parliament of 1861, three Jews were elected: Tullo Masarani, David Levi and Sansone D'Ancona, 'made famous in the struggle for the Risorgimento'; throughout Italy, Milano informs us, Jews were voted on to municipal councils, chambers of commerce and the like, even becoming mayors.[113] What he fails to mention is that in Prime Minister Bettino Ricasoli's 1861 cabinet, Sansone D'Ancona's nomination as minister of finance was opposed by Enrico Poggi, minister of justice, on the grounds that to appoint a Jew to a government post would offend public opinion and the Church. Poggi stipulated that he would step down unless D'Ancona was excluded, and Poggi's opinion prevailed. Despite this initial discrimination, D'Ancona enjoyed a successful political career.[114] Furthermore, Milano does not allude to the polemic that surrounded 'the Pasqualigo affair' which, according to Cantimori, 'does not deserve to be forgotten'.[115] Nevertheless, it has been expunged from a recent political appraisal.[116]

In July 1873, a Liberal member of parliament, Francesco Pasqualigo (1821–92) sent a telegram to King Vittorio Emanuele II – an unusual action in itself – strongly advising him not to accept the nomination of a Jew as minister of finance. The Jew in question was Isacco Pesaro Maurogonato (1817–92), who had a proven record as a patriot and as finance minister in the short-lived Venetian Republic of 1848/49. Indeed, such was his success in that post that when the Austrians regained possession of the Veneto, they recalled Maurogonato to assist them in other financial concerns. He had also served as an able member of parliament since 1866, working principally within the Treasury.[117] What were Pasqualigo's objections? In several articles and letters, he stated that Judaism had nationalist principles, and wherever Jews lived they constituted a religious and political community; complete identification with the Italian nation had not yet happened, partly due to the brief time of their emancipation, but it may never happen. 'A Minister of the kingdom of Italy must be *purely* Italian [*ha da essere uomo puramente italiano*]. Italian Jews have two nationalities.' He also stated categorically, apropos of Italian Jews in general, that 'you have been born and brought up in Italy, but you are Jews first and foremost [*prima di tutto*]; you are *legally* citizens of the State like anyone else, but in fact you are not Italian; when you become Italian and cease to be Jews, I will change my opinion', and he gave the salutary example of a Jewish colleague who had had his children baptized in order for them to completely identify (*immedesimarsi*) with the Italian people, a reference to Giuseppe Finzi.[118] In other words, Pasqualigo seemed to oppose Maurogonato's appointment on racial and political grounds, also adhering to the widely held concept that Jews formed 'a State within the State'.[119] What was disturbing about these views was that they were not those of a rabid Catholic anti-Semite, but of a Liberal member of parliament among whose number were eleven Jews.

Canepa contends that Pasqualigo was partly influenced by the religious fanaticism of his native Veneto – 'the centre of the Catholic movement and a focal point of anti-Semitism for the whole country' – which produced a ritual murder allegation in 1857 in Rovigo and, in the 1880s, a bishop at the Paduan seminary who read articles on this calumny with approval.[120] Throughout the polemic, Pasqualigo used the word *ebreo* (Jew), which had negative connotations when adopted by Catholic anti-Semites, rather than the liberal terminology *israelita*. Canepa also suggests that in the first decades of Unification, the Liberals were naturally apprehensive about the cohesion and stability of the new nation, its fragile Italian identity and its attendant economic and social problems, not to mention the Vatican's antagonism; thus the fear of a potentially divisive, distinctive Jewish presence was an underlying concern.[121] Toscano, on the other hand, views Pasqualigo's objections as 'a substantial deviation' from liberal values and emancipationist ideology. He rejects Canepa's hypothesis that they reflected a widespread preoccupation among the liberal ruling class, in favour of De Felice's postulation that the affair fell into oblivion and in no way impeded the process of integration.[122] The process was not impeded but it was not as smooth as he and others interpret it. Molinari is of the opinion that the Pasqualigo case was 'the first real demonstration of secular–liberal anti-semitism'.[123]

What was the Jewish response? Maurogonato declined the post, ostensibly on family grounds, but in a letter to the king, he expressed his disquiet about a minister who was not of the Catholic faith applying anti-clerical legislation, as this could be interpreted as an additional exacerbation to a delicate situation[124] (for example, under state legislation of 1871, ecclesiastical estates were to be sold and many male closed religious orders suppressed).[125] He, together with all the other Jewish members of parliament, had voted for the Law of Guarantees (1871) which made some concessions to the Church and accorded sovereignty to the pope. Canepa argues that from the 1860s, Jewish deputies of the moderate right of the Liberal Party disassociated themselves from anti-clericalism, adopting a low profile, fearing perhaps that they might be accused of favouring their own interests and of bitterness towards the Catholic Church after centuries of oppression. This policy led them to form frequent coalitions with moderate Catholic parties in the local elections and earned them derision from some sections of the Jewish press.[126] Giuseppe Levi, editor of *L'Educatore Israelita*, shared Maurogonato's concerns: a Jewish minister of finance would have placed an excessive burden on the incumbent at that time, precisely because the post had to do with finance and Jews; 'everything changes except prejudice', and it was prejudice that had led an educated Liberal member of parliament to claim that a Jew should not be a government minister. Pasqualigo's assumption stemmed from the misconception of equating religion with nationality, the temporal with the spiritual. No one, Levi argued, would dare to accuse French Protestants of not being as patriotic as French Catholics, and no one would expect French Protestantism to merge (*fondersi*) with Catholicism, as Pasqualigo demanded of the Jews.[127] And yet this is what Giuseppe Finzi (1815–86) attempted by having his children baptized. The motivation was also the consequence of discrimination: in a letter to Luigi Luzzatti of 13 September 1873, Finzi referred to a conversation with Pasqualigo in which he had explained his decision – 'we have to live in a predominantly Catholic society ... still full of prejudice ... many deep-rooted prejudices of all social classes' – and he did not wish his children to bear the burden of being part of a merely tolerated minority.[128] In hoping that baptism would protect his children from future anguish and humiliation, Finzi followed a familiar path of emancipated western European Jews.[129]

The lasting influence of a Catholic education permeated with anti-Semitism was acknowledged in the articles that Senator Giuseppe Musio wrote in defence of Maurogonato's appointment. Musio, a lawyer, pointed out the legal illogicalities of Pasqualigo's arguments and their significance not only for Italy but for international human rights. He also recalled the prejudices 'instilled in him by religious instruction [to the extent] that until maturity he thought he could see on a Jew's brow the brand of malediction' (*il marchio della maledizione*).[130] Musio was the most distinguished of Pasqualigo's adversaries, and the editors of *L'Educatore Israelita* and *Il Corriere Israelitico* paid him fulsome praise, as did the Venetian Jewish community and the Alliance Israélite Universelle in official letters of recognition for his authoritative intervention.[131] The Masonic Lodge of Rome also participated, with a lengthy debate in favour of the Jews. They also took the decision to write an open letter to Musio for his defence of human rights 'against the iniquitous and barbarous privilege of race'.[132] The Jewish lawyer Marco Diena dismissed Pasqualigo's notion of a political identity common to all Jews as 'a dream and a total anachronism' (Zionism was yet to come); emancipated Jews acknowledged as their country the one that had given them citizenship. He also took issue with Pasqualigo's use of the term *ebreo*, accusing him of being 'arm in arm with the most rabid theocrats', in spite of Pasqualigo's denials of any religious influence and his opposition to the Law of Guarantees.[133]

The only Jewish response that addressed the question of dual nationality raised by Pasqualigo was that of Marco Mortara (1815–94), chief rabbi of Mantua. His arguments were as follows: although the Jews had been a nation in the past, since the destruction of the Second Temple Judaism was totally detached from any nationalist aspirations. Jews throughout the world were in essence a religion and a race (*stirpe*); the modern ideology of nationhood was not based on these two concepts but on territory, language, traditions and a civil constitution – all elements that the Jews of Italy shared with other Italians. Judaism considered love for one's country as a moral obligation, which was respected even in times of persecution (*l'amore della patria, per quanto matrigna*). Pasqualigo had spoken of messianism as proof of the Jews' desire to reconstitute a nation of their own and of their transitory loyalty to particular countries. However, the messianic principles of Judaism lay in the ultimate triumph of monotheism, justice and universal brotherhood. Thus Judaism was the religion most suitable for modern society, equipping its adherents with an education which prepared them for complete integration in all sectors of Italian life. A Jew had no need to deny his own faith in order to feel and be fully Italian.[134]

Mortara's positive analysis of Judaism sparked a fierce and antagonistic reaction from a Jewish academic who hitherto had never publicly pronounced on Jewish affairs. Gustavo Uzielli (1839–1911) stated that he could understand the sense of repugnance to the idea of Jews in high office, since the Jewish race was 'historically reactionary', and the Jewish religion was obsolete and had failed to adapt its coarse and narrow precepts to the 'great social evolution of Christianity'. Jews had progressed only in a materialist sense, with their obsession with profit. He concluded by exhorting his co-religionists to abandon Judaism in favour of a higher, spiritualized form of Christianity. In his desire for assimilation, Uzielli had internalized the secular critique of Judaism as an anachronism, the anti-Semitic stereotype of the avaricious Jew, and he endorsed Pasqualigo's views.[135]

A postscript to the affair: in 1875, *Il Vessillo Israelitico* published a brief biographical sketch of Maurogonato in its series on Jewish members of parliament; no mention was made of the polemic, only that he had refused the ministerial post for family reasons. In the 1876 elections, Giuseppe Finzi encountered anti-Semitism from the opposition – so reported *Il Corriere Israelitico*: 'do not elect, do not have faith in Giuseppe Finzi who is a Jew'. In an attempt to counter these negative remarks, Finzi publicly repudiated his Jewish origins, instead, commented the editor, of fighting against such deep-rooted prejudice. The result was that the voters were not impressed by this abjuration and he was not elected, whereas others who declared themselves to be Jewish 'succeeded splendidly'.[136] *L'Educatore Israelita*, a few years earlier, had noted a growing tendency among a minority not to disclose their Jewish identity 'for fear of being noticed' (*per timore di farsi scorgere*) (1873, p.347).

Finzi was not the only Jew who faced anti-Semitic slurs: in 1879 and 1882 Edoardo Arbib (1840–1906) from Livorno, who had been one of Garibaldi's 'Thousand', stood as a parliamentary candidate for Viterbo. On both occasions, an anti-Semitic campaign was mounted against him, in particular by his opponent in the 1882 election, Enrico Pani Rossi ('Arbib was defeated because he was a Jew'); circulars and notices containing 'the whole arsenal of atrocious medieval accusations' were distributed to frighten the electorate.[137] During the national elections of 1880, Samuele Alatri, former president of the Rome Jewish community, was accused by the left-wing press of deliberately soliciting the moderate Jewish vote, as he was fighting a seat in the ghetto area of the city, thus appealing 'to sectarian solidarity', 'to caste solidarity'.[138] Alatri lost on the second ballot by a very small margin and his journalistic opponents were jubilant, as their tactics had clearly been effective. A decade later, the right-wing press used similar arguments when the same electorate, 'the whole tribe of Israel', supported a Jewish left-wing candidate.[139] Of whatever political colour, there was suspicion about potential Jewish separatism, which the Jews themselves attempted to guard against. Thus the Jewish community of Rome had second thoughts about planning exclusive celebrations to commemorate the twenty-fifth anniversary of liberation from papal rule in case the idea was misinterpreted. Instead, they ensured that their programme involved the whole of the district, 'to affirm shared civic aspirations and patriotism'.[140] In 1882, Medoro Savini, a deputy for the liberal Left, published two articles in a major Neapolitan daily on the Jews in which he articulated the anti-Semitic shibboleths of their extensive wealth, their exclusivity and lack of patriotism.[141] Giacomo Malvano (1841–1922), who became Secretary General at the foreign ministry between 1889 and 1907, was ousted from his diplomatic post in 1887 partly as a result of anti-Semitic slurs within the government and also in the press.[142]

ANTI-SEMITIC PUBLICATIONS

The most controversial manifestation of liberal anti-Semitism in the 1880s came from the noted physician–anthropologist, politician and senator, Paolo Mantegazza (1831–1910), who held the first Italian Chair of Anthropology in Florence. Between 1872 and 1885 he published a trilogy on love and sexuality; in a chapter in the third volume on 'the mutilation of the genitals', detailing rituals among 'savage tribes', including Jews, he attacked the perverse practice of male circumcision:

> [it] is a shame and an infamy ... I shall continue to shout at the Hebrews until my last breath: cease mutilating yourselves; cease imprinting upon your flesh an odious brand to distinguish you from other men; until you do this, you cannot pretend to be our equal. As it is, you, of your own accord ... proceed to proclaim yourselves a race apart, one that cannot, and does not care to, mix with ours.[143]

In September 1885, he reiterated these views in the popular Roman weekly, *Fanfulla della domenica*, in an article entitled 'The Anti-Semitic Question'. He emphasized the Jews' supranational separatism in pathological terms: 'they are excrescences, tumours ... preventing the free circulation of our forces. They are in a word the fat and nasty parasites of European life' (*i parassiti grassi e molesti della vita europea*).[144]

Mantegazza's article was one of many anti-Semitic publications which appeared in Italy, as elsewhere in Europe. A few years earlier, in 1879, Leonida Bissolati, future leader of Reformist Socialism, wrote a piece on racial anti-Semitism in the *Rivista Repubblicana* in which he expressed the view that the Jews' capacity for cognitive development is arrested at the age of 16 and therefore 'the Jew's brain is closed to science'.[145] An example of political anti-Semitism is *Gli usurai alla conquista del mondo: studio sociale* (The Usurers in the Conquest of the World: A Social Study), by 'Spartacus', published in Mantua/Cremona in 1880. It was a response to Osman Bey's 1871 pamphlet, *The Conquest of the World by the Jews*, which was translated into several languages as anti-Semitism gained momentum. The infamous forgery, *The Protocols of the Elders of Zion*, propagating the myth of a worldwide Jewish conspiracy, 'the most significant text in the history of twentieth-century anti-semitism',[146] did not appear in Italian translation until 1921, with a preface by the notorious anti-Semite, nationalist, fascist

Giovanni Preziosi, who claimed he was the instigator of political anti-Semitism in Italy.[147]

DISCRIMINATION IN PUBLIC LIFE

Was discrimination being experienced in other sectors of society in the first decades of the Italian nation? In the pages of *L'Educatore Israelita*, there are recorded cases of exclusion of entry to the navy corps and the military academy of Turin.[148] On 16 January 1860, the Milanese branch of the national bank opened its doors; among the board of directors nominated by the royal decree of 1 October 1859 no Jew figured. Maifreda's recent research has revealed 'mistrust on the part of government bodies towards the Jewish component'.[149] The appointment of Alessandro D'Ancona (younger brother of the politician Sansone) to the Chair of Italian at the University of Pisa was contested in 1861 by Catholic academics who questioned a Jew's competence to teach Dante. In 1864, Pasquale Villari, director of the Scuola Normale of Pisa, wrote to the minister of education opposing the nomination of D'Ancona as his successor, partly on the grounds that he was a Jew (he eventually took up the post in 1893). Villari also complained in a letter to a friend of 21 October 1861 that only Jewish students were attending D'Ancona's lectures. Isacco Artom wrote to D'Ancona requesting him to keep a protective eye on their mutual friend Salvatore De Benedetti, also an academic at the university, 'to avoid, if possible, a war with the priests'.[150] Much later, in 1907, D'Ancona was forced to resign as mayor of Pisa after only one year because of an anti-Semitic campaign in the local Catholic press.[151] *Il Vessillo Israelitico* reported on the initial refusal of Turin's city council to place a marble bust (commissioned by friends and admirers) of Giacomo Dina (1824–79), a leading emancipationist, journalist and politician, in one of the public gardens, as he was not worthy and was a Jew (*VI*, 1880, pp.256–7).

Antipathy did not only emanate from the ruling classes: in Rome in 1857, violent feuds broke out between Jewish and Catholic fishmongers, causing injuries and ten arrests; in 1873, the striking workers of the textile industry in Pisa, mostly Jewish-owned, wrote slogans such as 'Death to the Jews'.[152] With the secularization of schools in the post-Unification period and the admission of Jews, the Catholic Church initially attempted to undermine such changes through negative articles in their press. Thus the transformation of the Jesuit College in Rome into the Liceo E.Q. Visconti was contaminated by the presence of Jewish pupils and teachers who would jeopardize Christian principles and values; when in 1873 the girls' school of Tor de' Conti appointed the wife of the secretary of the Rome Jewish community, *L'Osservatore Romano* warned its readers of a liberal plot to deprive their children of a Christian education.[153] *L'Educatore Israelita* documented instances of discrimination: for example, in a primary school in Reggio Emilia, Catholic pupils taunted Jews, and in Modena a kindergarten continued to exclude them (1873, pp.148, 188). Conversely, the bishop of Treviso threatened to excommunicate the Istituto femminile S. Teoristo for admitting several Jewish girls (*VI*, 1879, p.60). *Il Corriere Israelitico* reported three anti-Semitic incidents, in Mantua, Rome and Venice: at Yom Kippur, congregations were insulted and women's clothing torn. The editor's comment was one of consternation that these excesses could happen in Italy (1876, p.141). As the century progressed, a note of alarm sounded at what was perceived as an increase in anti-Semitic manifestations in Italy.

In memoirs and autobiographies, mention is made of intolerance. Guglielmo Lattes, born in 1857 in Livorno, recalls 'barely concealed racial antipathy towards the Jewish students' on the part of members of the teaching staff at his secondary school and also at teacher training college in Pisa; others, in contrast, were 'very tolerant' and 'sincere liberals'. One of his fellow students, a 'fervent Catholic' tried to convert him and, when he qualified, he had difficulty in finding a job; he was told on more than one occasion that being a Jew was an obstacle in his future employment.[154] Jewish pupils were taunted in Luigi Luzzatti's high school in the 1850s in Venice.[155] However, Marco Momigliano, born in 1825 and writing in 1897, does not allude to anti-Semitism. Cavaglion, in his postface, suggests that the rabbi 'was resolved [*volle*] to conceal it out of love for his country'.[156] There is a suggestion that Tullo Massarani (1826–1905) was subjected to deliberate acts of cruelty as a child; as an adult, he adopted a defensive attitude. He was of the opinion that anti-Semitism had not taken root in Italy because most Jews did not accentuate their own physiognomy which marked them out as a race apart; everything that suggested separateness damaged 'that complete assimilation which should be the aim of every loyal citizen'.[157]

Evaluating these first decades of emancipation in Italy and Jewish reactions, various observations can be made: despite separation of Church and State, Catholic anti-Semitism through education, sermons and publications continued to have an impact on daily life at all levels, from the Cabinet office to the classroom; assimilatory pressure and aspiration to adhere to the majority, to identify with an as yet fragile notion of *italianità* was felt by many Jews; the stigma of otherness was experienced, hence the attitude of not wishing to be noticed, to remain in the shadow. Italian Jews had no central organization to represent them at national level and ensure that legislation was equitably applied; the 1863 and 1867 conferences had failed in this respect, and thus the Jewish press was an indispensable medium between them and the wider society, and played an active role in publicizing acts of discrimination and seeking redress. The difficulties on the part of the host society to accept diversity was partly derived from the ideology of the emerging nation states, which was predicated on similarity and conformity. Italian Jews will have looked with deep unease at the unfolding political events in Germany and Austria-Hungary where anti-Semitism was assuming mass proportions.

REPORTS FROM *IL CORRIERE ISRAELITICO*

The editors of *Il Corriere Israelitico* scrupulously recorded the inception, growth and spread of anti-Semitism worldwide. From the 1870s, there are frequent accounts of persecution against the Jews, from individual acts of prejudice to wholesale massacres such as the Russian pogroms; Romania is also frequently cited for its anti-Semitism – in 1879 there are reports in every issue.[158] In 1875, there appeared extensive extracts from a speech given in the Hungarian parliament by the leader of the anti-Semitic movement, Győző Istoczy, in which he warned of the pernicious influence of the Jews: 'They form a formidable caste, a powerful international body which aims to suppress other religions in order to gain world supremacy and create pan Judaism' (*CI*, 1875, p.3). By 1882, Istoczy was joined by a further five anti-Semitic deputies; by 1887 there were seventeen. He organized the first international anti-Semitic conference in Dresden.[159] In Germany in February 1879, Wilhelm Marr's pamphlet, *The Victory of Judaism over Germandom: Regarded from the Nondenominational Point of View*, became 'the first anti-semitic best-seller',[160] running to twelve editions in that year. As Pulzer points out, the significance is in the title: Jew is not contrasted to Christian but to German, and the two are deemed to be irredeemably incompatible, thus shifting the discourse against the Jews to one of race not religion.[161] 'I bow my head in admiration and amazement', wrote Marr, 'before this Semitic people, which has us under heel … We have among us a flexible, tenacious, intelligent, foreign tribe.'[162] The principal aim of Marr's League of Anti-Semites (1879) was to 'save our German fatherland from complete Judaisation'.[163] Alfred Stöcker (1835–1909), politician and Imperial Protestant Court chaplain from 1874, founded his Christian Social Workers' Party in 1878, the first political party to appeal to the masses on an anti-Semitic platform: in a rousing speech at a rally in Berlin on 19 September 1879, he called on his fellow Germans to rid themselves of the Jewish disease, the cancer that was destroying the Christian–German spirit.

At the other end of the social spectrum, the distinguished and influential nationalist historian, Heinrich von Treitschke (1834–96) of the University of Berlin, bastion of academic excellence and intellectual respectability, endorsed the anti-Semitic campaign in a series of articles of 1879/80 in which he reiterated fears of the Jews, particularly the many eastern European immigrants, as a danger to the new national life of Christian Germany. His statement 'the Jews are our misfortune' became a slogan of German anti-Semitism, later taken up by the Nazis. Theodor Mommsen (1817–1903), historian, liberal politician and colleague of Treitschke, condemned these anti-Semitic views (he was the only Christian to do so publicly) and he never forgave Treitschke for them. Nevertheless, he argued in an article of 1880 that 'admission into a great nation has its price', which the Jews must pay by eradicating all cultural and historical differences and converting to Christianity, reinforcing the emancipationist debates of a hundred years earlier.[164] Too often, as Arnaldo Momigliano remarked, Jews have been asked to deny their heritage in the name of an ill-conceived equality.[165] In the same year, an anti-Semitic petition, demanding the abrogation of civic equality for the Jews and restrictions on their immigration, attracted over 250,000 signatures and was debated in parliament over a period of two days. When a Liberal deputy asked what measures would be taken regarding the petition, the 'correct and cool response' from the vice-president of the Cabinet was merely to refer to the constitutional rights of all religious denominations. This was interpreted as a sign of encouragement by the organizers of the petition and more signatures were sought.[166] The view that Germany was a Christian nation gained popularity:

anti-Semitic tracts abounded and anti-Semitic associations were formed. The Deutsche schiller stiftung, a German writers' charitable foundation established in 1859 (the Schiller centenary), became increasingly ambivalent in its attitude towards the Jews from the 1870s, frequently awarding grants to well-known anti-Semitic writers such as Marr; if Jewish authors were recipients, doubts were raised regarding their eligibility.[167] Nationalist university student fraternities began to exclude Jews from the late 1870s; they were transformed into an anti-Semitic German Student Organization in 1881. This ban also affected gymnastic clubs and cultural societies.[168]

Il Corriere Israelitico, with increasing dismay, communicated these various manifestations of anti-Semitism in Germany, including a rally in Berlin on 18 December 1880 attended by 3,000 people; the speeches were accompanied by cries of 'Down with the Jews' and 'Out with the Jews' (1880, p.198). There was an arson attack on a synagogue in Stettin: 'the anti-semitic league is assuming ever more serious proportions, such as to awaken the deepest apprehension' (1880, pp.249–51). A baptized Jewish academic was prevented from giving a lecture at the University of Berlin by the vitriolic verbal abuse of 600 students: 'not even baptism can save; the race remains' (*neppure il battesimo può salvare; la razza rimane*).[169] In the eyes of these anti-Semites, nothing, neither assimilation nor conversion, could remove the stigma of being a Jew. The editor published statistics on the German population: out of a total of 47.7 million, 65 per cent were Protestant, 34 per cent Roman Catholic and 1.1 per cent Jewish, and yet, he commented, this 'tiny fraction so frightens the other 99 per cent!'[170]

How did the German Jews respond in the first decade of full emancipation to this hostility which was directed not only against recent immigrants from eastern Europe but also against patriotic assimilated Jews? As in Italy, there were no national, institutional structures to defend their civic rights and ensure equitable implementation. There was a reluctance to form such an organization; it ran counter to the integrationist ideology of being German (*Deutschtum*) and there was a fear that it would provoke anti-Semitism. Individual Jewish communities had reorganized themselves into purely religious bodies, and many were split into Orthodox, Conservative and Reform subgroups. Thus it was up to individuals to speak out. In October 1879, several members of the Berlin community protested about anti-Semitic incidents to the minister of the interior, but to no avail. Moritz Lazarus, a leading figure of Berlin Jewry, gave a public lecture in December 1879 on the definition of nationality, in which he rejected the criterion of race and emphasized the loyalty and patriotism of the German Jews. In 1880, after another spate of anti-Semitic agitation in Berlin, Treitschke's public utterances and the dispiriting outcome of the parliamentary debate, Lazarus held several meetings with leading Jews, the result of which was the creation of the Jewish Committee of 1 December 1890. Its principal aim was to defend Jews and promote Judaism. Although it remained in existence for ten years, it rarely convened, thus achieving very little. Many Jews were of the opinion that any unified response would be perceived as Jewish separatism.[171] There was a sense of anxiety and, for some, a profound depression. The well-known writer Berthold Auerbach (1812–82), a former friend of Treitschke (to whom he never spoke again), personally experienced anti-Semitism, and after attending the parliamentary debate during which anti-Jewish calls were made, he wrote to his brother: 'I have lived and laboured in vain ... the horrible fact remains that such crudity ... such hatred are still possible ... The consciousness of what is still preserved in the German man and what can explode unexpectedly – that is indelible.'[172]

The geographical and political position of Trieste ensured that the editors of *Il Corriere Israelitico* were always alert to what was happening in Austria, particularly the capital. As anti-Semitism waned in Germany in the 1880s and Stöcker's six Berlin candidates lost their seats in the 1881 elections, it gathered momentum in Austria.[173] Stöcker's counterpart was Karl von Vogelsang (1818–90), who from 1875 promoted a neo-feudal, conservative discourse as editor of the influential Catholic newspaper *Das Vaterland* in opposition to what he perceived as the Judaization of Europe. He laid the foundations for Lueger's Christian Social Party.[174] In contrast to the religious approach of Vogelsang was the pan-Germanic racial anti-Semitism of Georg Ritter von Schönerer (1842–1921), which was anti-Habsburg, anti-Austrian and directly influenced by German nationalism. He was active between 1882 and his arrest in 1888, but never achieved mass support; his lack of patriotism – he once shocked parliament with his cry, 'if only we already belonged to the German Empire' – alienated the middle classes and turned them towards Lueger's Christian Social ideas, which were beginning to take shape at the end of that decade with the establishment by two anti-Semitic priests of the Christlich–sozialer Verein (Christian–Social Union).[175] As in Germany, the university student societies in Vienna began to expel Jews from 1878; one of them invited Schönerer to become an honorary member and another issued a statement that 'Jews cannot be regarded as Germans, and not even when they are baptised.'[176] Nevertheless, through the pages of *Die Neuzeit*, organ of liberal Viennese Jewry, and the speeches of its leaders, a sense of optimism prevailed, combined with the belief that anti-Semitism was essentially a German nationalist import; no prominent figures such as Treitschke had embraced Jew-hatred; no brutal and violent outbreaks had occurred such as those in Berlin in 1880. They felt that, in contrast to Bismarck's ambivalence towards Jews in Germany, they had 'in the person his Holy Majesty Franz Joseph a guarantee of our protection'.[177] Therefore anti-Semitism was not perceived as a serious threat.[178]

The one exception to this sanguine stance was Dr Joseph Samuel Bloch (1850–1923), an orthodox rabbi from Galicia whose views were initially not welcomed in the capital since he criticized its Jewish establishment for their silence regarding anti-Semitism; they opposed his nomination to the Chair of Jewish Antiquities at the University of Vienna in 1884. However, as a member of parliament from 1883 to 1895, he became 'the foremost public defender of Jewish constitutional rights in Austria'.[179] In 1883, he brought a successful lawsuit against *Das Vaterland* for publishing an article on ritual murder, and in the same year he launched a robust attack, of which thousands of copies were distributed throughout Austria, against the infamous anti-Semitic tract, *Der Talmudjude* (The Talmud Jew), written by August Rohling, Catholic professor of Hebrew at the University of Prague, who was then involved in the Tisza–Eszlar trial as an 'expert' witness. Bloch 'became a hero of the Jewish cause', receiving many telegrams from the provinces.[180] In contrast, the leaders of the Viennese Jewish community restricted themselves to denying Rohling's defamations for fear of further reprisals; they also refused to acknowledge Bloch's involvement. In 1884, he founded a weekly journal, *Österreichische Wochenschrift* (Austrian Weekly), whose twin objectives were the fight against anti-Semitism and assimilationist tendencies. In the first issue he proposed the creation of a Jewish defence organization; two years later, the Österreichisch–Israelitische Union (Austrian Jewish Union) was set up under Bloch's guidance to foster Judaism and counter anti-Semitism.[181] By the end of the decade, the Viennese Jewish elite had come to accept this *Ostjude* from Galicia and to admire his courageous and bold stand as the anti-Semitic threat intensified in the 1890s. In addition, the international response to the 1881 Russian pogrom and the massive emigration that ensued brought with it Russian Jewish nationalism, which would take root in Vienna and elsewhere.

Il Corriere Israelitico naturally monitored the presence of anti-Semitism in Trieste itself. The first incident was in 1862: Jewish mourners were subjected to all kinds of insults from groups of men, women and children. The authorities were informed by the Jewish community but, judging by an article of 1887, such episodes had not been effectively contained – they had intensified in number and aggression as stones as well as insults were hurled at the processions, and 'this was threatening to be serious persecution' (1887, pp.213–14). The instigators of this increasing intolerance in the intervening decades could count on the tacit support of anti-Semitic politicians.[182] In 1870 there were incidents during Yom Kippur when Jewish shops were vandalized because they were closed. In the following year, four Jewish women had successfully passed public examinations enabling them to teach in elementary schools; one of them was the founding editor's daughter, Eugenia Morpurgo. The local populace did not approve and she was prevented from taking up her post as head teacher by a group of them who physically attacked her, shouting 'We don't want Jews, death to the Jews.' The police had to intervene. Restrictive legislation in 1883 on the number of Jewish teachers in Austrian state schools was greeted with approval by the Triestine Catholic press.[183] Also in 1883, a Jew was refused membership of a prestigious gentleman's club; all his papers were in order apart from a certificate of baptism. The event was reported in the local press and forty members resigned in protest. Despite the show of solidarity in this particular case, *Il Corriere Israelitico* observed that such exclusions were widely practised (1883, pp.235–7). Although Triestine Jews were successful in the economic sphere, they encountered social intolerance and also found it difficult to enter the higher echelons of politics, and when they did, they experienced discrimination.[184]

The most serious events of these decades occurred in 1882: during the celebrations marking the 500th anniversary of Trieste's annexation to Austria, a bomb exploded in a busy street on 2 August, killing one person and injuring many others. Although the victim was a Jewish boy, there were violent reactions and blame was imputed to the Irredentists, among whom were many Jewish activists. Thus Jewish shops and the synagogue were attacked, accompanied by the habitual slogan, 'Death to the Jews'.[185] In its account, *Il Corriere Israelitico* adhered to its editorial policy of abstaining from political comment and focused exclusively on the anti-Semitic dimension and the dangers it posed for the Jewish community. When communicating these manifestations of hatred, the editors depicted anti-Semitism as a foreign import – as did their co-religionists in Vienna: 'a hostile current coming from northern Europe' ... threatening 'the widespread spirit of tolerance ... in this wise and hospitable city' (*CI*, 1882, pp.114–15). To counteract and refute the prejudice, accusations and hostility, the Triestine journal offered its readers a series of scholarly apologetics, such as the one on usury by Leone Racah (*CI*, 1885, pp.177–81).

JEWISH RESPONSE

The first period of full civic equality for western and central European Jews witnessed spectacular success but also failure. The long-drawn-out and bitterly contested debates on emancipation ensured that the Jewish question remained a controversial issue; combined with centuries of anti-Jewish Catholic education these debates were a powerful reservoir on which to draw whenever there were crises, such as the economic depression of 1873 (the stock market crash in Berlin and Vienna), and a scapegoat was needed. The premises of emancipation were predicated on patronizing notions of the Jews' backwardness, inferiority and lack of education. It was thought they would not attain the high standards of Christian civilization for at least several hundred years. At the end of the eighteenth century, the majority of European Jews were arguably at their lowest ebb, in ghettos and excluded from all activity apart from usury and peddling second-hand goods. Thus condescension turned to dismay, envy and, in some quarters, hatred, when they progressed so swiftly within a matter of decades, given their pariah status a century before. The rapidity of their economic, social, political and cultural achievement 'has few parallels in history'; it was 'unprecedented in its scale and quality',[186] but it could not occur without negative repercussions. Indeed, Tsarist Russia, looking to the West, blocked the progress of the Jews (approximately 80 per cent of European Jewry lived within Russia's borders); were emancipation to be accorded them, one English observer remarked, within ten years 'every place of importance in the empire would be filled by a Jew'.[187] The anti-Semitism of these years displayed various disparate strands, but in essence they were the same: the concept that the Jews were an inassimilable and harmful presence. And yet, assimilationist ideology remained dominant among the Jews of central and western Europe, the eagerness to participate unquenched even at the expense of relinquishing cultural and ethnic difference, 'to be united with all mankind'; patriotic devotion was constantly articulated and fundamental belief in the Enlightenment ideals of freedom and equality before the law was undiminished.[188]

From the 1890s, such equanimity was to be severely tested. In Germany, in the last decade of the nineteenth century, there was a resurgence of anti-Semitism as new political parties such as Otto Böckel's Antisemitische Volkspartei and the Antisemitische Deutschsoziale Partei jostled for power in the 1893 national elections, and the Conservative Party confirmed its own anti-Semitic agenda. Sixteen seats were won by anti-Semite candidates; another was added two years later in a by-election; there were twenty-five by 1907. The Xanten ritual murder trial of 1891/92 stirred up further antagonism. In this period of nascent nationalism, the still-fragile German national identity favoured a Romantic *völkisch* conception of the pure Ayran race, and thus various views advocating segregation, exclusion or expulsion of the Jews gained currency; there was even belief that a scientist had invented a 'Judometer' that could measure the percentage of Jewish blood in an individual.[189] There was a realization among assimilated Jews that the strategy of avoiding action was no longer tenable; anti-Semitism was now too powerful. Thus the self-defence Centralverein deutscher Staatsbürger jüdischen Glaubens was founded on 26 March 1893 in Berlin. It was the largest organization in Germany, representing the majority of Jews. The name itself is significant: Central Association of German Citizens of the Jewish Faith, privileging patriotic *Deutschtum*; its middle-class members perceived themselves as Germans of the Jewish faith, not German Jews. One of its principal aims was to combat anti-Semitism by campaigning against anti-Semitic political candidates; reporting cases of discrimination to the police, the government, and the courts; publishing pamphlets and a monthly periodical, *Im deutschen Reich* (In the German Reich), containing detailed apologetics to counter anti-Semitic propaganda.[190] The orthodox Jews, through their journal *Der Israelit*, endorsed the Centralverein's policy regarding anti-Semitism but, for the ultra-orthodox, anti-Semitism was perceived as God's scourge on assimilated Jews for attempting to enter the Christian world; the only defence, in their eyes, was a retreat to traditional observance of the Torah.[191]

Despite religious equality established since 1871, government administration and the armed forces at the higher levels were largely closed to Jews. There were few professors in the universities but many Jewish *Privatdozenten* – unpaid qualified lecturers: Vital cites the case of Paul Ehrlich who, although awarded the Nobel Prize, was not given a full professorship until six years later, and then not at one of the prestigious state universities. Converted Jews often found promotion problematic as they were considered to be too Jewish and their very conversion enforced the stereotype of Jewish opportunism.[192] Birnbaum illustrates this phenomenon with the example of the sociologist Georg Simmel (1858–1918), a Protestant born to Jewish converts, who was nevertheless still considered a Jew. He faced virulent anti-Semitism and obstructions throughout his career, becoming a professor in Strasbourg only after a debate in the regional parliament concluded that he could not be considered Jewish.[193] The Centralverein's attempts to fight such discrimination were considered too moderate for the younger generation who joined the Zionist cause.

Karl Lueger's victory over the Liberals in the municipal elections of September 1895 transformed Vienna into the only city with an anti-Semitic administration. Herzl noted in his diary that there was 'wild cheering. A man next to me said with loving fervour, but softly, "That is our Leader" [*Das ist unser Führer*]. More than all the declamation and abuse, these few words told me how deeply anti-Semitism is rooted in the heart of the people.'[194] The Jewish question thus became central to the political agenda of the empire until Lueger's death in 1910. He and his Christian Social Party had the unequivocal support of the Catholic Church.[195] Among his policies, he advocated denominational education, restrictions on Jewish immigrants, a boycott of Jewish business and a diminution of Jewish influence in the public sphere. He employed rabble-rousing demagogues and neo-feudalist aristocrats to appeal to all social strata. He supported the founding of an Aryan theatre; he barred Gustav Mahler, director of the Vienna Court Opera, from conducting charity concerts sponsored by the city council; during the Russian revolution of 1905, he made a speech threatening a pogrom for Austria's Jews should they support the Social Democrats.

There was an increase of anti-Semitic abuse at the university, where even philo-Semitic Christian academics were considered legitimate targets, and Jewish students, who in Freud's words were 'expected to feel ... inferior and ... alien',[196] faced physical violence. A generally hostile atmosphere prevailed; the daily *Neue Freie Presse* was full of anti-Semitic reports. *Il Corriere Israelitico* communicated the comments of a Triestine deputy recently returned from the capital: 'anti-semitism is becoming ever more dangerous for public safety and threats are increasing on a daily basis.'[197] In the foreword to his autobiography, *My Youth in Vienna*, Arthur Schnitzler (1862–1931) wrote: 'in these pages a lot will be said about Judaism and anti-Semitism ... It was not possible, especially not for a Jew in public life, to ignore the fact that he was a Jew; nobody else was doing so, not the Gentiles and even less the Jews ... it was impossible to remain completely untouched'.[198] There was even greater discrimination against Jews for jobs, contracts and advancement: Freud had to wait seventeen years to be promoted in the medical faculty of the University of Vienna in 1902; the norm was eight.[199] An aspiring Jewish academic, Hans Kelsen, was advised not to apply to the university; when it was known that he was a convert, he was told he would still not get a post because of the students' anti-Semitism.[200] The civil service, the diplomatic corps and the higher echelons of the army remained closed to the Jews; anti-Semitism in the liberal professions, the aristocratic and clerical milieus was endemic.[201] Trieste had a taste of the anti-Semitism emanating from Vienna when Lueger made an official visit in 1898, during which anti-Italian demonstrations took place accompanied by shouts of 'Death to the Jews'.[202] In the Austrian provinces the situation was worse: in 1898 there were pogroms in Galicia, fomented by Catholic preachers, and the following year there were riots against pro-German Jews in Bohemia, exacerbated by the ritual murder trial. These uprisings were also linked to the bitter nationalist conflicts of the ethnic minorities such as the Czechs, Hungarians, Poles and Slavs.[203]

The Austrian Jewish establishment became more apprehensive. *Die Neuzeit* began to criticize the reticence of Austrian government ministers, who were contrasted unfavourably with the Hungarian prime minister's firm stand. Bloch continued his staunch defence of Jewish rights, brilliantly exposing the anti-Semitic slanders – his parliamentary speech of 11 February 1890 resulted in literally thousands of expressions of gratitude, and his one time adversary Adolf Jellinek described him as 'the Hercules of the anti-semitic Augean stable'.[204] He was the only Jewish deputy out of the twelve who upheld Jewish interests, but he was eventually silenced and defeated in the elections of 1895 by a Galician Polish–Christian–Social cabal. He continued to campaign against anti-Semitism through the pages of his journal.[205] In addition, the Austrian–Jewish Union, in the aftermath of

Lueger's ascent to power, set up a Legal Defence Committee in 1895, which in 1897 became a Legal Aid and Defence Bureau with representatives in sixty-two Austrian towns. Its multifarious activities included curbing the anti-Semitic press; responding to blood libel accusations, with limited success; thwarting Lueger's attempts at educational segregation; pressing the government to intervene in areas of anti-Semitic violence such as Galicia; and giving free legal aid to victims of discrimination.[206] Liberal Jews in Vienna thus responded robustly to anti-Semitic rule.

In Trieste, anti-Semitism also intensified with the formation of several associations, two of which were closely linked to Lueger's party: the Lega cristiano-sociale of 1897 and the Lega delle donne cristiano-sociali of 1899 for women; there was also a youth section. In 1903, Riccardo Camber and Vittorio Cuttin, both journalists, set up three organizations for Italian and Slovene workers, whose underlying ideology was anti-Irredentist and anti-Semitic. Their publications, *Il Sole* (The Sun) and *Il Figaro*, were secretly financed by the central government until Camber's death in 1907. There were also pan-German student societies which excluded Jews, and Slovene Catholic anti-Semitic factions. The anti-Semitic press was also very active in this period: alongside Camber's papers were those of the Lueger alliance, *L'Amico* (The Friend, 1896) and *L'Avvenire* (The Future, 1897). They all produced the usual shibboleths such as Jewish domination in every sphere, and ritual murder, drawing inspiration from Drumont, Rohling and other noted anti-Semites. *L'Amico* advocated boycotting Jewish businesses and avoiding all social contact; in this way 'our city will soon be free of Jewish exploitation, and the air will again be free from those microbes, *Judenrein*, as Lueger would say'.[207] They intensified their propaganda during the local elections of 1903 in an attempt to undermine the Irredentist National Liberal Party whose leadership was Jewish; they were subjected to racial abuse during council meetings. How did the Jewish community respond? When the old cemetery was vandalized, they took no action, which caused consternation among some of those who had been affected: in 1890, Lazzaro Cuzzi wrote to the leaders urging them not to permit such manifestations of intolerance to pass in silence; such reticence could be perceived as cowardice. The virulent anti-Semitism of *Il Sole* did arouse the concern of the Jewish community: at a meeting of June 1903, measures were discussed, including legal action, but again prudence prevailed for fear of provoking further antagonism. However, several members were not satisfied with this attitude. The National Liberals did protest at Camber and Cuttin's activities, but to no avail. It was left to *Il Corriere Israelitico* to record this atmosphere of intolerance amid increasing national tensions.[208]

As anti-Semitism posed a greater threat, the Enlightenment principles of freedom, equality and religious toleration, embodied in the Liberal Parties of Austria and Germany which were the political cornerstone of assimilated Jews, were being undermined, eroded and destroyed by the encroaching anti-Semitic nationalist parties. By 1914, through electoral defeats and alliances with Conservatives and anti-Semites, there was nothing left of liberalism in Austria or Germany.[209] It has been argued that anti-Semitism can be viewed as a 'crisis of modernity', arising as a consequence of political and socio-economic change brought about by industrialization, urbanization and extended electoral franchise, leading to 'a widespread antagonism to liberalism, democracy and the "ideas of 1789", which ... became identified with Jews and Judaism'.[210] In Italy in the 1890s, the Liberal regime, which had dominated the political landscape since Unification, was destabilized by the new Socialist Party (1892), the Italian Republican Party (1895), radical and anarchist groups, various financial scandals and riots, regional unrest and, above all, by the disastrous battle of Adowa in Abyssinia (1896), causing the fall of Francesco Crispi's government: 'it was the first time that an African army had defeated a European colonial power'.[211] Italy's incursions into Africa were to have bestowed on the country greater glory; instead, her fragile national identity received a devastating blow. A sense of shame, economic instability, military humiliation and a thirst for revenge became instrumental influences in the formation of a xenophobic nationalism in the first decades of the twentieth century.[212]

In such a climate of insecurity, anti-Semitism increased. In May 1892, Ugo Pisa, president of the Chamber of Commerce in Milan, gave a lecture on trade liberalization. A few weeks later, Luigi Gherini, a local landowner who favoured protectionism, viciously attacked Pisa's views in print, imputing them to his Jewish origins, accusing Jews of seeking to appropriate and dominate the financial and administrative sectors 'of the whole world', and of forming a formidable and rapacious caste. Significantly, Gherini did not perceive himself as belonging to 'that tyrannical party of ferocious anti-semites', as he thought there were some notable exceptions among 'the Jewish tribe'.[213] Maifreda argues that Gherini's anti-Semitism was representative of his social class, which had been badly damaged by the economic crisis of the 1880s; that it embodied a persistent distrust of the Jews, their supranationality and immense wealth, in spite of their integration, and Pisa was an exemplary figure, a patriot who had fought in the 1866 campaign, and a successful businessman who, a few years later, in 1898, was nominated a senator.[214]

The perception of Jewish solidarity beyond national boundaries was widespread: criticizing the press attention given to the violent attacks on the Jews of Corfu in 1891, the editor of *Il Popolo Romano* (Roman People) complained that 'we are at the stage that if a fly lands on a Jew's nose, all the telegraph wires are in action until the fly moves off ... We should stop all this news aimed at arousing pity for the Jews when they're better off than we are, otherwise, as I've said before, it will have the opposite effect and revive anti-semitism.'[215] In an article entitled 'Italian anti-semitism and ... Jewish weakness', *Il Corriere Israelitico* recounted the incident of a Jewish couple in the province of Mantua who went to the town hall to be married, but the Jewish mayor, Todeschini, was absent. They asked the *assessore* to take his place but he refused, as a Catholic, to unite Jews in matrimony. Todeschini wrote a letter of resignation which he then withdrew, 'convinced that it was a misunderstanding rather than a deliberate insult'. The editor commented: 'if they are even more offensive, will he still say it is just a misunderstanding?' (*CI*, 1902, p.156). The moral message to readers was the need to be more assertive in defence of their rights.

In many local elections, pro-Catholic and socialist candidates were openly hostile towards their Jewish opponents. In 1892 in Pesaro, a bitter offensive was launched against Ernesto Nathan (1845–1921), later to become the popular mayor of Rome (1907–13); he was tainted as a Jew, a Freemason and a foreigner (he was born in England; his father was German), and he lost by a few votes.[216] Sidney Sonnino (1847–1922) was baptized at birth into the Anglican Church and professed no religion. Nevertheless, he was a target for anti-Semitism: 'in both Catholic and secular milieux ... Sonnino's Jewish origins were constantly mentioned as his political career progressed'.[217] During electoral meetings in Padua, Catholics and socialists stated that Jews should not have the vote and that local affairs should be run exclusively by Catholics (*CI*, 1899, p.64). In Mantua in 1903, one of the most sustained campaigns was led by a priest, Don Venanzio Bini, who taught at the diocesan seminary and was editor of the religious periodical, *Il Cittadino* (The Citizen), which since its inception in 1896 had regularly published anti-Semitic articles. Don Bini, with his slogan 'Mantua for the Mantuans', based his manifesto largely on a policy of eradicating Jewish influence from the local economy, drawing inspiration from Karl Lueger, the anti-Semitic mayor of Vienna.[218] In the 1904 local elections, *Il Corriere Israelitico* noted that 'a militant clerical revival' in Milan, Naples, Venice, Florence, Bergamo and Livorno, evident in newspaper articles, posters and cartoons, 'has contaminated Italian life with anti-semitic hatred; and it is racial hatred that is the principal cause for the defeat of our co-religionists' (1904, p.196). *L'Idea Sionista* commented on 'the anti-Semitic movement which in Italy is rapidly increasing through the activities of the clerical nation and its allies', and cited the case of a small town in the Po valley, Monticelli d'Ongina, where for twenty years the local council had been in the hands of the 'clerical-conservatives' and had undertaken no reforms; they had been defeated two years previously; since then, sweeping changes had been made, such as the secularization of the schools. There had been an openly anti-Semitic backlash from the ousted clerical party, accusing the present incumbents – amongst whom there were one or two Jews – of a Jewish–Masonic plot to undermine Catholicism (*IS*, 1907, pp.98–9). Discrimination became endemic in schools and universities: Enzo Levi (1889–1947) recalled the insults and animosity he experienced at primary school in Modena; whenever he told his parents, he could see in their faces that they too had suffered 'because they were Jewish'.[219] Jemolo (1891–1981) evoked the anti-Semitism in Turin where even the most liberal families found it difficult to accept Jews socially and where Jewish university students kept together.[220]

Leading Italian academics such as Cesare Lombroso, an international figure in forensic medicine and criminal anthropology, were invited to consider the current 'scientific' theories of the racial degeneracy of the Jews. In Lombroso's case, the request came from the *Neue Freie Presse* of Vienna and the *Revue des revues* of Paris. The result was *L'antisemitismo e le scienze moderne* (Anti-Semitism and Modern Science), published in Italy and in German translation in 1894, in which he expressed his abhorrence of anti-Semitism, 'an icy wind, a savage hatred blowing across Europe'. He refuted the concept of a 'pure' race and rejected the racist ideology of the anti-Semites; he advocated a greater assimilation of Jews and Christians which, he claimed, could lead to a new religion, 'socialist

Christianity', that would respect scientific and social progress and contribute to the dissipation of anti-Semitism. Christians would have to shed their superstitions and prejudices and Jews must free themselves from their atavistic religious rites, but 'this was a utopia of which I see not even the initial traces'. He believed that anti-Semitism was ineradicable because it appealed to man's basest instincts. In a chapter entitled 'Defects of the Jews', Lombroso attributed to them – he at no point reveals his Jewish identity – many of the anti-Semitic stereotypes which, he stated, have contributed to their persecution. It is the assimilated, educated Jew's repudiation of his ancestral traditions in favour of scientific progress and a common civilization.[221] Jewish response within Italy was limited to hostile reviews in *Il Vessillo Israelitico* and *Il Corriere Israelitico*, whose editor, Curiel, accused Lombroso of ignorance and bad faith, condemning his violent attack on ancient religious traditions.[222]

A few years later, in 1897, Lombroso's son-in-law Guglielmo Ferrero (1871–1942) published a best-seller entitled *L'Europa giovane: studi e viaggi nei paesi del Nord* (Young Europe: Essays and Travels in Northern Countries). Several sections were based on national/racial types in which he delineated 'the great struggle [in Europe] between the Ayran and Semitic races' (*la grande lotta tra la razza ariana e la razza semitica*). He intimated that there was something in Jewish writers such as Heine that provoked not only admiration but also repugnance; that Heine was not 'authentically German'; that the Jews were a profoundly pessimistic and melancholy people. In Ferrero's opinion, there were in the Jewish character certain innate negative qualities which marked it out as 'foreign' and 'different' and thus inadaptable, in contradistinction to the superior, positive 'Aryan virtues'.[223] Cavaglion suggests that 'in the history of the first impact of the Jewish question on Italian public opinion, Ferrero's chapter on races represents one of the most characteristic moments'.[224] Dante Lattes commented extensively on an article that appeared in the literary journal *Nuova Antologia* in 1899, which gave a negative assessment of Italian Jews regarding their exclusivity and the persistence of usury. It also warned of the example of Dreyfus which should alert them to the extent of the hatred they engendered even in a civilized and progressive country such as France; and that they should guard against the defects and vices for which they were criticized. All this was conveyed 'in the interests of the Jews themselves and in the desire that anti-semitism did not take root in Italy'. Lattes, in the opening remarks of his critique, expressed his dismay that such ideas, which would not have been out of place in Drumont's *La Libre Parole*, should appear not in an obscure provincial magazine but in such a prestigious and influential periodical.[225]

THE DREYFUS AFFAIR

The Dreyfus Affair (1894–1906) was the most devastating blow to liberal ideology; it marked a defining moment in the history of anti-Semitism of the late nineteenth century. Not only did it tear France apart, dividing families and destroying friendships and alliances, but its impact on European Jewry as a whole cannot be overestimated. France was the cradle of human rights, the Enlightenment and emancipationist ideals, and now it was the scene of intense and prolonged anti-

Semitic violence. In the first two months of 1898, at the time of Zola's trial, sixty-nine riots took place, involving thousands; people were injured, Jewish property was vandalized and 'the whole of France appeared to be ablaze'. In French Algeria there were pogroms.[226] Maurice Barrès's infamous phrase would endure: 'That Dreyfus is guilty, I deduce from his race' (*Que Dreyfus est coupable, je le conclus de sa race*).[227] When Commandant Hubert-Joseph Henry, one of the principal conspirators, committed suicide, *La Libre Parole* set up a fund for his widow; not only did money flow in, but also messages of such virulence that even those Jews inured to this kind of vitriol were stunned: 'for the expulsion of the Yids'; from a priest 'who offers up the most ardent prayers for the extermination of the two enemies of France – the Jew and the Freemason'; from 'a section of officers ... who await with impatience the order to try new cannons ... on the ... Jews who poison the country'; from 'a future medical student, already sharpening his scalpels to dissect the Maccabee Dreyfus'; – 'finding not enough Jews to massacre, I propose cutting them in two'.[228] Drumont dubbed the Third Republic as *La République juive*,[229] identifying the regime with the Jews who had penetrated to its very heart, such as Joseph Reinach, 'the quintessence of the emancipated and republican state Jew'.[230] As the Dreyfus Affair gathered momentum it became a global phenomenon, and Dreyfus, at the time of the second trial in Rennes in 1899 with the second verdict of guilt, was 'the most famous man in the world'.[231] The honour of France, 'her very soul',[232] was in jeopardy: in Zola's words 'our noble and generous France has fallen to the bottom of the abyss'.[233] This period of French history has been amply documented, including the response of the Jews; recent research has revealed that they were not as passive as hitherto perceived.[234]

Initial investigations in Italy have shown that the majority of the non-Jewish press and leading intellectuals were Dreyfusards;[235] even D'Annunzio, who was no friend of the Jews, believed by 1899 that Dreyfus was innocent.[236] The exception was the Catholic Church, which supported the anti-Dreyfus campaign in France with all its authority. The principal periodicals, *Civiltà Cattolica* and *L'Osservatore Romano*, used the Affair to reiterate the shibboleths of Jewish domination, Jewish international conspiracy and the error of emancipation. They saw the anti-Semitism in France as a natural and healthy reaction of the masses, excessively oppressed by the spirit and power of the Jews; they hoped that Dreyfus's treachery would convince public opinion that Jews should not be considered as citizens; his condemnation contaminated the whole of Judaism. Even after his acquittal, *Civiltà Cattolica* continued to believe him guilty.[237] Zola's gesture – his open letter, *J'Accuse*, to the president of the Republic – was considered heroic by the secular Italian press; *Il Corriere della Sera* commented on the exceptionality of the event – that a novelist should intervene so publicly in politics. When French writers, artists and scientists rallied around Zola, signing petitions and demanding a retrial, many leading Italian figures including Boito, Carducci, De Amicis, Fogazzaro, Puccini and Verga followed suit.[238]

The coverage of *Il Vessillo Israelitico* focused on the enormity of the injustice meted out to Dreyfus and emphasized his unswerving patriotism and loyalty.[239] *Il Corriere Israelitico*, on the other hand, while also articulating these themes, extrapolated certain ideological issues on assimilation from the Zionist prespective. Dante Lattes, in a lecture on anti-Semitism given in Trieste in December 1899, stated: 'There are Jews who are non-Jews like Dreyfus, a modern assimilated Jew. He became a captain in the French army, but what did he gain? ... All these attempts at adaptation are of no use ... anti-semitism has won; it has defeated a man who got as close as possible to the French spirit ... How can we be optimistic when we see such wickedness?' (*CI*, 1900, pp.25–6). In the review of Dreyfus's memoir, *Five Years of My Life*, a criticism is made:

> [that] in his exalted patriotism ... Dreyfus has completely forgotten he is Jewish. In the whole book there is no reference at all to his people or his faith ... Is it a sign of weakness or the consequences of assimilation? ... When he writes of France, his whole soul vibrates and yet he has no word for his brothers who never abandoned him, even when the whole of France loathed him.[240]

ITALIAN NATIONALISM

In Italy, between 1903 and 1914, Giovanni Giolitti was the Liberal prime minister for most of the period. Despite his attempts to absorb the principal subversive groups, a new form of nationalism predicated on an ideology of ethnic chauvinism, imperialism and militarism began to emerge: 'it was the Nationalists who posed the biggest threat of all to "Giolittianism" ... by 1914 it [Italian nationalism] was a major force ... powerful enough to transform the whole political system'.[241] It began as a cultural revival: the first nationalist review *Il Regno* (The Kingdom, 1903–05), edited by Giovanni Papini and Enrico Corradini, the latter one of the founders of Italian nationalism, was followed by others such as *Il Leonardo* (1903–06), the editors of which were Papini and Giuseppe Prezzolini, and the avant-garde literary journal *La Voce* (The Voice, 1908–1916), also edited by Papini and Prezzolini. Between 1909 and 1910, nationalist publications appeared throughout Italy. *Il Tricolore* (Turin); *La Grande Italia* (Milan); *La Nave* (The Ship, Naples); *Mare Nostro* (Our Sea, Venice), and in 1911 the principal nationalist journal, *L'Idea Nazionale*, which became a daily in 1914. In addition there was the polemical and iconoclastic figure of Filippo Marinetti (1876–1944), whose 'Futurist Manifesto' was launched in Paris in 1909. The editors and contributors of all these literary and artistic initiatives caught what they perceived to be the public mood: a desire to be rid of Italy's sense of shame, lagging behind the other European nations, and to restore the past glories of Italy's greatness; 'they gave Italians a new image of themselves: active, passionate and warlike'.[242] In addition, mainstream national dailies, critical of Giolitti's policies, gave space, for example, to the nationalist views of the poet D'Annunzio and the future nationalist leader Luigi Federzoni; both were to have prominent positions in Mussolini's regime.

In December 1910, 300 nationalist sympathizers gathered in Florence and formed the Associazione Nazionalista Italiana (ANI); Scipio Sighele (1868–1913), the noted sociologist and Irredentist, was nominated president. Further conferences took place in Rome (1912) and Milan (1914), leading to the official establishment of the Nationalist Party, forerunner of Italian fascism. As with similar political movements elsewhere in Europe, Catholic support was fundamental to its success: the five nationalist deputies, who entered parliament in 1913, did so with Catholic votes; the election of Federzoni had the support of the Vatican.[243]

JEWISH RESPONSE IN ITALY

How did Italian Jews react to encroaching nationalism, which bore all the hallmarks of its counterpart in neighbouring countries in which anti-Semitism played a major role? Bearing in mind that they still did not have a central organization to publicize and coordinate their views, different responses emanated from various quarters. The Italian Zionist Federation, which had been in existence since 1901, held its fourth conference in March 1904. One of the speakers, Roberto Ascoli, a lawyer, conveyed a growing sense of unease in his assessment entitled 'Anti-Semitism in Italy'. He began by stating that there were still those who believed that Italy was free from anti-Semitism, yet recent episodes in the press and in local elections in Ancona, Ferrara, Florence and Mantua should have disabused them. In other cities, there were restrictions on the number of Jews in public office:

> as if we were a poison to be taken in small doses ... Daily life is but a sad confirmation of a painful truth: anti-Semitism exists, and it is deep-rooted and invincible; not persecutions or massacres, but persistent, erosive and active. We all vividly remember the aversion experienced at school ... Contempt and suspicion pervade our milieus: in cafes, trains and hotels we are never sure that an insult or disparaging remark will not be thrown at us.

When discussing the matter with non Jews, including friends, 'the reply was always the same: the anti-Semitic campaign was unjust; there were many decent, honest Jews, but ... taken all together, they arouse something that is not pleasant'. Ascoli then enumerated the causes of anti-Semitism, and like Lombroso, laid much of the blame on Jews themselves. He too believed that anti-Semitism was insoluble, but he thought that if Jews could improve their behaviour – be less arrogant, speak in more modulated tones, avoid a conspicuous and public display of wealth, be less avaricious, less ambitious (he even alluded to lack of personal hygiene and the *foetor judaicus*) – then 'the hatred, contempt and malice' could be attenuated. He added that the 'Jewish proletariat' must be helped to progress in their material and spiritual condition. He concluded by declaring that he was proud to be Jewish and that he deplored those Jews who concealed their origins and tolerated insults; Jews had a right to live among nations, but 'we have a duty to be better than others, because that is the role of all minorities'.[244] Ascoli had internalized anti-Semitic stereotypes and the emancipationist notion of *Bildung* ('self-formation'). Both he and Lombroso represented the educated, middle-class, assimilated Jew's strong identification with *italianità* at the expense of Jewish particularisms, although Lombroso went further, advocating the complete disappearance of Judaism. Ascoli, on the other hand, embodied the position of the majority of Italian Jews – a dual identity as Italian and Jewish. There was little discussion of Ascoli's lecture – he was given an ovation – apart from the president's brief comment that the Zionist Federation would, within its means, assist those who were subjected to discrimination, but there was no talk of setting up a defence or legal committee to deal with such cases. In December 1904, Gino Arias, a university professor and chairman of the Florence Zionist association, wrote in *Il Corriere Israelitico* that 'not even our free Italy' was without anti-Semitism, and he called for 'moral equality' to be incorporated with civil and political equality (*CI*, 1904, pp.215–16).

In Rome a few years later, two incidents occurred which, Caviglia claims, have left no trace in either local history or memoir, but they were mentioned in the Jewish press. In 1907, Beniamino Astrologo was manhandled in his shop by his employees because he insisted on closing on Saturday rather than Sunday (*VI*, 1907, p.536), and in July 1911, a Jewish boy, Alberto Fornari, was killed in the neighbourhood of the ghetto by 15-year-old Tullio Peroni, who stabbed his victim in the eye with an eleven-centimetre nail. Jewish boys were often attacked, but in this instance it led to a tragic death. Peroni was sentenced to five years' imprisonment. At the trial, his defence lawyer denied any anti-Semitic aspect – 'these boys have no understanding of race'.[245] According to Caviglia, there was widespread hatred of Jews among Rome's lower classes, ready to spill out into open hostility at any time.[246] A greater sense of violence seemed to be in the air; in a letter of 9 July 1906 from Udine (north-east Italy), Felice Momigliano wrote: 'It's a miracle that what happened to my co-religionists in Russia hasn't happened to me. There are five dailies here and all of them with admirable accord want me dead.' They hurled invective at him as a Jew, a socialist, a Freemason, a radical, an atheist.[247]

L'Idea Sionista dedicated considerable space to an anti-Semitic episode in Ferrara in 1907 which, in the way the local Jewish community reacted, contrasted sharply with the Ancona community's strong stance of 1900, and once again illustrated both the lack of compact support and of an organized response at national level. Jews were unjustly blamed for the authorship of two anti-clerical articles published in the local radical press; an anonymous anti-Semitic diatribe then appeared in a religious periodical. The leaders of the Jewish community appealed to the courts, but then acceded to the request of 'those Jews who are content with the appearance of liberty and tolerate the most terrible insults' and did not press charges. The editor of the Zionist journal criticized the leadership of the community for their lack of dignity, 'so necessary in these times of anti-semitic persecutions', and their passivity in the face of such attacks, and suggested they resign. In the same issue, a letter from Ferrara communicated the news that a petition had been drawn up to protest against the conduct of the Jewish council (*IS*, 1907, pp.96–7). Leone Ravenna, the long-serving president of the community – and, incidentally, father of the president of the Italian Zionist Federation – replied to the criticisms in an open letter. He explained the reasons for not pursuing the matter, after consultations with several eminent lawyers; it had been a difficult decision but 'we have been forced to bow our heads and abandon the idea of recourse to the law'; the petition had collected only twelve signatures. The editor of *L'Idea Sionista* had no right to doubt their integrity, to insinuate that they were ready to tolerate any abuse, or to give them lessons in human dignity. If others could do better, let them cast their votes and 'we will cede our posts with our heads held high' (*IS*, 1907, pp.117–18). In a lengthy riposte, the editor raised important issues regarding the conduct of the Jewish community: their action – or rather lack of it – was damaging and misguided and 'tainted with one of the greatest defects of Italian Judaism: a deficiency of collective dignity, of collective action'; as individuals, they would have behaved differently but as a group they succumbed to 'the usual reticence'. Their silence conveyed the message that Jews as a community ought always to submit to such derision and hatred, even though that was not the intention. Their failure to act left the community in a sorry state, unable to defend itself (*IS*, 1907, pp.113–15).

La Settimana Israelitica [*SI*] published a similar case 'because of its significance for the whole of Italian Jewry': the plans for a new synagogue were withdrawn by the Jewish community of Modena owing to insinuations and rumours about the contracts being 'those of usurers'. The editors took the same line as *L'Idea Sionista*: the Jews of Modena should have defended themselves; there was no sign of resistance, of solidarity, of the courage to fight for the protection of their rights and interests (*SI*, 4 [1912]). The diffidence of the communities' leadership, who feared disturbance and wished at all costs for tranquillity, contrasted sharply with the consternation of the Zionist press, whose editors – with a renewed sense of pride in their Jewish identity – conveyed their dismay at what they perceived as abject humiliation in the face of aggressive anti-Semitism. Had the Jews of Ferrara and Modena been more assertive, they would have found satisfaction in the law of the nation they so venerated. *La Settimana Israelitica* reported on a case before the magistrates in Lucca which 'could be replicated up and down the country': a Jew with all the right qualifications obtained a post in a primary school, but a local priest opposed his appointment, claiming that the teacher was an infidel and a heretic, and campaigned against him so successfully that parents removed their children from the institution (*SI*, 7 [1908]).

Initial response to the new Italian Nationalist Association was not entirely hostile: the youthful editors of *La Settimana Israelitica*, in their editorial of 2 December 1910, 'Nationalism and Us', at first presented a positive judgment on the basis of an article published in *Grande Italia* in which the military prowess of Jewish soldiers had been praised. This demonstrated, in their view, that Italian nationalism differed from that of France and Germany, since 'it cannot be based on racial or religious hatred ... If a party based on national pride was "anti-Jewish" it would be anti-Italian ... The Italian nationalists know that we are with them [*siamo con loro*] ... They know we are ready to fight for Italy ... We wish the new party which is meeting today in Florence good luck.' Such sanguinity was reiterated in April 1912: many Jews had signed up, motivated by their deep love for Italy. And yet, in the same issue, a letter was published warning young Jewish nationalists to be wary, to look to French nationalism and the Dreyfus Affair. Should Italian nationalism, whose ideology, according to its own leaders, was still 'chaotic', follow the anti-Semitic line, then *La Settimana Israelitica*'s advice was that Italian Jews should be against it (15 [1912]). A refutation of 'any anti-semitic manifestation' was published in the following issue in the form of another letter, from Alberto Musatti, the Jewish president of the Venetian nationalist group and a member of the central committee. *La Settimana Israelitica*'s position reflected the editors' *italianità*, but also their apprehension about nationalist ideology, influenced perhaps by what has become known as the 'Coppola affair'. It could also be argued that their response was a product of 'parallel nationalism', in that these young Jews, who were seeking to renew their own Jewish identity, saw in Italian nationalism a similar process.

In September 1911, Italy once again pursued her colonial aspirations by declaring war on Turkey and invading Libya. In November of that year, Francesco Coppola, one of the founder editors of the nationalist periodical *L'Idea Nazionale*, wrote two inflammatory articles, both with provocative titles. The first 'Israel against Italy', was an open letter to Charles Maurras (1868–1952), founder of the right-wing, anti-republican, anti-Semitic daily *Action Française* (1908–44), in which he accused the 'Jewish' press in Austria, England and Germany of promoting a 'formidable, disciplined and organized' anti-Italian pro-Turkish campaign, conducted 'by Jewish international financiers' in an attempt to crush the national spirit 'which is being revived so vigorously in Italy ... Superior civilizations rediscovering their traditional heroic values ... and mission ... are replacing wherever possible irremediably sterile races ... fatally condemned to die out' (*CI*, 1911, pp.128–9). And he invited Maurras to collaborate against the Jewish coalition. In making this gesture in such an unequivocally belligerent style, it seemed that Coppola fully endorsed French nationalist anti-Semitism. Uproar ensued: Musatti and another prominent Jewish nationalist, Raffaele Levi, resigned the day after the article appeared. In his resignation letter sent to the nationalist periodical and also published in *Il Corriere Israelitico*, which followed the 'affair' step by step, Musatti stated: 'I could not tolerate that beneath the Italian flag, anti-semitic propaganda is being made' (*CI*, 15 December 1911). At a meeting of the ANI's executive junta a few days later, Levi's resignation was rejected on the grounds that *L'Idea Nazionale* was not the official organ of the association, and therefore it could not assume responsibility for the personal opinions of the editors.[240] In the same issue, *Il Corriere* also reprinted several letters sent to *Il Giornale d'Italia* in which conflicting views were expressed: in the opinion of Heinrich Eisemann, a German Jew, the attacks in the Italian newspapers were directed against Judaism as a religion. In a reply to Eisemann, Gubello Memmoli, who was London correspondent for *Il Giornale d'Italia*, rejected the idea of a 'religious war' and categorically stated that 'there existed in the world semitism understood as a political force which is both master and slave to money', manipulated in the major European cities by 'a secret powerful consortium of Jewish bankers and businessmen'; Semitism and anti-Semitism represented two antithetical political ideologies, internationalism and nationalism.

Dante Lattes, one of *Il Corriere Israelitico*'s editors, robustly responded to 'a very violent letter' by Luigi Federzoni written under his nom de plume, Giulio De Frenzi, originally published in *Il Corriere di Tripoli* on 21 November 1911, from where Federzoni was reporting for *Il Giornale d'Italia*. In it, he expressed the view that the European anti-Italian press campaign was backed by 'Jewish thieves and usurers'. The Triestine journal also printed a more mild response to Federzoni sent to *Il Giornale d'Italia* from 'many Roman, but above all Italian Jews' (*molti ebrei italiani ma anzitutto italiani*), who wished to express their regret that the papers were continually full of phrases about Jewish usurers and Jewish bankers; instead, it would be gratifying to read about the bravery of the many Italian Jewish soldiers fighting for 'our beloved Italy' (*CI*, 15 December 1911). *Il Corriere Israelitico* also wrote a letter of protest to *L'Idea Nazionale* in which Coppola was accused of encouraging Italian nationalism to follow the French example, of attempting to set 'Italy against Israel' at such an historic time (*CI*, 1911, pp.129–30). The anti-Semitic polemic was taken up by other papers, including major dailies such as *La Stampa*, *Il Corriere della Sera*, and *Il Popolo Romano*, which made insinuations about the Jewish origins of the president of the Italian Press Federation, his position considered to be symptomatic of Jewish control of the European press.

As a result of these intense reactions, Coppola wrote a second piece, 'My "anti-semitism"', in which he declared that he had no wish to disseminate it in Italy; his intention was to denounce 'anti-Italian foreign Jewish cosmopolitan strategies against which every autochthonous nationalism had a right to defend itself if threatened'. He then distinguished between Italian Jews and those of Europe, stating that hitherto the former had not committed antinational gestures; 'for now there was no urgency to encourage anti-semitism in Italy', whereas in France, Germany and Russia it was 'a national necessity'. In Italy, Jews had also attained powerful positions in politics and finance, and although numerous they acted as individuals, but if they began to manifest 'a strong and deep racial solidarity' (*una ardente e profonda solidarietà di razza*) 'as in the manner of the protests about my recent article ... and demonstrate a collective conscience ... that is different from national interests', then it was 'our firm conviction to be vigilant in the future'.[249] Despite his protestations to the contrary, Coppola appeared once again to endorse an anti-Semitic nationalist policy in line with French nationalism; the potential enemy were the Jews within Italy. The editors of *Il Corriere Israelitico* responded with an open letter to Coppola of 5 December – their previous one to *L'Idea Nazionale* had not been published – in which they stated that Coppola had no reason to place his anti-Semitism within quotation marks as it was a very common form, a perfect example; a Russian correspondent had informed them that 'a rabid anti-semite' (*un feroce antisemita*) from his own country would have had no difficulty in subscribing to Coppola's views. They attacked him for calling anti-Semitism a 'necessity' and they made it plain there were proud, idealistic Jews ready to defend 'such offences against Israel' (*CI*, 1911, pp.149–50). Coppola responded a day later, refuting their accusations and reiterating his affirmation that in Italy there should be 'only one civilization and one form of solidarity and that was Italian'; Jews were free to cultivate their own, but if they did they should not be surprised that 'real Italians, of Italian blood and spirit' (*italiani veri, quelli di sangue e di animo*) were on guard 'for the health of *their* nation' (*CI*, 1911, pp.150–1). Again Coppola perceived the Jews within Italy as the adversary.

How did the other Italian Jewish periodicals react? Whereas *Il Corriere*

Israelitico conducted a relentless campaign against Coppola's overt anti-Semitism, also as an example to young Jews 'never to be supine in the face of offences against Israel' (*CI*, 15 December 1911), *Il Vessillo Israelitico* preferred to abstain from intervention, as the title of Guglielmo Lattes's article illustrated: 'We will not protest' (*Non protestiamo*). The anti-Semitic threats did not cause alarm, 'because Italy's sun has the virtue to destroy such evil seeds'; the Jews of Italy were fervent patriots: 'this they declaim loudly and courageously and name the heroes who shed their blood for Italy from the wars of the Risorgimento to redeemed Libya' (1911, pp.661–2). Confronted with such a crisis at a time of war, *Il Vessillo Israelitico* followed its standard strategy of stressing *italianità* and enduring patriotism, reflecting the views of the communities' leaders. The editors of *La Settimana Israelitica*, on the other hand, expressed their disquiet that the war with Turkey could have anti-Semitic repercussions when Jewish soldiers were dying, and to counter *Il Vessillo*'s response, they stated unequivocally: 'we do protest with all our force against those who insult Italy' and 'we protest again … Israel cannot be defined by Jewish gold'; they provided a synopsis of Coppola's first article for their readers (*SI*, 48 [1911]). The Italian Zionist Federation had closed down its journal, *L'Idea Sionista*, when the war began to avert accusations of divided loyalties – the Ottoman Empire was involved in Zionist negotiations over Palestine. The Coppola 'affair' concluded with his resignation from the ANI – although not from *L'Idea Nazionale* – and the reinstatement of Levi and Musatti's membership.

The controversy was reignited in April 1912 when Scipio Sighele, president of the ANI, presented his own resignation in a series of articles published in *La Tribuna* of Rome. He criticized the anti-democratic, reactionary aspects of the Italian nationalist movement, in particular its association with *Action Française*, and the anti-Semitism within its ranks; he deplored the direction that *L'Idea Nazionale* was taking; he pointed out the inconsistencies of Coppola's arguments. *Il Corriere Israelitico* once again closely followed the controversy, publishing lengthy analyses. In the first of such pieces, 'Jews and Nationalism' by Ugo Ayò, a regular Rome contributor, Sighele was praised for acknowledging the anti-Semitic trends within Italian nationalism as he had confirmed *Il Corriere*'s own stance since the inception of the movement when 'we took up our pen and warned the Jews of Italy … of its exclusionist ideas'. Ayò incorporated responses from other nationalists who refuted Sighele's claims – including Coppola who yet again denied the accusations levelled against him – and reports of the meeting of the ANI's executive junta which, in the light of Sighele's 'recent polemic', reiterated their previous position regarding views published in *L'Idea Nazionale*. Ayò concluded with the question: 'what are the Jews [of Italy] doing? Why are they leaving to others the defence of their Judaism and the task of combating that vile sentiment that is anti-semitism? And why has Musatti not reacted as he so courageously did last November?' (*CI*, 1912, pp.225–9).

In May 1912, in another article on Jews and nationalism, Ayò addressed critical remarks to Coppola and condemnatory words to Musatti for his continued commitment to the ANI, and he renewed his question, 'what are the Jews doing?' (*CI*, 15 May 1912). In June of the same year, under the identical heading, the editors deplored the continuing anti-Semitic campaign and also the nationalists' scaremongering propaganda of Jewish anti-patriotism which had subdued Italian Jews to yet more public protestations of loyalty to Italy. They added that not all spark of rebellion was extinguished, and they published a letter sent to them from a co-religionist from Bologna objecting to an anti-Semitic article in *Il Corriere di Livorno* (*CI*, 15 June 1912). Sighele failed to persuade his fellow nationalists and no one else resigned. Several leading members, including Coppola and Corradini, were confident that Sighele's departure had strengthened the ANI, and the anti-Semitic campaign continued.[250] *Il Corriere Israelitico*, in an article titled 'Our Brothers, Patriots of Italy', reported on Paolo Orano's essay in *L'Idea Nazionale* of 7 August 1913, in which he asserted that every Italian Jew was against the expansion in Libya and that their patriotism was always an effort, a dissimulated conviction: 'Jews are patriots of necessity, socialists out of expediency, subversives by tradition, instinctive enemies of western civilization.'[251] Orano was a regular contributor to *L'Idea Nazionale*, and in his own journal, *La Lupa* (The Wolf), he promoted the blood libel calumny.[252]

The large Jewish communities of Libya were not immune from antagonism: several articles in the Italian press, nationalist and otherwise, suspected them of preferring their Turkish masters; Italian soldiers in Libya had difficulty in distinguishing between Jews and Arabs, the latter being hostile to the Italian occupation. Thus Angelo Sereni, president of the Rome community and of the recently established Committee of Italian Jewish Communities, sent a telegram to the Jews of Tripoli in October 1911 expressing fraternal solidarity and advising them to discount any malign rumours of religious persecution on the part of the Italian government, which, on the contrary, would offer them equality. He thus urged them to unite 'with us in our fervent desire for the triumph of its civilizing mission'. Sereni received an immediate reply from the rabbi of Tripoli assuring him of total support for 'the new era of freedom and equality'. The rabbi of Benghazi also wrote to Sereni in the same vein in order to quash reports to the contrary in the Italian press.[253] During the 1914 conference of Jewish communities held in Milan, Angelo Sullam raised the question of 'Italian anti-semitism' with regard to the Jews in Libya, which was taken up by *Il Corriere Israelitico*[254] but glossed over by *Il Vessillo Israelitico* in its patriotic and prudent reportage: anti-Semites did exist even 'among us', but the government's position clearly demonstrated the enviable state of Italian Jews and nothing must jeopardize this (*VI*, 1914, p.295).

In the Italian national elections of 1913, which saw the introduction of universal male suffrage, increasing the electorate from three million to nine million, and the participation of Catholics, the ANI won its first seats. Thus a virulent and soon to be violent anti-Semitic ideology, bolstered by dissemination in the national press and public opinion, entered the mainstream of Italian politics. To counter it, the Jews of Italy had neither an association nor members of parliament to speak for them: *Il Corriere Israelitico* criticized the newly elected Jewish deputies, socialists, liberals and radicals for not promoting Jewish interests, but they reserved their 'profound disgust' for those Jews who had campaigned for the nationalists (*CI*, 1913, pp.121–4). The revival of traditional Catholic values emerged in the national elections of October 1913, combined with an aggressive anti-Semitism; these strategies were also effectively deployed at local levels. The principal targets for such propaganda were the small towns and villages of the countryside, where the Catholic Church wielded its greatest influence and where religious precepts were more potent than political argument.[255]

Canepa focuses on two electoral colleges to illustrate this: in Borgotaro (Parma), the radical Cavaglieri was accused, as a Jew, of innate hostility to Catholicism and the voters were called upon to defend their rural Christian community. *La Gazzetta di Parma* articulated the objections succinctly: 'the choice of a Jew [*israelita*] is not, in our opinion, an appropriate one; for the peasant, the Jew [*l'ebreo*] still represents the devil, which is even more terrifying when in the clothing of a freemason, as is professor Cavaglieri'.[256] He lost the election. In Borgo S. Dalmazzo (Cuneo) economic considerations prevailed over bigoted hyperbole. There were two main camps: agricultural, conservative and Catholic, represented by Count Alessandro Rovasenda di Rovasenda (1858–1943), against urbanization, modernization and industrialization, in the shape of the lawyer Marco Cassin (1859–1927), director of his family's bank, deputy mayor of Cuneo and president of the local Chamber of Commerce. Rovasenda had been the member of parliament since 1895 and had crushingly defeated Cassin in 1909. Thus Cassin's candidacy was not taken seriously, but gradually, through his efficient and effective canvassing, he became a serious threat. A major Catholic daily of Turin, *Il momento*, accused him of bribery and opportunism and claimed that there was a curse on his family, thus exploiting the superstitions of the largely peasant population, but the main thrust of the attack was that he was a Jew and therefore an outsider. In an open letter to Cassin, the editor of *Il momento* explained that among co-religionists and compatriots 'we are one family; those of another religion and country appear as intruders'; Jews always kept themselves apart, thus arousing the hostility which led to anti-Semitism; in Italy 'thank God [it] is not excessive ... but by what right can anyone deny Italians the freedom to entrust their representation to people of their own race and not to a foreign race?'[257] The leader of the clerical party, *Marchese* Filippo Crispolti, expressed similar sentiments in the same publication, which were robustly rebutted by Cassin in *Il Corriere Subalpino* (*VI*, 1913, p.587). The Catholic paper of Cuneo exhorted its readers not to vote for the Jewish candidate. Rovasenda himself was brutally blunt in his declaration: 'It would be too great an infamy and shame for Borgo San Dalmazzo, so noble in its traditions and Christian faith, to be represented by a Jew' (*VI*, 1913, p.587). In spite of a relentless campaign against him, Cassin won decisively. Contemporary accounts recorded his formidable organizational skills and the attractive proposals put forward for the peasants. *La Settimana Israelitica* reported another instance of anti-Semitism in the 1913 elections in the province of Reggio, where the *topos* of a powerful Jewish–Masonic conspiracy was utilized to whip up racial hatred against a Jewish candidate (*SI*, 8 [1913]). *Il Vessillo Israelitico* published a letter from Turin on the electoral contest in the fourth *collegio*, where a nationalist candidate, professing anti-Semitic sentiments through the pages of the local nationalist journal, was supported by a group of Jews. The Jewish correspondent wished to question these young men about 'their affiliation to a party which has an anti-Semitic programme and what they expect if it is victorious' (*VI*, 1915, p.17).

In Italy the convergence of the mass entry of Catholics into politics at national level with xenophobic nationalism would lead to the collapse of the Liberal State, the emergence of fascism and a new accord with the papacy, the Lateran Pacts of 1929. Thus Italy became part of the process in which 'Jew-hatred re-emerged as a powerful political presence at the same moment as manhood suffrage ... was introduced across western and central Europe.'[258] Nevertheless, there persisted the conviction among assimilated Jews that anti-Semitism was a reactionary phenomenon that would eventually disappear. With the rehabilitation of Alfred Dreyfus in France (1906), the landslide victory of the Liberal Party in Britain (1906), where political anti-Semitism was 'still-born',[259] the death of Karl Lueger in Austria (1910) and the lack of leadership among the anti-Semites of Germany (1910/11), they could be forgiven for thinking that it was 'moribund', rather than 'merely dormant'.[260] The leaders of the Jewish communities and the rabbis taught their members to have faith in the universalist ideals of the Enlightenment and in the dual conception as citizens and as Jews.[261] They never ceased in their commitment to the liberal values and emancipationist reforms that had transformed their lives, leading to participation and integration at the highest levels. It would therefore be an epistemological error to review this period of Jewish history from the perspective of the Shoah, as a 'rehearsal for destruction'.[262] The exemplars of liberal assimilated Jewry in Italy, such as Isacco Artom, Luigi Luzzatti, Ernesto Nathan and Alessandro D'Ancona, cannot be judged as guilty for not predicting the Racial Laws of 1938.[263] Dreyfus was not wrong to believe in his darkest hours on Devil's Island that 'Truth will finally triumph';[264] he was not to know that the nation for which he had unconditional loyalty was to betray the French Jews at Vichy. The profound belief in the symbiosis of *Deutschtum* and *Judentum* held by the majority of German Jews cannot be dismissed as 'a pathetic tale' or described as 'tragically naïve and even self-destructive'.[265] Jews sent their sons and daughters to Imperial Germany to live and study, as they considered it a country of prospects and freedom, despite the anti-Semitism; 'they were not simply blind or ignorant'.[266] As Volkov reminds us, it was from eastern Europe, from the pogroms of Russia, that new voices and new perspectives emerged: the perception of anti-Semitism as an incurable and irrational disease transmitted for 2,000 years, and the origins of Zionism.[267] Zionism also could not foresee 'the potential genocidal logic still only latent in the anti-Semitism of the nineteenth century'.[268]

NOTES

1. See Robert S. Wistrich, *Antisemitism: The Longest Hatred* (London: Methuen, 1991).
2. John Gross, *A Double Thread: A Childhood in Mile End – and Beyond* (London: Chatto & Windus, 2001), p.77.
3. Albert S. Lindeman, *Anti-Semitism before the Holocaust* (Harlow: Longman, 2000), pp.86, 91. See also Michael Stanislawski, *Zionism and the Fin de Siècle: Cosmopolitanism and Nationalism from Nordau to Jabotinsky* (Berkeley, LA, and London: University of California Press, 2001): 'the new nationalist movements ... tended to be antisemitic ... (at least outside of Italy)' (p.13).
4. See Cecil Roth, *The History of the Jews of Italy* (Philadelphia, PA: Jewish Publication Society of America, 1946), p.475, and Attilio Milano, *Storia degli ebrei in Italia* (Turin: Einaudi, 1963), p.693.
5. See, for example, Paolo Bernardini, 'The Jews in Nineteenth-Century Italy: Towards a Reappraisal',

Journal of Modern Italian Studies, 1, 2 (Spring 1996), p.295; and Alberto Cavaglion, 'L'Italia della razza s'è desta', *Belfagor*, 57 (January 2002), p.41.
6. Renzo De Felice, *Storia degli ebrei sotto il fascismo*, third edn (Turin: Einaudi, 1972 [1961]), pp.14–15. The words 'Jewish question' are italicized in the Italian text.
7. Ibid., pp.15, 20–1, 27–45.
8. Ibid., Preface, p.xii.
9. Ibid., p.iii. Between June 1944 (liberation of Rome) and 1949, several accounts of Italian Jewish experiences were published, and then silence until 1961, the publication year of De Felice's book. See Mario Toscano, *Ebraismo e antisemitismo in Italia: dal 1848 alla guerra dei sei giorni* (Milan: FrancoAngeli, 2003), pp.209, 214; and Alberto Cavaglion: 'in the years 1945 to 1949, there was a real interest [in the Jews], by far preferable to the reluctance and hypocritical censure of the 1960s, 1970s, and the early years of the 1980s' (cited in Toscano, *Ebraismo e antisemitismo*, p.211). See also Cavaglion's critical comments about much of the research published on the Racial Laws since 1988 in 'L'Italia della razza s'è desta': 'distortions ... interpretive rigidity due to ideological prejudices ... intellectual laxity ... unilateral reconstructions' (pp.28, 33, 35).
10. Andrew M. Canepa, 'Emancipation and Jewish Response in Mid-Nineteenth-Century Italy', *European History Quarterly*, 16, 4 (1986), p.410.
11. Mario Toscano, 'L'uguaglianza senza diversità: stato, società e questione ebraica nell'Italia liberale', *Storia contemporanea*, 25, 5 (1994), pp.686, 689. This article is reprinted in Toscano's collected essays, *Ebraismo e antisemitismo in Italia*, published in 2003.
12. Ibid., p.686.
13. Stefano Caviglia, *L'identità salvata: gli ebrei di Roma tra fede e nazione: 1870–1938* (Rome-Bari: Laterza, 1996), pp.5–7.
14. Gadi Luzzatto Voghera, *Il prezzo dell'eguaglianza: il dibattito sull'emancipazione degli ebrei in Italia (1781–1848)* (Milan: FrancoAngeli, 1998), p.15; Ester Capuzzo, *Gli ebrei nella società italiana: Comunità e istituzioni tra Ottocento e Novecento* (Rome: Carocci, 1999), p.78.
15. See, for example, Michele Sarfatti, *Gli ebrei nell'Italia fascista: vicende, identità, persecuzione* (Turin: Einaudi, 2000), p.11; Alberto Cavaglion, *ebrei senza saperlo* (Naples: l'ancora del mediterraneo, 2002), p.41; Alberto Burgio (ed.), *Nel nome della razza: il razzismo nella storia d'Italia 1870–1945* (Bologna: Il Mulino, 2000), pp.5–6. In Cavaglion's contribution to this large volume, 'Due modeste proposte', which examines Italian racist attitudes towards various ethnic groups, not only the Jews, he wisely notes that historians should not overlook 'the few noble figures who opposed racism' (p.379). See also Mario Toscano, 'L'antisemitismo nell'Italia contemporanea: note, ipotesi e problemi di ricerca', *Zakhor*, 6 (2003), pp.24–5; and by the same author, 'Italian Jewish Identity from the Risorgimento to Fascism, 1848–1938', in Joshua D. Zimmerman (ed.), *Jews in Italy under Fascist and Nazi Rule, 1922–1945* (Cambridge: Cambridge University Press, 2005), pp.35–53: 'Anti-semitism remained basically alien to the political views of the bourgeoisie and the ruling classes [in newly unified Italy]' (p.41).
16. Enzo Collotti, *Il fascismo e gli ebrei: le leggi razziali in Italia* (Rome-Bari: Laterza, 2003), pp.5–8. What is rather disconcerting is that Collotti contradicts himself within the space of a page: he states that political anti-Semitism must be considered as a sporadic and isolated phenomenon in liberal Italy, but also that there were episodes of intolerance against the Jews that 'perhaps were not so isolated' (p.9).
17. Alberto Cavaglion, 'Una famiglia ebraica fra Risorgimento e Resistenza', *Rassegna Mensile di Israel* [hereafter *RMI*], 64, 1 (1998), p.24.
18. Giovanni Miccoli, 'Santa Sede, questione ebraica e antisemitismo fra Otto e Novecento', in Corrado Vivanti (ed.), *Storia d'Italia, Annali 11, Gli ebrei in Italia*, vol. 2 (Turin: Einaudi, 1997), pp.1369–574; Ruggero Taradel and Barbara Raggi, *La segregazione amichevole: 'La Civiltà Cattolica' e la questione ebraica 1850–1945* (Rome: Riuniti, 2000); David I. Kertzer, *Unholy War: The Vatican's Role in the Rise of Modern Anti-Semitism* (London: Macmillan, 2002). See also the proceedings of the conference held in Rome in 2000: Catherine Brice and Giovanni Miccoli (eds), *Les racines chrétiennes de l'antisémitisme politique (fin XIX–XXe siècle)* (Rome: Publications de l'Ecole Française de Rome, 2003).
19. Romano Canosa, *A caccia di ebrei: Mussolini, Preziosi e l'antisemitismo fascista* (Milan: Mondadori, 2006), p.45: 'As Renzo De Felice has noted, for the whole of the second half of the nineteenth century, Italy experienced only one form of anti-semitism, that of the Catholics.'
20. See, for example, Gadi Luzzatto Voghera, 'Guerra e Pregiudizio: antisemitismo e islamofobia fra ostilità e convivenza'. This was a paper delivered at a conference in Rome in December 2005; Maleiha Malik, 'Muslims are now getting the same treatment Jews had a century ago', the *Guardian*, 2 February 2007, p.35. This is an edited version of a lecture presented at the 'Clash of Civilisations' conference in London in January 2007. I am grateful to Luisa Cheshire for bringing this article to my attention.
21. See, Robert S. Wistrich, *Between Redemption and Perdition: Modern Antisemitism and Jewish Identity* (London and New York: Routledge, 1990), p.195.
22. Jacob Katz, *From Prejudice to Destruction: Anti-Semitism, 1700–1933* (Cambridge, MA: Harvard

University Press, 1980), pp.260, 245. See also Lindeman, *Anti-Semitism before the Holocaust*, pp.59–60. Lindemann describes Marr as 'the patriarch of anti-Semitism'.
23. See, for example, Fabio Levi, 'Anti-Jewish Persecution and Italian Society', in Zimmerman (ed.), *Jews in Italy under Fascist and Nazi Rule*, pp.199–206: 'the clean break with the Church required by the liberal state during and after unification ... did much to ease the processes of Jewish integration' (p.199).
24. See Kertzer, *Unholy War*, pp.168–9. See also Martin Clark, *Modern Italy 1871–1982* (London and New York: Longman, 1984), p.85.
25. Katz, *From Prejudice to Destruction*, p.9.
26. Ismar Schorsch, *Jewish Reactions to German Anti-Semitism, 1870–1914* (New York and London: Columbia University Press, 1972), p.12.
27. Luzzatto Voghera, *Il prezzo dell'eguaglianza*, p.81.
28. Ibid., pp.66–7, 80–1. See also Valerio De Cesaris, *Pro Judaeis: il filogiudaismo cattolico in Italia (1789–1938)* (Milan: Guerini, 2006), pp.64–7.
29. See Rabbi I. Zoller, 'Per la storia del 28 giugno 1799 a Siena', *Rivista Israelitica*, 7, 4–6 (1910), pp.138–42, 191–3, 240–4 and 'Nuove fonti per la storia del 28 giugno 1799 a Siena', *Rivista Israelitica*, 8, 1 (1911), pp.30–2. See also Lionella Neppi Modona and Sonia Oberdorfer, '1799: un pogrom in Toscana', *RMI*, 53 (1988), pp.241–59. Their research brings to light documents forgotten for two centuries in the archives of the Jewish community of Florence; and Roberto G. Salvadori, *1799: gli ebrei italiani nella bufera antigiacobina* (Florence: Giuntina, 1999).
30. See Salvatore Foà, *Gli ebrei nel Risorgimento italiano* (Assisi and Rome: Carucci, 1978), pp.15–23; and Paolo Bernardini, 'The Jews in Nineteenth-Century Italy: Towards a Reappraisal', *Journal of Modern Italian Studies*, 1, 2 (Spring 1996), pp.295–6.
31. See Amos Elon, *The Pity Of It All: A Portrait of Jews in Germany, 1743–1933* (London: Allen Lane, 2003), pp.101–7; Wistrich, *Longest Hatred*, p.55; and David Vital, *A People Apart: The Jews in Europe, 1789–1939* (Oxford: Oxford University Press, 1999), pp.212–14.
32. See Canepa, 'Emancipation and Jewish Response', pp.410–11; and De Cesaris, *Pro Judaeis*, pp.150–2.
33. Enzo Levi, *Memorie di una vita (1889–1947)* (Modena: STEM Mucchi, 1972), pp.16–19
34. Andrew M. Canepa, 'Considerazioni sulla seconda emancipazione e le sue conseguenze', *RMI*, 47, 1–3 (1981), pp.75–6.
35. Augusto Segre, *Memorie di vita ebraica: da Casale a Gerusalemme* (Rome: Bonacci, 1979), pp.24, 42, 87. See also Guglielmo Lattes, *Memorie d'un insegnante* (Asti: Segre, 1922), pp.67–8, on these incidents in Pitigliano until the 1860s. Such restraint was also advocated by the German Jewish family magazine *Sulamith* in Germany at the time of the 1819 riots. See Elon, *The Pity Of It All*, p.106; and Vital, *People Apart*, p.215.
36. Andrew M. Canepa, 'Cattolici ed ebrei nell'Italia liberale (1870–1915)', *Comunità*, 32, 179 (1978), p.54. See also Maria Teresa Pichetto, *Alle radici dell'odio: Preziosi e Benigni antisemiti* (Milan: FrancoAngeli, 1983), pp.9–10, 103, 128.
37. Léon Poliakov, *The History of Anti-Semitism*, vol. 2 (London: Routledge & Kegan Paul, 1974 [1961]), p.221 (see also pp.220–32, 283–95). See also Hyam Maccoby, *Antisemitism and Modernity: Innovation and Continuity* (London and New York: Routledge, 2006), pp.30–8. The statutes were not repealed until 1865. The persistence of the stigma survives in the island of Majorca in the treatment of the *chuetas* (slices of bacon), so called because they are presumed to be of Jewish descent: see Poliakov, *History of Anti-Semitism*, p.289; and Maccoby, *Antisemitism and Modernity*, p.38.
38. See Kertzer, *Unholy War*, pp.205–12. See also Sander L. Gilman, *The Jew's Body* (New York and London: Routledge, 1991): the representation of the male Jew 'lies at the very heart of Western Jew-hatred' (p.5; see also pp.19, 35).
39. Kertzer, *Unholy War*, p.7. See also Wistrich, *Longest Hatred*, p.54: 'racial anti-semitism, grafted on to an older and still powerful Christian legacy of hate, served ... to uproot ... the modern dream of assimilation'; Sarfatti, *Gli ebrei nell'Italia fascista*, p.11: 'the new political anti-Judaism of the Church ... constituted the principal point of reference for other currents hostile to the Jews'; Michael Mack, *German Idealism and the Jew: The Inner Anti-Semitism of Philosophy and German Jewish Response* (Chicago, IL, and London: University of Chicago Press, 2003). Mack argues that 'to trace the ways in which pseudoscientific and pseudotheological versions of anti-semitism are mutually sustaining and reinforcing' will help us 'to understand the impact of both in generating the secularization and the politicization of religious oppositions between the Christian and the Jew in the social and intellectual history of the past three centuries' (pp.9–10). See also Sandro Servi, 'Building a Racial State: Images of the Jew in the Illustrated Fascist Magazine, *La Difesa della Razza*, 1938–1943', in Zimmerman (ed.), *Jews in Italy under Fascist and Nazi Rule*, pp.114–57: 'any analysis of ... *La Difesa della Razza* cannot help but confirm that the Fascist anti-Semitic campaign (like its Nazi counterpart) ... could only have been implemented due to the rich anti-Judaic heritage built over the centuries by the teachings of

the Christian churches' (p.122); and Maccoby, *Antisemitism and Modernity*, p.52: 'One of the central questions in the study of anti-semitism and modernity is the relation between modern anti-semitism and Christian anti-semitism'; the former, he argues, is 'almost entirely derived from Christian medieval demonization of the Jews' (p.52). The thesis of his book is that 'the root cause of the Holocaust was the deep hatred of the Jews which was the legacy of the Christian Middle Ages to the modern world' (p.49).
40. See Wistrich, *Longest Hatred*, pp.13–42.
41. Ferdinando Jabalot, *Degli ebrei nel loro rapporto colle nazioni cristiane del Reverendissimo padre F. Jabalot* (Rome: Poggioli, 1825), pp.11–12, 25–8, 44–5. This was first published in the third volume of the *Giornale Ecclesiastico di Roma*. See also Luzzatto Voghera, *Il prezzo dell'eguaglianza*, pp.71–2; and De Cesaris, *Pro Judaeis*, pp.87–90. Italianists may be interested to know that the poet Giacomo Leopardi's father, Monaldo, wrote an anti-emancipationist tract in 1829 (see Luzzatto Voghera, *Il prezzo dell'eguaglianza*, p.74).
42. Kertzer, *Unholy War*, p.65.
43. See David I. Kertzer, *The Kidnapping of Edgardo Mortara* (London: Picador, 1997); and D. Scalise, *Il caso Mortara: la vera storia del bambino ebreo rapito dal papa* (Milan: Mondadori, 1997).
44. Louis Loewe (ed.), *Diaries of Sir Moses and Lady Montefiore* (London: The Jewish Historical Society of England, 1983), p.96. See also pp.82–103.
45. Cited in Moretti, 'La dimensione ebraica di un maestro pisano', in Michele Luzzati (ed.), *Gli ebrei di Pisa (secoli IX–XX)* (Pisa: Pacini, 1998), pp.264–65. The words 'Jewish' and 'rabbis' are italicized in the original.
46. See, for example, the *Guardian*, 9 and 11 March 2000. Edgardo lived until the age of 88 and died in Belgium two months before the Nazi occupation. When an adult, he was permitted to see his relatives: a short piece in *Il Vessillo Israelitico* [*VI*] reports him visiting a kosher restaurant in Milan with members of his family (1904, p.249).
47. See Stefano Jesurum, *Essere ebrei in Italia* (Milan: Longanesi, 1987), p.125. See also Fausto Coen, *Una vita tante vite* (Catanzaro: Rubbettino, 2004). Coen was born in 1914, and he wrote this memoir for his grandchildren: 'in our house we too ... talked of ... the famous "Mortara case"' (p.15).
48. See Kertzer, *Kidnapping of Edgardo Mortara*, pp.34–56; and by the same author, *Unholy War*, Chapter 2, 'Forced Baptisms'. The acclaimed writer Alessandro Manzoni was in favour of conversion of the Jews as part of their regeneration, and was instrumental in the conversion of David Norsa (Tullo Massarani's tutor from Turin) and Marco Coen of Venice (see Luzzatto Voghera, *Il prezzo dell'eguaglianza*, pp.91–2).
49. *Civiltà Cattolica*, serie 3, 12 (1858), pp.385–416 (p.393).
50. Kertzer, *Kidnapping of Edgardo Morpurgo*, p.71.
51. Scalise, *Il caso Mortara*, p.113.
52. See *L'Educatore Israelita* [*EI*], 1864, pp.273–78, 303–6; 339–40. *Il Corriere Israelitico* reported similar incidents elsewhere in Europe, for example Poland and France (1877, p.211; 1878, p.240). On 15 September 1914, it carried a short piece entitled 'Blind Fanaticism', on an Italian Catholic teacher whose brightest pupil was a 6-year-old Jewish boy: 'it was a thorn in her side that that innocent creature belonged to the *hated* Jewish race!' (p.2). Thus, lacking the courage to have him secretly baptized, she taught him Catholic prayers and terrorized him with stories of the damnation of the Jews. The archives of the Jewish community of Florence document, among others, the case of Rosa Sadun, a 16-year-old from Pitigliano, who was abducted on 27 May 1861. Another case, dated October 1843, involved the secret baptism of Marianna Della Riccia, a woman who was a long-term patient in the lunatic asylum of Florence (ASCEF, Catecumeni 1831–1874, D.2.3/1 and 7).
53. See Canepa, 'Cattolici ed ebrei nell'Italia liberale', pp.74–5; and Clark, *Modern Italy*, p.157. The Catholics formed their own party, the Partito Popolare Italiano, in 1918. To compensate for this temporal deficit, at the first Vatican Council in 1870, a declaration of papal infallibility in spiritual matters was made. Church and State in Italy remained separate until the Lateran Pacts with Mussolini in 1929 (see Clark, *Modern Italy*, pp.154–6).
54. Kertzer, *Unholy War*, p.13.
55. Ibid., p.133.
56. Taradel and Raggi, *La segregazione amichevole*, p.5.
57. Ibid., pp.5–8. Subsequent popes similarly expressed their appreciation for their scrupulous fidelity to the Holy See's directives (pp.8–9). All articles were anonymous, but Kertzer and Taradel have identified the authors of some of them.
58. Seventy articles attacking Freemasonry appeared in the Jesuit journal in the first fifty years of its publication. See Canepa, 'Cattolici ed ebrei nell'Italia liberale', pp.88–93; Taradel and Raggi, *La segregazione amichevole*, pp.6–18.
59. *Civiltà Cattolica*, serie 8, 12 (1873), pp.340, 344, 666; serie 11, 3 (1880), p.130.
60. *Civiltà Cattolica*, serie 14, 8 (1890), pp.5–20, 385–407, 641–55. See also Kertzer, *Unholy War*,

pp.133–51; Taradel and Raggi, *La segregazione amichevole*, pp.25–35.
61. See Taradel and Raggi, *La segregazione amichevole*, pp.26, 45.
62. Cited in ibid., p.35.
63. See, for example, short pieces from 21 to 27 January 1898 in which the following views are expressed: anti-Semitism is a logical and inevitable result of emancipation; Christians have a natural repugnance and aversion to this deicide people, thus it is necessary that they should live apart; in addition to the usual diet of Masonic–Jewish and socialist–Jewish conspiracies.
64. See Canepa, 'Cattolici ed ebrei nell'Italia liberale', pp.77–81.
65. R. Po-chia, *The Myth of Ritual Murder: Jews and Magic in Reformation Germany* (New Haven, CT, and London: Yale University Press, 1988), pp.3–4. See also Hillel J. Kieval, 'The Importance of Place: Comparative Aspects of the Ritual Murder Trial in Modern Central Europe', in Todd M. Endelman (ed.), *Comparing Jewish Societies* (Ann Arbor, MI: University of Michigan Press, 1997), pp.135–65; Kertzer, *Unholy War*, Chapters 4, 7 and 11; De Cesaris, *Pro Judaeis*, pp.162–79; Marina Caffiero, 'Alle origini dell'antisemitismo politico: l'accusa di omicidio nel sei-settecento tra autodifesa degli ebrei e pronunciamenti papali', in Brice and Miccoli (eds), *Les racines chrétiennes de l'antisémitisme politique*, pp.25–59; and Francesco Crepaldi, 'l'omicidio rituale nella "moderna" polemica antigiu- daica di *Civiltà Cattolica* nella seconda metà del XIX secolo', also in Brice and Miccoli (eds), *Les racines chrétiennes de l'antisémitisme politique*, pp.61–78. For a recent controversial belief that groups of Ashkenazi Jews practised such blood rituals, see Ariel Toaff, *Pasque di Sangue: ebrei d'Europa e omicidi rituali* (Bologna: Il Mulino, 2007). For a negative review of this book, see David Abulafia, 'Libels of Blood', *Times Literary Supplement*, 2 March 2007, pp.11–12. Abulafia concludes: 'A his- torian who finds it so difficult to distinguish truth from fiction … is best advised to lay down his pen.' Such was the outcry in Italy that the publishers withdrew it.
66. See Kertzer, *Unholy War*, p.229. Oreglia, a principal contributor to the Jesuit journal at this time, claimed that some of the Papal Bulls were Jewish forgeries (see Taradel and Raggi, *La segregazione amichevole*, pp.22–3).
67. See Vital, *People Apart*, pp.323–44, 535–8. Vincenzo Manzini lists additional cases, including two in Italy (Mantua in 1824 and Rovigo in 1857) in *L'Omicidio rituale e i sacrifici umani, con particolare riguardo alle accuse contro gli ebrei* (Turin: Bocca, 1925), pp.134–45. See also Taradel and Raggi, *La segregazione amichevole*, who list over fifty cases between 1881 and 1900 (pp.183–4), and Kieval, 'Importance of Place', with 128 incidents between 1873 and 1900 (p.159).
68. See Kertzer, *Unholy War*, pp.86–105. See also Jonathan Frankel, *The Damascus Affair: 'Ritual Mur- der', Politics, and the Jews in 1840* (Cambridge: Cambridge University Press, 1997). *The Times*, one of the most influential papers in the world, stated in a leading article of 25 June 1840 that if the accusations were true, 'the Jewish religion must at once disappear off the face of the earth' (p.259); Samuel David Luzzatto exhorted Alessandro Manzoni to intervene. He made it known that he could not accede to this request, thus lending support to the accusations (see Luzzatto Voghera, *Il prezzo del- l'ugualianza*, p.92); Paul Mendes-Flohr and Jehuda Reinharz (eds), *The Jew in the Modern World: A Documentary History* (New York and Oxford: Oxford University Press, 1995), pp.313–15: a letter from the Elders of the Jewish Community of Damascus to the Elders of the Jewish Community of Con- stantinople giving details of the case and the atrocities to which their members were subjected in order to extract confessions of guilt.
69. See Frankel, *Damascus Affair*, pp.229, 269, 270, 379. On Damascus and other blood libel episodes in the Middle East in the nineteenth century, see Tudor Parfitt, *The Jews in Palestine 1800–1882* (Woodbridge: Boydell Press, 1987), pp.131–3, 186–97. Sir Richard Burton, British consul in Dam- ascus between 1869 and 1871, believed in the practice. His enquiries into the subject aroused the hos- tility of the Damascus Jews and were a factor in his recall from that post in 1871. See W.H. Wilkins's preface to Sir Richard F. Burton's *The Jew, The Gypsy and El Islam* (London: Hutchinson, 1898), pp.vii–viii. The book was published posthumously owing to its anti-Semitic tendency, but the appen- dix 'on the alleged rite of Human Sacrifice' was omitted 'in the exercise of the discretion given to me' (p.x). See also pp.121, 123, 128: 'The Jews crucified a boy at Norwich'; in 1288 'the Jews of Würzburg murdered a Christian'; 'The Jews murdered Padre Tomaso … at Damascus.'
70. See Frankel, *Damascus Affair*, pp.214–56. There were also fears and anxieties that such a public dis- play of Jewish solidarity would stir up fanaticism against them (see pp.237–40). See also Vital, *Peo- ple Apart*, pp.242–3, and Capuzzo, *Gli ebrei italiani*, pp.58–9.
71. Frankel, *Damascus Affair*, p.373. Herzl, founder of the Zionist movement, was to receive such adu- lation decades later. See also Loewe (ed.), *Diaries of Sir Moses and Lady Montefiore*, pp.208–61.
72. Frankel, *Damascus Affair*, pp.370–2.
73. Dan Cohn-Sherbok, *The Paradox of Anti-Semitism* (London and New York: Continuum, 2006). He gives historical examples, from biblical to modern times, to illustrate his thesis. The other part of the paradox, he argues, is that the absence of anti-Semitism 'may … lead to the disintegration of the

Jewish heritage' (p.2). The concept of the interrelation between anti-Semitism and Judaism is not new: on an individual basis, many have felt drawn to their Jewish identity when it is threatened by external circumstances. See Herzl's views and also those of Rabbi Bloch in Robert S. Wistrich, *The Jews of Vienna in the Age of Franz Joseph* (Oxford: Oxford University Press, 1989), pp.307–8. See also Nordau's comments in Michael Stanislawski, *Zionism and the Fin de Siècle*, in a letter of 1898: 'I am ... a Jew in response to the calumnies that afflict us, a Jew because of the tortures inflicted on those of my race. If the Jews were happy, I'd have very little to do with them, alas' (p.67). 'The freer the society in which we live, the weaker the links between the Jews become, but the spark of the sense of Jewish identity burns up in a crisis' (chief rabbi, Dr Immanuel Jakobovits, the *Observer*, 14 January 1979, p.3).

74. *Corriere Israelitico* [*CI*] 1865, pp.181–2, 241–4; 273–6. On Cohn, see Frankel, *Damascus Affair*, pp.84–5.
75. *CI*, 1883, pp.50–61, 80–5, 97–106, 121–8, 145–52, 168–76, 193–200, 217–22.
76. *CI*, 1899, p.128. See also pp.103–105, 127–32, 153–5, 178–9.
77. *CI*, 1913, pp.101–12, 124–7.
78. See *CI*, 1913, p.103; *Settimana Israelitica* [*SI*], 41 (1913); Luciano Tas, *Storia degli ebrei in Italia* (Rome: New Compton, 1987), p.116. On the Beilis case, see also Kertzer, *Unholy War*, pp.227–36; Taradel and Raggi, *La segregazione amichevole*, pp.46–7; and Mendes-Flohr and Reinharz (eds), *The Jew in the Modern World*, pp.367–71, 412–13. In the same year, the Milanese Zionist group also formally protested against the religious journal *Il Labaro* for defamation against the Jews (see *VI*, 1913, pp.509–10).
79. *VI*, 1913, pp.610–16, 671–4, 702–4; 1914, pp.14, 64, 254–5, 671–4. Beilis sent a letter of thanks from Jaffa for the 1,583 francs the Italian Jews had collected (pp.254–5). *La Settimana Israelitica* also reported extensively on the case, and in 1914 published an interview with Beilis from Palestine sent by their own correspondent, Maurice Slousch, in which Beilis spoke of his ordeal, saying that he had become very religious after the trial and speaking of his happiness at being in his native land and living a truly Jewish life (*SI*, 20 [1914]).
80. Mendel Beilis, *The Story of My Sufferings*, translated by Harrison Goldberg, with an introduction by Herman Bernstein and Arnold D. Margolin (New York: Mendel Beilis, 1926), p.219.
81. On Alexeyvitch's testimony, see Mendes-Flohr and Reinharz (eds), *The Jew in the Modern World*, pp.367–71.
82. In the 1899 Polna case, the accused was not pardoned until 1917.
83. See Taradel and Raggi, *La segregazione amichevole*, pp.22–35; Miccoli, 'Santa Sede, questione ebraica e antisemitismo fra Otto e Novecento', pp.1525–43; Charlotte Klein, 'Damascus to Kiev: *Civiltà Cattolica* on Ritual Murder', *Wiener Library Bulletin*, 27, 32 (1974), pp.18–25.
84. See Kertzer, *Unholy War*, pp.171–7; and Taradel and Raggi, *La segregazione amichevole*, p.28; *La Croix* was the most popular Catholic journal in France, reaching a circulation of 180,000 copies by 1893, double that of *Le Figaro* (p.175, n.86). The editors of *La Croix* described it in 1890 as 'le journal le plus antijuif de France' (cited in Miccoli, 'Santa Sede, questione ebraica e antisemitismo fra Otto e Novecento', p.1481).
85. See Kertzer, *Unholy War*, pp.163–4.
86. See Wistrich, *The Jews of Vienna*, pp.221–3; 260.
87. *Civiltà Cattolica*, serie 14, 12 (1891), p.497; serie 16, 6 (1896), p.113; see also Taradel and Raggi, *La segregazione amichevole*, pp.37–8, 41, 44.
88. Vital, *People Apart*, pp.538, 544. See also Kertzer, *Unholy War*: among the subscribers to *La Libre Parole* were 30,000 priests; '*La France juive* has been termed the most influential anti-Semitic work published in nineteenth-century Europe' (p.178). The two-volume work reached 200 editions by the end of the century, to be found 'next to the Bible ... of the most modest homes': Michael Burns, *France and the Dreyfus Affair: A Documentary History* (Boston, MA, and New York: Bedford/St Martin's, 1999), p.8.
89. Cited in Miccoli, 'Santa Sede, questione ebraica e antisemitismo fra Otto e Novecento', p.1528. On the many publications on ritual murder, see Frankel, *Damascus Affair*, Chapter 16.
90. *Civiltà Cattolica*, serie 14, 8 (1890), p.6. This remark is accompanied by a lengthy footnote helpfully listing the principal anti-Semitic publications, with suggestions on which to select for further reading.
91. Vital, *People Apart*, p.538. Propaganda about ritual murder was recycled by the fascist and Nazi regimes. See, for example, Sandro Servi, 'Building a Racial State': *La Difesa della Razza* published full-page illustrations of the Simon of Trent and Tisza–Eszlar cases with accompanying text (Fig. 3, Plate B).
92. Cited in Taradel and Raggi, *La segregazione amichevole*, p.178, n.106. On Benigni and his papal espionage ring, see Kertzer, *Unholy War*, pp.226–7. From 1920 to 1921, he published his own *Bollettino antisemita* (p.266). See also Pichetto, *Alle radici dell'odio:* Chapter 5; and Canepa, 'Cattolici ed ebrei nell'Italia liberale', who lists the principal Catholic journals for the period 1870–1915 (pp.61–2).
93. *CI*, 1872, pp.47–52; 1873, pp.16–18; 1885, pp.105–7.

94. *CI*, 1872, pp.156–57. See also De Cesaris, *Pro Judaeis*, pp.163–5.
95. Miccoli, 'Santa Sede, questione ebraica e antisemitismo fra Otto e Novecento', pp.1421–2.
96. See Bruno Di Porto, 'Gli ebrei a Pisa dal Risorgimento al fascismo tra identità e integrazione', in Luzzati (ed.), *Gli ebrei di Pisa*, p.301.
97. *CI*, 1900, pp.127–9, 152–3, 222; 1901, pp.32–3. See also Luigi Uretini, 'Stereotipi antisemiti ne "Il Mulo" (1907–1925)', in Burgio (ed.), *Nel nome della razza*, pp.293–308.
98. Canepa, 'Cattolici ed ebrei nell'Italia liberale', pp.97–8.
99. *L'Idea Sionista* [*IS*] reported on two other schools in Rome, run by nuns, where plays containing anti-Semitic material were performed (*IS*, 1904, p.83). See also *VI*, 1896, p.208, on another such publication distributed as a school prize, and approved by the ecclesiastical authorities, cited in Bruno Maida, *Dal ghetto alla città: gli ebrei torinesi nel secondo Ottocento* (Turin: Zamorani, 2001), p.317. On the fictional representation of Jews in Italy during this period, see, for example, Andrew M. Canepa, 'L'immagine dell'ebreo nel folklore e nella letteratura del postrisorgimento', *RMI* (5–6 1978), pp.383–99; and Lynn M. Gunzberg, *Strangers at Home: Jews in the Italian Literary Imagination* (Berkeley, CA: University of California Press, 1992). One of the most popular novels was written by a priest, Antonio Bresciani's *L'Ebreo di Verona* (The Jew of Verona), first published in instalments in *Civiltà Cattolica* in 1850/51. It was subsequently translated into French, German, English and Spanish.
100. See Kieval, 'Importance of Place', p.143, 160–1, citing the *Jewish Chronicle*, 29 July 1892, pp.5–6; and on Innsbruck, see Jacob Toury, 'Defense Activities of the Österreichisch-Israelitische Union before 1914', in Jehuda Reinharz (ed.), *Living with Antisemitism: Modern Jewish Responses* (Hanover, MD, and London: University Press of New England, 1987), p.181.
101. In their defence, the publishers stated that such definitions were routinely found in other Italian and foreign dictionaries (*VI*, 1910, pp.341–3, 416, 438–9).
102. Loewe (ed.), *Diaries of Sir Moses and Lady Montefiore*, p.287, cited in Kertzer, *Unholy War*, p.105. The private correspondence of the Vatican's Secretary of State and cardinal prefect illustrate their belief in the practice (pp.104–5).
103. *CI*, 1873, p.16. See also *EI*, 1873, p.121: 'in one of his usual allocutions the Pope hurled abusive words against the Jews and Jewish journalists … words which could ignite new hatreds'. See also Miccoli, 'Santa Sede, questione ebraica e antisemitismo fra Otto e Novecento', pp.1405–6.
104. See Kertzer, *Unholy War*, p.128.
105. See ibid., pp.214–17.
106. See ibid, pp.188–202; Taradel and Raggi, *La segregazione amichevole*, pp.36, 39, 44; Peter Pulzer, *The Rise of Political Anti-Semitism in Germany and Austria*, revised edn (London: Peter Halban, 1988) pp.175–8. In contrast to the pope's approval of Lueger, the emperor of Austria withheld his confirmation of Lueger as mayor until he was elected for the fourth time in 1897 (the first was in 1895).
107. 'Une visite à Léon XIII', *Le Figaro*, 15 March 1899, p.1.
108. Miccoli, 'Santa Sede, questione ebraica e antisemitismo fra Otto e Novecento', pp.1528–44. In his detailed account of this episode, Miccoli documents the Vatican's view that the leading English Catholics were pawns of the influential London Jews and therefore were regarded with suspicion (pp.1533, 1537). See also Kertzer, *Unholy War*, pp.218–20; and Taradel and Raggi, *La segregazione amichevole*, p.43.
109. Cited in Andrew M. Canepa, 'Pius X and the Jews: A Reappraisal', *Church History*, 61, 3 (1992), p.369.
110. See Kertzer, *Unholy War*, pp.228–36.
111. See Frankel, *Damascus Affair*, p.25; Kieval, 'Importance of Place', p.158; Klein, 'Damascus to Kiev', p.25; Miccoli, 'Santa Sede, questione ebraica e antisemitismo fra Otto e Novecento', p.1545.
112. Cited in Maida, *Dal ghetto alla città*, p.218. This exchange is not mentioned in Milano's *Storia degli ebrei*.
113. Milano, *Storia degli ebrei*, p.367.
114. Ulrich Wyrwa, 'Jewish Experiences in the Italian Risorgimento: Political Practice and National Emotions of Florentine and Leghorn Jewry (1849–1860)', *Journal of Modern Italian Studies*, 8, 1 (2003), p.26; and Cantimori, Preface, p.xviii.
115. Cantimori, Preface, p.xxi. De Felice, on the other hand, dismisses the Pasqualigo episode in a parenthesis, implying that the silence which followed 'these high-level anti-semitic manifestations clearly demonstrated that they were alien to Italian mentality' (*Storia degli ebrei sotto il fascismo* p.36).
116. Emilio Falco, 'Isacco Maurogonato Pesaro dalle prime esperienze politiche alla caduta della destra storica', *Clio*, 40, 3 (2004), pp.393–446.
117. See *VI*, 1875, p.79. See also Falco, 'Isacco Maurogonato Pesaro', pp.398–406.
118. See Cantimori, Preface, p.xix; Canepa, 'Il caso Pasqualigo', pp.168–70. Pasqualigo was accused of

plagiarism and distorting scholarly evidence to make his case: see *EI*, 1873, pp.342, 353, 357–8; *CI*, 1873, pp.155–7; and Canepa, 'Il caso Pasqualigo', p.170.
119. See Jacob Katz, *Out of the Ghetto: The Social Background of Jewish Emancipation, 1770–1870* (Cambridge, MA: Harvard University Press, 1973), pp.99–103. The slogan 'State within the State' 'became a kind of locus classicus in anti-Semitic literature' (p.100).
120. Canepa, 'Il caso Pasqualigo', p.181.
121. Ibid., p.189. See also by the same author, 'Emancipation and Jewish Response', p.429: 'Viewed in this light, the equivocal nature of emancipation formed the underlying, predisposing determinant of liberal anti-semitism'. See also Cavaglion, 'Una famiglia ebraica', p.25: 'the variable to emphasize, in order to understand the difficult historical process of integration [of the Jews], is the weakness of Italian identity as it was being formed, or not, in the liberal period'.
122. Toscano, 'L'ugualianza senza diversità', p.690.
123. Maurizio Molinari, *Ebrei in Italia: un problema di identità (1870–1938)* (Florence: Giuntina, 1991), p.38.
124. Cited in Canepa, 'Il caso Pasqualigo', p.177. Maurogonato became a senator in 1890.
125. See Clark, *Modern Italy*, pp.81–4.
126. Canepa, 'Il caso Pasqualigo', pp.177–8. On attacks from the Jewish press, see, for example, 'I cristianelli del ghetto' [The little Christians from the ghetto], *IS*, 1907, pp.25–8; *CI*, 1910, p.172: 'What are these Jews doing with our natural enemies?' However, *Il Vessillo Israelitico* viewed such alliances as an example of Jewish integration: 'why should not an Italian citizen – just because he is Jewish – work together with other citizens who share the same political platform?' (*VI*, 1905, p.333).
127. *EI*, 1873, pp.345–6, 353–6, 360.
128. Cited in Toscano, 'L'ugualianza senza diversità', p.690, n.18.
129. See Todd M. Endelmann, 'Conversion as a Response to Antisemitism in Modern Jewish History', in Reinharz (ed.), *Living with Antisemitism*, pp.68–9.
130. See *EI*, 1873, pp.358–9; *CI*, 1873, pp.202–3; Canepa, 'Il caso Pasqualigo', pp.170–1.
131. See *EI*, 1873, pp.358–9: 'no Jewish pen has written with such benevolence and with such enthusiasm about the Jewish people'; *CI*, 1873, pp.200–3; Canepa, 'Il caso Pasqualigo', p.171.
132. See *CI*, 1873, pp.200–1. Canepa suggests the Freemasons also used the occasion to make anti-clerical comments ('Il caso Pasqualigo', pp.171–2).
133. See Canepa, 'Il caso Pasqualigo', p.169; and Cantimori, Preface, p.xix.
134. See Canepa, 'Il caso Pasqualigo', pp.173–4. Mortara's article was published in *Il diritto*, 13–14 November 1873.
135. Uzielli's article was published in *Il diritto*, 18 November 1873. Uzielli was the son of a devoutly religious Jewish banker and philanthropist. See Canepa, 'Il caso Pasqualigo', pp.175–6. Alessandro D'Ancona, who was a friend and colleague, also an assimilated Jew who espoused *italianità*, found Uzielli's views offensive and wrote to tell him so (see Di Porto, 'Gli ebrei a Pisa dal Risorgimento', p.310).
136. *CI*, 1876, pp.177–9. *Il Vessillo Israelitico* also reported on Finzi's campaign, but in a more attenuated manner (*VI*, 1876, pp.413–14).
137. *CI*, 1882, p.211. See also Bruno Di Porto, 'Edoardo Arbib deputato di Viterbo', *RMI*, 40 (1973), pp.436–42. Pani Rossi cleverly exploited the inexperience of the voters which had increased that year due to electoral reform by distributing a circular on the eve of the elections purporting to be from the Vatican exempting them from the *Non expedit* to prevent a Jewish candidate from entering parliament (p.440). In 1886, Arbib was elected as deputy for Perugia, and was subsequently returned another four times to parliament; he became a senator in 1904.
138. Cited in Caviglia, *L'identità salvata*, p.68.
139. Cited in ibid., p.69.
140. *VI*, 1895, p.305. See also Caviglia, *L'identità salvata*, p.71.
141. See Canepa, 'Il caso Pasqualigo', p.187.
142. See Maida, *Dal ghetto alla città*, p.254.
143. Cited in Gilman, *The Jew's Body*, p.91. Gilman notes that in the medical literature of the late nineteenth century, circumcision was discussed within the context of hygiene and the transmission of syphilis: 'the Jews as the carriers of sexually transmitted diseases' was first associated with the Marranos of Spain in the fifteenth century. Jewish degeneration was central to Nazi discourse. Freud suggested that circumcision could be used to whip up anti-Semitism by reminding non-Jews of the fear of castration (pp.92–7). See also Sander L. Gilman, *Freud, Race and Gender* (Princeton, NJ: Princeton University Press, 1993), Chapter 2, 'The Construction of the Male Jew'.
144. Cited in Canepa, 'Il caso Pasqualigo', p.188. Canepa lists the names of other exponents of 'this liberal anti-semitic current' (p.189).
145. Bruno Di Porto, 'Dopo il Risorgimento, al varco del '900: gli ebrei e l'ebraismo in Italia', *RMI*, 47,

1–6 (1981), p.33. On other anti-Semitic articles in the socialist press, see Cavaglion, 'Gli ebrei e il socialismo: il caso italiano', in Francesca Sofia and Mario Toscano (eds), *Stato nazionale ed emancipazione ebraica* (Rome: Bonacci, 1992), pp.385–7.
146. Derek J. Penslar, 'Anti-Semites on Zionism: From Indifference to Obsession', in Jeffrey Herf (ed.), *Anti-Semitism and Anti-Zionism in Historical Perspective: Convergence and Divergence* (London and New York: Routledge, 2007), p.10. *The Protocols* have resurfaced throughout the Arab world: see Meir Litvak, 'The Islamic Republic of Iran and the Holocaust: Anti-Semitism and Anti-Zionism', in Herf (ed.), *Anti-Semitism and Anti-Zionism* pp.250–67: serial publication in two mainstream newspapers in the 1990s; a special government edition in 2000 (p.255); and Wistrich, *Longest Hatred*, pp.253–4.
147. See Pichetto, *Alle radici dell'odio*, p.29. In the 1930s, in order to influence Catholic opinion, Preziosi reprinted anti-Semitic articles of the 1890s from *Civiltà Cattolica* (pp.82–3). Pichetto provides a list of anti-Semitic publications in Italy between 1870 and 1945: see *Alle radici dell'odio*, pp.129–35. On Preziosi's fascist activities, see also Canosa, *A caccia di ebrei*.
148. *EI*, 1858, p.217; 1859, p.219, 317.
149. Germano Maifreda, *Gli ebrei e l'economia milanese: L'Ottocento* (Milan: FrancoAngeli, 2000), pp.175–6.
150. See Moretti 'La dimensione ebraica di un maestro pisano', p.244. The letter is dated 14 February 1862.
151. See ibid., pp.241–4, 350–1. Salvatore De Benedetti, who also aspired to the post of director, noted in two letters to D'Ancona (in 1867 and 1874) that 'there's the problem of being a Jew, but it will not be insuperable' (ibid., p.242). He added, in the letter of 23 September 1867, that certain influential Catholics whom he names 'deplore the fact that the Scuola Normale is tainted [*guasta*] by Jews' (ibid., p.241).
152. Canepa, 'Cattolici ed ebrei nell'Italia liberale', p.60; Luzzatti (ed.), *Gli ebrei di Pisa*, p.308.
153. Canepa, 'Cattolici ed ebrei nell'Italia liberale', pp.63–5. Canepa notes that this campaign ceased at the end of the decade due to the fact that Catholic instruction in state schools continued and thus the influence of the Catholic Church remained effective in the educational sphere (p.66).
154. Lattes, *Memorie d'un insegnante*, pp.42, 55, 70.
155. Luigi Luzzatti, *Memorie autobiografiche e carteggi* (Bologna: Zanichelli, 1929), p.6. Most of these confrontations ended in fights; Luzzatti once threw a student into a canal, but promptly rescued him as he could not swim (p.8). Both Lattes and Luzzatti also mention firm friendships with non-Jews.
156. Marco Momigliano, *Autobiografia di un rabbino italiano* (Palermo: Sellerio, 1986), p.57. The title itself is indicative of the author's patriotism.
157. Tullo Massarani, *Una nobile vita: carteggio inedito*, edited by Raffaello Barbiera (Florence: Le Monnier, 1909), vol. 1, p.v; vol. 2, pp.230–1.
158. Among the deliberations of an anti-Semitic congress held in Bucharest, supported by the Romanian government, was the statement that 'the Jews are unworthy to remain in Europe among civilized peoples and therefore ways must be found to drive them out of Europe and until then to deny them all rights' (*CI*, 1886, p.148). On the deteriorating conditions of the Romanian Jews after 1878, see David Vital, *The Origins of Zionism* (Oxford: Clarendon Press, 1975), pp.88–97.
159. *CI*, 1882, p.112. See also Wistrich, *The Jews of Vienna*, pp.208–9. The escalation of anti-Semitism in Hungary was linked to the Tisza–Eszlar ritual murder trial of 1882.
160. Katz, *From Prejudice to Destruction*, p.260.
161. Pulzer, *Rise of Political Anti-Semitism*, pp.47–8.
162. Wilhelm Marr, *The Victory of Judaism over Germandom*, in Mendes-Flohr and Reinharz (eds), *The Jew in the Modern World*, p.332.
163. Cited in Pulzer, *Rise of Political Anti-Semitism* p.49.
164. On Stöcker, Treitschke, Mommsen and other leading German anti-Semites such as Dühring, see, for example, Pulzer, *Rise of Political Anti-Semitism*, pp.50–90, 240–50; Vital, *People Apart*, pp.263–7; Mendes-Flohr and Reinharz (eds), *The Jew in the Modern World*, pp.333–4, 340–9; Elon, *Pity Of It All*, pp.214–20. On the problematic of Dühring's support for genocide, see Donald L. Niewyk, 'Solving the "Jewish Problem": Continuity and Change in German Antisemitism, 1871–1945', *Leo Baeck Institute Year Book* [hereafter *LBIYB*], 35 (1990), pp.360–1. See also Gilman, *Jewish Self-Hatred*, Chapter 5.
165. Momigliano, *Pagine ebraiche*, p.147. He had in mind not only Mommsen's views, but also those of Benedetto Croce. In the preface to a collection of essays by Cesare Merzagora published in 1947, which included two on the Jews in post-war Europe, Croce argued that the Jews should merge (*fondersi*) more fully with other Italians, and thus attempt to shed their distinctiveness in which they had persisted for centuries, and which had been the pretext for persecutions in the past, and 'it is to be feared in the future' (p.147). Momigliano commented: 'Only a complete lack of contact with Jewish culture can explain that not even Benedetto Croce managed to understand that Italian Jews

have the right (which subjectively can be a duty) to remain Jewish' (ibid.). As a result of these words Croce, who had an impeccable anti-fascist record, found himself at the centre of a bitter polemic. Dante Lattes responded with a lengthy article on the front page of *Israel*, 30 January 1947, provocatively titled 'Benedetto Croce and the worthless martyrdom of Israel' (*l'inutile martirio d'Israele*): he expressed his dismay that a man of his stature and reputation should impart such admonitions to the persecuted, rather than reserving them for the perpetrators; it would appear that Croce had no respect for the Jewish victims or their suffering, indeed he seemed to be blaming them for the atrocities and massacres. Croce's words clearly rankled not only with Lattes, but also with Momigliano who, more than thirty years later, returned to them. Scholars have attempted to exonerate Croce: Toscano, in his introduction to *Integrazione e identità*, writes of Croce's insufficient understanding of the post-war situation of the Jews (p.19). Gennaro Sasso, while admitting that the timing of such remarks was infelicitous, attempts to contextualize them within the universalist ideals of the Enlightenment and Croce's philosophical *Weltanschauung*. See Sasso, *Per invigilare me stesso: i taccuini di lavoro di Benedetto Croce* (Bologna: Il Mulino, 1989), pp.180–217. On the intellectual and political antipathies between Croce and Momigliano in the 1930s, see Simon Levis Sullam, 'Arnaldo Momigliano e la "nazionalizzazione parallela": autobiografia, religione, storia', *Passato e presente*, 25, 70 (2007), pp.71–5.

166. Sanford Ragins, *Jewish Responses to Anti-Semitism in Germany, 1870–1914: A Study in the History of Ideas* (Cincinnati, OH: Hebrew Union College Press, 1980), p.32. On Bismarck's ambivalent attitude to anti-Semitism, see Fritz Stern, *Gold and Iron: Bismarck, Bleichröder, and the Building of the German Empire* (London: Allen & Unwin, 1977), pp.494–531; and Wistrich, *The Jews of Vienna*, p.248: an Austrian Jewish contemporary observed that German anti-Semites regarded Otto von Bismarck 'as their silent but most helpful chief'.
167. See Jere H. Link, 'Semitism in German Literary Politics: The Special Case of the Deutsche Schillerstiftung', *LBIYB*, 35 (1990), pp.371–83. From the 1880s until the First World War, there was controversy among its members concerning the issue of Heine's place in Germany's literary canon. As a result there was a feeble centenary celebration in his native Düsseldorf in 1899 and protests against a statue (pp.381–2). The Schillerstiftung became Nazified and was closed down in 1945.
168. See, for example, Pulzer, *Rise of Political Anti-Semitism* p.248; Wistrich, *Between Redemption and Perdition*, p.201; and Vital, *People Apart*, p.270. In many of these university *Burschenschaften*, duelling was a prominent activity, and a scar on the face was therefore a visible sign of social acceptance into German culture, now denied to the Jewish students (see Gilman, *The Jew's Body*, pp.181–3).
169. *CI*, 1880, p.200. See also Todd M. Endelman, 'Memories of Jewishness: Jewish Converts and Their Jewish Pasts', in Elisheva Carlebach, John M. Efron and David N. Myers (eds), *Jewish History and Jewish Memory: Essays in Honour of Yosef Hayim Yerushalmi* (Hanover, MD, and London: Brandeis University Press, 1998), pp.311–29.
170. *CI*, 1880, p.238. The 1870s was also the decade of the struggle between the Catholic Church and the State, the *Kulturkampf*: see Wolfgang Altgeld, 'German Catholics', in Rainer Liedtke and Stephen Wendehorst (eds), *The Emancipation of Catholics, Jews and Protestants: Minorities and the Nation State in Nineteenth-Century Europe* (Manchester and New York: Manchester University Press, 1999), pp.100–21.
171. See Ragins, *Jewish Responses to Anti-Semitism in Germany* pp.28–35. On Lazarus's lecture, see also Gilman, *Jewish Self-Hatred*, pp.219–21.
172. Cited in Ragins, *Jewish Responses to Anti-Semitism in Germany* p.33.
173. See Pulzer, *Rise of Political Anti-Semitism*, p.98; Ragins, *Jewish Response to Anti-Semitism in Germany*, p.38.
174. See Pulzer, *Rise of Political Anti-Semitism*, pp.125–8; Wistrich, *The Jews of Vienna*, pp.224–6.
175. Cited in Pulzer, *Rise of Political Anti-Semitism*, p.144; see also pp.145–55, 161–2; Carl E. Schorske, *Fin-de-Siècle Vienna: Politics and Culture* (Cambridge: Cambridge University Press, 1981), pp.120–33: Schönerer 'elevated anti-Semitism into a major disruptive force in Austrian political life' (p.120); Wistrich, *The Jews of Vienna*, pp.206–19.
176. Cited in Pulzer, *Rise of Political Anti-Semitism* p.245. One of those expelled was Herzl.
177. Cited in Wistrich, *The Jews of Vienna*, p.272.
178. See ibid., pp.238–69.
179. Ibid., p.289; see also pp.270–309; and Walter R. Weitzmann, 'The Politics of the Viennese Jewish Community, 1890-1914', in Ivar Oxaal, Michael Pollak and Gerhard Botz (eds), *Jews, Antisemitism and Culture in Vienna* (London and New York: Routledge & Kegan Paul, 1987), pp.127–30.
180. Wistrich, *The Jews of Vienna*, p.283.
181. On the Union, see Wistrich, *The Jews of Vienna*, Chapter 10. The Union had no nationalist aspirations and there was cooperation with the Kultusgemeinde.
182. On these early incidents, see also Catalan, *La Comunità ebraica di Trieste*, pp.254, 292.

183. Elizabeth Schächter, *Origin and Identity: Essays on Svevo and Trieste* (Leeds: Northern Universities Press, 2000), pp.59–60.
184. See Tullia Catalan, 'Società e sionismo a Trieste fra XIX e XX secolo', in Giacomo Todeschini and Pier Cesare Ioly Zorattini (eds), *Il mondo ebraico: gli ebrei tra Italia nord-orientale e Impero asburgico dal Medioevo all'Età contemporanea* (Pordenone: Studio Tesi, 1991), p.464.
185. On the political repercussions of this incident, see John Gatt-Rutter, *Italo Svevo: A Double Life* (Oxford: Clarendon, 1988), pp.56–7.
186. Lindemann, *Anti-Semitism before the Holocaust*, p.53; Wistrich, *Longest Hatred*, p.54. See also Maccoby, *Antisemitism and Modernity*, pp.52–3, and S.N. Eisenstadt, *Jewish Civilization: The Jewish Historical Experience in a Comparative Perspective* (Albany, NY: State University of New York Press, 1992), pp.106–7.
187. Cited in Lindemann, *Anti-Semitism before the Holocaust*, p.53.
188. Frederic Raphael, *The Necessity of Anti-Semitism* (Southampton: University of Southampton, Central Printing Unit, 1989), p.7. This is the text of the Parkes Twenty-Fifth Anniversary Lecture. See also Wistrich, *Between Redemption and Perdition*, p.198, and Michael A. Meyer, *Judaism within Modernity: Essays on Jewish History and Religion* (Detroit, MI: Wayne State University Press, 2001), p.103: 'Jews entered German society under the aegis of Enlightenment rationality and universalism and remained true to these principles even when abandoned by a society in quest of its unique German soul.'
189. See Pulzer, *Rise of Political Anti-Semitism*, pp.102–19; Niewyk, 'Solving the "Jewish Problem"', pp.354–68. In his assessment of these late-nineteenth-century anti-Semites, Niewyk asserts: 'hence the seeds of genocide were planted' (p.368).
190. See Arnold Paucker, 'The Jewish Defense against Antisemitism in Germany, 1893–1933', in Reinharz (ed.), *Living with Antisemitism*, pp.104–32; Ragins, *Jewish Responses to Anti-Semitism in Germany*, pp.51–61; Jehuda Reinharz, *Fatherland or Promised Land: The Dilemma of the German Jew, 1893–1914* (Ann Arbor, MI: University of Michigan Press, 1975), pp.48–70; Schorsch, *Jewish Reactions to German Anti-Semitism*, pp.12–14; and Vital, *People Apart*, pp.272–3. Many aspects of the Jewish body were perceived to be different, and these included the notion that flat feet were a distinct racial feature which made Jews unfit for military service. The Centralverein enlisted the expertise of an orthopaedic surgeon on this matter, and in 1897 a history of *Die Juden als Soldaten* (Jews as Soldiers) was published in Berlin in order to chronicle their presence in the army throughout the nineteenth century. See Paucker, 'Jewish Defense against Antisemitism', p.116, and Gilman, *The Jew's Body*, Chapter 2, 'The Jewish Foot'.
191. See Ragins, *Jewish Responses to Anti-Semitism in Germany*, pp.91–102.
192. Vital, *A People Apart*, pp.268–9. See also Endelman, 'Conversion as a Response to Antisemitism', pp.77–83.
193. Pierre Birnbaum, 'In the Academic Sphere: The Cases of Emile Durkheim and Georg Simmel', in Michael Brenner, Vicki Caron and Uri R. Kaufmann (eds), *Jewish Emancipation Reconsidered: The French and German Models* (Leo Baeck Institute, London: Mohr Siebeck, 2003), pp.171–95.
194. Marvin Lowenthal (ed. and trans.), *The Diaries of Theodor Herzl* (New York: Dial Press, 1956), p.69 (20 September 1895).
195. See Kertzer, *Unholy War*, pp.192–5. See also Herzl's meeting with the anti-Semitic papal nuncio in Vienna, Agliardi, on 19 May 1896, in Lowenthal (ed. and trans.), *Diaries of Theodor Herzl*, pp.132–3.
196. Cited in Gilman, *Freud, Race and Gender*, p.16. 'For the young Freud, then, being Jewish meant being seen as different, as diseased, as culturally incomplete' (ibid.). See also, for example, Freud's letters to his wife, Martha Bernays, in Ernst L. Freud (ed.), *Letters of Sigmund Freud 1873–1939* (London: Hogarth Press, 1961), pp.93–4, 143; and Peter Gay, *Freud: A Life for Our Time* (London and Melbourne: Dent, 1988), pp.11–12.
197. *CI*, 1901, p.26. On Lueger, see, for example, Wistrich, *The Jews of Vienna*, pp.219–59; by the same author, *Longest Hatred*, pp.63–5: Lueger 'was the first political role model for the young Adolf Hitler' (p.63); Pulzer, *Rise of Political Anti-Semitism*, pp.156–83; Steven Beller, *Vienna and the Jews, 1867–1938: A Cultural History* (Cambridge and New York: Cambridge University Press, 1989), pp.193–200; Frederic V. Grunfeld, *Prophets without Honour: A Background to Freud, Kafka, Einstein and Their World* (New York: Holt, Rinehart & Winston, 1979), p.54; Weitzmann in Oxaal, Pollak and Botz (eds), *Jews, Antisemitism and Culture in Vienna*, pp.135–7; Schorske, *Fin-de-Siècle Vienna*, pp.133–46.
198. Arthur Schnitzler, *My Youth in Vienna*, translated by Catherine Hutter (London: Weidenfeld & Nicolson, 1971), pp.6–7. In his only novel, *Der Weg ins Freie* (Road to the Open, 1908), most of the characters are Jewish, and they articulate varied responses to their dilemma, from conversion to Zionism. On Schnitzler's novel, see, for example, Wistrich, *The Jews of Vienna*, Chapter 17.

See also Lowenthal (ed. and trans.), *Diaries of Theodor Herzl*, p.56, 8 July 1895: 'S[chiff] related that his brother-in-law, upon leaving the train at Kitzbühel, had been insulted by an anti-Semite ... There are a thousand such incidents every day.'
199. See Gay, *Freud*, p.139. See also Beller, *Vienna and the Jews*, pp.196–7; and George Clare, *Last Waltz in Vienna: The Destruction of a Family 1842–1942* (London: Macmillan, 1981), pp.21–3.
200. See Beller, *Vienna and the Jews*, p.205.
201. See Wistrich, *The Jews of Vienna*, p.299.
202. See Anna Millo, 'Elites politiche ed elites economiche ebraiche a Trieste alla fine del XIX secolo', in Todeschini and Zorattini (eds), *Il mondo ebraico*, p.397.
203. See, for example, Wistrich, *The Jews of Vienna*, pp.207–8.
204. Cited in Wistrich, *The Jews of Vienna*, p.294. See also pp.292–6, which contain extended extracts of Bloch's speeches.
205. Ibid., pp.297–301.
206. See Toury, 'Defense Activities', pp.167–92; Wistrich, *The Jews of Vienna*, pp.335–43.
207. Cited in Ellen Ginzburg Migliorino, 'L'Antisemitismo e la comunità ebraica a Trieste nei primi anni del Novecento', in Todeschini and Zorattini (eds), *Il mondo ebraico*, p.438.
208. See Catalan, *La comunità ebraica di Trieste*, Chapter 11; Ginzburg Migliorino, 'L'Antisemitismo e la comunità ebraica a Trieste', pp.435–41.
209. See, for example, Beller, *Vienna and the Jews*, pp.200–1; Pulzer, *Rise of Political Anti-Semitism*, pp.122–31, 185–228: 'Nationalism had, by the beginning of the twentieth century, become the main driving force behind anti-Semitism' (p.221); Wistrich, *The Jews of Vienna*, pp.301–2, 313–14, 325–6: 'European liberalism ... the spiritual asylum of the Jews, their protective haven ... was everywhere surrendering ... to the siren-call of nationalism' (p.301).
210. Christian Wiese, 'Modern Antisemitism and Jewish Reponses in Germany and France, 1880–1914', in Brenner, Caron and Kaufmann (eds), *Jewish Emancipation Reconsidered*, p.131. See also David Feldman, 'Was Modernity Good for the Jews?', in Bryan Cheyette and Laura Marcus (eds), *Modernity, Culture and 'the Jew'* (Cambridge: Polity Press, 1998), p.179.
211. Clark, *Modern Italy*, p.100; see also pp.69–80, 92–104, 112–17; Nicholas Doumanis, *Italy* (London: Arnold, 2001), pp.113–21.
212. See Clark, *Modern Italy*, p.101.
213. Maifreda, *Gli ebrei e l'economia milanese*, pp.279–80.
214. Ibid., p.281.
215. *Il Popolo Romano*, 18 May 1891, cited in Caviglia, *L'identità salvata* p.72.
216. Alessandro Levi, *Ricordi della vita e dei tempi di Ernesto Nathan* (Florence: La Nuova Italia, 1927), pp.209–14.
217. Paola Carlucci, *Il giovane Sonnino fra cultura e politica, 1847–1886* (Rome: Archivio Guido Izzi, 2002), pp.41–2; see also Capuzzo, *Gli ebrei italiani*, pp.91–2. Sonnino's father, Isacco, converted on his marriage in 1843.
218. See *IS*, 1903, p.75; *VI*, 1903, p.371; Canepa, 'Cattolici ed ebrei nell'Italia liberale', pp.67–8. There had been several outbreaks of anti-Semitic violence in Mantua: in 1824, 1842, 1874, and after the national elections in 1913. In other words, Bini's hatred of the Jews sprang from fertile ground.
219. Enzo Levi, *Memorie di una vita*, p.12.
220. Arturo Carlo Jemolo, *Anni di prova* (Verona: Pozza, 1969), p.95.
221. Cesare Lombroso, *L'antisemitismo e le scienze moderne* (Turin and Rome: Roux, 1894), pp.9, 108, 109. Lombroso is not wholly negative, as there is also a chapter on Jewish genius and modernity. See also David Forgacs, 'Building the Body of the Nation: Lombroso's *L'antisemitismo* and Fin-de-Siècle Italy', in Bryan Cheyette and Nadia Valman (eds), *The Image of the Jew in European Liberal Culture, 1789–1914* (London: Vallentine Mitchell, 2004), pp.96–110; Toscano, *Ebraismo e antisemitismo*, pp.33–8; Delia Frigessi, 'Cattaneo, Lombroso e la questione ebraica', in Burgio (ed.), *Nel nome della razza*, pp.247–64.
222. *VI*, 1894, p.63; *CI*, 1894, pp.200–2. See also Frigessi, 'Cattaneo, Lombroso e la questione ebraica', p.262. She notes that within a few years, Lombroso modified his views to the extent that he was invited to become honorary president of the Turin Zionist association (p.259).
223. Guglielmo Ferrero, *L'Europa giovane: studi e viaggi nei paesi del Nord* (Milan: Treves, 1897), pp.352–4, 362–8, 385–6.
224. Alberto Cavaglion, *Felice Momigliano (1866–1924): una biografia* (Bologna: Il Mulino, 1988), p.63. Cavaglion suggests (p.64) that James Joyce drew on Ferrero for the creation of the character of Bloom in *Ulysses*.
225. *CI*, 1899, pp.122–6, 148–52.
226. Pierre Birnbaum, *Anti-Semitism in France: A Political History from Léon Blum to the Present* (Oxford: Blackwell, 1992), p.1. See also Vital, *People Apart*, p.547.

227. Cited in Pierre Birnbaum, 'Les Juifs et l'Affaire', in Jean-Jacques Becker and Annette Wieviorka (eds), *Les Juifs de France de la Révolution française à nos jours* (Paris: Editions Liana Levi, 1998), p.82. Barrès, a novelist, journalist and nationalist politician, was a leading anti-Dreyfusard.
228. See Burns, *France and the Dreyfus Affair*, pp.130–1. These messages were published in book form, 'The Henry Monument', and filled more than 700 pages.
229. See Katz, *From Prejudice to Destruction*, p.297.
230. Birnbaum, *The Jews of the Republic*, p.146.
231. Burns, *France and the Dreyfus Affair*, p.143. See also James Wald, 'Periodicals and Periodicity', in Simon Eliot and Jonathan Rose (eds), *A Companion to the History of the Book* (Oxford: Blackwell, 2007), pp.421–33: 'Periodicals turned the Dreyfus case into "The Affair" that affirmed the power of the press and public intellectuals' (p.427).
232. Vital, *People Apart*, p.549.
233. Cited in Burns, *France and the Dreyfus Affair*, p.160.
234. On the reaction of French Jewry to the Dreyfus Affair, see, for example, Wiese, 'Modern Antisemitism and Jewish Reponses', pp.142–53; and Aron Rodrigue, 'Rearticulations of French Jewish Identities after the Dreyfus Affair', *Jewish Social Studies: History, Culture, and Society*, new series, 2 (Fall 1996), pp.3–4.
235. See *VI*, 1897, p.406: 'The Italian press, it has to be said, has done its duty … and apart from a few retrograde journals, it has sided in favour of the poor condemned man.' See also, for example, Maurizio Raspi (ed.), *L'Affaire Dreyfus in Italia* (Pisa: ETS Editrice, 1991), and Gian-Carlo Menichelli, 'La reception de l'Affaire en Italie', in Michel Drouin (ed.), *L'Affaire Dreyfus de A à Z* (Paris: Flammarion, 1994). This latter account contains some inaccuracies with regard to *Civiltà Cattolica*.
236. See Burns, *France and the Dreyfus Affair*, p.151.
237. See *L'Osservatore Romano*, 20 and 25 January 1898: 'the masonic and Judaic papers who defend Dreyfus and Zola accuse us of inciting hatred against the Jews'. See also Canepa, 'Cattolici ed ebrei nell'Italia liberale', pp.101–4; Taradel and Raggi, *La segregazione amichevole*, p.41; John Cornwell, *Hitler's Pope: The Secret History of Pius XII* (London: Viking, 1999), p.24. The role of the Church in the Dreyfus Affair, particularly the contributions of *La Croix*, precipitated the Law of Separation of the Church and State in 1905. Thousands of religious schools were closed, and France broke off diplomatic relations with the Vatican (see Burns, *France and the Dreyfus Affair*, p.171).
238. *VI*, 1898, pp.38–40, which gives a complete list; Italian university students sent Zola telegrams (*VI*, 1898, p.26); *CI*, 1902, p.132 on Zola as 'a hero of truth and justice … the interpreter of the cry of pain of the oppressed'. See also Scipio Sighele's article in *La Tribuna*, 15 February 1898, in Raspi (ed.), *L'Affaire Dreyfus in Italia*, pp.66–71.
239. See, for example, *VI*, 1897, p.353; 1898, pp.26–7; 1899, pp.177–9; 1906, p.434.
240. *CI*, 1901, pp.7–9. Bernard Lazare, French anarchist, writer, Jewish nationalist and one of the first Dreyfusards, gave a divergent interpretation of the work: he saw in Dreyfus's 'fatalistic resignation' the suffering of the Russian and Romanian Jews, the Algerian Jews 'beaten and pillaged' (see Burns, *France and the Dreyfus Affair*, p.170). In praise of Lazare's part in the Affair, see *CI*, 1896, pp.147–9. See also *CI*, 1899, pp.57–61, Dante Lattes on 'The Consequences of the Dreyfus Affair': the moral lesson to be drawn for Jews was never to forget their Jewishness; patriotism should not entail the sacrifice of one's religion and ideals; *CI*, 1899, pp.175–7 on the case of a new conscript to the French army, Gaston Bernard, who was brutalized by his superiors because he was a Jew, tarnished with the name of the traitor Dreyfus, with the result that within three weeks he was dead.
241. Clark, *Modern Italy*, p.150. On Giolitti, see pp.136–50.
242. Ibid., p.173; see also pp.150–6, 174–5; Doumanis, *Italy*, pp.121–31; Alexander De Grand, *The Italian Nationalist Association and the Rise of Fascism in Italy* (Lincoln, NE, and London: University of Nebraska Press, 1978), pp.10–40.
243. See Clark, *Modern Italy*, p.155; De Grand, *Italian Nationalist Association*, p.47; Doumanis, *Italy*, pp.123–8.
244. ACDEC, Fondo Sullam, 1.2.2.2.2, Convegni FSI, B.5, file 45, *Atti del IV Convegno Sionnistico Italiano* (Modena: Tipo-Litografia Modenese, 1904), pp.21–3. Ascoli's conference paper was published as a pamphlet, *L'Antisemitismo in Italia, cause e rimedi* (1904), by the Zionist journal *L'Idea Sionnista*.
245. *CI*, 1913, pp.189–90. See also *SI*, 28 (1911), on fights between Christian and Jewish boys in the vicinity of the Rome ghetto when regularly someone ended up in hospital; *VI*, 1912, pp.189–90; Caviglia, *L'identità salvata* pp.4–5.
246. Ibid., p.4.
247. Cited in Bruno Di Porto, 'Dopo il Risorgimento, al varco del '900. Appendice: Felice Momigliano ad Arcangelo Ghislieri. Lettere inedite', *RMI*, 47, 7–12 (1981) p.58.
248. *CI*, 15 December 1911. Until 1914, *L'Idea Nazionale* was independent of the ANI. The association's

structure comprised a twenty-one-member central committee and an executive junta which conducted the day-to-day business (see De Grand, *Italian Nationalist Association* p.26).
249. *CI*, 1911, pp.147–8. Both of Coppola's articles were published in *L'Idea Nazionale* on 16 and 30 November 1911, the former also in *Action Française*. See also Tullia Catalan, 'L'antisemitismo nazionalista italiano visto da un ebreo triestino: Carlo Morpurgo ed il "caso Coppola"', *Qualestoria*, 1–2 (1994), pp.95–118; Caviglia, *L'identità salvata* pp.140–3, and Toscano, *Ebraismo e antisemitismo*, pp.41–7.
250. See De Grand, *Italian Nationalist Association*, p.36.
251. *CI*, 15 August 1913. Paolo Orano (1875–1945) was one of the architects of the Racial Laws of 1938 in that his *Gli Ebrei in Italia* (1937) provided Mussolini with many of the political premises on which to base them. In the 1930s, Orano became professor of fascist history and doctrine at the University of Perugia.
252. See Toscano, *Ebraismo e antisemitismo*, p.47.
253. See Caviglia, *L'identità salvata* pp.145–6.
254. See *CI*, 15 April 1912; *CI*, 15 October 1912; *CI*, 15 May 1915.
255. See Zorzi's preface to Canepa, 'Cattolici ed ebrei nell'Italia liberale', pp.ix–x.
256. Cited in Canepa, 'Cattolici ed ebrei nell'Italia liberale', p.70.
257. Ibid., p.72.
258. Feldman, 'Was Modernity Good for the Jews?', p.179.
259. Ibid., p.183. See also David Vital, *Zionism: The Crucial Phase* (Oxford: Clarendon Press, 1987), p.104: 'Jews were not considered a *threat*. The English upper classes felt superior in every respect.' On the ongoing historiographical debate on Anglo-Jewry and anti-Semitism, see, for example, David Cesarani, 'British Jews', in Liedtke and Wendehorst (eds), *Emancipation of Catholics, Jews and Protestants*, pp.33–55, and Cheyette and Valman (eds), *Image of the Jew in European Liberal Culture*, Introduction, pp.2–4.
260. See Pulzer, *Rise of Political Anti-Semitism*, p.193. Böckel and Ahlwardt withdrew from politics; Stöcker died in 1909; two other prominent proponents died in 1910 and 1911.
261. See Stanislawski, *Zionism and the Fin de Siècle*, pp.11–12.
262. See Patrick Cabanel and Chantal Bordes-Benayoun (eds), *Un modèle d'intégration: juifs et israélites en France et en Europe (XIX–XX siècles)* (Paris: Berg, 2004), p.11; Shulamit Volkov, 'Readjusting Cultural Codes: Reflections on Anti-Semitism and Anti-Zionism', in Herf (ed.), *Anti-Semitism and Anti-Zionism*, p.47. Volkov's reference is to Paul W. Massing's *Rehearsal for Destruction: A Study of Political Anti-Semitism in Imperial Germany* (1949).
263. See Cavaglion, *ebrei senza saperlo*, p.101.
264. Dreyfus's words from his first diary entry of 14 April 1895, cited in Burns, *France and the Dreyfus Affair*, p.60.
265. Penslar, 'Anti-Semites on Zionism', p.16; Stansilawski, *Zionism and the Fin de Siècle*, p.12.
266. Volkov, 'Readjusting Cultural Codes', p.45.
267. Ibid., p.46; see also Wistrich, *Between Redemption and Perdition*, p.195.
268. Wistrich, *Between Redemption and Perdition*, p.204.

5

'We are a people – one people'

'The distinctive nationality of Jews neither can, will, nor must be destroyed.'[1]

The Russian pogroms of 1881, the consequence of the assassination of Tsar Alexander II, precipitated a turning point in modern Jewish history, bringing about 'a revolutionary change in Jewish politics'.[2] Jonathan Frankel contends that the responses from Jews worldwide were without precedent. There was overwhelming support for the victims, including the large influx of Jewish refugees from the Ukraine flooding into western Europe. Innovative intellectual manifestations included Leo Pinsker's proto-Zionist pamphlet, *Autoemancipation: An Appeal to His People by a Russian Jew* (published in German in 1882); the Hovevei Zion (Lovers of Zion) movement, founded in Russia in 1882, which by 1889 had 138 societies throughout Europe; and the Viennese Zionist student group, Kadimah (Forward) also founded in 1882, by newcomers from eastern Europe, with the exception of its leader, Nathan Birnbaum (1864–1937), who popularized the terms *Zionismus* and *zionistisch*.[3] Similar student bodies were established in Berlin and Paris in the early 1890s; membership comprised mostly Russian and Polish Jews.[4] Thus Herzl's Zionist movement was predominately east European in origin. It will be argued that in western Europe, political Zionist groups, wherever formed, were the initiative of Jews from eastern Europe, with the corollary that philanthropic Zionism was the prevailing ideology of emancipated Jewry.[5] Two other crucial but perhaps obvious points to make: political Zionism achieved its central aim with the foundation of the State of Israel in 1948; it was not a movement of the masses in the West. The leaders, from both East and West, were predominantly middle class and professional.[6] From the First Congress, a wide spectrum of ideological positions, conflicting factions and divisions of opinion emerged, reflecting, as David Vital so succinctly states, 'the fissiparity and heterogeneity of the Jewish people'.[7] These include, apart from Herzl's political and secular Zionism, cultural, practical, religious and socialist Zionism.

Zionism was a nineteenth-century nationalist movement and, as such, it had to invent appropriate myths and leaders. One 'foundation myth', perpetuated by Herzl and Nordau was that the Dreyfus Affair had transformed them into Zionists. However, it is the case that anti-Semitism forced them both to confront their Jewish identity and its significance.[8]

Herzl, as a young man, had 'fantasies of personal grandeur' – he confided to his diary that he wished to be a Prussian aristocrat[9] – and his initial, spectacular solution to the Jewish question was a mass baptism of the Jews in Vienna's St Stephen's Cathedral, orchestrated by him in agreement with the pope.[10] These qualities of theatricality and self-image were effectively harnessed to the Zionist cause. Herzl's impressive physical appearance (with his black beard he looked like a Hebrew prophet) had a powerful effect on those who encountered him. Journeying to Constantinople in June 1896, the train stopped at Sofia, where crowds thronged the platform to greet Herzl – 'I was hailed as Leader, as the Heart of Israel' – [11] and after a successful meeting with the immigrant Jews of London's East End in July of the same year, Herzl noted in his diary: 'I saw and heard my legend being made.'[12] When he rose to address the first Zionist Congress in 1897, a contemporary account recalls: 'That is no longer the elegant Dr Herzl of Vienna, it is a royal descendant of David arisen from the grave ... was it not a miracle that took place here? ... it was as if the Messiah, son of David, stood before us. A powerful desire seized me to shout through this tempestuous sea of joy: "Yechi Hamelech! Long live the King."'[13] In 1903, Herzl travelled to Russia to plead the cause of the Jews after the Kishinev atrocities; everywhere he stopped, people waited for him as for their deliverer. Herzl was particularly moved by the overwhelming ovations he was accorded in the Polish city of Vilna,[14] where police records state that he was 'received as a king'.[15] To perpetuate and commemorate the regal representation of Herzl in the minds of his followers, the artist Ephraim Moses Lilien (1874–1925) created a Zionist iconography with the figure of Herzl at its centre: the famous photograph of 1897 has Herzl looking like a prophet gazing at the Promised Land (this and other images were reproduced many times in a variety of formats as part of Zionist propaganda).[16] In Israel Zangwill's words, 'Herzl was the first Jewish statesman since the destruction of Jerusalem';[17] he was *primus inter pares*, negotiating with princes, popes and politicians. Apart from the political effect of his premature death at the age of 44 in 1904, the emotional impact was such that the president of the Italian Zionist Federation, for example, instructed his members to observe a one-year period of mourning and send letters of condolence to the family of *Il Grande Estinto*.[18] In 1913, at the Eleventh Congress held in Vienna, 10,000 people visited his graveside, 'the most profound Zionist demonstration in Europe before the First World War'.[19]

The careful cultivation of Herzl's image was part of a central goal of Zionism: the transformation of the ghetto and the bourgeois Jew; the regeneration of an oppressed, weak group on the one hand and complacent capitalists on the other into virile, heroic, strong men. The prime promoter of the new Zionist Jew was Max Nordau, Herzl's closest confidant.[20] Nordau coined the phrase *Muskeljudentum* (muscular Jewry) in his address to the Second Congress, and encouraged the establishment of Zionist sporting, gymnastics and hiking clubs which were named after legendary Jewish military heroes such as Bar Kochba and the Maccabees. This concept of masculinity was intended to instil a sense of pride and assertiveness in Jewish national identity.[21] It had to do with transforming the way Jews perceived themselves and projecting a positive image to counter the anti-Semitic stereotypes. In *The Jewish State,* Herzl stressed the importance of physical labour, and in his diary he wrote: 'I believe that a race of wonderful Jews will grow from the earth.'²² When he visited Palestine in 1898, among those he met were Jews on horseback and the sight of 'those fleet, daring horsemen' moved him to tears, 'proof that our young clothes-peddlers can be thus transformed'.²³ Herzl and Nordau's pursuit of regeneration, of *Bildung*, links back to the early debates on the emancipation of the Jews and Moses Mendelssohn's exhortations on moral and educational amelioration.²⁴

Another fundamental objective nurtured by the Zionist movement was a sense of solidarity and unity: 'the creation of the Jewish people as a national–cultural entity'.²⁵ At the First Congress, much was made of the firm friendship between Herzl and Nordau: they were often photographed together (Nordau with his white beard looked like an ancient sage) and thus they appeared as a forceful and united presence. Nordau, in his impressive opening speech, emphasized the common fate shared by the Jews: wherever they lived they suffered from physical or moral distress. In emancipated western Europe they experienced psychological anguish; in eastern Europe they endured persecution. He also praised the *Ostjuden*, who in their retention of traditional mores represented Judaism in all its authenticity.²⁶ Zionist ideology thus did much to construct a new image of eastern European Jewry in the eyes of their western counterparts. Among the 200 delegates, there were many strains of Jewry: orthodox, reform, secular, liberal, socialist and bourgeois. They were brought together in a spirit of fraternity through songs and symbols and, as they entered the congress building in 1897, they passed beneath the Zionist flag with a Star of David: 'with a flag you can lead men where you will – even into the Promised Land. Men will live and die for a flag.'²⁷ Another aspect that unified the movement and promoted a national spirit was the restoration of Hebrew as the language of the future Jewish State. This had not been part of Herzl's original plan: in *The Jewish State* he proposed a linguistic federation on the Swiss model; no one knew Hebrew well enough for it to be a viable option, and certainly not Yiddish or *Judendeutsch*, 'those miserable stunted jargons, those Ghetto languages'.²⁸ There were heated discussions on the *Kulturfrage* (the question of culture) at the Congresses, but at the outset in Basle in 1897 it was agreed to set up a committee for Hebrew literature, and by the 1911 Congress entire debates were conducted in Hebrew.²⁹

'At Basel I founded the Jewish State', wrote Herzl in his diary, and this statement formed part of the foundation myths of Zionism.³⁰ For the first time since Israel was exiled from its territory, noted one of the delegates, there had been a public dialogue about a Jewish homeland.³¹ East European Jews in their thousands were in favour – they had predominated in Basle, especially the Russians – and many were ready to emigrate.³² By the time of the Second Congress, there were 913 Zionist associations worldwide, 373 of which were in Russia and 250 in Austria-Hungary; by 1903 this number had risen to 1,000.³³ What were the views of the liberal, assimilated western European Jews? Herzl had failed to win over the wealthy philanthropists, as his many diary entries of 1896 reveal: 'the prosperous Jews are all against me'.³⁴ They were content to establish their own colonies in Palestine and elsewhere, but would not agree to finance Herzl's project. Herzl despised philanthropy, as he made clear in his discussion with Baron de Hirsch: 'You breed beggars … Philanthropy, it is apparent, debases the character of our people.'³⁵ Among their many objections, the most important, he noted, was patriotism, whether from the English or the French Jews. In 1895, he met the chief rabbi of France, Zadoc Kahn, and other leading Jews, five times. They 'harped on' their French nationality: 'As a body the French Jews are hostile to the matter ... Becker ... reeks of books and conventional patriotism.'[36] In May 1896, after a meeting between Nordau, Kahn and Baron Edmond de Rothschild, Herzl noted in his diary that the Baron refused to cooperate: 'what I am doing he considers dangerous, because I render the patriotism of the Jews suspect'.[37] Michael Berkowitz argues that Zionism 'invented a way for Jews to be good Zionists ... and good Germans, Austrians or Englishmen, apparently without conflict'.[38] Historical evidence suggests the contrary, raising the vexed question of patriotism and accusations of dual loyalties.

Zionist ideology radically rejected the assimilationist ideas held by the majority of western European Jews, claiming that racial and political anti-Semitism demonstrated the failure of Emancipation,[39] thus undermining the very basis on which they conducted their lives as citizens of the Jewish faith of the various nations in which they resided. The responses Herzl received in the 1890s reflect those which Pinsker encountered when he travelled to the West in 1882 in order to publicize his pamphlet, *Autoemancipation*. In Vienna, the prominent rabbi Adolf Jellinek told him that were he to agree with the Russian, he would have to repudiate everything the Jews had achieved since emancipation: 'We are at home in Europe ... We are Germans, Frenchmen, Englishmen ... down to the marrow of our bones.' In Bonn, it was explained to him that Jews 'had been fully integrated into civil society [*völlig eingebürgert*] and duly shared the national consciousness'.[40]

THE FIRST ZIONIST CONGRESS

Reactions to the announcement of the First Zionist Congress echoed these opinions. In June 1897, the English Hovevei Zion, whose leader, Colonel Goldsmid, had initially welcomed Herzl – 'we shall work for the liberation of Israel', he had declared in November 1895 – formally dissociated itself from the Congress.[41] In Austria, Dr Moritz Güdemann, chief rabbi of Vienna, published a violently anti-Zionist tract; Zadoc Kahn told Herzl his position was extremely difficult, as rabbis in France were government officials.[42] There were protests from the Jewish community of Munich, and on 11 June 1897 the executive committee of the German rabbinate – the *Protestrabbiner*, as Herzl dubbed them – publicly condemned the initiative as the dangerous work of fanatics, in the pages of the *Allgemeine Zeitung des Judentums*. They also stated that 'we comprise a separate community solely with regard to *religion*. Regarding nationality, we feel totally at one with our fellow Germans', striving towards the goals 'of our dear fatherland with an enthusiasm equalling theirs ... Thus will be demonstrated to the entire world that *German Jewry* has nothing in common with the intentions of Zionism.'[43] As a result of this intense opposition, the Congress was moved from Munich to Basle. Herzl noted in his diary: 'I gladly availed myself of the miserable patriotic protests of the Munich communal chieftains.'[44] The Centralverein, which represented the majority of German Jews, also denounced Herzl as a dangerous utopian who sought to jeopardize the hard-won emancipation of the Jews.[45] The *Neue Freie Presse,* the influential daily newspaper published in Vienna from 1864, for which Herzl was literary editor and political correspondent, completely ignored the Congress and never printed one word on the Zionist movement. The two publisher/proprietors, Eduard Bacher and Moritz Benedikt, both assimilated Jews, had tried unsuccessfully to prevent Herzl from bringing out *The Jewish State* the year before and to close the Zionist weekly, *Die Welt,* which Herzl had established in June 1897.[46] Paradoxically, since the *Neue Freie Presse* was an internationally renowned paper, it gave Herzl diplomatic and political status and therefore indirectly supported the Zionist cause.[47] In July 1897, the *Jewish Chronicle* carried two hostile articles, one entitled 'The Proposed "Zionist" Congress', although subsequent reports were more positive.[48]

France's Jewish community sent twelve delegates. However, several weeks later, an article appeared in the *Univers israélite* which embodied the opinion of assimilated Jews: 'great sympathy and support for the colonisation of Palestine for those who have no country, but we French Jews have our country and we intend to keep it' (*Mais nous, Israélites français, nous avons une patrie et nous entendons la garder*).[49] Italy sent not one delegate. Instead, in September 1897, a letter was addressed to the honourable members of the Zionist Congress in Basle, purporting to be an approved statement agreed upon by the Italian Jewish communities, in which they acknowledged the necessity of a safe haven for the persecuted Jews of eastern Europe as a praiseworthy and humanitarian project. They were convinced that the vast majority (*grandissima maggioranza*) of their co-religionists would proudly refuse to renounce their present *patria*. They, in their turn, expressed 'their indestructible devotion to a sole country, which is Italy, for whose happiness they intend to direct all their efforts ... ready to shed their blood on the battlefields ... They are convinced that no religious faith ... should incur anti-national aspirations.'[50] In Francesco Del Canuto's official history of the Zionist movement in Italy, no mention is made of the two letters from the secretaries of the Florence and Venice communities, dated 4 and 8 October 1897 respectively, which disclose that neither had been consulted on this matter; had they been, they would not have assented.[51] The originator of the document was the Jewish community of Casale Monferrato, the small town in Piedmont where *Il Vessillo Israelitico* was published by their chief rabbi, Cavaliere Flaminio Servi, whose opinion no doubt carried weight with the community's leaders. Moreover, Piedmontese Jews felt an especial devotion to Italy. In September 1897, Servi published a derisory account of the 'so-called Zionist Congress', recalling the *Jewish Chronicle*'s initial stance. The idea of a Jewish State was utopian, a reiteration of the Centralverein's judgement and that of the *Univers israélite*.[52] He also mentioned the dissent from elsewhere, adding that Italians did not need to protest as 'no Italian attended (and this fact is itself significant)'. He grudgingly accepted that the idea of helping the persecuted Jews of Russia and Romania to find a refuge in Palestine was admirable, but fraught with problems. His conclusion was one of alarm: 'anti-semitism has created Zionism; the infamous Drumont must be gratified to hear that Jews have no *patria* and are strangers everywhere, not citizens' (*Il Vessillo Israelitico* [*VI*], 1897, pp.286–9).

Thus the initial reactions from leading figures of west European Jewry to the

First Zionist Congress's programme – 'the creation of a home [*Heimstätte*] for the Jewish people in Palestine … The organizing and unifying of all Jewry … The strengthening of Jewish national feeling and consciousness',[53]– were compounded of misgivings and fear; rejection of the political perspective, but acceptance of the humanitarian dimension. They felt compelled to emphasize their patriotism and devotion to their respective father/motherlands in order to distance themselves from the notion of a supra-Jewish nationality. And yet, despite these reservations, Zionist organizations were established, and within each of them conflicts and tensions arose between the adherents of political and philanthropic Zionism.

ZIONISM IN WESTERN EUROPE

Before focusing on Zionism in Italy, a brief account of its development in western Europe will be given. Austria was the centre of the World Zionist Organization (WZO) and its official publication *Die Welt,* until Herzl's death in 1904. *The Jewish State* elicited hostile reviews from the West and the political establishment, but from the East it ignited an overwhelming fervour: adherents rushed to Vienna to meet Herzl, and in the shtetls of the Pale of Settlement, rumours spread that the Messiah had arrived, as David Ben-Gurion, the first prime minister of Israel (1948–63), then a 10-year-old boy, later recalled. The many letters of support Herzl received included the news that three million Polish Hassidim wished to join the movement. Chaim Weizmann from Russia, the first president of Israel (1948–53), then a university student in Berlin, wrote of the exhilaration he and his friends experienced.[54] In Vienna, Herzl's first followers were members of Kadimah, the student association.[55] Political Zionism appealed predominantly to the young and gave them a new form of Jewish identity in which they could feel a sense of pride. As university students they were in the front line of virulent anti-Semitism and were routinely excluded from other student bodies which were becoming progressively German nationalist in character.[56] These young Jews were also rebelling against the assimilationist trends of their parents, who wished to dissociate themselves from their eastern roots. To take a famous but emblematic example, Sigmund Freud (1856–1939): both his parents were from Galicia; the family had moved to Vienna when Freud was a child. As a student at the medical school in Vienna, he aspired to identify with German *Kultur* and distanced himself from his ties with the unassimilated Jews of eastern Europe.[57] A secular Jew, Freud eschewed both religion and Jewish nationalism, and yet one of his sons joined Kadimah and another was active in editing a Zionist periodical.[58]

Given the migration patterns of the 1880s to Vienna, it can be argued that the majority of Zionist supporters in the capital were of east European origin or birth.[59] They were galvanized by Herzl's charismatic leadership and lost no time in establishing Zionist chapters throughout Vienna. They also set up Hebrew-speaking groups, sports clubs, literary associations, lecture series on Jewish culture, kindergartens and concerts, appealing to all social strata. For example, in 1899, they formed the Vereinigung jüdischer Handlungsgehilfen und Privatbeamten (Organization of Jewish Shop Clerks and Business Employees).[60] All these activities were regularly reported in *Die Welt*. In order to officially register with the World Zionist Organization, one had to pay an annual subscription of a 'shekel', a small symbolic sum (equivalent to one lira or one Austrian schilling, for example). There were 872 shekel-payers in Vienna in 1902, more than in Bohemia, Bukovina, Moravia, Hungary, France or Italy. Though a minority, they played an active role in the Viennese Jewish community; the editors of *Il Corriere Israelitico* [*CI*] informed their readers that twenty Jewish journals were published in Austria-Hungary, the majority Zionist in orientation, an indicator of a flourishing organization (1907, p.200). The greatest number of subscribers within Austria-Hungary was in Galicia, comprising 60 per cent of affiliated Zionists.[61]

A political group in Austria which had no counterpart in other western European countries was Diaspora Jewish nationalism, also forged by young Jews. Their aim was the recognition of national Jewish autonomy within the multinational empire. They believed that the regeneration of Jewish national consciousness was imperative on Austrian soil; Herzl's vision might not materialize for some time. They founded a political party in 1898, which became the Jüdische Volkspartei in 1902, winning four seats in the general election of 1907. The four members of parliament came from Galicia and Bukovina (their candidate in Vienna lost very badly). In 1911 only one of them was re-elected; in that year there were eighteen Jews in the Austrian parliament but they rarely spoke on Jewish affairs. In their election campaigns the Jewish nationalists had joined forces with the Zionists, as they also did in their efforts to gain control of the Jewish community in Vienna, the Israelitische Kultusgemeinde, which they successfully achieved only in 1932. In attempting to infiltrate the official Jewish institution, they were responding to Herzl's call in the Second Congress to 'conquer the communities' (*eroberung der Gemeinden*) in order to further support for the Zionist cause.[62] In the intervening years there were acrimonious battles between the nationalists and Zionists on the one hand and the establishment figures on the other, the former accusing the latter of being assimilationist, elitist and estranged from Judaism, the latter denouncing the others for adopting tactics of which Karl Lueger would approve and of pandering to the anti-Semites' conviction of the Jews as a separate people. Throughout this period, and despite growing anti-Semitism, the leaders of the Jewish community continued to reiterate their loyalty to the emperor and the fatherland, while their opponents claimed that once elected they would create a truly Jewish entity, replacing the shallow 'Israelite Religious Community' with the more assertive Jüdische Volksgemeinde (Jewish People's Community). This change of nomenclature encapsulated the differing definitions of Jewish identity that the two groups represented: religious versus national. The conflict became so intense that within the Zionist/nationalist group the older Zionists resigned from the movement after Herzl's death, as they could not tolerate the militant radical behaviour of the younger members.[63] Such a generational split also occurred within the German Zionist party.

On Herzl's death, David Wolffsohn, a wealthy timber merchant from Cologne, the son of Lithuanian immigrants, and a close friend of the deceased, became the second president of the World Zionist Organization. Thus, from 1905, the official centre of the movement was transferred from Austria to Germany, where it remained until 1920. As in Austria, the first Zionists were student societies, mainly comprising Galician and Russian refugees who made contact with their counterparts in Vienna; the sixteen delegates to the First Congress were also predominantly from the East.[64] The Zionistische Vereinigung für Deutschland (The Zionist Organization of Germany, ZVfD) was established in 1897 and, in terms of their background, the leaders were similar to those of the Centralverein;[65] they were often members of both associations and therefore were able to work together amicably until 1912, when a younger and more radicalized group took over the running of the ZVfD. At its inception, the ZVfD promoted Palestine as a haven for the persecuted *Ostjuden*, not for German Jews who were dutiful citizens, devoted to the fatherland where they would continue to live. The German members felt compelled to reiterate their patriotism: they wished to be good Zionists and good Germans, but it was a problematic dual loyalty. Zionism gave them a renewed sense of pride in their Jewish heritage, but Germany remained their beloved homeland, birthplace of Goethe and Schiller. In other words, apart from their Zionist affiliation, they were no different from the majority of middle-class German Jews as represented by the Centralverein. Their stance is articulated in a key essay written by the noted economist Franz Oppenheimer which was published in *Die Welt* and the *Jüdische Rundschau* (Jewish Review, the official journal of the ZVfD) in 1910: 'We love our fatherland and the German *volk*, its culture and scenic landscape, we serve the cause of our fatherland with all our heart … we are … citizens who intend to remain for ever … Nevertheless, we remain Zionists.'[66] According to Oppenheimer, western European Jews did not need a land of refuge; this was for their brothers in the East, and it was they who comprised the rank and file membership of the movement in Germany.[67]

The second-generation Zionists who began to take over the leadership from 1909, when one of their number, Kurt Blumenfeld (1884–1963), became first party secretary, and another, a young lawyer, Arthur Hantke (1874–1955), was elected president, were not so accommodating. Like their counterparts in Austria, they had experienced vicious anti-Semitism at school and university and were inclined to believe it would increase. In addition, *völkisch* racial nationalism was gaining momentum, and in 1907, for the first time in national elections, German liberals made alliances with anti-Semitic parties. Thus Blumenfeld and his colleagues, although from affluent, middle-class, integrated backgrounds (Blumenfeld's father was a district judge), felt themselves to be strangers on German soil.[68] They rejected the Centralverein's firm belief in a synthesis between *Deutschtum* and *Judentum*, privileging the latter. They jettisoned philanthropic Zionism and in its place proposed 'postassimilationist' Zionism;[69] personal experience of Palestine became part of their ideology; the Jews from the East represented the ideal Jews, to be emulated.

Martin Buber (1878–1965), another key member of this group of Zionists who was an advocate of cultural Zionism, promoted the study of Hebrew and the rediscovery of Jewish ethnicity and heritage. In a controversial essay (1901) entitled *Gegenwartsarbeit* (implying Zionist work in the present time), which caused friction with Herzl, Buber emphasized the need for education on Jewish culture, and in the same year he established a section, 'Jewish Art and Knowledge', in the Berlin Zionist association.[70] Between 1910 and 1914, they attracted many young adherents, and membership of the movement rose from 6,000 in 1904 to nearly 10,000,[71] a minority within the total population of 500,000 German Jews, but one that was active and influential. At the Tenth Zionist Congress in Basle in 1911, Arthur Hantke was nominated to the Greater Actions Committee. Between 1897 and 1938, thirty-five Zionist journals appeared in Germany. There was also a Zionist publishing house, the Jüdischer Verlag (1902), in Berlin with Buber as one of the editors and in 1916 Buber founded the monthly *Der Jude*. Both Jehuda Reinharz and Amos Elon postulate that the radical Zionists were an inspiration to a generation of German Jews who were cut off from all traditions, espousing the Zionist cause in defiance of their assimilated, middle-class upbringing,[72] like their counterparts in Austria and Italy. A notable example of this disaffected cohort in Germany was Gershom Scholem (1897–1982), who came into contact with Buber while a student at the University of Berlin. He joined the Zionist movement in 1911, 'having been led there by my recognition of the self-deception practised by my family',[73] by which he meant their assimilationist values; for Scholem, 'German-Jew' was a 'doomed oxymoron'.[74]

In rejecting a synthesis between *Deutschtum* and *Judentum*, a rift opened up between the two Zionist factions, which in turn affected the relationship with the Centralverein. Between 1910 and 1911, the ZVfD attempted to infiltrate the elections of the Jewish community in Berlin by putting forward their own candidates. They were defeated, but obtained a sizeable vote, sufficient to alarm the Jewish liberal establishment. Tensions were such that in December 1912, an Antizionistisches Komitee (Anti-Zionist Committee) was formed by a group of liberals with the backing of all the leading Jewish organizations, which denounced Zionism as a danger in its advocacy of the separation of the Jews from other citizens and accusing the Zionists of aiding the anti-Semites with their assertion that the Jews did not belong in Germany. The views of this committee were reported in the Italian Jewish press.[75] In May the following year, the Centralverein passed a resolution stating that anyone who did not adhere to the *Deutsche Gesinnung* (German-mindedness) was no longer welcome as a member; it advised Jewish youth not to join the Zionist sports clubs. The Centralverein's resolution also made the distinction between 'good' Zionists, those who supported the philanthropic position regarding Palestine and the east European Jews, and the radicals who denied their attachment to the fatherland. In its turn, the ZVfD instructed its members to resign from the Centralverein. In 1914, at the fourteenth German Zionist conference, many of the older generation withdrew from active participation. The Centralverein's resolution signalled the complete rupture between the radical Zionists and the liberals, which was not rectified until – irony of tragic ironies – 1933, although during the First World War the two sides forgot their differences in order to fight for the fatherland.[76] The schism reflected divergent ideologies: for the Centralverein, the primacy of *Deutschtum* and the principle of assimilation; for the ZVfD, rejection of assimilation in favour of the ethnic and national bonds that unite all Jews.

In France, a similar dichotomy prevailed. Before the foundation of the Fédération Sioniste de France in 1901, various disparate groups were involved in Palestine:

the Hovevei Zion and their funds for Jewish colonists; Baron Edmond de Rothschilds's agricultural settlements; the Alliance Israélite Universelle's schools and agricultural colleges (the first one in Jaffa in 1870), all within the parameters of the French Jewish community. In addition, students in Paris, mainly from Russia and Poland, held regular meetings at the Société des étudiants israélites russes, formed in 1882 with Zadoc Kahn as honorary president. They were political but not active, conversant with the work of Pinsker and in contact with similar groups elsewhere. The Dreyfus Affair acted as a catalyst for a small group of French Jewish intellectuals, transforming them into Zionists: between 1897 and 1899 there was a flurry of Zionist activity, including three short-lived journals, two of which were co-edited by Bernard Lazare (1865–1903), a literary critic and journalist who was the first French Jew to make the transition from a conviction that total assimilation was the only solution to the Jewish question to a position of endorsing political Zionism. The impact of the Affair made him acutely aware of the hostile, anti-Semitic milieu in which the Jews of France lived: 'Le nouveau ghetto' was the title he gave to the article he published in *La Justice* in November 1894.[77] Lazare was also the first Dreyfusard in the public campaign to clear Dreyfus's name and became increasingly convinced that Jewish nationalism was the only valid response to anti-Semitism. He and his collaborators on the Zionist journals rejected assimilation and criticized the leaders of the French Jewish community for their perceived passivity and reticence in the wake of the Affair. Their positive objectives were to renew Jewish solidarity, cultivate Jewish culture and language, and encourage the colonization of Palestine.[78]

The Zionist movement in France was consolidated when a federation of the disparate groupings was formed in 1901. It also acquired a journal, *L'écho sioniste* (1899–1922), established by an Austro-Hungarian, Alexander Marmorek (1865–1923), a friend and collaborator of Herzl. The federation was essentially Paris-based with membership largely comprising east Europeans; the numbers increased with the new influx of Russian Jews after the failed revolution of 1905. They remained a small minority; Caterine Nicault estimates that before 1914, they numbered no more than 1,000, of whom 300 to 400 were militant.[79] There was competition from the various left-wing parties for the political commitment of the 30,000 or so east European Jews living in the capital. Many were influenced by Lazare's socialism; in 1899 he withdrew from the Zionist movement as it was too bourgeois and its leader too authoritarian. He gave lectures and was in close touch with immigrant student groups.[80] In 1902, the Université populaire juive was established in Paris for the Jewish east European immigrants and working men. It offered courses on Jewish history and literature, spoken Hebrew, the Bible, Zionism and Palestine. At the opening ceremony, Zadoc Kahn declared that Zionism had awakened '*le sentiment juif endormi*' in the young.[81]

The chief rabbi's presence at the opening of this educational institution leads to the consideration of the Jewish establishment's position with regard to Zionism. Herzl's negative assessment of the leadership in his meetings of 1895/86 did not alter. He had hoped to win over their support in his diplomatic negotiations, but this was not to occur. Further fruitless talks deepened his conviction that 'the French

Jews simply can't be counted on'.[82] The French rabbinate, under the guidance of Zadoc Kahn, attempted to steer a delicate balance between sympathy for Zionist activities in relation to the oppressed Jews of eastern Europe and reiteration of their confidence in the republican ideals of 1789 which would protect them from the temporary recurrence of anti-Semitism. Kahn did not attack Zionism as the German rabbinate had done; on the contrary, he saw its positive elements, if it helped French Jews to become more Jewish.[83] The Central Consistory and the Alliance Israélite Universelle, two bastions of assimilation and therefore ideologically opposed to political Zionism, treated the movement with condescension and indifference. Their philanthropic and patriotic views were articulated in the pages of the *Univers israélite* and *Archives israélites*. Other leading members of the Jewish establishment such as the Jewish politician Joseph Reinach, whose brother Salomon was vice-president of the Alliance (until 1912), when faced with the dual threat of anti-Semitism and Zionism, responded by defending liberalism and the universalist ideals of the Republic and rejecting the notion of ethnic solidarity as some kind of barbarous anachronism. The only solution was to assert one's devotion to the country that had emancipated them: 'We are French, and French we shall remain ... All our efforts, all our intellectual activity, all our love, the last drop of our blood belongs to France, and to her alone.'[84] The similar rhetoric in the patriotic protestations of the French and Italian Jews is striking. The fact that the majority of Zionists in France were eastern European added to the disquiet of the French-born Jews. Many of the leaders were also foreign: Marmorek and Nordau, for example, remained on the margins of French society and were expelled in 1914.[85]

It is significant that when *Il Corriere Israelitico* launched 'Letters from France' in 1908, beginning – not surprisingly – with 'Zionism in France', they contacted Marmorek, then president of the federation, who commissioned not a Frenchman to write the article but a Polish Jew, Baruch Hagani, resident in Paris. His analysis of Zionism's lack of success offers a contemporary insight from the perspective of an east European Zionist. The principal reason, in Hagani's opinion, was the monolithic homogeneity of French national culture which permitted no spiritual independence: '*un seul bloc ... son esprit, sa culture, son genie ... Tout est centralisé et tout est unifié*'.[86] Thus Zionist ideology positing a divergent historical past and future could not be acknowledged. In addition, the Jews (throughout he uses the word *juifs*, not *israélites*) had a sense of deep and exclusive gratitude towards the first country to emancipate them. This devotion, combined with assimilation and decline in religious observance, had led to progressive '*déjudaïsation*'; recent anti-Semitism, from which France 'has brilliantly recovered' (*elle s'est glorieusement ressaisie*), signalled a victory for the French Jews. The bourgeoisie was unwaveringly hostile to Zionism; they did not wish to hear of theories that undermined the way they had lived for over 100 years; the poor, in particular recent arrivals from eastern Europe, had other considerations such as earning a living. This left the students – all of them from abroad, mainly Russia – to create Zionist groups throughout Paris, augmented by the recruitment of petit-bourgeois Jewish immigrants. There was also a small cohort, thirty in number, of Poalei Zion (Workers of Zion) which was not part of the federation. Other

Zionist associations were to be found in Nancy, Montpellier and, outside France, in Algeria. The federation met regularly under the indefatigable Dr Marmorek, but the future of the movement in France was problematic.[87] Hence the apposite title of Nicault's book on Zionism in France: *Une rencontre manqué?* There is consensus among historians that the imperviousness of French Jewry, with few exceptions, to the Zionist discourse of Jewish nationalism was the result of their ineradicable bond to the French nation.[88] A postscript to the failure of pre-war Zionism on French soil is conveyed by Dreyfus's undiminished patriotism in his declaration after rehabilitation in 1906: 'It was a glorious day of reparation for France and the Republic ... for the ideas of liberty, justice and social solidarity.'[89]

Whereas France proved to be infertile ground for Herzl's project, England was another matter. From his first meeting with Zangwill in London in 1895 when he was introduced to influential figures of the Anglo-Jewish community, Herzl was received sympathetically. The *Jewish Chronicle* published a synopsis of Herzl's ideas, 'A Solution to the Jewish Problem', in January 1896, before they came out in book form later that year. Herzl loved England and even thought of moving to London in 1901. He was an Anglophile and admired, like so many others before and since, the sense of freedom. On meeting the Jewish member of parliament Sir Samuel Montagu at the House of Commons in July 1896, Herzl wrote: 'I came to understand why the English Jew should cling to a country where he can enter this house as one of its masters.'[90] England and Germany were the two countries that Herzl envisaged as supporters of his cause and, when diplomacy with the Kaiser failed, he turned to England.[91] The leaders of the English Zionist Federation (EZF), formed in 1898, who were also members of the principal institutions of Anglo-Jewry, played a prominent role in introducing Herzl to the relevant government ministers and the Rothschilds. His meetings in 1902 and 1903 with Joseph Chamberlain, Secretary of State for the Colonies, and Lord Lansdowne, Secretary of State for Foreign Affairs, were decisive: 'The British Government had recognized him, and the movement represented by him, as a negotiating party. In so doing Lansdowne had revolutionized Zionist fortunes.'[92]

The influence of individual senior members of the EZF, in particular Leopold Greenberg ('my faithful Greenberg' as Herzl called him[93]), was not reflected in the movement as a whole in the pre-war period: it lacked cohesive organizational structures; was riven by internal dissension; lacked its own journal; attracted only 4,000 paid-up members by 1914; made little effort to win over immigrant support, fearful of encouraging a 'revolt of the masses'; had few wholly dedicated staff (its leaders were principally businessmen); and the Herzlian strategy of infiltrating the major institutions of Anglo-Jewry had limited success.[94] An indication of the EZF's failings was the disaffection experienced by the Manchester branch: a dedicated group of young idealists who had enthusiastically endorsed the Basle Programme in 1897 – they called themselves Dorsho Zion, established in 1894 with a membership of over 800 by 1898 – had joined the EZF in 1899, but reluctantly, because 'we had no faith in the English Zionist Federation'.[95] Another exception to this ineptitude was none other than the future first president of Israel, Chaim Weizmann. He was also atypical in reaching the apex of the movement in which the rank-and-file members were from eastern Europe (his professional qualifications were also atypical). He came to England in 1904; by 1917 he was president of the EZF and led the negotiations that culminated in the Balfour Declaration: 'the man who precipitated the re-entry of Jewry into the world of politics … Herzl's first true successor'.[96]

Opposition to political Zionism from establishment figures such as members of the executive committees of the Board of Deputies and the Anglo-Jewish Association was vociferous and consistent; it could be compressed to a single statement: 'England is the Paradise of the Jew – Why help to lose it or be driven out?'[97] More sustained and scholarly objections were contained in Claude Montefiore's much publicized article, 'Nation or Religious Community?' (1900), in which he traced the historical process of the Jews. He argued, as had Reinach, that Jewish nationalism was part of a tribal past, an anachronism. Elsewhere, he rejected the Zionists' critique of assimilation by claiming that there was 'good' and 'bad' assimilation, the former being the beneficial absorption, without coercion, of cultural and social mores from the milieus in which Jews lived.[98] Others reiterated the views of their European counterparts that Zionism was dangerous and an ally of anti-Semitism; editorials of the *Jewish Chronicle*, such as that of 17 August 1900, asserted English Jews' patriotism and 'the absoluteness of their English citizenship and nationhood'.[99] Opposition to Zionism coalesced into the League of British Jews in 1917 in response to the Balfour Declaration.[100]

Rereading the Declaration,[101] in which the word 'Arab' is not mentioned, one has to consider the Zionists' attitude to the native population of Palestine. The Zionist movement, in its depiction of Palestine in photographs and reports, tended to diminish the Arab presence; it was idealized as a place where the new Zionist Jews would be in control of their lives (and where the Arabs would not be a problem) but would benefit from the Jewish colonies.[102] Herzl's response, when confronted by the advice of a distinguished civil servant from Jerusalem in 1899 that the Jews would never be masters in Palestine, that there would be uprisings against them and that they should find an uninhabited country elsewhere, was to state that the Arabs 'will acquire excellent brothers … who will cause the region, their historic motherland, to flourish'.[103] There were few voices of disquiet, such as Ahad Ha'am, who on a visit to Palestine in 1891 saw the immense obstacles, not least of which was the Arab population.[104] On the eve of the First Zionist Congress, the Allgemeine Zeitung des Judenthums questioned whether the Arabs would welcome large numbers of Jews, 'one of the earliest warnings against the widespread assumption that Palestine had … no politically conscious native population'.[105] Perhaps the most measured analysis came from Yitzhak Epstein in a lecture he gave at the Seventh Zionist Congress (1905), 'The Hidden Question', which was subsequently published in Odessa two years later in the Hebrew monthly *Hashiloah*. The issues he raised are as follows: the most pressing matter, relations with the Arabs, had gone unnoticed by the Zionists; 80 per cent of the half-a-million Arabs supported themselves by farming; there was no uncultivated land; methods of land acquisition hitherto had been questionable; 'we must not uproot people from land to which they and their forefathers dedicated their best efforts'; the power against the Jews must not be underestimated; there was general ignorance of everything regarding Arabs; the Jews must educate themselves and learn to understand their neighbours if there was to be a peaceful coexistence.[106] His words, it seems, went unheeded.

ZIONISM IN ITALY

The foremost spokesman for political Zionism in the Italian language was Dante Lattes. In 1928 he published a two-volume account of Zionism for the wider public; his views on the Arabs were naive and optimistic, in contrast to Epstein's. Under the section '*questione araba*', he wrote that the Arabs did not need Palestine as their national centre since they had other vast regions; those not affected by negative propaganda had welcomed Jewish immigration from which they had derived employment and good prices for their barren land (*terre coperte di sabbia*). He concluded by citing extracts from various speeches made in celebration of the Balfour Declaration, in which positive sentiments were expressed regarding the Arabs of Palestine.[107] For the Jewish readers of *Il Corriere Israelitico*, Lattes presented an idealized portrayal through a series of 'Letters from Palestine'. In the first one, the correspondent, David Krinkin, a young Russian Jew living in Italy and on a visit to Palestine, wrote enthusiastically of the 'miraculous progress' made by the Jewish colonists and the benefits they bestowed upon the Arabs. He described a dinner given by a group of Jews for the Arabs from whom they had purchased a large tract of terrain, during which one of the vendors, 'a notable from the city', made a speech 'in perfect Hebrew' welcoming the Jews to the land of their fathers: they had brought with them 'the beautiful gifts of their culture and their civilization' from which the Arabs would derive great recompense; the Jews had come peacefully without shedding blood. Prefacing the letter, Lattes commented that whoever read it would feel great comfort and pride at yet another demonstration of 'the victories of Zionism' (*CI*, 1912, pp.115–16).

In the period before the First World War, there were three broad groups committed to Zionism in Italy: the Federazione Sionistica Italiana (FSI) (1901–11) led by Felice Ravenna (1869–1937), its president; a group led by Rabbi Samuel Hirsch Margulies (1858–1922), from Polish Galicia, who was appointed chief rabbi of the Florentine Jewish community in 1890 and director of the Rabbinical College in 1899; and the editors, principally Dante Lattes, of the Triestine journal *Il Corriere Israelitico*.[108] There is consensus within the historiography of Italian Zionism that two central ideological strands prevailed: the humanitarian, philanthropic Zionism of the FSI, for whom the concept of a Jewish nation related only to the persecuted Jews of eastern Europe, and Herzl's political vision espoused in Florence and Trieste. However, this interpretation is problematic in that it belies the tensions within the FSI itself. Initial hostility from *Il Vessillo Israelitico* to the movement is also acknowledged, a hostility compounded of fears of anti-Semitism and accusations of dual loyalty. Patriotism also underpinned the ideology of the FSI. There is also agreement that Zionism generated a spiritual and cultural renewal of Judaism, particularly among the young.

Recent research has tended to privilege one of these areas and not the interaction between them. For example, David Bidussa and his co-authors examine perceptively the cultural formation of the leading editor of *Il Corriere Israelitico*, Dante Lattes, whose incisive and wide-ranging views shaped the Zionist orientation of the journal.[109] Tullia Catalan also focuses on Trieste and effectively presents the reasons for the journal's rejection of the FSI's timid Zionism in favour of a more aggressive and polemical approach.[110] Francesco Del Canuto charts the progress of the FSI and its periodical *L'Idea Sionista* from its hesitant beginnings.[111] He argues that Margulies's cultural initiatives were the backbone of the Zionist movement in Italy, not official Zionism. However, Margulies's role at the centre of international Zionism, particularly with regard to Herzl's visits to Italy, is not fully documented. Alberto Cavaglion revisits the chronology of institutional Zionism but concentrates on the dissent generated by Lattes and others, such as Felice Momigliano's socialist Zionism.[112] He emphasizes the need to assess the movement from outside the institutions: for example, the role of the Romanian Jew, Yosef Marcou Baruch (1872–99), also mentioned by Del Canuto. Unlike Del Canuto, Cavaglion is of the opinion that the Florentine initiatives had a broader impact, a view Mario Toscano shares.[113] Cavaglion also makes an interesting point about the intellectual role of outsiders and foreigners but does not expand on this; for example, although attention is given to Baruch and Lattes, Margulies is barely mentioned.[114]

Toscano assesses Italian press reactions to Zionism from 1896 to 1904: antagonism from Roman Catholic journals; a positive evaluation from the socialists, and sympathy for the humanitarian aspect from the major national papers. The period he covers does not include the polemics in the nascent nationalist publications, alluded to by Cavaglion and Del Canuto. He also examines the debates among Jewish intellectuals.[115] Toscano presents a somewhat contradictory interpretation of Margulies's role in the Jewish cultural regeneration: he sees him as a leader in the 'cultural desert' of Italian Judaism whose influence at a national level persisted until his death in 1922; and yet elsewhere he states that Margulies's initiatives 'remained absolutely minor and in no way representative of the social, religious and political orientation of the "mass" of Italian Jews who passively assisted in the disintegration of their own identity'.[116] These conflicting statements highlight several problematics: is it the case that on the one hand, there existed a renewed sense of Judaism, and that on the other, Zionism opened up 'irreparable scars' (*cicatrici immedicabili*) in assimilationist ideology and laid bare contradictions within the various Jewish communities and institutions?[117] Cavaglion and Toscano's analyses are too generalized; the process is more complex and nuanced. There were shifts in orientation over time; competing and contradictory ideologies coexisted. For example, particularly among the young, as elsewhere in western Europe, Zionism served not to weaken but to strengthen and reaffirm their Jewish identity, leading several to emigrate to Palestine. For others, members of the Jewish elite, ambivalence, even hostility towards Zionism was revealed, prompting them to affirm with greater insistency their patriotic loyalty to Italy to the extent that, for some, were they to choose between *ebraismo* and *italianità*, the latter would prevail. The parallel with German Jews, *Deutschtum* or *Judentum*, is striking. Dante Lattes, in the pages of *Il Corriere Israelitico*, insistently argued that Zionism and *italianità* were complementary. He did not deny the commitment to the newly unified Italian nation. He appealed to his fellow Italians' patriotic sentiment: as the Italian Risorgimento had given them freedom, so the Jewish Risorgimento would endow them with that national dimension that belongs to all peoples (*CI*, 15 April 1911). If we can accept that the views of the majority of assimilated middle-class Jews are reflected in the pages of *Il Vessillo Israelitico*,[118] with a change of editor a more moderate and sympathetic stance evolved amidst enduring love of Italy.

A close chronological focus reveals that of the three Zionist groups, the FSI was the weakest link; it collapsed in 1911 in the face of aggressive Italian nationalism. As Toscano suggests, the Florence group took over from the official organization with its series of national youth congresses which became progressively more Zionist in orientation;[119] Margulies's role was pivotal and, as such, was resented by the leaders of the FSI. The principal disseminator of political Zionism in Italy was Dante Lattes, another outsider, residing in Austria-Hungary's main seaport, a cosmopolitan metropolis open to myriad cultures which he brought to inward-looking Italy through the pages of *Il Corriere Israelitico*. Margulies and Lattes often collaborated (as the latter did with Alfonso Pacifici from 1916), not infrequently clashing with the FSI and their journal. Detailed analyses of the various permutations of Zionism will be given through the journals, conferences and correspondence, and the dynamics between the three groups. The ideological thread that linked them was their shared conviction that through Zionism, Jewish identity and culture were strengthened.

The initiator of Zionism on Italian soil was another east European Jew, the Romanian Yosef Marcou Baruch. In a dramatic gesture he sent a telegram of salutation to Basle on the first day of the First Congress in 1897, on behalf of himself and a few other young Zionist sympathizers in Rome, under the name 'Prisoners of Titus'.[120] Between 1897 and his suicide in 1899, he travelled throughout Italy establishing Zionist cohorts – for example, in Livorno where Dante Lattes was the secretary of one such group before he moved to Trieste in October 1898; in Ancona; in Turin, where one of Cesare Lombroso's daughters was among the fifty supporters; and in Florence.[121] Baruch attended the Second Zionist Congress in 1898 as a delegate, where it is said he had a significant verbal exchange with Herzl, who thought him somewhat disturbed.[122] However, in a short piece in *Il Vessillo Israelitico*, Lattes gives a sympathetic portrayal of a colourful conspirator without whom Zionism would not have taken root in Italy (*VI*, 1898, pp.10–13). Baruch's name was familiar to *Il Vessillo Israelitico*'s readers through the publication in 1898 of his reports on the military campaign in Greece, 'Gli israeliti nella campagna di Grecia: appunti d'un garibaldino'. With Baruch's premature death at the age of 27, Italian Zionism lost 'one of its most dynamic figures', whose activities *Die Welt* praised in its obituary.[123] Judging by the narrative written about him by Boris Rasmann at the request of Pietro Rabezzana and sent to Martin Buber, care of *Die Welt*, he was indeed a dynamic and courageous campaigner who travelled widely, inspiring those he met with his fiery eloquence but also incurring the displeasure of the Jewish establishment and in some instances the police: in Algeria, where he founded a journal, but was denounced as an anarchist; in Vienna, where he frequented the Kadimah society but had to leave in haste; also in Bulgaria, where he received threatening letters; and in Egypt, before arriving in Italy.[124]

As *Il Corriere Israelitico* has been included in this account of Zionism in Italy, it should be pointed out that the Triestine journal was in fact the first to publish on the movement. Prior to Dante Lattes's collaboration, two articles appeared: one in 1895 (*CI*, p.266), which was a short informative piece sent from Berlin by an unnamed correspondent; the second in 1896 (*CI*, pp.151–4), by Emilio Pincherle, a Triestine law student in Vienna, who attempted to give an exhaustive and enthusiastic explanation. The editor sent a representative to the First Congress, who gave extensive coverage of the proceedings.[125] 'Movimento sionistico' made its appearance as a standard rubric in every issue thereafter. The journal covered the subsequent international congresses, published articles by the prominent figures of political Zionism, such as Herzl, Nordau and Zangwill, translated extracts from *Die Welt*, and kept readers informed of other Zionist journals and activities. A lengthy essay was devoted to Herzl's death; another to Nordau's sixtieth birthday (*CI*, 1909, pp.41–2); an authorized translation of Nordau's play, *Il Dottor Kohn*, appeared in the 1901 issues. From the inception of the Zionist movement, the journal welcomed debates in which contributors aired their views. Thus we find from some Italian contributors the same reservations which were expressed in other western European countries. For example, in 1897 Rabbi Eude Lolli, chief rabbi of Padua, justified his negative attitude to Zionism on many grounds, including his opinion that Jewish national sentiment should be discouraged, that such separatist ideas would incite racial intolerance, and that *patria* for the Jews was their place of birth. In his reply to Rabbi Lolli in the following issue, Guglielmo Lattes rejected the former's criticism, declared his own support for philanthropic Zionism, concluding that 'Zionism does not suppress love of one's country ... therefore any fear on that count is unjustified.'[126]

Why was the Zionism propounded in Trieste more political than in Italy? Proximity to anti-Semitic Vienna and the first-hand experience of persecuted Jews from eastern Europe may account for the ideological divergence. Many of these emigrants were Zionists and would have had contact with local supporters.[127] In addition, there is the forceful approach of Dante Lattes. When he joined the editorial board, other initiatives were undertaken, permeating *Il Corriere*'s pages with his incisive, combative and spirited style and banishing erudite and sterile pedantry.[128] In 1900 he gave a lecture in Trieste entitled 'Anti-Semitism and the Jews' (published in the journal), in which he stated that the Jewish question would become an international one during the course of the twentieth century, and he warned with frightening prescience that 'all the peoples will be called upon to decide and it will end with the elimination and, if necessary, the extermination of the Jews' (*CI*, 1900, p.27). For Lattes, Zionism was above all a movement of spiritual and cultural renewal imbued with a national consciousness. In his emphasis on these dimensions, Luzzatto Voghera perceives the influence of his teacher at the Rabbinical College in Livorno, the distinguished scholar of Jewish mysticism, Rabbi Elia Benamozegh (1823–1900), and that of Ahad Ha'am, the foremost proponent of cultural Zionism; Lattes was also in contact with Martin Buber, who became a close friend.[129]

In 1905, Lattes began a new regular column on Jewish literature and art. His objective was twofold: to combat the assimilationist stance that Judaism was only a religious faith, and to introduce to Italian Jews the breadth of Judaic culture, privileging the works of Russian and Polish writers but also including those of western European Jews such as Edmond Fleg (pseudonym for Flegenheimer, 1874–1963), André Spire, Nordau and Zangwill. Thus *Il Corriere*'s readers were presented with the fiction of Shalom Aleichem and Shalom Asch, the essays of Ahad Ha'am and Joseph Klausner, literary reviews and reports on art exhibitions, and excerpts from other European Jewish journals.[130] In addition, to instil cultural pride, Lattes offered them essays such as 'Against Jewish Fear and Shame', in which he argued that just as Italians glorify, love and are familiar with Dante's *Divina Commedia*, so the Jews should promote the Bible; just as Dante's poetry is recited in squares, churches and theatres (Lattes had recently attended a reading in Florence's Or San Michele together with hundreds of others), the Jews should do the same with pages from the prophets. He also reminded them of their historic national mission, tracings its development from the post-biblical exilic era to post-emancipation, and of the need to fight for its fruition against those rabbis and community leaders who attempted to stifle and extinguish the regenerative power of moral and spiritual progress. He invited prominent Italian Zionists such as Gino Arias, Alfonso Pacifici and Felice Momigliano to contribute articles on similar themes.[131] In 1907, the journal underwrote the Florentine Pro Cultura Ebraica (Jewish Cultural) organization by assuming the role of its official representative. Lattes was very committed to this project and gave many lectures at its various centres, in particular Florence, Padua and Verona.

On 13 April 1904, the Circolo Sionistico Triestino (Zionist Association of Trieste) held its inaugural meeting, with Lattes as president. In his opening address he spoke of an era of renewal for Judaism as the prophetic ideal of national redemption was once again rekindled (*CI*, 1903, p.332). The objectives of the *circolo* were clearly defined: to campaign for the salvation of persecuted Jews; to raise funds for the Jewish colonization of Palestine; to educate the young in the spirit of modern Judaism, and to raise the dignity of Jews, both on a national and individual level. It had a full programme of political, cultural and social events which were reported in *Il Corriere Israelitico*. Membership rose from fifty to 121 within a few months. Leading Zionists from elsewhere gave talks, such as Gino Arias, Felice Momigliano and Margulies. In November 1904, Lattes, in his introduction to Margulies, praised him for revitalizing Jewish scholarship in Italy and concluded with the declamation: 'Long live Zionism! Long live Herzl! Long live the Jewish nation!' (*CI*, 1904, pp.198–9). Lattes's unwavering adherence to political Zionism was clearly articulated in the Triestine journal: Jews were a nation which must preserve its historical civilization; Jews must actively defend their nationalism and their traditions; Jews had a right to their *patria* (*CI*, 1907, p.109). Lattes's Zionist activities were not confined to his role as a journalist: he was a prolific author and indefatigable translator, particularly in the period between the two world wars.[132]

The year 1904 was also the one in which Jewish emigration through the port of Trieste intensified: every day, Jewish refugees fleeing persecution in eastern

Europe arrived in the city on their journey to Palestine or America. The Zionist group and the local Jewish community set up various committees in order to assist them. *Il Corriere Israelitico* reported on their activities, published details of embarkation times and the number of refugees in Trieste at a given period. Through these reports and the accounts of the pogroms in Russia and Romania, often in the same issue, the journal made its readers aware of the significance of Zionism as a salvation for their less fortunate co-religionists.

FELICE MOMIGLIANO AND FELICE RAVENNA

It was sympathy and solidarity for the persecuted Jews that led Felice Momigliano to accept the invitation of the socialist newspaper *Avanti!* to cover the Second Zionist Congress in 1898. Four articles were published between 2 and 5 September, printed on the first page. According to Cavaglion, they signified the period of maximum interest in the movement on the part of the newly formed Italian Socialist Party (1892); subsequent reports were not given the same exposure. For the socialists, Zionism was perceived as a movement in the defence of a new group of outcasts and pariahs.[133] Momigliano informed his readers of the vast numbers of the Jewish proletariat in eastern Europe in order to dispel the notion that Judaism was equated solely with the bourgeoisie and capitalism. He emphasized that the rank-and-file members of the Zionist movement ('the great Zionist army') were drawn from the millions of poor Jews from the East, and that they would be the ones to go to the Promised Land. He noted that at the Congress the majority of delegates comprised young enthusiasts from Russia and Poland who, excluded from the public and cultural life in the countries of their birth, longed for freedom and the possibility of fulfilling their ambitions. He stressed, in other words, the economic basis of Zionism: 'the economic question is the alpha and omega of the discussions'. He reported on the women delegates, mostly Russians studying in Germany or Switzerland, who had equal voting rights; one of them told him: 'I am a Jew and a Zionist; that is my distinction' (*je suis juive et sioniste; c'est mon titre de gloire*). He concluded that Zionism would not remedy anti-Semitism in western Europe, as western Jewish capitalists such as the Rothschilds would continue to prefer to live on the banks of the Seine. However, he adds, one could tend towards optimism and imagine the streets of Jerusalem filled with lively, active people who had achieved their emancipation through their own physical efforts.[134]

While Momigliano foregrounded the socialist aspects of Zionism for the readers of *Avanti!*, the sole Italian delegate at the Second Congress, Rabbi Sonnino of Naples, upheld the patriotic position of the majority of western Jewry, as *Il Corriere Israelitico*'s report of his speech to the Congress reveals: 'despite the apathy and even hostility to Zionism among not a few of my co-religionists, I who love beautiful Italy (*amantissimo della mia diletta patria*) and am a citizen of a free country where intolerance and anti-Semitism are almost unknown words, … feel an obligation to become involved in the fate of my suffering brothers … patriotism and philanthropy are synonyms'.[135] Another Italian presence at the Second Congress as an observer was the lawyer Felice Ravenna of Ferrara, future president of the FSI, delegate and, from 1900, a member of the Greater Actions Committee of international Zionism; in 1920, he succeeded his father Leone as leader of his Jewish community. In a front-page article in the Triestine journal he gives a positive account in order to counteract the antipathy towards the movement in Italy caused partly because of 'foolish accusations that the noble ideals of Zionism conflict with our feelings as Italians who love our beautiful country'. He comments that the number of Zionist associations in America, England and France, where Jews are free and have always been model citizens, should reassure Italians: they will not be required to sell up and move to the Holy Land; the creation of 'a Jewish centre' in Palestine (*un centro giudaico* – Ravenna does not use the word 'state' or 'homeland') is for those subjected to oppression and persecution. He makes an ideological distinction that would appease and appeal to potential Italian adherents: Zionism was a political and social movement for the Jews of eastern Europe, but was exclusively philanthropic and humanitarian for Italians, French and English of the Jewish faith. The sight of 800 people rejoicing in expansive solidarity, celebrating a proud Jewish spirit, was a moving and novel experience which he wishes his fellow Italians had witnessed.[136]

L'IDEA SIONISTA

There is something of a hiatus in this narrative. Scant documentation exists prior to the meeting in Ancona in September 1900 at which several leading members of Italian Zionism, such as Felice Ravenna and Carlo Conigliani, issued a statement to actively engage in Zionist propaganda on two fronts: on behalf of persecuted Jews and to raise the morale and dignity of Italian Jews.[137] To this end, on 31 January 1901, *L'Idea Sionista: Rivista Mensile del Movimento Sionista* (Monthly Review of the Zionist Movement, from 1904, *L'Idea Sionnista*, a more Italian orthography) was launched, a monthly journal which became the official organ of the FSI; its first editor was Carlo Conigliani from Modena. Baruch's activities between 1897 and 1899 and those of the first generation of political Zionists, the Prisoners of Titus, have been enveloped in silence by official Zionism,[138] although the Romanian was briefly acknowledged as 'the ardent apostle … the impassioned pioneer' by Ravenna in his article 'Il sionismo in Italia'.[139] In the opening editorial, Conigliani outlined the moderate position of the journal, shared by the majority of western Jews: the only way to combat anti-Semitism was 'to show solidarity to our distant brethren … Jerusalem is a symbol, nothing more than a very significant symbol [*nulla più che un simbolo significantissimo*] of this renewal of Judaism. It does not seek to give us a homeland, as we already have one, which is noble and beautiful' (*L'Idea Sionista* [*IS*], 1901, p.2). This ideological commitment to the Italian nation is reiterated throughout the journal's publication, as illustrated by the writer Enrico Castelnuovo's unequivocal statement: 'I was born a Jew, and I shall remain a Jew, but no one will force me to go to Jerusalem with the Chosen People. I am Italian and I do not understand what is meant by "Jewish nationality". These are my ideas on Zionism.'[140] A declaration such as this articulated the opinion of many Italian Jews.[141] Enzo Levi recalled his own family's acceptance of philanthropic Zionism, to give an oasis of peace to those born in barbarous lands.[142]

The dual role of Italian Zionism is reinforced in Ravenna's first article for *L'Idea Sionista*: the redemption of oppressed Jews and the renewal of Jewish pride among Italian Jews; to encourage those for whom being Jewish was 'an unbearable burden' (*un peso insopportabile*) to perceive themselves in a more positive light (*IS*, 1901, p.4). In this respect, Zionism in Italy was consonant with international Zionism, as expounded at the First Congress. It cannot be emphasized too strongly how often patriotism is mentioned in *L'Idea Sionista:* on nearly every page of the first few issues, 'the innate love of our beautiful land' is repeated together with the constant affirmation that Zionism was a humanitarian movement, 'not political in any way' (*per null'affatto politico*, *IS*, 1901, p.17). Ravenna commends Conigliani for distinguishing so clearly the humanitarian aspect of Zionism from the political dimension for the Jews of Italy, and he cites a letter from Nordau which states that no Jew who is fortunate enough to possess '*une patrie*' is asked to leave it (*IS*, 1901, p.25). Another contributor, Enea Vigevano, put the Italian case very bluntly: 'if German Zionism is nationalist, we are not ... we are not nationalist ... we are good Zionists and equally good Italians' (*IS*, 1901, pp.41–2).

FIRST CONFERENCES OF THE FSI

Conigliani, in his opening editorial, praised the role of 'our *Corriere Israelitico* which nobly supported the new idea [Zionism] and launched it in Italy' (*IS*, 1901, p.3). In its turn, the Triestine journal welcomed the Italian periodical and hoped that it would have the effect of renewing and reawakening Italy from the 'mists of assimilation' (*CI*, 1900, p.267). On 1 October 1901, in a letter to the Ferrara association, Conigliani called for a conference to consolidate and unify the various Zionist groups which then existed in Ancona, Ferrara, Livorno, Milan, Modena, Turin and Rome.[143] A few weeks later, on 23 October, a conference was held in Modena, where it was agreed to form a federation whose aims were threefold: to contribute to the work of the central committee in Vienna, defined as giving Jews who do not possess them full civil and political rights through the colonization of Palestine; to revive sentiments of solidarity among their co-religionists and raise their moral and intellectual condition; to promote Zionist propaganda in Italy (*nella patria italiana*). It was also agreed that a statement would be sent to the Fifth Zionist Congress (held in Basle in December 1901), 'solemnly reaffirming ... the perfect compatibility of the Zionist ideal with the most affectionate sentiments for Italy [*la patria italiana*], since Zionism is simply a manifestation of solidarity towards our brethren and a desire for justice and social progress'.[144] The motive for this declaration was to clarify publicly the nature and content of Zionist propaganda in Italy. It is clear that many Italian Jews were of the opinion that adherence to Zionism did conflict with patriotism. Thus a great deal of the publicity meted out by *L'Idea Sionista* and *Il Corriere Israelitico* treated this ideological impasse. Nordau's expositions on the subject, such as his article 'Patriotismo e Sionismo' were amongst the most frequently cited in order to defend Zionism's compatibility with love of one's country.[145] This particular piece was a translation from the French Zionist journal *L'Echo Sioniste*, an indication that French Jews also found this to be an intractable issue. Nordau's intention was to reveal the fallacious nature of the argument that Zionism and patriotism were antithetical by demonstrating the ways in which Zionist Jews were model citizens of the countries in which they resided. The most effective proof of their loyalty, he argued, was their readiness to shed their blood in the many wars that had been fought since the time of their emancipation. The Zionist Jew who enjoyed equality was able to fulfil his civic obligations without forgetting that he belonged to a people to whose glorious future he must contribute. 'This Zionist creed does not diminish his patriotism ... it is never in conflict with his patriotism. There is no need to sacrifice one to the other' (*CI*, 1902, p.220).

In December 1902, the Italian Zionists held their third meeting, the first of the federation, in Ferrara; Felice Ravenna was elected president. The aims were a variation of the previous conference of Modena: 'the redemption of the oppressed Jewish proletariat and the regeneration of Jewish life'. Among the conference papers was one by Dr Edgardo Morpurgo (1872–1942), secretary of the Milan association from 1903, on the need for physical exercise programmes for the young; Nordau's call for *Muskeljudentum* had resonated with him. Morpurgo also wrote a series of articles, published in both Zionist journals, on the psychic and somatic condition of European Jewry.[146] There were also reports from Vienna, discussions on various matters such as future activities, the 'Territorial Fund' (*Fondo territoriale*), by which they meant the Jewish National Fund[147] – *Il Corriere Israelitico* noted that Italian Zionists could not bring themselves to use the word 'national'. Greetings were received from Nordau and Zangwill.[148]

From April 1903, the Jewish papers were full of the horrifying details of the pogroms of Kishinev. The plight of the Russian Jews prompted an outpouring of sympathy and support: throughout Italy, for example, committees, and not just Zionist ones, were established. Public demonstrations took place in Milan, Modena and Turin.[149]

RABBI MARGULIES

Die Welt had reported favourably on Zionism in Italy, with particular reference to Margulies's 'lofty lecture' on the subject (*IS*, 1902, p.52). The name of the east European rabbi brings us to a crucial period for the Zionist movement in Italy and the *incipit* of tensions within it. Herzl's last diplomatic mission took place in Italy in January 1904, when he had audiences with King Victor Emanuel III, Pope Pius X and various government ministers.[150] Of relevance were the preparations for these meetings, as revealed in the correspondence between Herzl and his colleagues in Italy. Herzl's letters to Ravenna, which date from 16 December 1902 to 22 March 1904, survived the Second World War and were taken to Israel by one of Ravenna's daughters and given to the Italian synagogue in Jerusalem.[151] Those from Herzl to Margulies were donated to the Central Zionist Archives in Jerusalem by Margulies's widow after the war, when Carlo Alberto Viterbo, one of the rabbi's disciples, personally handed them over to the then director, Dr Alexander Bein, who was also Herzl's biographer.[152] The languages used were principally French, between Herzl and Ravenna, and German with Margulies. The tone of the letters on Herzl's part was friendly and cordial: *Mon cher Felice*, *Lieber Freund*! Ravenna, as would be expected, was more deferential and formal. Herzl and Margulies revealed mutual respect in their correspondence.

Although the letters deal mainly with Herzl's diplomatic mission in Italy, the earlier ones disclose Herzl's endeavours to energize Zionist activities in Italy; he was pleased with Ravenna's proposal to have his novel *Altneuland* translated into Italian and suggested the publisher Treves, but nothing came of it;[153] in January 1903, he asked Ravenna to bring influential Jews to the next Congress. In this, Ravenna succeeded: in 1901, there had been three Italian delegates but in 1903 there were six, indicating an increase in the number of *shekalim*.[154] These delegates included Ravenna and Angelo Sullam (1881–1971), a young Venetian Zionist who had completed his undergraduate thesis on Zionism and international law the year before.[155] In 1903 he was president of the Venice association; in 1906 he became treasurer of the FSI. Herzl liked Sullam sufficiently to give him a signed copy of the famous photograph of himself looking like a prophet.[156] The other delegate of interest was Rabbi Margulies; he clearly impressed Herzl by the impassioned speech he gave on the last day of the Congress in favour of the East Africa proposal, for which he received *applause vivissimi* (*IS*, 1903, pp.112–13). On 30 August 1903 – that is, two days later – Herzl requested him to arrange an audience with the king, but in consultation with 'my dear friend Dr Felice Ravenna, because I would be sorry if he thought that we wanted to disregard him'.[157] Herzl was right about Ravenna's feelings: he did feel neglected and he almost jeopardized the delicate negotiations owing to his resentment, an antipathy shared by Sullam who, in his private correspondence, referred to Margulies as 'excessively German and therefore treacherous, even though he has Italian citizenship' (*resta sempre arcitedesco e quindi un elemento infido*) and suggested that he should not be consulted.[158] Sullam constantly wished to exclude Margulies: with reference to a future meeting, Sullam wrote to Ravenna not to hold it in Florence as there 'they would be under the German surveillance of the German Margulies' (*sotto la sorveglianza tedesca del tedesco Margulies*).[159]

To return to Ravenna: it appears that Margulies's reputation with the World Zionist Organization preceded Herzl's meeting with him at the Sixth Congress. On 5 April 1903, Ravenna informed Sullam that with regard to Zionist activities in Florence, he had been instructed by Vienna to contact Margulies; he could hardly refuse, given the status Margulies enjoyed – the only rabbi in Italy to be thus respected – and Ravenna knew that the rabbi's support was equivalent to establishing a Zionist association. On 24 April 1903, he again told Sullam that Vienna requested him to make contact with Margulies in order to further the Zionist cause in Italy.[160] Margulies was aware of Ravenna's discontent and, rather than cause further friction, he notified Herzl, in a letter of 4 September 1903, that he was willing to hand over the assignment to Ravenna, who had asked him whether in his place he should feel humiliated that as president of the FSI he had not been entrusted with the task of negotiating an audience with the king.[161] In his reply of 7 September, Herzl showed sensitivity and tact: he urged Margulies to proceed but always in consultation 'with our friend Ravenna'.[162] Margulies was successful: he had an audience with the king on 11 October 1903, ostensibly to discuss the Zionist movement but in reality to prepare the ground for Herzl, and the meeting was widely reported in the national press. Margulies's account, which he sent to Herzl, is missing, but Herzl's reply of 14 October is fulsome in his praise for the 'brilliantly executed mission'.[163] On 13 December, Brusati, the king's chief aide-de-camp, informed Margulies that 'His Majesty the King was very willing to see Dr Theodor Herzl' (*Sua Maestà il Re vedrà molto volentieri il Dott. Teodoro Herzl*).[164] The audience was finally arranged for 23 January 1904 and, perhaps to placate Ravenna, it was he who accompanied Herzl to Rome: 'you will belong to me body and soul, my dear Felice, until we have completed our assignment', he wrote on 18 January.[165] Herzl also saw the minister of foreign affairs, Tittoni, at the king's request, and Giacomo Malvano, Secretary General at the foreign ministry, who could not refuse to see Herzl, given the circumstances. Malvano was a Jew but anti-Zionist, and therefore most unhelpful, as Herzl thought he might be; in a letter to Ravenna he commented that like all the other Malvanos he knew, this one would also be more patriotic than the king.[166] Margulies had dissuaded Herzl from organizing a meeting with Luigi Luzzatti, the new minister of finance (appointed in December 1903): 'It would be useless, even detrimental. He belongs to the most fanatical assimilationists' (*Egli appartiene ai più fanatici assimilazionisti*).[167]

Margulies's observation on Luzzatti brings us to the other important meeting Herzl had in Italy that January, with Pope Pius X, which took place three days after his audience with the king. Ravenna took upon himself the preparations for this significant event, as he was confident that his personal contacts with government ministers would prevail. Ravenna was a cousin of Malvano's sister, a family connection he communicated to Herzl. Ravenna told Herzl that a Jewish professor from the University of Padua had recently been favourably received by the pope; he happened to be a brother of one of Ravenna's aunts.[168] As a potential intermediary, Ravenna suggested another family friend, Leone Romanin Jacur (1847–1928), from a prominent Paduan Jewish family, a leading politician who had known the pope for thirty-six years. Despite Romanin Jacur's anti-Zionist views, which he divulged to Ravenna, Ravenna was convinced that 'Mr Romanin is the most appropriate person … no one else could carry out such a delicate mission … I am waiting for his prompt response.'[169] Ravenna's optimism, that Romanin Jacur's friendship with the pope would outweigh his Zionist stance, proved to be misplaced. Whereas Margulies triumphed with his negotiations, Ravenna was to fail completely. In a letter of 14 January 1904, Ravenna told Herzl that he was still waiting for a reply from the politician, despite several reminders.[170] Some days later, it arrived and was devastatingly negative: not only would he not intervene, but he firmly requested Ravenna 'to ensure that I do not have a meeting with the gentleman whose name you mention' (*Ma La prego di evitarmi un colloquio col Signore di cui Ella mi fa il nome*). Romanin could not bring himself to name Herzl. His conviction that Zionist activities were misguided made such an encounter impossible. Those sentiments were repeated in a letter written the following day.[171] In the event, it was a chance meeting that Herzl had with the papal count Lippay in Venice, en route for Rome, that led him to the pope.[172]

What conclusions can be drawn from this episode of Zionism in Italy? On the diplomatic front, despite cordial receptions, Herzl gained nothing. However, the favourable impression made by the founder of the movement led the king to view its aspirations with sympathy.[173] In his report for *Il Corriere Israelitico*, Dante Lattes surmised that the monarch would have admired the intimations of independence and Jewish national spirit, in sharp contrast to the conventional assimilationist protestations that he usually heard from leaders of the Italian Jewish communities. He added that in Ravenna's account of the proceedings for *L'Idea Sionista*, the king expressed displeasure that many Jews wished to conceal their origins. This criticism, writes Lattes, should galvanize those timid souls to stand up beneath the banner of the Jewish Risorgimento.[174] Margulies proved to have considerable political expertise and international status, and a significant role in the revival of Jewish culture in Italy which more than filled the vacuum left by the closure of the FSI. The negative repercussions were the envy and resentment that Margulies's privileged position, not least with Herzl, aroused in leading members of the FSI, which endured until the rabbi's death in 1922. In the meetings with Herzl and the king, 'Margulies acted as if he were the leader of the Jews in Italy, even though he had no official title.'[175]

These aspects of Margulies's contribution to Zionism in Italy have not been given sufficient consideration by Italian historians, nor have the failures of the FSI to capitalize on Herzl's presence in Italy to enhance its own political profile – after all, they did not even succeed in the small task of having Herzl's novel translated into Italian.[176] What Ravenna lacked in negotiating skills, he more than compensated for by his devotion to Herzl and the cause. On his way to Rome, Herzl visited the Ravenna household, where he met not only the immediate family but also Ravenna's father and several close Zionist friends. He was to stay only for a few hours but was persuaded to remain from 19 to 20 January. 'The rooms are cold and bare', he wrote in his diary, 'but the hearts are warm … The atmosphere reminded me a little of Vilna.'[177] It must have been an extremely emotional and heartening experience to recall the day in Vilna which, he noted, 'will remain engraved in my memory forever'.[178] As Giorgio Romano suggests, the loyalty, deference and dedication of the Italian Zionists were a welcome contrast to the recriminations, quarrels and hostilities which had been generated by the crisis over the Uganda project.[179] At least Herzl took away with him from Italy fond memories of friendship; a few months later, on 3 July 1904, he was dead, aged 44.

FOURTH CONFERENCE OF THE FSI

On 20 and 21 March 1904, the FSI held its fourth conference in Milan. There were delegates from eight regional associations: Ancona, Bologna, Ferrara, Milan, Modena, Padova, Venice and Naples; Rome did not send a representative as its group, although formed in 1902, was not officially affiliated to the FSI until

1904. All the delegates and participants were professional middle class; membership of the various groups shows this to be the case throughout Italy. For example, the list of 118 *shekalim* in Venice for 1907 contains lawyers, rabbis, engineers, academics, accountants and jewellers, and those with the title of 'Cavaliere'.[180] These were precisely the people whom Ravenna and his colleagues wished to attract to the movement, 'the most intellectual part of Italian Judaism' (*IS*, 1904, p.41). There were no rank-and-file cohorts from eastern Europe. In 1904, membership stood at 802 divided among nine groups; this was to rise to 1,200 among twelve groups in 1905.[181] The additions were Florence, Livorno and Mantua. The increase must in some measure be due to the success of the fourth conference and its subsequent propaganda drive.

In his opening address, Ravenna reiterated the original programme and 'the perfect compatibility of Italian patriotic sentiment with the classical ideal of Zionism'.[182] He added that despite opposition from orthodox and assimilated Jews, the Zionist cause was progressing slowly but surely: 'A Jew is a Zionist in as much as he is proud of being a Jew ... this pride has led us beneath the noble flag of Zionism'. He concluded with many words of praise for 'the sacred name of Herzl' (*IS*, 1904, p.5). The chief rabbi of Milan, Da Fano, in his welcoming speech, stressed the healing humanitarian work of the Zionists. Ravenna's report on the past year's activities of the FSI included their considerable involvement in Herzl's audiences with the king and the pope, 'to which our president attaches great importance; he hopes to continue the negotiations in the not too distant future' (Ravenna referred to himself in the third person in this part of the discourse, perhaps to give its portentous contents more gravitas; no mention was made of Margulies's part). He also mentioned the FSI's public demonstrations against the Kishinev pogroms, and the Sixth Zionist Congress. He announced to the conference that the Italian delegates at this congress, 'even though they admired the heroism of the numerous Russian representatives, who, in spite of the vision of the still warm blood of their massacred brethren, stubbornly refused to consider any proposal other than Palestine – the Italian delegates, I repeat, were unanimous in accepting with gratitude the offer of the British government' (*IS*, 1904, p.9). There were reports on Zionist propaganda in Italy – the figure of 'a few thousand' was given as the number of *Idea Sionista*'s readers (*IS*, 1904, p.16) – and on Italian Zionists' attitudes to the Jews in the East, in which once again the question of patriotism and Jewish self-esteem recurred: 'an Italian Jew is loyal to Italy and at the same time he is part of the great ethnic unity which he shares with Russian Jews ... to be a Zionist, the Italian Jew must feel pride in belonging to a noble race with ancient traditions' (*IS*, 1904, p.20).

The central Zionist tenet of renewed pride in one's Jewish identity, formulated at the First Congress, had been fully absorbed by the FSI and its adherents; so too had the Herzlian message to infiltrate the Jewish communities. In a series of papers on education, the regulation of charitable institutions and the vulnerability of the smaller communities, each speaker stressed the need for reform and transformation within the conservative administrations of the communities who were hostile to Zionist ideology. The proposal that the FSI should attempt to gain control of them in order to influence communal policy was greeted with loud applause.[183] It was also suggested that the French example of *università popolari* should be emulated to combat the general ignorance of Judaism, and that lectures and Hebrew classes should be established. These initiatives were not implemented by the Italian Zionist organization, but by Rabbi Margulies and a small group of devotees – yet another indicator of the FSI's failings. One speaker declared that it should be the responsibility of the federation to concern itself with Jewish studies; a new approach was needed to disseminate Jewish history, ethics, and so on. Just such an assignment had been undertaken by Rabbi Margulies: in January 1904, the first issue of *La Rivista Israelitica: Periodico Bimestrale per la Scienza e la vita del Giudaismo* appeared, and Margulies was the editor. He had notified Ravenna of this journal in December 1903.[184] It would seem that Ravenna chose not to inform the conference of this significant publication by a renowned rabbi and committed Zionist.

The last paper was that of Dr Edgardo Morpurgo, who presented his findings on the physical and psychical condition of Italian Jews in 1902 and 1903 from fifty-two communities. His recommendations that a special medical commission should be set up to study the problem of physical education among Italian Jews and promote good practice, and that charities should be involved, particularly on behalf of sick children, were approved unanimously.[185] During the various discussions, the question of a permanent centre for the FSI was raised, and it was agreed that locations should vary. This decision reflected the fragmentary structure of the FSI where no single association was dominant in influence or numbers – yet another weakness of the organization. At that time, the associations with the strongest membership were Milan (160),[186] Modena (128), Ferrara (119) and Ancona 111 (*IS*, 1904, p.17). Milan was chosen for the following year. Ravenna was re-elected president and a four-member council was nominated. The press who attended the conference were *Il Vessillo Israelitico*, *Il Corriere Israelitico*, *L'Echo Sioniste*, and a Polish paper from Warsaw, the *Sephirà*. Messages of support had been received from Herzl and Nordau.

The fourth conference represents the FSI at its most cohesive and effective: the president, fresh from his high-level meetings together with the founder of the movement, presented an authoritative presence; the delegates were few and united; discussions were friendly and constructive. The tensions with Margulies were not mentioned. Florence had not yet officially entered the FSI. All this was to change. In October 1904, the Gruppo Sionistico Fiorentino was formally constituted, with Gino Arias, a professor at the University of Rome, as its first president, and committee members who included Margulies and his Galician Polish colleague at the Rabbinical College, Rabbi Zevi Perez Chajes (1876–1925), who had been appointed by Margulies in 1902. In 1908, Chajes replaced Arias (*CI*, 1908, p.274). In 1905, membership stood at 138, making it the second-largest regional association.[187] A brief but relevant digression: it will be recalled that in 1903, Ravenna, in his capacity as president of the FSI, had been instructed by Vienna to contact Margulies concerning the establishment of a Zionist association in Florence. He did so, and Margulies, in his reply, explained that as a foreigner his position was a delicate one, but that once proceedings were underway he would cooperate and discuss matters, should Ravenna visit Florence.[188] In May 1903, Ravenna and

Sullam travelled to Florence – not, it seems, to see Margulies, but the lawyer and distinguished academic Cino Vitta (1873–1956).[189] Their attempts to enlist his support for the Zionist cause were not successful as his letter to Ravenna reveals; despite what Ravenna had been told about him, Vitta believed that he had no especial influence in either the city or the Jewish community. He had sympathy for their commitment, but the final objective of Palestine, however remote a possibility, put all Jews in a dilemma of choosing between the present and future *patria*. He was aware that Italian Zionists had made their choice of Italy, but there remained equivocations that needed to be clarified. He therefore ruled out the possibility of leading the movement in Florence; should he find that the idea had attracted individuals of worth and undisputed patriotism, he would become a humble follower; otherwise he would not offer his support.[190] Once again, it would appear, the FSI leadership failed to capitalize on Margulies's standing within international Zionism.

DISSENSION WITHIN THE FSI

Despite Vitta's qualms, reputable people were found in Florence and the group was formed. In contrast to *L'Idea Sionista*'s factual report (*IS*, 1904, pp.151–2), *Il Corriere Israelitico* gave generous publicity to its inauguration and Arias's opening address, in which he robustly declared that Zionism would restore Jewish pride and dignity, and that anyone who concealed their origins was a traitor to their ancestry (*un traditore della stirpe*). He dismissed claims that Italian Zionists were not loyal to their country (*CI*, 1904, pp.215–19). Despite the cursory concession to patriotism, Arias soon caused concern to his cautious colleagues in the FSI with his assertions that Zionism was a national movement, an epithet the FSI was loathe to acknowledge. 'Il movimento sionnista è movimento nazionale' was the title he gave to an article in the Italian Zionist journal (*IS*, 1905, pp.41–2), to which the editor responded by stating that Arias's views were not consonant with those of Italian Zionists. There followed a patriotic panegyric concluding with the oft-repeated phrase, 'our beautiful and beloved country' (*questa nostra dolce e diletta patria*) (*IS*, 1905, pp.79–80). Arias's opinions were given extensive coverage in the Triestine periodical, as they were shared by its editors.

Dissension also occurred between the Italian delegates at the Seventh Zionist Congress,[191] which took place in Basle in July 1905 and was reported in *Il Corriere Israelitico*. Two of the delegates, Edgardo Morpurgo – who would later lead the revolt of the Milan association – and Gino Arias, attempted to insist that the Italian contingent should conform to all the deliberations of the Congress, that there could not be 'a different Zionism' from that of other countries. The disagreement was once again over the thorny issue of Jewish nationality. Two special meetings were held during the Congress, on 28 and 31 July; at the second session Ravenna achieved conciliation with the promise that the matter would be discussed at the next FSI conference. The editors added that the 'special character' of Zionism in Italy had been noted by *Il Corriere*, but they had refrained from criticism (*CI*, 1905, pp.100–2). They also reiterated their own position in order to avoid misunderstandings: 'since the movement's inception, we are faithful to the *nationalist* [sic] programme' (*CI*, 1905, p.151). *L'Idea Sionista*, on the other hand, in its editorial 'After the Congress', asserted that 'there were no statements contradicting the ties that bind us to our *patria* Italy', therefore the FSI could 'tranquilly follow its course' (*IS*, 1905, p.94); and it also asserted that nothing in the Seventh Congress impinged upon patriotic sentiment, since 'the perfect compatibility of the Zionist ideal with sentiments of *italianità* were repeatedly affirmed; there may have been dissension about the essence of Zionism but not about our feelings of *italianità*' (*IS*, 1905, p.118). In other words, the tensions were edited out, as they were from Del Canuto's version.[192]

In the same issue of *L'Idea Sionista*, 1905, a 'Declaration' by Gino Arias was published, in which he once again referred to the serious accusation that Zionism was not compatible with the patriotic duties of Italian Jews. He rejected this without hesitation and declared that the two could coexist harmoniously; he added: 'I accept Primo Levi's formula published in the *Nuova Antologia: Italians first and then Jews*. I affirm that there is only one logical consequence of this formula: the Jewish idea must cede to the Italian idea, should a conflict arise' (*IS*, p.127).[193] It suggests a capitulation on Arias's part and again recalls the clash between *Deutschtum* and *Judentum*. However, a month later, in October, Arias, in a strongly worded article in the Triestine journal entitled 'After the Congress: the Obligations of Italian Zionism', attacked the concept of philanthropic Zionism as a continuation of a dishonourable tradition of 'mendicant Judaism' that begs for food and shelter. The Zionist agenda of the Seventh Congress had stated unequivocally that '*the Jewish people*' want '*a national abode* in Palestine, repudiating every other colonization'.[194] This 'virile and dignified language' should be adopted by Italian Zionism. 'Each nation has its country, for the Jewish nation it is Palestine.' He is mocking in his censure of fellow Italian Zionists and the dilution of Zionist ideology in the name of Italian patriotism (*CI*, 1905, pp.161–3). There are several other articles in this vein – that Zionism was a national movement and not humanitarian, and that if the FSI wished to remain within the organization it must adhere to the Basle programme; they include 'To Work' by Gino Racah of the Milan group (*CI*, 1905, p.170) and 'On the National Character of Zionism' by Umberto Cassuto of Florence: 'Zionism is the constant aspiration of the Jewish soul ... Herzl stated that "we are a people" ... we wish to affirm our ethnic unity' (*CI*, 1905, pp.171–3).

An explicit target of this critique of Zionism in Italy was *L'Idea Sionista* and its editor Amedeo Donati. Stung by the invective, he responded, reserving his most mordant remarks for Gino Arias, 'the illustrious professor', who clearly had 'a failing memory which required refreshing'; perhaps he had forgotten a certain declaration that he published at his own request in the pages of *L'Idea Sionista* a month earlier; how could it be interpreted in the light of all that he had written in *Il Corriere Israelitico*? (*IS*, 1905, pp.168–9). Thus by 1905 the two journals representing Zionism to the Italian public were engaged in an unseemly polemic and the FSI was riven with dissent.

The situation was further exacerbated when Carlo Francesco Gabba (1835–1920), a law professor from Pisa who was also a senator (from 1900) and thus an authoritative figure, wrote a damaging article in *La Rassegna Nazionale* published on 1 October 1905. In 'An Appeal to Italian Jews Concerning Zionism', he articulated the concerns of the nascent Italian nationalist movement about a separatist ideology in their midst which must be eradicated before it caused a schism tearing apart the very fabric of society. Gabba did not beat about the bush: at the last Zionist Congress, inflammatory proclamations of worldwide Jewish national unity were made amidst processions and even the waving of a special flag (this detail was highly significant for a nationalist such as Gabba). The unanimous solidarity of worldwide Jewry was a very serious challenge to Christian peoples. Zionism represented an assault on the very foundations of social order, and for Italians in particular, on the homogeneity, the solidity of national unity. He also suggested that the aberrant and dangerous Zionist ideology could foment latent anti-Semitism in many Christian nations, leading to civil war. He, of course, abhorred the hatred of the Jews, which had many causes such as racial antipathy and envy of the Jews' particular attributes which had led them to be among the richest and the dominant force of European finance. To openly declare a Jewish nationality and even the aspiration to form a state invited anti-Semitism. The majority of Italians were not anti-Semitic, he declared, and Jews in Italy had lived on Italian soil for centuries and were not proletariats who had recently arrived to parasitically exploit the host country with no desire to assimilate. Gabba then praised Italian Jews for their contribution to every sphere of public life. He cited, by way of example, his recently deceased good friend Tullo Massarani. The only difference between them and other citizens was their religious faith. The concept of a *Jewish nation*[195] made no sense to them; they recoiled from the suspicion that they might be less patriotic than Christian citizens. It was even possible, therefore, that a genuine 'fusion' would take place between Christians and Jews (in a footnote, he mentioned approvingly Pope Leo XIII's advocacy of mixed marriages, provided that the progeny receive a Catholic education). Thus Italy was in an enviable and unique position regarding their citizens of the Jewish faith; he had no doubt that the Italian government would block the immigration of proletariat Jews, as England had (a reference to the Aliens Act of 1905),[196] should the necessity arise. But can we hope, he asked, that Zionism does not take root in Italy to undermine the fraternal relations between Jews and Christians? He concluded:

> I therefore make my heartfelt and solicitous appeal to patriotic Italians of the Jewish faith that they should reassure the nation ... they should not restrict themselves to publicly repudiating and combating the criminal Zionist secession ... They must ensure that this iniquitous doctrine does not surreptitiously infiltrate Jewish schools. In this way they will add to the many worthy deeds undertaken for their country.[197]

Ten days later, on 10 October 1905, Ravenna wrote to Sullam that he had received two copies of Gabba's article and felt so angry that, had he responded on that day, he would have been capable only of writing insults, whereas because of Gabba's name and status he should receive a strongly worded but measured reply. Since the attack was so serious he wished Sullam to see a draft.[198] Ravenna's riposte was published in the December issue of *La Rassegna*

Nazionale as well as in *L'Idea Sionista*. He made the following points: if Jews were poor and persecuted, as in Russia and elsewhere in eastern Europe, what should they do but look to the land that once belonged to them (Gabba had suggested that the Russian Jews' adherence to Zionism was the cause of government anti-Semitism); 'this is the historical necessity, the economic and fated necessity of Zionism'. Gabba had stated that Zionism was a practical impossibility, but he should look at the facts: 100,000 Russian Jews had emigrated in the last five years; Zionism proposed a systematic emigration. East European Jews shared a language, a culture; they constituted a collective, 'a national consciousness'. The Zionist programme was peaceful and posed no threat to Christian peoples. The Jews of western Europe had a *patria*; should they deny it to those who did not? Did Italian Jews fail in their duties as citizens? Could they be accused of threatening national unity? Could their patriotism be doubted? Ravenna again reiterated the compatibility between Zionist ideals and 'our patriotism', which was solemnly acknowledged at the first Italian Zionist conference in 1901 and which had been demonstrated in their actions, statements and conduct. He concluded by pointing out that other journals were sympathetic to the Zionist cause, as was the king. The 1,000-strong membership of the FSI were cognizant of pursuing a great idea and yet remaining *italianissimi* (*IS*, 1905, pp.163–8). Cavaglion perceptively remarks on the FSI's political naivety and inability to sense the changing political climate in which, as elsewhere in western Europe, xenophobic nationalism was making its appearance; its aggressive, anti-Semitic views were gaining currency in such journals as *La Rassegna Nazionale*, *Il Regno*, and *L'Idea Nazionale*. By insisting on the equilibrium between Zionism and patriotism, Ravenna was unaware of the fine line he was walking; beneath lay an abyss into which Italian Zionism was eventually to fall.[199]

Il Corriere Israelitico, in its response to the Gabba polemic, attacked his ignorance of Zionism and robustly exhorted its readers to persevere and demonstrate to 'our enemies' how pointless their 'disgust' was that the Jews were gaining prominence. 'Our enemies say we are attempting to separate ourselves from others, as if ethnic diversity [*la diversità dei popoli*] was unheard of ... they want us to renounce our otherness' (*CI*, 1905, pp.196–9). These remarks reflect the different cultural context of the journal published in an empire where multiculturalism was accepted and where the Jews formed their own political party to promote Jewish national autonomy like the Hungarians, Poles and Czechs.

The 1906 January conference of the FSI held in Rome was dominated by a lengthy debate on Jewish nationalism. The federation's formal statement, which had been sent to the Fifth Congress, was confirmed in Rome.[200] The outcome of the Seventh Zionist Congress, with its clear mandate for a national homeland in Palestine, caused disquiet amongst many Italian Zionists, fearful of the consequences that might ensue in the shifting political landscape, Gabba's polemical article being symptomatic of it. Rabbi Chajes insisted on asking whether the Basle agenda was nationalist, and Professor Alessandro Levi argued that nationalist sentiment was justified for Jews without rights, especially for the Russians, but not in Italy, a view reiterated by Bernardo Dessau in his analysis of the last two years of Zionist activity in Italy. Professor Carlo Levi commented that Zionism could accommodate all opinions and tendencies, and Italian Zionists should not reveal divisions and appear vulnerable to their 'ever vigilant and implacable enemies' who were planning the dissolution of Zionism: why undermine years of effort? Sullam compared the endeavours of Zionism with those of Cavour in his struggles for the unity and independence of Italy. Ascoli stated that 'we are Italian and we intend to confirm that our Italian Zionist programme in no way contradicts our patriotic sentiments'. Ravenna expressed regret that doubts had been raised about Italian Zionists' patriotism. To Chajes's question, he replied rather evasively that 'whoever accepts the Basle agenda is a Zionist', and he concluded that Italian Zionism need change nothing in its work begun at the Modena conference (*IS*, 1906, pp.7–10). Conspicuous by their absence at this conference were the two delegates who had disagreed with their colleagues at the international congress, Gino Arias and Edgardo Morpurgo.[201] As *Il Corriere Israelitico* aptly observed in its report of the conference, no clear directive had emerged from the deliberations and no delegate in favour of the nationalist plan had been elected to the executive committee (*CI*, 1906, pp.22–3). One of them, Edgardo Morpurgo, was voted out of his position as FSI representative of the Jewish National Fund and the Jewish Colonial Trust to which he had been nominated in 1905. In a letter to Ravenna of 17 January 1906, he expressed his bitterness that four years of unstinting effort for the Zionist cause had been thus repaid by the federation, but he found comfort in the knowledge that his own group in Milan still supported him.[202]

During this conference, the fifth of the FSI, Ravenna had a private audience with the king, during which he wished to be fully informed by Ravenna of Zionist activities in Italy. He was pleased to have confirmation that western European Zionism was a movement of fraternal Jewish solidarity. He was delighted to hear that Zionists and Jews from other countries considered Italy to be 'the Paradise of the Jews', which he thought most appropriate, given that there was no racial or religious discrimination (*IS*, 1906, pp.13–14). Such a designation was also applied to England at this time. A clearer and more authoritative censure of Senator Gabba's views could not be found, observed *L'Idea Sionista*'s editor (*IS*, 1906, p.14).

Gabba was not mollified or reassured, and in April 1906 he launched another inflammatory attack on Zionism in Italy, also published in the nationalist journal *La Rassegna Nazionale*.[203] It is germane to dwell on the contents, given its author's stature and repute as a law professor and senator of the Realm. His public utterances on the Jews in Italy would have the same impact as those by the eminent historians Mommsen and von Treitschke in Germany. Gabba claimed to have received many letters of support for the views expressed in the first article, from Jews 'of all types'. Rabbis had written to reassure him that Zionism was a philanthropic operation for persecuted Jews, or that it was both a humanitarian movement and a revival of Jewish nationality that in no way diminished Italian patriotism. He had also heard from the president of the FSI. However, nothing he had read invalidated in any way the conclusions of the previous essay. The general public knew little about Zionism and he felt it his duty to publicize it more widely. The journal *L'Idea Sionista* had been brought to his attention, and in one issue the FSI stated their intention to extend operations to cities '*not yet won over*'[204] (*non ancora conquistate*). This *conquista* must be prevented at all costs. Zionism troubled many Jews because it placed in conflict two nationalities that were attributed to them, and this was the grave danger it posed. Zionism signified the affirmation of a Jewish nationality, distinct from and in contradistinction to the Christian nations among which the Jews lived. Those Zionists who denied these facts were ingenuous; Herzl's *Jewish State* was proof enough. Gabba then argued that the Jews could not constitute a nation as they had no language, literature or art and their traditions had been disrupted for nineteen centuries. The national contribution of the Jews was completed with the birth of Christianity:

> History teaches us what happens to minority races: first they are given inferior status and as such retain their distinctive characteristics; they then merge when no longer discriminated against, and finally disappear. This is the ineluctable fate of the semitic Jews [*Questo è appunto l'indeclinabile destino dei semiti ebrei*] ... In an unequal struggle between two races, history teaches us that it can only end with the extermination or the expulsion of the weaker one [*la lotta fra le due razze non finisce altrimenti che coll'esterminio, oppure colla espulsione della razza meno forte*].

The concept of dual nationality was 'a monstrosity in international law'. In order to demonstrate the dangers of Zionist propaganda, Gabba listed examples of violent separatist nationalist activities of Zionist Jews throughout Europe, including a proposal he had read in the *Irish World* of 15 December for an international Jewish parliament of 500 members! These facts illustrated that wherever Zionism took root, unrest and anti-Semitism ensued. As yet, he stated, there was no sign of anti-Semitism in Italy. Italian Jews were treated in the same way as their Christian compatriots, the only difference being their religious faith. This felicitous state of affairs must be maintained and nurtured. Zionism hitherto had had little success in Italy, and the principal reason was Zionism's incompatibility with love of one's *patria*. Italian Jews should dispel the equivocation that Zionism engendered: that it was one thing to help persecuted Jews and another to wish for a separation of the Jews from other nations; with the former everyone could participate; the latter was folly. In conclusion, Gabba again appealed to Italian patriots of the Jewish faith, in particular those who shared his views, to combat Zionism in the name of the nation's unity. All Italian patriots should take part.

In his critique of Gabba's ideas, Salvatore Mazzamuto argues that one cannot call him a 'real' racist or anti-Semite and that his assumption that the Jews will eventually disappear is but a continuation of the liberal ideology of national homogeneity. He omits any reference to the seditious passages and refers to those Jews who endorsed Gabba's battle against Zionist propaganda, including the editor of *Il Vessillo Israelitico*. He rather undermines his anodyne presentation of the Gabba polemic by citing a letter of 5 October 1887 written by a Jewish colleague at the University of Pisa, Salvatore De Benedetti, which alludes to Gabba as someone who one day would like to drive out Jewish academics. Moreover, Mazzamuto mentions that Gabba was considered a fascist *ante litteram* by supporters of the regime.[205] It is the case, nevertheless, that *Il*

Vessillo Israelitico approved of Gabba's stance, and chose to ignore, it seems, the anti-Semitic remarks camouflaged as concerns about Zionism. The editor's hostility since the inception of the movement continued in the reporting of the international congresses: Zionist aspirations were utopian and would give rise to anti-Semitism. Those aspects of Gabba's first piece which accorded with these firmly held views were given coverage with the additional comment that the journal 'had always seen the dangers of Zionist propaganda and had pointed them out courageously, convinced that they were thus undertaking an imperative of vital importance'. Affirmations of solidarity for 'our oppressed brethren' and of 'everlasting devotion to that country of which we are proud to be most loyal children' (*figli fedelissimi*) ended the article (*VI*, 1905, pp.579–81). In addition, an interview between the editor and the senator was published which was very favourable. The perils of Zionism were again reiterated. Gabba was asked whether Ravenna's statements regarding Zionists' patriotism had dispelled his doubts, to which the response was negative. He was asked whether it was not the duty of Italian Jews who had a *patria* they love to assist those who did not. 'Yes', was the reply, but there was no need to call such aid 'Zionism' and associate it with Jewish nationalism. He denied that anti-Semitism had anything to do with Roman Catholic intolerance and suggested that in Germany, where it was widespread, it originated principally from Protestant circles. Gabba ended the interview with expressions of admiration for many Jews. *Il Vessillo Israelitico* gave briefer treatment to Gabba's second article and dissented strongly from his view that the Jews would disappear.[206]

Despite this endorsement of Gabba's views, it is worth noting that there was a gradual shift of perspective from the time of Flaminio Servi's death in January 1904. When his son Ferruccio – also a rabbi – took over the editorship of *Il Vessillo Israelitico*, reports on Zionism were more conciliatory and constructive.[207] For example, there is a sympathetic obituary of Herzl (*VI*, 1904, pp.89–93); 'the utopian folly of Zionism' becomes 'a noble and beneficial utopia'; he acknowledges that one can be proud of one's Jewish ancestry and also love Italy, that 'beneath the symbol of Zionism, one can offer a hospitable land to those whose country is hostile towards them'; and that the FSI has effected a beneficial revival of Jewish culture in Italy.[208] A few years later, Ferruccio gave positive publicity to the work of the Jewish National Fund and its colonization of Palestine, and permitted a glowing first-hand account of the Eleventh Zionist Congress held in Vienna to be printed, describing the thousands of delegates, the city decked out with Zionist flags and posters, the numerous events in many locations, the sporting activities, the films on Palestine and plays and speeches in Hebrew: 'the great satisfaction of having lived eight intensely Jewish days … Had other Italian Jews been present their Jewish sentiment, which may be dormant but not extinguished, would have found a salutary reawakening.'[209] However, the issue of the compatibility of Zionism and *italianità* remained a leitmotif. The author was Anselmo Colombo, secretary of the recently established executive committee of the Jewish communities and also vice-president of the Rome community, who was thus an authoritative voice of Italian Jewry. The impact of the Zionist Congress led him to suggest in the article that *Il Vessillo Israelitico* should open its pages to a full and free discussion on the concepts of Jewish nationalism and universalism, on the position that 'official Judaism' ought to adopt and disseminate with regard to Zionism. In other words, he was arguing for a rapprochement between the FSI and community leaders which, hitherto, had not occurred, as the frequent references to the conservative, closed minds of the Jewish governing elite in *L'Idea Sionista* reveal. Unlike Austria, France, England and Germany, there was no coordinated response to Zionism from the Jewish communities, as they did not form a federation until 1914; the Piedmontese journal acted as a conduit for their views, hence the significance of Colombo's constructive approach.

In contrast to the considered attention to Gabba's articles by *Il Vessillo Israelitico*, *Il Corriere Israelitico* lambasted the professor for his unscholarly lack of documentation and numerous errors, concluding with fine irony that 'the destiny the good senator predicts for us with such evangelical sweetness [*dolcezza*] and in the name of Christian friendship really moves us, but we do not want to die!' Gabba was clearly incensed by the piece and demanded a right of reply, which was duly published. In addition, the editors reported a sitting of the Italian Senate of 7 May 1906, during which Gabba raised the question of dual nationality; in his second piece he had described it as 'a monstrosity of international law'. The reply he received from the Marchese di S. Giuliano made it apparent that the concept of dual nationality for Italians living abroad was legally acknowledged; therefore, argued *Il Corriere*, there was no contradiction between Jewish nationality and German, French or Italian citizenship.[210] Gino Arias, in his essays on Zionism, also attacked Gabba and unequivocally asserted the existence of a Jewish nationality 'which expresses one of the best aspirations of our modern society and is therefore destined to triumph' (*CI*, 1906, pp.44–8). Furthermore, to counter the negative image of Zionism disseminated by Gabba, several pieces sympathetic to the cause by eminent non-Jewish academics such as Vittorio Racca, professor of economics and international relations, were published.[211] Ravenna also responded to Gabba's second article, this time in a more robust and critical manner. He reiterated yet again the 'perfect compatibility of the Zionist ideal with our patriotism' (*IS*, 1906, pp.64–8). In spite of these damage limitation efforts, the harm was done and the fallout began.

Between 14 and 16 June 1906, another pogrom was perpetrated in Russia, injuring many and killing eighty people. Instructions from Zionist Central Office recommended public protests as before. Ravenna, in his circular to the regional Zionist presidents, suggested that such demonstrations might lead to unrest, and he therefore proposed a petition to parliament or a meeting with influential individual members. These alternative measures reflected timidity and a reluctance to expose Italian Zionists to political scrutiny.[212] On 27 June 1906, the secretary of the Livorno association wrote to Ravenna to inform him that despite great hopes and enthusiasm, his group – established the year before – had seen every initiative dashed by the deliberations of the Basle Congress, by the less than reassuring equivocations of the FSI Rome conference, and by '[the] hostility that has arisen from everywhere against Zionism … We, and the majority of Italian Jews, understand Zionism to be a social movement, devoid of any nationalist idea which we deem to be disastrous for its mission worldwide … The only alternative open to the group is its dissolution as we cannot work with any loyalty for an ideal that is contrary to our own.' A subsequent letter of 30 June confirmed its closure.[213]

In 1906, the World Zionist Organization established a commission to collate data, derived from a detailed questionnaire, on western European Jews, to be consigned to the Russian government in order to effect change in their policy towards Jews. Authoritative persons were required and in the letters sent to Ravenna by Nahum Sokolow, a Russian member of the Smaller Actions Committee, the names of '*le grand rabbin*' Margulies and another east European Jew residing in Florence – '*mon cher ami*', the renowned publisher Leo Olschki – were put forward with instructions to Ravenna to contact them; Margulies had recently taken part in an international conference held in Frankfurt concerning the Russian Jews.[214] Needless to say, given Ravenna's ambivalent attitude towards the chief rabbi, he gave the compilation of the questionnaire to another, an academic lawyer, Moise Finzi. The twenty-one page report on Italian Jews, dated 13 June 1906, contains few useful statistics and is economical with the truth. For example, it states that no social class in Italy was opposed to the emancipation of the Jews; there was no hostility, no antipathy; there never had been 'a Jewish question' in Italy; in no other country did the Jews so fully enjoy the benefits of freedom and equality; all had shown love for their country in peace and in war.[215] It is problematic to argue the counterfactual with any conviction, but one can only surmise that Margulies's analysis might have been more nuanced and informative.

Another blow to the authority of the FSI and its president was the creation in May 1907 of the first Comitato Pro Cultura Ebraica (Committee for Jewish Culture) in Florence, swiftly followed by others throughout the country. This was the initiative of Margulies; the Tuscan capital became the centre of a Jewish revival in Italy. This significant development will be examined in the following chapter. Suffice it to say that hitherto Zionism had lacked a permanent location; now the locus of influence shifted to Florence, where it remained. The FSI had no choice but to acknowledge the existence of this new organization; relations between the two were strained, although *L'Idea Sionista* was prompt in its praise for its objectives and conceded that Florence was the 'incontestable centre of our literary culture'.[216]

MINORANZA SIONISTA PURA

A further weakening of the FSI, precipitating a crisis, was the establishment in November 1907 of a splinter Zionist group in Milan, calling itself Minoranza sionista pura (MSP). At the Eighth Zionist Congress held in August of that year, Nordau, with his customary eloquence, had made it abundantly clear that Zionism was not a philanthropic movement; the Jews must now decide whether they were a nation and, if this were the case, every effort was to be made to attain the status of other nations.[217] The new group responded to Nordau's call. They were also reacting to the recent tensions within the FSI, as the article in *Il Corriere Israelitico* illustrates, written by one of their number under the pseudonym of Ben Zion. Aptly titled 'The Zionist Crisis in Italy', the author made the following points: only four Italian delegates were elected to attend the Eighth Congress; there was a disputed election in Milan between two delegates, one of whom espoused political Zionism; many members of the FSI were disillusioned after the Rome conference because of the polemics between the two ideologies, political and philanthropic, and the lack of consensus; the political faction comprising mostly young individuals – a similar radical generational divide as in Germany, France and Austria – wholly accepted the Basle programme and called themselves purists. He challenged the right of *L'Idea Sionista* to continue as the organ of the FSI, as it certainly did not reflect the views of the purist minority who would continue with actions of which they were proud and who would collaborate with the Triestine journal.[218]

The unsigned manifesto of the Minoranza sionista pura from Milan, dated 1 November 1907, was duly published in *Il Corriere Israelitico*. It appealed to the Zionists of Italy to accept the national significance of Zionism. The Jewish people had a specific national consciousness which they resolutely refused to renounce. 'This nationalist affirmation is highly significant for us ... We are convinced that in Italy too, indeed especially in Italy where assimilation spreads its insidious net, Zionism must be affirmed in all its purity and entirety.' They added that they sincerely loved the hospitable country of their birth, a love that was compatible with their fervent Zionist faith. They were not preoccupied by the harm this affirmation might cause and were determined to carry out the deliberations of the international congresses.[219] The purists subsequently acknowledged the Triestine journal as their official organ, and pledged their support for the Pro Cultura movement which was reinforced by the nomination of Aldo Sorani, president of Pro Cultura, to their provisional executive committee, which also included Eduardo Morpurgo. They would attempt to work within the FSI. Their educational and cultural objectives were far more ambitious and included international exchange visits for children of Zionist families and the publication of a *Piccola Biblioteca popolare di scienza dell'Ebraismo* along the lines of the German *Jüdische Bibliothek* (*CI*, 1907, pp.228, 261).

On 1 December 1907, Eduardo Morpurgo wrote to Ravenna informing him that support for the MSP was increasing, not only in Milan but also in Florence, Padua, Rome and Turin; the MSP would continue to work with the FSI on the Jewish National Fund.[220] In the pages of *L'Idea Sionista* there is no reference to this rebellion – the MSP's existence is barely mentioned. In his private correspondence with Ravenna, Sullam expressed his anger and frustration, tempered with some wit, about the new group: on 12 December 1907, the heading 'Minoranza sionista pura' was followed by twenty-one exclamation marks. He would ensure that the Venice group opposed them; their 'patent of purity' was offensive to other Zionists; on 2 January 1908, he commiserated with Ravenna on the visit from the Zionist purists and suggested that for future encounters he acquired a supply of straitjackets and other suitable appliances; on 14 February 1908, he told Ravenna that he had written a long letter to Morpurgo, advising him to desist and return to the fold: 'let's see how he replies. In any case I've got an excellent revolver!!!'[221] On a more serious note, the MSP's public endorsement of Jewish nationalism highlighted yet again the issue of dual nationality, which for Italian Zionists was a constant dilemma. At a meeting of the Venice group on 16 February 1908, attended by – among others – Edgardo Morpurgo, a discussion on the MSP led Sullam to state that their actions were deleterious for Italian Zionism, creating a conflict between patriotic and Jewish sentiments which would cause him profound anguish (*un gravissimo e doloroso stato d'animo*) and he would be forced to declare that he was more Italian than Jewish.[222] Dante Lattes posed the question apropos of Jewish nationalism: 'Are we firstly Italian and then Jews, or Jews and then Italian?' (*Noi siamo prima italiani e poi ebrei, o prima ebrei e poi italiani?*), to which a contributor, Edoardo Pirani, replied: 'Neither, but both in equal measure, that is Jewish Italians just as there are Christian Italians' (*Io credo nè prima nè dopo, ma contemporaneamente, cioè italiani ebrei come ci sono italiani cristiani*) (*CI*, 1907, pp.17–18). The dialectic paradigm of *Deutschtum/italianità* and *Judentum/ebraismo* was also being experienced in Italy.

SIXTH CONFERENCE OF THE FSI

Despite diminishing numbers and dissension, the FSI held its sixth conference in Venice in February 1908. In his opening speech, Ravenna conceded that Italian Zionism could not boast of great successes, but at least it had consistently adhered to its programme launched in 1901. During lengthy and heated discussions, this programme was reaffirmed and a proposal deploring 'the ambiguous declarations of the so-called purist groups' was carried twelve to three, with one abstention. A further proposal 'acknowledged the necessity of the Pro Cultura movement' and invited the executive committee of the FSI to assist it; this was carried unanimously. There were also encouraging reports of the reconstitution of the Livorno,[223] Rome and Florence groups that had languished, the last in all probability on account of other Jewish projects. In addition, Gino Arias announced the new monthly journal *L'Eco Sionista d'Italia* (*IS*, 1908, pp.35–7). It was based in Florence and propounded a political Zionist ideology, antithetical to *L'Idea Sionista*, and thus eroding still further the FSI. The first (unsigned) editorial of April 1908 was explicit: 'We do not conceive Zionism as a philanthropic, humanitarian movement … but as a movement that is intent upon "resolving the Jewish question" in all its complexity and giving to the Jews, not a refuge or a haven in Palestine, but a country governed by the rule of law where a full and free national life can unfold.' However, it was short-lived; by 1909 it had ceased publication; 'not even an echo could be heard', *L'Idea Sionista* commented rather unkindly (*IS*, 1909, p.74). Nevertheless it had strengthened, albeit briefly, the political wing of Zionism in Italy and also indicated Florence yet again as the centre of Jewish initiatives.

Il Corriere Israelitico's account of the sixth conference was positive: two constructive outcomes had resulted from the debates. Despite the negative comments on the MSP, a truce had been reached by which each faction would continue to function, thus leaving the majority to pursue their 'special form of Italian Zionism … that does not conflict, even in the minds of their enemies, with love of their country and their standing as Italian citizens'. The other was the recognition of the importance of the Pro Cultura movement. All that was necessary to give impetus to Italian Zionism was that these two associations should work together (*CI*, 1907, pp.320–2).

FAILURES OF THE FSI

Notwithstanding the Triestine journal's encouraging observations, the FSI was seriously debilitated by the divisions and continued to decline. In a dramatically-titled article, 'The End of Zionism?', the increase of clerical anti-Semitism was perceived as another reason for the desertion of the Zionist cause by its members (*IS*, 1908, pp.103–4). *L'Idea Sionista*'s regular reports on contributions to the Jewish National Fund revealed that for the last quarter of 1908, out of a total of 82,937.28 German marks, Italy had given nothing – the only country with a zero donation. In February 1908 Ravenna received an irate letter from Zionist Central Office deploring the 'shameful sum' received in the previous period; 'it was a matter of honour' to persuade contributors to pay more and a prompt reply from the recipient was expected with details of his efforts to enlarge the coffers. In December of the same year, another letter was sent stating that they were 'extraordinarily regretful' to have received no answers to their many letters; an urgent response was requested 'as it was not right that Italy should disappear from the lists'. In this instance, it was the shekel contributions that were lacking.[224] Thus even in the much vaunted activity of philanthropy, Italian Zionists were now failing. In addition, Ravenna's regular circulars to the regional groups revealed a lamentable lethargy, 'whereas the most admirable manifestations of Jewish renewal are to be found in the Pro Cultura of the young Florentines'.[225] On 9 February 1909, Sullam wrote to Ravenna: '*L'Idea Sionista* isn't going well ... I think everything about Italian Zionism is going badly'.[226] The divisive and radical agenda of the Minoranza sionista pura had also evaporated.

Ironically, while Felice Ravenna was struggling as president of the FSI,[227] his father Leone, in his capacity as facilitator of the federation of Jewish communities, was receiving accolades: after over forty years, many of the communities had decided to hold a conference (which took place in Milan in November 1909) to discuss again the possibility of cooperation. In an article in the Zionist journal on that conference, Leone Ravenna recalled his part in the conferences of the 1860s. He also acknowledged the FSI's debates on the problems of the communities (*IS*, 1909, pp.74–8). A further irony: the pages of *L'Idea Sionista*'s rather slim issues for 1910 contain several articles on the Pro Cultura's programmes and also on yet another of Margulies's journalistic endeavours – *La Settimana Israelitica (SI)* – to whom cordial greetings were sent. Sullam was not so genial: on 1 March 1909, he wrote to Ravenna in confidence that Aldo Sorani had contacted him requesting his assistance with a periodical that Margulies was planning:

> I told him it would be a pointless and damaging initiative and a waste of money ... For my part I wouldn't give a centime ... especially since Margulies is in charge, a German who has all the defects of a German and all the antipathy and presumption of a subject of the Emperor Joseph ... My

lively letter to Sorani will not prevent the journal's publication because Margulies is punctilious and aspires to excel in every possible way among Italian Jews.

He concluded gloomily that Italian Zionism seemed dead and the Venetian group moribund.[228] In his letter to Sorani of 27 February 1909, Sullam was scathing in his refusal to have anything to do with the new journal; indeed he was derisive in his comments about all the Jewish periodicals published in Italy: *Il Vessillo Israelitico* reported mainly 'gossip' about people, giving them the illusion that they, their friends and even their pets were famous;[229] *L'Idea Sionista* was a mere shadow; *La Rivista Israelitica* was a vehicle for Margulies and 'those Germans he has brought into Italy who have, like Germans generally, the greatest contempt for Italians and our culture ... they should publish their amusing elucubrations in their own language'. He suggested merging all the journals into one, as long as Margulies was not involved.[230]

Once again, a leading member of the FSI irrevocably damaged the movement in Italy by their repudiation of Margulies, the outsider, and those around him. And Margulies' disciples felt this rebuttal keenly. On 11 October 1909, Aldo Sorani, president of Pro Cultura, wrote to Ravenna wishing to know why every time they in Florence had done something for the common cause they were branded as 'schismatics and sowers of discord'. He referred to their attempts to discuss a possible merger between *L'Idea Sionista* and *L'Eco Sionista*, but there was no agreement from 'the other side'; thus their journal was forced to die and *L'Idea* continued 'its slow and painful death agony'. He added that Zionism was so diminished that the only way forward was through Jewish culture, Pro Cultura. Sorani offered to join forces with the FSI: 'you want a revival and so do I ... Modesty apart, if we all in Italy had attempted what we youngsters have done, we would have achieved something.'[231]

In December 1909, Margulies himself made another attempt to collaborate with the FSI: he also wrote to Ravenna, to inform him of the imminent publication of *La Settimana Israelitica*. It was common knowledge that *L'Idea Sionista* was failing, and thus the rabbi suggested that the Florentine journal should become the official organ of the FSI and would publish all communiqués and defend the ideals of Zionism.[232] This effort also fell on sterile ground: the president of the Padua Pro Cultura association, Giuseppe Morpurgo, notified Ravenna on 8 February 1910 that he had at last received a negative reply from the editor of *L'Idea Sionista* to the proposed merger between the two journals. He expressed his disappointment and also his opinion that the new publication would be very successful.[233] Again Florence was rebuffed to the disadvantage of the FSI.

As the activities of the FSI and the Florence group moved further apart, to the detriment of the former, external political events tested the federation's intractable dilemma of *italianità* and *ebraismo*. By 1910 the Italian nationalist movement had garnered sufficient momentum to generate the first Nationalist Congress; their principal journal, *L'Idea Nazionale* followed a year later. In September 1911 Italy declared war on Turkey and invaded Libya. In order to deflect accusations of unpatriotic actions – the Ottoman Empire was involved in Zionist negotiations over Palestine – the FSI suspended all public activity and closed down the ailing *Idea Sionista*. In November 1911, the 'Coppola affair' erupted. In the president's protocol of 31 March 1912, Ravenna informed the regional Zionist leaders of the reasons for not holding the Zionist conference in Milan the previous December: it might have been perceived as proof of tepid patriotism 'when all thoughts are turned to the war for Italy's political glory'; in addition, a cycle of propagandist lectures organized with 'the erudite and valiant Rabbi Armando Sorani of Florence' – not Margulies, but one of his students – had also been cancelled. 'This period of reflection' did not signify the end of the movement; it would resume when the political situation was more favourable. As a demonstration of 'our immutable Zionist sentiment which is not and can never be antithetical to patriotic manifestations', Ravenna requested that the annual shekel be collected as usual.[234]

Official Italian Zionism had capitulated to political pressures and withdrawn of its own volition from the public sphere, intimidated by the aggressive anti-Semitism of the nationalists. However, in Florence, the younger generation under Margulies's guidance proceeded with their work to promote Jewish culture in numerous ways, undaunted and unbowed. They organized conferences, continued their contributions to *Il Corriere Israelitico* and reported on Zionist matters in their own journal, *La Settimana Israelitica*, which was the principal conduit for the FSI – they even advertised a Zionist watch (*SI*, 43 [1913]). There was a sporadic recovery of the FSI with their conference in Milan in May 1913, but such was the secrecy surrounding it, of which Pacifici complained in a letter to Ravenna, that there were very few delegates.[235] In his opening speech, Ravenna acknowledged that Zionism in Italy was in crisis, with a rapidly declining membership and few financial resources. An illustration of the insoluble impasse of *ebraismo* and *italianità* was provided by Sullam's insistence that the federation must define precisely what was meant by Zionism in Italy, otherwise he would have to leave. The FSI had spent more than a decade doing almost little else but delineate its terms of reference. The most lively and radical speaker at the conference was Alfonso Pacifici who proposed, in an *echt* Herzlian manner, an assault on the aging, conservative community administrations through, for example, the introduction of the Zionist anthem in religious services in order to proclaim cultural and national renewal. Why not, he declared, undertake this little great revolution (*Perché non compiere questa piccola grande rivoluzione*, *SI*, 19 [1913])? It was sung in the Florence synagogue later that year (*SI*, 1 [1914]). He was applauded, and Ravenna conceded that in spite of Pacifici's rather intense and harsh expressions, such people were needed to rouse and stir the general apathy (*SI*, 19 [1913]). Although the conference was a modest affair, at least Zionism was once again being discussed publicly by the FSI after two years of silence. The last of its reports sent to the central committee before the outbreak of war made discouraging reading: very little progress; Zionist activity had been suspended during Italo-Turkish hostilities; this inactivity had spread to local groups with the result that membership had dropped to 600; only in Milan was there a thriving association with weekly meetings, lectures and collections for the National Fund. The youth movement, an indirect consequence of Zionism, would continue to have a beneficial effect (*SI*, 29 [1913]).

Il Corriere Israelitico, *La Settimana Israelitica* and *Il Vessillo Israelitico* informed their readers of the varied programme that the Milan group, 'always in the vanguard of Zionist propaganda' (*VI*, 1913, p.588), was planning for the winter of 1913: lectures, Hebrew classes, and concerts in aid of the Jewish National Fund. In addition, the group issued a manifesto on the much debated question of 'Zionism and *italianità*', which the Triestine journal hoped would conclude once and for all discussion on a question that had benefited neither Zionism nor Judaism (*CI*, 1913, p.103). The Italian periodicals published the manifesto, which reiterated yet again that there was no incompatibility between the two, and that no one had told or would tell Italians to abandon their country.[236] Max Nordau, on a visit to Milan for the Verdi celebrations, also addressed the local Zionists, and he too repeated his frequent message: Zionism was not a charitable organization, but a return to Judaism; Italians, although not returning to the land of their ancestors, could work on behalf of the dignity of their race and people; there was no conflict between Zionism and Italian patriotism.[237]

In the pre-First World War period, there were no further official meetings of the FSI. Just as the first stirrings of the Zionist movement in Italy had been the work of the flamboyant Romanian Yosef Marcou Baruch, so the last flurries of pre-war activity issued from the pen of another east European Jew, Pinhaus Rutenberg (1879–1942), whose dealings with Italian Zionists appear to have eluded Italian historians. Rutenberg, an engineer from the Ukraine, was one of four Russian 'activists' who were against the Zionist policy of inaction during the war. They envisaged supporting the Allies in word and deed with a Jewish fighting force. Rutenberg fled Russia after 1905 and sought support for his ideas from the Italians, the French and then the Americans. He returned to Russia in 1917. He was said to be an impressive man with a daunting mode of behaviour: thickset, always dressed in black, he would speak in a menacing manner through clenched teeth.[238] Between November 1914 and November 1915, Rutenberg conducted a frequent correspondence with Ravenna in an attempt to enlist the FSI for his cause. He had contacts with high-ranking government ministers, some of whom were dubious, such as Luigi Luzzatti, while others like Turati were more positive. In several letters, Rutenberg exhorted Ravenna to take the initiative, but it was the Russian who suggested forming a committee of influential Jewish and non-Jewish politicians sooner rather than later, 'because if there is war, we cannot do anything'. Italy entered the war in May 1915. The cautious Ravenna clearly had doubts and sought endorsements of Rutenberg's character, which he received from many quarters, including two from members of parliament who expressed their absolute respect, admiration and confidence in him.[239] Rutenberg travelled throughout Italy in enthusiastic and energetic pursuit of his goals, always informing Ravenna of his encounters. He was full of ideas: press releases; meetings in several cities; invitations to distinguished speakers. In his letter of 20 April 1915, he wrote, perhaps to motivate Ravenna, that in Russia the newspapers 'speak of the Jewish movement created by me [*sic*] in Italy in favour of the Palestinian state, and that Italy is favourable'.[240] Italy was sympathetic but nothing conclusive was achieved. This was largely as a result of the ever-threatening shadow of war and the indecision of the Italian government,[241] but also as a consequence of the tepid response from the FSI, as Sullam's letter to Ravenna of 14 February 1915 reveals:

> I am as convinced as you are that we will not get support for this committee and I think it is very debatable whether it should go ahead. At the moment everyone is saying Italians should remain united and think only of Italy's future. I do not believe we will find politicians willing to risk their position ... They might help us privately ... but not publicly.[242]

The Zionist Federation in Italy regained momentum when the Italian government recognized the Balfour Declaration in 1918. Ravenna resumed his role as president; he, Lattes and Sullam became key players in the immediate post-war period. In 1927, the first Italian pioneer, Enzo Sereni (1905–44), emigrated to Palestine where he devoted himself to establishing kibbutzim. During the Second World War he returned to Europe on missions to save Jews and take them clandestinely to Palestine. He was captured and deported in 1944 to Dachau where he perished.[243] The terrible and tragic irony of Zionist ideology was its transgression during those war years when the British Mandate in Palestine imposed stringent restrictions on the numbers of Jews permitted entry. And it was British Jews such as Nathan Mindel who had to enforce them.[244] Zionism, with its vision of a safe haven, a homeland for the Jews and reaffirmation of Jewish national identity, attempted to reverse the assimilatory process of the previous 100 years.

NOTES

1. Theodor Herzl, *The Jewish State: An Attempt at a Modern Solution of the Jewish Question*, 4th edn (London: Searl, 1946; first edn 1896), pp.14, 18. Seventeen editions of *Der Judenstaat: Versuch einer modernen Lösung der jüdischen Frage* were published in Herzl's lifetime in various languages. It was not translated into Italian until 1918.
2. Jonathan Frankel, 'The Crisis of 1881–82 as a Turning point in Modern Jewish History', in David Berger (ed.), *The Legacy of Jewish Migration: 1881 and its Impact* (New York: Brooklyn College Press, 1983), p.9.
3. See Frankel, 'Crisis of 1881–82', pp.12–19; on Kadimah and Birnbaum, see Robert S. Wistrich, *The Jews of Vienna in the Age of Franz Joseph* (Oxford: Oxford University Press, 1989), Chapters 11 and 12; see also David Vital, *The Origins of Zionism* (Oxford: Clarendon Press, 1975), pp.122–84, 212–23. For a comprehensive view of the international Zionist movement, see Vital's trilogy, of which this is the first volume. The others are: *Zionism: The Formative Years* (Oxford: Clarendon Press, 1982), and *Zionism: The Crucial Phase* (Oxford: Clarendon Press, 1987). On Moses Hess and other proto-Zionists, see, for example, Georges Bensoussan, *Une histoire intellectuelle et politique du Sionisme 1860–1940* (Paris: Arthème Fayard, 2002), pp.10–41.
4. See Jehuda Reinharz, *Fatherland or Promised Land: The Dilemma of the German Jew, 1893–1914* (Ann Arbor, MI: University of Michigan Press, 1975), pp.94–5; Michael Marrus, *The Politics of Assimilation: A Study of the French Jewish Community at the Time of the Dreyfus Affair* (Oxford: Clarendon Press, 1971), pp.252–3.
5. See Vital, *Origins of Zionism*, p.209: 'the philanthropic view was never fully eclipsed by any other and persisted well into the following century, until West European Jewry was itself engulfed in other horrors'; and Vital, *Zionism: Crucial Phase*, p.35: 'The springs of Zionism had always been in eastern Europe.'
6. See Vital's tables and analyses of the delegates to the Sixth Congress in *Zionism: Formative Years*, pp.482–94.
7. Vital, *Origins of Zionism*, p.374. On Zionist ideology from its inception to the establishment of the State of Israel, see, for example, Gideon Shimoni, *The Zionist Ideology* (Hanover and London: Brandeis University Press, 1995), and Jehuda Reinharz and Anita Shapira (eds), *Essential Papers on Zionism* (London: Cassell, 1996).
8. See Marvin Lowenthal (ed. and trans.), *The Diaries of Theodor Herzl* (New York: Dial Press, 1956), p.xix; and Michael Stanislawski, *Zionism and the Fin de Siècle: Cosmopolitanism and Nationalism*

from Nordau to Jabotinsky (Berkeley, LA, and London: University of California Press, 2001), pp.xvii, 13–14, 58–9.
9. Carl E. Schorske, *Fin-de-Siècle Vienna: Politics and Culture* (Cambridge: Cambridge University Press, 1981), p.161.
10. See Lowenthal (ed. and trans.), *Diaries of Theodor Herzl*, p.7.
11. Ibid., p.142.
12. Ibid., p.182. He addressed the Jews of the East End of London on several other occasions (see p.245).
13. Cited in Schorske, *Fin-de-Siècle Vienna*, p.171. See also Ritchie Robertson, *The 'Jewish Question' in German Literature 1749–1939: Emancipation and its Discontents* (Oxford: Oxford University Press, 1999), p.485: Max Brod described him as 'a king with a flowing Assyrian beard, a demi-god, but in modern dress'.
14. Lowenthal (ed. and trans.), *Diaries of Theodor Herzl*, pp.403–5. Herzl noted down verbatim Witte's solution to the Jewish question in Russia (Witte was minister of finance): 'I used to say to the late Emperor Alexander III: if it were possible to drown six or seven million Jews in the Black Sea, I should be perfectly satisfied. But if it is not possible, we must let them live' (p.395).
15. Vital, *Zionism: Formative Years*, p.264.
16. See Michael Berkowitz, *Zionist Culture and West European Jewry Before the First World War* (Chapel Hill, NC, and London: University of North Carolina Press, 1996), Fig. 14. See also Chapter 5 on visual culture in the Zionist movement, and Stanislawski, *Zionism and the Fin de Siècle*, Chapter 5, on the work of Lilien.
17. See Lowenthal (ed. and trans.), *Diaries of Theodor Herzl*, p.xxi. Zangwill (1864–1926) was a writer, an influential figure of Anglo-Jewry and within Zionism. In 1905, as a result of the Uganda affair, he withdrew from the movement to form the Jewish Territorial Organization whose aim (not successful) was to find an alternative site to East Africa. See also Michael Berkowitz, *The Jewish Self-Image: American and British Perspectives, 1881–1939* (London: Reaktion Books, 2000), p.55: 'Herzl embodied simultaneously a cultured Viennese, a dignified European statesman and the ideal new man that Zionism aspired to create.'
18. Central Zionist Archives, Jerusalem [hereafter CZA], Z1/402.
19. Berkowitz, *Zionist Culture*, p.103.
20. See Lowenthal (ed. and trans.), *Diaries of Theodor Herzl*, p.55, the entry of 6 July 1895: 'talked with Nordau about the Jewish question. Never before were we in such perfect accord ... I never felt so plainly that we belonged together.'
21. See Stanislawski, *Zionism and the Fin de Siècle*, pp.91–7. The Russian Jew Vladimir Jabotinsky campaigned for a militaristic Zionism during the First World War, which produced the first Jewish fighting unit in the British army, the Zion Mule Corps. In Palestine in 1920, Jabotinsky led the Haganah self-defence force and was hailed as the Jewish Garibaldi (p.208). The first Jewish gymnastic society in 'Italy' was established in Trieste in 1914. *Il Corriere Israelitico* (*CI*) reported on the second Jewish gymnastic convention held in Vienna in 1913: 1,200 gymnasts participated from twenty Austrian associations (*CI*, 1913, p.150).
22. Cited in Robertson, *The 'Jewish Question' in German Literature 1749–1939*, p.477.
23. Lowenthal (ed. and trans.), *Diaries of Theodor Herzl*, p.281. In an entry of 8 June 1895, after dining with his friends the Schiffs in Vienna, he wrote: 'they are Ghetto creatures, quiet, decent, timorous. Most of our people are like that. Will they understand the call to freedom and manliness?' (pp.38–9). The regeneration of the Jews in a future Jewish State is also articulated in Herzl's utopian novel *Altneuland* (1902).
24. Berkowitz, *Zionist Culture*, p.2.
25. Ibid., p.6.
26. See Stanislawski, *Zionism and the Fin de Siècle*, pp.88–9. Nordau also presented a very positive portrayal of the traditional Jew in his play *Doktor Kohn*, completed in the same year before the Congress (Stanislawski, *Zionism and the Fin de Siècle*, pp.82–6).
27. Lowenthal (ed. and trans.), *Diaries of Theodor Herzl*, p.22. See also Herzl, *The Jewish State*, p.72: 'The Flag ... we need one. If we desire to lead many men, we must raise a symbol above their heads.' On the author and text of the Zionist anthem, 'Hatikvah', see Berkowitz, *Zionist Culture*, pp.21–3.
28. Herzl, *The Jewish State*, pp.70–1. Moses Mendelssohn also despised Yiddish, describing it as 'a stammering, distorted and corrupt language', suggesting German in its place. See Ritchie Robertson, 'Reinventing the Jews. From Moses Mendelssohn to Theodor Herzl', in Ritchie Robertson and Edward Timms (eds), *Theodor Herzl and the Origins of Zionism* (Edinburgh: Edinburgh University Press, 1997), p.5.
29. See Berkowitz, *Zionist Culture*, Chapter 2. As Berkowitz notes, Herzl's attitude towards Hebrew became increasingly positive (p.51). In Jewish schools already established in Palestine the target language depended on the organizations that had founded them: French, English and German, although Hebrew was also taught. Only one or two lone voices suggested that Arabic and Islamic culture should form part of the curriculum in the creation of the new society (see Berkowitz, *Zionist Culture*, pp.113–14).

30. Lowenthal (ed. and trans.), *Diaries of Theodor Herzl*, p.224.
31. Vital, *Origins of Zionism*, p.373.
32. See Lowenthal (ed. and trans.), *Diaries of Theodor Herzl*, 10 March 1896: 'A fashion goods dealer in Semlin writes me that all the Semlin Jews are ready to emigrate' (pp.102–3).
33. See Vital, *Zionism: Formative Years*, pp.66, 412.
34. Lowenthal (ed. and trans.), *Diaries of Theodor Herzl*, p.199. See also Vital, *Origins of Zionism*, pp.14–19; 212–14; 269; 307–8; 334.
35. Lowenthal (ed. and trans.), *Diaries of Theodor Herzl*, p.16. In *The Jewish State*, Herzl writes: 'Beggars will not be endured. Whoever refuses to do anything as a free man will be sent to the workhouse' (p.55). Baron de Hirsch financed Jewish settlements in South America in the 1890s.
36. Lowenthal (ed. and trans.), *Diaries of Theodor Herzl*, pp.74–5. Also 16 November 1895: 'He [Kahn] professed himself to be a Zionist. But French "patriotism" also has its claims. Yes, a man has to choose between Zion and France … I shall be surprised if I get any serious help from him' (p.73).
37. Ibid., p.131. In *The Jewish State*, Herzl writes: 'In vain are we loyal patriots … in vain do we strive to increase the fame of our native land … we are denounced as strangers' (p.14).
38. Berkowitz, *Zionist Culture*, p.xv.
39. See Herzl, *The Jewish State*: 'modern anti-semitism … is as a result of the emancipation of the Jews' (p.25). See also Nordau's opening speech of the 1897 Zionist Congress in Stanislawski, *Zionism and the Fin de Siècle*, p.88.
40. Vital, *Origins of Zionism*, pp.135–6.
41. Lowenthal (ed. and trans.), *Diaries of Theodor Herzl*, pp.83, 212–13.
42. Vital, *Origins of Zionism*, p.335.
43. Paul Mendes-Flohr and Jehuda Reinharz (eds), *The Jew in the Modern World: A Documentary History* (New York and Oxford: Oxford University Press, 1995), pp.538–9.
44. Lowenthal (ed. and trans.), *Diaries of Theodor Herzl* p.218.
45. See Reinharz, *Fatherland or Promised Land*, p.182.
46. See Amos Elon, *Herzl: A Biography* (New York: Schocken Books, 1986), pp.166–9, 175–6, 246–7. See also Lowenthal (ed. and trans.), *Diaries of Theodor Herzl*, September 1898: when asked by Bülow, then German foreign minister, why the *Neue Freie Presse* was silent and the *Frankfurter Zeitung* was hostile about Zionism, Herzl replied: 'I explained that it was due to the fears of the Jewish liberal papers lest the anti-Semites question their patriotism' (p.235). In July 1902, he wrote that the owners of the Austrian paper were 'the mortal enemies of my Jewish project. The word Zionism has not been printed in its columns to this day' (p.365).
47. See Edward Timms, 'Ambassador Herzl and the Blueprint for a Modern State', in Robertson and Timms (eds), *Theodor Herzl and the Origins of Zionism*, p.20.
48. Vital, *Origins of Zionism*, p.336. See also David Cesarani, *The Jewish Chronicle and Anglo-Jewry, 1841–1991* (Cambridge: Cambridge University Press, 1994), pp.85–106, 122–7. See Elon, *Herzl*, pp.244–55, on the negative diplomatic reports on the First Congress; see John C.G. Röhl, 'Herzl and Kaiser Wilhelm II: A German Protectorate in Palestine?', in Robertson and Timms (eds), *Theodor Herzl and the Origins of Zionism*, pp.27–38, on the scribbled note from the kaiser in the margin of the German report: 'I am very much in favour of the Mauschels going to Palestine, the sooner they clear off there the better. I shall not put obstacles in their way' (p.29). As Röhl points out, one of Herzl's preferences was for a Jewish republic modelled on Imperial Germany and under German protection. How different the history of the Jews in the twentieth century would have been, he comments (p.27).
49. Cited in Caterine Nicault, *La France et le Sionisme 1897–1948: une rencontre manqué?* (Paris: Calmann-Lévy, 1992), p.22. See also Pierre Birnbaum, *Anti-Semitism in France: A Political History from Léon Blum to the Present* (Oxford: Blackwell, 1992), p.52: the Zionist cause 'shattered the unequivocal link binding every citizen to the state, because it revived the idea of a Jewish nation'.
50. Central Archives for the History of the Jewish People, Jerusalem [hereafter CAHJP], Territorial Collection, IT 79. A copy of the circular appealing to the Jewish communities to sign up to this letter was even sent to the Trieste community, an indication of its *italianità*. See Tullia Catalan, *La comunità ebraica di Trieste (1781–1914): politica, società e cultura* (Trieste: Lint, 2000), p.327.
51. CAHJP, IT 79.
52. See Marrus, *Politics of Assimilation*, p.274: Zionism was a useless diversion, utopian; it reinforced anti-Semitic charges of Jewish disloyalty to France (22 January, 1897). Marrus and also Nicault, in *La France et le Sionisme*, allude to several other articles in this vein.
53. Cited in Vital, *Origins of Zionism*, p.368.
54. See Elon, *Herzl*, pp.182–4.
55. See Wistrich, *The Jews of Vienna*: 'Kadimah … continued to play a crucial role as Herzl's lieutenants right up until the First Zionist Congress … The special rapport … the personal loyalty they felt towards him … enhanced still more the importance of the Austrian student cadre' (p.374).

56. See Marsha L. Rozenblit, *The Jews of Vienna 1867–1914: Assimilation and Identity* (Albany, NY: State University of New York Press, 1983), p.161.
57. See Robert S. Wistrich, *Between Redemption and Perdition: Modern Antisemitism and Jewish Identity* (London and New York: Routledge, 1990), p.77.
58. See Peter Gay, *Freud: A Life for Our Time* (London and Melbourne: Dent, 1988), pp.598–600; and Wistrich, *The Jews of Vienna*, pp.574–8.
59. See Steven Beller, 'Class, Culture and the Jews of Vienna, 1900', in Ivar Oxaal, Michael Pollak and Gerhard Botz (eds), *Jews, Antisemitism and Culture in Vienna* (London and New York: Routledge & Kegan Paul, 1987), pp.52–3.
60. See Rozenblit, *The Jews of Vienna*, pp.164–8: 'The large number of Zionist organizations in Vienna cannot suffice to indicate the extent to which Zionism attracted Viennese Jews in this period' (p.168). See also Appendix 2, pp.204–6, in which the Zionist organizations are listed.
61. See Rozenblit, *The Jews of Vienna*, pp.168, 243.
62. See Reinharz, *Fatherland or Promised Land*, p.112.
63. See Rozenblit, *The Jews of Vienna*, pp.170–93; and Walter R. Weitzmann, 'The Politics of the Viennese Jewish Community, 1890–1914', in Ivar Oxaal, Michael Pollak and Gerhard Botz (eds), *Jews, Antisemitism and Culture in Vienna* (London and New York: Routledge & Kegan Paul, 1987), pp.140–51.
64. See Amos Elon, *The Pity Of It All: A Portrait of Jews in Germany, 1743–1933* (London: Allen Lane, 2003), p.289.
65. The Centralverein did not take part in the objections of the *Protestrabbiner*.
66. Cited in Reinharz, *Fatherland or Promised Land*, p.132. The *Jüdische Rundschau*'s original title was *Israelitische Rundschau*; its name changed under a new editor in 1902. After *Die Welt* ceased publication in 1914, the German Zionist paper increased its influence (see Reinharz, *Fatherland or Promised Land*, p.106). See also Jehuda Reinharz, 'Ideology and Structure in German Zionism, 1882–1933', in Jehuda Reinharz and Anita Shapira (eds), *Essential Papers on Zionism* (London: Cassell, 1996), pp.268–97.
67. See Reinharz, *Fatherland or Promised Land*, pp.134–5.
68. Ibid, p.152, Elon, *The Pity Of It All*, p.290.
69. Elon, *The Pity Of It All*, p.291. See also Sandford Ragins, *Jewish Responses to Anti-Semitism in Germany, 1870–1914: A Study in the History of Ideas* (Cincinnati, OH: Hebrew Union College Press, 1980), pp.134–60.
70. See Christina Ujma, 'Political versus Cultural Zionism: Reflections on Herzl and Buber', in Robertson and Timms (eds), *Theodor Herzl and the Origins of Zionism*, pp.96–106. Buber was a disciple of the leader of cultural Zionism Ahad Ha'am, pen name of the Russian Jewish writer Asher Hirsch Ginsberg (1856–1927) with whom Herzl and Nordau clashed, particularly over Ahad Ha'am's review of Herzl's novel *Altneuland* (p.98). See also Steven J. Zipperstein, 'Ahad Ha'am and the Politics of Assimilation', in Jonathan Frankel and Steven J. Zipperstein (eds), *Assimilation and Community: The Jews in Nineteenth-Century Europe* (Cambridge: Cambridge University Press, 2004), pp.344–65.
71. Reinharz, *Fatherland or Promised Land*, p.155.
72. Ibid., p.150; Elon, *The Pity Of It All*, p.292.
73. Gershom Scholem, *Walter Benjamin: The Story of a Friendship* (New York: New York Review Books, 2003), p.10. See also Gershom Scholem, *From Berlin to Jerusalem: Memories of My Youth*, translated from German by Harry Zohn (New York: Schocken Books, 1980), the chapter entitled 'Student in Berlin'. Scholem emigrated to Palestine in 1923 and became the first professor of Jewish mysticism at the Hebrew University of Jerusalem in 1933.
74. Scholem, *Walter Benjamin*, Introduction, by Lee Siegel, p.x.
75. *Il Vessillo Israelititco* [*VI*], 1913, p.399.
76. See Reinharz, *Fatherland or Promised Land*, pp.162–8, 202–17.
77. Herzl wrote a play along similar lines, *Das neue Ghetto*, which he completed nine days before Lazare's article was published. At the time, he was the Paris correspondent for the *Neue Freie Presse*. See also Jörg Thunecke, '"Dynamite" or "Affront"? The Jewish Question in Herzl's play *Das neue Ghetto*', in Robertson and Timms (eds), *Theodor Herzl and the Origins of Zionism*, pp.62–73.
78. See Marrus, *Politics of Assimilation*, on Lazare, pp.164–88, 268–9; on the journals, pp.259–65. On Lazare, see also Aron Rodrigue, 'Rearticulations of French Jewish Identities after the Dreyfus Affair', *Jewish Social Studies: History, Culture, and Society*, new series, 2 (Fall 1996), p.2. Lazare was acclaimed at the Second Zionist Congress for his courageous fight for justice on Dreyfus's behalf (*CI*, 1898, p.121). Other prominent Jewish Dreyfusards were Julien Benda, Henri Bergson, Emile Durkheim and Marcel Proust. See H. Stuart Hughes, *Consciousness and Society: The Reorientation of European Social Thought 1890–1930* (London: Macgibbon and Kee, 1967), p.413.
79. Nicault, *La France et le Sionisme*, p.31.
80. See Birnbaum, *Antisemitism in France*, p.54: 'The period of the Dreyfus affair was vital because the temporary failure of the republican synthesis left the way open for both socialism and Zionism.'

81. Marrus, *Politics of Assimilation*, p.272.
82. Lowenthal (ed. and trans.), *Diaries of Theodor Herzl*, p.241. See also Herzl, *The Jewish State*, p.18: 'If French Jews protest – let them – because the whole thing does not concern them. They are Jewish Frenchmen, well and good!'
83. See Marrus, *Politics of Assimilation*, pp.278–80. Their position remained unchanged. In 1923, the Association of French Rabbis issued a statement in which they declared that 'the national and political doctrines of Zionism, of which they recognize the moral and ideal value for millions of their brethren, cannot be reconciled with the principles of French Judaism': Paula Hyman, *From Dreyfus to Vichy: The Remaking of French Jewry, 1906–1939* (New York: Columbia University Press, 1979), p.168.
84. Marrus, *Politics of Assimilation* p.276. From an interview Reinach gave to *Le Figaro* in the autumn of 1897. The two brothers were also among the first Dreyfusards. See also Jean-Jacques Becker and Annette Wieviorka (eds), *Les Juifs de France de la Révolution française à nos jours* (Paris: Editions Liana Levi, 1998), p.100.
85. Marrus, *Politics of Assimilation* p.265; Esther Benbassa, *The Jews of France: A History from Antiquity to the Present* (Princeton, NJ: Princeton University Press, 1999), p.146: 'Zionist leaders in France were foreign-born from the beginning'; Hyman, *From Dreyfus to Vichy*: 'The association of Zionism with immigrant activists accounts in part for the virulent and prolonged opposition of native French Jewry to the movement' (p.154).
86. *CI*, 1908, p.77. To retain the style, tone and form of the original, the editors published the piece in French. Hagani's words are a reflection of Ehrenfreund's study of the universalism of French culture and politics: 'every form of particularism was considered an attack on the "one and indivisible" character of the French republic'. See Jacques Ehrenfreund, 'Citizenship and Acculturation: Some Reflections on German Jews during the Second Empire and French Jews during the Third Republic' in Michael Brenner, Vicki Caron and Uri R. Kaufmann (eds), *Jewish Emancipation Reconsidered: The French and German Models* (Leo Baeck Institute, London: Mohr Siebeck, 2003), pp.155.
87. *CI*, 1908, pp.76–81. See also Baruch Hagani, *Le Sionisme politique et son fondateur* (Paris: Librairie Payot, 1917).
88. See Birnbaum, *Antisemitism in France*, p.52; Nicault, *La France et le Sionisme*, pp.235–6; Rodrigue, 'Rearticulations', p.21. Post-Balfour, Zionist activity increased in France.
89. Cited in Michael Burns, *France and the Dreyfus Affair: A Documentary History* (Boston, MA, and New York: Bedford/St Martin's, 1999), p.178. See also Stuart Hughes, *Consciousness and Society*, p.58: 'For them [French Jews] republican patriotism was a natural product of profound gratitude; the accusers of Captain Dreyfus committed a catastrophic error in imagining he could possibly betray his country.'
90. Lowenthal (ed. and trans.), *Diaries of Theodor Herzl*, p.177. On Montagu, see Vital, *Origins of Zionism*, pp.302–3.
91. See Steven Beller, 'Herzl's Anglophilia', in Robertson and Timms (eds), *Theodor Herzl and the Origins of Zionism* pp.54–61.
92. Stuart A. Cohen, *English Zionists and British Jews: The Communal Politics of Anglo-Jewry, 1895–1920* (Princeton, NJ: Princeton University Press, 1982), p.82; Vital, *Zionism: Formative Years*, pp.146–62. See Lowenthal (ed. and trans.), *Diaries of Theodor Herzl*, pp.364–6, 374–85. On Herzl, the British government and the East Africa proposal, see also Isaiah Friedman, 'Herzl and the Uganda Controversy', in Robertson and Timms (eds), *Theodor Herzl and the Origins of Zionism*, pp.39–53.
93. Lowenthal (ed. and trans.), *Diaries of Theodor Herzl*, p.361. Greenberg was editor of the *Jewish Chronicle* (1907–31) and the *Jewish World* (1913–31).
94. See Cohen, *English Zionists and British Jews*, pp.107–113, 321–2. Post-Balfour, the EZF was more effective: its members attained prominent positions in the major Jewish institutions where discussions on Palestine featured frequently on the agendas (p.323).
95. T.B. Herwald, 'Zionism in Manchester 1891–1900', http://www.art.man.ac.uk/RELTHEOL/JEWISH/EXHIBITION/5HERWALD.HTML (consulted 31/07/2006).
96. Vital, *Zionism: Crucial Phase*, pp.156–7. He became president of the WZO in 1920. 'He was deeply conscious of his origins at the heart of Jewry – Russia' (pp.157–8).
97. Cohen, *English Zionists and British Jews*, p.161.
98. See ibid., pp.163–73. Claude Montefiore (1858–1938), great-nephew of Sir Moses Montefiore, was president of the Anglo-Jewish Association, co-founder and co-editor of the *Jewish Quarterly Review*, and a preacher in Reform synagogues.
99. Cited in Cohen, *English Zionists and British Jews*, p.174.
100. On their objectives, see ibid., p.305.
101. In a letter to *The Times*, 20 July 2006, the present Lord Balfour states that 'many would say that a central tenet of the Balfour Declaration demanding mutual tolerance between Arabs and Jews was

always unattainable'.
102. See Berkowitz, *Zionist Culture*, Chapter 6.
103. Cited in Vital, *Zionism: Formative Years*, p.381. On the friction between Arabs and Jews in the 1890s, see pp.377–9.
104. See Vital, *Origins of Zionism*, pp.193–8.
105. Elon, *The Pity Of It All*, p.289.
106. See Mendes-Flohr and Reinharz (eds), *The Jew in the Modern World*, pp.558–62. Epstein (1862–1943), Hebrew writer and linguist of Russian origin, settled in Palestine in 1886.
107. Dante Lattes, *Il Sionismo* (Rome: Cremonese, 1928), vol. 2, pp.216–24.
108. Trieste was then part of Austria-Hungary; for the inclusion of *Il Corriere* as an 'Italian' publication, see Chapter 1.
109. David Bidussa, Amos Luzzatto and Gadi Luzzatto Voghera, *Oltre il ghetto: momenti e figure della cultura ebraica in Italia tra l'Unità e il fascismo* (Brescia: Morcelliana, 1992).
110. Tullia Catalan, 'Società e sionismo a Trieste fra XIX e XX secolo', in Todeschini and Zorattini (eds), *Il mondo ebraico*, pp.457–90; Catalan, *La comunità ebraica di Trieste*, pp.324–40.
111. Francesco Del Canuto, *Il movimento sionistico in Italia dalle origini al 1924* (Milan: Federazione Sionistica Italiana, 1972).
112. Alberto Cavaglion, 'Tendenze nazionali e albori sionistici', in Corrado Vivanti (ed.), *Storia d'Italia, Annali 11, Gli ebrei in Italia*, vol. 2 (Turin: Einaudi, 1997), pp.1291–320; Alberto Cavaglion, 'Il Sionismo nella stampa socialista di fine Ottocento: osservazioni preliminari', in Liliana Mezzabotta (ed.), *Italia Judaica: gli ebrei nell'Italia unita 1870–1945. Atti del IV convegno internazionale* (Rome: Pubblicazioni degli Archivi di Stato, 1993), pp.223–36. On post-First World War Zionism in Italy, see Simonetta Della Seta and Daniel Carpi, 'Il movimento sionista', in Vivanti (ed.), *Storia d'Italia, Annali 11, Gli ebrei in Italia*, vol. 2, pp.1321–68.
113. Toscano, *Ebraismo e antisemitismo*, p.71.
114. Cavaglion, 'Tendenze nazionali', pp.1309–14.
115. Toscano, *Ebraismo e antisemitismo*, pp.46–68.
116. Ibid., pp.72, 111–12. The first quotation comes from an article published originally in 1982, the second in 1990.
117. See Cavaglion, 'Tendenze nazionali', pp.1293, 1299.
118. Toscano is also of this opinion. See *Ebraismo e antisemitismo*, p.62.
119. Ibid., p.73.
120. See Del Canuto, *Il movimento sionistico*, p.25; Cavaglion, 'Tendenze nazionali', pp.1309–10. Titus, Roman emperor between 79 and 81 CE, destroyed Jerusalem in 70 CE when he was consul of Judea.
121. See Del Canuto, *Il movimento sionistico*, pp.36–8, and Cavaglion, 'Tendenze nazionali', p.1313. In July 1898, Baruch gave a lecture on Zionism in Florence (ASCEF, Gestione Comunità: Attività Sion Sionistiche 1898–1918, E.17.3).
122. See Elon, *Herzl*, pp.260–1, and Cavaglion, 'Tendenze nazionali', p.1314.
123. Del Canuto, *Il movimento sionistico*, p.38; Cavaglion, 'Tendenze nazionali', p.1314.
124. CZA, Baruch, A50/12. The letter, written in French, is not dated but was probably written soon after Baruch's death. Rabezzana was the brother of Baruch's erstwhile fiancée and Baruch's comrade in arms in the 'Garibaldi Legion' which fought in Crete. The slim file also contains Rabezzana's letter to Rasmann, dated 25 August 1899, and a letter of 10 January 1898, in rather poor Italian, from Baruch to Maria, his fiancée, begging her not to break off the engagement. See also Francesco Del Canuto and Riccardo di Segni, 'Una biografia inedita di Marcou Baruch', *RMI*, 46, 5–8 (1980), pp.220–8.
125. *CI*, 1896, pp.151–4; 1897, pp.97–105.
126. *CI*, 1897, pp.52–6; 1897, pp.74–7. Guglielmo Lattes, older half-brother of Dante Lattes, was a regular contributor to *Il Vessillo Israelitico* in which he also endorsed Zionism, as he did in his novel, *Tra la fede e l'amore: scene della vita ebraica moderna* (1903): a young rabbi has to conceal his Zionist sympathies as if they were contraband; another character, Giuseppe, lives in a Jewish community where there is a Zionist association of seventy members, mostly young, and no one suggests that there is a conflict between their patriotism and the Zionism promoted to assist their oppressed brethren.
127. See Catalan, 'Società e sionismo a Trieste fra XIX e XX secolo', p.459.
128. See Attilo Milano, 'Un secolo di stampa periodica ebraica in Italia', *RMI*, 12, 7–9 (April–June 1938), p.113. Lattes's first articles for *Il Corriere* date from 1896.
129. Gadi Luzzatto Voghera, 'La formazione culturale di Dante Lattes', in Bidussa, Luzzatto and Luzzatto Voghera, *Oltre il ghetto*, pp.69–70, 83, 93. See also *RMI*, 22, 9–10 (1976): these two issues are devoted to Lattes's Zionist essays and also contain articles on him. Lattes's own articles were published in French and German Jewish periodicals: for example, 'La nazione ebraica' (*CI*, 1900, pp.145–7) first

appeared in the Parisian *Univers israélite* and the *Jüdisches Volksblatt* of Vienna.

130. Shalom Aleichem (pseudonym of Sholem Yakov Rabinowitz, 1859–1916) was a popular Russian Jewish author who wrote primarily in Yiddish; the successful musical, *Fiddler on the Roof* (1964), is based on his short stories about Tevye the milkman. A curiosity: at a banquet held in his honour in New York, Aleichem was acclaimed as the Jewish Mark Twain, also present at the gathering. Twain responded by presenting himself as the American Shalom Aleichem (*CI*, 1907, p.289). Shalom Asch (1880–1957) is a Polish-born Jewish novelist and dramatist in the Yiddish language. Joseph Klausner (1874–1958) was a Zionist from Lithuania who emigrated to Palestine in 1919, where he became a professor of Jewish literature and subsequently of Jewish history at the Hebrew University in Jerusalem. Amos Oz, the renowned Israeli novelist, is his great-nephew. For a personal portrait of Klausner, see Oz's autobiographical work, *A Tale of Love and Darkness* (London: Vintage, 2005), first published in Hebrew in 2003. See also Luzzatto Voghera, 'La formazione culturale di Dante Lattes', pp.40–6.

131. *CI*, 1906, pp.112–14, 146–9; 1907, pp.2–9. For example, Gino Arias, 'Il Sionismo e le aspirazioni della società moderna', *CI*, 1906, pp.12–16, 44–8, 76–80; Felice Momigliano, 'Il proletariato ebraico e le aspirazioni messianiche', *CI*, 1904, pp.330–2 (first given as a lecture to the Zionist Association of Trieste); 'Ebrei in Italia e Ebrei in Russia', *CI*, 1907, pp.337–44; 'A proposito di modernismo ebraico', *CI*, 1909, pp.323–4. On Alfonso Pacifici's debates with Lattes in the 1911 and 1912 issues, see Luzzatto Voghera, 'La formazione culturale di Dante Lattes', pp.64–6.

132. On this period of Lattes's life when he returned to Italy, see Amos Luzzatto, 'Il rinnovamento culturale dell'ebraismo italiano tra le due guerre', in Bidussa, Luzzatto and Luzzatto Voghera, *Oltre il ghetto*, pp.97–153. See also Augusto Segre's recollections of Lattes as a friend and teacher (he taught Segre at the Rabbinical College in Rome), in his *Memorie di vita ebraica: da Casale a Gerusalemme* (Rome: Bonacci, 1979), pp.151–86, 369–77. Initially, Lattes was not welcomed by the Italian Jewish establishment, who did not share his Zionist views. However, post-Balfour, Lattes was at the centre of Zionist activities, becoming, in 1918, the secretary of the newly constituted FSI. Before leaving for Palestine in 1939, Lattes destroyed his entire archive (Segre, *Memorie*, p.185). On his return to Italy in 1946, Lattes became once again a prominent figure: from 1952 to 1956, he was vice-president of the Federation of Jewish Communities.

133. Cavaglion, 'Il Sionismo', pp.223–5. Momigliano wrote under the pseudonym of 'Eudemone', which is the Greek for Felice. See also Momigliano's article, 'Il proletariato ebraico e il sionismo', *La Nuova Antologia*, 1 October 1903 (cited in Cavaglion, 'Tendenze nazionali', p.1318), in which similar views are expressed. The Zionist movement was also reported in Filippo Turati's journal, *Critica sociale*. Turati was leader of the Socialist Party.

134. See Cavaglion, 'Il sionismo nella stampa socialista', pp.228–36. According to Cavaglion, Momigliano formed a small group of Zionist sympathizers in Milan but did not subscribe to the FSI. In a letter to Angelo Sullam he gives his reasons. See Alberto Cavaglion, *Felice Momigliano (1866–1924): Una biografia* (Bologna: Il Mulino, 1988), p.113.

135. *CI*, 1898, pp.133–5. *Il Vessillo Israelitico*'s account of the Second Congress was as dismissive as the first one: 'Thank God it's over. What confusion! What a babel.' Sonnino had offered his speech for publication, but the editor, in a note, indicated his decision to refuse it on the grounds that readers 'would be terribly bored' (*VI*, 1898, pp.297, 304).

136. *CI*, 1898, pp.121–3. In letters to Max Nordau, Ravenna expressed his regret that Zionism was not yet widespread in Italy and suggested that a French edition of *Die Welt* would be effective propaganda (letter dated 13 December 1898). In January 1899, he informed Nordau of the Zionist group in his city, Ferrara, with seventy members within a month of its establishment. He also communicated Rabbi Sonnino's difficulties in setting up an association in Naples, which was '*poco israelitico*'. CZA, A119/165. In 1907, the Naples group was 'in crisis', the effect of Rabbi Sonnino's departure (letter from Dario Ascarelli to Ravenna dated 24 December 1907; CZA, Ravenna, A353/17).

137. Archivio del Centro di Documentazione Ebraica Contemporanea, Milan [hereafter ACDEC], Fondo Angelo Sullam, I.2.2.2.2, Convegni/1.2.2, FSI (1902–32), B.5, file 44. See also Del Canuto, *Il movimento sionistico*, p.40.

138. See Cavaglion's comments, 'Tendenze nazionali', p.1319. In 1899, at the Third Congress, Italy was to be represented by three delegates: Vito Anau (Ancona), Felice Ravenna (Ferrara) and Rabbi Sonnino, but he was unable to attend (See Del Canuto, *Il movimento sionistico*, p.38).

139. *L'Idea Sionista* [*IS*], 1901, p.3.

140. *IS*, 1910, p.71. Castelnuovo was invited to be a founder member of the Venetian Zionist movement; he refused concisely but firmly. See his letter of 6 January 1903, cited in Simon Levis Sullam, *Una comunità immaginata: gli ebrei a Venezia (1900–1938)* (Milan: Unicopli, 2001), pp.36–7.

141. We have already noted Alessandro D'Ancona and Tullo Massarani's repudiation of Zionism in favour of wholehearted *italianità* (see Chapter 2). In 1902, *L'Idea Sionista* published a witty article on the var-

ious categories of 'non Zionists': the ignorant; the indifferent; the petty bourgeois; the rich ladies who frequent salons; the ambitious professionals, lawyers, civil servants or ministers of state, who are too busy to think about Zionism. All these groups have the potential to respond to judicious Zionist propaganda, with the exception of one type, 'those who are ashamed of being Jewish' (*IS*, 1902, p.19).
142. Enzo Levi, *Memorie di una vita (1889–1947)* (Modena: STEM Mucchi, 1972), pp.14–15.
143. CZA, Ravenna, A353/16. Ravenna lists these groups in his article in *L'Idea Sionista*, 1901, p.2. The statutes of the Ferrara group and their very name, Fratellanza Israelitica (Jewish Brotherhood), emphasize the philanthropic dimension. Its aims were twofold: to rekindle fraternal feeling in favour of oppressed Jews elsewhere and to contribute to the philanthropic work undertaken by the Zionist Committee of Vienna (Statutes published in 1899: see ACDEC, Fondo Sullam, I.3.1, Enti ebraici e/o sionistici, B.18, file 186).
144. *IS*, 1901, pp.73–7; *CI*, 1901, p.133.
145. *IS*, 1902, pp.17–19; *CI*, 1902, pp.217–21. See also Nordau on the same subject in *L'Idea Sionista*, 1903, pp.21–2.
146. See, for example, *L'Idea Sionista*, 1903, pp.42–6, 62–6, 88–91, 138–141. He also published a three-volume account of the Zionist movement, reviewed in *Il Corriere Israelitico* (1906, p.58).
147. The proposal for a Jewish National Fund to purchase land in Palestine was made at the First Zionist Congress (see Vital, *Origins of Zionism*, p.364).
148. *CI*, 1902, p.180; *IS*, 1903, pp.1–15.
149. *IS*, 1903, pp.39–41, 66–9. See CAHJP, IT 831; CZA, A353/16: the president of the Modena Zionist group sent Ravenna a money order of 1,189.75 lire, for the Russian victims, to pass on to the central committee of Vienna of which Ravenna was a member. These expressions of solidarity would, sadly, be repeated. They were also evident on behalf of the 1881 atrocities (CAHJP, IT 829).
150. See Vital, *Zionism: Formative Years*, pp.334–9; Lowenthal (ed. and trans.), *Diaries of Theodor Herzl*, pp.414, 417–34.
151. See Umberto Nahon, 'Le lettere di Teodoro Herzl a Felice Ravenna: il viaggio di Herzl a Roma nel gennaio 1904', *Rassegna Mensile di Israel* [hereafter *RMI*], 26, 6 (1960), p.236. Nahon relates that one of Ravenna's employees, knowing how important the letters were to his deceased boss, removed them from his office and handed them over to the daughter in 1945 before her departure for Israel.
152. See Giorgio Romano, 'I rapporti di Teodoro Herzl coi sionisti italiani (con trenta lettere inedite)', *RMI*, 26, 9 (1960), p.506. Margulies published a pamphlet on Herzl in 1904: *Herzl e il sionismo* (Florence: Galletti and Cassuto).
153. Nahon, 'Le lettere di Teodoro Herzl a Felice Ravenna', p.237; see Romano, 'I rapporti di Teodoro Herzl coi sionisti italiani', p.495, for Ravenna's letter. None of Herzl's work appeared in Italian translation until 1918.
154. See Nahon, 'Le lettere di Teodoro Herzl a Felice Ravenna', p.238. He gives the number of shekel contributors in Italy in 1903 as 654: Ancona 126; Modena 124; Ferrara 119; Milan 100; Venice 72; Bologna 57; Naples 56. For every 100 *shekalim*, one delegate was elected.
155. ACDEC, Fondo Angelo Sullam, I.1 Attività private; I.1.1, Scritti 1896–1922, B.1, file 2. From his student days, Sullam had subscriptions to *Die Welt* and *L'Echo Sioniste*; also catalogues from the *Jüdischer Verlag* and the Jewish Publication Society of America (see, I.1.2, Corrispondenza (1892–1937), B.2, file 11. He was also in correspondence with Nordau, requesting advice on what to read. See their exchange of letters between 1900 and 1904. Nordau was encouraging to '*mon cher jeune ami*', recommending Pinsker and Herzl's *Judenstaat* in the letter dated 23 December 1900; he expressed an interest in Sullam's article in *L'Idea Sionista*, which he hoped would revive Jewish consciousness in those of Sullam's readers in whom the Jewish sentiment was not completely extinguished (letter dated 9 August 1902). In CZA, AK433/3; A119/229. Sullam met Jabotinsky at the 1906 Zionist Congress and maintained a correspondence with him (See ACDEC, Fondo Sullam, I.1.2.2, B.3, file 18). On Sullam, see also Levis Sullam, *Una comunità immaginata*, pp.31–43.
156. A copy is among those included in Romano's article, dated 28 August 1903, with the words in Italian, 'memento of the sixth Congress in Basle to lawyer Angelo Sullam our friend'. Other photographs reproduced by Romano reveal that there were quite a few Italian observers at this Congress as well as the official delegates. See also Nahon, 'Le lettere di Teodoro Herzl a Felice Ravenna', p.239.
157. Nahon, 'Le lettere di Teodoro Herzl a Felice Ravenna', p.240.
158. ACDEC, Fondo Sullam, I.1.2.2, Corrispondeza generale (1903–35), B.3, file 14, Corrispondenza con Felice Ravenna 1910–35. These remarks were made in a letter dated 14 February 1915.
159. Ibid. This letter is dated 17 February 1915. Not surprisingly, these letters have not been mentioned in Italian accounts of the Zionist movement. It may be of interest to know that Sullam became a fascist and anti-Zionist, to the extent of rejecting even cultural Zionism (source: Simon Levis Sullam; Angelo Sullam was his great-grandfather).
160. Ibid.

161. See Romano, 'I rapporti di Teodoro Herzl coi sionisti italiani', pp.506–7. Of the tensions between Margulies and Ravenna, there is no reference in Del Canuto's official account of the Zionist movement in Italy.
162. Romano, 'I rapporti di Teodoro Herzl coi sionisti italiani', p.507.
163. Ibid., p.510.
164. Ibid., p.514.
165. Nahon, 'Le lettere di Teodoro Herzl a Felice Ravenna', p.250.
166. Ibid., p.244. The letter is dated 17 October 1903. Ravenna's reply of 21 October confirms Herzl's opinion of Malvano (see Romano, 'I rapporti di Teodoro Herzl coi sionisti italiani', p.501).
167. Romano, 'I rapporti di Teodoro Herzl coi sionisti italiani', p.516. The letter is dated 22 January 1904.
168. See ibid., p.501.
169. Ibid., pp.499–500. This information is contained in Ravenna's letter to Herzl of 12 October 1903. In another letter to Herzl, of 21 October, he reiterates his favourable comments about Romanin Jacur's goodwill and influence (p.502).
170. Romano, 'I rapporti di Teodoro Herzl coi sionisti italiani', pp.504–5.
171. Nahon, 'Le lettere di Teodoro Herzl a Felice Ravenna', pp.247–9. The letters are dated 15 and 16 January 1904.
172. See Vital, *Zionism: Formative Years*, p.337. These negotiations have been omitted from Del Canuto's account.
173. See Lowenthal (ed. and trans.), *Diaries of Theodor Herzl*, p.426: 'He [the king] said: "I am glad you have given up Uganda. I like this love of Jerusalem … I myself have seen the Jews at the Wailing Wall."'
174. *CI*, 1903, pp.260–1. The Italian Zionist journal produced a four-page supplement to the January 1904 issue on Herzl in Italy.
175. Alfonso Pacifici, 'Ha-rav Shemuel Zevì Margulies', *RMI*, 28, 6–7 (1962), p.254.
176. In 1913, Alfonso Pacifici wrote to Ravenna urging him, as president of the FSI, to find the funds for translations of Herzl's works. See CZA, Ravenna, A353/43: the letters are dated 12 August and 1 September.
177. Lowenthal (ed. and trans.), *Diaries of Theodor Herzl*, p.417.
178. Ibid., p.410.
179. Romano, 'I rapporti di Teodoro Herzl coi sionisti italiani', p.518. The Italian delegates voted in favour of Uganda (see ibid., p.519). On the crisis, see Vital, *Zionism: Formative Years*, Chapter 9.
180. CZA, Z2/65.
181. See *L'Idea Sionista*, 1904, p.34; 1905, pp.81, 102. In addition, there were those not yet affiliated – Rome, Turin and Vercelli – and small informal committees in Mantua and Verona (*IS*, 1904, p.17): paltry figures compared to the 1,572 associations in Russia (see *IS*, 1904, p.14). The official list of *shekalim* sent by Ravenna to Zionist Central Office in March 1906 is as follows: Ferrara 140; Modena 140; Venice 159; Florence 200; Ancona 106; Rome 90; Bologna 81; Naples 60; Milan 200; Livorno 18; Perugia 20; a total of 1,214 which, Ravenna predicted correctly, would be the highest they achieved. CZA, Z2/425.
182. *IS*, 1904, p.5. *L'Idea Sionista* published the proceedings of the conference, which constitute issues 3–5 of 1904.
183. In 1904, two Zionist supporters were elected to the Jewish community council in Rome, and yet, at the same time, the community's leaders did not permit the Zionist group in Rome to take part in their commemorations of Herzl's death, as they feared making Zionist propaganda. See CZA, A353/18; and Stefano Caviglia, *L'identità salvata: gli ebrei di Roma tra fede e nazione: 1870–1938* (Rome-Bari: Laterza, 1996), pp.110–13. In 1920, for a very brief period from January to May, eleven young Zionists – several of whom were Margulies's disciples, such as Alfonso Pacifici and Carlo Alberto Viterbo – gained control of the Florence community; a royal decree was needed to oust them. They produced a newsletter, *Comune Ebraico*, sold as a supplement with *Israel*. See Aldo Astrologo and Francesco Del Canuto, 'Firenze 1920: storia del "Comune ebraico"', *RMI*, 44, 1 (1978), pp.6–42. See also Carlo Alberto Viterbo's own recollections of that 'revolutionary time' in *Israel*, December 1974, p.7. We can note the change of name from 'comunità israelitica'. 'Comune ebraico' designated that it was part of the Jewish nation in the making, recalling the Austrian Zionists' Jüdische Volksgemeinde. See also the leading article in *Giovane Israele*, 4, 10 (1920), p.1: 'Zionism has officially been affirmed in an Italian community. In Florence the electoral battle for control [*conquista*] of the local Jewish administration has been won by the youthful and energetic Zionists … It is time to rid the communities of narrow-minded ideas, antiquated structures and aging personnel' (ACDEC, Fondo Sullam, I.3.1.1, B.18, file 205).
184. CZA, A353/39; the letter is dated 16 December 1903.

185. *IS*, 1904, pp.40–53, which include Morpurgo's data.
186. According to a handwritten list for the Seventh Zionist Congress in 1905, the membership for Milan was 188 (CZA, A353/ 15/A); Edgardo Morpurgo, in a letter to Ravenna of 29 November 1905, puts the figure at 205 (CZA, A353/40). After the war against Turkey, Italy acquired Libya and with it a sizeable Jewish community. In 1917 there was a Zionist group in Tripoli with 350 members (CZA, A353/5).
187. CZA, A353/14: handwritten membership list.
188. CZA, A353/39. The letter is dated 14 April 1903.
189. In 1910, Vitta became professor of law at the Istituto di Scienze Politiche e Sociali 'Cesare Alfieri' in Florence. He held a number of professorial posts at other institutions until 1938; he resumed his academic career after the war. He was president of the Jewish community in Florence during the Second World War.
190. CZA, A353/14. The letter is dated 6 June 1903. Vitta's name does not appear on the 1905 membership list.
191. On this Congress, see Vital, *Zionism: Formative Years*, pp.428–35. There was a two-day debate on the East African project, which was rejected. This time the Italian delegates voted in favour of Palestine.
192. Del Canuto, *Il movimento sionistico*, p.51.
193. Italics in the original. Primo Levi, who signed himself 'L'Italico' (the Italic), as if to cancel out his Jewish identity, was a follower of nationalism and an anti-Zionist. His article, 'Il sionismo e il suo congresso', to which Arias refers, was published in *La Nuova Antologia*, 16 August 1905. Another Jewish intellectual, the distinguished academic lawyer Ludovico Mortara, was also critical of Zionism. See Toscano, *Ebraismo e antisemitismo*, p.56.
194. Italics in the original.
195. Italics in the original.
196. Between 1880 and 1914, approximately 150,000 Jews emigrated to England, mostly from eastern Europe, two-thirds before the introduction of the Aliens Act. See Cohen, *English Zionists and British Jews*, p.18.
197. Carlo Francesco Gabba, 'Un appello agli israeliti italiani a proposito del Sionismo', *La Rassegna Nazionale*, 1 October 1905, pp.341–50.
198. ACDEC, Fondo Sullam, I.1.2.2, Corrispondenza generale, B.3, file 13. In another letter, dated 17 October 1905, Ravenna informed Sullam that he had written to the editor of *Il Resto Del Carlino* (a regional daily) expressing his regret that he had published part of Gabba's article when hitherto the paper had been positive in its reporting on Zionism. Sullam and Ravenna had been corresponding since 1902, when the former enquired whether the FSI might wish to publish his thesis on Zionism. By 1905, Sullam was one of Ravenna's trusted confidants. On 5 May 1904, Ravenna wrote to Sullam: 'I appeal to your well-known kindness and to the friendship that binds us'; on 11 December 1906: 'Dearest Angelo, you have really become an angel: all your letters are full of milk and honey' (B.3, file 13). At times there was an almost daily correspondence between them.
199. Cavaglion, 'Tendenze nazionali', pp.1301–2.
200. A copy of this statement on the compatibility between Zionism and Italian patriotism, is among Sullam's papers: ACDEC, Sullam, I. 2.2.2.2, Convegni, B.5, file 46.
201. *VI*, 1906, p.23. In several letters to Ravenna, Morpurgo expressed his dismay at the divergences from the Basle programme of *L'Idea Sionista* which, 'whether it likes it or not', was the official organ of the FSI (letter of 29 November 1905). On 17 December 1905 he informed Ravenna that he had seen Amedeo Donati, the editor. In the same letter he maintained that one could be Italian and retain intact Jewish national ideality, and it was vital to do so: 'the day that Jewish national sentiment disappears, Judaism will cease to exist'. CZA, A353/40. This was the view Nordau expressed at the Seventh Congress; there were two possibilities: either death through assimilation or redemption through Zionism (*IS*, 1905, p.120).
202. CZA, A353/40.
203. Carlo Francesco Gabba, 'Ancora del Sionismo in Italia', *La Rassegna Nazionale*, 1 April 1906, pp.353–68.
204. Italics in the original.
205. Salvatore Mazzamuta, 'I giuristi dell'ateneo pisano e la questione ebraica', in Luzzati (ed.), *Gli ebrei di Pisa*, pp.223–9. Other historians refer even more briefly to this polemic, hence its fuller treatment in this chapter.
206. *VI*, 1906, pp.94–7, 243.
207. From 1902, a similar change of direction occurred in the stance of Isaïe Levaillant, editor of *Univers israélite*. As a key spokesman for French Jewry, his change of attitude would have been influential. See Pierre Birnbaum, *The Jews of the Republic: A Political History of State Jews in France from*

Gambetta to Vichy (Stanford, CA: Stanford University Press, 1996), p.91.
208. *VI*, 1905, pp.459–61; 1910, p.52.
209. *VI*, 1913, pp.338–40, 505–8, 590–2.
210. *CI*, 1905, pp.383–4; 1906, pp.23–4; 164–6.
211. *CI*, 1906, pp.2–3, 109–111.
212. ACDEC, Fondo Sullam, 1.2.2.4, Corrispondenze, B.5, file 65. The circular, stamped as 'highly confidential', is dated 22 June 1906.
213. CZA, Ravenna, A353/14. The group consisted of thirty-two members. *L'Idea Sionista*'s comment on the low number of Zionist supporters from so large a community suggests that the middle classes' more frequent contact with non-Jews – there had never been a ghetto in the port city – rendered them uninterested in a movement that would accentuate racial differences (*IS*, 1905, p.83).
214. *IS*, 1906, p.105. CZA, Ravenna, A353/6. Several of the letters contain requests to Ravenna to hasten with the project.
215. CZA, Ravenna, A353/6.
216. *IS*, 1907, pp.110–12; 1908, pp.1–3, 63–5.
217. See Vital, *Zionism: Crucial Phase*, p.9.
218. *CI*, 1907, pp.101–2, 199–200.
219. *CI*, 1907, pp.215–16. In 1903, there had been dissent within the Milan group which had been resolved (*IS*, 1903, pp.88, 127, 145). See also Gino Racah's letter of 26 June 1903 to Ravenna 'on the strong currents of opposition to the executive committee'; but peace was restored with the election of a new committee (letter of 16 November 1903). CZA, A353/15/A. Del Canuto in *Il movimento sionistico in Italia* omits any reference to the MSP.
220. CZA, A353/40. Despite this opposition to the FSI, the correspondence between Morpurgo and Ravenna remained cordial.
221. In another letter, dated 6 February 1908, detailing the preparations for the Venice conference for which he was responsible, Sullam expressed the hope that he could keep 'that delightful Edgardo Morpurgo' on side, since 'by dint of doing new things, he kills off the old ones.' ACDEC, Fondo Sullam, I.1.2.2, Corrispondenza generale (1902–35), B.3, file 13; 1.2.2.2.2, Convegni, B.5, file 48.
222. ACDEC, Fondo Sullam, 1.2.4, Gruppo Sionistico Veneto (1903–11), B.7, file 80.
223. The Livorno group reformed in December 1907 with a reduced membership of twelve. They elected Eduardo Morpurgo as their delegate for the Venice conference, which suggests their Zionist perspective had shifted (*CI*, 1907, p.261).
224. In May 1910, a similar letter regarding the shekel funds was sent to Ravenna expressing displeasure that not even the smallest sum had been received. CZA, Z2/426 and Z2/425.
225. ACDEC, Fondo Sullam, 1.2.2.1, Federazione Sionistica Italiana, B.5, file 41. Protocol 2/1910, 14 January 1910.
226. ACDEC, Fondo Sullam, I.1.2.2, B.3, file 13.
227. Ravenna's colleagues began to complain of his silence: see letters from Roberto Ascoli (CZA, A353/28), Alfonso Pacifici (CZA, A353/43), and Aldo Sorani (CZA, A353/14).
228. ACDEC, Fondo Sullam, I.1.2.2, B.3, file 13.
229. Later that year, Sullam published such comments in *L'Idea Sionista* to which Ferruccio Servi strongly objected, citing 'the most renowned journal *The Jewish Chronicle* as an example of a paper that ran such items of news'. Servi wrote privately to Sullam 'to avoid public polemics ... There are so many common enemies to fight that I do not see the reason for us to tear each other to pieces' (*dilaniarci*). The letters are dated 9 and 13 October 1909. ACDEC, Fondo Sullam, I.1.2.2, B.3, file 16.
230. ACDEC, Fondo Sullam, I.1.2.2, B.3, file 18.
231. CZA, A353/14.
232. CZA, A353/39.
233. CZA, A353/40.
234. ACDEC, Fondo Sullam, I.2.2.2.1, B.5, file 41.
235. The letter is dated 27 April 1913. Pacifici protested against the clandestine nature of the conference, of no one knowing anything and thus losing its efficacy and importance (CZA, A353/43).
236. See *La Settimana Israelitica* [*SI*], 41 (1913); *VI*, 1913, pp.588–9.
237. See *CI*, 1913, p.103; *SI*, 41 (1913); *VI*, 1913, p.590.
238. See Vital, *Zionism: Crucial Phase*, pp.137–41.
239. The letters are dated 14 January 1914; 12 February 1915; CZA, A353/8/1. The members of parliament were Claudio Treves and Canepa.
240. All the letters are to be found in CZA, A353/8/1.
241. See Martin Clark, *Modern Italy 1871–1982* (London and New York: Longman, 1984), p.182. The Italian government negotiated with the *Entente* and the Triple Alliance in order to extract the largest

territorial concessions, regarding particularly Trent and Trieste. They eventually sided with the *Entente*.

242. ACDEC, Fondo Sullam, I.1.2.2, B.3, file 14. A month earlier, Sullam was writing to Ravenna in positive terms about Rutenberg's influence: 'In any case I would like Rutenberg to be there' (22 January 1915); 'We need some clear ideas ... we need Rutenberg to return' (26 January 1915); but by May, he was less enthusiastic: 'he is angry with us; he wants to make publicity ... but I told him to calm down because the Italian public has no time for Jewish problems'.

243. See Maurizio Molinari, *Ebrei in Italia: un problema di identità (1870–1938)* (Florence: Giuntina, 1991), pp.57–9; and Bidussa, Luzzatto and Luzzatto Voghera, *Oltre il ghetto*, pp.214–18.

244. See Jonathan Freedland, *Jacob's Gift: A Journey into the Heart of Belonging* (London: Hamish Hamilton, 2005), pp.222–3.

6
A Jewish Renaissance

The Italian Zionists, with their internal struggles and divisions, failed to provide a powerful presence and in 1911 they disbanded, even before the first intimations of hostility: the dual allegiance of *ebraismo* and *italianità* had not held; the former ceded to the latter. The Jewish communities were slow to organize themselves into a federation, achieving consensus only in May 1914. Unlike England and France, there was no chief rabbi in Italy to raise the prestige of the Italian rabbinate, which also revealed an incapacity for unity and leadership.[1] Thus Italian Jewry lacked a strong spiritual figurehead. The second half of the nineteenth century has been characterized as 'a cultural desert of Italian Judaism'.[2] The prominent figure of this period was Samuel Hirsch Margulies – Shemuel Zevì Margulies (his students preferred the Hebrew form of his name) – who was a Polish Jew from Brzezany, Galicia (then in Austria-Hungary, now Ukraine), educated in Germany.

Italian Jewish historiography has allocated to Margulies (1858–1922) an ever diminishing role: for Mario Toscano, he is both central (1982) and marginal (1990); for Alberto Cavaglion, he is barely acknowledged (1997);[3] for Gadi Luzzatto Voghera, he is conspicuous by his absence. In his recent article on nineteenth- and twentieth-century Italian Jewry (2004), Luzzatto Voghera mentions those few rabbis who contributed to the cultural life of the country and thus rose above the generally poor educational standards of their peers as mere employees of the Jewish communities: Elia Benamozegh, Dante Lattes, and Umberto Cassuto who was Margulies's student at the Rabbinical College of Florence, but not Margulies himself.[4] Why this omission? Cavaglion has suggested that a degree of parochialism crept into Italian scholarship and thus the innovative influence of outsiders was minimized.[5] It cannot be for lack of documentation, as is the case for Baruch. Margulies's significance for the Zionist movement in Italy was undervalued by his contemporaries (apart from his own circle), with the exception of Dante Lattes who was also an outsider at that time, and by historians; Margulies's correspondence with Herzl, for example, has only recently been reviewed within the context of international Zionism.[6] This chapter challenges the prevailing orthodoxy and re-presents Margulies as the dominant figure of his generation in Italy, the chief rabbi of Italy in all but name, and one of the most eminent representatives of the great rabbinical tradition. Through his achievements Florence became the centre of an intellectual and spiritual renaissance of Italian Judaism in the first decades of the twentieth century. Attilio Milano, in his seminal essay of 1938 on the Jewish press in Italy, held such a view, calling

Margulies 'Maestro' and acclaiming his scholarship, his authority and his audacious initiatives.[7] The date 1938 may help to explain the reason why Italian historians in the late twentieth and twenty-first centuries do not share this evaluation. It is, one could argue, a similar revisionist problematic as with Arnaldo Momigliano's 1933 concept of parallel nationalism. An external perspective can perhaps dispel the regnant negative assessment.

In 1889, the Jewish community of Florence found itself without a chief rabbi, having had difficulties in filling the post in the preceding decades. It was not the only community in this predicament: in Rome, owing to the lack of suitably qualified Italian candidates, the 71-year-old non-Italian director of the Rabbinical College, Mosè Levi Ehrenreich, was selected: (*Il Vessillo Israelitico* [*VI*], 1890, p.173). The committee responsible for the Florence appointment advertised not only in Italy but also abroad. By March of that year, seven Italians and one rabbi of Russian origin had applied, but none satisfied the stringent criteria (the seven Italians were already known to the committee, having applied unsuccessfully in the past). Then the name of Margulies was brought to their attention by an eminent German scholar, with additional glowing references from Paris, Budapest and Breslau. The president of the committee, the lawyer Moisè Finzi, travelled to Frankfurt to interview him in September 1889; he reported most favourably on the 31-year-old as an 'erudite, courteous, and experienced orthodox rabbi, but not intransigently so'.[8]

It is surprising that Margulies accepted; his east European background was so dissimilar. Alfonso Pacifici suggests it was the lure of Florence and Finzi's persuasive personality.[9] There was some opposition to his appointment on the grounds of his German education, and this resurfaced at the outbreak of the First World War, exacerbated by Margulies's open support for political Zionism.[10] Rabbi Flaminio Servi, editor of *Il Vessillo Israelitico*, indicated surprise and concern at the appointment: he queried Margulies's ability to preach in Dante's city, and suggested that Italy was gradually being filled with scholarly foreigners – a reference not only to Margulies, but also to a Russian rabbi who had occupied the vacant teaching post at the Rabbinical College in Rome.[11] However, after a visit to Florence in 1898, Servi expressed admiration for Margulies's influence and authority: every aspect of religious ritual and instruction was under his sole direction with no interference from the communal administration; he was an outstanding teacher; he had found an excellent kosher butcher – no mean feat in Italy – and supervised the baking of unleavened bread; he was scholarly and orthodox and accepted no half measures: 'he wants control and he is in control and has thus succeeded in obtaining the respect that no Italian rabbis have ever done … you can feel a religious spirit hovering everywhere' (*VI*, 1898, pp.54–6). This positive assessment is somewhat marred by prejudicial references to Margulies's inexhaustible Teutonic energy and inflexibility, as Servi erroneously thought that Margulies was born in Germany (*VI*, 1890, p.376). A few years later, the editor of *Il Vessillo Israelitico* expressed relief that Margulies had not taken a post in London, offered to him by 'the illustrious member of parliament, Sir Samuel Montagu', and suggested that the Jewish community of Florence should be similarly grateful (*VI*, 1901, p.29). Margulies's international stature is reflected in such an invitation, which was further enhanced not only through his role in the Zionist movement but also by his nomination in 1907 as president of the International Falasha Committee, established for the education of Ethiopian Jews; the activities of this committee were regularly reported in the Italian Jewish press. After the colonization of Libya in 1911, Margulies was one of the first to be sent by the Italian government to report on the conditions of the indigenous Jewish communities.

Margulies had studied at the renowned Jewish Theological Seminary of Breslau (Germany, now Wroclaw, Poland), founded in 1854, whose teachers had included many of the Wissenschaft des Judentums scholars. He also obtained a first-class honours degree in philosophy and Semitic languages from the University of Leipzig. By the time he arrived in Florence in 1890, he was fluent in Italian (the committee had also been concerned about his linguistic proficiency, since all the correspondence pertaining to the appointment was in German). In his inaugural address, he spoke of his principal duty to 'rekindle and nurture the religious spirit', especially among the young.[12]

In 1887 an Italian Rabbinical College had been established by royal decree in Rome, but by 1896 it was running into difficulties, with poor recruitment and resignations among the teaching staff. The commission set up to deal with the problem identified Margulies as the most suitable person to direct the college; they had been impressed by the success of his teaching at the Florentine Jewish community's school.[13] Independently, and in the same year, Margulies wrote to the poet David Levi, requesting a letter of recommendation to the minister of finance, Luigi Luzzatti (Levi's nephew by marriage), in order to discuss the possibility of establishing a rabbinical institute in Florence – an urgent necessity given 'the deplorable condition of Italian Judaism' (*le deplorabilissime condizioni in cui si trova il giudaismo italiano*). In Margulies's opinion there were few religious teachers or rabbis with the requisite intellectual and moral qualities and, unless the situation improved, the future looked grim.[14]

In 1899 the college moved to Florence under the directorship of Margulies. In that year Margulies appointed Dr Ismar Elbogen (1874–1943), also a graduate of the Jewish Theological Seminary of Breslau. In 1902 Elbogen left to take up a post in Berlin. He was replaced by the brilliant scholar Zevi Perez Chajes (1876–1925), then 26 years of age, who went on to become the chief rabbi of Trieste in 1912 and Vienna in 1918. The nomination of yet another foreigner aroused a certain amount of hostility in the Italian Jewish press. Curiously, *Il Corriere Israelitico* (*CI*), in its close identification with things Italian, published several antagonistic articles on Margulies, accusing him of not concerning himself with the future of the Italian rabbinate, of 'Germanizing' the Rabbinical College of Florence and of monopolizing Jewish scholarship.[15] In announcing the *concorso* for 1902, the editor of *Il Corriere* expressed the wish to have an Italian appointment; when this did not occur and another 'German' was chosen, he enquired as to the existence of Italian rabbis. Seven candidates had applied: three were Italians and two of them were immediately rejected owing to lack of documentation. Clearly there was dismay at the paucity of suitably qualified indigenous candidates and humiliation at being a mere outpost for foreign rabbis. There was satisfaction, therefore, when Giacomo Bolaffio was appointed chief rabbi of Turin: the editor states that 'after so many graduates from beyond the Alps, there is a Jewish community who finds an Italian rabbi' (*CI*, 1902, p.275). Bolaffio, from Gorizia, was in fact a citizen of Austria-Hungary. When the Rome community was once more without a chief rabbi in 1903 and all the Italian applicants had been discounted, the deputy rabbi of Trieste was appointed, Vittorio Castiglioni.[16]

Margulies succeeded in restoring the international reputation of the rabbinical college: its graduates, such as Elia Artom, Dario Disegni, David Prato, Angelo Sacerdoti and Umberto Cassuto, were 'symbols of Italian Judaism ... the distinguished rabbis of the twentieth century'.[17] Between 1907 and 1922, David Prato was director of the Talmud Torah in Florence. He improved standards and introduced curricula innovations such as the teaching of spoken Hebrew and Zionist ideology.[18] He later became chief rabbi of Alexandria in Egypt, returning to Italy in 1936 as chief rabbi in Rome, a position he resumed after the Second World War. Disegni was a rabbi in Turin where he remained for a long period, eventually becoming chief rabbi. He established and taught in a rabbinical college named in honour of Margulies. Cassuto was secretary of the Jewish community from 1906; he replaced Chajes at the Rabbinical College of Florence in 1912 until 1925; he was appointed as Margulies's successor in 1922, but resigned in 1925 to take the Chair in Hebrew language and literature at the Istituto di Studi Superiori in Florence; in Attilio Milano's opinion, Cassuto assumed the mantle of Samuel David Luzzatto.[19] Another of Margulies's students, Rabbi Gustavo Castelbolognesi, was nominated to fill the vacancy but, after having accepted, financial constraints compelled him to withdraw at the last moment; he later became chief rabbi of Milan. Cassuto's brother-in-law, Elia Artom, who was chief rabbi of Tripoli, succeeded Castelbolognesi in 1926 and stayed for a decade.[20] Angelo Sacerdoti was appointed chief rabbi of Rome in 1912; he remained in office until 1935. According to Stefano Caviglia, his influence and competence transformed the life of the community.[21] Thus it can be stated unequivocally that Margulies played a pivotal role in renewing and strengthening the rabbinate not only in Italy but also abroad.

Margulies's second significant achievement was the founding of the first Jewish academic journal in Italy, *La Rivista Israelitica. Periodico bimestrale per la scienza e la vita del Giudaismo*, which was published from 1904 until 1915.[22] His principal objective was to revitalize Italian Jewish scholarship which had languished since the death of Samuel David Luzzatto. In his first editorial, Margulies made clear that he intended to fill this lacuna, to create a rigorously scientific publication along the lines of the *Revue des études juives* in France, the *Monatschrift* in Germany, and the *Jewish Quarterly Review* in England.[23] Eminent scholars from abroad were invited to contribute articles on history, bibliography, literature, and rabbinical and biblical exegesis. It also contained book reviews, synopses of relevant foreign articles, and regular reports on the Zionist movement. In Attilio Milano's assessment, *La Rivista Israelitica* is worthy of occupying the highest place in the pantheon of publications on Judaism in Italy.[24]

Margulies's greatest and lasting legacy was perhaps the influence and inspiration that he exerted on his students, for whom he was 'Maestro' and 'a second father'.[25] His teaching was not restricted to the rabbinical college: he gave public lectures and also held private lessons (*conversazioni*) in his home. It was to such a meeting that the young Carlo Alberto Viterbo (1889–1974) was taken by fellow law undergraduate, Alfonso Pacifici (1889–1981). Viterbo came from an assimilated, middle-class family for whom Judaism was a painful reminder of the past. His friend Pacifici from a similar background had begun to discuss Judaism with him in their last year at school (1906/07) and later brought him into contact with Margulies, who accepted him unreservedly: 'It was the Maestro's lessons ... for over a decade ... that completed my "return".'[26] Pacifici also recalled the profound impact of those lessons 'from such a Maestro', whom he described as belonging to the category of 'mythical men' (*uomini mitici*), endowed with exceptional qualities, including outstanding oratorical skills, and a regal and imposing manner, 'born to command'.[27] He was one of Margulies's most beloved disciples, as the rabbi's correspondence reveals. The numerous letters Margulies wrote to 'My dearest Alfonso' (*Mio carissimo Alfonso*) attest to deep affection and paternal pride in the achievements of his 'son'; in a letter of 14 November 1911, he writes: 'I have read your wonderful article. It gave me great joy. Let me embrace you with a father's affection!'[28] Some of the letters and many postcards are in Hebrew; Margulies was delighted that Pacifici was learning the language. Viterbo recalls that the Maestro arranged for them to study Hebrew with 'an excellent teacher'.[29] Margulies's coteries, apart from his students at the rabbinical college, were these young men who were reacting against their assimilated bourgeois milieu in the same manner as their counterparts elsewhere in western Europe. Through Margulies's influence, they were encouraged to explore and experience their Jewish patrimony and reconnect with their Jewish identity.

In May 1907 the Comitato Pro Cultura Ebraica (Committee for Jewish Culture) was established in Florence: one can note the rejection of the adjective *israelitica* in favour of the more ethnically assertive *ebraica*. The inaugural programme devised by Aldo Sorani (1883–1945), the president, comprised a series of lectures given in May and June by Margulies's students: on the significance of Jewish culture (Sorani); the Maccabees (Sacerdoti); the destruction of the Second Temple (Prato); the Bar Kokhba revolt (Castelbolognsesi); the early history of the Florentine Jewish community (Cassuto). Both *Il Corriere Israelitico* and *Il Vessillo Israelitico* welcomed the initiative, regularly reporting on Pro Cultura's activities as it expanded throughout Italy. Sorani's inaugural lecture, published in full by the Triestine journal, conveys the motivations of the young Florentines to undertake such an enterprise: the inner necessity to search for meaning in their own lives through the study of their past history; to have fuller possession of their Jewish heritage; to identify with their forbears and clarify the significance of their Jewish identity; to redeem their ancestors from oblivion; the desire to live a Jewish life; to be actively involved and useful to their community; to communicate their knowledge and understanding to others. Their initiative was also borne of rebellion: to counteract 'with all the enthusiasm of our young hearts', the pseudo culture and religious apathy that in their opinion was pervading Italy (*CI*, 1907, pp.37–43). In a subsequent article, Sorani wrote of participating in a 'Jewish renewal', of hastening towards 'our spiritual reawakening' (*CI*, 1907, pp.106–7).

Il Corriere Israelitico became the official organ of Pro Cultura, and in August published its mission statement: to promote publicly Jewish culture, based on meticulous scholarly methodology, through lectures on history, literature and religion in order to disseminate such knowledge among their co-religionists, and to stimulate their interest in and understanding of the immense treasures of Judaism. The association also publicized its policy towards the Federazione Sionistica Italiana (FSI): it would collaborate on cultural matters while remaining independent.[30] These sentiments were reiterated by Aldo Sorani in *L'Idea Sionista* (*IS*), with more emphasis on the need for mutual support: 'Zionism's success among Italian Jews depends on the progress of Jewish culture' (*IS*, 1907, pp.110 12). This position was ratified at the sixth FSI conference held in Venice in March 1908. There was a lengthy debate and, although Felice Ravenna, president of the FSI, would have preferred the new association to be an 'emanation' of Zionism, Sorani's and Edgardo Morpurgo's (president of the Pro Cultura in Padua) proposal that 'the Venice conference, recognizing the necessity and usefulness of the Pro Cultura movement initiated in Florence, invites the federal council to assist its work in the most opportune way' was approved unanimously (*CI*, 1907, pp.319–20).

Throughout 1907, *Il Corriere Israelitico* published letters of support for Pro Cultura, such as Gino Arias' fulsome praise: 'The only beacon of Jewish culture in Italy is the Rabbinical College of Florence, but it is a very powerful beacon which radiates such a light that it is to be hoped will dispel the shadows which envelop Italian Judaism.' Arias was president of the Florence Zionist group and therefore saw the potential of this movement 'to win over new and faithful followers of Zionism' (*CI*, 1907, p.183). His reference to the Rabbinical College is a clear acknowledgement of Margulies's influence in the gestation of the new movement, an influence that others found irksome and therefore resented. Within a year of its foundation, Pro Cultura committees were established in Milan and Padua, and by 1910 throughout northern and central Italy, in Bologna, Ferrara, Livorno, Modena, Pisa, Rome, Venice and Verona, and there was the intention to establish a central committee.[31] Aldo Sorani was interviewed by *Il Corriere Israelitico*: the insistent questioning as to whether rabbinical authority was behind the movement, and whether the young Florentines 'were simply the mouthpiece of their masters', indicated a certain antagonism towards Margulies and his colleague Chajes, the two outsiders, whose impact on the Jewish milieu in Italy was so profound (*CI*, 1908, pp.33–5). However, it has to be said that leaders of the local Jewish communities were positive in their approach, and their goodwill was demonstrated in the loan of locales for the meetings and in active participation. The Committee of the Italian Jewish Communities was also favourably disposed: in their deliberations of 1912, it was recorded that the secretary Anselmo Colombo had been in contact with Aldo Sorani and David Prato about a cycle of lectures to be given in various communities (*CI*, 15 October 1912). There were, in effect, attempts by the president, Angelo Sereni, and the secretary to effect a rapprochement with the youth movement, Pro Cultura.

Padua was the first to follow Florence's example: at their initial meeting, the leaders of the local community and rabbis were invited to take part in the preliminary discussions. Their planned lecture programme for 1908 included Dante Lattes on Ahad Ha'am ('the greatest living Jewish writer'), Jews in medieval Spain, the democratic spirit in Jewish law, and a reading from Samuel David Luzzatto's publications (*CI*, 1907, p.257). Aldo Sorani, 'the indefatigable apostle' of Pro Cultura, 'the symbol of the renewed Jewish spirit', gave a speech at the inauguration of the Padua association in which he stated that the young had turned to the movement 'as to an anchor' when all else had failed (*CI*, 1908, p.208). In a provocatively-titled leading article, 'The Jewish Revolution: To Young Jews ... if there are any', in *Il Corriere Israelitico*, Sorani called upon Jewish youth to gather their forces 'as the hour of the Jewish revolution has arrived', and to attack the older generation, lost in their sleep and pointless wrangling. The young must unite and promote Jewish culture, the sole way to become Jews (*CI*, 1909, pp.321–2).

Pro Cultura was a wholly new direction for Italian Jews; it was without precedent.[32] It was generational, it was radical in its adherents' rejection of the status quo in which their elders were so entrenched, and in the positive rediscovery and re-evaluation of Judaism it was unequivocally anti-assimilationist. It was an inverse manifestation of Wissenschaft des Judentums: the German movement's principal objective was to show the world that Jewish scholarship and methodology were part of mainstream culture, a component of the German *Bildung*. Pro Cultura, on the other hand, intended to foreground its distinctive 'otherness' and its cultural diversity. Nearly a century had elapsed between the two movements, a period in which the high expectations of emancipation and integration had been revealed as flawed and, to some, illusory. To what extent were Sorani and his group not only influenced by Margulies's teachings, but also by the changing political and cultural climate in Italy and Europe? There is consensus among Italian historians that the transformation of the political scene – the erosion of the liberal regime in the Giolittian era, the growth of Italian socialism, the powerful alliances between Catholics and conservatives, and the emergence of a new form of reactionary nationalism, together with the affirmation of Zionism as an international movement – motivated Italian Jews to explore and reappraise their own national identity.[33] It was precisely Florence that was the centre of the Italian cultural revival predicated on nationalist ideology: the first nationalist reviews such as *Il Regno*, *Il Leonardo* and *La Voce* were published in the Tuscan capital, and it was in Florence in December 1910 that nationalist sympathizers held their first meeting.

It was against this background of cultural and political ferment that Margulies launched another project in his attempt to regenerate the Jewish spirit among the Jews of Italy: a new journal and the promotion of national conferences. *La Settimana Israelitica* (*SI*) – 'the first real journal, both for content and typography, to appear in Italy'[34] – was established on 1 January 1910. It was printed by the Tipografia Giuntina[35] which had been set up some years earlier by the Polish Jew, Leo Samuel Olschki, founder of the celebrated publishing house which is now in its fourth generation of the same family.[36] The printing works still exists under different owners, one of whom, Daniel Vogelmann, created Casa Editrice La Giuntina in 1980, which has become an internationally renowned publisher of every facet of Judaism. One could argue that Vogelmann is continuing in the twenty-first century the cultural tradition of the Pro Cultura movement. *La Settimana Israelitica* in its early years was quintessentially the publishing arm of Pro Cultura. It was edited under the auspices of Margulies until 19 December 1913, but the compilation was in the hands of his protégés; from that date the names of Alfonso Pacifici, Carlo Alberto Viterbo (then both 21 years of age), Quinto Senigaglia, and David Prato appeared for the first time on the front page. In its final year of existence, when only Pacifici remained, the journal's orientation was specifically Zionist.[37] It was a journal of and for the younger generation, written in a lively and persuasive style to celebrate and affirm a new sense of Judaism, of being Jewish.[38]

In the opening editorial, the principal aims were outlined: the dissemination of Jewish culture and the renewal of Jewish awareness. Articles on all aspects of Judaism would be published, on Jewish activities at home and abroad. A regular series in the first year comprised letters from correspondents in Berlin, Jerusalem, Lisbon, London, Polish Galicia, Romania, Trieste, Vienna, and the United States of America. Like Lattes in *Il Corriere Israelitico*, Margulies from the outset intended to develop the limited perspective of Italian Jews, bringing them detailed, contemporary accounts of their co-religionists' lives throughout the world in order to encourage intellectual and spiritual union among the Jews of the Diaspora and to publicize the prevailing issues and concerns. One could surmise that a Zionist agenda was behind such a decision: sympathy for the persecuted *Ostjuden* would be engendered by repeated narratives of their trials and tribulations. The first letter, from London, appearing in the second issue, described, inter alia, the various initiatives to help poor Jews, mainly from eastern Europe; the lengthy missive from Berlin (no. 4) presented many of the German Jewish associations, institutions and publications – 'an exuberance of energetic activity' – as a stimulus for the Italians; the communication from Galicia (no. 6) contained news of Zionist activities, the number of schools where Hebrew was the language of instruction, the poverty (no. 32); from Romania, the initial correspondence focused on Zionism and the success of Bezalel, the Arts Institute in Jerusalem (no. 14). Conversely, the Paris dispatch (no. 15) conveyed, perhaps as a warning to Italians, the paucity of Jewish life in the French capital: no traditions, ignorance of Jewish history and language, and indifference among the young.[39] The sheer size and variety of American Jewish life (two million Jews, of whom one million alone were in New York, no. 19), was contrasted to the new Jewish life taking root in Lisbon (500 people) after more than three centuries of exclusion (no. 23). Anti-Semitic manifestations in Germany, Austria, Hungary and Romania are reported. In addition to regular information on Pro Cultura, the Zionist movement, and the various Italian communities, a broad cultural perspective was provided through articles on Jewish history, on Jewish literature both ancient and modern, profiles of distinguished Jews, and politics from a Jewish perspective.

A sense of satisfaction of outcomes achieved informed the editorial of 6 January 1911. In order to consolidate this positive evaluation, an extensive interview with the eminent rabbinic scholar and president of the Jewish Theological Seminary of America, Romanian-born Solomon Schechter (1847–1915), was published in the spring.[40] This authoritative figure stated that on his last visit to Italy, fifteen years previously, he had thought that Judaism in Italy was in crisis, whereas now it was invigorated with new life, especially in Florence which had become its centre. He spoke in glowing terms of the Rabbinical College in Florence; of *La Rivista Israelitica*, 'the only Italian scholarly journal of Jewish studies'; of the 'noble enterprise' of *La Settimana Israelitica* 'to disseminate Jewish culture in Italy' (*SI*, 12 [1911]).

By the middle of the second year, on 14 July 1911, prompted perhaps by Margulies's youthful protégés and by the collapse of the Italian Zionist Federation, *La Settimana Israelitica* launched an appeal for unity, to assemble for the first time the young Jews of Italy in a spirit of renewal of their Jewish identity. The conference would encourage solidarity; it would signal the 'idealistic renaissance of young Italian Jews' (*il segno di una rinascita idealista fra i giovani ebrei italiani*); it would be a meeting based on friendship and debate, not a stuffy, bureaucratic, official congress.[41] For Pacifici, the key questions were: 'Who are we Jews? What do we signify? What does Judaism mean?' (*SI*, 41–2 [1911]). Letters of support poured in from the public articulating a variety of views: such a convention would validate Jewish culture at home and abroad; bring together isolated, small communities whose problems were ignored by the majority (a federation of the communities had not yet been established); associate the concept of a Jewish *risorgimento* with that of the Italian *Risorgimento*; help to combat assimilation and anti-Semitism.[42] The response to this initiative was also applauded by the foreign Jewish press in Austria-Hungary, England, Germany, Poland and Romania; the list was published on 1 December 1911. The only exception was *Il Vessillo Israelitico*: in the months between the appeal and the conference itself, and even after the conference had taken place, a bitter and protracted polemic ensued between this journal and *La Settimana Israelitica* on the subject of the genesis of the idea, with the Piedmontese journal's editor threatening lawsuits and demanding arbitration from a third party; even the president of the Committee of Italian Jewish Communities was requested to intervene to restore harmony.[43] Clearly the editor of the older established journal felt his role as representative of Italian Judaism had been usurped.

The first Convegno Giovanile Ebraico Italiano (Italian Jewish Youth Conference) took place at the Rabbinical College of Florence from 29 to 31 October 1911. David Prato presided and his welcoming message was: 'we are young and they say we represent the future ... the greatest hope for Italian Judaism'. Margulies, in his opening address, stated that 'nothing can be sweeter and more consoling for the person who has devoted his whole life to a high ideal than to see young people, the hope for the future, take the field'. Angelo Sullam conveyed greetings on behalf of the Italian Zionist Federation. Members of the foreign press, including a correspondent from *Die Welt*, were present. In the first paper, given by Aldo Sorani, 'Towards a New Jewish Apologetic', he conveyed his own way of perceiving Judaism: it was more than a religion, more than a nation; it had a unique life force (*una vita e una forza specifiche, una unicità incomparabile*). He was followed by Alfonso Pacifici, 'On Religious Practices': his scholarly disquisition on the longevity of the religion, the paradox of the Jewish exile, and the present crisis were exemplified in his own case – an atheist at secondary school, a mystic at high school and now an orthodox Jew who, through the Zionist movement, strongly felt a sense of national pride and a desire to proselytize. Religious practices would become a way of life, a return to traditional Judaism. Edgardo Morpurgo spoke about Pro Cultura, its organization and its significance for the younger generation and Umberto Cassuto spoke on his proposal for a history of Italian Jews. Elia Artom's thesis, 'On the Jewish Language', was that without Hebrew, 'without our language, we would not be nor could be Jews'; the study of Hebrew was a necessity and a duty. There were lively debates after each lecture and proposals were put forward: to set up a committee for the publication of historical research; to conduct a survey of Jewish schools; to strengthen Pro Cultura; to meet on an annual basis; to establish a secretariat in Florence.[44] Above all, a new, invigorated sense of Judaism had emerged, articulated with pride, passion and commitment, in 'a completely new language, which in its own way was revolutionary',[45] particularly from Sorani and Pacifici, the latter being the most charismatic of Margulies's disciples. Only a synopsis of his paper, which lasted two hours, could be given as his passionate, torrential manner of speaking could not be followed by the official stenographer. He later recalled the euphoria engendered at the first conference and his conviction that the 'volcanic' power of his words would transform at least some members of the audience: 'we ourselves were transformed, all united in one band of faith and action'.[46] Augusto Segre describes Pacifici: 'the immediate impression is of being in the presence of the traditional figure of a prophet that leaps from the pages of the Bible, not only because of his words and ideas, but also because of his long beard ... and clear, penetrating gaze'.[47] *Il Corriere Israelitico* devoted its lead article in the October issue to a detailed report of 'this first manifestation of youthful Jewish life', of which it was wholly supportive (*CI*, 1911, pp.105–11). The Committee of Jewish Communities, at their meeting in Florence, agreed to convey their congratulations to the organizers and also to send a synopsis of the proceedings to all communities (*CI*, 1911, p.131). The editor of *Il Vessillo Israelitico*, who had not been officially invited because of the acrimony, commented only briefly, criticizing the event as elitist, declaring that apart from the Florentine group only twenty delegates had attended (*VI*, 1911, p.621).

The editors of *La Settimana Israelitica* declared the conference a triumph, confidently stating that it signalled 'a significant and promising reawakening ... our generation must raise the banner of Judaism in this time of moral and spiritual renewal' (46 [1911]). Pacifici expanded his conference paper into a series of articles in the 1912 issues of the journal on the concept of 'integral Judaism' (*ebraismo integrale*), which were published as a monograph by the Tipografia Giuntina in the same year, with the title *Israele l'unico: ricerca di una definizione integrale dell'ebraismo*. This was a spiritual ideal of Judaism embracing religion, language and culture which gained currency and contributed to the formation of a stronger sense of national Jewish identity among the young Jews of Italy.[48] Another of Pacifici's initiatives was the Borsa di Studio Palestinese (Palestinian Scholarship Fund), which aimed to send one or more young Jews resident in Italy to Palestine to perfect their knowledge of spoken Hebrew, which they would then teach in Italian Jewish schools. It was launched in the pages of *La Settimana Israelitica* (37 [1912]) and *Il Corriere Israelitico* in September 1912, inviting subscriptions to be sent to Carlo Alberto Viterbo, who became the treasurer of the scholarship committee. In subsequent issues, the names, provenance and amount from each subscriber were published; by the end of March 1913, 1,908 lire had been collected (*SI*, 6 [1913]). *Il Vessillo Israelitico* also pledged its support, as did Felice Ravenna, president of the Italian Zionist Federation,[49] and the Committee of Jewish communities (*CI*, 15 December 1912).

The Borsa di Studio Palestinese was presented by Pacifici at the Second Italian Jewish Youth Conference, held in Turin in December 1912 and co-hosted by the leaders of the local Jewish community and the chief rabbi, Cav. Professor Giacomo Bolaffio. In the programme, the names of 123 participants from twenty-four communities are listed, including Trieste (Chajes and Lattes), Gorizia and Tripoli; the majority were naturally from Turin and Florence but Rome and Milan were also well represented, as were the other major centres, and several of the smaller ones such as Acqui, Cuneo and Vercelli, which also sent a delegate.[5] Many of the conference sessions were attended by an enthusiastic public of over 200 people (*VI*, 1912, p.802). Rabbi Bolaffio, in his opening address, praised the 'bold young men of Florence' who had organized the first convention and welcomed them to Turin, cradle of the Italian Risorgimento and now host to the Jewish renaissance (*il rinascimento ebraico*). Rabbi Umberto Cassuto, in his reply, enunciated a few words of Hebrew, 'the holy language of our fathers', concluding: 'our dream is this: the revival of Hebrew in every Jewish soul' (*VI*, 1912, pp.793–5). The first lecture by Pacifici expanded this theme: his aspiration was that all Jews should learn Hebrew, as reclaiming their linguistic patrimony was an essential aspect of his concept of integral Judaism. He later recalled the attempts of his group of friends to be bilingual: 'we were truly pioneers of spoken Hebrew in western Europe'.[51] He was followed by David Krinkin, a Jew of Russian origin residing in Rome, who gave an illustrated talk on Palestine, where he had spent several months. He spoke of the new Jewish life in the various colonies where Hebrew, 'our national language', was taught in the schools and spoken in the streets, and of the only country where you would find Jews who were not ashamed to publicly declare: 'I am a Jew and proud of it.' His final remarks were greeted with resounding applause: 'It was as if he were speaking for the millions of Russian Jews bowed beneath the yoke of an uncivilized government', wrote the correspondent for *Il Corriere Israelitico* (*CI*, 15 January 1913). Krinkin sang in Hebrew at the evening reception, and everyone was moved; he was the toast of the conference (*VI*, 1912, p.811). In his memoirs, Pacifici commented that Krinkin was an object of fascination because of his east European origin and his fluency in Hebrew.[52] Heated debates resulted from these two lectures, as both contained nationalist and Zionist sentiments. Krinkin and Lattes, during the discussion, also stated that Jews were in exile, a nomadic people. This view was categorically rejected by two officers of the Italian Zionist Federation, Felice Ravenna and Angelo Donati, who reiterated the official line that Zionism in Italy could only signify solidarity with the persecuted Jews; it could never entail renunciation of 'our Italian nationality'. A proposal put forward by Donati which reaffirmed the non-existence of Jewish nationalist sentiment among Italian Jews (*l'inesistenza negli Ebrei italiani di ogni preconcetto nazionalista*), was carried by thirty-seven votes, with twenty-eight against and twenty abstentions. That first day of the conference ended at midnight with the singing of the Zionist anthem.

The other key lectures were Dante Lattes on religious practices and Elia Artom on Jewish schools. Lattes approached the subject from a different perspective than Pacifici had done at the first conference. His thesis, *in nuce*, was that religious practices 'tacitly expressed the desire, the will, the need, the necessity to be Jews and to defend the ideal values of Jewish civilization'. They were an expression of cultural and national identity, of Zionist ideology; an articulation of a modern and dynamic Judaism. They were also indissolubly linked to biblical traditions: 'Above all other religious practices we should place justice, honesty and truth.'[53] Artom presented the findings of a survey on Jewish schools in Italy that he, Cassuto and Pacifici had conducted. In the ensuing discussion, it was agreed to set up a commission to investigate the issues raised in the report. Following a lecture by Emilio Bachi on the organizational structures of the youth movement, the election of members to the executive committee of the Federazione Giovanile Ebraica Italiana (Italian Federation of Jewish Youth) was carried out.[54]

Both *Il Corriere Israelitico* and *Il Vessillo Israelitico* published extensively and favourably on the Turin conference.[55] It had attracted a far greater number of participants than the first convention; the quality of the lectures, the freedom and breadth of the debates and the tangible proposals put forward all denoted the progress that had been achieved towards the moral and cultural renewal of Italian Judaism. In the following year, efforts were made to forge ahead with the various projects. The impressive promotional committee of the Society for the History of the Jews in Italy, whose thirty members were drawn from ten different cities, included not only academics and rabbis – Chajes, Cassuto and Margulies among the latter – but also a member of parliament and a member of the senate. The high-profile status of these individuals attests to the significance of the undertaking which brought together Jews and non-Jews in this collaboration. In April 1913, they issued a report in which they outlined their objectives. There had been a paucity of publications in this discipline in the preceding fifty years, of which little was of much value; and yet there was a wealth of documentation in archives and libraries, a prolific production of literary and scholarly material by Italian Jews. All of these sources awaited critical evaluation which would be of interest to scholars in many fields. They therefore invited all interested parties, irrespective of religion, to join them in forming the society.[56] *Il Vessillo Israelitico* hosted a leading article by Umberto Cassuto which emphasized the importance of this ambitious scheme to publish accessible texts and also to disseminate the research through series of popular lectures. As a gesture to the readership of the journal, Cassuto declared that none of this knowledge would obstruct or contrast in any way with the *italianità* 'of our roots of two millennia' (*VI*, 1913, pp.353–6). The major publication to come out of the project was Cassuto's monograph, *Gli ebrei a Firenze nell'età del Rinascimento* (1918), which has become a standard reference for Italian Jewish historiography.[57]

In May 1913, the Italian Federation of Jewish Youth also launched an appeal through their committee (which included Rabbi Elia Artom and Alfonso Pacifici), whose four fundamental premises were: the Hebrew language; Jewish culture; Palestine; and Jewish traditions (*CI*, 1913, p.227). In October 1913, Alfonso Pacifici, secretary of the Palestinian Scholarship Fund, issued a communiqué on its progress: a *concorso* for a scholarship of 500 lire was to be advertised, classes in spoken Hebrew had been introduced to the curriculum of Jewish schools in Florence, and the teacher's salary was to be financed by the fund: 'this bold innovation, planned some years ago by Rabbi Margulies, has now been put into effect'. The Jewish public in Italy was thus informed that the revival of Hebrew was not a thing of the future, but of the present. Hebrew courses were also being organized by the Pro Cultura groups, for example, in Florence, Ferrara and Milan. In Ferrara the teacher was Rabbi Artom, a former student of Margulies, and twenty members had enrolled.[58]

All three Jewish journals collaborated in promoting to a wider public the many initiatives which emanated from the small but dedicated group of Margulies's disciples. Such harmonious accord was marred in 1913 by another polemic between *Il Vessillo Israelitico* and *La Settimana Israelitica*, which had at its base the perennial conflict between *ebraismo* and *italianità* which had permeated the Zionist discourse of the FSI, and which had arisen in the conference debates in Turin. In June 1913, Emilio Bachi published an article in *Il Vessillo Israelitico* on the nascent Jewish Youth Federation, concluding with an exhortation to his peers to join the cultural clubs, where they would find 'purely Jewish milieus' (*ambienti puramente ebraici*), a sense of belonging 'to a race that is special, different, if not better and superior to the Latin race ... they will feel a renewed sense of pride in their race' (*orgoglio di razza*). Prefacing Bachi's Jewish separatist sentiments, the editor reminded the author and fellow members of the Federazione giovanile ebraica italiana that 'our *patria* is indissolubly Italy', inviting 'the dear children' (*figliuoli carissimi*) to be sensible (*VI*, 1913, pp.332–4). Pacifici replied to the prudent 'daddies' (*i babbi prudenti*) – the readers and the editor of *Il Vessillo* – who were so reluctant to recognize the political dimension of Zionism and were therefore concerned about the Jewish nationalism of the younger generation (*SI*, 24 [1913]). *Il Vessillo* reacted with an anonymous letter from a 'distinguished individual' of Italian Judaism who implicitly suggested that these young Zionists were fanning the flames of anti-Semitism, an accusation that the previous editor of the journal had levelled against the Zionist movement at its inception.[59]

In July, Ferruccio Servi, the editor, repeated his paternalistic admonition to the *figliuoli carissimi* to take care, and also acknowledged the *simpatia* he had for Pacifici, whose zeal and dedication he admired and for whom he had only one question: 'Which is your *patria*?' Within the same article Servi gave Bachi the right of reply to the 'distinguished individual'. Bachi, in his response, cites 'an even more authoritative' person, the chief rabbi of Florence 'whose intellect soars throughout the world': in a recent sermon, Margulies spoke of countries of adoption, such as Italy, where Jews were loyal and devoted citizens without, however, renouncing their dream of returning to Israel, 'our ancient land'. Bachi affirmed his *italianità* as a citizen, but also his race and his people as a Jew (*VI*, 1913, pp.386–8). In August, Pacifici answered the question posed by Servi with 'La mia patria' in *La Settimana Israelitica*: if by 'country' one means place of residence, communal life and language, 'then Italy is my country and it would be madness to deny it'; if it refers to 'that civilization, that ethnic group with whom one feels total identification … then Italy is not my country'.⁶⁰ Prefacing this piece is an editorial disclaimer expressing a complete divergence of views from those of our 'fervent and original friend', and adding that 'Italian Judaism cannot not consider [*non può non considerare*] Italy as their *patria* in which Jews have lived for centuries'; the double negative somewhat undermines the affirmation. The polemic was thus not solely generational, with the cautious, moderate *Vessillo* on the one side proclaiming primacy for *italianità* over *ebraismo*, but also existed within the group of young Zionists with some, like Pacifici, prepared to polemicize in order to broaden the debate still further and rouse the Jewish bourgeoisie from what he perceived as their assimilationist slumber. The two journalistic controversies are evidence of the increasing impact that Margulies's disciples exerted on mainstream Judaism as represented by *Il Vessillo Israelitico*.

In this climate of intense intellectual disputation, arrangements for the third Jewish Youth Conference were being made. Due to lack of documentation, it is not clear why Rome was chosen as the location.⁶¹ The Jewish community of the capital city had already shown its antagonism to Zionist activity 'on their doorstep'; the leadership had also initially obstructed the formation of a federation of Jewish communities and they were opposed to their vice-president, Anselmo Colombo, giving a lecture at the conference. The presence of David Krinkin, president of the Rome Pro Cultura association since its formation in December 1912, may have been a decisive factor; another may have been that the chief rabbi of Rome, Angelo Sacerdoti, was a former student of Margulies. The conference took place in February 1914. In January, a series of articles was published in *La Settimana Israelitica*, setting out the aims and objectives: a reaffirmation of the fundamental tenets – language, culture, tradition and Palestine – which for a committed young Jew were the 'four absolute, universal premises'; an assessment of communal administration, and their position with regard to the Jews of Libya (in the final programme this last item was omitted).⁶² In addition, there would be more robust coordination and discipline than at the previous two conventions: 'we hope that … a solid, practical, united youth organization will emerge' (*SI*, 5–7 [1914]).

Despite initial misgivings, the president of the Rome community, Angelo Sereni, was present to welcome the participants and praise 'the revival of Jewish youth'. However, it emerged from the discussion following the first lecture given by Colombo, on the Jewish communities and the areas where improvements were needed, that Sereni's 'official' greetings were not in fact supported by the community, which had not given their formal approval of the conference. There were also lectures on Agudath Israel, an international coalition of Orthodox Jewish bodies established in Germany to combat secularization and assimilation (Heinrich Eisemann),⁶³ and on the contemporary problems of Judaism, such as accusations of ritual murder, mass emigration of east European Jews, and mixed marriages, the solution to which was Zionism (David Krinkin). Pacifici's paper, 'The Organization of Jewish Youth', contained a reiteration of the four fundamental tenets: with regard to tradition, emphasis was given to observing the Sabbath as a group and sitting apart from others in the synagogue as a gesture of reaffirmation and renewal 'of our historic past'.[64] There was also a lecture on assimilation in its various manifestations, of which the remedy proposed was a precise and informed understanding of Judaism combined with a campaign against ignorance (Elia Artom). Artom spoke at such length and the discussion of Pacifici's proposals was so prolonged that Angelo Sullam did not present his paper on the synagogues and cemeteries of Italy. Instead, he protested vehemently against the conference organizers for not having the courage to confront the serious problem of Italian government policy towards the Libyan Jews, which he perceived as anti-Semitic.[65] His comments were applauded but not debated, and the conference closed.

The notable aspects of the conference were the conciliatory tone of Colombo when inviting the young to work in collaboration with the old, the ideological clash between Krinkin and Eisemann, and the opposition from some quarters to many of Pacifici's suggestions.[66] In their assessment of the proceedings, the editors of *La Settimana Israelitica* criticized the inconclusive, protracted discussions, the lack of a coherent structure, and the complete and 'deplorable' absence of participants from Milan, Turin and Padua; thus continuity with the previous conference had been lost. They were of the opinion that the dominance in the debates on the question of Jewish nationalism might have permeated the milieu of Italian Jewry as a whole; progress had been made to consolidate the organizational structure of the youth movement, to be called the Federazione giovanile ebraica d'Italia 'Giovane Israele'; and once again the conference had been a demonstration of 'Jewish vitality', the leitmotif of all the conferences (*SI*, 9 [1914]).

Despite its detailed report, *Il Vessillo Israelitico*'s verdict on the Rome meeting was negative: of the 150 delegates, the majority were Zionists; the rest had stayed away. Servi stressed the patriotic aspects of Colombo's paper, during which he had invited those present to affirm their affection for the king as 'most loyal Italians' (*fedelissimi italiani*). The editor's conclusion: yet another manifestation of Zionist Jews.[67] The Triestine journal was also not enthusiastic: the absence of members from the local community was noted; the 'poetic idealism' of Pacifici and his companions was perceived to be too abstract and theoretical, leaving the individual Jew to fend for himself. Lattes again emphasized the need to reach out to ordinary Jews in terms they would understand; to give them the culture they lacked and the language to appreciate that culture – in other words, to educate them – and then they would return to the synagogues and live a 'Jewish life'. Lattes was of the opinion that the strategy was misguided: too much discussion and too little action to attract the majority, to draw them in (*CI*, 15 March and 15 April, 1914). With hindsight, Pacifici concurred with Lattes's assessment: excessive passion and sentiment, not sufficient lasting achievement.[68] And yet they had affected the attitudes of some prominent individuals who in turn would influence others: in a leading article of April 1914 in *Il Vessillo*

Israelitico, 'From the Zionist Congress in Vienna to the Youth Congress in Rome', Anselmo Colombo described the process of transformation he had undergone as a result of these two events. He reiterated his admiration for the proud manifestation of Jewish identity that he witnessed in Vienna, at the heart of Christian Europe. Initially he had thought that the Jewish Youth Conference was inappropriate, given the nationalist political climate in Italy, but instead of fleeing from it as others had done, he took part with a lecture, the aim of which was the reconciliation of the young and the not so young to work together for the ideal of Jewish revival. The most significant outcome, in his view, was the decision to form an association which was to be independent of the communities, given the opposition from some quarters. However, as a result of the various debates, Pacifici et al. had understood the need for collaboration. Colombo's message was clear: the official representatives of Italian Judaism must understand that conflict with the Jewish Youth Movement would be detrimental; cooperation was imperative and the moment propitious. The Congress of Jewish Communities took place in May 1914 (*VI*, 1914, pp.177–80).

The immediate concern for Pacifici was the consolidation of the youth organization under its new title of Giovane Israele (Young Israel); the Federazione giovanile ebraica italiana had existed only on paper. As Toscano points out, Pacifici must have known about the Zionist group in Milan, which in October 1913 had established itself and a journal under the very same name, *Giovane Israele*.[69] After discussions lasting several months, Pacifici and Giuseppe Ottolenghi, editor of the Milanese periodical, joined forces: the two youth groups merged and the two editors ran both publications. Thus, from the first number in January 1915 of *La Settimana Israelitica*, the *direttore* was Pacifici and Ottolenghi the *redattore responsabile* (editor in charge) with office addresses in both Milan and Florence.[70]

These negotiations were overtaken by the First World War; its presence cast a shadow over the remaining issues. Whereas throughout the hostilities *Il Vessillo Israelitico* articulated an outpouring of patriotic fervour for the Jewish soldiers giving their lives as ultimate proof of their *italianità*, the young editors of the Florentine journal assumed a courageous stand from the outset, encapsulated in the title of the first article of 7 August 1914: 'In the Hour of Our Tragedy: Two Hundred Thousand Jews on the Battlefield Fighting against Each Other'. Without diminishing the duty of each loyal citizen to serve their country, they observed that in recent years a new sense of solidarity and brotherhood had developed between Jews of different countries through the growing awareness of a shared language, history and culture – 'this peaceful process of unity has been brutally shattered by destruction and bloodshed; yesterday conferences and meetings, today armed and ready to kill'. They reiterated their stance when Italy entered the war in May 1915; in 'The Hour of our Trial' (*L'Ora della Prova*), they exhorted their fellow Jews to remain steadfast in universal brotherly love, despite their obligation to fight: 'we must have the courage to proclaim that if war is necessary, hatred is not … every flag is the symbol of an ideal, every country is sacred … Let this be our humane motto … Brothers, do not hate each other' (*SI*, 21 [1915]). Thus, in contrast to *Il Vessillo Israelitico*, which published only the names of Italian Jewish soldiers who paid the ultimate price, *La Settimana Israelitica* listed the Jews from both sides of the conflict.

Although the war reduced the activities of the Jewish cultural revival, there was also continuity. In October 1915, the Florentine journal celebrated the twenty-fifth anniversary of Margulies as chief rabbi, the progenitor of the Jewish renewal (*SI*, 40 [1915]). The last issue of 23 December 1915 announced not the closure of the periodical but the appearance of a new one with the title of *Israel*, which was to signal 'new life', and at the same time 'the faithful continuation of *La Settimana Israelitica* and *Il Corriere Israelitico*', both of which ceased publication in that year. *Israel* brought together the talents of Lattes, Pacifici and Viterbo, three of the most influential individuals of Italian Judaism and Zionism.[71] The bold title, also in Hebrew, no longer used adjectivally, was a clear indication of its ideological position, a name that signified the combined components of Judaism: 'Israel is conceived historically as unity of race, tradition, civilization; aspirations, which, although today are scattered … await recognition of the right to exist among the peoples of the world.'[72] Such an audacious attitude was enhanced by the Balfour Declaration of 1917. Lattes and Pacifici were no longer sparring partners, the former setting his secular Zionism in opposition to the latter's predominantly religious concept of Judaism; they were two Jews working towards the same goal. Their voluminous private correspondence attests to their close collaboration and friendship.[73]

In *Israel*, Lattes maintained his cultural programme of *Il Corriere Israelitico*, broadening the literary perspective of its readers with extracts from the writings of east European authors such as Shalom Aleichem and Shalom Asch, and essays from his friend Martin Buber's periodical *Der Jude*, established in 1916.[74] Lattes and Pacifici also founded *Rassegna Mensile di Israel* in 1925, which is in existence to this day as the foremost scholarly journal of Italian Judaism.[75] In addition, Pacifici and Viterbo were involved in the very brief Zionist administration of the Florentine Jewish community which lasted from December 1919 until it was ousted in May 1920. In that year, Viterbo became vice-president of the Italian Zionist Federation; between 1931 and 1933 he was the president, a role he resumed after the Second World War. He inherited Margulies's interest in the Ethiopian Jews, and in 1936 he undertook a lengthy inspection of many Falasha villages as part of a government mission.[76] Together with Lattes and Pacifici he established the publishing house Casa Editrice Israel, an essential conduit not only for the dissemination of works by Italian Jewish authors such as Lattes but also for Italian translations of prominent foreign writers; the initial list of planned publications appeared in *Israel* in April 1921 (nos. 16–17). In 1919, David Prato and Nathan Shalem edited a bi-monthly magazine for children on Jewish life in Palestine, *Israel dei ragazzi*, at first distributed as a supplement with *Israel* and subsequently sold separately throughout Italy.[77] In 1921, the Convegno di Studi Ebraici was established in Florence; among its founders were several of Margulies's disciples: Elia Artom, Carlo Alberto Viterbo, Aldo Neppi Modona and Alfonso Pacifici. It was to some extent a continuation of the Pro Cultura precepts, with its emphasis on the study of language, culture and religious observance.[78] In the 1930s, Pacifici organized Jewish youth camping holidays, both summer and winter, one of the principal objectives being to escape 'the grey bureaucratic monotony of daily life under fascism'.[79] All Jewish activities that took place after 1924 were subject to police scrutiny.[80]

To effect closure of the pre-First World War era, mention must be made of the Fourth Jewish Youth Conference in Livorno at the beginning of November 1924, which should have taken place in 1915. It was a continuation of the three previous conventions but it also introduced new directions and new faces of Italian Judaism. Once again Pacifici was behind the initiative, and the local organizing committee obtained the support of Felice Ravenna, president of the FSI, and Angelo Sereni, president of the Consortium of Jewish Communities. However, as before, one of the persistently antagonistic voices was that of Angelo Sullam who, in a letter to Sereni of 24 September 1924, expressed his apprehension that the meeting would comprise the 'noisy and harmful minority' whose Jewish nationalism was not shared by the majority of Italian Jews, and reiterating yet again the underlying dialectic of *ebraismo* and *italianità*.[81] Despite an initial lack of enthusiasm when first propounded by Pacifici in the pages of *Israel*, Livorno proved to be the largest gathering, with 644 participants from all over Italy, and by all accounts it elicited the most powerful response, in which each speaker sought to find common ground and a sense of unity, despite differing ideological tendencies: 'three wonderful days that will not be forgotten by all those, young and old, who had the incomparable fortune to experience them. They will become part of the history of generations.'[82] Nearly half a century later, Viterbo wrote to Del Canuto that he could still feel the deep emotion, 'the warmth of the sincerity and effort to reach reciprocal understanding ... indelible words were spoken ... whose significance has remained with me throughout my life'.[83] Why was this meeting so memorable? There was awareness among the delegates of being part of the wider historical process:[84] the Balfour Declaration had strengthened Zionist resolve; the conflict between philanthropic and nationalist Zionism was surmounted; two years of fascist government had polarized political positions. According to Toscano, the three emblematic figures of the conference were Pacifici, Nello Rosselli and Enzo Sereni, each proposing significant modalities of Jewish identity. Pacifici pursued his concept of integral Judaism; for Rosselli, Judaism was perceived as an anti-fascist struggle for freedom and justice *tout court*; Sereni's solution was to proletarianize the Jewish people and emigrate to Palestine to work the land. The ideological choices of Sereni and Rosselli – the new men of the Livorno conference – shaped their futures and those of others.[85]

In a special issue of *Rassegna Mensile di Israel* devoted to the 1981 proceedings of a symposium on 'The Revival of Jewish Culture in Italy at the Beginning of the Twentieth Century', two crucial facts emerged: Florence was the centre of the revival and the reason was 'because Rabbi Margulies arrived in Florence in 1890'.[86] Can this interpretation be sustained? Can it be argued that Margulies achieved what Samuel David Luzzatto, by his own admission, had failed to accomplish, that is a 'School', a following, an enduring legacy? Despite forty or so graduates, the Rabbinical College of Padua had produced no scholarly Jewish tradition to emulate Luzzatto's own erudite and extensive publications. In a letter of 10 February 1857 to Marco Mortara, a former student, Luzzatto expressed his regret that only Mortara was interested in academic endeavour.[87] In the opinion of his disciples, Margulies's pivotal influence was indisputable: 'the importance of the "Margulies School" must be considered not only in the numbers of rabbis and teachers he trained for the many communities in Italy and abroad, but ... also in having formed directly and indirectly a new self-awareness within the whole of Italian Judaism'.[88] We could argue, with Pacifici, that while there was no influx of east European Jews in Italy, Margulies 'alone was for us all that mass immigration represented for other western European countries; he breathed new life into the moribund Jewish milieu'.[89] Even if, as some have posited, his sphere of influence did not extend beyond that of a middle-class minority,[90] Margulies transformed the way they perceived their Jewish identity: under his guidance they discovered culture, language, tradition and Jewish nationalism; they reconnected with their heritage and strengthened their religious belief beyond the merely formulaic.

Margulies died suddenly on 12 March 1922. Later that month, Chaim Weizmann, president of the World Zionist Organization and future first president of Israel, was in Italy on a diplomatic visit, as Herzl had been in 1904, involving audiences with the king, the Secretary of State for the Vatican and other distinguished dignitaries. He also met Italian Zionists. Sullam made every effort to prevent Weizmann from visiting the Tuscan capital, insisting that he should see only 'a certain type of Zionist' and have no contact with 'the people from Florence'.[91] Perhaps he hoped to succeed with Margulies no longer alive, but he was no longer vice-president of the FSI; that role was now taken by one of Margulies's disciples, Carlo Alberto Viterbo. Thus Weizmann did visit Florence, and it was the memory of his encounter with the small group of Zionists there that remained with him, as he recalls in his autobiography:

> [among them was] a young and ardent prophet of Zionism, Arnoldo [*sic*] Pacifici; and when they formed their society they went the whole way: they spoke Hebrew, they began to prepare themselves for life in Palestine; many of them – including Pacifici himself – became strictly orthodox; they edited one of the best Zionist papers of the day – *Israel*. Numerically insignificant, they were by the depth of their conviction and their absolute sincerity a great moral force. And though at first the community at large was inclined to resent them, they were so tactful, and at the same time so transparently honest in their faith, that even convinced anti-Zionists came to look upon them as something in the nature of 'apostles' of the Jewish revival, and to respect, if they could not understand, them ... The Italian Jewish community seemed to be a community of *sujets d'élite*. And the *élite* of that community, accustomed to enjoy in Italy every material and social advantage a man can ask, were turning their eyes to Palestine. I could not explain it. I could only thank God.[92]

NOTES

1. Two correspondents of *Il Vessillo Israelitico* (*VI*) had written in favour of such a post, to which the editor, himself a rabbi, demurred; autonomy had its advantages (*VI*, 1890, pp.105, 144). It was this

spirit of independence that prevented the individual Jewish communities from achieving a cohesive collaboration for many years.
2. Mario Toscano, *Ebraismo e antisemitismo in Italia: dal 1848 alla guerra dei sei giorni* (Milan: FrancoAngeli, 2003), p.72.
3. See ibid., pp.72, 111–12. Apart from Chapters 7 and 10, this volume is a collection of previously published articles; Alberto Cavaglion, 'Tendenze nazionali', in Corrado Vivanti (ed.), *Storia d'Italia, Annali 11, Gli ebrei in Italia*, vol. 2 (Turin: Einaudi, 1997), p.1311.
4. Gadi Luzzatto Voghera, 'L'Israélitisme en Italie aux xix e xx siècles', in Patrick Cabanel and Chantal Bordes-Benayoun (eds), *Un modèle d'intégration: juifs et israélites en France et en Europe (XIX–XX siècles)* (Paris: Berg, 2004), p.200. Samuel David Luzzatto was not a rabbi, hence his omission from the list. The exception to this increasing neglect is Massimo Longo Adorno, *Gli ebrei fiorentini dall'emancipazione alla Shoà* (Florence: Giuntina, 2003). This monograph's focus is from 1938, but in the first chapter Adorno acknowledges Margulies's role in the Jewish revival in Florence: see pp.9–16.
5. Cavaglion, 'Tendenze nazionali', p.1313.
6. See Chapter 5.
7. Attilio Milano, 'Un secolo di stampa periodica ebraica in Italia', *Rassegna Mensile di Israel* [hereafter *RMI*], 12, 7–9 (1938), pp.117–18. See also, by the same author, 'Gli enti culturali ebraici in Italia nell'ultimo trentennio (1907–1937)', *RMI*, 12, 6 (1938), pp.253–69. These two articles were published in April–June and February–March 1938 respectively. Racial legislation against the Jews came into effect in November 1938. The laws not only alienated large swathes of the Italian population, but were considered a source of shame by many fascists: see Martin Clark, *Modern Italy 1871–1982* (London and New York: Longman, 1984), p.258. Since Milano, the only historian to write at length on the Jewish revival centred in Florence is Mario Toscano: see Chapter 4, 'Fermenti culturali ed esperienze organizzative della gioventù ebraica italiana (1911–1925)', in Toscano, *Ebraismo e antisemitismo in Italia*, first published as an article in 1982. Cecil Roth also wrote briefly but positively about Margulies in his 1946 publication, *The History of the Jews of Italy* (Philadelphia, PA: Jewish Publication Society of America, 1946), pp.506–8.
8. Lionella Viterbo, 'La nomina del Rabbino Margulies: un *excursus* nella Firenze ebraica di fine Ottocento', *RMI*, 59 (1993), p.75. In fact, Margulies came from such a rigidly orthodox family that his request to study at a non-Jewish institution was regarded by his father as equivalent to apostasy – see his own autobiographical note cited by Carlo Alberto Viterbo in 'Un Maestro ancora presente', *RMI*, 38, 4 (1972), p.197. It is pertinent to mention that Lionella Viterbo is the archivist of the Jewish community of Florence, and that both her father, Aldo Neppi Modona, and her father-in-law, Carlo Alberto Viterbo, numbered among Margulies's disciples. They, together with Pacifici, formed a firm friendship: see Aldo Neppi Modona, 'Un testimone di anni lontani', *Israel*, December 1974, p.6.
9. Alfonso Pacifici, 'Ha-rav Shemuel Zevì Margulies', *RMI*, 28, 6–7 (1962), p.252.
10. L. Viterbo, 'La nomina del Rabbino Margulies', pp.68–9. See also Margulies's comments to the poet David Levi, in a letter of 20 March 1892, on the difficulties he encountered 'as a foreigner [which] ... I always have to face', in Leo Neppi Modona, '17 lettere di S.H. Margulies a David Levi', *RMI*, 27 (1961), p.505. See also Lionella Viterbo, 'Cronache dal passato fiorentino: la difficile successione del Rabbino Margulies (1920–26)', *RMI*, 60 (1994), pp.148–78: in 1921, the hostility of the community's administration compelled Margulies to consider taking up the prestigious post of director of the Jewish Seminary of Breslau. The president of the community congratulated him – eager, it would seem, to be rid of him. However, such was the outpouring of support from rabbis throughout Italy – many but not all of whom were his own students – that he was persuaded to remain. Angelo Sullam's intense antipathy to Margulies's perceived Germanic qualities has been noted in the previous chapter. At one of the first council meetings of the Florence Jewish community after the war, it was unanimously agreed that in future the chief rabbi should not only be an Italian citizen, which Margulies was, but also of Italian birth. Margulies was made aware of this decision. Aldo Neppi Modona was a member of the council and Margulies was saddened that one of his disciples, who had also known him as a family friend since childhood, had voted in favour of this motion. See Aldo Neppi Modona, 'Ricordi personali su S.H. Margulies', *RMI*, 38, 4 (1972), pp.217–18.
11. *VI*, 1889, pp.385, 422; 1890, p.270.
12. *Discorso inaugurale pronunziato dal Rabbino Maggiore, Dott. S.H. Margulies in occasione del suo Insediamento a Firenze* (Florence: Tipografia Cooperativa, 1890), p.7.
13. See Maddalena Del Bianco Cotrozzi, *Il Collegio Rabbinico di Padova: un'istituzione religiosa dell'ebraismo sulla via dell'emancipazione* (Florence: Olschki, 1995), p.334; *VI*, 1898, pp.50–1, 186–7, 217.
14. See Leo Neppi Modona, '17 lettere di S.H. Margulies a David Levi', *RMI*, 28, 2 (1962), pp.64–5. Margulies and the poet never met (Levi died in 1898) but they sustained each other through mutual

support and respect and shared Zionist convictions. Margulies championed the poet's oeuvre in Germany through his biography, *Dichter und Patriot: Eine Studie über das Leben und die Werke D. Levis* (1896); German translations of his poems and articles, for example in the *Allgemeine Zeitung des Judenthums* (June 1894). When Margulies was nominated Cavaliere, he felt that Levi was influential in the decision (letter of 25 December 1896).
15. *Il Corriere Israelitico* [*CI*], 1899, pp.132–4, 152–3. Margulies was accused by *Il Corriere* of not responding to overtures from the Rabbinical College of Livorno (*CI*, 1899, pp.132–4). Later attempts, reported by the Italian Jewish press, to merge the two colleges ended in failure, with Livorno rejecting the negotiations (*CI*, 15 April 1915).
16. On these appointments see *CI*, 1902, pp.82–3, 158; *VI*, 1903, pp.119, 179, 221.
17. L. Viterbo, 'La nomina del Rabbino Margulies', p.68.
18. See Silvia Guetta Sadun, 'L'educazione ebraica: il Talmud Torà di Firenze dal 1860 al 1922', in Liliana Mezzabotta (ed.), *Italia Judaica: gli ebrei nell'Italia unita 1870–1945. Atti del IV convegno internazionale* (Rome: Pubblicazioni degli Archivi di Stato, 1993), pp.82–96. From 1912, Prato employed Maestro Quittner, from Austrian Galicia, to teach modern Hebrew, and after the First World War, Nathan Shalem from Palestine replaced Quittner.
19. Attilio Milano, *Storia degli ebrei in Italia* (Turin: Einaudi, 1963), p.381. See also Adorno, *Gli ebrei fiorentini*, pp.25–9. Between 1931 and 1938, Cassuto was professor of Semitic Studies at the University of Rome, a post left vacant by Giorgio Levi Della Vida, who had refused to swear allegiance to the fascist regime and thereby lost the position he had held since 1920: see Alberto Cavaglion, *ebrei senza saperlo* (Naples: l'ancora del mediterraneo, 2002), p.146. In 1938, Cassuto emigrated to Palestine and was appointed to a Chair in Hebrew Studies at the Hebrew University of Jerusalem.
20. On the politics of these appointments, see Lionella Viterbo, 'Cronache dal passato fiorentino: la difficile successione del Rabbino Margulies (1920–1926)', *RMI*, 60 (1994), pp.158–63. Margulies had wanted Artom to return to Florence and work together with Cassuto, but Margulies's untimely death truncated the negotiations with the community's administration. I am grateful to Lionella Viterbo for information on Margulies's other students.
21. Stefano Caviglia, *L'identità salvata: gli ebrei di Roma tra fede e nazione: 1870–1938* (Rome-Bari: Laterza, 1996), p.127.
22. Samuel David Luzzatto and Lelio Della Torre of the Rabbinical College of Padua planned to establish such a journal in 1859, but nothing came of it: see Gadi Luzzatto Voghera, *Il prezzo dell'eguaglianza: il dibattito sull'emancipazione degli ebrei in Italia (1781–1848)* (Milan: FrancoAngeli, 1998), pp.163–4.
23. *La Rivista Israelitica*, 1, 1 (1904), p.1. From 1911, it became the organ of the Rabbinical College of Florence. A complete run of the journal is in the Biblioteca Nazionale, Florence.
24. Milano, 'Un secolo di stampa', p.118.
25. The paternal reference is that of Carlo Alberto Viterbo in 'Un Maestro ancora presente', p.199. Margulies died in Viterbo's presence on 12 March 1922. They, with others, were attending the prize-giving ceremony of the Talmud Torah. See C.A. Viterbo, 'Un Maestro ancora presente', pp.200–1. See also Neppi Modona's affectionate portrayal, 'Ricordi personali su S.H. Margulies', pp.214–21.
26. C.A. Viterbo, 'Un Maestro ancora presente', p.199; and Carlo A. Viterbo, 'Una vita per l'ebraismo', *Israel*, December 1974, p.6. In the *Israel* article, which is a brief, posthumous curriculum vitae (Viterbo died in August 1974), he reiterates his debt of gratitude and friendship to Pacifici, particularly for bringing him into contact with 'the great Maestro Margulies'. The entire December issue of *Israel* is devoted to the commemoration of Viterbo. See also Gershom Scholem's reconnection to Judaism through the 'wonderful teacher, to whom I for one owe infinitely much … Dr Isaak Bleichrode (1867–1954) … some of us came from quite irreligious homes, and yet he welcomed us with all his heart and without reservations', in *From Berlin to Jerusalem: Memories of My Youth*, translated from German by Harry Zohn (New York: Schocken Books, 1980), p.47.
27. Alfonso Pacifici, *Interludio: cinquant'anni intorno a un'idea. Lettere agli amici con ricordi personali e riflessioni e un'appendice di scritti scelti editi e inediti* (Turin: Toaz, 1959), pp.77, 85. See also pp.65–90, devoted to the figure of Margulies; and Pacifici, 'Ha-Rav Shemuel Zevi Margulies', p.254. On Pacifici's rich and varied life in Israel, to which he emigrated in 1934, see Renato Spiegel (ed.), *Archivio Alfonso Pacifici (1899–1974)*, Inventory no. 2 (Jerusalem: Central Archives for the History of the Jewish People, 2000).
28. Central Archives for the History of the Jewish People, Jerusalem [hereafter CAHJP], P172/132.
29. C.A. Viterbo, 'Una vita per l'ebraismo', p.7.
30. *CI*, 1907, pp.159–60. In his praise of the Pro Cultura programme, Lattes expressed the wish that in the pursuit of the highest levels of scholarship, the more humble Jews would not be forgotten, that the standard of dissemination would not exclude them (*CI*, 1907, pp.183–4). Sorani made clear that his target audience, those 'we need to attract to the cause', was the educated middle class, not *il pubblico minuto* (*CI*, 1907, p.106). The membership lists for the Florence association, 1911–15, contain the

names from this social stratum (CAHJP, P172/225). Pacifici believed that in Italy there was little possibility of 'mass action'; what was lacking in quantity was compensated by quality (See 'Un Ebraismo qualitativo', *Israel*, 26 June 1924).
31. The idea of a central committee or a federation of committees was never realized, although supported by several influential individuals apart from Sorani himself. See Sullam's letter to Ravenna of 28 September 1909: he thought the individual committees could link up with the Zionist groups (Archivio del Centro di Documentazione Ebraica Contemporanea, Milan [hereafter ACDEC], Fondo Angelo Sullam, I.1.2.2, B.3. file 13); and Edgardo Morpurgo's letter to Ravenna of 23 January 1910, 'a union of our forces' (Central Zionist Archives, Jerusalem [hereafter CZA], A353/40). In May 1909, the editors of *Il Corriere Israelitico* commented on the failure to coordinate as 'the typical Italian way which has so harmed Jewish life as a whole ... once again we recommend organization and co-operation' (15 May 1909).
32. See Attilio Milano, 'Gli enti culturali ebraici in Italia nell'ultimo trentennio (1907–1937)', *RMI*, 12, 6 (February–March 1938), p.254.
33. See, for example, Caviglia, *L'identità salvata*, p.122, and Toscano, *Ebraismo e antisemitismo*, p.76.
34. Milano, 'Un secolo di stampa', p.119.
35. The Tipografia was named after the famous sixteenth-century printer, Giunti. See Daniel Vogelmann, 'Breve storia della Giuntina', *UTZ Rivista degli Amici dell'Accademia dell'Ex Libris*, 3 (December 2000), pp.25–8.
36. Leo Olschki came from a family of printers from eastern Prussia. At the age of 25, he opened his first *bottega* in Venice, thence to Verona and finally Florence. See Klaus Voigt, 'Considerazioni sugli ebrei immigrati in Italia', in Sofia and Toscano (eds), *Stato nazionale ed emancipazione ebraica*, p.227.
37. In February 1914, David Prato resigned as administrator; in March 1914, Viterbo was forced to withdraw his name by his parents, who disapproved of his Jewish activities, as they deviated from the assimilatory trajectory of the family, but he remained behind the scenes (see 'Una vita per l'ebraismo', p.6); in January 1915, Senigaglia announced his departure, and Giuseppe Ottolenghi joined Pacifici.
38. See Milano, 'Un secolo di stampa', p.119, and Toscano, *Ebraismo e antisemitismo*, pp.76–7.
39. The correspondent would have been alluding to native-born French Jews; the east European Jewish immigrants of Paris established their own cultural associations and press, the main language of which was Yiddish. See, for example, Paula Hyman, *From Dreyfus to Vichy: The Remaking of French Jewry, 1906–1939* (New York: Columbia University Press, 1979), Chapter 3.
40. Prior to his post in America, Schechter was Reader in Rabbinical Studies at the University of Cambridge (1892) and Professor of Hebrew at University College, London (1899). He gained his international reputation through the identification of thousands of Hebrew manuscript fragments from the Cairo *Genizah*. The initial discovery in Cairo of the first fragment was made by two scholarly widowed sisters, friends of Schechter. See, for example, A. Whigham Price, *The Ladies of Castlebrae: The Life of Agnes Smith Lewis and Margaret Dunlop Gibson* (London: Headline, 1987). I am grateful to Marsha Taylor for this reference. In 1913, he was instrumental in the foundation of the United Synagogue of America, the principal organization of Conservative Judaism, the largest religious group of American Jewry. See Paul Mendes-Flohr and Jehuda Reinharz (eds), *The Jew in the Modern World: A Documentary History* (New York and Oxford: Oxford University Press, 1995), pp.497–9.
41. See *Settimana Israelitica* [*SI*], 28, 30, 36 (1911).
42. See *SI*, 29–35 (1911); see also Toscano, *Ebraismo e antisemitismo*, pp.74–5.
43. See, for example, *VI*, 1911, pp.470–1, 547–8, 607–10, 699–705; *CI*, 1911, pp.131–2; *SI*, 41–2 (1911); 3 (1912). As a result of the dispute, the Piedmontese journal was not invited to send a representative to the conference. *Il Vessillo Israelitico* asserted that in June 1911, Rabbi Dario Disegni of Verona had written to the editor about the idea of a conference; the editor had promised to support and publicize it, which he duly did a few days before the Florentine journal (*VI*, 1911, p.608). The irony is that Rabbi Disegni had been one of Margulies's students. However, from the correspondence with Rabbi Disegni that *Il Vessillo Israelitico* published, it appeared that Sorani did not want Disegni associated with the project, as a rabbi's name would discourage young people; therefore he, Sorani, insisted on claiming sole paternity and demanded that Disegni publish a disclaimer in either journal (*VI*, 1911, pp.608–9).
44. On the proceedings of the first conference, see *SI*, 44–5 (1911).
45. Toscano, *Ebraismo e antisemitismo*, p.76.
46. Pacifici, *Interludio*, p.88.
47. Augusto Segre, *Memorie di vita ebraica: da Casale a Gerusalemme* (Rome: Bonacci, 1979), p.375.
48. See Simonetta Della Seta Torrefranca, 'Identità religiosa e identità nazionale nell'ebraismo italiano del Novecento', in Mezzabotta (ed.), *Italia Judaica ... Atti del IV convegno internazionale* (1993), pp.263–72. See also David Bidussa, Amos Luzzatto and Gadi Luzzatto Voghera, *Oltre il ghetto: momenti e figure della cultura ebraica in Italia tra l'Unità e il fascismo* (Brescia: Morcelliana, 1992),

pp.195–209.
49. See Alfonso Pacifici's letter to Ravenna of 17 February 1913, thanking him for his authoritative and, he hoped, influential sponsorship (CZA, A353/43).
50. ACDEC, Fondo Sullam, I.3.1.1. Enti ebraici c/o Sionisti Italiani, B.18, file 204.
51. Pacifici, *Interludio*, pp.129–30.
52. Ibid., p.127.
53. See also Toscano's analysis, *Ebraismo e antisemitismo*, pp.81–2; and Bidussa, Luzzatto and Luzzatto Voghera, *Oltre il ghetto*, pp.60–1.
54. On the conference, see *SI*, 2–5 (1913).
55. See *VI*, 1912, pp.793–824: 'the sweetest impression [*dolcissima impressione*] remained with the participants'; *CI*, 15 January 1913: 'we returned from Turin with great joy in our hearts … the conference was an important manifestation of our national idea'. See also *CI*, 1912, pp.150–8.
56. ACDEC, Fondo Sullam, I.3.1.1, Enti ebraici c/o Sionistici Italiani, B.18, file 193. In England, France and Germany, similar societies were established in the 1880s and 1890s: the Jewish Historical Society of England; the Société des études juives; the Historical Commission for the History of the Jews in Germany. The Italian Protestants also had their Société d'histoire vaudoise (Waldensian History Society), which was subsequently changed to the Società di studi valdesi; see Gian Paolo Romagnani, 'Italian Protestants', in Liedtke and Wendehorst (eds), *Emancipation of Catholics, Jews and Protestants*, pp.160–1.
57. See Roberto G. Salvadori, *Gli ebrei di Firenze: dalle origini ai giorni nostri* (Florence: Giuntina, 2000), p.87. Adorno calls Cassuto 'the historical conscience of the Florentine Jewish revival' (p.25). See also Michele Luzzati, 'La ricerca storiografica sugli ebrei italiani del Medioevo e del Rinascimento tra la fine dell'800 e l'inizio del '900', *RMI*, 47, 7–12 (1981), pp.129–35. As Luzzatto Voghera observes, Cassuto's book is modest in comparison to Heinrich Graetz's eleven-volume *Geschichte der Juden* [*History of the Jews*] (1853–76); see *Il prezzo dell'eguaglianza*, p.164.
58. See *SI*, 44 (1913); *VI*, 1913, pp.573, 589, 593. See also the circular of the cultural association of Florence dated 27 October 1913, CAHJP, P172/225. The circular states that the principal focus of activity would be courses in spoken Hebrew (Pacifici was the secretary). See also *SI*, 41 and 44 (1913).
59. *VI*, 1913, pp.364–5, 389. Another correspondent, Giacomo Sacerdoti, also expressed this view: see *VI*, 1913, p.515.
60. *SI*, 31 (1913). An angry response from a correspondent, Arturo Orvieto, was published in *Il Vessillo*, in which he categorically rejected Pacifici's ideas and affirmed his own Italian patriotism in the name of the majority of Italian Jews (*VI*, 1913, pp.515–16).
61. See Toscano, *Ebraismo e antisemitismo*, p.85. Difficulties in the preparations for the conference are alluded to in *La Settimana Israelitica*, but no specific details are given (5 [1914]).
62. See programme of 6 February 1914 (ACDEC, Fondo Sullam, I.3.1.1, Entiebraici c/o Sionistici Italiani, B.18, file 204).
63. Its first conference, held in May 1912, was reported in *Il Corriere Israelitico* (1912, pp.47–9, 60–1, 72–3).
64. When the historian Cecil Roth visited Florence in 1920, he noted that although the synagogue was often half empty, at the back on the right 'the seats of the Zionists', as they were called, were always full; Pacifici and his companions could be found there. See *Israel*, 20 April, 27 April and 18 May 1961, cited in Adorno, *Gli ebrei fiorentini*, p.25.
65. His views were borne out by press reports (see, for example, *CI*, 15 April 1914).
66. *SI*, 9 (1914). The most vociferous opposition came from Angelo Sullam, whose antipathy to any Florentine initiative has already been noted.
67. *VI*, 1914, pp.93–109. An offshoot of the conference was an audience with the king on 22 March 1914 for Colombo, Sacerdoti and Alatri (a local member of the organizing committee), during which the monarch expressed his pleasure at this and other demonstrations of Jewish vitality (*VI*, 1914, pp.160–1).
68. Pacifici, *Interludio*, p.110.
69. Toscano, *Ebraismo e antisemitismo*, p.90. See also Milano, 'Un secolo di stampa', p.129.
70. See also Toscano, *Ebraismo e antisemitismo*, p.91. Few issues of *Giovane Israele* are extant; it ceased publication in 1923.
71. Various people collaborated on the editorial board of *Israel*, which ran from 1916 to 1938; from 1944 until his death in 1974, Viterbo was the sole editor.
72. This is a statement from the first editorial. On *Israel*, which like one of its predecessors was a weekly, see Milano, 'Un secolo di stampa', pp.121–3. According to him, it surpassed the sum of its two parts. See also Bidussa, Luzzatto and Luzzatto Voghera, *Oltre il ghetto*, pp.174–83. It was the first Jewish journal to be sold in newsagents in order to reach a non-Jewish readership (see the first issue of *Israel*, 'Our Programme', January 1916).
73. See CAHJP, P172/124.
74. Robertson has argued that Buber and his circle stimulated a 'Jewish Renaissance' in Germany at the

beginning of the twentieth century. See Ritchie Robertson, *The 'Jewish Question' in German Literature 1749–1939: Emancipation and its Discontents* (Oxford: Oxford University Press, 1999), pp.386–9. Moreover, Buber was in Florence in 1905 when he wrote several essays in which he drew analogies between the Jewish and Italian Renaissance. There seems to be no evidence that he met Margulies or any members of the Jewish community during his stay in the Tuscan capital. In a letter in December 1905, he wrote: 'Florence suits me ... we have no contact with other men at all and hardly miss it', cited by Christina Ujma, 'Political versus Cultural Zionism: Reflections on Herzl and Buber', in Robertson and Timms (eds), *Theodor Herzl and the Origins of Zionism*, p.102. There is consensus that in France the impact of the Dreyfus Affair effected a Jewish cultural renewal which is illustrated, in particular, in the poetry of Edmond Fleg and André Spire; the latter was also instrumental in the founding of the Association des jeunes juifs. See, for example, Aron Rodrigue, 'Rearticulations of French Jewish Identities after the Dreyfus Affair', *Jewish Social Studies: History, Culture, and Society*, new series, 2 (Fall 1996), pp.1–26; Michel Trebitsch, 'Les écrivains juifs français de l'affaire Dreyfus à la Seconde Guerre mondiale', in Jean-Jacques Becker and Annette Wieviorka (eds), *Les Juifs de France de la Révolution française à nos jours* (Paris: Editions Liana Levi, 1998), pp.169–95; Hyman, *From Dreyfus to Vichy*, pp.33–4, 153; and Colette Zytnicki, 'Itinéraire d'un poète, du symbolisme au Sionisme: Gustave Kahn (1859–1936)', in Cabanel and Bordes-Benayoun (eds), *Un modèle d'intégration*, pp.147–58. In a section entitled 'The high noon of Anglo-Jewry', the cultural activities of the 1880s and 1890s are described, such as the Maccabaeans, the Anglo-Jewish Historical Exhibition, and the publications of Claude Montefiore, Solomon Schechter and Israel Abrahams; see David Cesarani, *The Jewish Chronicle and Anglo-Jewry, 1841–1991* (Cambridge: Cambridge University Press, 1994), pp.88–91.
75. See Milano, 'Un secolo di stampa', pp.124–5.
76. See *Israel*, December 1974, p.7. See also Carlo Alberto Viterbo and Aharon Cohen, *Ebrei di Etiopia: due diari (1936 e 1976)* (Florence: Giuntina, 1993). Ethiopia was annexed to Italy in May 1936.
77. See Guetta Sadun, 'L'educazione ebraica', pp.94–5.
78. See Adorno, *Gli ebrei fiorentini*, pp.40–2. Adorno erroneously gives the year 1929 for the Convegno. I am grateful to Anna Teicher for the correct date based on archival material.
79. Adorno, *Gli ebrei fiorentini*, p.45. For other Jewish initiatives in Italy in the period between the two World Wars, see Milano, 'Gli enti culturali', pp.260–9, and 'Un secolo di stampa', pp.130–1; also Toscano, *Ebraismo e antisemitismo*, pp.93–109.
80. See Toscano, *Ebraismo e antisemitismo*, p.101. In June 1924, the Socialist leader and member of parliament, Giacomo Matteotti, was murdered by fascist thugs; he had denounced the May elections as a fraud. Having survived the crisis engendered by the assassination, Mussolini curbed all opposition. See Clark, *Modern Italy*, pp.224–30.
81. See Toscano, *Ebraismo e antisemitismo*, p.100. Ravenna and Sullam were members of the Consortium.
82. *Israel*, 6 November 1924. The 20 November issue of the journal contains the proceedings and the list of participants, including their place of residence.
83. Cited in Francesco Del Canuto, *Il movimento sionistico in Italia dalle origini al 1924* (Milan: Federazione Sionistica Italiana, 1972), pp.147–9.
84. See Viterbo's letter to Canuto; in May 1925, Enzo Sereni had been the Italian delegate at the first international congress of Jewish students in Antwerp (see *Israel*, 7 and 15 May 1924). See also Toscano, *Ebraismo e antisemitismo*, p.102.
85. On the Livorno conference, see, for example, Del Canuto, *Il movimento sionistico in Italia*, pp.137–49; in Bidussa, Luzzatto and Luzzatto Voghera, *Oltre il ghetto*, pp.244–74; Toscano, *Ebraismo e antisemitismo*, pp.99–107.
86. Giuseppe Laras, 'Il movimento sionistico', *RMI*, 47, 7–12 (1981), p.79.
87. See Samuel David Luzzatto, *Epistolario italiano francese latino pubblicato da' suoi figli* (Padua: Fratelli Salmin, 1890), vol. 2, pp.886–8. One young scholar, not a rabbinical student, with whom Luzzatto entered into correspondence in the guise of mentor, was the great philologist Graziadio Isaia Ascoli. In a long letter of 8 November 1846, in which he meticulously corrected Ascoli's errors on the Friuli dialect, Luzzatto wrote: 'you deserve much praise and encouragement for the long hours of study ... one day you will be honoured for your work on the Italian language' (pp.485–91). See also Luzzatto Voghera, *Il prezzo dell'eguaglianza*, p.148.
88. C.A. Viterbo, 'Un Maestro ancora presente', p.203.
89. Pacifici, 'Ha-rav Shemuel Zevì Margulies', p.256. See also C.A. Viterbo, 'Un Maestro ancora presente': 'It has been said – and it is true – that he [Margulies] was, for the enfeebled Jewish life in Italy, what mass emigration from the East was for other western European countries, which we did not have.'
90. See Toscano, *Ebraismo e antisemitismo*, p.83.
91. Simonetta Della Seta, 'Il movimento sionistico', in Vivanti (ed.), *Storia d'Italia, Annali 11, Gli ebrei*

in Italia, vol. 2, pp.1329–30. See also Archivio Storico della Communità Ebraica di Firenze, Gestione Comunità : Attività Sionistiche, E.17.1, 1898–1922, on the correspondence concerning Weizmann's visit on 23 April, which was scaled down because of Margulies's recent death.
92. Chaim Weizmann, *Trial and Error: The Autobiography of Chaim Weizmann* (London: Hamish Hamilton, 1949), pp.356–7. Weizmann visited many Italian cities in the company of David Prato, one of Margulies's former students.

Conclusion

'The historian must first endeavor to show similarity and commonality before he or she can speak with any conviction about difference, let alone singularity.'[1]

The ideology of emancipatory discourse was similar throughout western Europe; the same issues and concepts of the ways in which minorities were to be incorporated into the host society prevailed. Emancipation was a European process. Nevertheless, the contexts and chronology were diverse. In France a 'big bang' emancipation occurred: Jews were accorded political equality within a year, 1790/91.[2] In Italy, there was a brief period of freedom in those territories under Napoleonic rule, followed by a more protracted progress from 1848 to 1870, when the Statuto Albertino was extended in synchrony with the Unification of Italy, culminating in the liberation of the Rome ghetto in 1870. In Germany, where opposition was more bitterly contested than elsewhere in the West, the debates on emancipation lasted nearly a century.[3] It was 'emancipation by instalments', with a gradual extension of rights in the various states, a precedent set by Joseph II's *Toleranzpatent* of 1781.[4] In all cases, however, the religion of the minorities was to be relegated to the private sphere: French, German, Italian citizens of the Jewish faith. Chapter 2 discusses how citizenship and religion were negotiated, highlighting the complex transition from tradition to modernity, the many individual narratives illustrating the myriad modalities of Jewish identity.

The impact of nation-building also played its part in the development of the minorities. France had been a strong political nation state since the Revolution, fostering unwavering adherence of the Jews who were at the very centre of power – the 'State Jews', as Birnbaum defined them. The Unification of Germany rested on a shifting, insecure national identity which evolved as exclusively Christian (Protestant), in opposition to 'others' such as the Jews and the Roman Catholics.[5] Notwithstanding this ambivalence, German Jews sought to diminish any conflict between their Jewishness and *Deutschtum*. Italy, too, possessed a fragile national conscience, but one in whose creation the Jews were actively involved, believing themselves to be among the founding fathers of their nation. Their participation in the wars of independence and their allegiance to the Risorgimento ideals bound them to Italy in a unique way: in no other territory did the Jews fight for its deliverance from foreign domination. The dialectic of nationhood and emancipation favoured a more rapid and complete process of integration.[6] Other factors such as the exiguous number of Italian Jews, the length of time they had lived in various regions of Italy, the lack of linguistic barriers, and the absence of mass immigration from eastern Europe also support the singularity of the Italian Jewish experience. Despite these differences, demonstrations of patriotism followed a uniform pattern: Jews of the countries in which they resided affirmed their loyalty through repeated displays, concluding with their participation in the First World War: 'one sees ... the same desire of Jewish minorities to prove their fidelity to the nation'.[7]

The socio-economic profile of Jews in western Europe during this period is comparable: migration to the cities and upward social mobility; 'embourgeoisement went hand in hand with progressive urbanization'.[8] By 1900, a quarter of German Jews lived in Berlin; two-thirds of French Jews lived in Paris. However, in Italy there was no such demographic concentration: Italian Jews were dispersed among several cities in northern and central Italy, while the Rome community, though large, remained an anomaly. The Jews of France and Italy entered the government apparatus at the highest levels, while at the same time retaining their Jewish identity and communal ties. For the Jews in Germany and Austria-Hungary the state sector was closed to them until 1914 unless they converted, and even then access remained problematic.[9] Thus they progressed *outside* institutional structures, channelling their energies into business, industry, cultural and intellectual arenas to the extent that they reshaped the economy, politics and culture of these empires,[10] engendering, for example, the paradox of Heine's poetry, considered the highest expression of *Deutschtum*, yet rejected by the Germans themselves despite his conversion.

As individual Jews negotiated the complex process of assimilation, so too Jewish communities came to terms with their modified status. Throughout Europe, analogous wide-ranging programmes of education and 'regeneration' were established to assist adaptation to the demands of modern society. Community leaders and rabbis monitored liturgy and observance: in France and Italy, traditional orthodoxy remained intact, while in Germany reform movements split the collective. Through continued philanthropy and patronage, western European Jews shared in the fate of their co-religionists elsewhere, and in the Jewish press they were informed of renewed oppression, persecution and pogroms. This international commonality found expression in institutions such as the Alliance Israélite Universelle: 'the old solidarity between Jews remained'.[11]

The persistent prejudice about Jewish world domination (to name but one of the numerous calumnies), together with the burgeoning successes of emancipated Jews, fuelled new forms of intolerance underpinned by centuries-old Christian antagonism. Anti-Semitism manifested itself throughout Europe, but it varied in form and degree: in Germany and Austria-Hungary it assumed more virulent characteristics, generating political parties whose very ideology was anti-Semitic. In France and Italy, despite the separation of Church and State, everyday life was steeped in Christian values, and thus Catholic anti-Semitism was intense, although political anti-Semitism was not as violent until the eruption of the Dreyfus Affair.[12] Despite Drumont, no anti-Semitic party was formed in France; the Ligue antisémitique of 1888 lasted less than a year. In Italy also there was no such party.

Nevertheless, from 1908, as Charles Maurras's Action Française gathered momentum with its youth gangs of thugs, so too the militancy of the Italian Nationalist Association began to flex its muscles. Despite the disparate forms of anti-Semitism in different countries, the Jews of Europe tragically shared the same terrible fate.

Political Zionism was one of the major responses to the impact of anti-Semitism and the 'erosion' (from the Zionist perspective) of assimilation. A worldwide movement, it affected all Jews in varying ways. Many Jews from eastern Europe were eager to emigrate to Palestine; the leaders of the Zionist associations in western Europe espoused a philanthropic stance in support of their persecuted brethren – for themselves, they could not conceive of an identity separate from their beloved motherlands. The younger generations in the West in reaction to the assimilationism of their elders, endorsed political Zionism and, with it, a renewed interest in their Jewish heritage, inspiring new associations, journals and creative thought in a veritable Jewish cultural renaissance, not least in Italy.

Italy has always been on the margins of Jewish historiography, with Germany serving as the pre-eminent paradigm: 'when one thinks of assimilation in European Jewish history, indeed in the modern Jewish experience, one thinks of German Jewry'.[13] However, contemporary sources and recent Italian scholarship demonstrate that as individuals and as communities, the Jews of Italy shared the same concerns, tensions and aspirations; they underwent the same 'complex and multifaceted transformation'[14] as their co-religionists elsewhere. Birnbaum has argued that the France of the Third Republic 'seems to be the best available model of real integration of Jews into a state',[15] to which Italy of the liberal period can be added, producing Europe's first Jewish prime minister, Luigi Luzzatti, in 1910;[16] France had to wait until 1936 for Léon Blum. No longer can Italy be considered an anomaly within European Jewish history.

NOTES

1. David Sorkin, 'Enlightenment and Emancipation: German Jewry's Formative Age in Comparative Perspective', in Todd M. Endelman (ed.), *Comparing Jewish Societies* (Ann Arbor, MI: University of Michigan Press, 1997), p.90.
2. Comment by Peter Pulzer, pp.195–8 (p.196), on Pierre Birnbaum, 'In the Academic Sphere: The Cases of Emile Durkheim and Georg Simmel', in Michael Brenner, Vicki Caron and Uri R. Kaufmann (eds), *Jewish Emancipation Reconsidered: The French and German Models* (Leo Baeck Institute, London: Mohr Siebeck, 2003), pp.171–95.
3. See Endelman (ed.), *Comparing Jewish Societies*, Introduction, p.5.
4. See Andrew M. Canepa, 'Emancipation and Jewish Response in Mid-Nineteenth-Century Italy', *European History Quarterly*, 16, 4 (1986), p.430.
5. See, for example, Comment by Jakob Vogel, pp.73–8 (p.77), on Richard I. Cohen, 'Celebrating Integration in the Public Sphere in Germany and France', in Brenner, Caron and Kaufmann (eds), *Jewish Emancipation Reconsidered*, pp.55–73; see also, in the same volume, Jacques Ehrenfreund, 'Citizenship and Acculturation: Some Reflections on German Jews during the Second Empire and French Jews during the Third Republic', p.157: 'over the course of the nineteenth century the German people interrogated themselves a great deal about their national identity'. The Jews in Austria-Hungary had a tripartite identity: Austrian by political loyalty; Czech or Pole or Hungarian, etc., by cultural affiliation, and Jewish in ethnicity. However, the Jews within the Empire were regarded solely as adherents of a particular religious faith. See Marsha L. Rozenblit, *Reconstructing a National Identity: The Jews of Habsburg Austria during World War I* (Oxford: Oxford University Press, 2001), pp.4, 19.
6. See Toscano (ed.), *Integrazione e identità: l'esperienza ebraica in Germania e Italia dall'Illuminismo al fascismo* (Milan: FrancoAngeli, 1998), Introduction, pp.16–18.

7. Ehrenfreund, 'Citizenship and Acculturation', p.157.
8. Ibid., p.156.
9. See Birnbaum, 'In the Academic Sphere', p.175, citing Peter Pulzer from his book *Jews and the German State*: 'at no stage in German history between 1871 and 1933 was there a consensus that the Jew was a citizen like any other'. Roman Catholics in Germany were also excluded from the upper strata of the civil service, the universities and the army.
10. See Robert S. Wistrich, *Antisemitism: The Longest Hatred* (London: Methuen), p.54.
11. Jacob Katz, *Out of the Ghetto: The Social Background of Jewish Emancipation, 1770–1870* (Cambridge, MA: Harvard University Press, 1973), p.215.
12. See, for example, Pierre Birnbaum, *Anti-Semitism in France: A Political History from Léon Blum to the Present* (Oxford: Blackwell, 1992), p.19.
13. David Sorkin, 'The Impact of Emancipation on German Jewry: A Reconsideration', in Jonathan Frankel and Steven J. Zipperstein (eds), *Assimilation and Community: The Jews in Nineteenth-Century Europe* (Cambridge: Cambridge University Press, 2004), p.177.
14. Ibid., p.179.
15. Birnbaum, *Anti-Semitism in France*, p.17. See also by the same author 'Between Social and Political Assimilation: Remarks on the History of Jews in France', in Pierre Birnbaum and Ira Katznelson (eds), *Paths of Emancipation: Jews, States, and Citizenship* (Princeton, NJ: Princeton University Press, 1995), pp.115, 117: 'in no other country in the world were there as many Jews exercising political functions so crucial to the implementation of the state and the general control of society ... The strong French state was the only one in modern history, indeed in all history, to open its *Grands Corps* to Jewish statesmen.'
16. Benjamin Disraeli (1804–81), British prime minister in 1868 and from 1874 to 1880, had been baptized as a child.

Bibliography

ARCHIVAL MATERIAL

Archivio del Centro di Documentazione Ebraica Contemporanea, Milan
    Fondo Angelo Sullam
Archivio Storico della Comunità Ebraica di Firenze
    B.8.1–5 Opere Pie: Salomone Lampronti
    B.13.1 Opere Pie: Alberto Levi
    B.123 Opere Pie: Giuseppe Vivanti
    D.2.3 Catecumeni, 1831–74
    D.8.1 Congresso di Ferrara
    D.8.2 Congresso di Firenze
    E.17 Attività Sionistiche, 1898–1918
    E.19 Attività Culturali–Enti Vari Ebraici, 1918–35

Central Archives for the History of the Jewish People, Jerusalem
    IT 79 Territorial Collection
    IT 829, 831, 832, 868 – Italy
    P 172 Alfonso Pacifici

Central Zionist Archives, Jerusalem
    A50 Yosef Marcou Baruch
    A353 Felice Ravenna
    Z1 Central Zionist Office, Vienna, 1897–1905
    Z2 Central Zionist Office, Cologne, 1905–11

CONTEMPORARY PERIODICALS (1848–1915)

Civiltà Cattolica (1850–)
Il Corriere Israelitico (1862–1915)
L'Educatore Israelita (1853–74)
L'Idea Sionista (1901–11) (NB: This spelling is used throughout even though it changed to *Sionnista* after 1904)
Israel (1916–38; 1944–74)
L'Osservatore Romano (1861–)
La Settimana Israelitica (1910–15)
Il Vessillo Israelitico (1874–1922)

PRIMARY AND SECONDARY SOURCES

Abulafia, David, 'Libels of Blood', *Times Literary Supplement*, 2 March, 2007, pp.11–12.

Adorno, Massimo Longo, *Gli ebrei fiorentini dall'emancipazione alla Shoà* (Florence: Giuntina, 2003).

Alderman, Geoffrey, 'English Jews or Jews of the English Persuasion?', in Birnbaum and Katznelson (eds), *Paths of Emancipation* (1995), pp.128–56.

Allegra, Luciano (ed.), *Ebrei a Torino: ricerche per il centenario della sinagoga 1884–1984* (Turin: Allemandi, 1984).

Altgeld, Wolfgang, 'German Catholics', in Liedtke and Wendehorst (eds), *Emancipation of Catholics, Jews and Protestants* (1999), pp.100–21.

Anselmi, Sergio and Bonazzoli, Viviana (eds), *La presenza ebraica nelle Marche: Secoli XIII–XX* (Ancona: Quaderni monografici 'Proposte e ricerche', 1993).

Apih, Elio, *Trieste* (Rome-Bari: Laterza, 1988).

Arian Levi, Giorgina and Disegni, Giulio, *Fuori dal ghetto: il 1848 degli ebrei* (Rome: Riuniti, 1998).

Armani, Barbara, 'L'identità sfidata: gli ebrei fuori dal ghetto', *Storica*, 5, 15 (1999), pp.69–103.

Armani, Barbara and Schwarz, Guri, 'Ebrei borghesi: identità famigliare, solidarietà e affari nell'età dell'emancipazione', *Quaderni storici*, 38, 3 (2003), pp.621–51.

Artom, Eugenio, *Un compagno di Menotti e di Mazzini: Angelo Usiglio* (Modena: Soliniani, 1949).

Artom, Guido, *I giorni del mondo* (Brescia: Morcelliana, 1997).

Ascoli, Albert Russell and Von Henneberg, Krystyna (eds), *Making and Remaking Italy* (New York and Oxford: Berg, 2001).

Astrologo, Aldo and Del Canuto, Francesco, 'Firenze 1920: storia del "Comune ebraico"', *Rassegna Mensile di Israel*, 44, 1 (1978), pp.6–42.

Ballini, Pier Luigi (ed.), *Fiorentini del Novecento* (Florence: Polistampa, 2002), 2 vols.

Ballini, Pier Luigi and Pecorari, Paolo (eds), *Luigi Luzzatti e il suo tempo* (Venice: Istituto Veneto di scienze lettere ed arti, 1994).

Balsamo, Luigi and Cremente, Renzo (eds), *Angelo Fortunato Formiggini un editore del Novecento* (Bologna: Il Mulino, 1981).

Banks, Marcus, *Ethnicity: Anthropological Constructions* (London and New York: Routledge, 1996).

Barnard, Alan and Spencer, Jonathan (eds), *Encyclopedia of Social and Cultural Anthropology* (London and New York: Routledge, 1998).

Bauman, Zygmunt, *Modernity and Ambivalence* (Cambridge: Polity Press, 1991).

Becker, Jean-Jacques and Wieviorka, Annette (eds), *Les Juifs de France de la Révolution française à nos jours* (Paris: Editions Liana Levi, 1998).

Beilis, Mendel, *The Story of My Sufferings*, translated by Harrison Goldberg, with an introduction by Herman Bernstein and Arnold D. Margolin (New York: Mendel Beilis, 1926).

Belforte, Francesca, 'Una famiglia medio-borghese: i Belforte', in Luzzati (ed.), *Ebrei di Livorno* (1990), pp.91–106.

Beller, Steven, 'Class, Culture and the Jews of Vienna, 1900', in Ivar Oxaal, Michael Pollak and Gerhard Botz (eds), *Jews, Antisemitism and Culture in Vienna* (London and New York: Routledge & Kegan Paul, 1987), pp.39–58.

Beller, Steven, *Vienna and the Jews, 1867–1938: A Cultural History* (Cambridge and New York: Cambridge University Press, 1989).

Beller, Steven, 'Herzl's Anglophilia', in Robertson and Timms (eds), *Theodor Herzl and the Origins of Zionism* (1997), pp.54–61.

Bemporad, Memo, *La Macine: storia di una famiglia israelita negli ultimi 60 anni di vita italiana* (Rome: Carucci, 1984).

Benbassa, Esther, *The Jews of France: A History from Antiquity to the Present* (Princeton, NJ: Princeton University Press, 1999).

Benbassa, Esther and Attias, Jean-Christophe (eds), *The Jew and the Other* (Ithaca, NY, and London: Cornell University Press, 2004).

Bensoussan, Georges, *Une histoire intellectuelle et politique du Sionisme 1860–1940* (Paris: Arthème Fayard, 2002).

Benussi, Cristina (ed.), *Storie di ebrei fra gli asburgo e l'Italia: Diaspore/Galuyyot* (Udine: Gaspari, 2003).

Berengo, Marino, 'Luigi Luzzatti e la tradizione ebraica', in Ballini and Pecorari (eds), *Luigi Luzzatti e il suo tempo* (1994), pp.527–41.

Berger, David (ed.), *The Legacy of Jewish Migration: 1881 and its Impact* (New York: Brooklyn College Press, 1983).

Bergonzoni, Daniela, *Storia degli ebrei di Scandiano* (Florence: Giuntina, 1998).

Bergonzoni, Daniela and Padoa, Lazzaro, *Le comunità ebraiche di Scandiano e di Reggio Emilia* (Florence: Giuntina, 1993).

Berkowitz, Michael, *Zionist Culture and West European Jewry Before the First World War* (Chapel Hill, NC, and London: University of North Carolina Press, 1996).

Berkowitz, Michael, *The Jewish Self-Image: American and British Perspectives, 1881–1939* (London: Reaktion Books, 2000).

Bernardini, Paolo, *La questione ebraica nel tardo illuminismo tedesco: studi intorno allo 'Ueber die bürgerliche Verbesserung der Juden' di C.W. Dohm (1781)* (Florence: Giuntina, 1992).

Bernardini, Paolo, 'The Jews in Nineteenth-Century Italy: Towards a Reappraisal', *Journal of Modern Italian Studies*, 1, 2 (Spring 1996), pp.292–310.

Besso, Marco, *Autobiografia* (Rome: Fondazione Marco Besso, 1925).

Betri, Maria Luisa and Maldini Chiarito, Daniela (eds), *'Dolce dono graditissimo': la lettera privata dal Settecento al Novecento* (Milan: FrancoAngeli, 2000).

Bidussa, David, *Il sionismo politico* (Milan: Edizioni Unicopli, 1993).

Bidussa, David, 'Luoghi della memoria e percorsi dell'identità: note di lavoro', *Rassegna Mensile di Israel*, 71, 1 (2005), pp.125–46.

Bidussa, David, Luzzatto, Amos and Luzzatto Voghera, Gadi, *Oltre il ghetto: momenti e figure della cultura ebraica in Italia tra l'Unità e il fascismo* (Brescia: Morcelliana, 1992).

Birnbaum, Pierre, *Anti-Semitism in France: A Political History from Léon Blum to the Present* (Oxford: Blackwell, 1992).

Birnbaum, Pierre, 'Between Social and Political Assimilation: Remarks on the History of Jews in France', in Birnbaum and Katznelson, *Paths of Emancipation* (1995), pp.94–127.

Birnbaum, Pierre, *The Jews of the Republic: A Political History of State Jews in France from Gambetta to Vichy* (Stanford, CA: Stanford University Press, 1996).

Birnbaum, Pierre, 'Exile, Assimilation, and Identity: from Moses to Joseph', in Carlebach, Efron and Myers (eds), *Jewish History and Jewish Memory* (1998), pp.249–70.

Birnbaum, Pierre, 'Les Juifs et l'Affaire', in Becker and Wieviorka (eds), *Les Juifs de France de la Révolution française à nos jours* (1998), pp.75–101.

Birnbaum, Pierre, 'In the Academic Sphere: The Cases of Emile Durkheim and Georg Simmel', in Brenner, Caron and Kaufmann (eds), *Jewish Emancipation Reconsidered* (2003), pp.171–95.

Birnbaum, Pierre and Katznelson, Ira, 'Emancipation and the Liberal Offer', in Birnbaum and Katznelson (eds), *Paths of Emancipation: Jews, States, and Citizenship* (1995), pp.3–36.

Birnbaum, Pierre and Katznelson, Ira (eds), *Paths of Emancipation: Jews, States, and Citizenship* (Princeton, NJ: Princeton University Press, 1995).

Boccara, Elia, 'La comunità ebraica portoghese di Tunisi (1710–1944)', *Rassegna Mensile di Israel*, 66, 2 (2000), pp.25–98.

Bonilauri, Franco and Maugeri, Vincenza (eds), *Le comunità ebraiche a Modena e a Carpi: dal medioevo all'età contemporanea* (Florence: Giuntina, 1999).

Boralevi, Alberto, 'Angiolo Orvieto, "Il Marzocco", la società colta ebraica', in Del Vivo (ed.), *Il Marzocco* (1985), pp.213–33.

Brenner, Michael, Caron, Vicki and Kaufmann, Uri R. (eds), *Jewish Emancipation Reconsidered: The French and German Models* (Leo Baeck Institute, London: Mohr Siebeck, 2003).

Brice, Catherine and Miccoli, Giovanni (eds), *Les racines chrétiennes de l'antisémitisme politique (fin XIX–XXe siècle)* (Rome: Publications de l'Ecole Française de Rome, 2003).

Burgio, Alberto (ed.), *Nel nome della razza: il razzismo nella storia d'Italia 1870–1945* (Bologna: Il Mulino, 2000).

Burns, Michael, *France and the Dreyfus Affair: A Documentary History* (Boston, MA and New York: Bedford/St Martin's, 1999).

Burton, Richard F., *The Jew, The Gypsy and El Islam* (London: Hutchinson, 1898).

Cabanel, Patrick and Bordes-Benayoun, Chantal (eds), *Un modèle d'intégration: juifs et israélites en France et en Europe (XIX–XX siècles)* (Paris: Berg, 2004).

Caffiero, Marina, 'Alle origini dell'antisemitismo politico: l'accusa di omicidio nel sei-settecento tra autodifesa degli ebrei e pronunciamenti papali', in Brice and Miccoli (eds), *Les racines chrétiennes de l'antisémitisme politique* (2003), pp.2–59.

Calimani, Riccardo, *Di ebrei, di cose ebraiche e del resto* (Florence: Giuntina, 1984).

Canepa, Andrew M., 'Emancipazione, integrazione e antisemitismo liberale in Italia: il caso Pasqualigo', *Comunità*, 29, 174 (1975), pp.166–203.

Canepa, Andrew M., 'L'immagine dell'ebreo nel folklore e nella letteratura del postrisorgimento', *Rassegna Mensile di Israel*, 5–6 (1978), pp.383–99.
Canepa, Andrew M., 'Cattolici ed ebrei nell'Italia liberale (1870–1915)', *Comunità*, 32, 179 (1978), pp.43–109.
Canepa, Andrew M., 'Reflections on Antisemitism in Liberal Italy', *Wiener Library Bulletin*, 31, 47–8 (1978), pp.104–11.
Canepa, Andrew M., 'Considerazioni sulla seconda emancipazione e le sue conseguenze', *Rassegna Mensile di Israel*, 47, 1–3 (1981), pp.45–89.
Canepa, Andrew M., 'Emancipation and Jewish Response in Mid-Nineteenth-Century Italy', *European History Quarterly*, 16, 4 (1986), pp.403–39.
Canepa, Andrew M., 'Pius X and the Jews: A Reappraisal', *Church History*, 61, 3 (1992), pp.362–72.
Canosa, Romano, *A caccia di ebrei: Mussolini, Preziosi e l'antisemitismo fascista* (Milan: Mondadori, 2006).
Capuzzo, Ester, *Gli ebrei nella società italiana: comunità e istituzioni tra Ottocento e Novecento* (Rome: Carocci, 1999).
Capuzzo, Ester, *Gli ebrei italiani dal Risorgimento alla scelta sionista* (Florence: Le Monnier, 2004).
Capuzzo, Ester, 'La famiglia Sereni e l'ambiente ebraico italiano', *Clio*, 41, 3 (2005), pp.469–84.
Capuzzo, Ester, 'Risorgimento, liberalismo e ebraismo nell'esperienza di Eugenio Artom', *Clio*, 43, 2 (2007), pp.207–27.
Carlebach, Elisheva, Efron, John M. and Myers, David N. (eds), *Jewish History and Jewish Memory: Essays in Honour of Yosef Hayim Yerushalmi* (Hanover, MD, and London: Brandeis University Press, 1998).
Carlucci, Paola, *Il giovane Sonnino fra cultura e politica, 1847–1886* (Rome: Archivio Guido Izzi, 2002).
Carocci, Giampiero, *Storia degli ebrei in Italia: dall'emancipazione a oggi* (Rome: Newton & Compton, 2005).
Castelli, Rita, 'Una testimonianza', in Luzzati, *Ebrei di Livorno* (1990), pp.120–3.
Castelnuovo, Enrico, *I Moncalvo* (Rome: Lucarini, 1989).
Castignoli, Paolo, 'Fonti per la storia degli ebrei a Livorno: gli archivi locali', in Scandaliato Ciciani (ed.), *Italia Judaica* (1989), pp.183–90.
Catalan, Tullia, 'Società e sionismo a Trieste fra XIX e XX secolo', in Todeschini and Zorattini (eds), *Il mondo ebraico* (1991), pp.457–90.
Catalan, Tullia, 'L'antisemitismo nazionalista italiano visto da un ebreo triestino: Carlo Morpurgo ed il "caso Coppola"', *Qualestoria*, 1–2 (1994), pp.95–118.
Catalan, Tullia, 'L'organizzazione delle comunità ebraiche dall'Unità alla prima guerra mondiale', in Vivanti (ed.), *Storia d'Italia, Annali 11, Gli ebrei in Italia*, vol. 2 (1997), pp.1243–90.
Catalan, Tullia, 'Una scelta difficile: gli ebrei triestini fra identità ebraica e identità nazionale (1848–1914)', *Annali dell'Istituto storico italo-germanico in Trento*, 23 (1997), pp.335–57.
Catalan, Tullia, *La comunità ebraica di Trieste (1781–1914): politica, società e cultura* (Trieste: Lint, 2000).
Catalan, Tullia, 'Il Quarantotto fra Austria e Italia: le lettere alla famiglia di

Giacomo Venezian', in Betri and Maldini Chiarito (eds), *'Dolce dono graditissimo'* (2000), pp.254–70.

Catalan, Tullia, 'La "primavera degli ebrei": ebrei italiani del Litorale e del Lombardo Veneto nel 1848–1849', *Zakhor*, 6 (2003), pp.35–66.

Cavaglion, Alberto, *Felice Momigliano (1866–1924): una biografia* (Bologna: Il Mulino, 1988).

Cavaglion, Alberto, 'Gli ebrei e il socialismo: il caso italiano', in Sofia and Toscano, *Stato nazionale ed emancipazione ebraica* (1992), pp.377–92.

Cavaglion, Alberto, 'Il Sionismo nella stampa socialista di fine Ottocento', in Mezzabotta (ed.), *Italia Judaica ... Atti del IV convegno internazionale* (1993), pp.223–36.

Cavaglion, Alberto (ed.), *La moralità armata: studi su Emanuele Artom 1915–1944* (Milan: FrancoAngeli, 1993).

Cavaglion, Alberto, 'Tendenze nazionali e albori sionistici', in Vivanti (ed.), *Storia d'Italia, Annali 11, Gli ebrei in Italia*, vol. 2 (1997), pp.1291–320.

Cavaglion, Alberto, 'Una famiglia ebraica fra Risorgimento e Resistenza', *Rassegna Mensile di Israel*, 64, 1 (1998), pp.23–9.

Cavaglion, Alberto, 'Qualche riflessione sulla "mancata Riforma"', in Toscano, *Integrazione e identità* (1998), pp.152–66.

Cavaglion, Alberto, 'L'Autobiografia ebraica in Italia fra Otto e Novecento. Memoria di sé e memoria della famiglia: osservazioni preliminari', *Zakhor*, 3 (1999), pp.171–7.

Cavaglion, Alberto, 'Due modeste proposte', in Alberto Burgio (ed.), *Nel nome della razza: il razzismo nella storia d'Italia 1870–1945* (Bologna: Il Mulino, 2000), pp.379–86.

Cavaglion, Alberto, 'L'Italia della razza s'è desta', *Belfagor*, 57 (January 2002), pp.27–42.

Cavaglion, Alberto, *ebrei senza saperlo* (Naples: l'ancora del mediterraneo, 2002).

Cavaglion, Alberto, *Gli ebrei in Piemonte* (Turin: AEC, 2003).

Cavaglion, Alberto, *il senso dell'arca: ebrei senza saperlo: nuove riflessioni* (Naples: l'ancora del mediterraneo, 2006).

Cavarocchi, Francesca, *La comunità ebraica di Mantova fra prima emancipazione e unità d'Italia* (Florence: Giuntina, 2002).

Caviglia, Stefano, *L'identità salvata: gli ebrei di Roma tra fede e nazione, 1870–1938* (Rome-Bari: Laterza, 1996).

Cedarmas, Adonella, *La comunità israelitica di Gorizia (1900–1945)* (Pasian di Prato: Istituto Friulano per la Storia del Movimento di Liberazione, 1999).

Celata, Giuseppe, *Gli ebrei a Pitigliano: i quattro secoli di una comunità diversa* (Pitigliano: Laurum, 1995).

Cesarani, David, 'British Jews', in Liedtke and Wendehorst (eds), *Emancipation of Catholics, Jews and Protestants* (1999), pp.33–55.

Cesarani, David, *The Jewish Chronicle and Anglo-Jewry, 1841–1991* (Cambridge: Cambridge University Press, 1994).

Cheyette, Bryan and Marcus, Laura (eds), *Modernity, Culture and 'the Jew'* (Cambridge: Polity Press, 1998).

Cheyette, Bryan and Valman, Nadia (eds) *The Image of the Jew in European Liberal Culture, 1789–1914* (London and Portland, OR: Vallentine Mitchell, 2004).

Cipolla, Gaetano, 'The Jews of Sicily', in DiNapoli (ed.), *Italian Jewish Experience* (2000), pp.51–64.
Ciuffoletti, Zeffiro, 'Amelia Rosselli', in Ballini (ed.), *Fiorentini del Novecento* (2002), vol. 2, pp.147–55.
Clare, George, *Last Waltz in Vienna: The Destruction of a Family 1842–1942* (London: Macmillan, 1981).
Clark, Christopher, 'German Jews', in Liedtke and Wendehorst, *Emancipation of Catholics, Jews and Protestants* (1999), pp.122–47.
Clark, Martin, *Modern Italy 1871–1982* (London and New York: Longman, 1984).
Coen, Fausto, *Una vita tante vite* (Catanzaro: Rubbettino, 2004).
Cohen, Richard I., 'Celebrating Integration in the Public Sphere in Germany and France', in Brenner, Caron and Kaufmann (eds), *Jewish Emancipation Reconsidered* (2003), pp.55–73.
Cohen, Richard I., 'Nostalgia and "Return to the Ghetto": A Cultural Phenomenon in Western and Central Europe', in Frankel and Zipperstein (eds), *Assimilation and Community* (2004), pp.130–55.
Cohen, Stuart A., *English Zionists and British Jews: The Communal Politics of Anglo-Jewry, 1895–1920* (Princeton, NJ: Princeton University Press, 1982).
Cohen Albert, Phyllis, 'Israelite and Jew: How Did Nineteenth-Century French Jews Understand Assimilation?', in Frankel and Zipperstein (eds), *Assimilation and Community* (2004), pp.89–109.
Cohn-Sherbok, Dan, *The Paradox of Anti-Semitism* (London and New York: Continuum, 2006).
Colbi, Paolo S., 'Un "capitolo glorioso" di vita culturale ebraica triestina dei secoli passati', *Rassegna Mensile di Israel*, 66, 1 (2000), pp.105–117.
Collotti, Enzo, *Il fascismo e gli ebrei: le leggi razziali in Italia* (Rome-Bari: Laterza, 2003).
Colorni, Vittore, *Judaica Minora: saggi sulla storia dell'ebraismo italiano dall'antichità all'età moderna. Nuove Ricerche* (Milan: Giuffrè, 1991).
Comba, Augusto, 'Giuseppe David Levi profeta del Risorgimento', in Mola (ed.), *Isacco Artom e gli ebrei italiani* (2002), pp.109–16.
Conti, Fulvio (ed.), *La massoneria a Livorno: dal Settecento alla Repubblica* (Bologna: Il Mulino, 2007).
Cornwell, John, *Hitler's Pope: The Secret History of Pius XII* (London: Viking, 1999).
Crepaldi, Francesco, 'L'omicidio rituale nella "moderna" polemica antigiudaica di *Civiltà Cattolica* nella seconda metà del XIX secolo', in Brice and Miccoli (eds), *Les racines chrétiennes de l'antisémitisme politique* (2003), pp.61–78.
Dainotto, Roberto Maria, 'The Jewish Risorgimento and the Questione Romana', in DiNapoli (ed.), *Italian Jewish Experience* (2000), pp.107–15.
D'Ancona, Alessandro, *Ricordi ed Affetti. In memoria d'illustri italiani. Ricordi di Maestri, Amici e Discepoli. Ricordi di Storia. Ricordi Autobiografici e Affetti* (Milan: Treves, 1902).
De Benedetti, Rodolfo, *Nato ad Asti: vita di un imprenditore* (Genoa: Marietti, 1989).

De Benedetti, Salvatore, *Marianna Foà Uzielli: ricordo biografico* (Livorno: Vigo, 1880).
De Benedetti, Salvatore, *Giuseppe Levi: ricordo biografico*, published in the same volume with Giuseppe Levi, *Autobiografia di un padre di famiglia* (Florence: Le Monnier, 2003; first edn 1868).
De Cesaris, Valerio, *Pro Judaeis: il filogiudaismo cattolico in Italia (1789–1938)* (Milan: Guerini, 2006).
De Felice, Renzo, *Storia degli ebrei sotto il fascismo*, third edn (Turin: Einaudi, 1972 [1961]).
De Felice, Renzo, 'Stato, società e questione ebraica nell'Italia unita', in Sofia and Toscano, *Stato nazionale ed emancipazione ebraica* (1992), pp.421–32.
De Grand, Alexander, *The Italian Nationalist Association and the Rise of Fascism in Italy* (Lincoln, NE, and London: University of Nebraska Press, 1978).
De' Paratesi, Nora Galli, 'Il giudeo-italiano e i dialetti giudeo-italiani', in Bice Migliau (ed.), *La cultura ebraica nell'editoria italiana (1955–1990)* (Rome: Ministero per i Beni Culturali e Ambientali, 1992), pp.131–48.
Del Bianco Cotrozzi, Maddalena, *Il Collegio Rabbinico di Padova: un'istituzione religiosa dell'ebraismo sulla via dell'emancipazione* (Florence: Olschki, 1995).
Del Bianco Cotrozzi, Maddalena, 'Ebraismo italiano dell'Ottocento: *La educazione della donna* di David Graziadio Viterbi', in Luzzati and Galasso (eds), *Donne nella storia degli ebrei d'Italia* (2007), pp.329–45.
Del Canuto, Francesco, 'La stampa ebraica in Italia dall'emancipazione alla seconda guerra mondiale', in Miglau (ed.), *La cultura ebraica nell'editoria italiana* (1992), pp.67–78.
Del Canuto, Francesco, *Il movimento sionistico in Italia dalle origini al 1924* (Milan: Federazione Sionistica Italiana, 1972).
Del Canuto, Francesco, 'La soppressione della stampa ebraica in Italia e la sua ripresa (1938–1944)' in Mezzabotta (ed.), *Italia Judaica ... Atti del IV convegno internazionale* (1993), pp.464–73.
Del Canuto, Francesco and di Segni, Riccardo, 'Una biografia inedita di Marcou Baruch', *Rassegna Mensile di Israel*, 46, 5–8 (1980), pp.220–8.
Della Pergola, Sergio, *Anatomia dell'ebraismo italiano: caratteristiche demografiche, economiche, sociali, religiose e politiche di una minoranza* (Assisi and Rome: Carucci, 1976).
Della Pergola, Sergio, 'Quantitative Aspects of Jewish Assimilation', in Vago (ed.), *Jewish Assimilation in Modern Times* (1981), pp.185–206.
Della Pergola, Sergio, 'Precursori, convergenti, emarginati: trasformazioni demografiche degli ebrei in Italia, 1870–1945', in Mezzabotta (ed.), *Italia Judaica* (1993), pp.48–91.
Della Pergola, Sergio, 'La popolazione ebraica in Italia nel contesto ebraico globale', in Vivanti (ed.), *Storia d'Italia, Annali 11, Gli ebrei in Italia*, vol. 2 (1997), pp.895–936.
Della Peruta, Franco, 'Gli ebrei nel Risorgimento fra interdizioni ed emancipazione', in Vivanti (ed.), *Storia d'Italia, Annali 11, Gli ebrei in Italia*, vol. 2 (1997), pp.1135–67.

Della Seta, Simonetta and Carpi, Daniel, 'Il movimento sionistico', in Vivanti (ed.), *Storia d'Italia, Annali 11, Gli ebrei in Italia*, vol. 2 (1997), pp.1321–68.

Della Seta Torrefranca, Simonetta, 'Identità religiosa e identità nazionale nell'ebraismo italiano del Novecento', in Mezzabotta (ed.), *Italia Judaica* (1993), pp.263–72.

Del Regno, Filomena, 'Un archivio ottocentesco: le carte di Isacco Artom presso il centro bibliografico', *Rassegna Mensile di Israel*, 64, 1 (1998), pp.13–22.

Del Vivo, Caterina (ed.), *Il Marzocco: carteggi e cronache fra Ottocento e Avanguardie (1887–1913). Atti del seminario di studi (12–14 dicembre 1983)* (Florence: Olschki, 1985).

Deustcher, Isaac, *The Non-Jewish Jew and Other Essays*, edited with an introduction by Tamara Deutscher (London: Oxford University Press, 1968).

Di Porto, Bruno, 'Edoardo Arbib deputato di Viterbo', *Rassegna Mensile di Israel*, 40 (1973), pp.436–42.

Di Porto, Bruno, 'Dopo il Risorgimento, al varco del '900: gli ebrei e l'ebraismo in Italia', *Rassegna Mensile di Israel*, 47, 1–6 (1981), pp.19–41.

Di Porto, Bruno, 'Dopo il Risorgimento, al varco del '900. Appendice: Felice Momigliano ad Arcangelo Ghislieri. Lettere inedite', *Rassegna Mensile di Israel*, 47, 7–12 (1981) pp.42–62.

Di Porto, Bruno, 'Gli ebrei a Pisa dal Risorgimento al fascismo tra identità e integrazione', in Luzzati (ed.), *Gli Ebrei di Pisa* (1998), pp.283–340.

Di Porto, Bruno, 'Il giornalismo ebraico in Italia: un primo sguardo d'insieme al "Vessillo Israelitico"', *Materia giudaica*, 6, 1 (2001), pp.104–109.

Di Porto, Bruno, 'Apporti e posizioni di ebrei nella vita e nella cultura politica italiana', in Mola (ed.), *Isacco Artom e gli ebrei italiani* (2002), pp.59–107.

DiNapoli, Thomas P. (ed.), *The Italian Jewish Experience* (Stony Brook, NY: Forum Italicum Publishing, 2000).

Dinelli, Laura and Bernardini, Luciano (eds), *I laboratori toscani della democrazia e del Risorgimento: la 'repubblica' di Livorno, 'l'altro' Granducato, il sogno italiano di rinnovamento* (Pisa: ETS, 2004).

D'Innocenzo, Michael and Sirefman, Josef P. (eds), *Immigration and Ethnicity: American Society – 'Melting Pot' or 'Salad Bowl'* (Westport, CT, and London: Greenwood Press, 1992).

Dionisotti, Carlo, 'Appunti su Ascoli', in Gavazzeni and Gorni (eds), *Le tradizioni del testo* (1993), pp.419–32.

Dohm, Christian Wilhelm von, *Ueber die bürgerliche Verbesserung der Juden* (Berlin and Stettin: Friedrich Nicolai, 1781/83).

Doumanis, Nicholas, *Italy* (London: Arnold, 2001).

Drouin, Michel (ed.), *L'Affaire Dreyfus de A à Z* (Paris: Flammarion, 1994).

Dubin, Lois C., 'Trieste and Berlin: The Italian Role in the Cultural Politics of the Haskalah', in Katz (ed.), *Toward Modernity* (1987), pp.189–224.

Dubin, Lois C., *The Port Jews of Habsburg Trieste: Absolutist Politics and Enlightenment Culture* (Stanford, CA: Stanford University Press, 1999).

Dubin, Lois C., 'The Jews of Trieste: Between Mitteleuropa and Mittelmeer, 1719–1939', in Klopp (ed.), *Bele Antiche Stòrie* (2008), pp.69–90.

Ehrenfreund, Jacques, 'Citizenship and Acculturation: Some Reflections on

German Jews during the Second Empire and French Jews during the Third Republic' in Brenner, Caron and Kaufmann (eds), *Jewish Emancipation Reconsidered* (2003), pp.155–63.
Eisenstadt, S.N., *Jewish Civilization: The Jewish Historical Experience in a Comparative Perspective* (Albany, NY: State University of New York Press, 1992).
Eliot, Simon and Rose, Jonathan (eds), *A Companion to the History of the Book* (Oxford: Blackwell, 2007).
Elon, Amos, *Herz: A Biography* (New York: Schocken Books, 1986).
Elon, Amos, *The Pity of It All: A Portrait of Jews in Germany, 1743–1933* (London: Allen Lane, 2003).
Endelman, Todd M., 'Native Jews and Foreign Jews in London, 1870–1914', in Berger (ed.), *Legacy of Jewish Migration* (1983), pp.109–29.
Endelman, Todd M., 'Conversion as a Response to Antisemitism in Modern Jewish History', in Reinharz (ed.), *Living with Antisemitism* (1987), pp.59–83.
Endelman, Todd M., (ed.), *Comparing Jewish Societies* (Ann Arbor, MI: University of Michigan Press, 1997).
Endelman, Todd M., 'Memories of Jewishness: Jewish Converts and Their Jewish Pasts', in Carlebach, Efron and Myers (eds), *Jewish History and Jewish Memory* (1998), pp.311–29.
Eriksen, Thomas Hylland, *Ethnicity and Nationalism: Anthropological Perspectives* (London and East Haven, CT: Pluto Press, 1993).
Facchini, Cristiana, *David Castelli: ebraismo e scienze delle religioni tra Otto e Novecento* (Brescia: Morcelliana, 2005).
Falco, Emilio, 'Isacco Maurogonato Pesaro dalle prime esperienze politiche alla caduta della destra storica', *Clio*, 40, 3 (2004), pp.393–446.
Feldman, David, 'Was Modernity Good for the Jews?', in Cheyette and Marcus (eds), *Modernity, Culture and 'the Jew'* (1998), pp.171–87.
Ferrara degli Uberti, Carlotta, 'La questione dell'emancipazione ebraica nel biennio 1847–1848: note sul caso livornese', *Zakhor*, 6 (2003), pp.67–91.
Ferrara degli Uberti, Carlotta, '"Laboriose, educatrici e saggie": sulla corrispondenza femminile al "Vessillo Israelitico" all'alba del Novecento', in Luzzati and Galasso (eds), *Donne nella storia degli ebrei d'Italia* (2007), pp.403–26.
Ferrara degli Uberti, Carlotta, *La 'Nazione Ebrea' di Livorno dai privilegi all'emancipazione (1814–1860)* (Florence: Le Monnier, 2007).
Ferrara degli Uberti, Carlotta, 'Rappresentare se stessi tra famiglia e nazione. Il "Vessillo Israelitico" alla soglia del '900', *Passato e Presente*, 70 (2007), pp.35–58.
Ferrero, Guglielmo, *L'Europa giovane: studi e viaggi nei paesi del Nord* (Milan: Treves, 1897).
Filippini, Jean-Pierre, 'La nazione ebrea di Livorno', in Vivanti (ed.), *Storia d'Italia, Annali 11, Gli ebrei in Italia*, vol. 2 (1997), pp.1045–66.
Filippini, Jean-Pierre, 'Il ceto mercantile ebraico di Livorno dall'Unità d'Italia alle leggi razziali del 1938', in Mezzabotta (ed.), *Italia Judaica* (1993), pp.236–44.
Foà, Chiara, *Gli ebrei e i matrimoni misti: l'esogamia nella comunità torinese (1866–1898)* (Turin: Zamorani, 2001).

Foà, Salvatore, *Gli ebrei nel Risorgimento italiano* (Assisi and Rome: Carucci, 1978).
Forgacs, David, 'Building the Body of the Nation: Lombroso's *L'antisemitismo* and Fin-de-Siècle Italy', in Cheyette and Valman (eds), *Image of the Jew in European Liberal Culture* (2004), pp.96–110.
Formiggini, Gina, 'Documenti e Testimonianze: Ricordo di Carlo e Nello Rosselli', *Rassegna Mensile di Israel*, 34, 6 (1968), pp.351–8.
Frankel, Jonathan, 'The Crisis of 1881–82 as a Turning Point in Modern Jewish History', in David Berger (ed.), *The Legacy of Jewish Migration: 1881 and its Impact* (New York: Brooklyn College Press, 1983), pp.9–22.
Frankel, Jonathan, *The Damascus Affair: 'Ritual Murder', Politics, and the Jews in 1840* (Cambridge: Cambridge University Press, 1997).
Frankel, Jonathan, 'Assimilation and the Jews in Nineteenth-Century Europe: Towards a New Historiography?', in Frankel and Zipperstein (eds), *Assimilation and Community: The Jews in Nineteenth-Century Europe* (2004), pp.1–37.
Frankel, Jonathan and Zipperstein, Steven J. (eds), *Assimilation and Community: The Jews in Nineteenth-Century Europe* (Cambridge: Cambridge University Press, 2004).
Frattarelli Fischer, Lucia, 'Reti toscane e reti internazionali degli ebrei di Livorno nel Seicento', *Zakhor*, 6 (2003), pp.93–116.
Frattarelli Fischer, Lucia and Vaccari, Olimpia (eds), *Sul filo della scrittura: fonti e temi per la storia delle donne a Livorno* (Pisa: Edizione Plus, 2005).
Freedland, Jonathan, *Jacob's Gift: A Journey into the Heart of Belonging* (London: Hamish Hamilton, 2005).
Freud, Ernst L. (ed.), *Letters of Sigmund Freud 1873–1939* (London: Hogarth Press, 1961).
Friedman, Isaiah, 'Herzl and the Uganda Controversy', in Robertson and Timms (eds), *Theodor Herzl and the Origins of Zionism* (1997), pp.39–53.
Frigessi, Delia, 'Cattaneo, Lombroso e la questione ebraica', in Burgio (ed.), *Nel nome della razza* (2000), pp.247–64.
Fubini, Guido, *La condizione giuridica dell'ebraismo italiano* (Turin: Rosenberg and Sellier, 1998).
Funaro, Liana Elda, '"Vita e legge": note per una storia della comunità ebraica livornese nel secondo Ottocento', *Rassegna Storica Toscana*, 48, 1 (2002), pp.145–73.
Funaro, Liana Elda, '"Speculiamo, amiamo, combattiamo": lettere inedite di Elia Benamozegh', *Nuovi Studi Livornesi*, 10 (2002–2003), pp.131–48.
Funaro, Liana Elda, 'Il ruolo degli ebrei livornesi: due percorsi individuali su uno sfondo mediterraneo', in Dinelli and Bernardini (eds), *I laboratori toscani della democrazia e del Risorgimento* (2004), pp.79–98.
Funaro, Liana Elda, '"Compagna e partecipe": donne della comunità ebraica livornese nel secondo Ottocento', in Frattarelli Fischer and Vaccari (eds), *Sul filo della scrittura* (2005), pp.319–39.
Funaro, Liana Elda, 'Massoneria e minoranze religiose nel secolo XIX', in Conti (ed.), *La massoneria a Livorno* (2007), pp.343–416.

Funaro, Liana Elda, 'A Mediterranean Diaspora: Jews from Leghorn in the Second Half of the Nineteenth Century', in Petricioli (ed.), *L'Europe méditerranéenne: Mediterranean Europe* (2008), pp.95–110.
Gabba, Carlo Francesco, 'Un appello agli israeliti italiani a proposito del Sionismo', *La Rassegna Nazionale*, 1 October 1905, pp.341–50.
Gabba, Carlo Francesco, 'Ancora del Sionismo in Italia', *La Rassegna Nazionale*, 1 April 1906, pp.353–68.
Garti, Isacco, 'Il carteggio Ascoli-Luzzatto', *Italia*, 1, 1 (1976), pp.70–92.
Gatt-Rutter, John, *Italo Svevo: A Double Life* (Oxford: Clarendon, 1988).
Gavazzeni, Franco and Gorni, Guglielmo (eds), *Le tradizioni del testo: studi di letteratura offerti a Domenico De Robertis* (Milan and Naples: Ricciardini, 1993).
Gay, Peter, *Freud: A Life for Our Time* (London and Melbourne: Dent, 1988).
Ghisalberti, Carlo, 'Sulla condizione giuridica degli ebrei in Italia dall'emancipazione alla persecuzione: spunti per una riconsiderazione', in Mezzabotta (ed.), *Italia Judaica* (1993), pp.19–31.
Gilman, Sander L., *Jewish Self-Hatred: Anti-Semitism and the Hidden Language of the Jews* (Baltimore, MD, and London: Johns Hopkins University Press, 1986).
Gilman, Sander L., *The Jew's Body* (New York and London: Routledge, 1991).
Gilman, Sander L., *Freud, Race and Gender* (Princeton, NJ: Princeton University Press, 1993).
Ginzberg Migliorino, Ellen, 'L'Antisemitismo e la comunità ebraica a Trieste nei primi anni del Novecento', in Todeschini and Zorattini (eds), *Il mondo ebraico* (1991), pp.433–55.
Ginzburg, Natalia, *Lessico famigliare* (Turin: Einaudi, 1963).
Giribaldi Sardi, Maria Luisa, *Scuola e vita nella comunità ebraica di Ast (1800–1930)* (Turin: Rosenberg and Sellier, 1993).
Gordon, Milton M., *Assimilation in American Life: The Role of Race, Religion and National Origins* (New York: Oxford University Press, 1964).
Graetz, Michael, 'The History of an Estrangement between Two Jewish Communities: German and French Jewry during the Nineteenth Century', in Katz (ed.), *Toward Modernity* (1987), pp.159–69.
Graetz, Michael, 'Jewry in the Modern Period: The Role of the "Rising Class" in the Politicization of Jews in Europe', in Frankel and Zipperstein (eds), *Assimilation and Community* (2004), pp.156–76.
Greilsammer, Ilan, 'Réflexions sur l'identité juive de Léon Blum', in Cabanel and Bordes-Benayoun (eds), *Un modèle d'intégration* (2004), pp.159–67.
Gross, John, *A Double Thread: A Childhood in Mile End – and Beyond* (London: Chatto & Windus, 2001).
Grunfeld, Frederic V., *Prophets without Honour: A Background to Freud, Kafka, Einstein and Their World* (New York: Holt, Rinehart & Winston, 1979).
Guetta, Alessandro, *Filosofia e qabbalah: saggio sul pensiero di Elia Benamozegh* (Milan: Thalassa de Paz, 2000).
Guetta Sadun, Silvia, 'L'educazione ebraica: il Talmud Torà di Firenze dal 1860 al 1922', in Mezzabotta (ed.), *Italia Judaica* (1993), pp.82–96.
Gunzberg, Lynn M., *Strangers at Home: Jews in the Italian Literary Imagination* (Berkeley, CA: University of California Press, 1992).

Hagani, Baruch, *Le sionisme politique et son fondateur* (Paris: Librairie Payot, 1917).
Herf, Jeffrey (ed.), *Anti-Semitism and Anti-Zionism in Historical Perspective: Convergence and Divergence* (London and New York: Routledge, 2007).
Herzl, Theodor, *The Jewish State: An Attempt at a Modern Solution of the Jewish Question*, 4th edn (London: Searl, 1946; first edn 1896).
Herwald, T.B., 'Zionism in Manchester 1891–1900', http://www.art.man.ac.uk/RELTHEOL/JEWISH/EXHIBITION/5HERWALD.HTML (consulted 31/07/2006).
Hobsbawm, E.J., *The Age of Capital 1848–1875* (London: Abacus, 1995).
Honess, Claire E. and Jones, Verina R. (eds), *Le donne delle minoranze: le ebree e le protestanti d'Italia* (Turin: Claudiana, 1999).
Hyman, Paula, *From Dreyfus to Vichy: The Remaking of French Jewry, 1906–1939* (New York: Columbia University Press, 1979).
Hyman, Paula E., *Gender and Assimilation in Modern Jewish History: The Roles and Representation of Women* (Seattle, WA, and London: University of Washington Press, 1995).
Hyman, Paula E., 'The Social Contexts of Assimilation: Village Jews and City Jews in Alsace', in Frankel and Zipperstein (eds), *Assimilation and Community* (2004), pp.110–29.
Jabalot, Ferdinando, *Degli ebrei nel loro rapporto colle nazioni cristiane del Reverendissimo padre F. Jabalot* (Rome: Poggioli, 1825).
Janik, Allan, 'Viennese Culture and the Jewish Self-Hatred Hypothesis: A Critique', in Oxaal, Pollak and Botz (eds), *Jews, Antisemitism and Culture in Vienna* (1987), pp.75–88.
Jarrassé, Dominique, 'Le temple israélite. Approche comparative d'un symbole et d'un instrument de l'israélitisme dans l'Europe et l'Amerique du XIX siècle', in Cabanel and Bordes-Benayoun (eds), *Un modèle d'intégration* (2004), pp.65–75.
Jemolo, Arturo Carlo, *Anni di prova* (Verona: Pozza, 1969).
Jesurum, Stefano, *Essere ebrei in Italia* (Milan: Longanesi, 1987).
Kaplan, Marion A., *The Making of the Jewish Middle Class: Women, Family and Identity in Imperial Germany* (Oxford: Oxford University Press, 1991).
Katz, Jacob, *Emancipation and Assimilation: Studies in Modern Jewish History* (Farnborough: Gregg, 1972).
Katz, Jacob, *Out of the Ghetto: The Social Background of Jewish Emancipation, 1770–1870* (Cambridge, MA: Harvard University Press, 1973).
Katz, Jacob, *From Prejudice to Destruction: Anti-Semitism, 1700–1933* (Cambridge, MA: Harvard University Press, 1980).
Katz, Jacob (ed.), *Toward Modernity: The European Jewish Model* (New Brunswick, NJ, and Oxford: Transaction Books, 1987).
Kertzer, David I., *The Kidnapping of Edgardo Mortara* (London: Picador, 1997).
Kertzer, David I., *Unholy War: The Vatican's Role in the Rise of Modern Anti-Semitism* (London: Macmillan, 2002).
Kieval, Hillel J., 'The Importance of Place: Comparative Aspects of the Ritual Murder Trial in Modern Central Europe', in Endelman (ed.), *Comparing Jewish Societies* (1997), pp.135–65.

Klein, Charlotte, 'Damascus to Kiev: Civiltà Cattolica on Ritual Murder', *Wiener Library Bulletin*, 27, 32 (1974), pp.18–25.
Klopp, Charles (ed.), *Bele Antiche Stòrie: Writing, Borders, and the Instability of Identity: Trieste, 1719–2007* (New York: Bordighera, 2008).
Laras, Giuseppe, 'Il movimento sionistico', *Rassegna Mensile di Israel*, 47, 7–12 (1981), pp.74–80.
Lattes, Dante, *Il Sionismo* (Rome: Cremonese, 1928), 2 vols.
Lattes, Giuseppe, *Due Discorsetti letti nel tempio israelitico di Chieri dal Rabbino Giuseppe Lattes richiesti da alcuni suoi diletti Alunni e stampati a loro diligenza e spese in atto di stima* (Turin: Tipografia di Giuseppe Coen, 1848).
Lattes, Guglielmo, *Catechismo israelitico pratico proposto per le scuole elementari religiose* (Livorno: Belforte, 1895).
Lattes, Guglielmo, *Tra la fede e l'amore: scene della vita ebraica moderna* (Florence: Paggi, 1903).
Lattes, Guglielmo, *Cuore d'Israele: libro per ragazzi israeliti* (Livorno: Belforte, 1908).
Lattes, Guglielmo, *Dall'East End ... al Cantico dei Cantici: Scritti e racconti del Novellatore Israelita* (Casale Monferrato: Rossi & Lavagno, 1910).
Lattes, Guglielmo, *Memorie d'un insegnante* (Asti: Segre, 1922).
Lepschy, Giulio, *Mother Tongues and Other Reflections on the Italian Language* (Toronto: University of Toronto Press, 2002).
Levi, Alessandro, *Ricordi della vita e dei tempi di Ernesto Nathan* (Florence: La Nuova Italia, 1927).
Levi, Alessandro, *Ricordi dei fratelli Rosselli* (Florence: La Nuova Italia, 1947).
Levi D'Ancona, Luisa, '"Notabili e dame" nella filantropia ebraica ottocentesca: casi di studio in Francia, Italia e Inghilterra', *Quaderni storici*, 38, 3 (2003), pp.741–76.
Levi, David, *Ausonia. Vita d'Azione (dal 1848–1870)* (Rome: Loescher, 1882).
Levi, Enzo, *Memorie di una vita (1889–1947)* (Modena: STEM Mucchi, 1972).
Levi, Fabio, 'Gli ebrei nella vita economica dell'Ottocento', in Vivanti (ed.), *Storia d'Italia, Annali 11, Gli ebrei in Italia*, vol. 2 (1997), pp.1171–210.
Levi, Fabio 'Anti-Jewish Persecution and Italian Society', in Zimmerman (ed.), *Jews in Italy under Fascist and Nazi Rule* (2005), pp.199–206.
Levi, Giuseppe, *Autobiografia di un padre di famiglia* (Florence: Le Monnier, 2003; first edn 1868).
Levis Sullam, Simon, *Una comunità immaginata: gli ebrei a Venezia (1900–1938)* (Milan: Unicopli, 2001).
Levis Sullam, Simon, '"La loro *vera* lingua": storia e memoria linguistica degli ebrei in Italia tra Ottocento e Novecento', *Rassegna Mensile di Israel*, 69, 1 (2003), pp.49–72.
Levis Sullam, Simon, 'Arnaldo Momigliano e la "nazionalizzazione parallela": autobiografia, religione, storia', *Passato e presente*, 25, 70 (2007), pp.59–82.
Levis Sullam, Simon, '"Their *True* Tongue": History, Memory, Language, and the Jews of Italy', in Myers, Ciavolella, Riell and Symcox (eds), *Acculturation and Its Discontents* (2008), pp.183–202.

Liedtke, Rainer and Wendehorst, Stephen (eds), *The Emancipation of Catholics, Jews and Protestants: Minorities and the Nation State in Nineteenth-Century Europe* (Manchester and New York: Manchester University Press, 1999).

Lindeman, Albert S., *Anti-Semitism before the Holocaust* (Harlow: Longman, 2000).

Link, Jere H., 'Anti-Semitism in German Literary Politics: The Special Case of the Deutsche Schillerstiftung', *Leo Baeck Institute Year Book*, 35 (1990), pp.371–83.

Litvak, Meir, 'The Islamic Republic of Iran and the Holocaust: Anti-Semitism and Anti-Zionism', in Herf (ed.), *Anti-Semitism and Anti-Zionism* (2007), pp.250–67.

Livi Bacci, Massimo, 'La demografia degli ebrei italiani agli inizi del secolo', *Rassegna Mensile di Israel*, 47, 7–12 (1981), pp.81–5.

Loewe, Louis (ed.), *Diaries of Sir Moses and Lady Montefiore* (London: The Jewish Historical Society of England, 1983).

Lombroso, Cesare, *L'antisemitismo e le scienze moderne* (Turin and Rome: Roux, 1894).

Lombroso, Paola and Gina, *Cesare Lombroso. Appunti sulla vita. Le Opere* (Milan, Turin and Rome: Bocca, 1906).

Lowenthal, Marvin (ed. and trans.), *The Diaries of Theodor Herzl* (New York: Dial Press, 1956).

Luzzati, Michele, 'La ricerca storiografica sugli ebrei italiani del Medioevo e del Rinascimento tra la fine dell'800 e l'inizio del '900', *Rassegna Mensile di Israel*, 47, 7–12 (1981), pp.129–35.

Luzzati, Michele (ed.), *Gli ebrei di Pisa (secoli IX–XX)* (Pisa: Pacini, 1998).

Luzzati, Michele (ed.), *Ebrei di Livorno tra due censimenti (1841–1938): memoria familiare e identità* (Livorno. Belforte, 1990).

Luzzati, Michele, 'Integrazione e assimilazione nella Livorno ebraica: proposte per una discussione', in Luzzati (ed.), *Ebrei di Livorno tra due censimenti (1841–1938)* (1990), pp.9–22.

Luzzati, Michele and Galasso, Cristina (eds), *Donne nella storia degli ebrei d'Italia. Atti del IX convegno internazionale Italia Judaica* (Florence: Giuntina, 2007).

Luzzatti, Luigi, *Dio nella libertà: studio sulle relazioni tra lo Stato e le Chiese* (Bologna: Zanichelli, 1926).

Luzzatti, Luigi, *Memorie autobiografiche e carteggi* (Bologna: Zanichelli, 1929), 2 vols.

Luzzatto, Amos, 'Il rinnovamento culturale dell'ebraismo italiano tra le due guerre', in Bidussa, Luzzatto and Luzzatto Voghera, *Oltre il ghetto* (1992), pp.97–153.

Luzzatto, Samuel David, *Epistolario italiano francese latino pubblicato da'suoi figli* (Padua: Fratelli Salmin, 1890), 2 vols.

Luzzatto Voghera, Gadi, 'Aspetti della cultura ebraica in Italia nel secolo XIX', in Vivanti (ed.), *Storia d'Italia, Annali 11, Gli ebrei in Italia*, vol. 2 (1997), pp.1211–41.

Luzzatto Voghera, Gadi, *Il prezzo dell'eguaglianza: il dibattito sull'emancipazione degli ebrei in Italia (1781–1848)* (Milan: FrancoAngeli, 1998).

Luzzatto Voghera, Gadi, 'Italian Jews', in Liedtke and Wendehorst (eds), *Emancipation of Catholics, Jews and Protestants* (1999), pp.169–87.

Luzzatto Voghera, Gadi, 'Per uno studio sulla presenza e attività di parlamentari ebrei in Italia e in Europa', *Rassegna Mensile di Israel*, 69, 1 (2003), pp.73–92.

Luzzatto Voghera, Gadi, 'L'Israélitisme en Italie aux xix e xx siècles', in Cabanel and Bordes-Benayoun (eds), *Un modèle d'intégration* (2004), pp.197–207.

Maccoby, Hyam, *Antisemitism and Modernity: Innovation and Continuity* (London and New York: Routledge, 2006).

Mack, Michael, *German Idealism and the Jew: The Inner Anti-Semitism of Philosophy and German Jewish Response* (Chicago, IL, and London: University of Chicago Press, 2003).

Maida, Bruno, *Dal ghetto alla città: gli ebrei torinesi nel secondo Ottocento* (Turin: Zamorani, 2001).

Maifreda, Germano, *Gli ebrei e l'economia milanese: L'Ottocento* (Milan: FrancoAngeli, 2000).

Malino, Frances and Sorkin, David (eds), *From East to West: Jews in a Changing Europe, 1750–1870* (Oxford: Blackwell, 1990).

Malino, Frances, 'French Jews', in Liedtke and Wendehorst (eds), *Emancipation of Catholics, Jews and Protestants* (1999), pp.83–99.

Manzini, Vincenzo, *L'Omicidio rituale e i sacrifici umani, con particolare riguardo alle accuse contro gli ebrei* (Turin: Bocca, 1925).

Margolies, Morris B., *Samuel David Luzzatto: Traditionalist Scholar* (New York: Ktav, 1979).

Margulies, S.H., *Discorso inaugurale pronunziato dal Rabbino Maggiore, Dott. S.H. Margulies in occasione del suo Insediamento a Firenze* (Florence: Tipografia Cooperativa, 1890).

Margulies, S.H., *Parole dette dal Rabb. Magg. Cavaliere Dott. S.H. Margulies nella solenne commemorazione del 50 anniversario dello Statuto nel tempio israelitico di Firenze* (Florence: Galletti and Cassuto, 1898).

Margulies, S.H., *Herzl e il sionismo* (Florence: Galletti and Cassuto, 1904).

Marrus, Michael, *The Politics of Assimilation: A Study of the French Jewish Community at the Time of the Dreyfus Affair* (Oxford: Clarendon Press, 1971).

Massarani, Tullo, 'Notizie autobiografiche d'un patriota', in Raffaello Barbiera (ed.), *Ricordi cittadini e patriottici* (Florence: Le Monnier, 1908), vol. 2, pp.3–20.

Massarani, Tullo, *Ricordi cittadini e patriottici*, edited by Raffaello Barbiera (Florence: Le Monnier, 1908), 2 vols.

Massarani, Tullo, *Una nobile vita. Carteggio inedito*, edited by Raffaello Barbiera (Florence: Le Monnier, 1909), 2 vols.

Materini Zotta, Maria Fausta, *L'Ente comunitario ebraico: la legislazione negli ultimi due secoli* (Milan: Giuffrè, 1983).

Mayer Modena, Maria, 'Le parlate giudeo-italiane' in Vivanti (ed.), *Storia d'Italia, Annali 11, Gli ebrei in Italia*, vol. 2 (1997), pp.937–63.

Mazzamuto, Salvatore, 'Ebraismo e diritto dalla prima emancipazione all'età repubblicana', in Vivanti (ed.), *Storia d'Italia, Annali 11, Gli ebrei in Italia*, vol. 2 (1997), pp.1767–827.

Mazzamuto, Salvatore, 'I giuristi dell'ateneo pisano e la questione ebraica', in Luzzati (ed.), *Gli ebrei di Pisa* (1998), pp.211–39.

McClymer, John F., 'The Paradox of Ethnicity in the United States: The French-Canadian Experience in Worcester, 1870–1914', in D'Innocenzo and Sirefman (eds), *Immigration and Ethnicity* (1992), pp.15–23.

Mendes-Flohr, Paul and Reinharz, Jehuda (eds), *The Jew in the Modern World: A Documentary History*, second edn (New York and Oxford: Oxford University Press, 1995).

Menichelli, Gian-Carlo, 'La reception de l'Affaire en Italie', in Drouin (ed.), *L'Affaire Dreyfus de A à Z* (1994).

Meriggi, Marco, 'Bourgeoisie, bürgertum, borghesia: i contesti sociali dell'emancipazione ebraica', in Sofia and Toscano (eds), *Stato nazionale ed emancipazione ebraica* (1992), pp.155–69.

Meyer, Michael A., *The Origins of The Modern Jew: Jewish Identity and European Culture in Germany, 1749–1824* (Detroit, MI: Wayne State University Press, 1967).

Meyer, Michael A., *Response to Modernity: A History of the Reform Movement in Judaism* (New York and Oxford: Oxford University Press, 1988).

Meyer, Michael A., *Judaism within Modernity: Essays on Jewish History and Religion* (Detroit, MI: Wayne State University Press, 2001).

Mezzabotta, Liliana (ed.), *Italia Judaica: gli ebrei nell'Italia unita 1870–1945. Atti del IV convegno internazionale* (Rome: Pubblicazioni degli Archivi di Stato, 1993).

Miccoli, Giovanni, 'Santa Sede, questione ebraica e antisemitismo fra Otto e Novecento', in Vivanti (ed.), *Storia d'Italia, Annali 11, Gli ebrei in Italia*, vol. 2 (1997), pp.1369–574.

Migliau, Bice (ed.), *La cultura ebraica nell'editoria italiana (1955–1990)* (Rome: Ministero per i Beni Culturali e Ambientali, 1992).

Milano, Attilio, 'Gli enti culturali ebraici in Italia nell'ultimo trentennio (1907–1937)', *Rassegna Mensile di Israel*, 12, 6 (February–March 1938), pp.253–69.

Milano, Attilio, 'Un secolo di stampa periodica ebraica in Italia', *Rassegna Mensile di Israel*, 12, 7–9 (April–June 1938), pp.96–133.

Milano, Attilio, *Storia degli ebrei in Italia* (Turin: Einaudi, 1963).

Milano, Attilio, 'La Costituzione "Livornina" del 1593', *Rassegna Mensile di Israel*, 34, 7 (1968), pp.394–410.

Milano, Roberto, 'Dal diario di Elia Tagliacozzo volontario garibaldino', *Rassegna Mensile di Israel*, 64, 1 (1998), pp.87–93.

Millo, Anna, 'Elites politiche ed elites economiche ebraiche a Trieste alla fine del XIX secolo', in Todeschini and Zorattini (eds), *Il mondo ebraico* (1991), pp.381–401.

Mincer, Laura, 'La tradizione rivisitata nel teatro Yiddish di Moni Ovadia',

Rassegna Mensile di Israel, 66, 20 (2000), pp.145–54.
Miniati, Monica, 'Le "emancipate": le ebree italiane fra Ottocento e Novecento', in Honess and Jones (eds), *Le donne delle minoranze* (1999), pp.243–54.
Miniati, Monica, *'Les Emancipées': les femmes juives italiennes aux XIXe e XXe siècles (1848–1924)* (Paris: Honoré Champion, 2003).
Mola, Aldo A. (ed.), *Isacco Artom e gli ebrei italiani dai Risorgimenti al fascismo* (Foggia: Bastogi, 2002).
Mola, Aldo A., 'Lelio Della Torre: un rabbino tra Risorgimento e Terza Italia', in Mola (ed.), *Isacco Artom e gli ebrei italiani* (2002), pp.27–38.
Molinari, Maurizio, *Ebrei in Italia: un problema di identità (1870–1938)* (Florence: Giuntina, 1991).
Momigliano, Arnaldo, 'The Jews of Italy', *New York Review of Books*, 24 October 1985, pp.22–6.
Momigliano, Arnaldo, *Essays on Ancient and Modern Judaism*, edited and with an introduction by Silvia Berti, translated by Maura Masella-Gayley (Chicago, IL, and London: University of Chicago Press, 1994) (*Pagine ebraiche*, Turin: Einaudi, 1987).
Momigliano, Marco, *Autobiografia di un rabbino italiano* (Palermo: Sellerio, 1986).
Monti Orel, Silvana, *I giornali triestini dal 1863 al 1902* (Trieste: Lint, 1976).
Morpurgo, Marina, 'Ebraismo reform: un'ora con rabbi Barbara', *Keshet*, 3, 1 (2005), pp.75–8.
Moretti, Mauro, 'La dimensione ebraica di un maestro pisano: documenti su Alessandro D'Ancona', in Luzzati (ed.), *Gli ebrei di Pisa* (1998), pp.241–82.
Morris-Reich, Amos, *The Quest for Jewish Assimilation in Modern Social Science* (London: Routledge, 2008).
Mosse, George L., 'Jewish Emancipation: Between *Bildung* and Respectability', in Reinharz and Schatzberg (eds), *The Jewish Response to German Culture* (1985), pp.1–16.
Mosse, George L., 'Gli ebrei e la religione civica del nazionalismo', in Sofia and Toscano (eds), *Stato nazionale ed emancipazione ebraica* (1992), pp.143–54.
Mosse, Werner E., 'Problems and Limits of Assimilation: Hermann and Paul Wallich 1833–1938', *Leo Baeck Institute Year Book*, 33 (1988), pp.43–65.
Mosse, Werner E., 'Terms of Successful Integration: The Tietz Family 1858–1923', *Leo Baeck Institute Year Book*, 34 (1989), pp.131–61.
Mosse, Werner E., 'Integration through Apartheid: The Hirschs of Halberstadt 1780–1930', *Leo Baeck Institute Year Book*, 35 (1990), pp.133–50.
Mosse, Werner E., 'Integration and Identity in Imperial Germany: Towards a Typology', *Leo Baeck Institute Year Book*, 42 (1992), pp.83–93.
Mosse, Werner E., 'From "Schutzjuden" to "Deutsche Staatsbürger Jüdischen Glaubens": The Long and Bumpy Road of Jewish Emancipation in Germany', in Birnbaum and Katznelson (eds), *Paths of Emancipation* (1995), pp.58–93.
Myers, David N., '"The Blessing of Assimilation" Reconsidered: An Inquiry into Jewish Cultural Studies', in Myers and Rowe (eds), *From Ghetto to Emancipation* (1997), pp.17–35.

Myers, David N. and Rowe, William, V. (eds), *From Ghetto to Emancipation: Historical and Contemporary Reconsiderations of the Jewish Community* (Scranton, PA: Scranton University Press, 1997).
Myers, David N. and Ruderman David B. (eds), *The Jewish Past Revisited: Reflections on Modern Jewish Historians* (New Haven, CT, and London: Yale University Press, 1998).
Myers, David, N., Ciavolella, Massimo, Riell, Peter H., and Symcox, Geoffrey (eds), *Acculturation and Its Discontents: The Italian Jewish Experience between Exclusion and Inclusion* (Toronto: University of Toronto Press, 2008).
Nahon, Umberto (ed.), *Scritti in memoria di Sally Mayer (1875–1953): saggi sull'Ebraismo italiano* (Jerusalem: Fondazione Sally Mayer, 1956).
Nahon, Umberto, 'Le lettere di Teodoro Herzl a Felice Ravenna. Il viaggio di Herzl a Roma nel gennaio 1904', *Rassegna Mensile di Israel*, 26, 6 (1960), pp.235–56.
Neppi Modona, Aldo, 'Ricordo di Angiolo Orvieto', *Rassegna Mensile di Israel*, 34, 1 (1968), pp.3–10.
Neppi Modona, Aldo, 'Ricordi personali su S.H. Margulies', *Rassegna Mensile di Israel*, 38, 4 (1972), pp.214–21.
Neppi Modona, Aldo, 'Un testimone di anni lontani', *Israel*, December 1974, p.6.
Neppi Modona, Leo, '17 lettere di S.H. Margulies a David Levi', *Rassegna Mensile di Israel*, 27 (1961), pp.502–12.
Neppi Modona, Leo, '17 lettere di S.H. Margulies a David Levi', *Rassegna Mensile di Israel*, 28, 2 (1962), pp.62–75.
Neppi Modona, Lionella and Oberdorfer, Sonia, '1799: un pogrom in Toscana', *Rassegna Mensile di Israel*, 53 (1988), pp.241–59.
Nicault, Caterine, *La France et le Sionisme 1897–1948: une rencontre manqué?* (Paris: Calmann-Lévy, 1992).
Niewyk, Donald L., 'Solving the "Jewish Problem": Continuity and Change in German Antisemitism, 1871–1945', *Leo Baeck Institute Year Book*, 35 (1990), pp.335–70.
Nordau, Max, *Zionistische Schriften* (Cologne and Leipzig: Jüdischer Verlag, 1909).
Orvieto, Angiolo, *Poesie scelte*, with an introduction by Carlo Pellegrini (Florence: Olschki, 1979).
Ottolenghi, Luisa Mortara, 'Figure e immagini dal secolo XIII al secolo XIX', in Vivanti (ed.), *Storia d'Italia, Annali 11, Gli ebrei in Italia*, vol. 2 (1997), pp.965–1008.
Oxaal, Ivar, Pollak, Michael and Botz, Gerhard (eds), *Jews, Antisemitism and Culture in Vienna* (London and New York: Routledge & Kegan Paul, 1987).
Pacifici, Alfonso, *Israele l'unico: ricerca di una definizione integrale dell'ebraismo* (Florence: Tipografia Giuntina, 1912).
Pacifici, Alfonso, *Interludio: cinquant'anni intorno a un'idea. Lettere agli amici con ricordi personali e riflessioni e un'appendice di scritti scelti editi e inediti* (Turin: Toaz, 1959).
Pacifici, Alfonso, 'Ha-rav Shemuel Zevì Margulies', *Rassegna Mensile di Israel*, 28, 6–7 (1962), pp.251–61.

Pagis, Dan, 'Caratteri generali della poesia ebraica italiana', *Rassegna Mensile di Israel*, 60, 1–2 (1994), pp.6–21.
Parfitt, Tudor, *The Jews in Palestine 1800–1882* (Woodbridge: Boydell Press, 1987).
Paucker, Arnold, 'The Jewish Defense against Antisemitism in Germany, 1893–1933', in Reinharz (ed.), *Living with Antisemitism* (1987), pp.104–32.
Pavan, Ilaria, '"Ebrei" in affari tra realtà e pregiudizio: paradigmi storiografici e percorsi di ricerca dall'Unità alle leggi razziali', *Quaderni storici*, 38, 3 (2003), pp.777–821.
Pellegrini, Paolo, 'Una storia, tante storie: famiglie ebraiche a Terni fra Otto e Novecento', *Rassegna Mensile di Israel*, 70, 2 (2004), pp.63–114.
Penslar, Derek J., 'Anti-Semites on Zionism: From Indifference to Obsession', in Jeffrey Herf (ed.), *Anti-Semitism and Anti-Zionism in Historical Perspective: Convergence and Divergence* (London and New York: Routledge, 2007), pp.1–19.
Pesciatini, Daniela, 'Tra emancipazione e assimilazione: i Cingholi-Ottolenghi', in Luzzati (ed.), *Ebrei di Livorno* (1990), pp.157–71.
Petricioli, Marta (ed.), *L'Europe méditerranéenne: Mediterranean Europe* (Brussels: Peter Lang, 2008).
Pezzino, Paolo and Tacchini, Alvaro (eds), *Leopoldo e Alice Franchetti e il loro tempo* (Città di Castello: Petruzzi Editore, 2002).
Pichetto, Maria Teresa, *Alle radici dell'odio: Preziosi e Benigni antisemiti* (Milan: FrancoAngeli, 1983).
Plati, Gioietta and Sturmann, Carmela, 'I Piperno, i Cave e i Disegni: storie di famiglia', in Luzzati (ed.), *Ebrei di Livorno* (1990), pp.65–74.
Po-chia, R., *The Myth of Ritual Murder: Jews and Magic in Reformation Germany* (New Haven, CT, and London: Yale University Press, 1988).
Poliakov, Léon, *The History of Anti-Semitism* (London: Routledge & Kegan Paul, 1974 [1961]), 2 vols.
Pugliese, Stanislao G. (ed.), *The Most Ancient of Minorities: The Jews of Italy* (Westport, CT, and London: Greenwood Press, 2002).
Pulzer, Peter, *The Rise of Political Anti-Semitism in Germany and Austria*, revised edn (London: Peter Halban, 1988).
Ragins, Sanford, *Jewish Responses to Anti-Semitism in Germany, 1870–1914: A Study in the History of Ideas* (Cincinnati, OH: Hebrew Union College Press, 1980).
Raphael, Frederic, *The Necessity of Anti-Semitism* (Southampton: University of Southampton, Central Printing Unit, 1989).
Raspi, Maurizio (ed.), *L'Affaire Dreyfus in Italia* (Pisa: ETS Editrice, 1991).
Reinharz, Jehuda, *Fatherland or Promised Land: The Dilemma of the German Jew, 1893–1914* (Ann Arbor, MI: University of Michigan Press, 1975).
Reinharz, Jehuda (ed.), *Living with Antisemitism: Modern Jewish Responses* (Hanover and London: University Press of New England, 1987).
Reinharz, Jehuda, 'Ideology and Structure in German Zionism, 1882–1933', in Reinharz and Shapira (eds), *Essential Papers on Zionism* (1996), pp.268–97.
Reinharz, Jehuda and Schatzberg, Walter (eds), *The Jewish Response to German Culture: From the Enlightenment to the Second World War* (Hanover, MD, and London: University Press of New England, 1985).

Reinharz, Jehuda and Shapira, Anita (eds), *Essential Papers on Zionism* (London: Cassell, 1996).
Richarz, Monika, 'Un profilo sociale degli ebrei tedeschi 1850–1933', in Toscano (ed.), *Integrazione e identità* (1998), pp.73–83.
Righini, Eugenio, *Antisemitismo e Semitismo nell'Italia politica moderna* (Milan-Palermo: Sandron, 1901).
Robertson, Ritchie, 'Reinventing the Jews. From Moses Mendelssohn to Theodor Herzl', in Ritchie Robertson and Edward Timms (eds), *Theodor Herzl and the Origins of Zionism* (Edinburgh: Edinburgh University Press, 1997), pp.3–11.
Robertson, Ritchie, *The 'Jewish Question' in German Literature 1749–1939: Emancipation and its Discontents* (Oxford: Oxford University Press, 1999).
Robertson, Ritchie and Timms, Edward (eds), *Theodor Herzl and the Origins of Zionism* (Edinburgh: Edinburgh University Press, 1997).
Rodrigue, Aron, 'Abraham de Camondo of Istanbul: the Transformation of Jewish Philanthropy', in Malino and Sorkin (eds), *From East to West* (1990), pp.46–56.
Rodrigue, Aron, 'From *Millet* to Minority: Turkish Jewry', in Birnbaum and Katznelson (eds), *Paths of Emancipation* (1995), pp.238–61.
Rodrigue, Aron, 'Rearticulations of French Jewish Identities after the Dreyfus Affair', *Jewish Social Studies: History, Culture, and Society*, new series, 2 (Fall 1996), pp.1–26.
Rodrigue, Aron, 'Totems, Taboos, and Jews: Salomon Reinach and the Politics of Scholarship in Fin-de-Siècle France', *Jewish Social Studies: History, Culture and Society*, new series, 10 (Winter 2004), pp.1–19.
Rogoni, Sandro, 'Eugenio Artom', in Ballini (ed.), *Fiorentini del Novecento* (2002), pp.11–21.
Röhl, John C.G., 'Herzl and Kaiser Wilhelm II: A German Protectorate in Palestine?', in Robertson and Timms (eds), *Theodor Herzl and the Origins of Zionism* (1997), pp.27–38.
Romagnani, Gian Paolo, 'Italian Protestants', in Liedtke and Wendehorst (eds), *Emancipation of Catholics, Jews and Protestants* (1999), pp.148–68.
Romanelli, Raffaele, 'Urban Patricians and "Bourgeois" Society: A Study of Wealthy Elites in Florence, 1862–1904', *Journal of Modern Italian Studies*, 1, 1 (1995), pp.3–21.
Romano, Giorgio, 'I rapporti di Teodoro Herzl coi sionisti italiani (con trenta lettere inedite)', *Rassegna Mensile di Israel*, 26, 9 (1960), pp.494–520.
Ronchetti Vitaloni, Mirella, 'Fonti archivistiche sull'evoluzione demografica economica e culturale della comunità israelitica di Livorno tra '800 e '900', in Mezzabotta (ed.), *Italia Judaica* (1993), pp.245–55.
Rosselli, Amelia, *Memorie*, edited by Marina Calloni (Bologna: Il Mulino, 2001).
Rossi Artom, Elena, *Gli Artom: storia di una famiglia della comunità ebraica di Asti attraverso le sue generazioni (XVI–XX secolo)* (Turin: Zamorani, 1997).
Roth, Cecil, *The History of the Jews of Italy* (Philadelphia, PA: Jewish Publication Society of America, 1946).
Roth, Leon, *Jewish Thought as a Factor in Civilization* (Paris: Unesco, 1961).
Rozenblit, Marsha L., *The Jews of Vienna 1867–1914: Assimilation and Identity* (Albany, NY: State University of New York Press, 1983).

Rozenblit, Marsha L., *Reconstructing a National Identity: The Jews of Habsburg Austria during World War I* (Oxford: Oxford University Press, 2001).
Rozenblit, Marsha L., 'Jewish Assimilation in Habsburg Vienna', in Frankel and Zipperstein (eds), *Assimilation and Community* (2004), pp.225–45.
Ruffini, Francesco, *La libertà religiosa: storia dell'idea* (Milan: Feltrinelli, 1967).
Rürup, Reinhard, 'Verso la modernità: l'esperienza ebraica in Europa dagli inizi dell'emancipazione', in Toscano (ed.), *Integrazione e identità* (1998), pp.32–48.
Sabatello, Eitan F., 'Trasformazioni economiche e sociali degli ebrei in Italia nel periodo dell'emancipazione', in Mezzabotta (ed.), *Italia Judaica* (1993), pp.114–24.
Sacerdoti, Giancarlo, *Ricordi di un ebreo bolognese: illusioni e delusioni 1929–1945* (Rome: Bonacci, 1983).
Salah, Asher, 'Livorno: un convegno internazionale di studi su Elia Benamozegh', *Rassegna Mensile di Israel*, 66, 3 (2000), pp.113–24.
Salvadori, Roberto G., *La comunità ebraica di Pitigliano: dal XVI al XX secolo* (Florence: Giuntina, 1991).
Salvadori, Roberto G., *1799: gli ebrei italiani nella bufera antigiacobina* (Florence: Giuntina, 1999).
Salvadori, Roberto G., *Gli ebrei di Firenze: dalle origini ai giorni nostri* (Florence: Giuntina, 2000).
Salzano, Teresa, 'Un "libro cuore" ebraico', *Rassegna Mensile di Israel*, 47, 7–12 (1981), pp.159–66.
Sarfati, Georges-Elia, *Discours ordinaires et identités juives: la représentation des Juifs et du judaisme dans les dictionnaires et les encylopédies de langue français (du Moyen Age au XX siècle)* (Paris: Berg, 1999).
Sarfatti, Michele, *Gli ebrei nell'Italia fascista: vicende, identità, persecuzione* (Turin: Einaudi, 2000).
Sasso, Gennaro, *Per invigilare me stesso: i taccuini di lavoro di Benedetto Croce* (Bologna: Il Mulino, 1989).
Sassoon, Donald, *The Culture of the Europeans: From 1800 to the Present* (London: Harper, 2006).
Savelli, Laura, 'Una città e i suoi ebrei: Pisa tra le due guerre mondiali' in Luzzati, *Gli ebrei di Pisa*, pp.347–73.
Scalise, D., *Il caso Mortara: la vera storia del bambino ebreo rapito dal papa* (Milan: Mondadori, 1997).
Scandaliato Ciciani, Isotta (ed.), *Italia Judaica: gli ebrei in Italia dalla segregazione alla prima emancipazione. Atti del III convegno internazionale* (Rome: Pubblicazioni degli Archivi di Stato, 1989).
Scardozzi, Mirella, 'Una storia di famiglia: i Franchetti dalle coste del Mediterraneo all'Italia liberale', *Quaderni storici*, 38, 3 (2003), pp.697–740.
Scardozzi, Mirella, 'Amiche: lettere di Marianna, Regina e Lina Uzielli a Emilia Toscanelli Peruzzi', in Luzzati and Galasso (eds), *Donne nella storia degli ebrei d'Italia* (2007), pp.373–402.
Scardozzi, Mirella, 'Da merciai "con fagotto" a industriali del cotone', in Luzzati (ed.), *Gli ebrei di Pisa*, pp.159–209.

Schächter, Elizabeth, *Origin and Identity: Essays on Svevo and Trieste* (Leeds: Northern Universities Press, 2000).
Schächter, Elizabeth, 'Perspectives of Nineteenth-Century Italian Jewry', *Journal of European Studies*, 31 (2001), pp.29–69.
Schächter, Elizabeth, 'The Consequences of Unification for the Italian Jewish Communities: The Conferences of Ferrara (1863) and Florence (1867), *The Italianist*, 23 (2003), pp.245–57.
Schnitzler, Arthur, *My Youth in Vienna*, translated by Catherine Hutter (London: Weidenfeld & Nicolson, 1971).
Scholem, Gershom, *From Berlin to Jerusalem: Memories of My Youth*, translated from German by Harry Zohn (New York: Schocken Books, 1980).
Scholem, Gershom, *Walter Benjamin: The Story of a Friendship* (New York: New York Review Books, 2003).
Schorsch, Ismar, *Jewish Reactions to German Anti-Semitism, 1870–1914* (New York and London: Columbia University Press, 1972).
Schorske, Carl E., *Fin-de-Siècle Vienna: Politics and Culture* (Cambridge: Cambridge University Press, 1981).
Schwarz, Guri, 'A proposito di una vivace stagione storiografica: letture dell'emancipazione ebraica negli ultimi vent'anni', *Memoria e Ricerca*, 19 (2005), pp.159–74.
Sciloni, Gaio, 'Scrittori ebrei nell'Italia dell'Unità: reciproche influenze o assimilazione? Un caso Pascoli-Orvieto', in Mezzabotta (ed.), *Italia Judaica* (1993), pp.97–113.
Scocchi, Angelo, *Gli ebrei di Trieste nel Risorgimento italiano* (Trieste: Mazziniana, 1952).
Segre, Augusto, *Memorie di vita ebraica: da Casale a Gerusalemme* (Rome: Bonacci, 1979).
Segre, Dan Vittorio, *Memoirs of a Fortunate Jew: An Italian Story*, translated by the author (London: Paladin, 1988).
Segre, Dan V. 'The Emancipation of the Jews in Italy' in Birnbaum and Katznelson (eds), *Paths of Emancipation* (1995), pp.206–37.
Seroussi, Edwin, 'Singing Modernity: Synagogue Music in Nineteenth- and Early Twentieth-Century Italy', in Myers, Ciavolella, Riell and Symcox (eds), *Acculturation and Its Discontents* (2008), pp.164–82.
Servi, Elena, *Pitigliano ebraica* (Pitigliano: 2002).
Servi, Flaminio, *Gli Israeliti d'Europa nella civiltà. Memorie storiche, biografie e statistiche dal 1789 al 1870* (Turin: Tipografia Foa, 1871).
Servi, Sandro, 'Building a Racial State: Images of the Jew in the Illustrated Fascist Magazine, *La Difesa della Razza*, 1938–1943', in Zimmerman (ed.), *Jews in Italy under Fascist and Nazi Rule* (2005), pp.114–57.
Shimoni, Gideon, *The Zionist Ideology* (Hanover, MD, and London: Brandeis University Press, 1995).
Silber, Michael K., 'The Entrance of Jews into Hungarian Society in *Vormärz*: The Case of the "Casinos"', in Frankel and Zipperstein (eds), *Assimilation and Community* (2004), pp.284–323.
Sofia, Francesca, 'Su assimilazione e autocoscienza ebraica nell'Italia liberale', in Mezzabotta (ed.) *Italia Judaica* (1993), pp.32–47.

Sofia, Francesca and Toscano, Mario (eds), *Stato nazionale ed emancipazione ebraica* (Rome: Bonacci, 1992).
Sori, Ercole, 'Una "comunità crepuscolare": Ancona tra Otto e Novecento', in Anselmi and Bonazzoli (eds), *La presenza ebraica nelle Marche* (1993), pp.189–278.
Soria, Marco, 'I (De) Soria di Livorno: genealogia e storia famigliare', *Rassegna Mensile di Israel*, 72, 1 (2006), pp.136–58.
Sorkin, David, 'Emancipation and Assimilation: Two Concepts and their Application to German-Jewish History', *Leo Baeck Institute Year Book*, 35 (1990), pp.17–33.
Sorkin, David, 'Enlightenment and Emancipation: German Jewry's Formative Age in Comparative Perspective', in Endelman (ed.), *Comparing Jewish Societies* (1997), pp.89–112.
Sorkin, David, 'The Impact of Emancipation on German Jewry: A Reconsideration', in Frankel and Zipperstein (eds), *Assimilation and Community* (2004), pp.177–98.
Speelman, Raniero, 'La lingua della letteratura italo-ebraica contemporanea fra prestiti e traduzione', *Rassegna Mensile di Israel*, 70, 1 (2004), pp.47–77.
Spiegel, Renato (ed.), *Archivio Alfonso Pacifici (1899–1974)* (Jerusalem: Central Archives for the History of the Jewish People, 2000).
Spini, Giorgio, *Risorgimento e protestanti* (Turin: Claudiana, 1998).
Stähler, Axel, 'Orientalist Strategies of Dissociation in a German "Jewish" Novel: *Das Neue Jerusalem* (1905) and its Context', *Forum for Modern Language Studies*, 45, 1 (2008), pp.51–89.
Stanislawski, Michael, *Zionism and the Fin de Siècle: Cosmopolitanism and Nationalism from Nordau to Jabotinsky* (Berkeley, CA, and London: University of California Press, 2001).
Stern, Fritz, *Gold and Iron: Bismarck, Bleichröder, and the Building of the German Empire* (London: Allen & Unwin, 1977).
Stille, Alexander, *Benevolence and Betrayal: Five Italian Jewish Families Under Fascism* (London: Jonathan Cape, 1992).
Stuart Hughes, H., *Consciousness and Society: The Reorientation of European Social Thought 1890–1930* (London: Macgibbon & Kee, 1967).
Stuart Hughes, H., *Prisoners of Hope: The Silver Age of the Italian Jews 1924–1974* (Cambridge, MA and London: Harvard University Press, 1983).
Symcox, Geoffrey, 'The Jews of Italy in the *Triennio Giacobino* 1796–1799', in Myers, Ciavolella, Riell and Symcox (eds), *Acculturation and Its Discontents* (2008), pp.148–63.
Taradel, Ruggero and Raggi, Barbara, *La segregazione amichevole: 'La Civiltà Cattolica' e la questione ebraica 1850–1945* (Rome: Riuniti, 2000).
Tas, Luciano, *Storia degli ebrei in Italia* (Rome: New Compton, 1987).
Thunecke, Jörg, '"Dynamite" or "Affront"? The Jewish Question in Herzl's play *Das neue Ghetto*', in Robertson and Timms (eds), *Theodor Herzl and the Origins of Zionism* (1997), pp.62–73.
Timms, Edward, 'Ambassador Herzl and the Blueprint for a Modern State', in Robertson and Timms (eds), *Theodor Herzl and the Origins of Zionism* (1997), pp.12–26.

Toaff, Ariel, *Pasque di sangue: ebrei d'Europa e omicidi rituali* (Bologna: Il Mulino, 2007).
Todeschini, Giacomo and Ioly Zorattini, Pier Cesare (eds), *Il mondo ebraico: gli ebrei tra Italia nord-orientale e Impero asburgico dal Medioevo all'Età contemporanea* (Pordenone: Studio Tesi, 1991).
Tosatti, Giovanna, 'Comunità israelitica ed amministrazione pubblica nei documenti dell'Archivio Centrale dello Stato', in Mezzabotta (ed.), *Italia Judaica* (1993), pp.142–51.
Toscano, Mario, 'L'uguaglianza senza diversità: stato, società e questione ebraica nell'Italia liberale', *Storia contemporanea*, 25, 5 (1994), pp.685–712.
Toscano, Mario (ed.), *Integrazione e identità: l'esperienza ebraica in Germania e Italia dall'Illuminismo al fascismo* (Milan: FrancoAngeli, 1998).
Toscano, Mario, 'L'antisemitismo nell'Italia contemporanea: note, ipotesi e problemi di ricerca', *Zakhor*, 6 (2003), pp.21–34.
Toscano, Mario, *Ebraismo e antisemitismo in Italia: dal 1848 alla guerra dei sei giorni* (Milan: FrancoAngeli, 2003).
Toscano, Mario, 'Storiografia e identità: revisione e critica dell'autorappresentazione degli ebrei in Italia: alcune considerazioni introduttive', in Benussi (ed.), *Storie di ebrei fra gli asburgo e l'Italia* (2003), pp.45–56.
Toscano, Mario, 'Italian Jewish Identity from the Risorgimento to Fascism, 1848–1938', in Zimmerman (ed.), *Jews in Italy under Fascist and Nazi Rule* (2005), pp.35–54.
Tosh, John, *The Pursuit of History: Aims, Methods and New Directions in the Study of Modern History*, third edn (London and New York: Longman, 2000).
Toury, Jacob, 'Defense Activities of the Österreichisch-Israelitische Union before 1914', in Reinharz (ed.), *Living with Antisemitism* (1987), pp.167–92.
Trebitsch, Michel, 'Les écrivains juifs français de l'affaire Dreyfus à la seconde guerre mondiale', in Becker and Wieviorka (eds), *Les Juifs de France de la Révolution française à nos jours* (1998), pp.169–95.
Ujma, Christina, 'Political versus Cultural Zionism: Reflections on Herzl and Buber', in Robertson and Timms (eds), *Theodor Herzl and the Origins of Zionism* (1997), pp.96–106.
Uretini, Luigi, 'Stereotipi antisemiti ne "Il Mulo" (1907–1925)', in Burgio (ed.), *Nel nome della razza* (2000), pp.293–308.
Vago, Bela (ed.), *Jewish Assimilation in Modern Times* (Boulder, CO: Westview Press, 1981).
Ventura Avanzinelli, Milka, 'Gravidanza, parto, allattamento: testimonianze di donne ebree fiorentine del Novecento', in Luzzati and Galasso (eds), *Donne nella storia degli ebrei d'Italia* (2007), pp.505–47.
Vital, David, *The Origins of Zionism* (Oxford: Clarendon Press, 1975).
Vital, David, *Zionism: The Formative Years* (Oxford: Clarendon Press, 1982).
Vital, David, *Zionism: The Crucial Phase* (Oxford: Clarendon Press, 1987).
Vital, David, *A People Apart: The Jews in Europe, 1789–1939* (Oxford: Oxford University Press, 1999).
Viterbo, Carlo A., 'Un Maestro ancora presente', *Rassegna Mensile di Israel*, 38, 4 (1972), pp.195–206.

Viterbo, Carlo A., 'Una vita per l'ebraismo', *Israel*, December 1974, pp.6–8.
Viterbo, Lionella, 'La nomina del Rabbino Margulies: un *excursus* nella Firenze ebraica di fine Ottocento', *Rassegna Mensile di Israel*, 59 (1993), pp.67–89.
Viterbo, Lionella, 'Cronache dal passato fiorentino: la difficile successione del Rabbino Margulies (1920–1926)', *Rassegna Mensile di Israel*, 60 (1994), pp.148–78.
Vivanti, Corrado (ed.), *Storia d'Italia, Annali 11, Gli ebrei in Italia*, vol. 1, *Dall'alto Medioevo all'età dei ghetti*; vol. 2, *Dall'emancipazone a oggi* (Turin: Einaudi, 1996 and 1997).
Vogelmann, Daniel, 'Breve storia della Giuntina', *UTZ Rivista degli Amici dell'Accademia dell'Ex Libris*, 3 (December 2000), pp.25–8.
Voigt, Klaus, 'Considerazioni sugli ebrei immigrati in Italia', in Sofia and Toscano (eds), *Stato nazionale ed emancipazione ebraica* (1992), pp.223–43.
Volkov, Shulamit, 'Readjusting Cultural Codes: Reflections on Anti-Semitism and Anti-Zionism', in Herf (ed.), *Anti-Semitism and Anti-Zionism* (2007), pp.38–49.
Wald, James, 'Periodicals and Periodicity', in Eliot and Rose (eds), *Companion to the History of the Book* (2007), pp.421–33.
Wassermann, Jakob, *My Life as German and Jew* (London: Allen & Unwin, 1934).
Waters, Mary C. and Jiménez, Tomás R., 'Assessing Immigrant Assimilation: New Empirical and Theoretical Challenges', *Annual Review of Sociology*, 31 (2005), pp.105–25.
Weitzmann, Walter R., 'The Politics of the Viennese Jewish Community, 1890–1914', in Oxaal, Pollak and Botz (eds), *Jews, Antisemitism and Culture in Vienna* (1987), pp.121–51.
Weizmann, Chaim, *Trial and Error: The Autobiography of Chaim Weizmann* (London: Hamish Hamilton, 1949).
Wendehorst, Stephen, 'Emancipation as a Path to National Integration', in Liedtke and Wendehorst (eds), *The Emancipation of Catholics, Jews and Protestants*, pp.188–206.
Wertheimer, Jack, *Unwelcome Strangers: East European Jews in Imperial Germany* (New York and Oxford: Oxford University Press, 1987).
Wiese, Christian, 'Modern Antisemitism and Jewish Reponses in Germany and France, 1880–1914', in Brenner, Caron and Kaufmann (eds), *Jewish Emancipation Reconsidered* (2003), pp.129–53.
Wistrich, Robert S., *Revolutionary Jews from Marx to Trotsky* (London: Harrap, 1976).
Wistrich, Robert S., *Socialism and the Jews: The Dilemmas of Assimilation in Germany and Austria-Hungary* (London and Toronto: Associated University Presses, 1982).
Wistrich, Robert S., *The Jews of Vienna in the Age of Franz Joseph* (Oxford: Oxford University Press, 1989).
Wistrich, Robert S., *Between Redemption and Perdition: Modern Antisemitism and Jewish Identity* (London and New York: Routledge, 1990).
Wistrich, Robert S., *Antisemitism: The Longest Hatred* (London: Methuen, 1991).

Woolf, Judith, *The Memory of the Offence: Primo Levi's If This is a Man* (Market Harborough: Troubador, 2001).

Wyrwa, Ulrich, 'Jewish Experiences in the Italian Risorgimento: Political Practice and National Emotions of Florentine and Leghorn Jewry (1849–1860)', *Journal of Modern Italian Studies*, 8, 1 (2003), pp.16–35.

Yerushalmi, Yosef Hayim, *Zakhor: Jewish History and Jewish Memory* (Seattle, WA, and London: University of Washington Press, 1982).

Zimmerman, Joshua D. (ed.), *Jews in Italy under Fascist and Nazi Rule, 1922–1945* (Cambridge: Cambridge University Press, 2005).

Zipperstein, Steven J., 'Ahad Ha'am and the Politics of Assimilation', in Frankel and Zipperstein (eds), *Assimilation and Community* (2004), pp.344–65.

Zoller, I., 'Per la storia del 28 giugno 1799 a Siena', *Rivista Israelitica*, 7, 4–6 (1910), pp.138–42, 191–3, 240–4.

Zoller, I., 'Nuove fonti per la storia del 28 giugno 1799 a Siena', *Rivista Israelitica*, 8, 1 (1911), pp.30–2.

Zweig, Stefan, *The World of Yesterday* (Lincoln, NE, and London: University of Nebraska Press, 1964).

Zytnicki, Colette, 'Itinéraire d'un poète, du symbolisme au Sionisme: Gustave Kahn (1859–1936)', in Cabanel and Bordes-Benayoun (eds), *Un modèle d'intégration* (2004), pp.147–58.

Index

abduction of Jewish children, 65, 102
acculturation, 4, 14, 20, 53n
Acqui, educational institutions, 76
Action Française, 133, 135
Adorno, Massimo Longo, 225n
Agudath Israel, 219
Ahad Ha'am, 164, 168, 169, 197n, 212
Aiello, Barbara, 71
Alatri, Samuele, 113
Aleichem, Shalom, 169, 200n, 222
Alexander II, Tsar (assassination of), 152
Alexeyevitch, Ivan, 106
Aliens Act (1905), 181
Alliance Israélite Universelle, 6, 29, 39, 63, 64, 65, 69, 87, 232; and anti-Semitism, 102, 112; and Zionism, 161, 162
Almagià, David, 70, 91n
Ancona Jewish community, 2, 42, 54n, 64, 68, 72, 74, 87, 89n, 90n, 91n
Anglo-Jewish Association, 164
Anti-Semitic League (Antisemiten-Liga), 99, 117
anti-Semitism, 5, 85, 97–138; Austrian, 99, 116, 119-20, 122–4, 125; blood libel/ritual murder allegations, 6, 100, 101, 104–9; discrimination in public life, 115–16; French, 133; German, 99, 104, 108, 117–18, 119, 121–2, 138; Italian, 97–100, 107–8; 113–14; 125–7; 129–38; 180–2; 183–5; and Jewish identity, 27–8; Jewish responses, 118–21; origins of term 'anti-Semite', 99; paradox of, 105; Pasqualigo, Francesco (case of), 110–14; political, 7, 98, 100, 140n; publications, 114–15; religious/Catholic Church, 6–7, 97, 98, 100–1, 107, 109, 116, 124; reports of, 116–21
Anti-Zionist Committee, Germany, 160
Archives Israélites, 62n, 162
Arab population, Palestine, 164–5
Arbib, Edoardo, 113
Arias, Gino, 131, 169, 178–80, 183, 186, 189, 211
Armani, Barbara, 54n, 55n
Artom, Beniamin, 77, 84
Artom, Elia, 209, 215, 217, 220, 222
Artom, Eugenio, 17, 50n
Artom, Guido, 28
Artom, Isacco, 15, 21, 28–9, 30, 56n, 76, 110, 115, 138
Artom, Raffaele, 28
Artom family, 28–9, 35, 56n, 84

Asch, Shalom, 169, 200n, 222
Aschenheim, Steven, 3
Ascoli, Graziadio Isaia, 16, 21, 30, 36, 229n
Ascoli, Roberto, 130–1
assimilation, 3–4, 5, 22, 33; civic, 4; cultural, 4, 14; marital, 4, 42–4; structural, 4; Zionist perspective, 42, 129, *passim*
Associazione Nazionalista Italiana (ANI), 129, 132, 135, 233
Asti Jewish community, 78, 83, 84
Auerbach, Berthold, 118–19
Austria: anti-semitism in, 99, 116, 119–20, 122–4, 125; Austrian-Israelite Union, 120, 123–4; as centre for World Zionist Organization, 157, 158–9; Liberal Party, 124; *see also* Vienna
Austrian-Israelite Union, 120, 123–4
autobiographies, 29–31, 116
Autoemancipation (Pinsker), 152
Avanti! (socialist newspaper), 170
Ayò, Ugo, 135–6

Bacher, Eduard, 156
Bachi, Emilio, 217, 218
Balfour Declaration, 164, 165, 194, 199n, 222, 223
Ballerini, Raffaele, 107
Barrès, Maurice, 128
Baruch, Yosef Marcou, 166, 167, 171, 193, 206
Bauman, Zygmunt, 24, 54n
Beilis, Mendel, 106, 143n
Bein, Alexander, 174
Bemporad, Memo, 34, 35
Benamozegh, Elia ben Abraham, 15–16, 37, 48n, 49n, 67, 168, 206
Benedikt, Moritz, 156
Ben-Gurion, David, 157
Benigni, Umberto, 107
Berkowitz, Michael, 155, 195n
Berr, Berr Isaac, 24–5
Besso, Marco, 30–1, 34
Bidussa, David, 165–6
Bildung (self-formation), 3, 17, 76, 130, 154, 212
Bini, Venanzio, 126
Birnbaum, Nathan, 152
Birnbaum, Pierre, 53n, 122, 196n, 198n, 233, 234n
Bissolati, Leonida, 114
Bloch, Joseph Samuel, 119, 120, 123

blood libel accusations, 6, 100, 101, 104–9, 121–2
Blum, Léon, 233
Blumenfeld, Kurt, 159
Board of Deputies of British Jews, 63, 164
Böckel, Otto, 121
Bolaffio, Giacomo, 209, 216
Bologna Jewish community, 74; Congress (1917), 76; re-establishment of community in, 85
Borsa di Studio Palestinese (Palestinian Scholarship Fund), 214, 216
Bromley, Yulian, 5
Buber, Martin, 159–60, 167, 168, 222, 229n
Budapest, anti-Semitic riots, 106

Camber, Riccardo, 124
Canepa, Andrew, 98, 100, 108, 109, 111, 137, 146n
Canosa, Romano, 98
Cantimori, Delio, 97, 110
Cantoni, Alberto, 37, 59n
Cantoni, Lelio, 15, 41, 48n, 56n, 57n, 72, 73, 74
Capuzzo, Ester, 52n, 98
Carlo Alberto, 3, 20
Carpi Jewish community, 83
Casa Editrice Israel, 222
Casa Editrice La Giuntina, 212
Casale Monferrato Jewish community, 33, 77, 156
Cassin, Marco, 137
Cassuto, Umberto, 180, 206, 209, 215, 216, 217
Castelbolognesi, Gustavo, 209
Castelli, David, 30
Castelnuovo, Enrico, 37, 171, 200n
Castiglioni, Vittorio, 209
Catalan, Tullia, 42, 67, 75, 166
Catholic Church: anti-Semitism, 6–7, 97, 98, 100–1, 103, 107, 109, 111, 115, 116, 122, 124, 128, 137, 150n; Papal Bulls, 105; press, 103–4, 107
Cavaglion, Alberto, 30, 39, 98, 116, 127, 139n, 145n, 150n, 166, 170, 182, 206
Caviglia, Stefano, 4, 25, 51n, 52n, 76, 98, 131, 209
Cavour, Camillo Benso di, 15, 18, 29, 48n, 52n, 110, 183
Central Association of German Citizens of the Jewish Faith (Centralverein deutscher Staatsbürger jüdischen Glaubens), 122, 155–6, 160
Central Consistory, France, 63, 73, 162
Cesarani, David, 62n, 229n
Chajes, Zevi Perez, 178, 182, 183, 208, 209, 211, 216, 217
Civiltà Cattolica (Jesuit journal), 6, 102, 103, 104, 106, 107, 108, 109, 128
Coen, Fausto, 34–5
Coen, Giuseppe, 102
Cohn, Albert, 'Jewish Letters', 105
Cohn-Sherbok, Dan, 105
Collotti, Enzo, 98, 139n
Colombo, Anselmo, 86, 87, 88, 185, 211, 219, 220, 221

Comitato Pro Cultura Ebraica (Committee for Jewish Culture), Florence, 187, 190, 210, 211, 212, 215
Committee of Italian Jewish Communities, 87, 136, 214, 215
Conferences of Italian Jewish communities: from 1909 to 1914, 63, 85–9; Ferrara 1863, 64–7, 74, 84; Florence 1867, 67–73, 84; Jewish Youth, 78, 214–20, 223
Conigliani, Carlo, 171, 172
conversion, 44–5, 65
Coppola, Francesco/Coppola affair (1911), 133, 134, 135, 136, 192
Corradini, Enrico, 129, 136
Crémieux, Adolphe, 21, 53n, 63, 69, 105
Crispi, Francesco, 125
Crispolti, Filippo, 137
Croce, Benedetto, 147n
Curci, Carlo Maria, 103
Curiel, Aron di Shemuel, 40, 70, 127
Curiel, Riccardo, 40
Cuttin, Vittorio, 124

d'Adria, Rocca (Cesare Algranati), 107
Damascus Affair (1840), 63–4, 105, 108
D'Ancona, Alessandro, 15, 26–7, 36, 55n, 115, 138; as editor of *La Nazione*, 102
D'Ancona, Sansone, 29, 110
Das Vaterland (Catholic newspaper), 119
D'Azeglio, Massimo, 3, 15
De Benedetti, Rodolfo, 2, 34, 56n, 61n
De Benedetti, Salvatore, 15, 29, 30, 80, 115, 146n, 184
De Felice, Renzo, 1–2, 97, 98, 111, 139n, 144n
Del Canuto, Francesco, 156, 166, 180, 202n, 204n, 223
Della Pergola, Sergio, 4–5, 34, 52n, 53n
Della Torre, Lelio, 37, 41, 70–1, 72
Der Israelit (journal), 122
Desportes, Henri, 108
Deutsche Schillerstiftung (German writers' charitable foundation), 118
Die Neuzeit, 119, 123
Die Welt, 156, 157, 158, 159, 167, 168, 173, 214
Diena, Marco, 112
Dina, Giacomo, 15, 36, 48n, 76
Disegni, Dario, 209, 227n
Dohm, Christian Wilhelm von, 3
Donati, Amedeo, 180, 216–17
Doumanis, Nicholas, 51n
Dreyfus, Alfred/Dreyfus Affair (1894–1906), 20, 24, 27, 28, 109, 132, 138, 152, 161, 163, 229n, 231; details of case, 127–9
Drumont, Edouard-Adolphe, 107, 124, 127, 128, 156, 231
dual nationality issues, 112, 131, 184, 186, 188

Eastern European Jews, 38
Edict of Tolerance (1781), 7, 231
educational system, Italian Jewish, 13, 76–9
Ehrenfreund, Jacques, 233n

Ehrlich, Paul, 122
Eisemann, Heinrich, 133, 219, 220
Elbogen, Ismar, 208
Elon, Amos, 160
emancipation of Jews: consequences, 81; debates on, 10n, 121; first, 3, 14, 20; post-emancipation period, 4–5; process, 16; second, 3, *passim*
Endelman, Todd M., 8
English Zionist Federation (EZF), 163, 164
Enlightenment, 3, 99, 121, 123, 124, 127, 138, 148n; and German Jews, 13
Epstein, Yitzhak, 164, 165
Estatutos de limpieza de sangre, 100
Euchel, Isaac, 14

Fanfulla della domenica, 114
Fano, Enrico, 25
Federazione Giovanile Ebraica Italiana (Italian Federation of Jewish Youth), 217, 218, 220, 221
Federazione Rabbinica Italiana (Italian Rabbinical Federation), 76
Federazione Sionistica Italiana (FSI), 2, 7, 33, 87, 88, 165, 166, 167, 211; first conference, 172–3; fourth conference, 176–9; fifth conference, 183; sixth conference, 189–90; dissension within, 179–87; failures, 190–4
Federzoni, Luigi, 129, 130, 133, 134
Ferrara: anti-Semitism in, 99, 130, 131, 132; Conference (1863), 64–7, 74, 84; educational institutions, 77
Ferrara degli Uberti, Carlotta, 48n
Ferrero, Guglielmo, 127
Finzi, Giuseppe, 15, 111, 112, 113
Finzi, Ida, 37
First World War, 45–6, 221, 232
Fleg, Edmond (Flegenheimer), 169, 229n
Florence Jewish community, 23, 36; Conference (1867), 67–73, 84; educational institutions, 77, 79; synagogue, 84
Foà, Arturo, 43
Foà, Chiara, 44
Foà, Giuseppe, 20, 42
France: Association of French Rabbis, 198n; Central Consistory, 63, 73, 162; and Dreyfus affair *see* Dreyfus, Alfred/Dreyfus case (1894–1906); Zionism in, 160–3; *see also* Alliance Israélite Universelle
Franchetti, Augusto, 31, 36
Franchetti, Leopoldo, 31
Franchetti, Raimondo, 31
Franchetti family, 31–2
Frankel, Jonathan, 152
Freedland, Jonathan, 11n
Freemasons, 103
Freud, Sigmund, 5, 123, 145n, 148n, 157
FSI *see* Federazione Sionistica Italiana (FSI)
Funaro, Angiolo, 23, 54n
Funaro, Liana Elda, 23, 50n, 94n

Gabba, Carlo Francesco, 180–1, 182, 183, 184, 185, 186

Gambini, Francesco, 99
Gans, Herbert, 35
Garibaldi, Giuseppe, 16, 17, 19, 20, 82
Gentiloni Pact, 103
Germany: anti-Semitism in, 99, 104, 108, 117–18, 119, 121–2, 122, 138; Unification, 231; Zionism/Zionist organizations, 158, 159, 160
Gherini, Luigi, 125
ghettos, 14, 99, 101–2, 108, 121
Gilman, Sander L., 140n, 145n
Giovane Israele (journal), 202n, 221
Gordon, Milton M., 3–4
Gougenot des Mousseaux, Henri, 108
Gramsci, Antonio, 18
Grande Italia, 132
Greenberg, Leopold, 163
Gregory XVI, Pope, 108
Grunfeld, Federic V., 58–9n
Güdemann, Moritz, 155

Hagani, Baruch, 162, 198n
Halakah, 4, 5
Hantke, Arthur, 159, 160
Hashiloah, 164
Haskalah movement, 13, 14
Heine, Heinrich, 61n, 231
Henry, Hubert-Joseph, 128
Herzl, Theodor, 7, 122, 178, 224; and Zionism, 152–3, 154, 156, 157, 158, 163, 174, 175, 196n, 197n
Holocaust, papal silence on, 6, 7
Houses of the Catechumens, 65, 102
Hyman, Paula E., 34, 198n

identity, Jewish, 4–5, 13–62; Eastern European Jews, 38; family life, 34–6; and First World War, 45–6; integration, 21–5; Jewish culture, 37–8; memoirs and autobiographies, 29–31; narratives, 25; national culture, 36; periodical press, 2, 22, 38–42, 46; post-emancipation period, 4–5; religious conversion, 44–5; Risorgimento movement, 14–20, 78
Il Corriere Israelitico (The Jewish Courier), 2, 6, 7, 8; on anti-Semitism, 116–21, 131, 136, 141n; on assimilation, 40–2; on discrimination in public life, 115–16; on Dreyfus Affair, 129; and Ferrara Conference (1863), 67; and First World War, 46; on French Zionism, 162; and Jewish identity, 22, 25, 29; and Jewish press, 39, 40, 41; and marital assimilation, 43; philanthropy, 80–1; on religious conversion, 44, 45; ritual murder allegations, 105, 107, 108; and social and demographic change, 64, 86; on synagogues, 84; on Turin conference, 217; and Zionism, 166, 167, 168, 170, 179, 182, 183, 187, 188, 189, 192
Il Giornale d'Italia, 133, 134
Il Momento, 137
Il Popolo Romano (Roman People), 125, 134
Il Regno, 129, 182, 212
Il Sole (The Sun), 124

INDEX

Il Vessillo Israelitico (The Jewish Banner), 2, 7, 78, 87, 221–2; on anti-Semitism, 106, 108, 115, 135, 137; on Dreyfus Affair, 128; on First World War, 45, 46; and Jewish press, 40, 41; and Pasqualigo case, 113; philanthropy, 81; on Turin conference, 217; and Zionism, 156, 165, 167, 185, 191, 200n
Im deutschen Reich (In the German Reich), 122
integration, 21–5, *passim*
International Falasha Committee, 208
Irredentism, 19n, 31, 46, 49n, 120, 124
Israel (journal), 7, 222
Israélite (as term), 25
Israelitische Kultusgemeinde (Vienna Jewish community), 62n, 158
Istituto Seghetti, 108
Istoczy, Győző, 117
Italian Nationalist Association, *see* Associazione Nazionalista Italiana
Italian Zionist Federation, *see* Federazione Sionistica Italiana

Jabalot, Ferdinando, 101
Jabotinsky, Vladimir, 195n
Jacur, Leone Romanin, 109, 175
Jarrassé, Dominique, 95n
Jellinek, Adolf, 123, 155
Jemolo, Arturo Carlo, 20, 30, 126
Jewish Chronicle, 52n, 62n, 156, 163, 164, 204n
Jewish communities, regulations (Italy), 73–6
Jewish National Fund, 33, 173, 185, 188, 190, 193
Jewish State, The (Herzl), 153, 154, 156, 157, 195n, 196n, 198n
Jewish Youth Conferences in Italy, 78, 214–20, 223
Jewish-Masonic conspiracy allegations, 100, 103, 104, 126, 137
John Paul (Pope), 6–7
journals *see* periodical press
Judentum, synthesis with *Deutschtum*, 138, 159, 160, 166, 189, 231
Judeo-Italian dialect, 13, 14
Jüdische Rundschau (Jewish Review), 159
Jüdische Volksgemeinde, 158, 202n
Jüdische Volkspartei, 158
Juif (as term), 25

Kadimah (Viennese Zionist student group), 152, 157, 168, 197n
Kahn, Zadoc, 155, 161, 162
Kaplan, Marion, 34
Katz, Jacob, 11n, 63
Kelsen, Hans, 123
Kertzer, David, 98, 109
Kishinev pogroms, 153, 173, 177
Klausner, Joseph, 169, 200n
Krinkin, David, 165, 216, 219, 220

La Croce pisana (The Pisan Cross), 107
La Croix, 106, 150n

La Libre Parole, 107, 127, 128
La Nazione (Florentine newspaper), 102
La Patria, 107
La Rassegna Nazionale, 181, 183
La Rivista Israelitica (1845–1847), 38–9, 40
La Rivista Israelitica (1904–1915), 178, 191, 209, 214
La Settimana Israelitica (The Jewish Weekly), 2, 86, 88, 132–3, 135, 190, 192, 212, 213, 219
L'Amico, 124
Lampronti, Salomone, 80
L'Apostata smascherato, 44–5
Lattes, Dante, 7, 37, 42, 49n, 82, 206, 212, 217; and anti-Semitism, 127, 129, 133; as editor, 40, 166–7; and leading figure, 26, 27, 28, 33; and Zionism, 165, 167, 168, 169, 176, 189
Lattes, Guglielmo, 43, 61n, 77, 116, 135, 168, 199n
L'Avvenire, 124
Law of Guarantees (1871), 75, 111, 112
Lazare, Bernard, 150n, 161
Lazarus, Moritz, 118
League of Anti-Semites *see* Anti-Semitic League (Antisemiten-Liga)
L'écho sioniste, 161
L'Eco Sionista d'Italia, 189
L'Educatore Israelita (The Jewish Educator), 2, 6, 8, 29, 39, 40, 63, 64; and discrimination, 115; and Ferrara Conference (1863), 65, 67; Levi as editor, 66; Mortara's letter to, 75; and Pasqualigo case, 113; and Risorgimento, 17; ritual murder allegations, 107; *see also Il Vessillo Israelitico* (The Jewish Banner)
Leo XII, 101
Leo XIII, 103, 106, 108, 109, 181
Lepschy, Giulio, 47n
Levi, Alberto, 80
Levi, David, 67, 68, 71, 72, 84
Levi, David (poet), 15, 18, 30, 36, 48n, 72, 92n, 110, 208; and Margulies, 225n, 226n; and Massarani, 26
Levi, Enzo, 20, 32–3, 35, 44, 46, 83, 100, 126, 171–2
Levi, Fabio, 22
Levi, Giuseppe, 29, 30, 39, 41, 64, 66, 70, 77, 92n, 111–12
Levi, Primo, 47n
Levi, Raffaele, 133
Levi, Salvador Vita, 15
Levis Sullam, Simon, 18, 47n
Liberal Party of Italy: anti-Semitism of, 100, 103; in Britain, 138; and Catholic Church, 111; Liberal Parties of Austria and Germany, 124
Libya, acquisition as Italian colony (1911), 87, 135; Jewish community in, 136, 203n, 208, 220
L'Idea Nazionale, 129, 133, 134, 135, 136, 191
L'Idea Sionista (The Zionist Idea), 2, 131, 132, 172, 176, 180, 182, 186, 189, 190; *L'Eco Sionista*, possible merger with, 191
Lilien, Ephraim Moses, 153
L'Israélite français, 25

265

Livorno, 14, 16, 23, 67, 69, 70, 223; educational institutions, 77, 78, 79; exodus of Jews from, 84; Jewish community; 2, 19, 22, 24, 71, 80
Lolli, Eude, 168
Lombroso, Cesare, 19, 36, 126, 127, 130, 167
Lopez, Sabatino, 28
L'Osservatore Romano (Vatican daily), 103, 104, 106, 115, 128
Lovers of Zion (Hovevei Zion) movement, 152, 155, 161
Lueger, Karl, 106–7, 108–9, 119, 123, 126, 138, 144n, 158; political victory, 122, 124
L'Univers israélite, 156, 162, 200n, 204n
Luzzati, Michele, 19, 51n
Luzzatti, Luigi, 21, 27–8, 34, 112, 116, 138, 175, 193, 208, 233
Luzzatto, Samuel David (Shadal), 16, 40–1, 72, 90n, 142n, 209, 212, 223, 229n
Luzzatto Voghera, Gadi, 1, 19, 24, 53n, 98, 139n, 168, 206, 228n

Maccoby, Hyam, 140n
Mack, Michael, 140n
Mahler, Gustav, 59n, 123
Mahler, Raphael, 13
Maifreda, Germano, 115, 125
Malvano, Alessandro, 75
Malvano, Giacomo, 114, 175
Mantegazza, Paolo, 114
Mantua Jewish community, 54n, 74, 85
Margotti, Giacomo, 107
Margulies, Samuel Hirsch, 2, 8, 27, 33, 37, 76, 87, 167, 206, 207–8, 209, 210, 214, 218, 223, 224, 225n; and Zionism, 165, 166, 173–6, 191
marital assimilation, 4, 42–4
Marmorek, Alexander, 161, 162, 163
Marr, Wilhelm, 99, 117, 118
Marrano Jews, 36, 145n
Massarani, Tullo, 15, 19, 21, 26, 27, 36, 52n, 55n, 110, 116, 181
Maurogonato, Isacco Pesaro, 16, 31, 110, 111, 112, 113
Maurras, Charles, 133, 233
Mazzamuto, Salvatore, 184
Mazzini, Giuseppe, 14, 15, 19, 51n, 52n
Memmoli, Gubello, 133
memoirs, 29–31, 98, 116; Dreyfus, 129
Mendelssohn, Moses, 13, 154, 195n, 197n
Merzagora, Cesare, 147n
Meyer, Michael A., 90n, 148n
Miccoli, Giovanni, 98, 144n
migration, internal, 81–5
Milan Jewish community, 22, 23, 71, 74, 84, 85, 86
Milano, Attilio, 39, 97, 206–7, 209, 211, 225n
Mindel, Nathan, 194
Miniati, Monica, 34
Minoranza sionista pura (MSP), 187–9
Modena Jewish community, 67, 84
Molinari, Maurizio, 24, 111
Momigliano, Arnaldo, 18, 21, 32, 34, 117, 207

Momigliano, Attilio, 34, 36, 93n
Momigliano, Felice, 19, 52n, 131, 166, 169, 170
Momigliano, Marco Mordechai, 30, 57n, 85, 116
Mommsen, Theodor, 117, 183
Mondovi Jewish community, 30, 83–4
Montagu, Samuel, 163, 207
Monte San Savino, 99
Montefiore, Claude, 164, 198n
Montefiore, Moses, 80, 101–2, 105, 108
Montessori, Maria, 31
Morpurgo, Abram Vita, 40, 41, 44–5
Morpurgo, Edgardo, 173, 178, 179, 183, 189, 211, 215
Morpurgo, Eduardo, 188
Morpurgo, Giuseppe, 191
Morpurgo, Rachele, 37
Mortara, Edgardo, 65, 101–2
Mortara, Elena, 102
Mortara, Ludovico, 21–2, 30
Mortara, Marco, 16, 30, 60n, 66, 67, 70, 71, 75, 91n, 223; and anti-Semitism, 112, 113
Mosse, Werner E., 11n, 55n
Musatti, Alberto, 133, 135
Musio, Giuseppe, 112

Naples Jewish community, 70, 84, 85
Nathan, Ernesto, 19, 46, 52n, 126, 138
Nathan-Rosselli family, 15
Neppi Modona, Aldo, 37, 222, 225n
Neppi Modona, Lionella, 140n
Neue Freie Presse, 123, 156
Nicault, Caterine, 161, 163
Nordau, Max, 32, 57n, 143n, 152, 153, 154, 155, 162, 168, 169, 172–3, 178, 187, 193, 201n
Nuova Antologia, 127

Olper, Samuele Salomone, 67, 72, 75
Olschki, Leo Samuel, 187, 212, 227n
Oppenheimer, Franz, 159
Orano, Paolo, 136
Orciani, Andrea, 107
Orvieto, Adolfo, 36
Orvieto, Angiolo, 36, 37, 52n, 59n
Österreichische Wochenschrift (Austrian Weekly), 120
Österreichisch-Israelitische Union (Austrian Israelite Union), 120
Ostjuden, 38, 154, 159, 213
Ottolenghi, Bonajut, 100
Ottolenghi, Giuseppe, 221
Ottolenghi, Giuseppe (General), 21, 25
Ottolenghi, Lazzaro, 42, 43, 44
Ottolenghi, Leonetto, 56n, 78
Ottolenghi, Zaccaria, 28
Ovadia, Moni, 38
Ovazza, Ernesto, 46, 55n
Ovazza, Vitta, 19, 23

Pacifici, Alfonso, 33, 167, 169, 192, 202n, 207, 210, 213, 214, 217, 220, 221, 222–3

Padua, Pro Cultura, 211–12; anti-Semitism in, 107, 111, 126; Rabbinical College, 68, 69, 71, 72
Palestine, Zionists' attitude to, 164–5
Papini, Giovanni, 129
parallel nationalization, 18, 133
Paris, Gaston, 27
Pasqualigo, Francesco (case of), 110–14
periodical press: anti-Semitic, 114–15; Catholic, 103–4, 107; Jewish, 2, 22, 38–42, 46; *see also specific journals*
Peroni, Tullio, 131
Peruzzi, Ubaldino, 31
philanthropy, 79–81
Pincherle, Emilio, 168
Pincherle, Leone, 16, 19
Pinsker, Leo, 152, 155, 161
Pisa Jewish community, 22, 23, 27, 68, 74
Pisa, Israele Luigi, 20
Pisa, Ugo, 125
Pitigliano Jewish community, 20, 81, 82, 87
Pius IX, 6, 100, 101, 102, 103, 108
Pius X, 107, 109, 173, 175
Poalei Zion (Workers of Zion), 162
Poggi, Enrico, 110
pogroms, 38, 81, 104, 117, 120, 123, 128, 138, 152, 170, 186; Kishinev, 173, 177
Pomponesco Jewish community, 83
Pontremoli, Esdra, 39
Prato, David, 209, 210, 211, 213, 214, 222, 227n
press *see* periodical press
Preziosi, Giovanni, 98, 115, 146n
Prezzolini, Giuseppe, 129
Pro Cultura *see* Comitato Pro Cultura Ebraica (Committee for Jewish Culture)
Protocols of the Elders of Zion, The (forgery), 114–15, 146n

Rabezzana, Pietro, 167
Racah, Gino, 180
Racah, Leone, 7, 121
Racca, Vittorio, 186
Racial Laws (1938), 6, 34, 38, 97, 138
Raggi, Barbara, 98
Rasmann, Boris, 167
Rattazzi, Urbano (law of), 73, 74, 86
Ravenna, Felice, 165, 170–4, 177–8, 182, 186, 190, 192, 194, 216, 223
Ravenna, Leone, 26, 49n, 63, 64, 68, 70, 86, 87, 88, 91n, 95n, 131, 190
Reinach, Joseph, 21, 51n, 53n, 128, 162, 164
Reinach, Salomon, 21, 162
Reinharz, Jehuda, 160
religious reforms, debates on (Italy), 70–1
Revere, Giuseppe, 15, 36, 48n
Ricasoli, Bettino, 110
Rignano, Isacco, 15
Risorgimento movement, 14–20, 78, 214, 216, 231
ritual murder allegations, 100, 101, 104–9, 121–2
Robertson, Ritchie, 10n, 195n, 229n

Rodrigue, Aron, 89n
Rohling, August, 119–20
Romania, anti-Semitism of, 116–17, 146n
Romano, Giorgio, 176
Rome Jewish community, 2, 13, 19, 22, 23, 52n, 68, 71, 74, 84, 113–14; conference (1914), 88; ghetto in, 101–2, 108
Rosselli, Amelia, 19
Rosselli, Nello, 35, 223
Rosselli family, 15, 19
Rossi Artom, Elena, 9n, 35
Roth, Cecil, 1, 58n, 225n, 228n
Rothschild, Carlo Mayer De, 85
Rothschild, Edmond de, 155, 161
Rothschild, Sara Louise, 31
Rothschild families, 29, 80, 85, 94n, 163, 170
Rovasenda di Rovasenda, Alessandro, 137
Rovighi, Cesare, 38–9
Rozenblit, Marsha L., 54n, 197n
Rutenberg, Pinhaus, 193, 205n

Saba, Umberto, 37
Sabbioneta Jewish community, 83
Sacerdoti, Angelo, 76, 209, 219
Sacerdoti, Giancarlo, 33–4, 58n
Salvadori, Roberto, 36, 48n, 82
Sarfatti, Michele, 18, 51n, 140n
Savini, Medoro, 114
Scandiano Jewish community, 68, 83, 87
Scardozzi, Mirella, 31
Schechter, Solomon, 213–14
Schnitzler, Arthur, 123, 149n
Scholem, Gershom, 57n, 160, 197n, 226n
Schönerer, Georg Ritter von, 119
Schwarz, Guri, 9n, 54n, 55n
Sciloni, Gaio, 37
Segre, Augusto, 1, 14, 33, 45, 77, 100, 215
Segre, Dan Vittorio, 17, 23, 25, 32, 35
Senigaglia, Quinto, 213
Sereni, Angelo, 20, 45, 86, 136, 211, 219, 223
Sereni, Enzo, 35, 194, 223
Servi, Elena, 82, 94n
Servi, Ferruccio, 218
Servi, Flaminio, 39–40, 41, 42, 71, 75, 76, 80, 81, 156, 185, 207, 220; *Jews in European Civilization*, 75
Shalem, Nathan, 222
Sighele, Scipio, 129, 135, 136
Simmel, Georg, 122
Simon of Trent, 104
Sinigaglia Jewish community, 79, 87; ghetto in, 99
social and demographic change, 63–89; community regulations, 73–6; education, 13, 76–9; Ferrara Conference (1861), 64–7; Florence Conference (1867), 67–73; internal migration, 81–5; philanthropy, 79–81
Sokolow, Nahum, 187
Sonnino, Sidney, 31, 46, 126
Soragna Jewish community, 68, 82–3
Sorani, Aldo, 188, 190–1, 210, 211, 212, 214
Soria, Marco, 20

Sorkin, David, 3, 4, 6
Spire, André, 169, 229n
Statuto Albertino, 3, 15, 231
Stern, Fritz, 4
Stille, Alexander, 11n, 19, 55n
Stöcker, Alfred, 117, 119
Stuart Hughes, H., 5, 198n
Sulamith (journal), 17
Sullam, Angelo, 86, 136, 174, 183, 188, 189, 190, 194, 201n, 214, 220, 223
Svevo, Italo, 37, 59n

Tagliacozzo, Elia, 17
Taradel, Ruggero, 98
Tedeschi, Marco, 77
Terracini, David, 66, 68, 69, 71, 78
Tisza-Eszlar trial, 105–6
Toaff, Elio, 36
Toscano, Mario, 18, 50n, 98, 111, 139n, 166, 167, 206, 221, 225n
Treitschke, Heinrich von, 117, 118, 119, 183
Treves, Marco, 75
Trieste, 2, 7, 8, 37, 40, 84; anti-Semitism in, 120–1, 124; Triestine community, 64; Zionist Association, 169
Tripoli Jewish community, 46, 84, 87, 88, 136
Turin Jewish community, 20, 22, 24, 32, 44, 54n, 69–70, 73, 87; educational institutions, 76, 79; Supreme Court, 74; synagogue, 84–5

Umberto I, 20
Unità Cattolica, 106, 107
Usiglio, Angelo, 15
Uzielli, Gustavo, 113
Uzielli, Marianna Foà, 18

Venezian, Felice, 19, 49n
Venezian, Giacomo, 16, 45
Vercelli Jewish community, 15, 30, 39, 64, 69, 92n, 95n; conference (1856), 73; educational institutions, 76
Verona Jewish community, 68, 84
Vienna, 7, 38, 81, 91n, 122; Eleventh Zionist Congress, 153, 185
Vigevani, Alberto, 102

Villari, Pasquale, 115
Vital, David, 1, 24, 42–3, 44, 59n, 61n, 122, 151n, 152
Viterbo, Carlo Alberto, 32, 33, 57n, 173–4, 202n, 210, 213, 216, 222, 223, 224, 227n, 228n, 229n
Viterbo, Lionella, 225n, 226n
Vitta, Cino, 179
Vittorio Emanuele II, 19, 20, 27, 110
Vittorio Emanuele III, 20, 173
Vivanti, Giuseppe, 80
Vogelmann, Daniel, 212, 213
Vogelsang, Karl von, 119
Voghera, Giorgio, 37
Volkov, Shulamit, 3, 138

Waldensians (Italian Protestants), 3, 52n, 65, 73, 78
Weininger, Otto, 41
Weizmann, Chaim, 157, 163, 224
Wissenschaft des Judentums, 41, 60n, 208, 212
Wistrich, Robert S., 91n, 140n, 148n, 149n, 197n
Wolffsohn, David, 158
World Zionist Organization (WZO), 157, 158, 174, 187

Yiddish, 13, 14, 38, 47n, 154, 195n, 227n
'Young Italy' (*La Giovine Italia*) movement, 14, 15

Zangwill, Israel, 153, 163, 168, 169, 173
Zionism, 7, 138, 154; First Congress, 155–7, 167, 172; Second Congress, 167, 170; Fifth Congress, 172; Seventh Congress, 179, 180, 182; Eighth Congress, 187, 188; Eleventh Zionist Congress, 153, 185; and anti-Semitism, 181; in Austria, 152, 157–9; in England, 163–4; in France, 160–3; in Germany, 158, 159, 160; international, 172; in Italy, 165–94; Palestine, attitudes to, 164–5; philanthropic, 159, 172, 180; political, 152, 157, 161, 164, 167, 233; post-assimilationist, 159; socialist, 166, 170; in Western Europe, 152–65
ZVfD (Zionist Organization of Germany), 159, 160